THE WYCLIFFE EXEGETICAL COMMENTARY

Kenneth Barker, General Editor

NAHUM, HABAKKUK, ZEPHANIAH

Richard D. Patterson

MOODY PRESS

CHICAGO

© 1991 by
THE MOODY BIBLE INSTITUTE
OF CHICAGO

All Scripture quotations, unless otherwise noted, are the author's translation.

Library of Congress Cataloging in Publication Data

Patterson, Richard Duane.
    Habakkuk, Nahum, Zephaniah / Richard D. Patterson.
        p.   cm. — (The Wycliffe exegetical commentary)
    Includes bibliographical references and indexes.
    ISBN 0-8024-9264-9
    1. Bible. O.T. Habakkuk—Commentaries. 2. Bible. O.T. Nahum—Commentaries. 3. Bible. O.T. Zephaniah—Commentaries.
I. Bible. O.T. Habakkuk. English. Patterson. 1991. II. Bible.
O.T. Nahum. English. Patterson. 1991. III. Bible. O.T.
Zephaniah. English. Patterson. 1991. IV. Title. V. Series.
BS1635.3.P37   1991
224'.9—dc20   91-20962
                                                CIP

1 2 3 4 5 6 7 8 9 Printing/AK/Year 94 93 92 91

Printed in the United States of America

To Ann,
a wife of noble character,
who is worth far more than rubies
(Prov. 31:10)

THE WYCLIFFE EXEGETICAL COMMENTARY

The Wycliffe Exegetical Commentary provides a scholarly, thorough analysis of every passage in every book of Scripture. Written especially for the informed layman, student, and scholar, all exegesis and exposition is based on the original languages of the Bible books. Translations used are those of the authors. Textual criticism and word study are included where appropriate.

This in-depth commentary also includes extended excursuses on important topics of theological, historical, and archaeological interest.

The text is interpreted according to a historical, critical, grammatical hermeneutic and propounds a conservative, evangelical theology. But the reader will not get a narrow view of problem passages. This commentary interacts with a range of major views, both evangelical and nonevangelical.

Leading conservative scholars from many denominations have contributed. These scholars represent a cross-section of respected evangelical seminaries and colleges.

General Editor
Kenneth L. Barker (B.A., Northwestern College; Th.M., Dallas Theological Seminary; Ph.D., Dropsie College for Hebrew and Cognate Learning) is executive director of the NIV Translation Center (a ministry of the International Bible Society) in Lewisville, Texas, and former academic dean and professor of Old Testament literature and exegesis at Capital Bible Seminary, Lanham, Maryland.

Old Testament Editors
Richard Patterson (A.B., Wheaton College; M.Div., Northwest Baptist Theological Seminary; Th.M., Talbot Theological Seminary; M.A., Ph.D., University of California—Los Angeles) is chairman of the Department of Biblical Studies and professor of Semitic languages and literatures at Liberty University, Lynchburg, Virginia.

Ronald Youngblood (B.A., Valparaiso University; B.D., Fuller Theological Seminary; Ph.D., Dropsie College for Hebrew and Cognate Learning) is professor of Old Testament and Hebrew at Bethel Theological Seminary West, San Diego.

New Testament Editor
Moisés Silva (B.A., Bob Jones University; Ph.D., University of Manchester, England; B.D., Th.M., Westminster Theological Seminary) is chairman of the New Testament department and professor of New Testament at Westminster Theological Seminary, Philadelphia.

NAHUM

When God revealed to Nahum the coming doom of Assyria and Nineveh, Nahum relayed that message to his countrymen with a poetic skill that is unequaled among the other Minor Prophets. His powers of description are so superb that readers in all ages have marveled at the forcefulness and accuracy of his words. Nahum's good news of Nineveh's fall has not only reverberated across the pages of time but stands both as a reminder that God is in control of the flow of history and as a harbinger of the good news of God's ultimate purpose to sum up all history in His Son.

HABAKKUK

Habakkuk wrestled with the perennial problem of the operation of God's holiness and justice in a world of spiritual and moral decay. Unable to resolve his problem apart from divine instruction, he came to God with hard questions. Habakkuk learned what every believer must come to realize: that Israel's Redeemer is in control of earth's history and does have a plan for its people; that God's high ethical standards are normative for all persons; and that mature believers will live their lives in total faith and trust in God, who alone is a sufficient guide and resource for life's changing fortunes.

ZEPHANIAH

Zephaniah is best remembered for his teachings concerning the Day of the Lord. But Zephaniah should also be remembered as a prophet of hope who looked beyond the impending judgment of mankind to an age when a purified and faithful people will serve God in truth and rejoice in the everlasting blessings of His love. Zephaniah's teachings remind all believers not only of God's standards and purposes but of the positive difference one believer can make in an unbelieving and materialistic society. His timeless warnings and message of hope need to be boldly proclaimed once again in today's self-serving world.

About the Author
Richard D. Patterson (A.B., Wheaton College; M.Div., Northwest Baptist Theological Seminary; Th.M., Talbot Theological Seminary; M.A., Ph.D., University of California—Los Angeles) is chairman of the Department of Biblical Studies and professor of Semitic languages and literatures at Liberty University, Lynchburg, Virginia. He contributed to *The Expositor's Bible Commentary* and has written articles for *Grace Theological Journal*, the *Journal of the Evangelical Theological Society*, and other scholarly journals.

Table of Contents

General Editor's Introduction   xiii

Preface   xv

Abbreviations   xvii

References   xix
   General Works   xix
   Nahum   xxi
      Commentaries and Special Studies
      Articles
   Habakkuk   xxii
      Commentaries and Special Studies
      Articles
   Zephaniah   xxiv
      Commentaries and Special Studies
      Articles

NAHUM

Introduction to Nahum   3
   Historical Context   3

Setting	3
Authorship	7
Literary Context	8
Literary Features	8
Outline	11
Unity	11
Occasion and Purpose	12
Text and Canonicity	13
Theological Context	14

1. The Doom of Nineveh Declared
   (Nahum 1:1-15 [HB 1:1–2:1]) 17
   Superscription (1:1) 19
   A. Theme (1:2) 21
   B. Development: A Hymn to the Sovereign God (1:2-10) 27
      1. Who defeats His foes (1:2-6) 28
      2. Who destroys the plotters (1:7-10) 36
   C. Application: God's Justice for Nineveh and Judah
      (1:11-15 [HB 1:11–2:1]) 42

2. The Doom of Nineveh Described, Part One
   (Nahum 2:1-13 [HB 2:2-14]) 53
   A. Theme (2:1-2 [HB 2:2-3]) 54
   B. Development: First Description of Nineveh's Demise
      (2:3-10 [HB 2:4-11]) 60
   C. Application: The Discredited City (2:11-13 [HB 2:12-14]) 74

3. The Doom of Nineveh Described, Part Two (Nahum 3:1-19) 81
   D. Development: Second Description of Nineveh's Demise
      (3:1-7) 81
   E. Application: The Defenseless Citadel (3:8-19) 93
      1. A comparison of Nineveh and Thebes (3:8-13) 94
      2. A concluding condemnation of Nineveh (3:14-19) 102

HABAKKUK

Introduction to Habakkuk	115
Historical Context	115
Setting	115
Authorship	117
Literary Context	119
Literary Features	119

Outline   126
Unity   127
Occasion, Purpose, and Teachings   129
Text and Canonicity   132

Theological Context   134

1. The Prophet's Perplexities and God's Explanations,
   Part One (Habakkuk 1:1–2:1)   135
   Superscription (1:1)   136
   A. First Perplexity:
      How Can God Disregard Judah's Sin? (1:2-4)   138
   B. First Explanation:
      God Will Judge Judah Through the Chaldeans (1:5-11)   144
   C. Second Perplexity:
      How Can God Employ the Wicked Chaldeans? (1:12–2:1)   154

2. The Prophet's Perplexities and God's Explanations,
   Part Two (Habakkuk 2:2-20)   169
   D. Second Explanation:
      God Controls All Nations According to His Purposes
      (2:2-20)   169
      1. Preliminary instructions (2:2-3)   170
      2. Guiding principles (2:4)   176
      3. Specific applications (2:5-20)   179
         a. The case of the Chaldeans (2:5)   179
         b. The first woe: The plundering Chaldean will be
            despoiled (2:6-8)   183
         c. The second woe: The plotting Chaldean will
            be denounced (2:9-11)   190
         d. The third woe: The pillaging Chaldean will be
            destroyed (2:12-14)   193
         e. The fourth woe: The perverting Chaldean will
            be disgraced (2:15-17)   198
         f. The fifth woe: The polytheistic Chaldean will be
            deserted by his idols (2:18-20)   205

Excursus on Habakkuk 2:4   211

3. The Prophet's Prayer and God's Exaltation
   (Habakkuk 3:1-19)   225
   A. The Prophet's Prayer for the Redeemer's Pity (3:1-2)   226
   B. The Prophet's Praise of the Redeemer's Person (3:3-15)   230
      1. The Redeemer's coming (3:3-7)   230

      a. His appearance (3:3-4)   231

      b. His actions (3:5-7)   234

    2. The Redeemer's conquest (3:8-15)   238

      a. His power as seen at the waters (3:8-9*b*)   238

      b. His power as seen in the natural world (3:9*c*-11)   242

      c. His power as seen by the enemy (3:12-15)   246

  C. The Prophet's Pledge to the Redeemer's Purposes

    (3:16-19)   254

    1. A statement of the prophet's trust in the Redeemer

      (3:16-18)   255

    2. A concluding note of praise to the Redeemer (3:19)   261

Excursus on Habakkuk 3   267

ZEPHANIAH

Introduction to Zephaniah   275

Historical Context   275

  Setting   275

  Authorship   279

Literary Context   281

  Literary Features   281

  Outline   289

  Unity   290

  Occasion and Purpose   292

  Text and Canonicity   294

Theological Context   294

1. The Announcement of the Day of the Lord

  (Zephaniah 1:1–2:3)   297

  Superscription (1:1)   297

  A. Pronouncements of Judgment (1:2-6)   299

    1. On all the earth (1:2-3)   299

    2. On Judah and Jerusalem (1:4-6)   303

  B. Exhortations Based on Judgment (1:7-13)   307

  C. Teachings Concerning the Day of the Lord (1:14–2:3)   319

    1. Information concerning that day (1:14-18)   319

    2. Instructions in the light of that day (2:1-3)   328

2. Additional Details Concerning the Day of the Lord,

  Part One (Zephaniah 2:4–3:7)   335

  A. Further Pronouncements of Judgment (2:4–3:7)   336

    1. On the nations (2:4-15)   336
       a. Philistia (2:4-7)   337
       b. Moab and Ammon (2:8-11)   343
       c. Cush (2:12)   348
       d. Assyria (2:13-15)   350
    2. On Jerusalem (3:1-7)   356

3. Additional Details Concerning the Day of the Lord,
   Part Two (Zephaniah 3:8-20)   365
   B. An Exhortation Based on Judgment (3:8) 366
   C. Additional Teachings Concerning the Day of the Lord
     (3:9-20)   368
     1. Information concerning that day (3:9-13) 368
     2. Instructions in the light of that day (3:14-20) 376

Selected Index of Subjects   389

Index of Authors   393

Selected Index of Scripture   401

Selected Index of Hebrew Words   415

General Editor's Introduction

John Wycliffe (c. 1320-1384) is widely known as "the Morning Star of the Reformation." One of the reasons for that reputation was his great concern for the translation, sufficiency, and understanding of Holy Scripture. Since that is also one of the chief concerns of this commentary series, it is appropriate that it be named after him.

The key descriptive term in the series title, however, is *Exegetical.* While the various areas of biblical criticism receive at least brief treatment, the principal emphasis of the commentary is exegesis. By exegesis we mean the application of generally accepted hermeneutical principles to the original (Hebrew, Aramaic, and Greek) biblical text with a view to unfolding (lit. "leading out," Gk. *exēgeomai*) its correct, contextual meaning. The method followed is commonly referred to as grammatico-historical exegesis. A more complete designation would be the grammatical-historical-literary-theological method.

To facilitate the reader's most effective use of the *Wycliffe Exegetical Commentary* (WEC), it will be helpful to delineate here some of its policies and practices:

1. This is a commentary on the Hebrew, Aramaic, and Greek texts of the Bible, not on an English translation. Consequently Hebrew, Aramaic, and Greek words and phrases appear in their original scripts, but with English transliterations and translations provided at their first occurrence. After that, transliterations alone normally suffice. However, only the original scripts are employed in the Addi-

tional Notes and footnote discussions, since scholars and specialists would be the ones most interested in that more technical material (e.g., word studies, grammatical or syntactical points, etymologies, textual variants in the original languages, specialized bibliographies, etc.). Unless otherwise indicated, all Scripture translations are those of the authors of the individual volumes.

2. WEC stresses the development of the argument of a given book and its central theme(s). An attempt has been made to show how each section of a book fits together with the preceding and following sections. We do not want the reader to become so preoccupied with the trees (analysis) that he fails to see the forest (synthesis).

3. Some flexibility has been allowed in the introductions to the books of the Bible—and even in the exegetical approach—in order to reflect the strengths and interests of the various commentators as well as the nature and purpose of the material.

4. Most of the abbreviations and transliterations follow the guidelines of the *Journal of Biblical Literature* (*JBL*). Usually the only abbreviations listed are those not found in *JBL*.

5. Asterisks in either the Translation or the Exegesis and Exposition section refer the reader to discussions of text-critical problems in the Additional Notes section, though these are not the only kinds of discussions one will encounter in the Additional Notes sections (see above, under 1).

I wish to express my gratitude to Moody Press for inviting me to edit this entire series and particularly to Greg Thornton and Garry Knussman for their assistance. Special thanks go to Richard Patterson and Ronald Youngblood (Old Testament co-editors) and Moisés Silva (New Testament editor). Grateful acknowledgment is also given to all the contributors of the individual volumes; they are to be commended especially for their cooperation and patience with the editors. All of us trust and pray that WEC will be used by God to advance the cause of a more exegetically-based, and so more accurate, biblical interpretation and biblical theology. In other words, we hope that this series will be an example of "correctly handling [lit. "cutting straight," Gk. *orthotomeō*] the Word of truth" (2 Tim. 2:15).

Paul's parting words to the Ephesian elders seem apropos here: "Now I commit you to God and to the word of his grace, which can build you up and give you an inheritance among all those who are sanctified" (Acts 20:32, NIV).

KENNETH L. BARKER
General Editor

Preface

At the outset, I wish to express my thanks to Moody Press and to general editor Kenneth L. Barker for inviting me to join in the production of the WEC series and to write this particular volume. Unfortunately, the books of Nahum, Habakkuk, and Zephaniah are often neglected by pastor and people alike, to the loss of all concerned. These prophets were not only astute observers of their time and authors of literary distinction, they were also spiritually sensitive men who held a high concern for God's person and reputation. Their pronouncements on the greed, materialism, and spiritual and moral decay that beset seventh-century-B.C. Judahite society are no less valid in today's world. Careful consideration of these books will, therefore, pay rich spiritual dividends to their readers.

My hope is that those who interact with this commentary will come to love these prophets as I have. In carrying out the aims of the series I have attempted to follow faithfully the WEC format. My translations are intended to be neither strictly literal nor highly literate. Rather, my goal is to give a faithful translation of the MT that reflects the conclusions given in the exegetical discussions. Particularly important or disputed areas are marked by an asterisk and referred to in the Additional Notes by the symbol †.

Preceding each translation I have provided an opening overview of the section under consideration. Consequently the reader becomes aware at the beginning of the discussion of where he is in the book's flow of thought and of what might lie ahead. The Exegesis and Exposition section is devoted to the larger issues controlling the interpretation of the passage. It is my conviction that the chair of proper exegesis rests upon the four evenly balanced legs of grammatical precision, historical accuracy, literary conventions, and proper theological conclusions. Therefore, matters relative to all four areas will be found, though in varying degrees, throughout the exegetical discussions. In utilizing these exegetical tools, however, my aim has been always to avoid technical jargon so that the comments will be useful to all of God's people. At times, matters brought up in this section will receive fuller attention in the Additional Notes. Such items are marked by an asterisk and indicated in the Additional Notes by italics.

The Additional Notes section is reserved for matters of concern to scholarly precision. While they often contain information useful in understanding or amplifying the conclusions reached in the Exegesis and Exposition, they at times contain details not mentioned previously. Although original text citations are not generally transliterated here, as in the Exegesis and Exposition, they are usually translated so that the material under consideration will be understandable to all readers. Likewise, comments and citations in extrabiblical foreign languages are customarily translated or summarized for the benefit of all.

My special thanks go to Ronald Youngblood for his many helpful suggestions and to my dear wife, Ann, who painstakingly (and painfully) prepared this commentary from my handwritten draft. Only my students and secretary can begin to appreciate the herculean nature of that task! My fondest hope is that the result of our labors has been the production of a commentary that is readable and helpful and not given to a display of erudition. Remembering Hitzig's observation that we accomplish nothing in our own strength (*Mit unserer macht is nichts getan*), to the extent that this has been achieved the final credit belongs to Him who is the source of all true wisdom. Above all, may this book be honoring to Him "who loved [us] and gave himself for [us]" (Gal. 2:20, NIV).

Abbreviations

The following abbreviations have been adopted for this commentary in addition to or in modification of those found in the *Journal of Biblical Literature:*

COT   C. F. Keil and F. Delitzsch, Commentaries on the Old Testament

DSS   The Dead Sea Scrolls

EBC   *The Expositor's Bible Commentary*

GTJ   *Grace Theological Journal*

ISBE-1   *The International Standard Bible Encyclopaedia* (1939 edition)

KB-3   L. Koehler und W. Baumgartner, *Hebräisches und Aramäisches Lexikon zum Alten Testament* (3d edition)

NKJV   *New King James Version*

Pesh.   The *Peshitta*

RSP   Loren R. Fisher, ed., *Ras Shamra Parallels,* Analecta Orientalia 49, 3 vols. (Roma: Pontificium Institutum Biblicum, 1981)

TWOT   *Theological Wordbook of the Old Testament*

WEC   Wycliffe Exegetical Commentary

ZPEB   *The Zondervan Pictorial Encyclopedia of the Bible*

References

General Works

Baker, David W. *Nahum, Habakkuk, Zephaniah*. TOTC. Downers Grove, Ill.: InterVarsity, 1988.

Bewer, Julius A. *The Literature of the Old Testament*. 3d ed. New York: Columbia U., 1962.

Bullock, C. Hassell. *An Introduction to the Old Testament Prophetic Books*. Chicago: Moody, 1986.

Chisholm, Robert B., Jr. *Interpreting the Minor Prophets*. Grand Rapids: Zondervan, 1989.

Contenau, Georges. *Everyday Life in Babylon and Assyria*. New York: W. W. Norton and Co., 1966.

Craigie, Peter C. *Twelve Prophets*. 2 vols. Philadelphia: Westminster, 1985.

Delaporte, L. *Mesopotamia*. Translated by V. Gordon Childe. New York: Barnes and Noble, 1970.

Driver, S. R. *An Introduction to the Literature of the Old Testament*. Rev. ed. New York: Scribner's, 1950.

Eissfeldt, Otto. *The Old Testament: An Introduction*. Translated by P. R. Ackroyd. New York: Harper & Row, 1976.

Feinberg, C. L. *The Minor Prophets*. Chicago: Moody, 1976.

Freeman, Hobart E. *An Introduction to the Old Testament Prophets*. Chicago: Moody, 1971.

_____. *Nahum Zephaniah Habakkuk.* Everyman's Bible Commentary. Chicago: Moody, 1973.

Hailey, Homer. *A Commentary on the Minor Prophets.* Grand Rapids: Baker, 1972.

Harrison, R. K. *Introduction to the Old Testament.* Grand Rapids: Eerdmans, 1971.

Hummel, Horace D. *The Word Becoming Flesh.* St. Louis: Concordia, 1979.

Jastrow, Morris, Jr. *Hebrew and Babylonian Traditions.* New York: Charles Scribner's, 1914.

Keil, C. F. *The Twelve Minor Prophets.* COT. 2 vols. Grand Rapids: Eerdmans, 1954.

Laetsch, Theo. *The Minor Prophets.* St. Louis: Concordia, 1956.

Larue, Gerald A. *Babylon and the Bible.* Grand Rapids: Baker, 1969.

Layard, Austen H. *Nineveh and Its Remains.* 2 vols. New York: Putnam, 1849.

Lehman, Chester K. *Biblical Theology: Old Testament.* Scottdale, Pa.: Herald, 1971.

Lehrman, S. M. *The Twelve Prophets.* Soncino Books of the Bible. 12th ed. Edited by A. Cohen. New York: Soncino, 1985.

Luckenbill, Daniel David. *Ancient Records of Assyria and Babylonia.* 2 vols. Chicago: U. of Chicago, 1926-27.

Olmstead, A. T. *History of Assyria.* Chicago: U. of Chicago, 1951.

Parrot, André. *Babylon and the Old Testament.* New York: Philosophical Library, 1958.

_____. *Nineveh and the Old Testament.* New York: Philosophical Library, 1955.

Pritchard, James B., ed. *Ancient Near Eastern Texts.* 3d ed. Princeton: Princeton U., 1969.

Pusey, E. B. *The Minor Prophets.* 2 vols. Grand Rapids, Baker, 1953.

Rice, T. T. *The Scythians.* London: Thames and Hudson, 1957.

Robertson, O. Palmer. *The Books of Nahum, Habakkuk, and Zephaniah.* NICOT. Grand Rapids, Eerdmans, 1990.

Robinson, T. H. *Prophecy and the Prophets.* 2d ed. London: Duckworth, 1953.

Saggs, H. W. F. *Assyriology and the Study of the Old Testament.* Cardiff: U. of Wales, 1969.

_____. *Everyday Life in Babylonia and Assyria.* New York: G. P. Putnam's, 1965.

_____. *The Greatness That Was Babylon.* New York: Hawthorn, 1962.

_____. *The Might That Was Assyria.* London: Sidgwick & Jackson, 1984.

Schoville, Keith N. *Biblical Archaeology in Focus.* Grand Rapids: Baker, 1978.

Smith, George Adam. *The Book of the Twelve Prophets*. Rev. ed. 2 vols. Garden City, N.Y.: Doubleday, 1929.

Smith, Ralph L. *Micah–Malachi*. WBC. Waco: Word, 1984.

Vermes, G. *The Dead Sea Scrolls in English*. Baltimore: Penguin, 1962.

von Rad, Gerhard. *Old Testament Theology*. 2 vols. New York: Harper, 1965.

von Orelli, C. *The Twelve Minor Prophets*. Translated by J. S. Banks. Reprint. Minneapolis: Klock and Klock, 1977.

Wiseman, D. J. *Chronicles of Chaldaean Kings*. London: British Museum, 1956.

_____, ed. *Peoples of Old Testament Times*. Oxford: Clarendon, 1973.

Nahum

Commentaries and special studies

Armerding, Carl E. "Obadiah, Nahum, Habakkuk." In *EBC*, vol. 7. Grand Rapids: Zondervan, 1985.

Cathcart, Kevin J. *Nahum in the Light of Northwest Semitic*. Rome: Biblical Institute Press, 1973.

Haldar, Alfred. *Studies in the Book of Nahum*. Uppsala: Lundequistska Bokhandeln, 1947.

Kohlenberger, John R. III. *Jonah and Nahum*. Everyman's Bible Commentary. Chicago: Moody, 1984.

Maier, Walter A. *The Book of Nahum*. Grand Rapids: Baker, 1959.

Schulz, Hermann. *Das Buch Nahum*. Berlin: Walter de Gruyter, 1973.

Smith, John M. P. *A Critical and Exegetical Commentary on Zephaniah and Nahum*. ICC. Edinburgh: T. & T. Clark, 1911.

Articles

Allis, O. T. "Nahum, Nineveh, Elkosh." *EvQ* 27 (1955): 67-70.

Becking, Bob. "Is het boek Nahum een literaire eenherd." *NedTTs* 32 (1978): 107-24.

Cathcart, Kevin J. "More Philological Studies in Nahum." *JNSL* 7 (1979): 1-12.

_____. "Treaty Curses and the Book of Nahum." *CBQ* 35 (1973): 179-87.

Christensen, D. L. "The Acrostic of Nahum Reconsidered." *ZAW* 87 (1975): 17-30.

_____. "The Acrostic of Nahum Once Again." *ZAW* 99 (1987): 409-15.

_____. "The Book of Nahum: The Question of Authorship within the Canonical Process." *JETS* 31 (1988): 51-58.

Delcor, Matthias. "Allusions a la deese Istar, Nahum 2:8." *Bib* 58 (1977): 73-83.

Florit, Josep Ribera i. "La versión aramaica del profeta Nahum." *Anuario* 6 (1980): 291-322.

Levenson, J. D. "Textual and Semantic Notes on Nahum 1:7-8." *VT* 25 (1975): 792-95.

Patterson, Richard D., and Michael E. Travers. "Literary Analysis and the Unity of Nahum." *GTJ* 9 (1988): 45-58.

_____. "Nahum: Poet Laureate of the Minor Prophets." *JETS* 33 (1990): 437-44.

Renaud, Bernard. "La composition du livre de Nahum." *ZAW* 99 (1987): 198-219.

Rowley, H. H. "Nahum and the Teacher of Righteousness." *JBL* 75 (1956): 188-93.

Saggs, H. W. F. "Nahum and the Fall of Nineveh." *JTS* 20 (1969): 220-25.

Tsumura, David T. "Janus Parallelism in Nah 1:8." *JBL* 102 (1983): 109-11.

Weiss, R. "A Comparison Between the Masoretic and the Qumran Texts of Nahum III, 1-11." *RQ* 4 (1963-64): 433-39.

Woude, A. S. van der. "The Book of Nahum: A Letter Written in Exile." *OTS* 20 (1977): 108-26.

Yoder, P. B. "A-B Pairs and Composition in Hebrew Poetry." *VT* 21 (1971): 470-89.

Habakkuk

Commentaries and special studies

Armerding, Carl E. "Obadiah, Nahum, Habakkuk." In *EBC*, vol. 7. Grand Rapids: Zondervan, 1985.

Brownlee, W. H. *The Text of Habakkuk in the Ancient Commentary from Qumran*. JBL Monograph XI. Philadelphia: Society of Biblical Literature, 1959.

_____. *The Midrash Pesher of Habakkuk*. Missoula, Mont.: Scholars, 1979.

Hiebert, Theodore. *God of My Victory*. Harvard Semitic Monographs 38. Atlanta: Scholars, 1986.

Humbert, P. *Problèmes du livre d'Habacuc*. Neuchatel: Secretariat de L'Universite, 1944.

Ward, W. Hayes. *A Critical and Exegetical Commentary on Habakkuk*. ICC. Edinburgh: T. & T. Clark, 1911.

Articles

Ahuviah, A. "'Why Do You Countenance Treachery?' A Study in the Oracle Which Habakkuk the Prophet Saw (1:1–2:4)." *Beth Mikra* 31 (1985/86): 320-27.

Albright, W. F. "The Psalm of Habakkuk." In *Studies in Old Testament Prophecy Dedicated to T. H. Robinson,* edited by H. H. Rowley, pp. 1-18. Edinburgh: T. & T. Clark, 1950.

Cassuto, U. "Chapter III of Habakkuk and the Ras Shamra Texts." In *Biblical and Oriental Studies,* translated by Israel Abrahams, vol. 2, pp. 3-15. Jerusalem: Magnes, 1975.

Cathcart, Kevin J. "Legal Terminology in Habakkuk 2:1-4." *Proceedings of the Irish Biblical Association* 10 (1986): 103-10.

_____. "A New Proposal for Hab 1,17." *Bib* 65 (1984): 575-76.

Dahood, Mitchell. "Two Yiphil Causatives in Habakkuk 3:13a." *Or* 48 (1979): 258-59.

Day, John. "New Light on the Mythological Background of Allusion to Resheph in Habakkuk iii 5." *VT* 29 (1979): 353-55.

Eaton, J. H. "The Origin and Meaning of Habakkuk 3." *ZAW* 76 (1964): 144-71.

Emerton, J. A. "The Textual and Linguistic Problems of Habakkuk II.4-5." *JTS* 28 (1977): 2-17.

Gowan, D. E. "Habakkuk and Wisdom." *Perspective* 9 (1968): 157-66.

Gunneweg, A. H. J. "Habakuk und das Problem des leidenen ṣdyq." *ZAW* 98 (1986): 400-15.

Harris, J. G. "The Laments of Habakkuk's Prophecy." *EvQ* 45 (1973): 21-29.

Janzen, J. Gerald. "Habakkuk 2:2-4 in the Light of Recent Philological Advances." *HTR* 73 (1980): 53-78.

Johnson, Marshall D. "The Paralysis of Torah in Habakkuk I 4." *VT* 35 (1985): 257-66.

Koch, Dietrich-Alex. "Der Text von Hab 2 4b in der Septuaginta und im Neuen Testament." *ZNW* 76 (1985): 68-85.

Longman, Tremper III. "The Divine Warrior: The New Testament Use of an Old Testament Motif." *WTJ* 44 (1982): 290-307.

Margulis, Baruch. "The Psalm of Habakkuk: A Reconstruction and Interpretation." *ZAW* 82 (1970): 409-39.

Otto, E. "Die Stellung der Wehe-Worte in der Verkündigung des Propheten Habakuk." *ZAW* 89 (1977): 73-106.

Patterson, Richard D. "The Psalm of Habakkuk." *GTJ* 8 (1987): 163-94.

Peckham, Brian. "The Vision of Habakkuk." *CBQ* 48 (1986): 617-36.

Prinsloo, W. S. "Die boodskap van die boek Habakuk." *Nederduits Gereformeerde Teologiese Tydskrif* 20 (1979): 146-51.

Rast, Walter E. "Justification by Faith." *Cur TM* 10 (1983): 169-75.

Scott, James M. "A New Approach to Habakkuk ii 4-5a." *VT* 35 (1985): 330-40.

van der Wal, A. J. O. "*Lō' Nāmūt* in Habakkuk I 12: A Suggestion." *VT* 38 (1988): 480-82.

Verhoef, P. A. "Habakkuk." In *ZPEB*, edited by Merrill C. Tenney. Vol. 3, pp. 1-5. Grand Rapids: Zondervan, 1975.
Walker, H. H., and N. W. Lund. "The Literary Structure of the Book of Habakkuk." *JBL* 53 (1934): 355-70.
Zemek, George, Jr. "Interpretive Challenges Relating to Habakkuk 2:4b." *GTJ* 1 (1980): 43-69.

Zephaniah

Commentaries and special studies

Fausset, A. R. "Zephaniah." In R. Jamieson, A. R. Fausset, and David Brown, *A Commentary Critical, Experimental and Practical on the Old and New Testaments.* 6 vols. Grand Rapids: Eerdmans, 1948.
Kapelrud, A. S. *The Message of the Prophet Zephaniah.* Oslo-Bergen-Troms: Universitetsforlaget, 1975.
Sabottka, L. *Zephanja.* Rome: Biblical Institute Press, 1972.
Smith, John M. P. *A Critical and Exegetical Commentary on Zephaniah and Nahum.* ICC. Edinburgh: T. & T. Clark, 1911.
Walker, Larry. *Zephaniah.* In *EBC*, vol. 7. Grand Rapids: Zondervan, 1985.

Articles

Anderson, George W. "The Idea of the Remnant in the Book of Zephaniah." *Annual of the Swedish Theological Institute* 11 (1977-78): 11-14.
Baldacci, Massimo. "Alcuni nuovi esempi di taw infisso nell'ebraico biblico." *Bibbia e Oriente* 24 (1982): 107-14.
Cazelles, H. "Sophonie, Jérémie et les Scythes en Palestine." *RB* 74 (1964): 24-44.
Christensen, Duane L. "Zephaniah 2:4-15: A Theological Basis for Josiah's Program of Political Expansion." *CBQ* 46 (1984): 669-82.
Clark, David. "Of Beasts and Birds: Zephaniah 2:14." *BT* 34 (1982): 243-46.
Clark, David. "Wine on the Lees." *BT* 32 (1981): 241-43.
Delcor, M. "Les Kerethim et les Cretois." *VT* 28 (1978): 409-22.
De Roche, Michael. "Zephaniah I 2-3: The 'Sweeping' of Creation." *VT* 30 (1980): 104-9.
Donner, H. "Die Schwellenhüpfer: Beobachtungen zu Zephanja 1, 8f." *JSS* 15 (1970): 42-55.
Eiselen, F. C. "Book of Zephaniah." *ISBE-1* 5:3144-45.
Elliger, K. "Das Ende der 'Abendwolfe' Zeph 3, 3, Hab 1, 8." In *Festschrift A. Bertholet*, edited by W. Baumgartner, pp. 158-75. Tübingen: J. C. B. Mohr, 1950.

Fensham, F. C. "Book of Zephaniah." *IDBSup*, pp. 983-84.

Gordis, Robert. "A Rising Tide of Misery." *VT* 37 (1987): 487-90.

Gozzo, Serafino M. "Il profeta Sofonia e la dottrina teologica del suo libro." *Antonianum* 52 (1977): 3-37.

Hyatt, J. P. "The Date and Background of Zephaniah." *JNES* 7 (1948): 25-29.

Hoffman, Y. "The Root QRB as a Legal Term." *JNSL* 10 (1982): 67-73.

Ihromi. "Die Haufung der Verben des Jubelns in Zephanja iii 14f., 16-18: *rnn, rwʿ, śmḥ, ʿlz, śwś* und *gîl*." *VT* 33 (1983): 106-10.

Lemaire, Andre. "Note sur le titre *bn hmlk* dans l'ancien Israël." *Sem* 29 (1979): 59-65.

Lohfink, Norbert. "Zefanja und das Israel der Armen." *BK* 39 (1984): 100-108.

Nel, J. P. "A Structural and Conceptual Strategy in Zephaniah, chapter 1." *JNSL* 15 (1989): 155-67.

Oeming, Manfred. "Gericht Gottes und Geschichte der Völker nach Zef 3, 1-13." *TQ* 167 (1987): 289-300.

Olivier, J. P. J. "A Possible Interpretation of the Word *ṣiyyâ* in Zeph. 2, 13." *JNSL* 8 (1980): 95-97.

Renaud, B. "Le Livre de Sophonie. La Theme de YHWH structurant de la Synthese Redactionnelle." *RevScRel* 60 (1986): 1-33.

Rice, Gene. "The African Roots of the Prophet Zephaniah." *The Journal of Religious Thought* 36 (1979): 21-31.

Schneider, D. A. "Book of Zephaniah." *ISBE* 4:1189-91.

Seybold, Klaus. "Text und Auslegung in Zef 2, 1-3." *Biblische Notizen* 25 (1984): 49-54.

Smith, L. P., and E. R. Lacheman. "The Authorship of the Book of Zephaniah." *JNES* 9 (1950): 137-42.

Stuhlmueller, Carroll. "Justice toward the Poor." *TBT* 24 (1986): 385-90.

von Rad, G. "The Origin of the Concept of the Day of Yahweh." *JSS* 4 (1959): 97-108.

Williams, D. L. "The Date of Zephaniah." *JBL* 82 (1963): 77-88.

Zalcman, Lawrence. "Ambiguity and Assonance at Zephaniah ii 4." *VT* 36 (1986): 365-71.

NAHUM

Introduction to Nahum

The aim of this chapter and succeeding introductory chapters is to acquaint the reader with the crucial questions that have affected the interpretation of the biblical passages under consideration. Because proper hermeneutical procedure rests primarily upon a basis of historical, grammatical, literary, and theological data, each of the introductory chapters will focus on the crucial problems associated with those areas. Since the solutions suggested in each case are those drawn from the exegesis of the text, the introductions should be considered as an integral part of the expositions that follow.

HISTORICAL CONTEXT

SETTING

The *terminus a quo* for the origin and setting of Nahum's prophecy can be deduced from the mention (3:18) of the fall of Thebes (663 B.C.), whereas the *terminus ad quem* is the date of the fall of Nineveh (612 B.C.), an event that is predicted throughout the book. During these five decades the ancient Near East was to witness a great transition. The Assyrian king who ruled through most of this long period was Ashurbanipal (668-626 B.C.). Although he fought some nine military campaigns that advanced the sphere of Assyrian control or influence, from Persia on the east to Arabia and Egypt on the south and southwest, he was largely the heir of the accomplishments of the great Sargonid kings who preceded him. Accordingly, Ashurbanipal could increasingly turn his attention to such internal matters as great building projects, religious pursuits, and the cultivation of the Assyrian *beaux arts* and *belles lettres*. Indeed, his reign was the zenith of an Assyrian imperialism, cultural flowering, and socio-political system that spanned the length and breadth of the Fertile Crescent and has been termed the *Pax Assyriaca.*

The land of Judah, which had resisted successfully a formal takeover by King Sennacherib of Assyria during the days of Hezekiah (2 Kings 18-19; 2 Chron. 32:1-23; Isa. 36-37), had also been able to maintain its independence during the reign of Sennacherib's son Esarhaddon (681-668 B.C.). Manasseh (698/97-640 B.C.) then ruled over Judah and was evil to the point of total apostasy. His early spiritual degradation is carefully detailed in the Scriptures (2 Kings 21:1-11, 16; 2 Chron. 33:1-9, 19). Because of his wickedness, the nation of Judah was doomed to divine judgment (2 Kings 21:12-15). Manasseh's capitulation to Ashurbanipal during his first Egyptian campaign (AR 2:876) only plunged him into deeper sin until at last (c. 648 B.C.) his duplicity caused him to be summoned to an audience before the Assyrian king. Ashurbanipal had just subdued his seditious brother Shamash-shum-ukin and was then occupying his brother's base of support in Babylon. After being called there, Manasseh repented and was subsequently released and returned to Judah. But although the Chronicler reports Manasseh's spiritual transformation at that time, few lasting gains were made in Judah despite the reforms that Manasseh attempted. True reform would tarry until the reign of his grandson Josiah (640-609 B.C.).

With the accession of Josiah, Judah's fortunes experienced political, economic, and spiritual reversal. Because the young king was a godly man, his rule was marked by repeated periods of reform and iconoclastic purge. His order for the repair of the Temple in 621 B.C. occasioned the "chance" finding of a copy of the Book of the Law (2 Kings 22:8-13), an event that brought further royally initiated spiritual reforms and religious celebration to Judah (23:1-25; 2 Chron. 34:32–35:19).

By the mid-640s Ashurbanipal's campaigning was over, and he began increasingly to enjoy the fruits of the long years of Assyrian expansion. Ashurbanipal mentions spending much time in the care and aggrandizement of Nineveh. By the last decade of his reign, signs of Assyrian weakness began to surface. Ancient sources suggest that Ashurbanipal himself grew indolent and degenerate. At any rate, with his death in 626 B.C. Assyrian fortunes took a sharp decline. Very shortly the Chaldean Nabopolassar succeeded in gaining independence for Babylon and, having found common cause with the Medes

judge Nineveh and restore His people (2:1-2). All of this is immediately carried forward in a visionary rehearsal of the attack against Nineveh (2:3-10) and is closed by a taunt song in which Assyria is compared to a lion trapped in Nineveh, its own lair (2:11-13). The theme
is developed further in a second description of the fall of Nineveh
(given in the form of a pronouncement woe) but with emphasis upon
the reasons for Nineveh's fall, particularly its lustful rapacity (3:1-7).
This section, too, is closed by a taunt song in which Nineveh is declared to be no better than mighty Thebes. Thebes had boastfully
counted on her basic defensive features, yet her recent fall is known to
all. Accordingly, Nineveh's fate is all the more certain. A sovereign
God is about to judge the Assyrians and Nineveh for their endless
cruelty (3:8-19).

Thus Nahum's central message concerning the doom and demise
of Nineveh proceeds in a bifid structure (1:2-15; 2:1–3:19) that is
patterned in accordance with theme (1:2; 2:1-2), development
(1:2-10; 2:3-10; 3:1-7), and application (1:11-15; 2:11-13; 3:8-19).
Nahum closes each major section (1:15; 3:18-19), as well as two subsections (2:13; 3:7), with a refrain concerning the activity/inactivity
of a messenger.

This bifurcation of theme finds corroboration in the canonical
form of the book. The author has developed his work in accordance
with principles of compilation and composition known to the Semitic
world and demonstrably practiced by the Old Testament writers.[4] In
addition to the wedding of structure with theme and development
mentioned above, Nahum makes good use of such compilational
techniques as bookending/enveloping to enclose whole sections (e.g.,
"scattering"—2:1; 3:18-19), subsections (בְּלִיַּעַל [bĕliyya'al], "wick-
ed(ness)"—1:11, 15), and even individual cola (יהוה [YHWH], "Yah-
weh/The LORD"—1:3). He also employs hooking/stitching to link together the distinctive units at various levels. That the major
subsections are thus connected may be seen in that the opening statement of theme (1:2) is hooked to the following thematic development
via the catchword "LORD" and the theme of divine wrath (1:3-10); the
idea of plotting links 1:3-10 with 1:11-15, and "destroying" binds
1:11-15 and 2:1-2. Further hooks can be shown to link the following
units: attacking (2:1-2; 2:3-10), plundering (2:3-10; 2:11-13), "chariots" and the phrase "I am against you" (2:11-13; 3:1-7), and death
and destruction (3:1-7; 3:8-19). Hooking words (stitch words) or ideas
also connect not only major sections but also subsections (e.g., "fire,"
3:13, 15).

---

4. See my discussion in R. D. Patterson and M. E. Travers, "Literary Analysis
and the Unity of Nahum," *GTJ* 9 (1988): 48-50.

In addition to the previously mentioned instances of refrain to mark major sections or subsections, Nahum at times employs refrain and repetition to signal either the beginning or ending of a smaller unit. Examples include "not (again)/no (one)" (1:15; 2:9, 13; 3:3, 7(?), 19), הִנֵּה (*hinnēh*), "behold/lo" (1:15; 2:13; 3:5, 13), the motif of "fire" that "consumes" (1:6, 10; 2:3, 13; 3:13, 15), and the use of rhetorical question (1:6; 2:11; 3:8, 19).

Both broad types of literary form are attested in this short prophecy: prose (e.g., 2:1-10) and poetry (e.g., 1:2-10). There is also an abundance of literary tropes and features, such as metaphor and simile (1:3*b*, 6, 10, 13; 2:4, 7, 8, 11-13; 3:4, 5-6, 12, 13, 15, 17, 18, 19), synecdoche (2:4, 10, 13; 3:13), picturesque brevity (2:1, 9, 10*b*; 3:2-3), rhetorical question (1:6; 2:11; 3:8, 19), irony (2:1, 8; 3:14, 15), satire (2:11-13; 3:8-13, 14-19), woe (3:1-7), enjambment (2:12; 3:7), chiasm (1:2; 3:1-7), staircase parallelism (3:15), terraced parallelism (1:2), pivot-pattern parallelism (2:4), an acrostic poem (1:2-10), and numerous examples of alliteration and assonance that can be seen in the Hebrew text (e.g., 1:2-3*a*, 4*b*, 5; 2:1, 2, 6-7, 9, 11, 12, 13; 3:4, 7, 10, 18). Though this is not an exhaustive list of Nahum's literary devices, it is obvious not only that they span the entire length of the book (thereby arguing for the unity of the whole prophecy) but that his praise as a poet is well deserved. Bewer remarks: "Nahum was a great poet. His word pictures are superb, his rhetorical skill is beyond praise."[5] J. M. P. Smith observes:

> Though the rhythm and metre of Nahum are not so smooth and regular as is the case with some Heb. prophets, yet in some respects the poetry of Nahum is unsurpassed in the OT. His excellence is not in sublimity of thought, depth of feeling, purity of motive, or insight into truth and life. It is rather in his descriptive powers. He has an unexcelled capacity to bring a situation vividly before the mind's eye. . . . Accurate and detailed observation assists in giving his pictures verisimilitude. Lowth rightly said, "Ex omnibus minoribus prophetis nemo videtur aequare sublimitatem, ardorem et audaces spiritus Nahumi."[6]

It can be said with good reason, then, that Nahum was the poet laureate among the Minor Prophets.

Even more important for exegetes of the book is the realization that Nahum's literary skill is not merely a display of his craftsmanship for his readers or a means of enlivening an otherwise colorless statement. Rather, his literary figures not only assist and enrich the understanding of the meaning of the text but are the very form

---

5. J. A. Bewer, *The Literature of the Old Testament*, 3d ed. (New York: Columbia U., 1962), p. 147.
6. J. M. P. Smith, *A Critical and Exegetical Commentary on Micah, Zephaniah and Nahum*, ICC (Edinburgh: T. & T. Clark, 1911), pp. 273-74.

and content in which its meaning is to be apprehended. Further, they demand that the reader respond to their message in the totality of his being. One will not appreciate so fine a piece of literature as Nahum's prophecy unless he approaches it with his whole person—intellectually, emotionally, and volitionally, and, above all, in full dependence upon the Holy Spirit.

OUTLINE

In accordance with its theme, development, and structural guidelines, the book may be outlined as follows:

Superscription (1:1)
I. The Doom of Nineveh Declared (1:2-15 [HB 1:2–2:1])
   A. Theme: God Is a God of Justice Who Will Punish the Wicked and Avenge His Own (1:2)
   B. Development: A Hymn to the Sovereign God (1:2-10)
      1. Who defeats His foes (1:2-6)
      2. Who destroys the plotters (1:7-10)
   C. Application: God's Justice for Nineveh and Judah (1:11-15 [HB 1:11–2:1])
II. The Doom of Nineveh Described (2:1–3:19 [HB 2:2–3:19])
   A. Theme: God Is a Just Governor of the Nations Who Will Punish Wicked Nineveh and Restore His Own (2:1-2 [HB 2:2-3])
   B. Development: First Description of Nineveh's Demise (2:3-10 [HB 2:4-11])
   C. Application: The Discredited City (2:11-13 [HB 2:12-14])
   D. Development: Second Description of Nineveh's demise (3:1-7)
   E. Application: The Defenseless Citadel (3:8-19)
      1. A comparison of Nineveh and Thebes (3:8-13)
      2. A concluding condemnation of Nineveh (3:14-19)

UNITY

Every one of the forty-seven verses of this short prophecy has been attacked by higher critics as being spurious. Contemporary critical scholarship tends to hold that at least one-third of the material was written by someone other than Nahum. Special targets for the attack center in parts of the title, the acrostic poem (1:2-10), the "hopeful sayings" (1:12-13; 2:1, 3), and the closing dirge (3:18-19). The result has been a rather uniform denial of the unity of the book.[7]

---

7. For details, see Bewer, *Literature*, p. 147; Smith, *Nahum*, pp. 268-70; R. H. Pfeiffer, *Introduction to the Old Testament* (New York: Harper, 1941), pp. 594-95; G. A. Smith, *The Book of the Twelve Prophets*, rev. ed. (New York: Doubleday, 1929), 2:81-88.

All of this, however, rests on the shakiest of premises. The rejection of part of the superscription because it is a double title flies in the face of the same phenomenon elsewhere (e.g., Hos. 1:1, 2; Amos 1:1; Mic. 1:1; cf. Isa. 13:1). The supposedly interpolated acrostic hymn of praise can be seen as part and parcel of the message and development of the entire book and integral to the words directed toward Nineveh and Judah that follow (1:11-15). Rejecting the genuineness of the "hopeful sayings" would necessitate doing so in virtually every prophetic book, for the prophets uniformly combine condemnation and comfort in their messages. It must be added that the messages of hope in Nahum depend not only on the process of Nineveh/Assyria's downfall but also on God's use of nations, which He will ultimately judge, to bring conditions favorable to Judah's restoration. Judgment and hope are thus inextricably intertwined; both are integral to the theme, development, and applications found in the book. The attempt of several critics to deny the closing dirge to Nahum is subjective at best and erroneous in fact, for it forms a proper ending refrain not only to the previous taunt song (3:8ff.) but also to the entire second half of the book (2:1–3:19).

The various denials of the unity of the book are thus arbitrary and without foundation. As the previous discussion has shown, a demonstrable unity of theme and development is wedded to the structure of the entire prophecy. Further, there is thematic unity to the book in the author's employment of several key words and at least ten literary motifs sprinkled throughout.[8] Indeed, Nahum's literary genius has enabled him to write a carefully composed and tightly structured prophecy that is unsurpassed by any of the writing prophets. The logical conclusion is that the book of Nahum is a unified literary piece, the product of one skilled author—the prophet Nahum.

OCCASION AND PURPOSE

It would seem apparent that it was revealed to Nahum, who lived in the dark times of the wicked Manasseh and witnessed the reduction of his nation to vassalage during the early campaigns of Ashurbanipal (which eventuated in the fall of Thebes), that Israel's God was yet in control of earth's history and still its sovereign despite all that had so recently come to pass. Further, these events were but a prelude and a means to the judgment of both Judah and Nineveh and were, in turn, part of the process that would accomplish the restoration of God's people. Accordingly Nahum writes his short prophecy (1) to

---

8. See Carl E. Armerding, "Nahum," in *EBC* (Grand Rapids: Zondervan, 1985), 7:451-52.

announce the doom of Nineveh and the demise of the mighty Assyrian empire and (2) to bring a message of consolation to a sin-weary and oppressed Judah.

Some critical scholars, however, have suggested that Nahum's writings originated as part of a liturgical celebration (von Rad). Various forms of this view exist, with some (Humbert) postulating that the prophecy was composed for use in a liturgical setting at a New Year's festival celebrating Nineveh's capture in 612 b.c. The opening hymn and those verses containing rhetorical questions have been cited as proof of a series of solo recitatives and antiphonal responses designed to dramatize the fall and destruction of Nineveh. Others (Sellin, Fohrer) isolate several separate liturgical fragments or find a celebration of late liturgical poems commemorating the event. (Haupt even suggests that two of the conjectured four poems were written as late as the Maccabean era.) A further variation proposes that this prophetic material had much in common with Near Eastern mythological motifs celebrating the death and revivification of a cult god that were dramatized in an annual festival, especially in Mesopotamia, and adapted for use in the worship of Yahweh (Haldar, Mowinckel).[9]

All such theories, ingenious as some may be, are foundationless (only 1:15 bears any resemblance to a liturgical observance) and fail to deal adequately with the fact that Nahum's prophecy looks forward to the distant fall of Nineveh and bears little resemblance to such celebrations as the Babylonian *Akītu* festival. Such theories attest the stubborn persistence of a sort of pan-Babylonianism that has increasingly been rejected by Assyriologists and Biblicists of all persuasions. Thus H. W. F. Saggs declares, "The extravagant and indiscriminate enthusiasm with which its proponents argued for the Pan-Babylonian Hypothesis led to its rejection, both from the Old Testament and from the Assyriological side, though it did not pass without leaving some effects upon the course of Biblical Studies."[10]

TEXT AND CANONICITY

The MT of Nahum is especially well preserved, with possible corruptions being cited in few places (e.g., 1:4*b*; 3:18). Cathcart's pronouncement remains true:

Recently discovered witnesses of the text of Nahum, including the Pesher

---

9. For details, see Ralph L. Smith, *Micah–Malachi*, WBC (Waco, Tex.: Word, 1984), pp. 65-67.
10. H. W. F. Saggs, *Assyriology and the Study of the Old Testament* (Cardiff: U. of Wales, 1969), p. 13.

of Nahum (4QpNah) found at Qumran; the Hebrew scroll of the Minor Prophets from Wadi Murabba'ât, and fragments of a Greek text of the Minor Prophets from Naḥal Hever, indicate that the consonantal text found in the Hebrew Bible today has been handed down with incredible accuracy for nearly two thousand years at least.[11]

Most critical suggestions therefore deal with such details as proper pointing or word division rather than with the reading of the consonantal text and revolve around matters of Semitic cognates and questions of Northwest Semitic grammar. Reference to the LXX and Syriac versions has proved to be of limited value.

The canonicity of the book has never been seriously questioned. Its prevalence among biblical manuscripts from the intertestamental period, its utilization by the sectaries at Qumran as a source for application to certain events in their own day (probably in the days of the Jewish priest/king Alexander Jannaeus [103-76 B.C.] and Demetrius III, king of Syria [c. 95-83 B.C.]), and its employment by the early church Fathers (e.g., Tertullian, Lucian) give witness to its acceptance and usage. Doubtless it was known to the apostle Paul as well (cf. Rom. 10:15 with Isa. 52:7; Nah. 1:15). These facts concerning the canonicity of Nahum are in harmony with Beckwith's conclusion:

> Looking back over all this evidence (nearly the whole of which dates from before the 'Council' of Jamnia, where the Jewish canon is usually supposed to have been closed), one notes that, with the exception of the three short books Ruth, Song of Songs and Esther, the canonicity of every book of the Hebrew Bible is attested, most of them several times over.[12]

THEOLOGICAL CONTEXT

Perhaps the most basic theological perspective of Nahum is that of God's sovereignty. God is seen as supreme over nature (1:4-6, 8), nations (1:15; 2:1, 3-7)—including Nineveh/Assyria (1:11-12a, 14; 2:8-10, 11-13; 3:5-7, 11-19), Judah (1:12b-13; 2:2), and Thebes/Egypt (3:8-10)—and all people (1:3, 6, 7-10). As a sovereign God He is also the controller of earth's history (1:12; 2:13; 3:5-7), who moves in just judgment against His foes (1:2-3a, 8-10, 14; 2:13; 3:5-7, 11-19) but with saving concern for those who put their trust in Him (1:7-8a, 12b-13, 15; 2:2). God is shown also to be a God of revelation (1:1) who, although He is a jealous (1:2) and omnipotent God (1:3) who abhors

---

11. Kevin J. Cathcart, *Nahum in the Light of Northwest Semitic* (Rome: Biblical Institute Press, 1973), p. 13.
12. Roger Beckwith, *The Old Testament Canon of the New Testament Church* (Grand Rapids: Eerdmans, 1985), p. 76.

sin (3:4-6, 19), is also long-suffering (1:3) and good (1:7) and has distinct purposes for His redeemed people.

In that regard, many have suggested that in adapting Isaiah's messianic promise (Isa. 52:7) to his message concerning Nineveh's downfall (Nah. 1:15), Nahum understands that God's dealings with Judah and Assyria were part of His teleological purposes in the Messiah. In any case, it is certain that the messianic import of Nah. 1:15 was utilized by the early church and has brought comfort to the saints throughout the succeeding ages, who, while keeping their spiritual exercises, look forward with confidence and in expectation to that One who shall reign in righteousness and execute perfect peace.

One final note might be raised with regard to Nahum's theological perspective. For in employing such literary devices as satire (2:11-13; 3:8-13, 14-17) and woe (3:1-7) to predict the doom of Nineveh, his language borders on the use of imprecation and is thus reminiscent of the tone of many psalms (e.g., Pss. 35, 58, 59, 69, 83, 109, and 139). The problem with all such cases is as J. G. Vos points out, "How can it be right to wish or pray for the destruction or doom of others?"[13]

A number of solutions may be suggested. (1) The prayers are uttered by men of faith who are concerned not for personal vengeance but for God's holy reputation. Thus C. K. Lehman, who says, "The defeat of Israel would be a reproach to God's name."[14] (2) Such men wrote under the influence of the Holy Spirit and were looking at the whole situation from God's point of view. Gleason Archer remarks,

> As long as the wicked continued to triumph their prosperity seemed to refute the holiness and sovereignty of the God of Israel. A Hebrew believer in the Old Testament age could only chafe in deep affliction of soul as long as such a state of affairs continued. Identifying himself completely with God's cause, he could only regard God's enemies as his own, and implore God to uphold His own honor and justify His own righteousness by inflicting a crushing destruction upon those who either in theory or in practice denied His sovereignty and His law.[15]

(3) The imprecator shared God's hatred of sin and longed to see God's righteousness vindicated. Numerous cries in the Psalms (e.g., Pss. 7:9; 28; 45:1, 13; 59:13; 69:6; 139:23-24) as well as several places in Job, Proverbs, and Ecclesiastes attest this truth. (4) The imprecator was concerned with a *"zeal for God and God's kingdom. . . . And as he*

---

13. J. G. Vos, "The Ethical Problem of the Imprecatory Psalms," *WTJ* 4 (1942): 123.
14. C. K. Lehman, *Biblical Theology* (Scottsdale, Pa.: Herald, 1971), 1:439.
15. Gleason Archer, Jr., *A Survey of Old Testament Introduction*, rev. ed. (Chicago: Moody, 1974), pp. 452-53.

was God's representative, his enemies . . . must be accounted the enemies of God himself and his cause on earth."[16] (5) Such prayers are often evangelistic. Although they justly denounce the enemies of God and invoke His wrath against them, they at times provide a sounding board for the God who cares for the souls of all men and peoples (cf. Ps. 58:11; Jonah 4:11). (6) Imprecations can be in part *"prophetic teachings as to the attitude of God toward sin and impenitent and persistent sinners."*[17] They remind their hearers that a holy God will yet put down all personal and corporate sin and reign in righteousness over all the earth. (7) The judgment of the wicked and the vindication of the faithful would "provide an opportunity for the righteous to praise God ([Pss.] 7:17; 35:18, 28)."[18]

It is evident that Nahum's outlook on the fate of wicked Nineveh bears a strong resemblance to that of the imprecators. It is a good Lord who must and will take vengeance, not Nahum or his people (1:2-4, 7, 14; 2:13; 3:5-6). Essentially it is God's sovereign authority and reputation for righteousness that are at stake in Judah's controversy with Nineveh (1:2-6). Nineveh's idolatry, rapacity, inordinate pride, and endless cruelty were so great that they called for divine intervention (1:11, 14; 2:11-13; 3:4-7, 19). Indeed such would give the prospect of genuine peace, rejoicing, and the renewed opportunity to worship God in perpetuity (1:7-8, 12-13, 15; 3:19).

If Nahum's words seem harsh, then, it is because he must use appropriate literary convention to express the seriousness of the situation. As one who understands the divine perspective and senses the issues in God's teleology that are at stake, he cannot do otherwise. For while "the Lord is good" (1:7, NIV) and patient, He "will surely not leave (the guilty) unpunished" (1:3). Whatever they plot against the Lord, "He will make an end (of it); trouble will not arise a second time" (1:9). Nahum's assurances reinforce the twin truths of God's justice against sinners and care for "those who seek refuge in him" (1:7), at the same time looking forward longingly to that final message of good news when the Ninevehs of this world have been silenced and believing people may live in peace and everlasting felicity.

---

16. Chalmers Martin, "Imprecations in the Psalms," in *Classical Evangelical Essays in Old Testament Interpretation*, ed. W. C. Kaiser, Jr. (Grand Rapids: Baker, 1972), pp. 123-24. For his excellent discussion, see pp. 128-30.
17. Martin, "Imprecations," p. 128.
18. J. Carl Laney, "A Fresh Look at the Imprecatory Psalms," *BS* 138 (1981): 44. Laney's treatment (e.g., pp. 35, 45) is particularly penetrating and should be consulted in any study of imprecation. Martin's remarks on the subject are also highly beneficial.

1

The Doom of Nineveh Declared (Nahum 1:1-15 [HB 1:1–2:1])

Nahum begins his prophecy with a notice of its central focus—Nineveh (1:1)—and then turns his attention to a description of Nineveh's certain doom (1:2-15; see n. 2 in the introduction). Throughout the book Nahum's prophecies deal with Nineveh's doom, its eventual defeat, and its destruction. In the opening section, doom is declared to be certain, because it has been decreed by the sovereign and just Judge of the world, who deals equitably with all.

Nahum begins his prophecy with a two-part hymn that sets forth the theme of the section and depicts selected key elements of God's nature. The hymn emphasizes that God is a God of justice who will punish the wicked and avenge His own (1:2). Further, He is a sovereign and mighty God who, although He is long-suffering, will defeat His guilty foes (1:3-6) and who, though He is beneficent, will destroy those who plot against Him (1:7-10). The rehearsal of these general truths concerning the character and work of God provides a foundation for their application to the world situation of Nahum's day. Nineveh, the plotter against and afflicter of God's people, will experience the just judgment of God, while a previously punished Judah will know relief from affliction and be restored to peace and joy (1:11-15).

In recording his opening prophetic remarks Nahum uses several literary devices. In addition to the initial double psalm of praise (1:2-10), the first chapter displays chiasmus (1:2, 3), terraced structure (1:2), and various forms of paronomasia, including plays on words (1:2, 3, 15), sounds (1:2, 3, 4*b*, 10), and even letters (', *n*, *q*

[1:2-3*a*], *g* [1:5], *s* [1:10], *ṣ* [1:15]). Metaphor (1:3), simile (1:6), and rhetorical question (1:6*a*, 10) are also in evidence.

Critical scholars have recognized in the majestic hymn to Yahweh in 1:2-10 the skeleton of an acrostic poem added by a later editor that has suffered some corruption and displacement in the course of transmission. Thus, for example, J. M. P. Smith places v. 2*b* after v. 9 in order to have an *n* line in proper place. He also drops v. 3*a* as a gloss. Because varying results have been arrived at by different scholars[1] in recasting the proposed acrostic, most conservative commentators have rejected the theory altogether.[2] But the hymnic nature of vv. 2-10 is undeniable. Though it may be impossible to recover the "lost acrostic" with demonstrable certainty, the task may not be totally without merit. As I have pointed out elsewhere,

> if, then, rather than resorting to wild emendations and wholesale transpositions one views the beginning and ending of the canonical poem to be deliberately weighted so as to form a distinct frame for the psalm, a fairly consistent picture emerges: *aleph*, six lines (vv. 2-3*a*), *beth—yodh*, two lines each, and eight lines of *kaph* (perhaps to balance the six lines of *aleph* plus the two lines of superscription). The point would be that in Nahum's acrostic arrangement, the prescribed letter of the alphabet need only occur within (not necessarily only as the first letter of the first word; cf. *zayin* and *yodh* lines) the line, although in several cases there is a deliberate concatenation of the letter in question in the line(s) devoted to it.[3]

The data may be conveniently tabulated in the following chart:

Verses	Letter	Lines	Occurrences
1-3*a*	*aleph*	6(+)2	6(+)2
3*b*	*beth*	2	3
4*a*	*gimel*	2	1
4*b*	*daleth*	2	(1)‡
5*a*	*he*	2	3
5*b*	*waw*	2	4
6*a*	*zayin*	2	1
6*b*	*ḥeth*	2	1
7*a*	*ṭeth*	2	1
7*b*-8*a*	*yodh*	2	1
8*b*-10	*kaph*	8	7

‡Accomplished via text-critical methods.

1. See the discussion in J. M. P. Smith, *Micah, Zephaniah, and Nahum*, ICC (Edinburgh: T & T Clark, 1911), pp. 295-97.
2. See, e.g., Gleason Archer, *A Survey of Old Testament Introduction* (Chicago: Moody, 1974), p. 353. See also Walter A. Maier, *The Book of Nahum* (Grand Rapids: Baker, 1980), pp. 52-62.
3. R. D. Patterson and Michael E. Travers, "Literary Analysis and the Unity of Nahum," *GTJ* 9 (1988): 56-57; see also Hummel, *The Word Becoming Flesh* (St. Louis: Concordia, 1979), p. 339.

SUPERSCRIPTION (1:1)

Translation

An oracle concerning Nineveh;
The book of the vision of Nahum the Elkoshite.

Exegesis and Exposition

The superscription to Nahum's prophecy is unusual in that it is doubly constructed. The prophecies that follow are termed both מַשָּׂא (*maśśā'*, "an oracle"*) and חָזוֹן (*ḥăzôn*, "a vision"). Because the former term is derived from the Hebrew verb נָשָׂא (*nāśā'*, "lift up"), two meanings have traditionally been assigned to the derived noun: (1) "burden" and (2) "oracle." Those who favor the first translation (e.g., Calvin, Hengstenberg, Keil, Luther, Maier) call attention to the more natural reading of the root in the idea of a burden that is carried, whether that of animals (2 Kings 5:17) or men (Jer. 17:21, 22; cf. Deut. 1:12), and to the customary following of the term by an objective genitive ("the burden of/concerning X"). Those who take the noun to mean something like "oracle," "utterance," or simply "prophecy" (e.g., Laetsch, E. J. Young) point out that the term is used often to introduce nonburdensome prophecies (e.g., Zech. 12:1; Mal. 1:1) and that the associated verb is used of speaking in such cases as lifting up the voice (Isa. 3:7; 42:11), of lifting/taking up a parable (Num. 23:7), proverb (Isa. 14:4), prayer (Isa. 37:4), lamentation (Amos 5:1), or the name of God (Ex. 20:7).[4] The strength of the Ugaritic parallels as well as the many biblical examples of *nāśā'* used in a context of "lifting up the voice" appear to tip the weight in favor of the latter suggestion. Thus Barker remarks:

> The verb is used of lifting up or uttering a *māšāl* ("oracle") in Numbers 23:7, 18; 24:3, 15, 20, 21, 23, and of lifting up the voice (NIV, "shouted") in Judges 9:7 ("voice" is omitted from the Hebrew idiom in Isa 3:7; 42:2). *Nāśā'*, then, means not only "to carry," hence the meaning "burden" for *maśśā'*, but also "to lift up" in a more general sense. Therefore *maśśā'* could refer to the "lifting up" of the voice—i.e., to utter an oracle, hence the meaning "oracle."[5]

By also calling his prophecy a vision, Nahum underscores the fact that what he says is not of his own invention but is that which God has specially revealed to him (cf. Num. 24:4, 16; 2 Chron. 32:32; Isa. 2:1; Dan. 2:26; 4:10 [HB 4:7]; Amos 1:1; Obad. 1; cf. Mic. 1:1). At the

---

4. See Kevin J. Cathcart, *Nahum in the Light of Northwest Semitic* (Rome: Biblical Institute Press, 1973), pp. 36-37; KB-3 2:604.
5. Kenneth L. Barker, "Zechariah," in *EBC* (Grand Rapids: Zondervan, 1985), 7:657; see also W. C. Kaiser, Jr., "נָשָׂא," *TWOT* 2:602.

outset, then, Nahum makes clear that his words were not his own insights based upon his observations of the events of his time. Rather, they were nothing less than the message given to him by the sovereign God whose Word he must deliver, however difficult it might be.

Nahum's prophecy is directed at Nineveh.* The mention of Nineveh in the superscription is significant in that without this notation the direction of the message of the entire first chapter could be unclear. Indeed, Nineveh is not specifically named in the original text until 2:9 (English 2:8). The inclusion of the Assyrian capital in the superscription, therefore, identified the object of the announcement of God's judgment with which the book begins.

Additional Notes

1:1 The term מַשָּׂא can stand at the head of individual oracles (e.g., Isa. 13:1; 14:28; 15:1; 17:1; 19:1; 21:1, 11, 13; 22:1; 23:1; 30:6; Ezek. 12:10; Zech. 9:1; 12:1) or whole books (e.g., Hab. 1:1; Mal. 1:1), as here. Nahum takes his place beside Isaiah (13:1) and Habakkuk (1:1) in linking מַשָּׂא with some form of the root חזה ("see"; cf. Lam. 2:14). Perhaps the latter root[6] and its derivatives, while dealing primarily with the communication of received revelation, also imply that the prophet or חֹזֶה ("seer") was one who as God's chosen servant saw things from God's point of view and attempted to get others to see them too.[7] The word "seer" may further indicate that Nahum was allowed a visionary foreglimpse of Nineveh's actual siege and fall.[8]

The appearance of the double title has caused many to question the authenticity of the superscription and to carry their suspicions to other portions of the book as well.[9] As Maier points out, however, the parts of the double title complement one another and are, in any case, similarly paralleled in the headings to Amos, Micah, and Isaiah's prophecy against Babylon (Isa. 13:1).

Nineveh: Because the name of the Assyrian capital occurs in the superscription, the NIV has not gone beyond the bounds of translational propriety in inserting "Nineveh" into the text in at least three places before 2:8 (HB v. 9) (1:11, 14; 2:1 [HB v. 2]). Similar to this

---

6. See A. Jepsen, "חזה," *TDOT* 4:280-90.
7. See further Abraham J. Heschel, *The Prophets* (New York: Harper & Row, 1962), 1:24.
8. See the additional note at Hab. 1:1 and the discussion of C. F. Keil, *The Twelve Minor Prophets*, COT (Grand Rapids: Eerdmans, 1954), 2:9.
9. See the discussion in J. M. P. Smith, *Nahum*, p. 285. Many scholars suggest that part of Nahum's oracles are "vision reports"; see M. Sister, "Die Typen der prophetischen Visionen in der Bibel," *MGWJ* 78 (1934): 399-430; A. S. Van der Woude, *Jona, Nahum: Prediking Old Testament* (Nijkerk: Callenbach, 1978), p. 97.

insertion at obvious places is the NIV inclusion of "O Judah" at 1:12, a text that clearly anticipates the statement of 1:15 (HB 2:1). The NIV could just as well have read "Nineveh" rather than "the city" at 2:7 (HB v. 8).

Like Obadiah, who prophesied against Edom, Nahum's prophecy is single-minded, envisioning the judgment of but one city/nation— Nineveh/Assyria. Unlike the slim hope that Obadiah holds out for Edom at the last (vv. 19-21), Nahum has no such comfort for Nineveh.

סֵפֶר ("book"): Keil's suggestion that the inclusion of the word "book" in the superscription indicates that the prophecy was written but never delivered orally is perhaps an overstatement. The use of the term may simply suggest that Nahum's burdensome vision, whether delivered orally or not, has now under divine inspiration been committed to a permanent record that all may read (cf. Hab. 2:2).

Nahum: H. Hummel suggests that the meaning of Nahum's name ("comfort") is quite apropos:

> It may be accidental (some critics think it deliberately artificial), but the name "Nahum" superbly summarizes the book's message. God's justice means judgment on the enemy, but "comfort" to the faithful. The book thus exemplifies the role which "Gentile oracles" play in all the prophets. The point is not that God's people go scot-free, but precisely the reverse: if God so judges those whom He employs temporarily as instruments of His judgment upon His unfaithful people, how much more fearful the judgment upon His own people if they finally miss the message.[10]

For the term "Elkoshite," see the introduction under Authorship. It may be added here that there seems to be little warrant for following Schulz's conjecture that the second half of the superscription ("the book of the vision of Nahum the Elkoshite") indicates the existence of a postexilic author who, basing his own redaction on an earlier poem aimed at the doom of Nineveh, whose fall he saw as related to an eschatological process that means salvation for Israel, created a final edition that both spoke to the situation of his own day and was intended to be read as a whole in a worship ceremony.[11]

A. THEME (1:2)

Nahum's prophecy begins with an indication of its theme: God is a God of justice who will punish the wicked and avenge His own (1:2). That theme dominates not only the hymnic material in which it is set (1:2-10) but also the whole first section of the book (1:2-15).

---

10. Hummel, *The Word*, p. 342.
11. Hermann Schulz, *Das Buch Nahum* (Berlin: Walter de Gruyter, 1973), pp. 67, 131-33.

Translation

A jealous* God
  and an avenger is Yahweh;
Yahweh is an avenger
  and Lord of wrath.
An avenger is Yahweh to His foes,
  and He is a keeper* (of wrath) against His enemies.

Exegesis and Exposition

The words that form both the opening lines of Nahum's hymn of praise and the statement of theme of that hymn as well as the whole first section are punctuated by the threefold repetition of the name of Yahweh over four lines of poetry dealing with God's avenging wrath: (1) Yahweh is a jealous God and an avenger; (2) Yahweh is an avenger and Lord of wrath; (3) Yahweh is an avenger against His foes and is a keeper of wrath against His enemies (1:2). He is described at the outset as being a "jealous and avenging God" (NIV). The first term can be understood here either in the sense of being jealous or of being zealous. The latter idea appears to be the original significance from which either the positive (zeal, jealousy) or negative (envy) connotations arose. Normally its use with God and Israel rests upon the basis of the covenant, especially as expressed by the figure of the marriage relationship.* As a jealous husband, Israel's covenant God abhors spiritual adultery (cf. Ex. 20:4-5; 34:14; Deut. 4:23-24; 5:8-9 with Jer. 2:1–3:5; Ezek. 16:35-42; 23:25). Indeed, a jealous God's righteous wrath would one day effect an apostate people's judgment and exile from the land (cf. Deut. 6:13-15; Josh. 24:19-20; Ps. 79:5). In all of this, however, God's jealous wrath is also maintained for action on behalf of His own, particularly after they have repented and so been restored to His favor (Isa. 59:17; Ezek. 5:13; 36:6-7; 38:17-23; 39:25-29; Zeph. 3:8-17; Zech. 8:2-3).

Nahum's employment of the idea of jealousy, then, is in harmony with the familiar scriptural motif of the husband and the wife. This motif is often applied to God's relation to Israel. Israel had been the object of God's eternal love. She had been brought into the family of God in the Exodus from Egypt. He had cared for her and nourished her in the testings of the wilderness and had brought her safely into the land of inheritance. Well did God recall her total devotion and the loving warmth and pristine purity of those early wedding days. Living in the land of promise, a thoughtful and happy wife ought to have been what God had intended her to be: holy to the Lord (Jer. 2:2-3). But such scarcely had been the case. Jeremiah 2:4–3:5 recounts the sorry tale of the bride who had become God's wayward wife.

Jeremiah's portrayal of the spiritual odyssey of Israel/Judah is in harmony with the same theme sung by other prophets. Hosea's marriage was to picture God's relation to Israel. It emphasized that Israel's wanton apostasy would gain her only the loss of her freedom, until God would pay the price for her sin and bring her back to Himself in the latter days (Hos. 1–3).

Isaiah (Isa. 54:4-17) relates that Israel had been forsaken by God because of her wickedness. Nevertheless she was yet God's wife and, as a repentant nation, would yet be forgiven and regathered in righteousness and so enjoy the everlasting acceptance and protection of her divine husband.

Ezekiel 16 is devoted to the same theme. Jerusalem is likened to a bride (v. 8) who had become a brazen harlot (vv. 15, 43), even outdoing Sodom in her iniquity (vv. 44-52). Because she had broken her marriage oath, she incurred God's chastisement (vv. 53-59). But God, a forgiving and loyal husband, would yet receive her back and remove her humiliation forever (vv. 60-63).

It is no surprise, then, that the theme of the bride is taken up again by Christ and the apostles, whose Bible was largely still the Old Testament. The relationship now, however, is between Christ and the church (cf. Mark 2:19) and, as such, complements the relationship of God the Father with Israel.

Paul reminds the Ephesians that Christ loved the church as a husband loves his bride. Accordingly He sacrificed Himself for her so that she might be pure and holy and seen in all her God-given beauty (Eph. 5:25-27). Paul rehearses to the Corinthian believers how he (the friend of the bridegroom) had intoduced them (the bride) to Christ (the groom). Although she had been a pure virgin, Paul found that the Corinthian church had been susceptible (like Eve) to the serpent's bite of false gospels. Thus the Corinthians stood in particular need of his ministry to them lest they stray further (2 Cor. 11:1-4).

The Revelation given through John pictures the joy of heaven at the proclamation of that great wedding supper of the Lamb for His waiting bride: "Let us be glad and rejoice and give honor to him; for the marriage of the Lamb *has* come, and his wife has made herself ready" (Rev. 19:7). Certainly it is true that, although she has been wedded to Christ, the church His bride awaits His coming to take her to His home and to the full joy of that festive occasion. Of that coming of the bridegroom, Christ Himself warns a waiting generation to be ready and watching, longing for His coming (Matt. 25:1-13).

Paul reminds his readers, who make up the waiting bride of Christ, that the church is to have a faithful and productive marriage. For that reason she has been married to her saving husband and has become one spirit with Him, her body having become the temple of the Holy Spirit (1 Cor. 6:15-19). As His bride, who both expects His imminent return and is mindful of her union with Christ, the church is to keep herself pure (1 John 3:1-3), remembering the wedding price that Christ Himself has paid (1 Cor. 6:20).

The use of the word "wrath" in the last line of the initial couplet is doubtless designed to form an inclusion with v. 6. It also anticipates Ezekiel's familiar pairing of wrath and jealousy (e.g., Ezek. 16:38; cf. 5:13; 36:6; 38:18-19).

The occurrence here of the set parallel terms אֵל (*'ēl*, "El/God") and בַּעַל (*ba'al*, "Baal/lord") in these lines strengthens the suggestion of a deliberately formed chiasmus designed not only to strike a responsive chord in Nahum's readers but to call attention to the double assertion concerning the Lord's being an avenger that is sandwiched between them. As a God of holiness and justice, God reserves the right of vengeance to Himself. However the course of history might seem to be unfolding, God observes it all and will ultimately take proper action against all sin (cf. Isa. 34:8; 61:2; 63:4). Such the Lord is about to do in the case of Nineveh/Assyria. The three ideas (jealousy, wrath, vengeance) bound together in these opening lines form the groundwork for all of Nahum's prophecy. As a jealous God, Yahweh demands the absolute devotion that the only true and sovereign God deserves; in His righteous wrath, Yahweh alone can and will deal justly with all who sin, even as His justice dictates; and as an avenging God, Yahweh will discipline, defend, or deliver according to the demands of His holiness.

The theme is filled out in two further lines (connected asyndetically and constructed as terraced poetry) elaborating on the centerpiece of the previous chiasmus: Yahweh is an avenger* against His foes and a keeper (of wrath) against His enemies. Because Assyria (represented by Nineveh its capital) will be the focus of Nahum's attention, these words take on a distinctive importance. The previous chiasmus had stressed the fact that Yahweh, a jealous God and Lord of wrath, is an avenger. His vengeance against foes is further underlined here. If, as is well known, God's jealous wrath has brought vengeance against His own apostate Israel, how much more ought those who are not His own—His foes—to fear?

Thus vengeance* becomes a key to unlocking the door of understanding to Nahum's prophecy. In reading of God's vengeance, however, one must not think of the familiar human vindictiveness of spirit so often condemned in the Scriptures (cf. Deut. 32:35; Prov. 25:21-22 with Rom. 12:19-20; Lev. 19:18 with Matt. 19:19). Although God may delegate the operation of vengeance to constituted authority (cf. Num. 31:1; Josh. 10:13; Esther 8:13), it primarily belongs to Him (Deut. 32:35-43; Heb. 10:30-31). Indeed, man is cautioned against a spirit of wrath that can so easily lead to taking vengeance (cf. Eph. 4:26-27). Because God is holy, He cannot let sin go un-punished; because only God is perfectly holy and just, as well as all-wise, only He can exact the proper punishment (Ps. 94).

The last line of verse 2 is important for understanding the process of God's vengeance: His judicial wrath is not always immediate. At times He holds in reserve His wrath against His foes until the proper occasion. God's government, including His judicial processes, is on schedule, even though to an awaiting mankind His timing may seem to lag. This thought anticipates that of the next line, serving notice that the theme of the book is also the theme of the hymn in which it is located (1:2-10).

Additional Notes

1:2 †קַנּוֹא: Though this adjective appears only here and in Josh. 24:19, קַנָּא occurs five times (Ex. 20:5; 34:14; Deut. 4:24; 5:9; 6:15) and the noun קִנְאָה more than three dozen times, many of which refer to God. Cathcart calls attention to Albright's contention that the out-standing characteristic of God in the prophets was His jealousy and suggests that the use of אֵל and בַּעַל with קַנּוֹא and חֵמָה may be reflective of Canaanite hymnody, wherein El and Baal often occur in paral-lelism. But the fact that Nahum's hymn has similar sentiment to poems ascribed to the Canaanite storm-god could indicate no more than Nahum's considerable literary skill in utilizing old themes in composing his psalm of praise to Yahweh. Certainly there is no need to see wholesale adoption of a Canaanite composition dedicated to Baal, as some suggest.[12] God's own self-assertion is that He is a jeal-ous God (Ex. 20:4; Deut. 5:8).

> Attributing jealousy to the Lord poses no problem, for in OT usage jeal-ousy is but the intolerance of rivalry or unfaithfulness. How one ex-presses that intolerance determines whether or not it is sin. When ap-plied to the Lord, it usually concerns Israel and carries with it the notions of the marriage or covenant relationship and the Lord's right to exclusive possession of Israel.[13]

Nevertheless the double parallelism of קַנּוֹא||חֵמָה and בַּעַל||אֵל to frame an intervening repeated couplet indicates a deliberate chias-mus built upon familiar traditional literary motifs, including Ca-naanite ones. Further, the mention of בַּעַל may have wider connota-tions. In addition to being the name of the Canaanite storm-god, the

---

12. See Theodor H. Gaster, *Thespis* (New York: Harper & Row, 1961), p. 143; J. Gray, "The Hebrew Concept of the Kingship of God: Its Origin and Devel-opment," *VT* 6 (1956): 280.
13. Barker, "Zechariah," in *EBC*, 7:612. See also the discussion in Maier, *Nahum*, pp. 159-60.

25

noun may refer to an owner (Ex. 22:7), master (Isa. 1:3), or ruler (Isa. 16:8). Because Yahweh is redeemed Israel's owner, master, and husband, His wrath can be either spent against her or extended on her behalf. By the word בַּעַל Nahum could also be reporting that despite the rampant idolatry initiated by King Manasseh, Yahweh (not Baal) is the true Lord of the universe (cf. vv. 3*b*-5) who will deal in righteous wrath with sin and rebellion. It may also be a veiled attack on Hadad, the Assyrian storm-god.

The introduction of the last two lines of Nah. 1:2 asyndetically makes the contrast with the preceding chiasmus all the more dramatic. In such cases, a crispness and vividness characteristically attends the author's words. The thought here is that the thrust of God's *vengeance* (v. 2*a*) is immediately to be qualified by seeing that this aspect of His character is aimed at his foes. Even here, however, the emphasis needs to be qualified by the full scriptural teaching concerning God's vengeance, a doctrine that is often misunderstood. Indeed, a complete analysis of the data makes clear that vengeance is often integral to the biblical teaching on grace, mercy, and judgment (e.g., Ex. 20:3-4; Deut. 5:7-8). As Smick (*TWOT* 2:599) so aptly points out:

> The Bible balances the fury of God's vengeance against the sinner with greatness of his mercy on those whom he redeems from sin. God's vengeance must never be viewed apart from his purpose to show mercy. He is not *only* the God of wrath, but must be the God of wrath in order for his mercy to have meaning.

צָר and אֹיֵב: These are recognized set parallel pairs.[14]

†וְנוֹטֵר has been much discussed. Like the preceding "takes vengeance" (NIV), it is technically a participle; God is "a maintainer (of wrath)." In common with the Syriac *něṭar*, the root means basically to "keep," "guard," "maintain" and hence has the same semantic range as Heb. נָצַר (cf. Old Aramaic נְצַר with classical Aramaic נְטַר) and also שָׁמַר with which it occurs in parallel in Jer. 3:5; Amos 1:11. Because נָטַר appears to bear the meaning "be angry," "bear a grudge" in several contexts (e.g., Lev. 19:18; Ps. 103:9; Jer. 3:5, 12), a significance seemingly shared on occasion by its parallel שָׁמַר (Jer. 3:5; Amos 1:11), some scholars have suggested that both verbs know a second root signifying "rage," "be in fury." M. Held has provided impressive evidence that these postulated roots (*šmr* II‖*nṭr* II) are stative verbs, whereas the synonymous pair *šmr* I‖*nṣr* (guard) are transitive. Thus *nṭr* I ("guard") may owe its origin to Aramaic/Syriac נְטַר whereas *nṭr*

---

14. P. B. Yoder, "A-B Pairs and Composition in Hebrew Poetry," *VT* 21 (1971): 475-76.

II may be cognate with the Akkadian *nadāru* ("be angry/furious," "be in rage").[15] But despite the arguments of Held and of such scholars as G. R. Driver[16] and Cathcart, the conclusion of Maier—that all of the suggested instances where *šmr*/*nṭr* seem to be stative are simply cases of elliptical constructions (i.e., the verbs themselves meaning "maintain/reserve," with the idea of anger being supplied by the context)—is on the whole the simplest answer to the problem. It does not need to posit a conjectured root that has undergone phonetic change, and it has the advantage of being contextually more sound in that the traditional meaning anticipates the sentiment of the next verse.

B. DEVELOPMENT: A HYMN TO THE SOVEREIGN GOD (1:2-10)

Having drawn the reader's attention to a sovereign and just God who deals in judgment with the ungodly (v. 2), Nahum develops this theme in a twofold hymn to Yahweh concerning the character and work of God: (1) although the Lord is long-suffering, He will assuredly judge the guilty with all the force that a sovereign God can muster (1:3-6); and (2) although the Lord is good and tenderly cares for the righteous (particularly in times of affliction), He will destroy those who plot against Him (1:7-10).

Verse 2, at once theme and opening hymnic expression, is doubly indicated in the Outline (see introduction) and in the present discussion (i.e., 1:2-6; 1:7-10). After the statement of the thesis, the hymn is developed around two nonverbal sentences setting forth two aspects of Yahweh's character: (1) "The Lord is slow to anger and great in power" (v. 3, NIV); (2) "The Lord is good, a refuge in times of trouble" (v. 7, NIV). These two statements serve as headings to units that amplify the thematic sentiment in v. 2. The two sections thus formed are likewise composed in a similar format: (1) descriptive statement(s) followed by conjunctive *waw;* (2) further development given in controlling introductory forms: prepositional phrase (v. 3*b*), emphatic accusative (v. 8*b*); (3) conclusion marked by rhetorical questions (vv. 6*a*, 9) and figurative reinforcement (vv. 6*b*, 10).

In composing his hymn, Nahum has drawn upon familiar motifs long used in the worship of Yahweh. His indebtedness to the religious literature utilized in the worship of Yahweh can be seen by comparing the hymn with other ascriptions of praise to the Lord. It is evi-

---

15. M. Held, "Studies in Biblical Homonyms in the Light of Akkadian," *JANESCU* 3 (1971): 46-55, as cited by Cathcart, *Nahum,* p. 43.
16. G. R. Driver, "Studies in the Vocabulary of the Old Testament III," *JTS* 36 (1935): 361-66.

dent, for example, that vv. 2-6 are dependent on images and phrases drawn from the epic traditions commemorating the Exodus (a compositional plan also followed by Habakkuk [3:3-15]):

V.	Motif	Texts
2	God is a jealous God	Ex. 30:5; Josh. 24:19
3	God's long-suffering patience	Ex. 34:6, 7
	Theophany in the storm	2 Sam. 22:10; Ps. 68:4 (HB 68:5)
4	God's rebuke of the sea and	2 Sam. 22:16; Ps. 77:16 (HB 77:17);
	drying it up	Hab. 3:15; Ex. 14:21-22
5	Violent shaking of nature	Judg. 5:4-5; 2 Sam. 22:8; Pss. 68:8
		(HB 68:9); 77:18 (HB 77:19);
		114:6; Hab. 3:6
6	God's mighty wrath topples	Ex. 15:14ff.; Hab. 3:10
	the enemy	
	Even rocks burnt	Deut. 32:22

Verses 7-10, however, are drawn largely from various standard expressions in mainstream Israelite theology found in various places in the Psalms and particularly in the prophet Isaiah (esp. Isa. 8). As well, Armerding demonstrates that several prominent ideas found in vv. 2-6 are also held in common with Isaiah (in one instance, Nah. 1:4b, the closest parallel is in Isa. 33:9). Though most of these parallels are somewhat general and may indicate nothing more than that both Isaiah and Nahum were familiar with the same traditional material, Armerding has made an interesting point.[17]

It does seem certain, then, that Nahum's hymn falls into two portions, as seen not only structurally but in the type of material contained in each of the two poetic sections. The first (vv. 2-6), drawn largely from traditional Exodus themes, underscores God's wrath against an unbelieving enemy; the second (vv. 7-10) comes from a wider spectrum of praises to God for His defense of His own, while defeating the enemy. Although his familiarity with Isaiah may account somewhat for the selection of some of the material, it was all at his disposal (as is the case also with Habakkuk), and his own unique genius accounts for its presentation in the form of an acrostic (or semiacrostic) hymn.

1. WHO DEFEATS HIS FOES (1:2-6)

Translation (vv. 3-6)
Yahweh is slow to anger* but great in power
   and will surely not leave (the guilty) unpunished*.
His way is in the whirlwind and the storm,
   and clouds are the dust of His feet.

---

17. Carl E. Armerding, "Nahum," in *EBC*, 7:454-56.

⁴He rebukes the sea and dries it up,
  and He makes all the rivers run dry.
Bashan and Carmel are withered,
  and the flower of Lebanon fades.
⁵The mountains tremble because of Him,
  and the hills melt away*;
also the earth quakes before Him,
  yea, the world* and all who dwell in it.
⁶Before His indignation who can stand?
  And who can endure His fierce anger?
His wrath is poured out like fire,
  and the rocks are shattered by Him.

Exegesis and Exposition

Nahum's opening thesis—that God as a God of justice will punish the wicked and avenge His own—is developed when the prophet notes that this means God will surely defeat His foes. In so arguing Nahum remarks first of all that the Lord is "slow to anger." Although he takes righteous vengeance on His foes (v. 2), this does not always mean instant retaliation. Rather, His justice may be "slow" in coming, for He is a God of infinite patience who has an overriding concern for the souls of people (cf. 2 Pet. 3:9-15). Instructive in understanding God's patience is its appearance in combination with phrases such as "great in lovingkindness" (Ex. 34:6; Num. 14:18; Neh. 9:17; Pss. 86:15; 103:8; 145:8; Joel 2:13). Far from being simply an omnipotent sovereign who executes justice with rigid disinterest, God is a God of truth and love who, because He longs to bring people into a family relationship, abounds in forbearance toward those who deserve only judgment (cf. Ex. 34:6-7).

The concluding part of the sentence, however, keeps a needed balance in proper perspective: Despite His infinite patience (cf. Joel 2:13), a God of truth and justice (Pss. 9:9 [HB 9:10]; 31:5 [HB 31:6]) will not acquit the guilty but must ultimately confront unrepented sin so that justice triumphs in the punishment of the guilty (Ex. 34:7; Num. 14:17-18; Deut. 28:58-68; Isa. 24:14-24; Jer. 30:11; 46:28; Joel 3:4-8, 19 [HB 4:4-8, 19]). Moreover, God is not only just (Rom. 3:26), but as an omnipotent sovereign He has the inherent strength to effect His justice: He is "great in power," as the following lines demonstrate (vv. 3b-6).

The description of God that proceeds in amplifying the statement concerning God's strength contains striking poetic imagery. The tropes found here include metaphor (v. 3b), graphic image (vv. 4-5), rhetorical question (v. 6a), and simile (v. 6b). All are chosen not just for dramatic effect but as the most appropriate form for conveying the author's intended meaning.[18] As poetic devices they intensify the emotive response of the reader by presenting carefully designed word pictures. Thus God's omnipotence and approach are represented by the whirlwind and the storm (v. 3), the earthquake (v. 5), and fire (v. 6). M. Travers's remarks are to the point: "It is through such tropes as the metaphor, image and simile that Nahum establishes the thorough destructiveness, the utter terror of God's wrath: who can withstand him?"[19]

The theophany portrayed in the metaphor of v. 3*b* is a familiar one in the Old Testament: God is the God of the storm. The figure is often utilized for contexts dealing with judgment (e.g., Isa. 29:6; 66:15; Zech. 9:14). Perhaps in contrast to the impotent pagan storm-gods, God had appeared since the time of Israel's redemption out of Egypt and conquest of Canaan as the mighty controller of the tempest and all the forces of nature (Ex. 15:1-18; 19:16-19; Judg. 5:4-5; 2 Sam. 22:8-16; Pss. 68:7-8 [HB 68:8-9]; 77:17-20 [HB 77:18-21]; 144:5-6; Hab. 3:3-15).[20] Therefore Yahweh alone is in control of the natural world as well as of the affairs of mankind (Job 37:1-24; 38:1–42:6; Ps. 104; Acts 17:24-28).

Nahum's description of God's omnipotence and sovereignty that follows is in harmony with mainstream Hebrew orthodoxy and is phrased in familiar imagery: God is in the whirlwind* and the storm* (cf. Ps. 83:16; Isa. 29:6); He treads the lofty clouds* under His feet (cf. Ex. 19:16-19; 2 Sam. 22:10; Pss. 68:5 [HB 68:6]; 97:2; 104:3; Isa. 14:14; 19:1; 66:15; Matt. 24:30; 26:64; Mark 13:26; 14:62; 1 Thess. 4:17; Rev. 1:7); He controls the rivers and seas* (cf. Ex. 14:21-22; 15:8; Judg. 5:21; 2 Sam. 22:16; Pss. 66:6; 77:16 [HB 77:17]; 106:9; 114:3-5; Isa. 42:15; 44:27; 50:2; 51:10; Jer. 51:36; Hab. 3:15); He can make desolate* the most luxurious of lands (e.g., Bashan and Carmel;* cf. Isa. 16:8; 19:7; 29:17; 33:9; 42:15; Jer. 4:26; 48:31-33; Mic. 7:13); the mountains* and earth quake and collapse at His presence (cf. Judg. 5:4-5; 2 Sam. 22:8, 16; Job 28:9; Pss. 46:6 [HB 46:7]; 77:18 [HB 77:19]; 114:4-7; Isa. 13:13; 42:15; 64:11; Jer. 4:24; Joel 3:16 [HB 4:16]; Mic. 1:4; Hab. 3:6, 10; Zech. 14:4) so that the world and its inhabitants are helpless before Him—even the most impenetrable of rocks

---

18. For the statement that metaphor as an example of a trope constitutes meaning, see Paul Ricoeur, "The Metaphorical Process as Cognition, Imagination, and Feeling," in *On Metaphor*, ed. Sheldon Sacks (Chicago: U. of Chicago, 1979), pp. 141-57. Ricoeur's thesis is that metaphor creates meaning rather than embellishes it.
19. Patterson and Travers, "Literary Analysis," p. 51.
20. See further my remarks in "The Song of Deborah," in *Tradition and Testament: Essays in Honor of Charles Lee Feinberg*, ed. John S. Feinberg and Paul D. Feinberg (Chicago: Moody, 1981), pp. 130-31; see further R. D. Patterson, "The Psalm of Habakkuk," *GTJ* 8 (1987): 163-70.

lies shattered before His fiery wrath (cf. Deut. 32:22; 1 Kings 19:11; Jer. 23:29; Matt. 27:51).

In all this Nahum gives a graphic picture of the limitless and invincible power of God. Accordingly he can ask whether any could stand in the face of such an almighty One when He executes His wrath.* The answer is "No one, no one at all!" By implication this anticipates the subject of his prophecy: Not even mighty Nineveh, home of the Assyrian world empire, would be able to withstand the sovereign God of all nature. The Creator, controller, and consummator of this world and its history is the same one who will not leave the guilty unpunished.

Additional Notes

1:3 †אֶרֶךְ אַפַּיִם: This phrase is appropriately translated in LXX in each of the instances cited in the Exegesis and Exposition by the Greek adjective μακρόθυμός ("patient"). The corresponding noun, μακροθυμία ("patience"), is often used in the New Testament. Peter in particular applies the term to God who, in the days of Noah, endured a world of spiritual bankruptcy (1 Pet. 3:20). Peter reports that He similarly delays the great day of judgment so as to prolong the day of salvation (2 Pet. 3:15). Because God is patient, believers ought to be also (cf. Matt. 18:21-25). The Christian has a source of aid in being "long-suffering," for it is a fruit of the Spirit (Gal. 5:22). Not only the Christian minister (2 Cor. 6:6), who most assuredly must develop this trait (1 Tim. 1:16), but every Christian should be marked by godly patience toward all (1 Thess. 5:14), which allows him to walk worthy of his Christian calling (Eph. 4:2; Col. 3:12), thus reproducing in his life the same performance of faith as his spiritual predecessors (Heb. 6:11-12).

It is instructive that in several cases μακροθυμία is juxtaposed with such words as χρηστό(τητο)ς ("[loving]kind[ness]," 2 Cor. 6:6; Gal. 5:22) and ἀγάπη ("love"; 2 Tim. 3:10). God is not only patient; God is love (1 John 4:8). It is no surprise, then, that as Christians are charged to love one another (1 John 4:7-12) they are reminded that true Christian love is characterized by both long-suffering (1 Cor. 13:4) and endurance in all things (13:7). Christians, of all people, ought to be patient. Thus Paul rightly charges believers to "put on love, which is the bond of perfectness" (Col. 3:14).

†The verb נקה ("be innocent") is related to Semitic cognates in Akkadian, Arabic, and Aramaic meaning "be clean/pure" (cf. Dan. 7:9). In the piel stem the verb becomes declarative:[21] "declare inno-

---

21. For the declarative use of the piel stem, see Delbert Hillers, "Delocutive Verbs in Biblical Hebrew," *JBL* 6 (1967): 320-24.

cent," "acquit" (cf. Job 9:28; Joel 3:21 [HB 4:21]). As such, it is characteristically reserved for the divine prerogative (e.g., Ex. 20:7; 34:7; Num. 14:18; Job 9:28; Jer. 30:11; 46:28; but note 1 Kings 2:9). The employment of יהוה here in enveloping structure calls further attention to this latter fact.

לֹא: Although A. Haldar[22] argues for reading an emphatic *lamedh* here, such scarcely makes good sense contextually. Moreover, the scriptural parallels cited above (note especially Ex. 34:7; Num. 14:18) argue strongly for the retention of the MT negative particle. Translating the verb with the addition of an accusative "the guilty" is a natural translation *ad sensum*. Cathcart (*Nahum*, p. 45) calls attention to Cross's reading of a Hebrew inscription from Khirbet Beit Lei:

> *nqh yh 'l ḥnn*   Absolve (us) O Merciful God!
> *nqh yh yhwh*   Absolve (us) O Yahweh!

Some critical scholars (e.g., J. M. P. Smith) have suggested that v. 3*a* be treated as a gloss, possibly supplied from Num. 14:17, so as to soften the force of God's wrath just recorded. Quite the contrary, the scriptural parallels, the flow of the context, and the authorial design in the concatenation of the letter *aleph* argue for the retention of the line. Further, as Cathcart points out, the essential integrity of vv. 2-3*a* is supported by the heaping up of the consonants *n* and *q* (six times) and the combination of the ideas of strength/wrath and gentleness/mercy found in such extrabiblical literary sources as the Babylonian *Ludlul Bēl Nēmeqi*, where Marduk is described as one

> Whose fury surrounds him like the blast of a tornado,
> Yet whose breeze is as pleasant as a morning zephyr;
> His anger is irresistible, his rage is a hurricane,
> But his heart is merciful, his mind forgiving,
> The . . . of whose hands the heavens cannot hold back,
> But whose gentle hand sustains the moribund.[23]

All this also speaks against Smith's suggestion that the MT reading גְּדוֹל־כֹּחַ, found uniquely here as opposed to the more usual רַב חֶסֶד ("abounding in lovingkindness"), if to be retained at all must refer to God's moral strength, for "the thought probably is that Yahweh's self-control is too great to permit him to act upon the impulse of sudden outbursts of wrath."[24] The thought perhaps parallels that of Ps. 147:5:

---

22. A. Haldar, *Studies in the Book of Nahum* (Uppsala: Lundequistska Bokhandeln, 1947), p. 18. For emphatic *lamedh*, see Mitchell Dahood, *Psalms*, AB (Garden City, N.Y.: Doubleday, 1970), 3:406-7.
23. Cathcart, *Nahum*, pp. 46-47; for the full text of *Ludlul Bēl Nēmeqi*, see W. G. Lambert, *Babylonian Wisdom Literature* (Oxford: Clarendon, 1960), pp. 30-62.
24. J. M. P. Smith, *Nahum*, p. 289.

Great is our Lord   גָּדוֹל אֲדוֹנֵינוּ
and abundant in strength.   וְרַב־כֹּחַ

סוּפָה ("*whirlwind*") occurs also in Hos. 8:7 in a context of judgment and in parallel with עָנָן ("cloud") in Jer. 4:13. שְׂעָרָה ("*storm*") is
a biform of סְעָרָה ("[wind]storm"), both of which are related to Akkadian *šārum* ("windstorm"). Both nouns occur together in Isa. 29:6 in a
context of judgment. סוּפָה is paired with the masculine noun form סַעַר
("storm") in Ps. 83:15 (HB 83:16). Yahweh's power over the storm
could be viewed as a veiled denunciation of both the Canaanite Baal
(who was often worshiped in poetic lines of similar sentiment and
whose worship was even then rampant in Judah) and Haddu/Hadad,
the Assyrian storm-god.

The occurrence of these two terms for storm, as well as the image
of the God of the clouds shared in common between Isaiah and
Nahum, underscores Armerding's contention that Nahum had a
strong literary dependence on Isaiah:

> The evidence for literary interdependence between Isaiah and Nahum is
> thus founded on unique, multiple verbal repetitions linking specific pas-
> sages (e.g. Nah 1:2 and Isa. 59:17-19; 1:3-6 and 29:6; 1:4 and 33:9; 50:2;
> 1:4-5 and 42:15; 1:15 and 52:1, 7; 2:9-10 and 24:1, 3; 2:10 and 21:3-4;
> 3:5-7 and 47:2-3; 3:7 and 51:19). It is reinforced by the extensive con-
> tinuity of imagery in other related passages (e.g., drought, earthquake,
> fire, stubble, burial, lions). And it is corroborated to the point of virtual
> certainty by the shared pattern of oppression, deliverance, and judgment
> experienced specifically in relation to Assyria (cf. Isa. 5:26-30; 7:17-20;
> 8:4-8; 9:1; 10:5-34; 11:11, 15-16; 14:24-27; 19:23-25; 20:1-6; 27:13;
> 30:27-33; 31:1-9; 36:1–37:38; 38:6; 51:17–52:7).[25]

Armerding suggests that the ubiquity of the interrelationship between Isaiah and Nahum may well provide corroborative evidence of
Isaiah's authorship of all the prophecy that bears his name.

W. G. E. Watson may be correct in suggesting that the use of the
two words for storm here is an example of hendiadys. He translates
the line "In the tempestuous whirlwind his road."[26]

God's *treading* upon the *clouds* is reminiscent of the title "rider on
the clouds" (Ps. 68:4 [HB 68:5]). רכב with עַל often means "mount up
upon" (cf. Akkadian *rakābu*). One may note especially 1 Sam. 25:42; 2
Sam. 19:27; 1 Kings 13:13-14; 18:45; 2 Kings 9:16, where רכב is used
of mounting together with an accompanying activity. Such familiar
phrases as רֹכֵב בָּעֲרָבוֹת ("rider on the clouds," Ps. 68:4 [HB 68:5]; cf.
Ugaritic *rkb ʿrpt*) and רֹכֵב הַשָּׁמַיִם ("he who rides upon the heavens"; cf.
Deut. 33:26), as well as רֹכֵב עַל־עָב קַל ("he who rides upon a swift

---

25. Armerding, "Nahum," in *EBC*, 7:455.
26. W. G. E. Watson, *Classical Hebrew Poetry* (Sheffield: JSOT Press, 1986), p.
196.

cloud," Isa. 19:1), may all likewise be understood as "he who mounts/is mounted upon the clouds/heavens." The traditional meaning "ride upon" is, of course, equally possible.[27] In this word there may again be a veiled reference to Hadad who appears in Ugaritic texts as "Hadad, lord of the storm clouds" and in the Assyrian recension of the Atraḥasīs Epic as the one who "rode on the four winds, (his) asses."[28]

1:4a Many find in these parallel lines a further adoption of an original Canaanite setting. The juxtaposition of יָם and יַבֵּשׁ may compose a merismus made up of polar word pairs. יָם ("sea") and נָהָר ("river") are familiar set parallel pairs in both the Ugaritic texts and the OT.[29]

1:4b The mention of *Bashan, Carmel,* and *Lebanon* is reminiscent of a similar context in Isa. 33:9. All three were noted for being places of special fertility. Bashan (south of Mount Hermon on the east side of the Jordan) was fabled for the productivity of its land and therefore its fine cattle (Mic. 7:14); Carmel (the promontory along the Mediterranean Sea in central Canaan south of the Bay of Acre) was prized for its beauty and its fruitfulness (Song of Sol. 7:5; Jer. 50:19); and Lebanon (home of the lofty mountains of coastal Syria) was famed for its great cedars (1 Kings 5:14-18; Isa. 2:13). The conquering Mesopotamian kings frequently boasted of traveling to the forests of Lebanon.[30] Cathcart notes that the double parallels Lebanon/Bashan and mountains/hills have a counterpart in Isa. 2:13-14.[31]

For the relation of the double אֻמְלַל in the reconstruction of the proposed acrostic in vv. 2-10, see the note on v. 2. That the first occurrence of the word was originally written as a similar parallel root, such as דָּלַל or דָּמְלַל, rests upon not only the needs of the acrostic pattern but also the fact that the ancient versions uniformly used two different words to express the Hebrew word(s) in question.[32] In the absence of further evidence in the Hebrew manuscript tradition, however, the case for an unbroken acrostic must remain unproved

---

27. See *AHW*, p. 944; G. Liedke, "רכב," *THAT*, 2:777-82. See also R. D. Patterson, "A Multiplex Approach to Psalm 45," *GTJ* 6 (1985): 37 n. 35.
28. See further Cathcart, *Nahum*, p. 48.
29. See the full discussion in A. Cooper, "Divine Names and Epithets in the Ugaritic Texts," *RSP*, 3:369-83.
30. See, e.g., Sennacherib's penetration of this area as recorded in D. D. Luckenbill, *AR*, 2:161-62. Sennacherib's boast is also noted in 2 Kings 19:23. See further A. Heidel, *The Gilgamesh Epic and Old Testament Parallels* (Chicago: University Press, 1963), pp. 6-7.
31. K. Cathcart, "Kingship and the Day of Yahweh in Isaiah 2:6-22," *Hermathena* 125 (1978): 52, 55.
32. For details, see J. M. P. Smith, *Nahum*, p. 298. For the existence of pulal forms in Hebrew, see GKC par. 55d.

due to the absence of a *daleth* in v. 4. In fact, Joel's use of אֻמְלָל in parallel with יָבֵשׁ ("be dried up," Joel 1:10, 12) in his description of a devastating drought may argue for Nahum's adaptation of Joel's language, resulting in a deliberately formed broken acrostic. Such a broken alphabetic acrostic occurs in Pss. 9-10 where ד is likewise missing.

1:5 The figure of the divine shaking of the *mountains* (cf. Jer. 4:24; Hab. 3:6) is found also in Canaanite texts praising Baal/Hadad.[33] גִּבְעָה/הַר is a common parallel pair in Isaiah (e.g., Isa. 2:2, 14; 10:32; 30:17; 42:18).

†The usual translation of מוּג as "melt" has met with some discussion. Because the other lines in v. 5 contain the picture of shaking/trembling, some have suggested that consistency of image demands a similar sense for מוּג. Thus the NEB reads "heave and swell" and the NJB "reel." Support for such renderings comes from the ancient versions: LXX ἐσαλεύθησαν ("are shaken," "sway") and Pesh. 'etparaq ("be rent/broken"). Possible etymological support may also be found in Arabic *māja* ("surge"). This thought is supported further by such poetic parallels as Jer. 4:24; Hab. 3:6; Ps. 18:7 (HB 18:8). Conversely, the more usual translation of מוּג as "melt" is favored by a comparison with Ps. 97:5; Mic. 1:4. The hithpael of מוּג (as here) is read elsewhere only in Ps. 107:26; Amos 9:13. In the former case it could best be understood either as trembling (so AB) or "melted" (NIV). In the latter text, "melting" or "flowing" is clearly appropriate. Accordingly a final decision as to the precise nuance of מוּג here is elusive.

Compounding the problem in understanding the verb מוּג is וַתִּשָּׂא ("and [the earth] quakes") in the next line. Cathcart suggests reading וַתִּשָּׁא, "and (the earth) is laid waste" (cf. RSV, NEB), from the root שָׁאָה ("roar," "crash into ruins"), a suggestion that finds support in Pesh. If Cathcart's proposal is followed, it would make an interesting parallel with the Vg reading in the parallel line: *desolati sunt* ("are desolate," "laid waste"). The MT, however, is fully defensible here both contextually and in the light of the intransitive use of נָשָׂא elsewhere (cf. Ps. 89:9 [HB 89:10]; Hos. 13:1; Hab. 1:3) and has the general support of LXX ἀνεστάλη ("was raised up") and Vg *contremuit* ("trembles violently"). Thus the various emendations are unnecessary.[34]

†וַתֵּבֵל: The last line has also undergone critical examination. Particular attention has been paid to the two conjunctions, the first of which is missing in LXX and Pesh. and the second of which has

---

33. See Cathcart, *Nahum*, p. 53.
34. For full details, see Maier, *Nahum*, pp. 170-71.

been considered awkward. W. F. Albright proposes the deletion of the second waw so that the line reads *wattêbal* (from אָבַל, "mourn") כָּל יֹשְׁבֵי בָה, "and all its inhabitants drooped" (cf. Amos 8:8; 9:5). W. L. Moran takes the second waw with תֵּבֵל, viewing the resultant reconstruction as a remnant of an ancient *taqtulū(na)* form and reading *têbālû* "(all its inhabitants) mourned."[35] Ingenious as these suggestions are, there is no reason to reject the MT. תֵּבֵל is a common set synonym with אֶרֶץ ("earth"), which is found in the parallel line (cf. 1 Sam. 2:8; Isa. 18:3; 24:4; 26:9, 18; 34:1). Further, as Maier points out, the double occurrence of *waw* in the disputed line is probably intentional, yielding "not only the earth but all who dwell in it."

1:6 זַעְמוֹ: Those who see a rigid acrostic in vv. 2-10 usually transpose זַעְמוֹ to the first slot in a sentence, thus forming a case of anticipatory emphasis. Although such a procedure may preserve the desired alphabetical sequence, such may not be necessary to Nahum's poetic scheme, as noted previously. The order of the MT is reminiscent of Ps. 147:17 and may be intentionally formed so as to emphasize the juxtaposed verbal phrases that follow, while leaving *wrath* as a frame for the double rhetorical question that it encloses (זַעְמוֹ . . . בַּחֲרוֹן אַפּוֹ). If so, the utter hopelessness of Nineveh's situation is stressed. The use of זַעַם with חֲרוֹן אַף is attested also in Pss. 69:24 (Heb. 69:25); 78:49; Zeph. 3:8.

The use of rhetorical question in a hymn of praise is common enough (cf. Ps. 113:5). עָמַד and קוּם may find a parallel use as a set pair in Job 8:15.

1:6b The figure of wrath is continued in the first of the couplets that makes up v. 6b. It is a wrath that burns so intensely that even usually impenetrable rocks are broken up before it (cf. Deut. 32:22; 1 Kings 19:11; Jer. 4:26; 23:29; 51:26; Mic. 1:4). Cathcart calls attention to the combination of נָתַךְ and חֵמָה in contexts of divine judgment elsewhere in the OT and notes the use of נָתַךְ in the pouring out of Hadad's wrath in the Panammū I inscription. The employment of נָתַץ in the parallel line leaves a picture of a wrath so great that it is like an intense fire that shatters solid rock. God's judgment melts all opposition before it.

2. WHO DESTROYS THE PLOTTERS (1:7-10)

Translation
Good (better) is Yahweh as (than) a fortress
   in the day of distress,

---

35. See further Cathcart, *Nahum*, p. 53; W. L. Moran, "The Hebrew Language in Its Northwest Semitic Background," in *The Bible and the Ancient Near East*, ed. G. Ernest Wright (Garden City, N.Y.: Doubleday, 1965), pp. 71, 83 n. 108.

and He knows* those who seek refuge in Him
  in the overwhelming flood*.
⁸He makes a(n) (complete) end of those who rise up against Him*
  and pursues His foes into darkness*.
⁹What(ever) (will) you plot against Yahweh(?)
He will make an end* (of it);
  trouble* will not arise a second time.
¹⁰Indeed, they shall be as (totally) consumed
  as a completely entangled thorn bush,
(or) as those utterly satiated with their drink,
(or) as fully dry stubble.

Exegesis and Exposition

Nahum begins the latter portion of his hymn with the second of his statements regarding God's nature. He points out that God's goodness and concern for His own do not diminish His power and determination to judge the wicked (cf. Ps. 145:7-9). Rather than being a weakening quality, God's goodness assures all people that He will execute His judgment equitably (cf. Pss. 98:9; 145:17-20).

Verse 7 stresses the positive aspect. Like those within a fortress on the day of siege, so those who trust* in God's goodness and loving concern for them may rest secure. The verse provides a dramatic contrast with v. 6 in that Nahum moves from the subject of wrath to that of compassion. God is compared metaphorically to a refuge (cf. Ps. 37:37-40), and the effect is to make Israel a literary foil to Nineveh. Thus, in the midst of a context emphasizing vast destruction, a picture that will quickly be applied to Nineveh, the scene takes a momentary shift to assure God's people of His goodness and protection. The practical result will be to place in stark contrast Israel's blessedness and Nineveh's defenselessness before God's all-consuming wrath (cf. Ex. 15:7; Isa. 5:21-25; 33:11-12).

Having painted such a poignant portrait, Nahum returns to the subject of the destruction of God's foes (vv. 8-10). God, in His judicial wrath, will come against them like a victorious commander pursuing his foes to the farthest recesses of the earth. Indeed, God's enemies will come to understand that He will overturn their insolent plotting against Him so thoroughly that, like men entangled in thorns or overcome with their own drunkenness, they will be easily overthrown. As dry stubble is devoured by fire, God's fiery wrath will consume them. They will not devise their devious plot a second time.

The contrast between the fortunes of believers and the wicked is often drawn in the Scriptures (e.g., Psalms 1; 37; Prov. 4:10-19; Matt. 7:13-14, 24-27). He who trusts in God is the one who knows and believes in Him (cf. Gen. 15:6) and hence has the assurance (Isa. 26:3) that God will take note of him in the adversities of life (Pss. 17:7; 18:30 [HB 18:31]; 31:19-20 [HB 31:20-21]), when life's circumstances rush in upon him like an overwhelming flood (Pss. 18:1-6 [HB 18:2-7]; 32:6-7; 124). Indeed, to all such believers God's goodness reaches out, and He becomes their fortress in distress (Ex. 15:2; Pss. 27:1-3; 28:8; 91:2; Isa. 25:4; Jer. 16:19). Conversely, those who trust in self, who rise up against God, will find that He will in turn stand against them. Those who plot against Him (Pss. 1:1; 2:1-3; 21:11 [HB. 21:12]), among whom Assyria was often named (e.g., Ps. 83:5-8 [HB 83:6-9]), can be assured that their plot not only will not succeed (cf. Pss. 1:4-5; 2:12; Hos. 7:15-16), but it will also self-destruct, leaving them in danger of certain judgment.

The figures that Nahum has chosen to use in these verses are particularly apropos. Because proud Nineveh plotted against God (cf. v. 11) instead of trusting in Him, she would know no safety in the overwhelming floods of life that were to come. Both tradition and archaeological excavations record that Nineveh's fall was enhanced physically by the weakening effect of floodwaters. Likewise, historical traditions recount that on the night of the city's capture its defenders, convinced of Nineveh's impregnability, were engaged in eating and drinking. Thus Diodorus (*Bibliotheca historica* 2.26.4) reports:

> It happened at this very time that the king of the Assyrians . . . turned to indulgence and divided among his soldiers for a feast animals and great quantities of both wine and all other provisions. Consequently, since the whole army was carousing, Arbaces, learning from some deserters of the relaxation and drunkenness in the camp of the enemy, made his attack upon it unexpectedly in the night.

The reference to fire not only echoes the concluding lines of the first portion of the hymn (v. 6) and adds dramatic pathos to the divine sentence of judgment in this section but is also distinctly appropriate. The ruins of Nineveh show abundant evidence of the intensity of the conflagration that consumed the fallen city. Whatever application these verses have to God's enemies in general, it is obvious that Nahum's prophetic pronouncements have a particular relevance for Nineveh.

Additional Notes

1:7 A contrast in subject matter (wrath in v. 6 vs. goodness in v. 7) and syntactic structure (note the employment of an intentional asyndeton to introduce v. 7) indicate the initiation of a new portion in the hymn.

†טוֹב יהוה לְמָעוֹז† has been variously rendered. לְמָעוֹז is commonly taken as apposition and placed in a separate line:

> The Lord is good,
>   a refuge. . . . (NIV)
> The Lord is good,
>   a stronghold. . . . (KJV, NASB, NKJV, RSV).

Leaving לְמָעוֹז in the first line makes the second line short. Some alleviate the situation by inserting into the line such phrases as "for those who trust in him" (Brockington). *BHS* solves the problem by rearranging the words in the verse and augmenting it to read: "The Lord is good to those who wait for him, a fortress in the day of distress." NJB takes the *lamedh* as a comparative particle and translates the line "Yahweh is better than a fortress," thus leaving the phrase in question with the first poetic line. Cathcart at first translated the words similarly, calling attention to Song of Sol. 1:2*b*-3*a* as support.[36] On the whole, the retention of לְמָעוֹז with the first line would seem to make both good sense and better literary style, whether or not one takes the *lamedh* to be a comparative particle. Thus construed, the resultant two lines give a good balance with the following couplet, yield good sense, and furnish additional evidence for an acrostic in vv. 2-10. The end result is reflected in my translation above. NJB, while translating differently, follows the same poetic arrangement:

> Yahweh is better than a fortress
> in time of distress;
> he recognises those who trust in him
> even when the flood rushes on.

†וּבְשֶׁטֶף: The *waw* is an example of explicative *waw*.[37]

†וְיֹדֵעַ: Several suggest an expanded use of ידע here, such as "care for" (NIV, NEB) or "recognize" (NJB). Because this verb has a wide semantic range when used of divine knowledge, however, it is perhaps better to translate "and He knows" and leave the precise nuance to the expositor.[38]

As for חָסָה ("trust"), though Girdlestone reports that, of the many synonyms employed to render the idea of trust, this verb is used when the concept of God as a refuge is intended or where God is compared

---

36. Cathcart, *Nahum*, p. 55. Cathcart subsequently changed his mind and translated the passage in question as follows: "Yahweh is good, indeed a fortress"; for details, see K. Cathcart, "More Philological Studies in Nahum," *JNSL* 7 (1979): 4.
37. See further M. Pope, "'Pleonastic' Waw before Nouns in Ugaritic and Hebrew," *JAOS* 73 (1953): 95-98; D. W. Baker, "Further Examples of the WAW EXPLICATIVUM," *VT* 30 (1980): 129-36.
38. For details, see G. F. Botterweck, "ידע," *TDOT* 5:448-54.

to a rock or shield, Gamberoni suggests that extensive use of the word has developed a strong concept of the believer's absolute and exclusive trust in Yahweh.[39] Thus, for those who put their total trust in the Lord and in him alone, God is a strong fortress. Such a person can stand the test even in the day of adversity, when the troubles of life come rushing in like an overwhelming flood. Isaiah (Isa. 25:4) employs similar language to praise God for His power in the stresses of life: "For You have been a refuge/fortress [מָעוֹז] for the poor, a refuge/fortress [מָעוֹז] for the needy in his distress, a refuge/shelter [מַחְסֶה] from the storm, and a shade from the heat."

1:8 †מְקוֹמָהּ: The MT "her place" has been taken to refer to Nineveh (1:1). However, the LXX τοὺς ἐπεγειρομένους, "those who rise up" (against Him; cf. NJB, "those who defy him"), suggests a different reading, perhaps מְקִימֶיהוּ. Cathcart proposes *miqqômêhû*, "of his assailants." Either reading would make a more suitable parallel with אֹיְבָיו than the pointing of the MT. Similar in sentiment are the instances of the use of the qal participle of קוּם in parallel with אֹיֵב ("enemy"; e.g., Ps. 18:39-40 [HB 18:40-41]) and the cases where the two are utilized in close proximity (cf. Deut. 28:7; Ps. 18:48 [HB 18:49]; Mic. 7:6). Note also Ps. 59:2 where the hithpael participle of קוּם stands in parallel with אֹיֵב. The MT reading "her place" has its able defenders, however (e.g., Keil, Maier).

The phrase *"and pursues his foes into darkness"* has occasioned some controversy due to the lack of a clear precedent for the use of רָדַף with a double accusative. The translation suggested here (cf. NIV) nevertheless makes good contextual sense, especially in view of the parallel with the thought of God's making a complete end of His enemies. "Darkness" can be construed either as the land of death (the final end of the wicked), a·thought found in such texts as Job 10:20-22; 17:13; 18:18; Ps. 35:6, 8, 10-12 (HB 35:7, 9, 11-13), or simply as an idiom for God's relentless pursuit that brings punishment in a final extermination of His foes (Isa. 8:22; Zeph. 1:15). In the light of v. 9 the latter suggestion is perhaps better. Maier's "with darkness" appears forced.

1:9 †מַה־תְּחַשְּׁבוּן has been taken either as a rhetorical question, "Why/what will you plot against Yahweh?"—a question directed at the heathen (= Nineveh) or at Judah—or as an indirect question, "Whatever you plot against Yahweh" (cf. NIV, NASB). In light of the following verse, it is perhaps better to adopt the latter alternative. The verbal form could also be viewed as a piel imperfect 3d masc. pl. archaistically constructed (or retained) in poetic fashion in confor-

---

39. See R. Girdlestone, *Synonyms of the Old Testament* (Grand Rapids: Eerdmans, 1956), pp. 103-4; J. Gamberoni, "חסה," *TDOT* 5:64-75.

mity to a Northwest Semitic *tĕqaṭṭĕlû(na)* form, "(whatever) they will plot." In any case, whether the clause is viewed as a direct or indirect question, it answers schematically to a similar development in the first section of the hymn (cf. v. 6).

†With כָּלָה "(make) an end (of)," cf. Ugaritic *kly*, "finish off," "destroy"; Akkadian *kalû.*

†צָרָה ("trouble/opposition") has been emended by some (e.g., *BHS*) to read צָרָיו ("his enemies/adversaries"; e.g., NJB, NEB) on the basis of its frequent association with קוּם (cf. Pss. 3:1 [HB 3:2]; 44:5 [HB 44:6]; 74:23). But no manuscript evidence exists for such an emendation, and the MT makes good sense as it stands. The use of קוּם here in conjunction with the previous כָּלָה . . . עֹשֶׂה argues strongly for the reading of a verbal form in v. 8 (קוּם) rather than the noun מָקוֹם ("place"). The thought reemphasizes that of v. *9a:* God's just judgment will bring a total end to the opposition of His foes. There will be no second rebellion.[40]

1:10 †Verse 10 is an often debated *crux interpretum.* Cathcart affirms: "This must be one of the most difficult texts in the Old Testament. No satisfactory translation of the passage has been offered to date."[41] Each line of the verse, as well as the sense of the whole, has been subjected to critical scrutiny. The first two images have been particularly troublesome: (1) סִירִים סְבֻכִים ("entangled thorns") has met with such despair of solution that many (e.g., Ehrlich, J. M. P. Smith) have dubbed it hopelessly corrupt. Various textual emendations and rearrangements have been attempted, none of which appears to be an improvement upon the basic figure given in the MT. (2) וּכְסָבְאָם סְבוּאִים ("and like those drunken from their drink") is usually translated so as to yield a rendition that emphasizes becoming totally drunk. Although numerous conjectures have been put forward, none has proved to be entirely satisfactory.[42]

Not only must the difficulty of establishing the precise meanings of the words involved in the two figures be solved, but once the meanings are established the resultant figures must be related to the third image of the verse: "like fully dry stubble." Some common ground of comparison must be found if one is to make good sense of the three parallel lines in the verse. Although certainty regarding the verse's flow of thought is problematic, it is simplest to follow the MT and find the clue to the solution of the total picture in the introductory

---

40. For *ṣārâ* as "rebellion" or "opposition," see T. H. Gaster, *Myth, Legend and Custom in the Old Testament* (New York: Peter Smith, 1969), p. 665.
41. Cathcart, *Nahum*, p. 60.
42. For details, see Maier, *Nahum*, pp. 193-95; J. M. P. Smith, *Nahum*, pp. 294-95, 301-2.

double particle כִּי עַד (lit. "for unto"; cf. LXX). Unfortunately these words have proved to defy smooth interpretation, causing them to be variously rendered, emended, or even left untranslated. Three syntactic factors must be kept in mind: (1) עַד usually carries with it the recognition of the farthest point to which the action/thought has come and often occurs in contexts demanding a note of emphasis (e.g., Ex. 9:7; 14:28; Judg. 4:16; 2 Sam. 17:22; Job 25:5; Ps. 147:15; Hag. 2:19).[43] (2) כִּי is often used in poetic structures to emphasize the preceding material, while signaling the conclusion of the whole thought, or to bring the poem/hymn to a close.[44] (3) Verse 10 must be contextually related in meaningful fashion to v. 9 but not to v. 11. (See the introductory remarks to vv. 11-15.) Taking account of these data and following the MT (although ignoring the placement of the *athnaḥ*), the translation given at the beginning of this unit emerges.

The point of the comparison in all three seemingly unrelated cases is that of total consumption: the bush by its thorns, the drunkard by his drink, the stubble by fire. The effect is heightened by the use of the prophetic perfect of אֻכָּל (significantly in the pual stem, unless this is a qal passive[45]) and the piling up of the *s* sound (6 times) in this otherwise *k* verse. Doubtless each of the lines belongs to the proverbial literature, and the three are brought together by Nahum as a fitting conclusion to the hymn proper in such a way as to re-emphasize the impossibility of God's enemies ever rising up again after He has judged them. The verse and the whole hymn look forward to God's judgment of Nineveh. He will make a complete end of the proud city.

C. APPLICATION: GOD'S JUSTICE FOR NINEVEH AND JUDAH (1:11-15 [HB 1:11–2:1])

With the completion of the hymn, Nahum turns to the two nations and their capitals that are the subject of his prophecies. The latter half of his hymn had been directed against those who plot against God. Keying in on that term, Nahum turns to the supreme example of such activity: Assyria and its capital city of Nineveh. In four short verses Nahum brings God's charges against Nineveh for

---

43. See BDB, p. 724.
44. For details, see R. Gordis, "The Asseverative Kaph in Ugaritic and Hebrew," *JAOS* 63 (1943): 176-78; M. Dahood, *Psalms*, 3:402-6.
45. For the existence of the qal passive in biblical Hebrew, see R. J. Williams, "The Passive *Qal* Theme in Hebrew," in *Essays on the Ancient Semitic World*, ed. J. W. Wevers and D. B. Redford (Toronto: University Press, 1970), pp. 43-50.

which it will be judged (v. 11) regardless of its seemingly limitless strength (vv. 12a, 14), a judgment that will result in a respite for Judah in its affliction (vv. 12b-13). The section is closed with a stirring message of good news: Because wicked Nineveh has been judged, a repentant Judah may once again worship God in peace (v. 15).

From a literary perspective this narrative unit is characterized by such features as the stitch-word "one who plots" (v. 11; cf. v. 9), a monocolon (v. 12), and a concluding refrain (v. 15). That these verses compose a single literary unit is guaranteed not only by the presence of an initial stitch-word and closing refrain but also by the employment of the enveloping/bookending word בְּלִיַּעַל (bĕliyyaʿal, "wicked[ness]") in verses 11, 15. This short section is thus distinct from the previous hymn in 1:2-10 and from the announcement in 2:1ff. Schematically it forms the application of Nahum's stated theme (v. 2) and hymn of praise (vv. 2-10).

Translation

From you has come forth one who plots evil against Yahweh, a counselor of wickedness*.
¹²Thus says Yahweh*,
"Even though they have allies* and are very numerous, so much the more will they be cut off* and pass away. Although I have afflicted you, I will not afflict you again.
¹³But now I will break his yoke from upon you, and I will tear your shackles away."
¹⁴Yahweh has issued a command concerning you*: "None of your name will be sown again;
I will cut off the (carved) images and (molten) idols, and I will make* your grave, for you are vile*."
¹⁵Behold*, on the mountains the feet of one who brings glad tidings, who proclaims peace!
Celebrate your festivals, O Judah, fulfill your vows! For the wicked one shall never again pass through you; he is completely cut off.

Exegesis and Exposition

In a dramatic structural shift from hymnic to narrative style, Nahum turns to Nineveh in application of the teaching of his hymn. Nineveh/Assyria is identified as a plotter*, an identification that seems obvious in the light of the military exploits of its most prominent kings. The primary reference may well be to Sennacherib, who launched his infamous third campaign against the western countries of the Fertile Crescent in general and Judah in particular. According to his own records, having subdued the northern lands, he took Eltekeh, Timnah, and Ekron on the Philistine coast and some 46 cities of Judah. Although he failed to subdue Jerusalem, the booty that he carried away from the campaigning was enormous. The scriptural record likewise indicates that the Judahite king paid a huge tribute to Sennacherib and that the Assyrian king spent considerable time in taking the key towns of Lachish and Libnah in the western Shephelah (2 Kings 18:13–19:8). The writer of Kings also records something of Sennacherib's own secret plottings against the Lord at that time (2 Kings 19:21-28). Because of the viciousness of the plotter's thoughts, he is aptly termed "one who counsels wickedness." The word translated in v. 11 as "wickedness" (NIV) is בְּלִיַּעַל (*bĕliyya'al*) and is often translated "worthlessness." It speaks of a character of life so totally reprobate that the term came ultimately to be applied to Satan himself (2 Cor. 6:15). Whether or not directly applicable to Sennacherib, Nahum's words would doubtless be welcomed by God's people, many of whom had been alive during Sennacherib's campaigns and in whose memories the horror of those earlier days was etched indelibly.

The initial phase of Nahum's messages against Nineveh follows in vv. 12-14. As the opening monocolon declares, Nahum's words were nothing less than a solemn pronouncement from the Lord. However flawless and numerous Nineveh's armies might be, it was also true that God could cut them off so that the Assyrian forces would melt away. It had happened previously (2 Kings 19:32-36). Such a fact could serve as a guarantee that the Assyrian menace would never again bring affliction* to God's people. Indeed, the Lord had a personal word for each of the parties involved. For Judah there was reassurance that its Assyrian vassalage* would soon pass away, a condition that became a virtual reality during the latter days of Josiah's reign. In contrasting Judah's previous and future situations, Nahum compares Judah's unjust treatment to a yoke and shackles, all of which shall be broken (v. 13). For Nineveh there was the solemn affirmation that her long night of cruel domination was soon to end. This vile and ruthless nation would shortly pass from the scene of earth's history and leave it without any to carry on its political identity.

The gravity of the sentence against Nineveh/Assyria is underscored by Nahum's use of a different figure, that of sowing. The pronouncement that Nineveh would lack descendants to bear her name* reads literally in the MT "There shall not be sown (any) of your name again/anymore." As a farmer sows his seed in anticipation of harvest, so a man's posterity is viewed as his seed (e.g., Gen. 13:16). The metaphor is common in the Old Testament.[46] Stress is laid here on the

---

46. See H. D. Preuss, "זָרַע," *TDOT* 4:150-62.

impossibility of Nineveh's recovery. Never again will it know its former fame, for it will have neither status nor descendant to perpetuate
its name.

Along with the idea of sowing, Nahum's use of the word "name"*
is particularly appropriate. Whereas the term often carries with it
the nuances of "character" and "reputation" it also connotes "existence." In this case, to "cut off the name" was to destroy a person or
leave him without descendant (cf. 1 Sam. 24:21; Job 18:17; Isa. 14:22).
Conversely a man continued to exist in his posterity, for it was his
name and seed (Isa. 66:22; cf. Jer. 13:11). Alas, Nineveh/Assyria would
never again have its name sown!

The pathos of Assyria's demise is further deepened by the notice
that none of her vaunted gods, so long venerated in Mesopotamia,
would be able to deliver her from God's sentence of death. Rather,
their limitations are clearly spelled out. These "gods" are what they
appear to be—mere temple "images"* and "idols"* that could never
be of help (cf. Isa. 44:9-20) to a doomed Nineveh. Worse still, those
same gods will be cut off, doubtless as an indication of the usual
custom in the ancient world whereby the victor desecrated the temples of the conquered foe and carried off the idols. The Assyrians
themselves were past masters of such activities. Now it was their turn
to suffer such indignities. Maier reports concerning the time-honored
temples of Nineveh:

> Some sections of the Nabu temple were so completely overturned that
> competent investigators decided further exploration of these sites would
> not pay. Slabs written by Ashurbanipal have been found at Nineveh in
> both temples, Ê-mash-mash and Ê-zida. On one with official repetition
> the king asks Ishtar (and Nabu on the other) "For all time, O Ishtar, look
> upon it (the temple) with favor." The utter devastation of this sanctuary
> only fourteen years after Ashurbanipal's death proved Ishtar's impo-
> tence.[47]

Armerding adds, "The statue of Ishtar was discovered, prostrate and
headless, amid the ruins of her temple, which had stood at Nineveh
for almost fifteen centuries."[48]

The divine sentence ends with a dreadful dictum. So hopeless was
Nineveh's case and so devastating would be her demise that she
would not even have a memorial left to her greatness (cf. Ps. 49:16-17
[HB 49:17-18]), nor would anyone erect a monument to her memory.
So poor and wretched will she be that only the God who planned her
doom will be there to mark out her lowly grave in the ruins of the
once proud city. Further reason for the necessity of the divine inter-

---

47. Maier, *Nahum*, pp. 212-13.
48. Armerding, "Nahum," in *EBC*, 7:469.

ment is given in the observation that none will want to preserve Nineveh's remembrance, for she is utterly reprobate. Because of her debased activity she has gained such contempt for herself that her demise will bring to the lips of the observers of her fall a sigh of relief and a song of rejoicing (v. 15; cf. 3:19).

With the pronouncement of the irreversible decision of divine judgment, once again there is a word for Judah. Again there is a change of figure—from that of bondage (v. 13) to that of a herald. It is a message of good news.* A messenger comes (from Nineveh?) bearing the glad tidings of peace, not only relief from warfare but also restoration of prosperity. Once again conditions will be favorable for the resumption of Judah's sacrifices and feasts.* So, too, the many promises made to God, doubtless made mostly during the dark days of the Assyrian presence, could be carried out. Likewise, thanksgiving could be rendered to God, for the wicked Assyrian invader has been destroyed, never again to be a threat to God's people.

Nahum's prophecy is a near historical realization of Isaiah's prophecy relative to the eschatological scene. Isaiah foresees the day when an oppressed Israel shall be freed at last from oppressors and invaders, and its people shall not only hear the message of the Lord's salvation but also experience the everlasting serenity that comes with His presence in royal power in their midst (Isa. 52:1-10; cf. Joel 3:18-20 [HB 4:18-21]). Jerusalem shall be holy (cf. Jer. 33:16) and in turn bear the good news of the tender care of her saving shepherd to the other cities of Judah (Isa. 40:9-11). Under the direction of the Messiah (Isa. 52:13–53:12) Zion will be rebuilt and her enemies subdued, and she shall live in everlasting felicity with her God (Isa. 61:1-7).

The emphasis of Isaiah and Nahum on God's good news becomes an important motif for the New Testament revelation. Jesus' birth was thus announced as an occasion of glad tidings (Luke 2:10), and Christ announced that His ministry was in initial fulfillment of the message of salvation and joy that Isaiah prophesied (cf. Luke 4:16-21 with Isa. 61:1-2). Peter makes clear to Jew and Gentile alike that Christ has effected their full salvation, with the result that God's full peace can be enjoyed by all (Acts 10:34-43), a message of good news that Paul likewise affirms (Eph. 2:14-18). It is no wonder, then, that Paul later builds on the theme of the message of good news and peace that Christ has provided both as scriptural evidence for the Jew and as a challenge to all believers to bear the gospel to a needy mankind (Rom. 10:9-15; cf. Isa. 52:7; Nah. 1:15 [HB 2:1]).

Nahum's prophecy, together with that of Isaiah 52:7, is thus related not only to Paul's missionary challenge but also to the theme of the good news of Christ's saving work. But in contrast to Isaiah, who uses the motif of good news to depict those eschatological events so important to the purposes of God, which begin with Christ's first advent and are exhausted only in His second, Nahum employs the theme to depict events in the near historical scene. In a sense, Nahum's prophecy of the joyous news of the impending demise of Assyria/Nineveh and of Judah's subsequent peace stands as a harbinger of the defeat of the "Assyrians" and of the great promises of God that shall be realized by the Zion of the eschatological era. Because of the saving work of Israel's Messiah and the earth's Lord Jesus Christ, all can rejoice in the essence of Nahum's great prophecy. P. C. Craigie puts it well:

> Thus, although Nahum spoke of Nineveh's defeat before the event had happened, his faith here outstrips the contemporary realities of his time. A messenger would indeed come one day soon, and his message would be one of peace.
> Nahum . . . here anticipates the Gospel. . . . The message is one of peace, a peace from external oppression and a new kind of peace with the God who is the giver of all life.[49]

May the saints of all ages take up Nahum's challenge to those of his day to maintain their spiritual commitment!

Additional Notes

1:11 The participle חֹשֵׁב ("plotter") is the literary hook between this section and the preceding hymn (cf. תְּחַשְּׁבוּן, v. 9). As in the case with narrative structure, where the existing conditions under which the account proceeds are given with a suffix-conjugation verb, so here the Lord's charges against Nineveh are rehearsed with the facts being introduced by the phrase מִמֵּךְ יָצָא, after which the divine pronouncement is made.[50] The employment of this phrase represents a clear structural break with the preceding hymn. There is also a thematic shift from a hymn of general application to the specific case of Nineveh.

†The term יֹעֵץ בְּלִיַּעַל ("one who counsels wickedness") stands in stark contrast to the coming Messiah, who will be a פֶּלֶא יוֹעֵץ ("wonder of a counselor," Isa. 9:6 [HB 9:5]). The word בְּלִיַּעַל emphasizes the worthlessness of the counsel that is given. Although the etymology of the word is uncertain, causing בְּלִיַּעַל to receive varying and even contradictory translations, the term has unsavory associations in the OT.

---

49. P. C. Craigie, *Twelve Prophets* (Philadelphia: Westminster, 1985), 2:66-67.
50. For details as to the use of the suffix conjugation in narrative verbal sequence, see W. L. Moran, *A Syntactical Study of the Dialect of Byblos as Reflected in the Amarna Tablets* (Ann Arbor: University Microfilms, 1950), pp. 36-39; S. Schrader, "Was the Earth Created a Few Thousand Years Ago?—Yes," in *The Genesis Debate*, ed. R. Youngblood (Grand Rapids: Baker, 1991), pp. 76-77.

It is used of utter reprobates (Judg. 19:22; 1 Sam. 10:27), serving as an appropriate designation for Jezebel's two false witnesses against Naboth (1 Kings 21:10).

1:12 †While a prophet's words are often introduced by some such phrase as "thus says the LORD," this phrase occurs only here in Nahum.[51] The singular use of so common a formula argues for a certain deliberate emphasis, perhaps expressing Nahum's sense of the awesomeness of the Lord's pronouncement that he was about to deliver.

†The divine sentence is expressed in the form of a condition whose protasis is formed with the particle אִם and a participle. Such constructions usually have a present or immediate future time reference and express a real contingency or possibility.[52] Therefore, the likelihood of a strong and sizeable military force at the disposal of the Assyrians is in view. That army is described as being שְׁלֵמִים וְכֵן רַבִּים, a difficult phrase that has been variously translated and emended. The problem centers in the first word, which can bear such nuances as "health," "completeness," "safety," "prosperity." Cathcart, citing a Ugaritic text where *šlm* occurs in parallel with *ʿzz* ("strengthen"), proposes the translation "be strong" here.[53] The NIV translation "allies" depends on a study by D. J. Wiseman[54] and is perhaps the best solution to the time-honored crux. Together with the following וְכֵן רַבִּים (Ex. 1:12), it suggests the thought "even though they will have allies and so be all the more numerous."[55] Thus construed, the following apodosis becomes an argument *a fortiori:* "so much the more will they be cut off and their armies pass away."

†נָגֹזּוּ is usually understood as coming from the root גָּזַז, which is customarily employed for the shearing of sheep or the cutting of human hair. The unpointed form, however, could also be explained as coming from גָּזָה ("cut/cut off") or גּוּז ("pass over/away"), either of which would yield a suitable sense here. The concluding עבר may be a collective perf. sing. (so Keil) or be repointed as an infinitive absolute or 3d masc. pl. perf. (so Cathcart). The MT is perfectly understandable as it stands and may indicate a change in emphasis from the

---

51. For *'āmar* as a term of divine communication, see S. Wagner, "אָמַר," *TDOT* 1:335-41.
52. For details, see R. J. Williams, *Hebrew Syntax*, 2d ed. (Toronto: University Press, 1976), p. 85; A. B. Davidson, *Hebrew Syntax*, 3d ed. (Edinburgh: T. & T. Clark, 1958), p. 176.
53. Cathcart, *Nahum*, p. 63.
54. D. J. Wiseman, " 'Is It Peace?' Covenant and Diplomacy," *VT* 32 (1982): 311-26.
55. For כֵּן used as an adverbial particle of degree, see BDB, p. 486.

cutting off of the individual soldiers/units to the resultant demise of the entire army.

The following line forms a second portion of the divine decree (hence the *waw*) and is a suppressed condition formed by deletion of the particle. The protasis is constructed with a perfect to express a condition assumed to be true: "If it is true that I have *afflicted* you (i.e., Judah), I will *afflict* you no longer." The NIV not inappropriately translates the two conditional sentences in v. 12 as introductory concessive clauses. Certainly a clear contrast is envisioned in each case. However many the enemy might number, they will be reduced to zero; however much God might have used the Assyrians to chastise His people, such would no longer be the case. For עָנָה ("afflict") in contexts of God's judicial punishment of His people, see Deut. 8:2-3; Pss. 90:15; 119:75. Joel reports that the Assyrians would be used as instruments of God's chastisement if no repentance was forthcoming in Judah and Jerusalem (Joel 2:1-27). Habakkuk (Hab. 1:5-11) similarly warns of God's use of the Chaldeans. Armerding sees a reflection of Isa. 51:22–52:1 in the changed circumstances given here and in the following verses.

1:13 וְעַתָּה ("and/but now") is used in cases of rhetorical analysis to introduce the next point in consequence. Not only will conditions between Assyria and Judah be reversed; God's people will also be set free of Assyrian *vassalage*. "Yoke" and "shackles" (or "bonds") are common terms to depict the fate of those held in vassalage by treaty arrangement with their overlord (cf. Jer. 27:1-10). Although מוֹט refers properly to the "bar" of the yoke, Nahum is using the word synecdochically (the bar for the whole yoke). The yoke itself is often a figure of servitude or vassalage (cf. Lev. 26:13; Isa. 14:25; Jer. 28:10-12; Ezek. 30:18). Similar language abounds in the secular literature of the period. Thus Nabopolassar boasts: "As for the Assyrians who since distant days had ruled over all the people and with heavy yoke had brought misery to the people of the land, from the land of Akkad I banished their feet and cast off their yoke."[56] The Lord's promise of freedom from chains for those who follow Him stands in bold contrast with the complaint of those who would refuse His rightful sovereignty over them (Ps. 2:1-2).

1:14 †Just as the divine decree concerning Judah's changed status had been specially introduced with Yahweh's name (v. 12), so also here. What follows is a clear command from Yahweh for Nineveh. The variation in addressee is accomplished via a contrast in subject mat-

---

56. Stephen Langdon, "Die Neubabylonischen Königsinschriften," *Proceedings of the Society of Biblical Archaeology* (1912): 17ff.

ter and a change in the gender of the persons addressed. Although the promise to Judah was constructed with a 2d fem. sing. objective suffix, a 2d masc. sing. suffix is employed here, probably either in reference to Nineveh's king or in personification of Assyria or Nineveh. The shift in gender as well as in tone (from promise to threat) indicates a shift in referent.

The loss of *name* and seed would mean total annihilation for Nineveh. Armerding rightly remarks:

> The "name" of a population represented its living identity, perpetuated in its "descendants"; to be destitute of descendants therefore represented obliteration of identity and of life itself (cf. Deut 7:24; 9:14; 1 Sam 24:21; et al.). The root underlying "descendants" (*zrʿ*, "seed," "sow") is used of physical and particularly dynastic succession. It implies the eradication of Nineveh's dynastic rule, therefore, and of the nation whose cohesion derived from the Neo-Assyrian monarchy now centered at Nineveh; a similar sentence is passed on Babylon and its king in Isaiah 14:4, 20-23.[57]

The term "name" also has important connotations for the understanding of God, for it calls attention to His revealed character and reputation. It eventually became a technical term for God (cf. Dan. 9:18-19; Amos 2:7; 9:12) and hence was applied by the writers of the NT and the early church Fathers to Christ (e.g., Acts 4:12; 5:41; 3 John 7; Ign. *Eph.* 3:1; 7:1; *Phil.* 10:1; *2 Clem.* 13:1, 4; and often in Hermas).[58] It is still used to this day and may be frequently heard in the Hebrew equivalent of the phrase "God willing" (*ʾim yirṣeh haššēm*, "If the Name is willing").

The מ with מִשְּׁמְךָ ("of/from your name") can be viewed either as a partitive use of the preposition or as an enclitic *mem* after the preceding verb.[59] The critical emendations of this line usually drop *m* and read יִזָּכֵר instead of יִזְרַע, thus changing the image from sowing to remembering.[60] J. M. P. Smith calls this conjectured emendation "gratuitous" but goes on to restructure the section so as to bring vv. 11 and 14 together with 2:2 and 2:4-14 as part of a series of five strophes pointing to the destruction of Nineveh.

פֶּסֶל and מַסֵּכָה are usually taken to refer to carved and molten *images* respectively. As such, they constitute two of several words for

---

57. Armerding, "Nahum," in *EBC*, 7:468.
58. See further G. Vos, *Biblical Theology* (Grand Rapids: Eerdmans, 1954), pp. 76-77; M. Jastrow, *A Dictionary of the Targumim, the Talmud Babli and Yerushalmi, and the Midrashic Literature* (New York: Pardes, 1950), 2:1590.
59. For enclitic *-m*, see H. D. Hummel, "Enclitic MEM in Early Northwest Semitic, Especially Hebrew," *JBL* 76 (1957): 85-107; M. Pope, "Ugaritic Enclitic -m," *JCS* 5 (1951): 123-28.
60. See *BHS*; J. M. P. Smith, *Nahum*, pp. 327-28.

idols and images in the OT.[61] But the usual definitions do not always apply, and we cannot be certain concerning the original significance of the two terms.

†For אָשִׂים ("I will make/set") Cathcart prefers the root שָׁמַם ("to devastate"), relating the thought here to the widespread ancient fear of tomb desecration. The contextual stress, however, appears to focus on God's personal preparation of Nineveh's grave rather than on Nineveh's dread of the destruction of her grave. Although J. M. P. Smith declares that the thought "make your grave" is not "used elsewhere as the equivalent of 'put to death' or 'bury thee,' " Maier appears to be correct in asserting that "these passages with a markedly similar point of view should be noted: Isa. 53:9; Ezek. 39:11."[62] The MT, then, should be retained.

†כִּי קַלּוֹתָ: The charge "for you are vile" represents a moral extension of the meaning of the root קָלַל ("be light"). It is used of a person's slighted reputation (2 Sam. 6:22) and also of actively treating someone contemptuously (2 Sam. 19:44; Isa. 23:9), hence of cursing (Gen. 12:3; 1 Sam. 17:43; 2 Sam. 16:5). Some have suggested taking the form as a pual (Horst) or relating it to the Ugaritic *qll*, "fall" (Haldar), while others have emended the text into a noun, for example *qîqālôt*, "dung heap" (*BHS*), or *qlyt*, "shame" (G. R. Driver). J. M. P. Smith resolves the felt need for an active meaning here by omitting the כִּי and reading קָלוֹן ("dishonor"), thus translating the whole line, "I will make thy grave a dishonour." In the light of the context, it is best to retain the MT and translate the form "you are vile" (lit. "of little account," hence "contemptible").

1:15 (HB 2:1) †Nahum uses the particle הִנֵּה to call attention to key descriptive statements in his prophetic discourses. Here it introduces the close of the first portion of the book.

The verb בִּשַּׂר does not necessarily mean a message of *good news* but simply indicates the bearing of a message (cf. 1 Sam. 4:17-18). Similarly, the Akkadian cognate *bussurum* means basically "bring a message."[63] Nevertheless, it is most often used in the OT, as in Ugaritic, of bearing glad tidings, hence is translated that way in most

---

61. See further J. Gray, *I & II Kings*, 2d ed. (Philadelphia: Westminster, 1970), p. 337; "Idol," *IDB* 2:673-75; F. B. Huey, Jr., "Idolatry," *ZPEB* 3:242-48; R. D. Patterson, "סֶמֶל," *TWOT* 2:628.
62. J. M. P. Smith, *Nahum*, p. 312; Maier, *Nahum*, p. 215.
63. See A. L. Oppenheim, "The Archives of the Palace of Mari II," *JNES* 13 (1954): 145; H. S. Pelser, "The Verbal Roots bśr/bšr/bsr (!) and sbr in the Semitic Languages," *O.T. Werk Suid A* 15 (1972): 68-73; R. W. Fisher, *A Study of the Semitic Root BSR to Bring (Good) Tidings* (Columbia: University Press, 1966).

English versions. For the combination of good news and peace, see Isa. 52:7; Luke 2:10, 14; Acts 10:36.

חָגִּי . . . חַגַּיִךְ ("celebrate your feasts/festivals"): The noun is cognate accusative. The great yearly feasts (perhaps often curtailed during the years of Assyrian oppression) centered on God's saving acts in behalf of His people (Deut. 16:16).

Votive offerings were a matter of the believer's free will, but once made they were to be kept and were to be of high quality (cf. Lev. 22:18-25; 27:1-13; Num. 15:2-16; Deut. 12:6-7; 23:21-23 [HB 23:22-24]; Prov. 20:25; Eccles. 5:4-7 [HB 5:3-6]). Gordon Wenham's remarks on Leviticus 27 are most appropriate:

> Vows are made in the heat of the moment. In retrospect, when the crisis is over, they may well seem foolish and unnecessary, and the person who made the vow may be tempted to forget it or only fulfil it partially. Scripture includes a number of warnings about such an attitude. . . . It may well be part of the purpose of this chapter to discourage rash swearing by fixing a relatively high price for the discharge of the vows, and penalizing those who change their minds.[64]

נְדָרָיִךְ ("your vows") rhymes with חַגַּיִךְ ("your feasts") of the preceding line, a fact that probably accounts for the sandwiched position of "Judah" between חַגַּיִךְ and חָגִּי.

כֻּלֹּה נִכְרָת: This line not only illustrates the familiar poetic device of ending a stanza with a short line; its brevity also gives the effect of an action that is quick and thorough. The promise of complete annihilation of the enemy such that it could never again invade Jerusalem/Judah, together with the promise of peace and prosperity for God's people, is repeated elsewhere in the prophets (e.g., Isa. 52:1, 7; Joel 3:17 [HB 4:17]). The prophecy of certain judgment and sure deliverance is basic to the scriptural teaching concerning the Day of the Lord.[65]

---

64. G. J. Wenham, *The Book of Leviticus*, NICOT (Grand Rapids: Eerdmans, 1979), p. 337. For short lines to mark a stanza ending, see Watson, *Poetry*, p. 165.
65. See R. D. Patterson, "Joel," in *EBC*, 7:256.

2

The Doom of Nineveh Described, Part One (Nahum 2:1-13 [HB 2:2-14])

Having declared Nineveh's certain doom and Judah's sure relief, Nahum turns to the chief consideration of his prophecy: the fall of Nineveh. Chapters 2 and 3 will again be punctuated with a style of alternating considerations. None of this bears the slightest resemblance, however, to theories of a sort of pan-Babylonian prophetic liturgy proposed by men like Sellin and Fohrer who isolate some three groups of liturgical material in Nahum. Bullock correctly points out that

> an alternating pattern between addresses to Nineveh and Judah is identifiable in chapter 2, but the kind of responses one would expect in a liturgy are hard to find in the book. Further, the superscription calls it an "oracle" and a "vision," terms that hardly qualify for a liturgical composition.[1]

Rather, the alternating considerations take the form of an introductory theme that once again traces the respective fortunes of Nineveh and Judah (2:1-2), followed by a pair of descriptions of Nineveh's fall (2:3-10; 3:1-7), and capped by concluding taunt songs (2:11-13; 3:8-19) that underscore the helplessness of Nineveh's situation. The whole section, then, flows from an introductory reiteration of the book's basic thesis: God is a just governor of the nations who will punish wicked Nineveh and restore His own people. This theme is

---

1. C. Hassell Bullock, *An Introduction to the Old Testament Prophetic Books* (Chicago: Moody, 1986), p. 220.

developed with regard to Nineveh by means of a long narrative section (2:3-10) and a woe oracle (3:1-7) and is specifically applied in the form of taunt songs, a literary technique well attested in ancient victory songs (2:11-13; 3:8-19). Graphic literary figures abound in these two chapters, discussions of which can be found in the introductory remarks to the individual units.

A. THEME (2:1-2 [HB 2:2-3])

Translation

A scatterer has come against you*.
"Guard* the fortress,
  watch the road,
strengthen your loins,
  summon all your strength!"
²For Yahweh will restore the splendor of Jacob
  like* the splendor* of Israel;
for plunderers have plundered them
  and destroyed their vines.*

Exegesis and Exposition

The fate of plotting Nineveh (cf. 1:11-15) is carried forward in the announcement of the arrival of its attacker. Nineveh's besieger is called literally "a scatterer."* The reference is doubtless to the coming army composed of Chaldeans, Medes, and Ummanmanda (Scythians?) before whom Nineveh eventually fell.

The demise of the decaying Assyrian empire was assured from the moment of Ashurbanipal's death in 626 B.C. In the following year the Chaldean king Nabopolassar would gain independence for Babylon and initiate the Neo-Babylonian kingdom. Over the course of the next dozen years Nabopolassar would succeed in gradually reducing the Assyrian hold on Mesopotamia, especially as he would finally make common cause with his allies. The ancient capital city of Ashur was to fall in 614 B.C.; Nineveh's own fall would take place a scant two years later. Because the Assyrians would survive to fight two still later campaigns (Haran, 609 B.C.; Carchemish, 605 B.C.), "scatterer" (cf. 3:18) is an appropriate designation for Nineveh's attackers. Nahum's prophecy centers on the fall of Nineveh, for its capture would mark the end of an era and the onset of the Neo-Babylonian empire, whose greatest king, Nebuchadnezzar II (605-562 B.C.), would prove to play a dramatic role in Judah's own later history (2 Kings 24:1–25:26; 2 Chron. 36:5-21; Jer. 37-39; 52:1-30; Ezek. 24; Dan. 1-4).

In the light of the critical announcement, Nahum issues a fourfold command. Each of the imperatives is expressed asyndetically, thus producing a staccato effect and lending urgency and dramatic appeal to the scene. Nahum's admonitions are probably to be understood as irony, perhaps with a touch of sarcasm. The four lie in a double set of brief commands, the first pair of which concerns the city itself and the second its citizens. The defenders are to "guard the fortress" and to "watch the road."* They are urged to make Nineveh's fortifications secure, at the same time watching closely the routes that would lead the enemy to the city. Having seen to the city's protection, they are to draw up their courage (lit. "strengthen your loins"*) and gather all their strength in order to be ready for instantaneous action, mentally and physically. Because Nineveh's doom had already been announced (chap. 1), all such efforts were obviously destined for failure. Mighty Nineveh would be powerless before its assailants, despite any and all efforts to defend it.

In contrast to the certain destruction of Nineveh, oft-destroyed Israel/Judah, whose defeat had frequently been reported in the Assyrian annals, would know the restoration* and splendor that only a sovereign and beneficent God can give. Indeed, the prophets frequently predict that God will yet "restore the fortunes" of His people (cf. Hos. 6:11; Joel 3:1 [HB 4:1]; Amos 9:14; see also Jer. 30:18; 31:23; 32:44) in an era of renewed refreshment, prosperity, and happiness. The promise harks back to God's people as heirs of the Abrahamic Covenant (Gen. 17:3-8; 22:17-18; 28:13-15). The play on words here, Jacob/Israel, is probably not to distinguish between the northern and southern kingdoms, for only Judah now existed, but rather, as Cyril suggested so long ago, to emphasize the great future revival and blessing of God. As a disciplined, repentant, and more matured Jacob had been given reassurance of his participation in God's covenant with Abraham, signified by his receiving the new name Israel (Gen. 32:28; 35:9-15), so God's people would yet know the glorious provisions of His irrevocable promises. Keil expresses it well:

> Both names stand here for the whole of Israel. . . . Jacob is the natural name which the people inherited from their forefather, and Israel the spiritual name which they had received from God. . . . He will exalt the nation once more to the lofty eminence of its divine calling.[2]

The realization of Israel's full covenant blessings will find fulfillment in a great future day when the glorious one (Isa. 24:14-16) will dwell (cf. Joel 3:17, 21 [HB. 4:17, 21]; Ezek. 48:35) in the midst of His people, thus giving glory to His nation and land (cf. Deut. 33:27-29; Isa. 4:2; 60:15).

---

2. C. F. Keil, *The Twelve Minor Prophets*, COT (Grand Rapids: Eerdmans, 1954), 2:19.

Additional Notes

2:1 (HB 2:2) †The announcement of the advance of the *"scatterer"* provides a thought that is bookended in 3:18-19 by the mention of the scattered refugees. The thought of destruction in 2:1-10 forms a literary link with 1:11-15 (cf. v. 14). The identity of the scatterer has been discussed often. Because the hiphil is regularly used of God as the disperser of nations (cf. 2 Sam. 22:15; Ps. 144:6; Isa. 24:1; Hab. 3:14), the possibility must be entertained that God could be intended here. But human agency is also expressed by the stem of this verb (cf. Jer. 23:1-2) and seems clearly the intent (although under the control of God) of the description that follows (cf. 3:5-7). Likewise, the synonym פָּזַר ("scatter") is used of both divine (Ps. 89:10 [HB 89:11]) and human (Jer. 50:17) agency. Attempts to identify any one particular scatterer (e.g., Cyaxeres the Mede, Nabopolassar, or Nebuchadnezzar) are pointless, the masc. sing. participle being either the common collective singular or simply singular because the precise enemy was not further identified in Nahum's predictive perception. If Nahum had been written later, as some critics affirm, more than likely the foe(s) would have been clearly designated. Attempts to emend the text to read "hammerer" (cf. *BHS*) are not suitable to the context.

†The phrase עָל . . . עָלָה ("come up against") is often used as part of the technical vocabulary for military action (cf. Isa. 7:1; Joel 1:6). It occurs with place names 12 times in the OT and with general designations 8 times.

†נָצוֹר ("guard") is an infinitive absolute, used here as a substitute for an imperative to give greater vividness. Accordingly Cathcart may be correct in suggesting that the three succeeding verbal forms (צַפֵּה, חַזֵּק, and אַמֵּץ) are also to be so identified. If so, all four verbal forms refer to the near antecedent "you" (i.e., Nineveh). Nevertheless, because it is true that an infinitive absolute when used as a substitute for a finite verbal form will often be constructed with a following required finite form, Gesenius considers the three verbal forms in question to be imperatives.[3] If Gesenius is right, since they are masc. sing. they could refer to the army of Nineveh or to the citizenry as a whole. Armerding's suggestion that they must refer to the "scatterer" (a masc. sing. participle), although yielding tolerable sense, is unnecessary and unsuitable both on the basis of the perceived literary structure of the book, which views vv. 1-2 as a restatement of the theme, and because the simplest understanding of the command

---

3. See A. B. Davidson, *Hebrew Syntax*, 3d ed. (Edinburgh: T. & T. Clark, 1901), p. 122.

takes them to refer to the defenders. Moreover, although the latter pair of imperatives might apply equally well to attacker or defender, the former pair seems clearly to be related to matters of defense.

צָפָה ("*watch*," cf. Akkadian *ṣapû*, "watch," "look out") carries with it the idea of an intense gazing (Ps. 66:7; Prov. 15:3). As a substantive it is used of a watchman, one usually stationed on a wall, whose duties included that of informing his superiors of impending danger (e.g., 2 Kings 9:17-20). The LXX ἐχ θλίψεως ("out of tribulation") arises from a wrong understanding of the MT.

"*Strengthening the loins*" implies not only the more familiar "girding up the loins" (i.e., of the full-flowing garment so as to be ready for action) but also gathering all of one's personal and physical strength, as the parallel line makes clear.

2:2 (HB 2:3) The phrase "*restore* the splendor" carries with it the more usual thought of "restore the fortune." The latter phrase is at times rendered "bring again the captivity" (KJV), an idea supported by the LXX and Pesh.[4] The thoughts are supplementary: A repentant, redeemed Israel will be freed from exile and restored to its promised land to enjoy an era of peace and prosperity permeated by the glorious presence of her heavenly Redeemer. It is small wonder, then, that Nahum can speak of the restored glory of Jacob or that Daniel can speak of the land of Israel as "the beautiful land" (Dan. 11:41).

†כִּגְאוֹן: The כ is customarily taken as a comparative particle, "like," even though Cathcart insists that the whole sentence be translated "for Yahweh is restoring the glory of Jacob, indeed the glory of Israel"[5] (i.e., rendering the particle as emphatic). גָּאוֹן can be translated positively ("splendor"), as here, or negatively ("pride"; cf. Prov. 8:13; 16:18; Isa. 16:6). Because of the occurrence of "their vines" in the latter part of the verse, some (cf. *BHS*) have suggested that the proper reading here should be גֶּפֶן ("vine"). Thus J. M. P. Smith declares: "The following line demands the mention of a vine here as the antecedent of its thought. The words 'vine' and 'pride' in Hebrew vary only in one consonant; hence confusion in copying was easy."[6] Some suggest that the "their" of the last line logically calls for an antecedent that is best provided by reading "vine" instead of "splendor" in the earlier parallel line. The proper antecedent of "their vines," however, as well as for the previous "plundered them," is the earlier occurring pair "Jacob" and "Israel." Those two names, though

---

4. For the phrase "restore the fortunes," see my remarks on Joel 3:1 in "Joel," in *EBC* (Grand Rapids: Zondervan, 1985), 7:259.

5. Kevin J. Cathcart, "More Philological Studies in Nahum," *JNSL* 7 (1979): 6.

6. J. M. P. Smith, *Micah, Zephaniah and Nahum*, ICC (Edinburgh: T. & T. Clark, 1911), p. 305.

mentioned individually for the purpose of drawing an analogy between Jacob/Israel and present/future Judah (see Exegesis and Exposition), taken together traditionally symbolized "all Israel." A logical plural, Jacob/Israel forms a proper antecedent for the pronouns "them" and "their" in the last two lines of v. 2. It may be added that the plurals in both cases could also refer to the people of Jacob/Israel.

Still further, the occurrence of "vines" does not necessitate a change of גָּאוֹן to גֶּפֶן, for obvious progression of thought is intended by introducing the subject of vines. The vine was a well-known symbol of the covenant relation between God and Israel (Isa. 5:1-7; Ezek. 17; cf. Ps. 80:8 [HB 80:9]). Together with the fig tree, the vine was symbolic of God's blessing upon His people (Hos. 2:12; Amos 4:9; Mic. 4:4; cf. 1 Kings 4:25 [HB 5:5]; 2 Kings 18:31; see also Ps. 105:33; Isa. 36:16; Jer. 5:17; 8:13; Hag. 2:19; Zech. 3:10). The point of the flow of thought in the verse is not repetition of figure but advance. Israel's glory/splendor lay in her relation to the glorious One. The evidence of His presence and blessings consisted in the fruitfulness of the vine. When the vine lay devastated by plague (e.g., Joel 1:4) or the invader's heel (as here), it was indicative of God's chastisement of His people. God used such means and symbols to bring His people to repentance and spiritual growth, from being "Jacob" to being "Israel." With repentance and restoration would come renewed splendor and fruitfulness.

†Some have seen in וּזְמֹרֵיהֶם ("and their vines") an indication of the meaning "branches/shoots" and hence another need for reading גֶּפֶן for גָּאוֹן in the earlier part of the verse. But Cathcart is probably right in suggesting that this is simply a case of *pars pro toto*, with a whole plant (vine and branches) being intended. Cathcart's own further suggestion of relating the word to the root *dmr* ("protect") and to an Ugaritic word for a class of soldiers seems forced, as does Stonehouse's proposal to translate the phrase "their oliveyards."[7] It is interesting to note, however, that גָּאוֹן and the root *dmr* occur in close proximity in Ex. 15 where, after Moses says, "Yah is my strength and power" (זִמְרָת, v. 2), he tells of the greatness of God's majesty (גָּאוֹן). It is of course impossible to ascertain whether Nahum was drawing upon the Exodus hymn (as did Isaiah [Isa. 12:2] and the psalmist [Ps. 118:14]), but if he was indebted to such a setting, the argument for

---

7. See Kevin J. Cathcart, *Nahum in the Light of Northwest Semitic* (Rome: Biblical Institute Press, 1973), pp. 85-86; G. G. V. Stonehouse, *The Books of the Prophets Zephaniah and Nahum*, Westminster Commentaries (London: Methuen, 1929), p. 115. For literature and examples of this root, see H. B. Huffmon, *Amorite Personal Names in the Mari Texts* (Baltimore: Johns Hopkins, 1965), pp. 187-88.

retaining גָּאוֹן would be further strengthened and the final זְמֹרֵיהֶם could be translated "their defenses." Significantly, שָׁחַת, which follows, is often used in military contexts by the prophets (cf. Isa. 14:20; Jer. 48:18; Ezek. 26:4).

It should be noted in passing that Maier attempts to build a case for the negative use of גָּאוֹן here by postulating that the previous verb is not derived from שׁוּב ("return/restore") but from שָׁבַב ("cut off/destroy"). Although this makes for a tolerable translation and allows the image of destroying to form an inclusio for the verse, it does not yield the smoothest exegetical sense. Verses 1-2 are clearly a reiteration of the theme of the book and thus contain, as traditionally affirmed, a contrast between the fate of Nineveh and that of Judah. Both instances of the particle כִּי are to be taken causally, the information contained in the second כִּי clause deriving from that introduced by the first.

†בְקָקוּם בֹּקְקִים ("plunderers have plundered them"): Two roots have generally been seen to lie behind these words: *bqq* I, "lay waste," and *bqq* II, "be luxuriant."[8] Because the reasons for the restoration of God's people/land are being introduced, the former root is the more appropriate one. It will figure prominently again in v. 11. The repetition of the root reflects Nahum's literary flair (cf. נָצוֹר מְצֻרָה in v. 2). Nahum's piling up of similar sounds is also to be noticed, *s* occurring eight times (cf. five uses of *ṣ* in v. 1). Because the chief emphasis of the judgment is directed against Nineveh, "the plunderers" are probably the Assyrians primarily, even though Israel had known the incursion of many invaders from all sides. Since Nahum prophesied during the reign of wicked Manasseh, the recent campaigns of Sennacherib and Esarhaddon would have been fresh in the memories of Nahum and all Judah. The annals of Sennacherib's third campaign report the following:

> As to Hezekiah, the Jew, he did not submit to my yoke. I laid siege to 46 of his strong cities, walled forts and to the countless small villages in their vicinity, and conquered (them) by means of well-stamped (earth-)ramps, and battering-rams brought (thus) near to the walls (combined with) the attack by foot soldiers, (using) mines, breeches as well as sapper work. I drove out (of them) 200,150 people, young and old, male and female, horses, mules, donkeys, camels, big and small cattle beyond counting and considered (them) booty.[9]

Esarhaddon records that he summoned his vassal Manasseh to Nineveh: "And I summoned the kings of the Hittiteland (Syria) and (those)

---

8. See KB-3, 1:144.
9. *ANET*, p. 288.

across the sea,—Ba'lu, king of Tyre, Manasseh, king of Judah. . . ."[10] If Nahum's prophecy dates from as late as Ashurbanipal's later western campaigns (650-648 B.C.), his words would be all the more vivid.[11]

B. DEVELOPMENT: FIRST DESCRIPTION OF NINEVEH'S DEMISE (2:3-10 [HB 2:4-11])

Nahum turns from his introductory theme to the first of two descriptions of Nineveh's certain destruction. The section contains two parts: (1) a description of the attackers of Nineveh (vv. 3-6), and (2) the consequences of the attack for Nineveh (vv. 7-10). It is marked by several distinctive literary features (references are to the MT) such as the use of simile (vv. 5, 8, 9), metonymy (v. 4), and synecdoche (v. 5), chiasmus (vv. 5, 8), enjambment (v. 8), and especially paronomasia, by which the poet makes skillful plays on words (vv. 9, 10, 11), sounds (vv. 5, 9, 10, 11), and even letters (vv. 5-6: *y, q, ḥ*; 9: *m*; 10: *k, q*; 11: *b*). There may be an instance of irony in v. 9.

Translation

The shields of the soldiers are red(dened),
   the warriors are dressed in scarlet;
the coverings* on the chariot are like fire in the day of its
      preparation,
   and the spears* are brandished.
⁴Through the streets the chariots race wildly,
   they rush to and fro through the squares.
Their appearance is like (flaming) torches;
   like (streaking) lightning they flash here and there.
⁵He gives orders to* his mighty men*,
   they stumble forward* on their way;
they hasten to the wall*,
   and the protective shield* is put in place*.
⁶The river gates are opened,
   and the palace collapses and crumbles.
⁷Her exiles* are carried away,
   and her handmaidens moan*—
like the sound of doves
   (while) beating* on their breasts.
⁸As for Nineveh, her waters* are like a pool* of water,
   and they (her citizens) are fleeing away.

---

10. *AR*, 2:265.
11. Cf. 2 Chron 33:11; see further R. D. Patterson and H. J. Austel, "1, 2 Kings," in *EBC*, 4:277-80.

"Stop! Stop!"* But no one turns around*.
9"Plunder* the silver! Plunder* the gold!"
For there is no end* to the treasure*,
   the abundance/wealth of all its precious things*.
10 She is destroyed, despoiled, and denuded*;
   hearts melt and knees shake;
there is trembling in all the loins,
   and all faces grow pale*.

Exegesis and Exposition

Nahum's description of the attack against Nineveh begins with a consideration of its attackers (vv. 3-6). The invading army's attire and equipment are described first (v. 3). They are clad in scarlet* and carry reddened* shields, all of which would not only give a distinctive color to the army in the hand-to-hand combat that was sure to come but would also provide a grim forecast of the shedding of the defenders' blood that would soon be mingled with the reddish clothing and equipment of the striking force. Adding to the awesome appearance of the "scatterer" was the terrifying sight of its chariotry. With horse and chariot bedecked with highly polished metal that gleamed like fire in the brilliant Near Eastern sunlight and with soldiers equipped with polished cypress spears (which often give a reddish appearance) that they brandished smartly (perhaps at first in military drill, but soon in battle), the effect of the whole spectacle was designed to strike terror into the stoutest of hearts.

A well-known question arises concerning the description of the chariots: Does the activity of the chariots continue the depiction of the basic preparatory actions of the besiegers (v. 3), or does it constitute the first movement in the attack against the city's walls (vv. 5-6)? The solution to the problem probably lies in viewing v. 4 as a hinge, a unit of thought that has individual existence and yet binds two portions of a narrative together. That such is the case may be corroborated by noting the designed stitching effect of the word "chariot" (v. 3) and the image of hurrying (cf. v. 5). The transitional nature of v. 4 as a hinge may be further seen in the employment of a first-slot preposition to introduce new, yet related, material (cf. 1:11) and the use of pivot-pattern parallelism, a feature often utilized in introducing a new unit.[12] The result is a clear pattern describing the siege of Nineveh: the enemy's assembling of his forces (v. 3), the initial advance (v. 4), and the all-out attack (vv. 5-6) and its aftermath (vv.

---

12. For details, see W. G. E. Watson, *Classical Hebrew Poetry* (Sheffield: JSOT Press, 1986), pp. 214-20.

7-10). Thus the hurrying and scurrying of men and chariots described in v. 4 constitute the preparatory stage that will lead to the opening assault. What a sight it must have been for the defenders, with metallic trappings sending back the sun's rays in such reflective splendor that they doubtless seemed to the observing eye to be now like a gleaming torch* and now like a flash of lightning!*

The scene progresses from one of preparation and advance to one of conflict (vv. 5-6). With the staging operations completed, the enemy commander gives the order to charge the wall. The seasoned warriors respond instantly. Hastening forward, they reach Nineveh's massive city wall where they put in place the mantelet that will give them protection from Nineveh's defenders during the siege operations (cf. Jer. 52:4; Ezek. 4:2). Thus protected from the flying arrows, falling stones, and lighted torches that came down from the city's protectors atop the wall, the process of breaching the city could begin. Typically this would include the use of siege mounds and towers, scaling ladders and tunneling operations, battering rams and axes, and the torching of the city gate. For Nineveh the means of defeat, however, came from an unexpected source. Nineveh trusted not only in her massive walls that Sennacherib had begun and named "The Wall That Terrifies the Enemy" (outer wall) and "The Wall Whose Splendor Overwhelms the Foe" (inner wall) but also in her surrounding moat and the proximity of the Tigris River. Yet ironically these defenses would work against the proud city. Diodorus reports that a series of torrential downpours swelled the "Euphrates" (i.e., the city's river systems: the Khosr, which flowed through the city, and the Tigris) and flooded Nineveh, thereby undermining its wall and causing the collapse of a significant part of it.

Sennacherib had also built a double dam for the Khosr River to form a reservoir for Nineveh's populace. This was augmented by a series of dam gates or sluices to regulate the supply of water to the city. Maier may be right in suggesting that the primary intent of Nahum's prediction is that the advancing enemy would shut the sluices, thereby cutting off the city's drinking supply. But with the reservoir full, the gates would again be opened, causing the already flooded Khosr to destroy the surrounding walls where it entered the Ninlil Gate. Furthermore: "The Quay Gate, at which the Khosr left the city, might also be devastated and in the intervening city much serious damage done. After the flow subsided, the entrance to Nineveh would have been made much easier for the besiegers."[13]

---

13. W. A. Maier, *The Book of Nahum* (Grand Rapids: Baker, 1980), p. 253. For full details relative to warfare in the ancient Near East, see Y. Yadin, *The Art of Biblical Warfare* (New York: McGraw-Hill, 1963); see also R. DeVaux, *Ancient Israel*, trans. John McHugh (New York: McGraw-Hill, 1961), pp. 215-57.

Perhaps these data are to be received as representing the true intent of the prophecy. In any case, biblical evidence (cf. 3:8ff.) and historical tradition combine to indicate that neither wall nor water would deliver the seemingly impregnable city. Accordingly, Zephaniah's prophecy takes on a touch of poignancy and pathos: "He will stretch out his hand against the north and destroy Assyria, leaving Nineveh utterly desolate and as dry as the desert" (Zeph. 2:13).

Nahum next envisions the subsequent collapse of Nineveh's magnificent palace. As the account unfolds, entrance to the city has been gained by the attackers, for the Assyrians are seen as being captured and led away into exile, while the women, pleading for mercy and bewailing their fate, are being led away moaning plaintively. Michael Travers aptly remarks:

> It is in this narrative unit that Nahum creates one of his most pathetic scenes, that of the terror of the innocent people of Nineveh. In a simile, Nahum depicts the anguish of the innocent slave girls of the city as the moan of doves (2:7). The slave girls are helpless victims of their masters' demise. The simile evokes pathos, compassion for the slaves' imminent deaths.[14]

Whether the magnificent north palace (recently built by Ashurbanipal and furnished with stunning examples of Assyrian *beaux artes*) or the south palace (built by Sennacherib and restored by Ashurbanipal, who kept most of the documents of his famous library there) is meant is not certain. Obviously, however, the city has been breached and the end is near.

The inevitable consequences that follow upon a city's capture are then detailed (vv. 8-10). The progression in the scene is heightened through anticipatory emphasis: "As for Nineveh." Henceforth the fate of the fallen city is in view. Conquered Nineveh is said to be "like a pool of water." The simile is both effective and apropos. Mighty Nineveh was situated in a favorable location that blessed her with an adequate water supply, one made more abundant by wise administrative leadership. But now the blessing has turned into a curse at the hands of the enemy whose siege operations have left Nineveh a veritable "pool of water." From the waters and the crumbling city the masses flee away in sheer panic.

In the midst of the clamor of the departing throng an impassioned voice rings out: "Stop! Stop!" Whether the person crying out is an Assyrian civil or military official, or whether the words were uttered by Nahum himself and intended to be taken as irony, is not certain. One thing is sure: No one turns around, much less halts, in his desperate flight. Another cry is heard (the entire scene is depicted

---

14. Richard D. Patterson and Michael E. Travers, "Literary Analysis and the Unity of Nahum," *GTJ* 9 (1988): 53.

with the author's characteristic picturesque brevity): "Plunder the silver! Plunder the gold!" Are they the words of the invaders, the prophet, or God Himself? Regardless, it is ultimately the certain judgment of God. Nineveh, who had heaped up hordes of captured treasure, would now face despoliation. The precious possessions of nations that poured into the Neo-Assyrian capital as a result of trade, tribute, and booty were almost beyond counting. Now Nineveh in turn would have her riches taken away. Maier's observations are once again to the point:

> In remarkable agreement with Nahum's prophecy that "there is no end to the store" is the factual account in the *Babylonian Chronicle* that the spoil taken at Nineveh's capture was "a quantity beyond counting." To understand that this statement was not a conventional exaggeration but that the plunder in the city which once plundered the adjacent world was fabulous in amount and value, one need but scan the records of the Sargonide dynasty to find the lists of heavy loot exacted by Nineveh. During Ashurbanipal's long reign the wealth of Babylon, Thebes, and Susa were brought to the capital. Significantly, little gold or silver has been discovered in the Kouyunjik mounds. The city was completely sacked.[15]

The call to loot the great city does not go unanswered. The final description comes to its readers like the repeated tolling of a bell in dirge-like wailing: *bûqâ! ûmĕbûqâ! ûmĕbullāqâ!* Nineveh was "destroyed, and despoiled, and denuded." The sight would send such a shudder through the strongest people that uncontrollable trembling would seize the entire body and their faces blanch. The portrayal is one of abject terror, painted again in synecdoche and picturesque brevity: melting hearts, knees knocking together, bodies writhing, faces made colorless with fright. Laetsch describes it well:

> The heart of the people, their spirit, once so fearless, so proud, so indomitable, now is melted like wax. Alarm, fear, terror, consternation, black despair grip them. No longer can they form any plan of resistance; their knees tremble; sickening anguish, nauseating horror grips their loins. Their faces "gather blackness," assume the livid, ashen color of people frightened to death.[16]

Additional Notes

2:3 (HB 2:4) The *reddened* shields refer perhaps to highly polished metal fittings that gleamed in the sunlight or to the dyeing of the shields with red color so as to strike terror into the hearts of

---

15. Maier, *Nahum*, p. 270. Maier devotes several pages (pp. 268-70) to documenting from the Assyrian records the immense riches acquired by the Assyrians in tribute and booty.
16. T. Laetsch, *The Minor Prophets* (St. Louis: Concordia, 1956), p. 305.

the enemy. Some have suggested that it might be a veiled reference to the Assyrians' blood that would yet be splattered on them. The adjective מְאָדָּם ("red") is sing., agreeing with מָגֵן, which, though sing., must be translated as a pl. in accordance with the demands of the context. Singular construct nouns followed by plurals may be translated as plurals. Interestingly enough, Nahum utilizes the opposite structure to express the pl. in the parallel line, the construct pl. being followed by a sing. noun אַנְשֵׁי־חַיִל ("warriors").[17]

"Redness" is also indicated in the parallel line by the adjective מְתֻלָּעִים ("scarlet," a plural in agreement with אַנְשֵׁי), referring to the attire of the soldiers. Some evidence exists for the wearing of reddish or purple dress into combat, perhaps to strike awe and terror into the hearts of the enemy (see Xenophon, *Cyropaedia* 6.4.1; cf. Ezek. 23:5-6). It is possible, of course, that this term may have simply been selected as a suitable parallel for מְאָדָּם, both words being used metonymically for the effects that the enemy's spattered blood had on the warriors' shields and garments.[18] Final interpretation must be correlated with the succeeding lines, which appear to focus on the description of the army at the outset of the campaign (v. 3b) before moving on to detail its approach (v. 4) and attack (vv. 5-6). If so, the scenario of "spattered blood" is probably out of synchronization.

†The translation of the word פלדות has been much disputed. On the basis of the Arabic *fûlād* (cf. Syriac *pûlād*, "steel"), it is often taken to mean some such metal (cf. NASB, NIV, NJB). Others have suggested a transposition of the first two consonants to read *lappîdôt* ("torches"; cf. *BHS*, Pesh., KJV), which, with the preceding "fire," can be rendered something like "flash like fire" (RSV). Some have suggested a complete transposition of the consonants to read *dlpt* (from the root דָּלַף, "drop") and propose the meaning "flickering" (thus NEB, "like flickering fire"). The difficulty of this well-known crux and the uncertainty reflected in the ancient versions (cf. LXX αἱ ἡνίαι and Vg *habenai*, "[the] reins") have brought forward many guesses. One of the more interesting is that of Cathcart who relates the word to Ugaritic *pld*, a type of covering, and takes the following "chariots" to be metonymy for the harnessed chariots. He therefore translates the clause as "fiery are the caparisons of the horses." Final certainty still escapes the expositor. Perhaps Cathcart and *BHS* are on the right track in relating the term to the Ugaritic word. Accordingly I have

---

17. For the pl. in compound expressions, see Davidson, *Syntax*, par. 15. For the parallel terms גְּבוֹרִים ‖ אַנְשֵׁי חַיִל, see the remarks of H. Eising, "חַיִל," *TDOT* 4:350.
18. See further T. H. Gaster, *Myth, Legend and Custom in the Old Testament* (New York: Peter Smith, 1969), p. 727.

provisionally translated the line "the coverings on the chariot are like fire." Thus construed, the thought is that the reflected gleam of the bedecked horses and chariots would strike yet further terror into the hearts of those who beheld the sight "on the day of its preparation" (i.e., for battle; cf. Prov. 21:31). Stylistically the whole thought is contained in two full lines that constitute a clear case of designed enjambment.

†וְהַבְּרֹשִׁים† has likewise been the subject of debate. The mention of a chariot in the previous clause has suggested to some the possible confusion of *b* and *p* in this one, thus an original וְהַפָּרָשִׁים ("steeds"; cf. NEB, RSV; or "horsemen," NJB, LXX). One may note the combination of רֶכֶב and פָּרָשִׁים in Isa. 21:7. Because the connection of the word in the MT with cypress wood seems inescapable, however, the idea of highly polished spears or lances being brandished by the accompanying infantry or by the members of the chariot team seems to be most likely.[19] The whole picture in verse 3*b* is clouded at best, with uncertainty attaching not only to the proper reading of the words in question but to the understanding of the final text. The difficulty of these lines was already apparent by the time of the ancient versions, as underscored by the great confusion evidenced in the LXX translation: ". . . with fire. In the day of his preparation the reins of their chariots and the horsemen will be disordered in their ranks."

2:4 (HB 2:5) בַּחוּצוֹת ("through the streets"): As the note in *The NIV Study Bible* points out, the scene of the action described in this verse has been understood as that of the attackers or the defenders.[20] The parallel term רְחֹבוֹת basically means "open places" and is used most often for wide places within a city or village (cf. Deut. 13:16 [HB 13:17]; Ezra 10:9; Neh. 8:1; Esther 4:6) but may possibly designate open places outside the city as well.[21] The flow of thought in the passage appears to demand a location outside Nineveh proper. Therefore, "streets/squares" should probably be understood of the surrounding villages that made up Nineveh's suburbs. The two words are used in parallel in such texts as Prov. 5:16; 7:12; 22:13; 26:13; Jer. 5:1; 9:20; Amos 5:16.

†יִתְהוֹלְלוּ† ("[the chariots] race wildly"), יִשְׁתַּקְשְׁקוּן ("they rush to and fro"), and יְרוֹצֵצוּ ("they flash here and there") are all alternate D-stem verbs (hithpolel, hithpalpel, and polel respectively) expressing

---

19. For suggestions on the various elements of the whole line, see *The Preliminary and Interim Report on the Hebrew Old Testament Text Project*, ed. Barthélemy et al. (New York: United Bible Societies, 1973-80), 5:342-43.
20. For full details, see the discussion in Maier, *Nahum*, pp. 243-44.
21. So BDB, p. 932a.

intensity of motion or special energy.[22] Certainly each is well utilized by Nahum, who again demonstrates his literary expertise in choosing not only words but also forms that stress the activity and movement of the advancing chariotry. The first verb is found in a similar context in Jer. 46:9; the other verbal forms are *hapax legomena*, although their roots are attested elsewhere in the MT.

The swift movement of the chariots with their polished metal glistening in the sunlight makes an appearance כַּלַּפִּידִם ("like [flaming] torches") and כַּבְּרָקִים ("like [flashing] lightning"). Again the whole effect produces awe and fright in the sight of all who beheld the spectacle. That vv. 3-4 have been preparatory to the actual attack to follow in vv. 5-6 is evident from Nahum's employment of the unit-ending pivot device combined with a double chiasmus.[23]

2:5 (HB 2:6) †יִזְכֹּר ("he remembers"; cf. LXX, Vg; NASB, NKJV) seems to make little sense in the context unless, as some suggest, Yahweh is the subject, not the attacking enemy. The difficulty has occasioned numerous alternative suggestions for understanding the verb, such as "summon" (NIV, RSV; cf. NJB) or "recount" (KJV), as well as several conjectural emendations.[24] Because the subject of the chapter thus far has been the "scatterer" and it would thus appear somewhat forced to suggest God as the subject here, because the usual meaning of the verb seems to be inappropriate if the "scatterer" is the subject, and because none of the conjectured readings can be viewed as satisfactory, some such alternative meaning as those suggested by several of the English versions needs to be found. "Recount" (KJV) gives little sense to the context; "summon" (NIV, RSV), while not attested elsewhere in the OT for this verb (unless perhaps Job 14:13), yields tolerable sense here. Perhaps the best solution is to see the precise nuance as something like "(give) order(s) (to)," a meaning found in the Akkadian cognate *zakāru*,[25] the thought being that of the commander giving the order to charge (the wall, v. 6*b*).

†יִכָּשְׁלוּ ("they stumble") has proved no less difficult. As Cathcart points out, the verb *kāšal* is customarily used in military contexts to indicate weariness and lack of progress. Since none of the conjectural emendations rests on authoritative grounds or appreciably improves

---

22. See J. Muilenburg, "Hebrew Rhetoric: Repetition and Style," in *Congress Volume*, VTS 1 (Leiden: E. J. Brill, 1953), p. 101.
23. For details, see Watson, *Hebrew Poetry*, pp. 214-21.
24. See further Maier, *Nahum*, pp. 247-48; Cathcart, *Nahum*, pp. 92-93. Maier concludes that "the variety and mutual exclusiveness of these emendations testify to their unsoundness." J. M. P. Smith (*Nahum*, p. 330) observes that "none of the emendations offered can be considered satisfactory."
25. See *CAD*, 21:16-17.

the sense, the nuance of the verb in this context must be decided in accordance with its normal semantic range. Because the following lines, like the one preceding this verb, envision the attacking force, it cannot be the defenders who "stumble on their way." Although a final solution is not yet forthcoming, it may be helpful to view the stumbling as occurring among the attacking soldiers. Thus, if the command to charge the wall has just been given (as suggested above), an overzealous response might well occasion a first stumbling, much as an athlete often stumbles by an initial overstride from a standing start. Even normally quick movements can cause stumbling. This idea is supported by the report of the next line: "They hasten to the wall."

†The sense of אַדִּירָיו ("his great ones") is not necessarily the more usual "officers/nobles/chieftains" or "picked troops" of the NIV, for the word probably refers to the magnificently attired (v. 3) general soldiery, here designated according to their established reputation, hence "his mighty men."

†חוֹמָתָהּ: Although some have suggested a repointing of the word to yield a directive *he* at its end (cf. *Tg. Neb.*, Pesh.), the MT is fully defensible as an adverbial accusative with 3d fem. sing. suffix, "(to) her (Nineveh's) walls (cf. LXX)."[26]

†וְהֻכַן הַסֹּכֵךְ ("and the protective shield is put in place"): Although Cathcart proposes repointing the verbal form וְהֻכַן to a hiphil infinitive absolute (to continue a preceding verbal clause, as is common in Northwest Semitic), the shift from an active verb to a passive one in parallelism is not without precedent (cf. Pss. 24:7; 69:14 [HB 69:15]; Jer. 31:4; Hos. 5:5). An emendation to a 3d masc. pl. verb (cf. LXX) is also not necessary. The shift from prefix- to suffix-conjugation verb not only brings the bicolon to an end but also portrays the result of the action of the initial surge to the wall.

The *hapax legomenon* הַסֹּכֵךְ must refer to some type of covering, as a glance at its cognates shows.[27] The consistent attention directed to the activities of the scatterer suggests a mantelet, or large protective shield, used by the attackers to shield them from the arrows and missiles of the defenders on the wall. Laetsch points out that

> the Assyrians used smaller, hutlike shelters which could be readily carried by a few men, or larger, towerlike structures rolled on wheels to the top of the embankments built round about the besieged city. The sheds offered protection to the soldiers while building these embankments, and later while seeking to undermine the foundations of the walls to hasten their collapse. The towers were provided with machines hurling stones

---

26. See further GKC par. 118d.
27. See R. D. Patterson, "סָכַךְ," *TWOT* 2:623-24.

and firebrands against the walls and into the city, in order to smash the fortifications and start conflagrations. Moved close to the walls, they also offered vantage points for attack by the soldiers.[28]

The presence of the double *k* in this word is a reminder of the prophet's frequent use of the repetition of a particular consonant for sound effect. (*k* is employed six times in this verse, three occurrences being found in this clause alone.) Such assonance not only links the action more closely but underscores dramatically the rushing movement to the wall.

2:6 (HB 2:7) †With the Hebrew שְׁעָרִים ("sluice/dam gates") compare Old South Arabic *t'rt* ("sluices"). For the root מוג ("melt"), see the discussion in the note on 1:5. The "melting" here could be viewed as a description of the fear aroused among the inhabitants of the palace or as the collapsing of the palace walls (so the ancient versions) due to flooding or fire. The noun הֵיכָל (cf. Sumerian *É·GAL;* Akkadian *ēkallu*), "large house," "palace," "temple," was also used in the OT for the holy place of the Solomonic Temple (1 Kings 6:17).[29] The definite article here renders it probable that the reference is to the king's palace rather than to one of Nineveh's several temples.

†והצב occurs as the first word in v. 7 (HB v. 8). It has proved to be a time-honored *crux interpretum.* Maier provides a list of more than a dozen suggestions that have been put forward as a sample of the many ideas that have been proposed. The ancient versions are likewise in disagreement. Basically three positions have been taken. (1) The form is a noun (*huṣṣāb*) meaning something like "beauty," "lady," "mistress" and refers either to Nineveh itself or to the statue of Ishtar that was housed there (Cathcart). (2) The form is a verb that is to be translated either "it is decreed" (NIV, NKJV) or "dissolved" (NASB; i.e., the palace or its column base[30]). (3) The form should be emended entirely.[31] The problem is heightened by the two feminine verbs that follow. J. M. P. Smith declares the form "insoluble" and the meaning of the whole line "hopelessly obscured."[32] Although final certainty continues to escape Nahum's interpreters, perhaps the solution lies along literary lines in (1) understanding (with Saggs) הֻצַּב in the sense of "dissolved" (cf. Akkadian *naṣābu,* "suck out," or Arabic *ḍabba,* "to hew to the ground") and (2) placing the word in v. 6 (HB v. 7), a

---

28. T. Laetsch, *The Minor Prophets,* p. 302. See for full details A. H. Layard, *Nineveh and Its Remains* (New York: Putnam, 1849), 2:281-86.
29. For details, see M. Ottosson, "הֵיכָל," *TDOT* 3:382-88.
30. See H. W. F. Saggs, "Nahum and the Fall of Nineveh," *JTS* 20 (1969): 221-22.
31. See further J. M. P. Smith, *Nahum,* pp. 320-21.
32. For suggestions as to solving the several problems in the whole line, see *Old Testament Text Project,* 5:343-45.

procedure that would yield a poetic 3/3 structure for this verse and a resultant double set of 2/2 in the following verse. This procedure would also provide a second consecutive verse that is closed by a passive suffix-conjugation verb. Thus construed the verse yields good sense: "The palace collapses and crumbles."

2:7 (HB 2:8) †It is better to point the MT גֻּלְּתָה ("[she was] stripped") as גָּלְתָה ("her exiles/captives").[33] Such a reading nicely anticipates the employment of the same figure in 3:10. By taking וְהֻצַּב with v. 6 and by following the pointing suggested here, v. 7, though in narrative structure, takes on poetic proportions as a deliberately designed instance of enjambment. Not only does such a procedure allow Nahum's literary abilities to be seen more clearly and provide a smooth translation of vv. 6 and 7, but there is also no interpretive need for the supposed presence of a stripped Assyrian queen, as suggested by some. Nor is there need for seeing the statue of Ishtar being carried away. The NIV translation "(the city) be exiled" rests on a repointing of MT to גָּלְתָה (cf. Vg *captivus abductus est*, "is carried away captive," and NEB "[the train of captives] goes into exile").

†The root נָהַג ("moan") is a *hapax legomenon*, although it is well attested in Syriac and Arabic. מְתֹפְפֹת ("beating") is a denominative from תֹּף ("tambourine"), here in the polel stem to indicate the women's repeated striking of their breasts in lamentation. Cathcart appropriately calls attention to a similar sentiment in the *Curse of Agade*. Such actions were typically carried out by women who were pleading for mercy in situations like these.[34]

2:8 (HB 2:9) †כִּבְרֵכַת־מַיִם ("like a pool of water"): The word for pool is frequently attested in the OT and appears in the Siloam inscription (line 5)[35] as well as in Ugaritic, South Arabic, and Egyptian (= *brkt*). Recent scholarship has tended to suggest a second root alongside the more customary one that yields בָּרַךְ ("bless").[36] It at times implies an artificial pool (Neh. 3:16), a meaning that is appropriate here.

†מֵימֶי הִיא ("her waters"): These words have occasioned numerous comments. Among those that attempt to retain the consonantal text of the MT, two primary ideas have been put forward. (1) Some have opted for dividing the two words as מִן ("from") plus the pl. of יוֹם

---

33. For the collective meaning "exiles" here, see BDB, p. 163b.
34. See S. N. Kramer's translation of "The Curse of Agade" in *ANETS*, p. 214. The figure of the weeping woman is abundantly attested in the literature and artistry of the ancient Near East and the OT, as is the action of beating the breast in contrition (cf. Jer. 31:15; Luke 18:13; 23:27). For weeping women pleading for mercy and subsequently lamenting their captured state, see Layard, *Nineveh*, 2:286-87.
35. *KAI*, no. 189.
36. See, e.g., KB-3, 1:154.

("day") plus הָ (= 3d fem. sing. pronominal suffix) and translating "throughout her days" (NASB; cf. KJV, "of old"). (2) Most view the first word as the pl. construct of מֵי ("waters"), as suggested by the ancient versions. But, because the pl. construct form is followed by a fem. sing. independent pronoun, a construction that grammarians have generally considered to be "evidently corrupt,"[37] critical scholars have tended to emend the text to read מֵימֶיהָ ("her waters").[38] This approach, combined with the following phrase, has produced translations such as "whose waters run away" (RSV; cf. NJB). As Cathcart demonstrates, however, precedent for the reading found in the MT is attested amply in Ugaritic, where the independent pronoun in such cases is found in both the genitive and accusative.[39] Taking the MT at face value and following Keil's observation that the next clause deals with Nineveh's citizens, not water,[40] the whole idea makes good sense by rendering it according to the translation provided at the beginning of this section. The effect is again almost poetic, yielding three lines composed as 3/2/2, with enjambment over lines one and two.

עִמְדוּ עֲמֹדוּ† ("Stop! Stop!"): The second imperative is pausal. NIV inserts "they cry" after the two imperatives *ad sensum*, a proposal put forward by several critics who insert some such form as אָמַר ("say/cry") or זָעַק ("cry/yell") before or after the imperatives. The compressed speech and asyndetically juxtaposed imperatives of the MT are far more dramatic as the text stands.

וְאֵין מַפְנֶה† ("but no one turns around"): The words are reminiscent of Jer. 46:5, 21. Cathcart perspicaciously calls attention to the heaping up of the letter *m* in this verse (nine times), an assonance that enhances dramatic effect.

2:9 (HB 2:10) בֹּזּוּ† ("plunder!"): The double imperative doubtless answers to the pair in the previous verse. LXX reads διήρπαζον ("they seized"), suggesting an original suffix-conjugation in their exemplar.

---

37. For details, see GKC par. 130d (n.); note also the remarks of J. M. P. Smith, *Nahum*, pp. 322, 332; A. R. Hulst, *Old Testament Translation Problems* (Leiden: E. J. Brill, 1960), pp. 247-48.
38. See the critical note in *BHS*.
39. See for further details C. Gordon, *Ugaritic Textbook* (Rome: Pontifical Biblical Institute, 1965), pp. 34-36; M. Dahood, "The Independent Personal Pronoun in the Oblique Case in Hebrew," *CBQ* 32 (1970): 86-90; *Psalms*, AB (Garden City, N.Y.: Doubleday, 1970), 3:374. Maier's suggestion (*Nahum*, p. 266) to read the independent pronoun as הִי ("lamentation"), here written with an added *aleph* due perhaps to a scribal corruption (cf. GKC par. 23i), rests on a *hapax legomenon* in Ezek. 2:10, which itself is a *crux interpretum* that has occasioned much controversy. The proposal has little to commend it. For the Ezekiel problem, see the remarks of M. Greenberg, *Ezekiel, 1-20*, AB (Garden City, N.Y.: Doubleday, 1983), p. 67.
40. C. F. Keil, *Minor Prophets*, 2:25.

Although this reading is followed by some critics, it is unnecessary and at variance with the dramatic effect in the MT. Silver and gold often appear as set pairs to express wealth or booty (Gen. 24:34; Josh. 6:19).[41]

†אֵין קֵצֶה ("there is no end"; cf. 3:3, 9) occurs in the OT outside Nahum only in the remarkable parallel in Isa. 2:7. Armerding points this out as one of many texts that show a literary interdependence between the two prophets.

†כְּלִי חֶמְדָּה ("precious things") occurs elsewhere with silver and gold (2 Chron. 32:27; Dan. 11:8; Hos. 13:15). The root *ḥmd* connotes a strong desire, hence "desirable/precious things," and as such was intended possibly as a suitable literary envelope with the earlier כֶּסֶף ("silver").

†תְּכוּנָה ("treasure," from כוּן ["be established," "prepare"]) refers to the furnishings of proud Nineveh. The booty to be taken from Nineveh thus included not only its precious metals but also the many objects and utensils made from them. Together with the next line, the general sense is that Nineveh possessed untold wealth of every conceivable kind. *Tĕkûnâ* also performs a rhyming function with *ḥemdâ*.

2:10 (HB 2:11) † בוּקָה וּמְבוּקָה וּמְבֻלָּקָה ("destroyed and despoiled and denuded"): The assonance and alliteration are striking. Cathcart calls attention to a stylistic resemblance with Isa. 22:5 as well as to the employment of the root בָּלַק with בָּקַק in Isa. 24:1 followed by the use of בָּקַק and בָּזַז two verses later. Although this type of paronomasia is common enough in the OT (e.g., Joel 2:2; Mic. 1:10ff.; cf. Nah. 2:2 [HB 2:3]), the parallels with Isaiah are striking and may point to a further literary relationship between the two prophets.

†The appearance of the root חוּל ("tremble") in parallel with קִבְּצוּ פָארוּר ("[all faces] grow pale") recalls Joel 2:6.[42] Though the first root is common enough, the word פָארוּר is a rare and somewhat troublesome word. Several etymologies have been proposed. (1) פָרוּר ("pot"). Combined with קְבָץ, the thought is assumed to be describing a reaction of terror. Much as one gathers blackness from the burned part of a pot, so terrified faces "gather blackness" (KJV).[43] (2) פָרַר ("break in pieces"). Due to great fear, all faces have gathered wrinkles (Ehrlich).[44] (3) פַארוּר ("glow," "red/crimson"). Faces glow with excite-

---

41. See M. Dahood, "Ugaritic-Hebrew Parallel Pairs," *RSP*, 1:234-35. Note also the several entries on the black obelisk of Shalmaneser III, in *ANET*, p. 231; *AR*, 1:211 (pars. 589, 590, 592, 593).
42. For discussion of the use of these words in Joel 2:6, see my note in "Joel," in *EBC*, 7:249.
43. This derivation is followed by J. A. Thompson in his comments on Joel 2:6 (*IB*, p. 745); cf. LXX.
44. The image is thus that of the puckered forehead. For details, see S. M. Lehrman, "Joel," in *Soncino Edition of the Bible*, ed. A. Cohen (New York: Soncino Books, 1948), p. 66.

ment due to the press of the fierce battle (KB).[45] (4) פָּאַר ("beautify"). Combined with the verb קְבַץ the idea would be "to draw in beauty," "to withdraw (healthy) color," hence "grow pale" (NASB, NIV; S. R. Driver).[46] On the whole the last alternative seems the simplest and has been followed in the translation above.[47]

Cathcart demonstrates the close connection of the last three lines of v. 10 with the thought of Isa. 13:7-8:

> Both texts mention the melting of hearts. . . . In Nahum, there is mention of the trembling of the knees; in the Isaiah text, the feebleness of the hands. Anguish in the loins and the change of the colour of the face are found in both passages. For anguish in the loins, compare also Is. 21:3.[48]

Once again a connection between Isaiah and Nahum seems certain.

Nahum's first description of Nineveh's fall ends on a tragic but powerful note. Herbert Marks captures it well: "The description culminates in a magnificent cadence in which the repetition of 'all' enforces the note of finality, and the conversion of splendor to ruin is represented not in itself, but more powerfully by its effect on those who suffer it."[49]

---

45. KB, p. 750. Although differing etymological associations are put forward to substantiate the position, several scholars favor the idea of redness; cf., e.g., L. C. Allen, *The Books of Joel, Obadiah, Jonah and Micah*, NICOT (Grand Rapids: Eerdmans, 1976), p. 65; Julius A. Bewer, *Obadiah and Joel*, ICC (Edinburgh: T. & T. Clark, 1985), pp. 101-2. One may also note W. Rudolph, who has defended this idea in several publications; for bibliographical data, see KB-3, 3:860.

46. Among those advocating paleness as the thought here, see S. R. Driver, *The Books of Joel and Amos* (Cambridge: University Press, 1915), p. 53; C. F. Keil, *Minor Prophets*, 1:192-93; A. Haldar, *Studies in the Book of Nahum* (Uppsala: Lundquistska Bokhandeln, 1947), p. 59.

47. Numerous miscellaneous attempts have been made to solve this *crux interpretum*. To my knowledge no one has suggested viewing the *p* in *pā'rûr* as the Semitic conjunctive particle "and (then)" (cf. Ugaritic *p*; Arabic *f*) prefixed to the verb *'ārar* (cf. Akkadian *arāru* II, "fear"). Together with the previous קִבְּצוּ, the twice occurring phrase (Joel 2:6; Nah. 2:10) could be an example of hendiadys that became idiomatic, "convulsed with fear." Although such a meaning is unattested in the OT for *'ārar*, the idiom as such could be a borrowed one. With repointing, the usual understanding of the verb ("curse") would also yield tolerable idiomatic sense, the whole line reading, "every face contracts/is contracted and curses." קִבְּצוּ here could of course also be repointed as a qal passive. An intransitive sense is known in Arabic (*qabaḍa*, V form). For proposed examples of conjunctive *p* in the OT, see M. Dahood, *Psalms*, 3:410. The phrase remains an insoluble crux; I have followed the majority of scholars in translating (*ad sensum*), "all faces grow pale."

48. Cathcart, *Nahum*, p. 104.

49. Herbert Marks, "The Twelve Prophets," in *The Literary Guide to the Bible*, ed. Robert Alter and Frank Kermode (Cambridge: Harvard U., 1987), p. 215.

C. APPLICATION: THE DISCREDITED CITY
(2:11-13 [HB 2:12-14])

If the prophet's own words were not evident in the preceding cries (vv. 9b-10), they surely come forward here. Contemplating the demise of arrogant Nineveh, Nahum utilizes a taunt song, a literary form that was common in the ancient Near East. As a taunt song it takes its place as a subtype of satire, the first of three such pieces directed against Nineveh (cf. 3:8-13; 3:14-19). The satirical tone is Juvenalian. Using an extended metaphor (or allegory), Nineveh is ironically compared to a lion's den, now no longer the lair of an invincible predator or a den of refuge for its cubs but reduced to ashes. The point of the satirical taunt song is clear. Nineveh shall be judged for its self-ishness, rapacity, and cruelty. Other literary features include rhetorical question, enjambment, and paronomasia (v. 11), chiasmus (v. 12), *oratio variata* and synecdoche (v. 13), and the employment of repetition and refrain: "behold" (v. 13; cf. 2:1; 3:5, 13), "I am against you" (v. 13; cf. 3:5), and the motif of the message/messenger (v. 13; cf. 2:1; 3:7, 19).

Translation

Where* is the dwelling place* of the lion*,
  the place* for the young lions*,
where the lion, the lioness* went,
  the lion cub, and none made (them) afraid*?
¹²The lion tore for the sake of his cubs*
  and strangled* for his lionesses;
yes, he filled his lair* with prey
  and his dens* with torn flesh.
¹³Behold*, I am against you—
  the declaration of Yahweh Sabaoth:
I will burn up her chariots in smoke*,
  and a sword will devour your young lions*;
I will cut off your prey from the earth,
  and the voice of your messengers*
  will be heard no more.

Exegesis and Exposition

The lion motif is particularly appropriate. History attests that Sennacherib compared himself to a lion,[50] decorating his palace free-

---

50. See *AR*, 2:129. J. M. P. Smith (*Nahum*, p. 324) properly remarks: "The lion was the favourite animal for artistic and decorative purposes in Assyria; hence the figure is peculiarly fitting."

ly with sphinxlike lion statues. Other Assyrian kings referred to themselves as lions and adorned their palaces with various artistic representations of the lion. Reliefs of the Assyrian kings on the lion hunt appear frequently on the palace walls.

With the description of the demise and despoliation of the supposedly invincible city of Nineveh given and the notice of the plight of its citizenry completed, Nahum can now ask, "Where?" The mighty lion of the nations (Assyria) used to proceed at will from its impenetrable lair (Nineveh) to return its prey to its pride (the citizens of Nineveh). Where is all of that now? Once Nineveh bulged with the bounteous booty that her kings had brought within its walls. The annals of the Assyrian kings repeatedly report the ravenous rapacity of the Assyrian conquerors and the barbaric cruelty with which they acquired their ill-gotten gain. Thus Assyria's great king Ashurbanipal boasts of his subjugation of Akkad:

> As for those men . . . I slit their mouths (*v.*, tongues) and brought them low. The rest of the people, alive, by the colossi, between which they had cut down Sennacherib, the father of the father who begot me,—at that time, I cut down those people there, as an offering to his shade. Their dismembered bodies (lit. flesh) I fed to the dogs, swine, wolves, and eagles, to the birds of heaven and the fish of the deep.[51]

And in a campaign against Elam he reports:

> At the command of Assur and Ishtar, I entered into its palaces and dwelt there amidst rejoicing. I opened his treasure-houses, wherein were heaped up the silver, gold, property and goods, which the former kings of Elam, down to (and including) the kings of these (present) days, had gathered and laid up, and into which no foe other than myself had ever brought his hand,—(these treasures) I carried out and counted as spoil.[52]

In the light of such brutality God's pronouncement again is heard: "Behold, I am against you." Such is the solemn utterance of the Lord of Hosts (Yahweh Sabaoth). This term (found about 260 times in the OT) declares God's sovereignty not only over creation (Amos 4:13) but also over all nations and over earth's history (Isa. 37:16). Although God had used Assyria as His agent to punish an unrepentant Israel, He could and would use still another army (who in turn will one day suffer God's chastisement for its own sin, Jer. 50:18) to effect the just judgment of haughty Assyria (Zeph. 2:13-15), the very nation for whom a merciful God had earlier been so concerned (Jonah 4:2, 11). Ultimately Israel herself will triumph through

---

51. *AR*, 2:304.
52. *AR*, 2:309; for other examples of Assyrian cruelty and rapacity, see H. E. Freeman, *Nahum Zephaniah Habakkuk*, Everyman's Bible Commentary (Chicago: Moody, 1973), pp. 36-38; Maier, *Nahum*, pp. 281-83.

her Lord of Hosts, who will rule everlastingly over all forces, heavenly and earthly alike (1 Sam. 17:45; Isa. 24:21-23; 34:1-10).

The results of the divine sentence for Nineveh are spelled out: The city will go up in smoke*, her citizens will be put to the sword, and her immense treasures will be carried off, never to be replenished. The voice of those messengers who carried the words and business of the Assyrian king to the far-flung provinces of the once mighty empire will be heard no more.

In v. 13, several of Nahum's themes come temporarily to the surface before finding their final expression in chap. 3: "declares the LORD" (cf. 1:12 with 3:5), "against/concerning you" (cf. 1:14 with 3:5), "fire" (cf. 1:6; 2:4 with 3:13, 15), "devouring" (cf. 1:14-15 with 3:15), cruelty/wickedness (cf. 1:11 with 3:19), "no one/none" (cf. 1:14-15 with 3:6-7, 18-19), and the motif of the messenger/message (cf. 1:15 with 3:5, 19). Armerding's observation is well taken:

> This verse draws together the major motifs and vocabulary of Nahum's prophecy: the Lord's inexorable opposition to Nineveh; the destruction of its military resources; the role of "sword" and "fire" that "consume" the enemy; the cutting off of Nineveh and its "prey"; the termination of its cruelty, symbolized by the "young lions"; and the reversal of fortunes that awaits Assyria and Judah, exemplified in the fate of the "heralds."[53]

Just as in this section, so Nahum's first oracle (chap. 1) had ended with a pronouncement of judgment for Nineveh/Assyria but had included a message of hope for Judah as well (vv. 12-15). Nahum's second oracle is not yet through, however, and before he adds a further note of good news (3:19) he will again consider the defeat and demise of Nineveh, detailing the reasons for the divine sentence (3:1-7, 8-19).

Additional Notes

2:11 (HB 2:12) †אַיֵּה ("where?"), besides its use as an interrogative particle requesting information, can be used, as here, to introduce a taunt (cf. Jer. 2:28). It was also commonly utilized in forming personal names (e.g., אִיּוֹב = 'ayya 'abu(m), "Where Is the Father?" [= Job]).

†מָעוֹן ("dwelling place"), while used of God's habitation, whether in heaven (Deut. 26:15) or in the Temple (2 Chron. 36:15), can also be used, as here, for the lair of animals. In the latter instances the masc. noun is consistently used by the prophets to depict the haunt of desolate cities (e.g., Jer. 9:10; 10:22; 49:35; 51:37), but such is not the case with fem. forms (cf. Job 38:40; Amos 3:4).

†מִרְעֶה ("pasture") in the parallel line has met with considerable

---

53. C. Armerding, "Nahum," in *EBC*, 7:479.

controversy. Because the reading מְעָרָה ("cave"; cf. *BHS*) would seem to make a more suitable parallel with the "dwelling place" (or den) of the first line, many modern translations have decided for such an emendation (NJB, NEB, RSV). The change requires simply a transposition of two letters. But the proposed alternative reading lacks textual support and would be ungrammatical due to the presence of the following masc. pronouns. Moreover, the proposed word does not appear in the OT in the sense of a den for animals. The MT should be retained—but in what sense? Some decide for the sense of "feeding place" (from the root רָעָה, "to feed"; e.g., Keil, NASB, NIV), others for the food grown there, hence "fodder" (Maier). מִרְעֶה, however, can designate not only a pasture but open country. Consequently the word may intend simply the district where the lion's cave was found. The translation "place" is a contextual one that leaves the final decision open. In any case, Keil's remarks remain valid: "The point of comparison is the predatory lust of its rulers and their warriors, who crushed the nations like lions, plundering their treasures, and bringing them together in Nineveh."[54]

The several words for lion here seem intended to represent the whole family (or pride) of lions: אַרְיֵה ("lion"), לָבִיא ("lioness"), גּוּר אַרְיֵה ("lion cub"), and כְּפִיר ("young lion"). The ancient versions, however understand לָבִיא as an infinitive construct, apparently reading לָבוֹא from בּוֹא ("enter"). Accordingly some (Ehrlich, Haldar, Maier) take the MT as a hiphil infinitive construct form shortened from לְהָבִיא ("to bring"; cf. Jer. 27:7).

†וְאֵין מַחֲרִיד ("none made [them] afraid"; "with nothing to fear" [NIV]): The phrase is reminiscent of the often repeated description of those undisturbed by danger, whether men (Mic. 4:4) or animals and birds (Deut. 28:6; Isa. 17:2; Jer. 7:33; Ezek. 34:28; Zeph. 3:13). The אֲשֶׁר . . . שָׁם ("where . . . there") in the previous line is a relative clause introduced by a relative particle and closed by a resumptive adverb. The clause has locative force. The relative pronoun here betrays its Akkadian origin as a noun (*ašru* [construct *ašar*], "place"; cf. Aramaic/Syriac אֲתַר/*'ătar* with secondary development into a locative relative "place where," with further development in Hebrew as a general relative particle). A similar nominal origin and development has been suggested for Phoenician *'ēš* from West Semitic *'iš*, "man (who)," but this remains unproved. The Semitic languages also know of a double particle series to express the relative idea, the demonstrative/explicative particles *du* and *tu*, both of which are attested in the MT (particularly in older poetic material) as זוּ (e.g., Ex. 15:13)

---

54. Keil, *Minor Prophets*, 2:27.

and שׁ (e.g., Num. 24:15).[55] The final two lines of v. 11 provide a case of progressive enjambment.[56]

2:12 (HB 2:13) †גְּרוֹתָיו ("his cubs"): גּוּר ("whelp") and גֹּר ("lion cub") are attested. Since masc. sing. Hebrew nouns frequently take fem. plurals, there is no need to emend the text to a masc. pl. as some (e.g., Duhm) have done.

†מְחַנֵּק ("strangled"): Although it has been charged by some that the idea of lions strangling their prey is unrealistic,[57] with the result that some such translation as "tore up" (NJB) has been substituted, the verb means "strangle" throughout the Semitic family of languages and is consistently so used in the OT. As Cathcart observes:

> Lions do strangle their prey and we have excellent representations from the Near East of lions strangling their prey. Most impressive is a Phoenician ivory (c. 715 B.C.) in the British Museum which shows a lioness standing over a man with its left paw around his neck. Even older, on a shell, dating from the 3rd millennium B.C., and excavated at Lagash, there is a scene of a lion attacking a bull. The lion has its paw and foreleg right around the bull's neck, and its teeth buried in the back of its neck.[58]

The root *ṭrp* ("tear/rip open") occurs three times in this verse ("tore," "prey," "torn flesh"), strategically placed in poetic parallelism and in chiasmus so as to emphasize the viciousness of the lion with regard to its prey. The usual distinction between the two words for prey (טֶרֶף and טְרֵפָה) is that the latter word lays more stress on the torn condition of the victim.[59]

†חֹרָיו וּמְעֹנֹתָיו ("his lairs/caves . . . his dens"): The plurals here may indicate the change of location that a lion makes at times, or they may reflect popular speech dealing with general activities: (a) lion(s) bring(s) the prey into his (their) lair(s). In any case, Nineveh is still in view.

2:13 (HB 2:14) †הִנְנִי (lit. "Behold me"): Nahum uses the particle הִנֵּה several times at strategic points as a transitional device (cf. 1:15; 3:5, 13). This particle is often used to introduce divine pronouncements and to authenticate a prophet's words.[60] The phrase "I am

---

55. Note also the employment of the explicative/relative particle in Judg. 5:5; see R. D. Patterson, "The Song of Deborah," in *Tradition and Testament: Essays in Honor of Charles Lee Feinberg*, ed. John S. Feinberg and Paul D. Feinberg (Chicago: Moody, 1981), pp. 127, 131, 154 n. 31. For examples of the possibility of Hebrew אִישׁ employed as a relative pronoun, see 1 Sam. 22:2; 2 Sam. 23:7; Ps. 112:1; Prov. 26:19. The possible relatival use of אִישׁ has been suggested in recent years by R. Gelio, "È possibile un 'îš relativo/demonstrativo in ebraico biblico?" *RivB* 31 (1983): 410-34.
56. For progressive enjambment, see Watson, *Hebrew Poetry*, p. 334.
57. See J. M. P. Smith, *Nahum*, pp. 325, 333.
58. Cathcart, *Nahum*, pp. 107-8.
59. See BDB, p. 383.
60. See D. Vetter, "הִנֵּה," *THAT*, 1:505-7.

against you" contains a 2d fem. sing. pronoun referring to Nineveh, the intended comparison in the allegory. It recurs with הִנְנִי in 3:5. The introductory particle is reinforced by the noun נְאֻם ("declaration of"; cf. NIV, "declares") that so frequently is used to confirm the divine source of a prophet's message (cf. Jer. 9:22; 23:31; Ezek. 20:3; Zech. 12:1).[61]

†בֶּעָשָׁן ("in the smoke"), a form of zeugma (or synecdoche), stresses the burning of the vaunted Assyrian war chariots.[62]

†כְּפִירָיִךְ ("your young lions"): The metaphor of calling royalty, leaders, or warriors by animal names is common in both Ugaritic and Hebrew.[63] The figure of devouring the prey (vv. 11-12) is continued here, but with image transfer: the young lions are now the prey devoured by the enemy's sword. With the reintroduction of direct discussion with Nineveh, the poet returns to using a 2d fem. sing. suffix (cf. "against you" in line 1 of this verse), thus making a shift from the 3d fem. sing. suffix with "her chariot(s)" in the parallel line. Such cases of *oratio variata* (or enallage) are common in Semitic poetry (cf. Ps. 23) and often employed by the prophets (e.g., Isa. 1:29; Jer. 22:24; Mic. 7:19). Proposed emendations to "your chariots" (cf. *BHS*) are therefore unnecessary.[64]

†מַלְאָכֵכֵה ("your messengers"): The MT is strange; one would expect מַלְאָכַיִךְ. The form in the text has been taken as a dialectal variant, an Aramaism, or unusual pronominal form, or has been understood as being derived from מְלָאכָה ("work"; cf. LXX, Pesh.). The poet's use of the messenger/message motif to end each principal section gives assurance of the meaning of the term, even though the form remains somewhat of an enigma. Maier may be correct in viewing it as a unique form that is not without a reasonable basis:

> There is an unusual latitude in the form of the nominal suffixes for the second person singular. If this person in the masculine may take the ending כָה ("(Ps 139:5, with the verbal suffix counterpart ָ-ךָ, Gen 27:7); if the second sing. fem. suffix may be כִי ("(Jer 11:15, with the same form for the verbal suffix, Ps 103:4), or יְכִי ("(2 Kings 4:3), is it unreasonable to assume that מַלְאָכֵכֵה is a unique suffix of the second sing. fem., the gender and number required by the context?[65]

---

61. See further L. J. Coppes, "נְאֻם," *TWOT* 2:541-42.
62. A similar use of "fire" in synecdoche occurs at 3:5.
63. See Watson, *Hebrew Poetry*, p. 268.
64. Note that the LXX reads πληθός σου, "your multitude" (cf. 4QNah rwbkh, "your abundance"). For *oratio variata* in change of discourse in Greek, see A. T. Robertson, *A Grammar of the Greek New Testament in the Light of Historical Research* (Nashville: Broadman, 1934), pp. 442-43; for its employment in the Song of Solomon, see M. H. Pope, *Song of Songs*, AB (Garden City, N.Y.: Doubleday, 1977), p. 297.
65. Maier, *Nahum*, p. 289.

3

The Doom of Nineveh Described, Part Two (Nahum 3:1-19)

With the completion of the first description of Nineveh's doom, which has been capped by a taunt song castigating the discredited city (2:3-13), Nahum turns once again to developing the theme (2:1-2) of the section (2:1–3:19). The demise of Nineveh is rehearsed again (3:1-7), this time however underlining the reasons that necessitate such a devastation. Nahum will again build upon that description with another taunt song, which will occupy the greater portion of the third chapter (vv. 8-19) and flow in two movements. The first unit compares Nineveh's situation to that of once-proud Thebes, which also fell despite its seeming impregnability (vv. 8-13); the second constitutes a stinging concluding condemnation of Nineveh itself (vv. 14-19). Since this chapter (like the preceding) forms a part of the second half of the book, the headings of the individual units will reflect the outline given in the Introduction.

D. DEVELOPMENT: SECOND DESCRIPTION OF NINEVEH'S DEMISE (3:1-7)

Nahum writes his second description of Nineveh's certain doom in the form of a woe oracle. The initial "woe" is a word drawn from a lamentation liturgy for the dead. As utilized by the prophet, while containing a prophetic declaration and description of the coming judgment, it also constitutes a formal denunciation of the doomed city. Woe oracles normally contain three elements: invective, criticism, and threat. Here these are arranged in chiasmus: invective (vv. 1, 7), threat (vv. 2-3, 5-6), criticism (v. 4). This betrays a deliberate design that imparts information for understanding the author's intentions not only in the whole unit but also in the well-known *crux interpretum* at v. 4 (see Exegesis and Exposition). Other literary features in this section include merismus (v. 1), picturesque brevity (vv. 2, 3), alliteration and staircase parallelism (v. 4), metaphor (vv. 4, 5-6), paronomasia, *oratio variata*, enjambment, and refrain (v. 7).

Translation

Woe* to the city of blood,
   all of it a lie;
full of plunder*,
   it never lacks* prey*.
²The crack* of whips*
   and the rumble of wheels;
galloping horses*
   and jolting chariots*;
³charging calvalry*,
   flashing* swords,
   and gleaming* spears;
an abundance of slain
   and a multitude of corpses.
There is no end to the bodies;
   they stumble over the dead.
⁴(It is) because of* the numerous harlotries of the harlot,
   she who is graciously fair*,
   the mistress of sorceries*;
(it is) she who makes merchandise* of the nations by her
      harlotries,
   and peoples* by her sorceries.
⁵"Behold I am against you"—
   the declaration of Yahweh Sabaoth:
"I will lift* your skirt over your face,
   and I will show the nations your nakedness
   and kingdoms your shame.
⁶I will pelt you with filth*
   and make you a contemptuous* spectacle*.
⁷And it shall come to pass that all who see you
   will flee* from you and say,
'Nineveh is ruined*;
   who will mourn* for her?'
Where shall I seek*
   comforters for you?"*

Exegesis and Exposition

In pronouncing his woe against Nineveh, Nahum begins with an invective that singles out Nineveh's established reputation. Nineveh was, first of all, a city of blood.* Keil suggests that Nineveh is being accused of being a murderous city. Certainly Nineveh's bloody activities are well documented. The extreme cruelties perpetrated by Ashurnasirpal II, Shalmaneser III, and Ashurbanipal are especially notorious. Among many examples the following may be cited:

> I [Ashurnasirpal II] took the city, and 800 of their fighting men I put to the sword, and cut off their heads. Multitudes I captured alive, and the rest of them I burned with fire, and carried off their heavy spoil. I formed a pillar of the living and of heads over against his city gate, and 700 men I impaled on stakes over against their city gate. The city I destroyed, I devastated, and I turned it into a mound and ruin heap. Their young men and their maidens I burned in the fire.[1]

> Like Adad I [Shalmaneser III] rained destruction upon them. With their blood I dyed [the mountain] like red wool. . . . His cities I turned to wastes. Arzashku, together with the cities of its neighborhood, I destroyed, I devastated, [I burned with fire]. Four (?) pyramids (pillars) of heads I erected in front of its gate. Some (of his people) I fastened alive into these pyramids, others I hung up on stakes around the pyramids.[2]

> As for those men . . . I [Ashurbanipal] slit their mouths (v., tongues) and brought them low. The rest of the people, alive, by the colossi, between which they had cut down Sennacherib, the father of the father who begot me,—at that time, I cut down those people there, as an offering to his shade. Their dismembered bodies (lit. flesh) I fed to the dogs, swine, wolves, and eagles, to the birds of heaven and the fish of the deep.[3]

Maier appropriately remarks:

> The atrocious practice of cutting off hands and feet, ears and noses, gouging out eyes, lopping off heads and then binding them to vines or heaping them up before city gates; the utter fiendishness by which captives could be impaled or flayed alive through a process in which their skin was gradually and completely removed—this planned frightfulness systematically enforced by the "bloody city" was now to be avenged.[4]

Further, the city was characterized as being a place of total deceit; it was full of lies*—"all of it a lie." The description depicts the Assyrians' use of treachery and alluring platitudes to gain others' loyalty. They also employed psychological warfare, couching their words in false promises and outright lies to gain the submission of

---

1. *AR*, 1:156.
2. *AR*, 1:219-20.
3. *AR*, 2:304.
4. W. A. Maier, *The Book of Nahum* (reprint, Grand Rapids: Baker, 1980), p. 292.

enemy cities in times of siege (cf. 2 Kings 18:28-32).[5] Their idolatry, arrogant pride (cf. Zeph. 2:15), and misrepresentation of God Himself (2 Kings 19:21-27) were particularly loathsome. Nineveh's ravenous appetite for robbery and plunder is also mentioned, a trait that harks back to the preceding taunt song and the figure of Nineveh as a lion's den to which her ill-gotten prey was taken. In every way, then, Nineveh was known to all as a wicked city (cf. Jonah 1:2).

In vv. 2-3 Nahum moves on to a vivid description of the coming battle. Whether Nahum is reporting what he has seen in a vision or merely himself envisions the future scene, his portrayal is done with picturesque brevity that utilizes a number of vivid images. Michael Travers puts it well:

> The writer portrays a number of graphic images of the impending military destruction. In the first image, whips crack, wheels clatter, horses gallop, and chariots jolt (3:2). This opening image draws the reader's attention to the machines of war, the horses and chariots; the poet uses this picture to heighten the terror which he shows most graphically in the next image.[6]

Once again a poignant portrait of the battle scene and its din is drawn: the cracking whip that signals the chariots' movement, the rumble of the chariots together with the pounding of the horses' hoofs, the advance of cavalry and infantry, the battle engagement itself. And then, ever so quickly, it is over, and all the commotion is followed by a scene of deafening silence, with the slain* strewn across the battle area. It is a macabre and melancholy setting.

So many have lost their lives—and for what? Because an unalterably proud, selfish, and unholy people had come to the time of divine judgment. She who had brought havoc and ruin to so much of the ancient Near East would now face death and destruction. Here again a notable crux occurs. Does the statement (v. 4) relative to Nineveh's harlotry explain the death and destruction described in the previous verses, or does it initiate the following declaration of God's judgment against the city? The problem is heightened in that 3:4 is not an independent sentence and therefore would normally need to be related grammatically either with what precedes or with what follows.

Once more (cf. 2:4) the problem is solved by viewing this verse as a hinge binding two portions together with vividness and smoothness of succession. That the verse is so constructed may be noted in the use of the subunit terminator 'ēn qēṣeh ("there is no end"; NIV "without

---

5. See further H. W. F. Saggs, *The Might That Was Assyria* (London: Sidgwick & Jackson, 1984), pp. 256-57.
6. R. D. Patterson and M. Travers, "Literary Analysis and the Unity of Nahum," *GTJ* 9 (1988): 53.

number") in v. 3, and the picking up of the image of harlotry in what follows. The transitional nature of the hinge verse may be further seen in the employment of a first-slot preposition to introduce new, yet related, material (cf. 1:11). Perhaps the conclusive fact is that, as indicated at the beginning of this section, the customary three elements of woe oracles are arranged chiastically so that the poet's criticism of Nineveh (v. 4) is located centrally between the invective (vv. 1, 7) and the threat (vv. 2-3, 5-6).

Accordingly the reader is presented with a statement related to what precedes and anticipating/initiating the discussion that follows. There is thus a smooth transition from one subunit to another, the mention of Nineveh's harlotry and witchcraft accounting for the grisly death scene that precedes, while providing the critical basis for the Lord's judicial pronouncement that follows.

The prophet reveals the causes of Nineveh's condemnation for which God's judgment must inevitably come. Nineveh was a city of beauty and splendor. It was adorned with temples, palaces, parks, a botanical garden, and even a zoo. It was guarded by massive fortifications and walls. Access to the well-laid-out cosmopolitan center with its broad streets was gained via 15 gates protected by colossal stone bulls. Fresh water was brought into the city by means of a system of dams and an aqueduct. It was truly a splendid and sophisticated metropolis, but it had gained its wealth and grandeur by making merchandise of other nations through either military might or economic exploitation. Further, it had enslaved many with its sociopolitical seductions, most of which were connected with its religious harlotry. Armerding observes:

> Nineveh is here seen as using both immoral attractions (the city was a center of the cult of Ishtar—herself represented as a harlot) and sorcery (Assyrian society was dominated by magic arts; IDB, 1:283-87) as a means to enslave others. The metaphor is very close to the reality.[7]

Truly, then, Nineveh/Assyria was a "mistress of sorceries."

Once again (cf. 2:13) the prophet turns to threat in a declaration of divine judgment befitting the harlot Nineveh. Yahweh of Hosts Himself was against her (cf. 2:13) and would mete out a punishment corresponding to her conduct. In a simile depicting Nineveh as a harlot, Nahum declares that Nineveh, like any prostitute, will be exposed to public shame (cf. Hos. 2:3; Ezek. 16:37) by having the borders of her garment thrown violently over her face (cf. Jer. 13:26), thus fully revealing her nakedness. Her seemingly impregnable defenses will be thrown down and her substance exposed to all. A help-

---

7. C. Armerding, "Nahum," in *EBC* (Grand Rapids: Zondervan, 1985), 7:481.

less Nineveh, a city that had so disgraced others, will herself be put to open shame.

Further, Nineveh will be pelted with filth. The word translated "filth" denotes that which is detested. A strong word, it is usually reserved for contexts dealing with aberrations connected with pagan worship. The word carries with it the idea of the loathing all such detestable practices produce; the thought is that despoiled Nineveh will be treated as a detested and abominable thing. Condemned for her abhorrent idolatrous worship, a thing of incredible filth in God's sight, she is treated as an object of revulsion by having dirt heaped upon her. It is an action denoting intense disrespect (2 Sam. 16:13; cf. Mal. 2:3). The image is heightened by the further statement that Nineveh would be treated contemptuously, being made a spectacle in the sight of the nations.

The woe reaches its climax with a return to invective. It takes the form of a sarcastic appraisal of Nineveh's hopeless plight: Nineveh is destroyed, destitute, devoid of mourners. The verse begins with a striking play on words. Nahum has prophesied that Nineveh will become a sorry sight, a horrendous spectacle (rōʾî, v. 6); he reports now (v. 7) that "all who see you" (rōʾayik) will flee from ruined Nineveh in disgust. Those who flee, bearing the news of a devastated Nineveh, will proclaim not only the city's demise but that they can find for her neither mourners nor comforters.*

Once again Nahum ends a section or subsection with the motif of a message/messenger (cf. 1:15; 2:13; see 3:18-19), but this time with the added feature of a literary foil: a play on the word for comfort and the prophet's name. Whereas Judah/Jerusalem had its Nahum (nahûm), Assyria/Nineveh could boast no comforters (měnahămîm) whatever.

Additional Notes

3:1 הוֹי ("woe"): This interjection is a strong word used with precision by the prophets. Zobel's analysis leads him to point out that

> fundamentally, hôy forms part of laments for the dead; in the prophetic literature it occurs as an element of prophetic invective. There is a formal similarity between the use of hôy in laments for the dead and its use in invective: in both contexts it is followed by a nominal construction. In invective, however, these nominal forms do not define the relationship of the mourner to the subject of his lament as they do in laments for the dead. They describe instead the reprehensible conduct of men toward Yahweh, thus motivating the threat that follows (Isa. 1:4; 5:8, 11; 18:1; 28:1; 45:9, 10; Amos 6:1; Mic. 2:1; Nah. 3:1; Zeph. 2:5; 3:1).[8]

---

8. On הוי, see R. J. Clifford, "The Use of *hôy* in the Prophets," *CBQ* 28 (1966): 458-64. For the consideration of this particle as an extrametrical element, see W. G. E. Watson, *Classical Hebrew Poetry* (Sheffield: Sheffield U., 1986), p. 110.

הוֹי normally introduces a new section, frequently as poetic anacrusis. עִיר־דָּמִים ("*city of blood*"; cf. Ezek. 22:2; 24:6, 9): The plural may be explained as indicating an abstract idea, "bloodshed," or the result of an action involving the matters at hand, "blood that is shed."[9]

כֻּלָּהּ כַּחַשׁ ("all of it a lie"): The basic idea is that of total falsehood; Nineveh is "*full of lies*" (NIV). The thought of absolute falsehood is established by such passages as Ps. 59:13; Hos. 7:3; 10:13; 12:1. The Assyrian practice of using deception as a psychological tool to gain the submission of a besieged city can be illustrated from the archives of Tiglath-Pileser III (745-727 B.C.), as pointed out by H. W. F. Saggs, who finds in all of this an interesting parallel with Sennacherib's siege of Jerusalem in 701 B.C. (cf. 2 Kings 18:15–19:37):

> On the 28th we came to Babylon. We stood in front of the Marduk gate. We negotiated with the Babylonian ruler [who at that time was a Chaldaean usurper named Ukin-zer]. . . . A servant of Ukin-zer the Chaldaean was at his side. They came out with the Babylonian citizens and were standing in front of the gate. We spoke in these terms to the Babylonian citizens: "Why should you act hostilely to us for the sake of them? . . . Let Babylon agree [to *surrender*(?)]. I am coming to Babylon to confirm your citizen-privileges." We spoke many words with them. . . . They would not agree. They would not come out; they would not talk with us. They kept sending us messages. We said to them: "Open the great gate; let us enter Babylon."[10]

†פֶּרֶק ("plunder") and טֶרֶף ("prey"; cf. NIV "victims") may as Cathcart suggests be chiastically placed and may together form a sort of merismus.[11] One could argue, however, that there is here, rather, an enveloping between lines 1 and 4, with lines 2 and 3 being a case of enjambment via asyndeton and הוֹי viewed as anacrusis:

Woe!	הוֹי
City of blood,	עִיר דָּמִים
All of it with deceit	כֻּלָּהּ כַּחַשׁ
(and) plunder filled;	פֶּרֶק מְלֵאָה
(Its) prey does not depart.	לֹא יָמִישׁ טָרֶף

†לֹא יָמִישׁ ("lacks"; lit. "does not depart"): Although the verb is hiphil, the masc. sing. subject noun that follows and with which it agrees makes it intransitive. Were the verb to be viewed as transitive with the following noun as its object, the verb would need to be fem. so as to agree with עִיר ("city"). The translation for all of v. 1 given at

---

9. For details, see R. J. Williams, *Hebrew Syntax*, 2d ed. (Toronto: U. of Toronto, 1976), p. 6; GKC, par. 124n.
10. H. W. F. Saggs, *Assyriology and the Study of the Old Testament* (Cardiff: U. of Wales, 1969), p. 17.
11. Kevin J. Cathcart, *Nahum in the Light of Northwest Semitic* (Rome: Biblical Institute Press, 1973), p. 126. For the use of merismus here, see Watson, *Hebrew Poetry*, p. 323.

the beginning of this section follows the usual syntactic arrangement of modern English versions (NIV, NASB).

3:2-3 The short phraseology that makes up vv. 2-3 yields a dramatic effect. The verses are characterized by a staccato style and filled with words that take on an almost onomatopoeic quality. It is a fine example of picturesque brevity. There is also progression in the individual lines that compose the passage, providing a strong touch of realism.

3:2 †שׁוֹט ("whip") is rendered as a pl. in LXX (cf. NIV). While the MT noun here and in the following phrases is sing., it is doubtless a collective sing. and thus translated as a pl. What happens with individual battle chariots is reproduced by the whole chariot force.

†קוֹל ("crack," "sound"; with רַעַשׁ = "rumble"), like some of the words in the description that follows (e.g., לַהַב רֶקֶד), is found in a similar martial context in Joel 2:5. Whereas Joel speaks of the horse of the chariot, Nahum focuses on the rumbling of the chariot wheels. Although רַעַשׁ ("shake"; with קוֹל = "rumble") is at times used for the din of battle (Isa. 9:4; Jer. 10:22), it is often used for the shaking of the earth (Amos 1:1; cf. the verbal root in Judg. 5:4; Pss. 68:8 [HB 68:9]; 77:18 [HB 77:19]; 2 Sam. 22:8). Together with קוֹל here, the translation "rumble" best serves to reproduce the force of the sound.

†וּמֶרְכָּבָה מְרַקֵּדָה ("and jolting chariots") exhibits both alliteration and assonance. The verb *rāqad* is related to Akkadian *raqādu* ("leap/skip"; cf. also Ugaritic *rqdm*, "dancers"; Arabic *raqada*, "leap"). The Assyrian battle chariot was feared far and wide. Sennacherib called his private war chariot "The Vanquisher of the Wicked and Evil" (*sāpinat raggi u ṣēni*) and also "The Vanquisher of the Enemy" (*sāpinat zāʼiri*).[12] דהר ("galloping") in the previous line occurs also in Judg. 5:22.[13]

3:3 †פָּרָשׁ ("horse") again provides a literary correspondence with Joel (cf. Joel 2:4). Although the term can also mean "horseman," together with the following participle the resultant phrase is probably best rendered, with the NIV, "charging cavalry."[14]

†לַהַב ("flashing" [sword]; lit. "flame") and בָּרָק ("gleaming" [spear]; lit. "lightning") provide two picturesque images of awesome battle weapons, reflecting the sunlight in their wielders' hands. Both

---

12. For the text, see R. Borger, *Babylonisch-Assyrische Lesestücke* (Rome: Pontificium Institutum Biblicum, 1963), Table 49, V:70; Table 50, VI:8; for a translation, see *AR*, 2:126-27.
13. For discussion, see R. D. Patterson, "The Song of Deborah," in *Tradition and Testament: Essays in Honor of Charles Lee Feinberg*, ed. John S. Feinberg and Paul D. Feinberg (Chicago: Moody, 1981), p. 139.
14. For various suggestions as to the force of מַעֲלֶה (lit. "bringing up"), see Maier, *Nahum*, pp. 299-300.

are used frequently in military contexts under various figures (cf. Deut. 32:41; Judg. 3:22; Job 39:23; Ezek. 21:15; Joel 2:5; Nah. 2:4 [HB 2:5]; Hab. 3:11).

The next four lines contain three terms for the bodies of those *slain* in battle: חָלָל ("slain"), פֶּגֶר ("corpse"), גְּוִיָּה ("dead body," "cadaver"). One is reminded of the frequent Assyrian boast of leaving behind after the battle a host of dead bodies. For example Ashurnasirpal reports,

> With the masses of my troops and by my furious battle onset I stormed, I captured the city; 600 of their warriors I put to the sword; 3,000 captives I burned with fire; I did not leave a single one among them alive to serve as a hostage. Hulai, their governor, I captured alive. Their corpses I formed into pillars; their young men and maidens I burned in the fire. Hulai, their governor, I flayed; his skin I spread upon the wall of the city of Damdamusa; the city I destroyed, I devastated, I burned with fire.[15]

The repetition of the last word and the presence of the last phrase have drawn criticism. Thus J. M. P. Smith says,

> It is probable that these words are a marginal note which has found its way into the text; they may have been intended as a cross-reference to 2[6], or they may be only a variant of the preceding clause. That they do not belong here appears not only from the fact that they are superfluous in the poetic form, but also from the additional fact that they introduce a verb for the first and only time into a series of phrases thrown off in ejaculatory fashion one after the other, like a series of stereopticon views.[16]

Nahum, however, often uses repetition for effect (cf. 2:3, 9 [HB 2:4, 10]), even in this unit (vv. 2, 4). Moreover, he has already used a verbal sentence in this section (v. 1). Indeed, the description of the battle for Nineveh (vv. 2-3) is both opened and closed by repetition. Further, the shift from the staccatolike phrases of the previous nine lines to a nonverbal and a verbal sentence in the two lines involving the repetition of גְּוִיָּה provides climactic force to the whole scene. Nahum's readers are thus presented with a somber view of a ghastly sight. The employment of the verb כָּשַׁל ("stumble") provides a literary echo of the description in 2:5 (HB 2:6). In the previous account the attacking soldiers stumbled in their haste to reach the city wall; here they stumble over the defenders' slain bodies. A further literary connection with chap. 2 may be seen in the phrase אֵין קֵצֶה לְ ("there is no end to"; 2:9 [HB 2:10]).

3:4 †מֵרֹב ("[it is] because of"): The causal use of מִן is attested amply in the OT (e.g., Ex. 2:23; Deut. 7:7; 2 Sam. 3:11; Isa. 43:4; Zech.

---

15. *AR*, 1:146.
16. J. M. P. Smith, *Micah, Zephaniah and Nahum*, ICC (Edinburgh: T. & T. Clark, 1911), p. 337.

2:8). "Harlotry" is often used figuratively in a religious sense, particularly of the apostasy of God's covenant nation. Noteworthy is the case of Hosea's relationship to Gomer as a symbol of God's relation with Israel (Hos. 1:2; 2:6, 15 [HB 2:4, 13]). Some texts appear to use the figure in a commerical sense (e.g., Isa. 23:16-17; Mic. 1:7). Perhaps both ideas are latent here, although the parallel with כְּשָׁפִים ("sorceries") would seem to indicate that Nahum's chief complaint against Nineveh is for its spiritual atrocities. Perhaps, as J. M. P. Smith cautions, we should not attempt to isolate any one specific feature of Nineveh's international harlotry but rather affirm that "using all of her manifold and multiform attractions, she has succeeded in bringing nations into subjection, only to use them for the furtherance of her own selfish ends."[17] Maier adds: "As a lewd woman deceitfully displays her charms, uses enticements to deceive and ruin men, so Assyria has beguiled nations and lured them to their downfall."[18]

The problem of the grammatical relationship of the full phrase is resolved in the LXX by including it with v. 3 and then beginning a new sentence with a vocative—"O comely harlot" (v. 4)—that continues into v. 5, which contains the apodosis, "Behold, I am against you." As suggested in the Exegesis and Exposition, the solution to the grammatical relationship of v. 4 may well lie in treating it as a transitional hinge composed of an independent sentence with elided subject/conclusion (aposiopesis).[19] The difficulty of determining the precise syntactical relationship of v. 4 is doubtless the cause for some modern renderings. For example, *La Sainte Bible* translates the MT as "*C'est à cause des*" rather than utilizing the more familiar comparative causal particle *parce que* whether in postpositive (e.g., Jer. 14:4, 5, 6) or initial (e.g., John 20:29) position.

†טוֹבַת חֵן ("graciously fair"; lit. "good of grace"): The phrase is constructed as an attributive genitive and is descriptive of Nineveh. The following phrase בַּעֲלַת כְּשָׁפִים ("mistress of sorceries") makes an interesting contrast with Nahum's earlier בַּעַל חֵמָה ("lord of wrath," 1:2) as a description of Yahweh. Cathcart calls attention to the designation of the witch of Endor (1 Sam 28:7) as בַּעֲלַת אוֹב ("medium") and of the Canaanite Anat as *b'lt mlk* ("mistress of kingship"), *b'lt drkt* ("mistress of dominion"), and *b'lt šmm rmm* ("mistress of the high heavens"). Nineveh is the enchantress par excellence.

†הַמֹּכֶרֶת ("she who makes merchandise"; lit. "who sells") has been rejected by many expositors either as unsatisfactory or as a gloss.

---

17. Ibid.
18. Maier, *Nahum*, p. 302.
19. For literary hinging, see H. Van Dyke Parunak, "Transitional Techniques in the Bible," *JBL* 102 (1983): 540-41.

Cathcart points out that wherever this verb is constructed with the following בְּ plus a noun, as here, it usually means "sell for" (cf. Ps. 44:12 [HB 44:13]; Joel 3:3 [HB 4:3]; Amos 2:6). Accordingly he follows M. Dahood in repointing the form as *hammukkeret* (hophal fem. sing. participle from נָכַר, "know"), translating "who is known by."[20] The simplest solution, however, is to retain the MT but to understand the verb in the sense of "make merchandise of" (cf. Akkadian *makāru*, "use in business"). Nineveh is thus described as "she who makes merchandise of the nations" by her numerous harlotries and sorceries. Thus construed, it is another picture of Nineveh's selfish and cruel exploitation.

†מִשְׁפָּחוֹת ("peoples"; lit. "families"): The word is often used in a sense wider than the English term, meaning "clan," "kindred." In Josh. 7:16-18 it designates one of the clans of the tribe of Judah. BDB suggests that it also can refer to still smaller subdivisions. At times it forms a subunit of the terms גּוֹיִם ("nations," Ps. 22:27 [HB 22:28]) and עַמִּים ("peoples," Ps. 96:7) or even appears as a parallel term to גּוֹיִם (Jer. 10:25; Ezek. 20:32). Therefore, the noun can refer to familial relations at several levels or have a still wider use (cf. Gen. 12:3; 28:14; Zech. 14:17). But, since in cases where מִשְׁפָּחָה occurs in parallel with גּוֹיִם it always is found in the second of the two parallel members, perhaps these cases indicate intensification by diminution.[21] If so, such situations may actually intend a smaller rather than a larger unit. Nahum, then, may mean here both nations and the peoples that compose them—perhaps, even as H. J. Austel suggests, those with strong blood ties.[22]

3:5 For the statement "Behold I am against you," see the note at 2:13.

†וְגִלֵּיתִי ("and I will lift/uncover"): The verb means basically "uncover" but is used in a wide variety of contexts and displays many nuances. In a context similar to this one where, as here, the word "skirt" is used, the verb חָשַׂף ("make bare," "expose") is employed (Jer. 13:26-27), which may cast light on the meaning here (cf. also Jer. 13:22). The use of either verb makes it possible that "skirt" is used euphemistically for what is otherwise concealed (cf. LXX τὰ ὀπίσω σου, "your backward parts"; Vg *pudenda tua*, "your shameful parts"), the whole phrase thus designating the exposure of one's private parts. The literal translation given at the beginning of the section makes

---

20. For details, see Cathcart, *Nahum*, pp. 129-30. For good discussions on the form, see J. M. P. Smith, *Nahum*, p. 365; Maier, *Nahum*, pp. 304-6.
21. For discussion of methods of intensification in Hebrew parallel structures, see Robert Alter, *The Art of Biblical Poetry* (New York: Basic Books, 1985), pp. 13-26, 62-84.
22. H. J. Austel, "שׁפח," *TWOT* 2:947.

perfect sense. In any case, the violent action contemplated here leaves its recipients with a great sense of shame. Such actions were often applied as punishment for prostitution (cf. Jer. 13:22, 26-27; Ezek. 16:37-39; 23:10, 29; Hos. 2:3, 9-10 [HB 2:5, 11-12]). Several scholars have followed the lead of D. R. Hillers in seeing a relation between the biblical data cited here and the curse pronounced in an Aramaic inscription of Sefîre: "[And just as] a [ha]r[lot is stripped naked], so may the wives of Matî''el be stripped naked, and the wives of his offspring and the wives of [his] no[bles]."[23] The extended figure in the parallel lines shows a progressive heightening of the thought, thus providing an intensification of the theme.

3:6 †שִׁקֻּצִים ("filth") is used here either as a plural of intensification or to indicate an abstraction.[24]

†נָבַל (lit. "be foolish") means in the piel "treat as a fool," hence "treat contemptuously." כְּרֹאִי ("as a spectacle") has occasioned some controversy. The proposed noun רְאִי ("seeing") seldom occurs elsewhere in the OT (all cases may, perhaps, be explained as participles in the genitive case) and comes from the root רָאָה ("see"). Literally translated, the line would read something like "I will treat you with contempt and make you a spectacle" (thus NIV). The translation suggested at the beginning of this section treats the two verbs (נָבַל and שִׂים) as hendiadys: "and make you a contemptible spectacle." Verse 6 continues to heighten the effect: Nineveh will be treated as that which is detestable, as an utter disgrace and a public spectacle. Nahum plays on the root רָאָה in these verses: וְהַרְאֵיתִי ("and I will show," v. 5), כְּרֹאִי ("as a spectacle," v. 6), רֹאַיִךְ ("who see you," v. 7).

3:7 †יִדּוֹד ("will flee"): Although one might expect a suffix-conjugation verb after וְהָיָה ("and it shall come to pass"), the prefix conjugation is common enough.[25] The Greek tradition renders the MT by such verbs as ἀποπηδήσεται ("will leap away"), καταβήσεται ("will descend"), and ἀναχωρήσει ("will draw back"), suggesting uncertainty in the exemplar or lack of understanding of the root.

†שָׁדְּדָה ("ruined/laid waste"): A pual perfect from שָׁדַד ("deal violently with"), the verb is related to the Akkadian šadādu ("devastate").[26]

---

23. Basing his conclusions on the study of this verse in Nahum, D. R. Hillers (*Treaty-Curses and the Old Testament Prophets* [Rome: Pontifical Biblical Institute, 1964], pp. 58-60) has suggested the reading of the Sefîre inscription given in the note. See also J. A. Fitzmyer, *The Aramaic Inscriptions of Sefîre* (Rome: Pontifical Biblical Institute, 1967), pp. 14-15, 56-57.
24. See further A. B. Davidson, *Hebrew Syntax*, 3d ed. (Edinburgh: T. & T. Clark, 1901), pp. 18-19.
25. See GKC, par. 112y.
26. For its use in the divine title El Shaddai, see my remarks in "Joel," in *EBC*, 7:243 n. 15.

†מִי יָנוּד ("who will mourn?"): The verb נוד means basically "move to and fro," "wander." In contexts of sadness it is used for shaking the head in grief. Its employment here forms a word and sound play with the previous יְדוֹד. Thus a shaking or fluttering movement can be seen in both words. As for sound play, men may "shake loose" (*yiddôd*) from Nineveh (i.e., flee), but they will not shake the head in grief (*yānûd*) for it (i.e., mourn). The poet intentionally heaps up the letters *d* and *n*, each occurring some five times in this verse.

†אֲבַקֵּשׁ ("shall I seek"): This verb lays stress on individual initiative in seeking persons or things and displays a wide variety of nuances depending on the object sought or the emphasis of the context (e.g., "seek/seek out," "search for," "long for"; also "desire," "ask," "demand," etc.).[27] The most common significance of the root ("seek") is the best meaning here.

מְנַחֲמִים ("comforters"): Grieving and comforting naturally occur together (cf. Job 2:11; Isa. 51:19; Jer. 15:5). The ancient versions read a singular here, perhaps taking the MT plural as an abstract noun ("comfort/consolation").

†לָךְ ("for you"): The form is frequently emended to 3d fem. sing. לָהּ ("to her") so as to agree with the previous line. The MT can be defended, however, on the grounds that the shift in persons may represent a change from the fleeing exiles' words (לָהּ) to Nahum's own words (לָךְ). Whether such is the prophet's intention, such shifts in gender or person (enallage or *oratio variata*; cf. 2:13) are common in poetry and prophetic discourse.[28]

E. APPLICATION: THE DEFENSELESS CITADEL (3:8-19)

With his woeful description of Nineveh's destruction completed, Nahum once again uses a taunt song to depict Nineveh's dire plight. The section flows in two movements. The first, opening with a rhetorical question, reminds Nineveh that she is no more secure than once-proud Thebes, which also fell. Rather, her allegedly impregnable defenses will fall as easily as ripe figs shaken from the tree by the eater, and her most virile champions will prove to be little more than helpless women (vv. 8-13). In the second portion the prophet ironically ridicules Nineveh's defenders, urging them to make all necessary preparations. It will be to no avail, for her protectors will be shown to be inept at best, deserters at worst. In the end, the message of her fall will be rehearsed to a rejoicing mankind (vv. 14-19).

Both halves of the taunt, like the taunt song in 2:11-13, are splen-

---

27. For a full discussion, see S. Wagner, "בָּקַשׁ," *TDOT* 2:229-41.
28. See n. 64 in chap. 3 and GKC, par. 144p.

did examples of satire. Both contain a specific object of satirical attack: Assyria/Nineveh (vv. 8, 19); both provide a vehicle for carrying forward the satire: portraiture (vv. 8-10), irony (vv. 14, 15), simile (vv. 15-17), and metaphor (vv. 18, 19); both have a satirical tone: Juvenalian attack (vv. 11, 13) and sarcasm (vv. 13, 14-19); and both reveal a distinct trait that merits correction: Nineveh's pride as seen in her trust in her vaunted defenses (vv. 11-13) and Nineveh's haughtiness as evidenced in her disdainful cruelty toward others (v. 19). Other literary features in this section include alliteration and assonance (vv. 8, 10, 11, 18), rhetorical question (vv. 8, 19), synecdoche (v. 13), staircase parallelism accompanied by hyperbole (v. 15), enjambment (vv. 8, 9, 10, 12, 16, 17, 18, 19), *oratio variata* (v. 9), and refrain (v. 19).

1. A COMPARISON OF NINEVEH AND THEBES (3:8-13)

Translation

Are you better than Thebes*
  that sat by the Nile*,
  with water surrounding her,
whose (outer) wall* was the sea,
  with water her rampart*?
⁹Cush and Egypt were her boundless*
  strength*;
Put and Libya were among your helpers*.
¹⁰Yet she went into exile*,
  she went into captivity;
yet her infants were dashed to pieces*
  at the head of every street;
they cast lots for her nobles*,
  and all her leading men* were bound in chains.
¹¹You too* will become drunk*,
  you will go into hiding*;
you too will seek refuge* from the enemy.
¹²All your fortresses* are fig trees
  with* first-ripe fruit;
if they are shaken, they fall
  into the mouth of the eater*.
¹³Behold*, your troops* in your midst are women;
  to your enemies* the gates of your city* are wide open,
  (for) fire consumes your bars.

Exegesis and Exposition

Thebes was the illustrious and time-honored capital of Egypt. Situated on both sides of the Nile in Upper Egypt, it achieved its greatest fame as the political, religious, and cultural center of Egypt's great New Kingdom dynasties (18-20). Its former greatness is still attested by such impressive ruins as Karnak, Luxor, and Medinet Habu, so that Armerding justifiably observes: "Its temples and palaces are said to have found no equal in antiquity, and they are still regarded by some as the mightiest ruins of ancient civilization to be found anywhere in the world."[29]

Thebes was still a thriving metropolis in the waning days of Egypt's twenty-fifth (Nubian) dynasty (c. 751-656 B.C.), even though the dynastic capital appears to have been situated farther north in Memphis. After Esarhaddon of Assyria defeated Pharaoh Taharqa (690-664 B.C.) at Memphis in 671 B.C., the final king of the dynasty, Tanwetamani (664-656 B.C.), eventually abandoned Egypt in the wake of the advance of Ashurbanipal. This Assyrian king conquered Thebes in 663 B.C., taking vast plunder and leaving behind a client kingdom that would ultimately develop into Egypt's last great flourishing kingdom, the twenty-sixth (Saite) dynasty.

Before Ashurbanipal's victory, Thebes had seemed unconquerable. Surrounded by a strong defensive wall and a water system that included lakes, moats, canals, and the Nile, Thebes had been able to boast of the help of not only all Egypt but also its seventh-century allies: Sudanese Cush, Put (perhaps the fabled land of Punt in coastal Somaliland), and Libya. None of these, however, was to prove effective in protecting Thebes. Indeed, none of them supplied a source of strength for Thebes at all.

In point of fact Egyptian and Libyan relations were always somewhat tenuous, and in the future (c. 568 B.C.) a falling out between these allies would spell the end of the twenty-sixth-dynasty Pharaoh Hophra. Jeremiah (Jer. 46:9-10) likewise prophesied that Egypt's allies—Cush, Put, and Libya—would be no deterrent to defeat in the day of the Lord's judgment against Egypt.

Moreover, at the crucial hour, Tanwetamani so feared the power and wealth of Ashurbanipal that he left Thebes to its fate and fled for his life to the safety of the more inaccessible haunts of his Nubian homeland. Assurbanipal goes on to report:

> That city (i.e. Ni') my hands captured in its entirety,—with the aid of Assur and Ishtar. Silver, gold, precious stones, the goods of his palace, all there was, brightly colored and linen garments, great horses, the people, male and female, two tall obelisks, made of shining electrum (*ahalê*), whose weight was 2,500 talents, (and) which stood by the gate of the temple, I removed from their positions and carried them off to Assyria. Heavy plunder, and countless, I carried away from Ni'. Against Egypt and Ethiopia I waged bitter warfare and established my might.[30]

---

29. Armerding, "Nahum," in *EBC*, 7:484.
30. *AR*, 2:296.

The scriptural account adds that the fallen city experienced the customary fate of captured cities: Those who were not killed were captured, and many were exiled; its nobility were enslaved, most via the casting of lots,* and its infants* were cruelly dashed to pieces at prominent places in the streets. All of this was designed to strike terror into the hearts of those the conquerors left behind. Thus was once mighty Thebes taken and its surviving inhabitants either exiled or reduced to captivity.

Although Tanwetamani kept up the claim of being pharaoh of Egypt after Ashurbanipal's departure, he did not return there but retired to his Nubian capital at Napata where he died (c. 653 B.C.). With Ashurbanipal's victory, the installation of an Assyrian client kingdom, and the death of Tanutamun, Nubia's experiment in northward imperialism was over. Historical notices of contacts between the two nations cease except for brief mentions of Egyptian campaigns against Nubia in the early years of Psamtik I (655-610 B.C.) and the later years of his grandson Psamtik II (594-588 B.C.).[31]

If, as the Assyrians themselves knew full well, great Thebes, despite all of her natural defenses and vast network of allies, had not escaped such ignominy, could Nineveh expect to do better? The answer is a resounding negative. Nineveh, like Thebes, would know the terror of all-out attack. Nahum prophesies that Nineveh "will become drunk." The stupefying effect of intoxicating drink is often applied figuratively to threats of military defeat (e.g., Jer. 25:27; Lam. 4:21; Ezek. 23:33; Hab. 2:16). At such times the military and civilian personnel in a besieged city often resort to drunkenness. Accordingly, because the Assyrians were well known for their drinking habits, it comes as no surprise to learn that an early tradition (preserved in Diodorus Siculus, *Bibliotheca Historia* 2.24-27) records that the smug and debased Assyrians feasted and became drunk on the very night of the city's fall. Whether Nahum's words are intended to be taken figuratively or literally, the fact remains that Nineveh was to know even more fully than Thebes full and certain destruction before a besieging army. Tottering and reeling before the enemy, the Ninevites, whether those left in the city or those in headlong flight, would attempt to hide themselves in places of secure refuge.

Verses 12-13 depict the hopelessness of Nineveh's defensive measures. Nahum blends simile and metaphor to point out that the city's massive fortifications would crumble as readily before the eager attackers as first-ripe figs fall into the mouths of those who shake the

---

31. For details, see A. H. Gardiner, *Egypt of the Pharaohs* (Oxford: Clarendon, 1961), pp. 349-50; K. A. Kitchen, *The Third Intermediate Period in Egypt* (Warminster: Aris & Phillips, 1973), pp. 394-406.

trees. Further, its famed defenders would prove to be no more successful in protecting the city than would untrained and weak women.* Although some ancient traditions report a strong measure of degenerate effeminacy among the Assyrian leadership in the closing days of the empire, Nahum's words emphasize the relative weakness of the doomed defenders (cf. Isa. 19:16; Jer. 50:37; 51:30). The main point is that neither defenses nor defenders would be effective in the face of the coming onslaught.

The idea of a consuming fire in the last line of v. 13 is, as Armerding properly points out, a familiar key word for Nahum (cf. 1:10; 2:13; 3:15). One is reminded of the similar phraseology in the Phoenician Kilamuwa Inscription: "And I was in the hands of the kings like a fire that eats the beard and (like) a fire that eats the hand."[32] The burning of captured cities (Josh. 6:24; Judg. 18:27) and their gates (Neh. 1:3; 2:3, 13, 17) is widely attested in the records of the ancient Near East. An interesting parallel to vv. 11-13 occurs in connection with Ashurbanipal's campaign against his rebellious brother Shamash-shum-ukin, in which mention is made of bars to the city gate, the term "my enemy" with regard to the flight of the citizens of Babylon, and the use of fire in punishing the foe.[33] With fire having consumed the (bars of the) gates ("bars" being used synecdochically for the whole gate), entrance to the city would be easily gained. The addition of this line asyndetically gives a dramatic climax to the unit.[34]

Additional Notes

3:8 †אָמוֹן נֹא (Nō' 'āmôn, "City of Amun," i.e., Thebes): The Assyrians knew the city as Niʾu (Amarna Nî), and the Greeks called it Διὸς Πόλις ("Divine City"). In Egypt itself it was known as n'iwt rst ("Southern City") or as simply n'iwt ("The City"). Accordingly Ezekiel (Ezek. 30:14-16) can also call it just Nō'. Amun (Egyptian 'Imn) rose to prominence in Egypt's twelfth dynasty and, after subsequently being assimilated with the sun-god Rēʿ, became the principal national deity Amun-Rēʿ, "king of the gods," patron deity during the New Kingdom era (c. 1570-1085 B.C.).

†יְאֹרִים: The root appears to be Egyptian ('itrw, "river"). In the OT

---

32. For the text and commentary, see H. Donner and W. Röllig, *Kanaanäische und Aramäische Inschriften* (Wiesbaden: Harrassowitz, 1966), 1:5; 2:32-33; for English translation, see *ANET*, p. 654.
33. See *AR*, 2:300-4.
34. For similar use of asyndeton in Akkadian, see my remarks in *Old Babylonian Parataxis* (Ann Arbor: University Microfilms, 1971), pp. 167-69.

it is most often utilized to designate the Nile (e.g., Ex. 1:22) and/or its arms/canals (e.g., Isa. 19:6).[35] The plural here is generally taken to refer to the Nile's canals around Thebes, although some suggest that the form is a plural of majesty. The former understanding seems more appropriate and is supported by the line that follows: "(with) water around it." This line may be viewed as a case of periodic enjambment (cf. NIV) or as a nominal sentence (so Maier), introducing the succeeding two lines.

†חוֹמָתָהּ . . . חֵיל ("[outer] wall . . . her rampart"): Cathcart made a good case for translating these words as "outer wall" and "ramparts" and for reading מַיִם ("water") for the MT מִיָּם ("from [the] sea/river"). His suggestions have been followed here. Thebes counted heavily on its watery position for its defense. Cathcart goes on to cite R. Berger's comparison of these lines with an inscription from Esarhaddon that reads:

| ša dūrānūšunu tâmtumma | whose walls are the sea and |
| edû salḫūšun | whose rampart is the high water. |

Those who follow the MT in reading מִיָּם suggest that the intent of the text is to indicate either substantially the same idea as the proposed emendation—that is, that the wall consisted of the sea itself (so Armerding, Keil)—or that מִן ("from") prefixed to "sea/river" denotes origin or direction, thus "arising out of the sea" (Maier). יָם, generally translated "sea," can at times have a wider semantic range, as when referring to the Euphrates River (Isa. 27:1; Jer. 51:36) or to the famed place of the Israelite crossing, יַם־סוּף ("Sea of Reeds," "Red Sea"), probably one of Egypt's eastern lakes.[36] The suffix in חוֹמָתָהּ functions as a double-duty suffix, hence "(her) outer wall . . . her rampart."

3:9 †עָצְמָה ("her strength"): The form is probably to be understood as the masc. sing. noun עֹצֶם with the 3d fem. sing. suffix. Thus the suffix is written without *mappiq* as is often the case before following soft sounds.[37]

†The NIV is doubtless correct in translating Nahum's oft-used phrase וְאֵין קֵצֶה (lit. "and there is no end") as an adjective, "boundless" (or "limitless/immeasurable").

†בְּעֶזְרָתֵךְ ("among your helpers") may have been placed last in its line by Nahum so as to serve as a bookend to עָצְמָה. If so, Nahum has

---

35. See T. O. Lambdin, "Egyptian Loan Words in the Old Testament," *JAOS* 73 (1963): 151; see also H. Eising, "יְאֹר," *TDOT* 5:359; R. D. Patterson and H. J. Austel, "1, 2 Kings," *EBC* (Grand Rapids: Zondervan, 1988), 4:269-70.
36. See R. D. Patterson, "סוּף," *TWOT* 2:620.
37. See GKC, par. 91e. Note also the renderings of the ancient versions: LXX: ἰσχὺς αὐτῆς; Vg: *fortitudo eius*, both of which may be translated "her strength."

once again employed *oratio variata*. Cathcart, having noted a relation between this verse and Ezek. 27:10, at first suggested that עֶזְרָה is derived from a second root related to the Ugaritic noun *ġzr* ("warrior") and translated the whole phrase "in your army." Later, however, he properly changed his mind.[38] Indeed, although military might is envisioned here, the Hebrew phrase is far more wide-ranging and includes all sorts of supporting resources. Thus the translation "helpers" (so NASB) remains a convenient rendering of the MT, although the NIV "allies" is not without merit. The change *ad sensum* from "your" to "her" helpers/allies (NASB, NIV) is unnecessary and destroys the enallage (her . . . your) that is so characteristic of Nahum (cf. 2:13; 3:7).

3:10 †לַגֹּלָה† ("into exile"): Since the normal idiom is בַּגּוֹלָה (hence the reading of 4QNah), it may be that the presence of בַשְּׁבִי ("into captivity") may have occasioned the prophet's use of stylistic variation in the shift from בַ to ל. Although the meaning "in/into" is attested for both prepositions, M. D. Futato has suggested that, even though the semantic range of בַ and ל may overlap and therefore yield the same English translation, the distinctive nuance of each may always be felt: בַ = position within the confines of; ל = position at, or pertaining/belonging to.[39] Although the verb הָלַךְ ("went") is to be taken with both prepositional phrases, it is possible that there may be more than stylistic variation here. Thus, the citizens of Thebes went into that which belongs/pertains to exile (ל) and went into the confines of captivity (בַ).

†יְרֻטְּשׁוּ† ("were dashed to pieces"): The form is a preterite.[40] The practice of exterminating *infants* is recorded elsewhere in the Scriptures (2 Kings 8:12; Ps. 137:9; Isa. 13:16, 18; Hos. 10:14; 13:16; cf. Matt. 2:16-18). The perpetration of barbaric acts of cruelty against captive cities is abundantly attested in the Assyrian annals. Ashurbanipal reports that in the Elamite War

> I cut off the head of Teumman, their king,—the haughty one, who plotted evil. Countless of his warriors I slew. Alive, with (my) hands, I seized his fighters. With their corpses I filled the plain about Susa as with *baltu* and *ashagu*. Their blood I let run down the Ulai; its water I dyed (red) like wool.[41]

---

38. Kevin J. Cathcart, "More Philological Studies in Nahum," *JNSL* 7 (1979): 10.

39. M. D. Futato, "The Preposition 'Beth' in the Hebrew Psalter," *WTJ* 41 (1978): 68-83.

40. For the use of the Hebrew preterite, see Williams, *Syntax*, pp. 32-33; see also Z. S. Harris, *Development of the Canaanite Dialects* (New Haven: American Oriental Society, 1939), pp. 47-48.

41. *AR*, 2:300.

In a later Elamite campaign against Bit-Imbi:

> The people dwelling therein, who had not come forth and had not greeted my majesty, I slew. Their heads I cut off. (Of others) I pierced the lips (and) took them to Assyria as a spectacle for the people of my land.[42]

To these may be added the examples of Assyrian cruelty mentioned earlier in the additional note on 3:2-3 and the exposition of 3:1-7.

†As for the casting of lots for captives and their possessions, one may note Obad. 11; Joel 3:3 (HB 4:3).[43] The practice is also documented in extrabiblical literature, as is the binding in chains of captured nobility (cf. 2 Kings 25:7; Isa. 45:15; Jer. 40:1, 4). Ashurbanipal boasts:

> I entered that city; its inhabitants I slaughtered like lambs. Dunanu (and Sam'gunu, . . . in shackles, fetters of iron, bonds of iron, I bound them hand and foot. The rest of the sons of Bêl-ikîsha, his family . . . I carried off from Gambulu to Assyria.[44]

As for נִכְבַּדֶּיהָ ("her nobles"), note the appellation of the merchants of Tyre as "renowned in the earth" (Isa. 23:8). The meaning "nobles" is assured both from its relation to its root and from the contextual parallel "leading men" (lit. "great ones"). רְתְּקוּ may form an enveloping paronomasia with יְרְטְּשׁוּ. Cathcart calls attention to the play on the consonants *d* and *q* in the second half of the verse.

3:11 †גַּם ("too") is a flavoring particle whose exact nuance needs to be felt in individual contexts. Together with its occurrences in the previous verse ("yet") it is found four times in close proximity. Its recurrence has the effect of the clarion peal of a bell dolefully sounding out the awful truth that Nineveh, too, must surely reenact the tragic experience of Thebes.

†For MT תִּשְׁכְּרִי ("you will become drunk") several scholars suggest תִּשָּׂכְרִי ("you will hire yourself out," i.e., as a prostitute), citing the familiar example of wartime conditions described in the KRT epic (lines 97-98).[45] By adopting this reading one is forced also to understand differently the following נֵעֲלָמָה ("hiding"). Cathcart follows Dahood[46] in understanding this latter word as being related to עלמה ("maiden") and translates the whole phrase, "you will become young again." Although the Ugaritic parallel is interesting, the pointing of both verbs in the MT makes sense as it stands and is appropriate to

---

42. *AR*, 2:306.
43. See my remarks in "Joel," in *EBC*, 7:261-62.
44. *AR*, 2:300.
45. For the text, see C. H. Gordon, *Ugaritic Textbook* (Rome: Pontifical Biblical Institute, 1965), p. 250.
46. M. Dahood, "Review of T. H. Robinson, F. Horst, *Die Zwölf Kleinen Propheten*," *CBQ* 17 (1955): 104.

the desperate conditions described here. Moreover Nahum has mentioned the problem of drunkenness earlier in another connection (in 1:10). Still further, the idea in the parallel line of seeking refuge from the enemy favors the thought of going into hiding for נֶעֱלָמָה. Maier's suggestion to take the form נַעֲלָמָה as a passive, "be hidden" (i.e., under the collapsing rubble), appears unlikely in light of the following line.

†The MT מָעוֹז ("refuge") comes from the root עוז ("seek refuge"). The use of the verb בִּקֵּשׁ ("seek")[47] rather than any of its numerous synonyms may suggest the earnest and frantic search by the fleeing exiles for a place of safety. Note, however, that Nahum never uses the common synonym דָּרַשׁ ("seek"), so that his employment of בִּקֵּשׁ may indicate a stylistic preference.

3:12 †מִבְצָר ("fortress") is generally taken to come from the root בָּצַר ("restrain/cut off," hence "fortify"), although Cathcart relates the Hebrew root to Cyrus Gordon's suggestion for the Ugaritic verb *bṣr* ("soar"). The idea behind the word "fortress" would then be derived from the act of "raising defenses higher." André Parrot unnecessarily understands the fortresses here to refer to Nineveh's supporting towns of Ashur and Tarbiṣu, which fell in 614 B.C., two years before Nineveh itself was captured.[48]

†For עִם ("with") in such types of subordinate structure, see Song of Sol. 4:13. For the image of early ripe figs taken into the mouth of the eater, see Isa. 28:4. יִנּוֹעוּ וְנָפְלוּ provides another example of alliteration and assonance.

3:13 †הִנֵּה ("behold") is again used in drawing a unit to its close (cf. 1:15; 3:5). This particle stands outside the parallel structure of the verse as anacrusis.[49]

†עַמֵּךְ ("your troops"): The military situation involved here has led several commentators (e.g., Cathcart, R. L. Smith) and modern versions (e.g., NIV, RSV; cf. NEB) to abandon the traditional understanding of the word as "people" (e.g., KJV).

Nahum's taunt concerning Nineveh's warriors becoming women is illuminated by D. R. Hillers's reminder of Near Eastern treaty curses in which warriors are compared to women, especially in the treaty between Ashurnirari V of Assyria and Mati'ilu of Arpad, where the curse of warriors becoming women is juxtaposed with that of Mati'ilu's wives becoming prostitutes.[50] J. M. P. Smith arbitrarily omits עַם as a "misplaced correction of עִם in v. 12" and translates:

---

47. See footnote 27.
48. André Parrot, *Nineveh and the Old Testament* (New York: Philosophical Library, 1955), p. 279.
49. See Watson, *Hebrew Poetry*, p. 110.
50. See D. R. Hillers, *Treaty-Curses*, pp. 66-68.

"Behold, women are in the midst of thee!"[51] But such a suggestion is at variance with both the reading of the passage and the secular parallels, and it upsets the syntax and structure of the traditional texts.

לְאֹיְבַיִךְ† ("to your enemies") stands in emphatic position at the head of the second line of the verse. The emphatic position has been retained in the translation both to reflect the sentiment of the Hebrew and to maintain the force of the parallel pair "gates/bars" in the closing lines.

אַרְצֵךְ† ("your city"): I have related the noun to the Akkadian cognate *erṣetu* ("city quarter"). Thus "gates" probably refers to the gates of (sections of) Nineveh. If one follows the traditional understanding for אֶרֶץ ("land"), the reference would probably be to the fortified cities leading to Nineveh.

2. A CONCLUDING CONDEMNATION OF NINEVEH (3:14-19)

Translation

Draw for yourself water for the siege;
  strengthen your defenses;
go to the clay
  and tread the mortar
  —strengthen* the brickwork!
¹⁵There* the fire will consume you,
  the sword will cut you down,
  it will devour you like a grasshopper*.
Multiply* yourselves like grasshoppers,
  swell your ranks like locusts*.
¹⁶You have increased your merchants
  more than the stars of the heavens;
(they are) grasshoppers (that) strip (the land) and fly away.
¹⁷Your guards* are like locusts,
  your officials like a swarm of locusts that settle on the walls* on
  a cold day;
(when) the sun rises, they flee*,
  and their place is unknown.
¹⁸Where* are your shepherds slumbering, O king of Assyria,
  your nobles taking their rest?
Your people are scattered* upon the mountains
  with no one to gather (them).

---

51. For translation of the text of the treaty between Ashurnirari and Mati'ilu, see *ANET*, p. 533.

¹⁹There is no healing* for your fracture;
    your injury is severe*.
All who hear the news about you
    will clap (their) hands over you;
for on whom has not passed
    your evil continually*?

Exegesis and Exposition

With v. 14 Nahum approaches the end of his prophecy. The verses that follow form the second portion of an extended taunt song that again functions as satire. Although the closing verses constitute one literary unit, several movements are discernible. Thus, this short pericope contains two short commands given in irony (vv. 14-15*a*; 15*b*-17) and a final gibe that forms both a concluding denunciation and a doleful dirge (vv. 18-19).

The first movement emphasizes the futility of physical preparations in view of the coming siege. Nahum's sarcasm is evident throughout. He tells the Ninevites first of all to lay in a good water supply. Maier points out the lack of natural water resources for Nineveh, a fact that heightens the force of Nahum's taunting exhortation:

> This scarcity of potable water in Nineveh itself gives unusual force to the prophet's urging, "Draw thyself water for a siege." If the invaders followed the usual strategy of hostile forces in antiquity, one of their first actions would have been to cut off the water supply furnished by Sennacherib's dam and its reservoir. Nahum foreseeing that the water would be withheld from the city, and inferring a long, protracted siege, tauntingly directs the Ninevites to lay up stores for the beleaguered days.[52]

Similarly Nahum urges the citizens of Nineveh to strengthen the strategic points of the city's defenses.* That would mean giving particular attention to repairing the brickwork of the fortifications and key pressure points in the wall, such as at the city gates, where the walls were doubly thick. It is known that both Esarhaddon and Ashurbanipal devoted considerable effort to matters of repair and to the strengthening of Nineveh's defenses, including its walls. The force of the irony becomes immediately apparent. In those matters where the most extensive preparations are urged to be taken—water and walls—the city was to meet its demise (see the exposition of 2:6-7).

Nahum prophesies that Nineveh would know the besieger's fiery* torch and sword as the enemy sweeps through the city like a horde of devouring locusts. The devastation wrought by locusts was well-

---

52. Maier, *Nahum*, pp. 339-40.

known to the ancients and is amply chronicled in many sources.[53] The dreaded locust attack became a ready point of literary comparison to a military assault. One is reminded of Joel 2:2-11, where attacking Assyrians are compared to a locust invasion.

The mention of the fearsome locusts occasions Nahum's shift in the use of irony. Once again the figure of the locusts is utilized. Locusts—how appropriate! You too, Nineveh, should perform like locusts, multiplying your defensive forces to locustlike proportions. Should that not be easy for Nineveh? Indeed, it could be truly said of the city that she had acted before like a locust. As a result of her far-flung conquests, Nineveh had become filled with booty and with the famed Assyrian merchant* who, plying his trade, filled the city with every conceivable commodity. But with the coming of the threat of invasion, Nineveh's merchants will take their wares and flee, leaving the city deprived of its provisions, many of which would be so desperately needed in the ensuing struggle. As locusts who come only to satisfy their insatiable appetites and then fly off, so her merchants would take their goods and go, leaving a needy populace behind.

Likewise, Nineveh's trusted officials could be likened to locusts that come out of the ground in great swarms, lodge during the cooler part of the day on walls, and then, with the rising of the sun, fly away. Ancient sources record the flight of the Assyrian nobility with the advance of the combined enemy force against Nineveh.[54] The Assyrian kings repeatedly boasted that, on hearing of the advance of the Assyrian monarch, the enemy king and his officials fled for their lives. Particularly instructive are the words of Ashurbanipal:

> In my second campaign I made straight for Egypt and Ethiopia. Tandamanê heard of the advance of my army and that I was invading the territory of Egypt. He forsook Memphis and fled to Ni', to save his life.[55]
>
> Ummanaldasi, king of Elam, heard of the entrance of my armies into the midst of Elam, forsook Madaktu, his royal city, fled and went up into the (*lit.*, his) mountain(s). Umbahabua, who, after Elam had risen in revolt, had fled to the city of Bubilu, and had seated himself on the throne of Elam in place of Ummanaldasi, heard, like that one, (of my invasion), forsook Bubilu, the city that was his royal seat, and like a fish betook (himself) to the depth of the distant waters.[56]

---

53. See the valuable excursus in S. R. Driver, *The Books of Joel and Amos* (Cambridge: Cambridge U., 1915), pp. 64-93.
54. See Diodorus Siculus, *Bibliotheca historica*, 2.26.8; the text and its translation are given in the *Loeb Classical Library*, ed. E. H. Warmington, translated by G. H. Oldfather (Harvard: University Press, 1933), p. 439. See also D. J. Wiseman, *Chronicles of Chaldaean Kings* (London: Trustees of the British Museum, 1956), p. 61.
55. *AR*, 2:295.
56. *AR*, 2:306.

Now the Assyrian king and his officials would be cast in the same role. With the heat of the day's battle, Nineveh would be left without her leadership to provide her defense. How skillfully Nahum has played upon the figure of the locust! Like locusts her merchants and officials flee and leave Nineveh alone, leaderless, ill-equipped to meet the advance of the locustlike army that was even now about to surround her. M. Travers puts it well:

> No defense and no government. Stripped within and under siege from without, Nineveh stands defenseless. Nahum emphasizes the absolute vulnerability of Nineveh with these few brief similes. It is too late for Jonah's invitation to repentance.[57]

As Nahum approaches the end of his prophecy he changes the figure one last time. Nineveh's leaders are now compared to shepherds* (cf. Jer. 23:1-2) who have nodded off to sleep and allowed the sheep (the Ninevites) to be scattered (in flight or in exile) and subjected to harm. Even worse, no one comes to regather them. The choice of this motif as the final one for the book may suggest, as many commentators have observed, that the "sleep" of the shepherds/officials is the sleep of death (cf. Jer. 51:57). With its officialdom dead in battle, Nineveh's citizens have fled or been captured. With all leadership lost, there was none left to gather them. The "scatterer" (2:1) had come and done his work.

It was Nineveh's final hour. The once mighty city had fallen and would soon become a ghost town; it would become a ruins, haunted only by wild animals moving through the rubble (cf. Zeph. 2:13-15). Nahum's final denunciation of the city tolls out like a bell for a state funeral: Gone! Gone! Both city and citizenry, gone! Nineveh's last wound had been the *coup mortel.* But there would be no lamentation over the deceased city, only universal relief and rejoicing. She who had so cruelly treated mankind had reaped the reward of her evil deeds (cf. Hos. 8:7).

Before listening to the last words of the messenger, it is appropriate to give a summary word concerning the accuracy of Nahum's prophecies. As indicated in the various preceding comments, Nahum's words have been dramatically precise in their fulfillment. Indeed, the prophecies concerning the siege and fall of Nineveh stand as a remarkable example of fulfilled prophecy.

(1) The fact of an intense siege (3:14) is validated both in the Babylonian Chronicles and by Diodorus Siculus. Although Diodorus tells of a protracted siege of more than two years, Assyriologists sug-

---

57. Patterson and Travers, "Literary Analysis," p. 55.

gest that the evidence indicates a campaign that took little more than three months. H. W. F. Saggs maintains that

> Greek tradition speaks of Scythians eventually coming into alliance with the Medes, and Nabopolassar must have been a party to this, for in 612 he joined the Ummanmanda and the Medes in besieging Nineveh. The city fell within three months, a surprisingly brief period in view of the fact that the comparable city of Babylon withstood the Assyrian army, masters of siegecraft, for well over a year.[58]

In any case, Nahum's taunting words concerning siege preparations find corroboration in the findings of archaeologists who note the hasty strengthening of the walls at strategic defensive positions.

(2) The fall of the city due to water (1:8; 2:7, 9) has been attested both by archaeologists and the ancient historians Xenophon and Diodorus. The latter, reporting that an oracle had predicted Nineveh's defeat only when the river declared war on it, subsequently adds, "It came to pass that the Euphrates, running very full, both inundated a portion of the city and broke down the walls for a distance of twenty stades."[59] Unusually heavy rains were known to have given difficulty to Nineveh, which was served by three rivers: the Tigris, the Khosr, and the Tebiltu. A high-water season and a sudden storm, accompanied by the swelling of any or all three rivers, would account for the fulfillment of Nahum's prophecy as confirmed by Diodorus. Maier suggests that an added dimension could have been the opening of the sluice gates along the second and third rivers, thereby increasing the already dangerous floodwaters.

(3) Nahum also predicts the burning of the city (1:10; 2:13; 3:3, 15; cf. 1:6), a fact confirmed by archaeological excavation. Diodorus Siculus charges that the reigning king, a depraved and effeminate man, acted out of fear and superstition:

> At this the king, believing that the oracle had been fulfilled and that the river had plainly become the city's enemy, abandoned hope of saving himself. And in order that he might not fall into the hands of the enemy, he built an enormous pyre in his palace, heaped upon it all his gold and silver as well as every article of the royal wardrobe and then, shutting his concubines and eunuchs in the room which had been built in the middle of the pyre, he consigned both them and himself and his palace to the flames.[60]

Nahum's emphasis on the destruction of Nineveh's temples (1:14) is also confirmed by the excavations at Nineveh.[61]

---

58. Saggs, *The Might That Was Assyria*, p. 120.
59. *Bibliotheca historica*, 2.27.1, *LCL*, pp. 440-41.
60. *Bibliotheca historica*, 2.27.2, *LCL*, pp. 440-41.
61. Details as to the destruction of Nineveh may be found in R. Campbell Thompson and R. W. Hamilton, "The British Museum Excavations on the

(4) Minute details concerning the events of the final days before Nineveh's fall, such as the drunkenness (1:10; 3:11), cowardice, degeneracy (3:3), and the desertion (2:9; 3:17) of the city by its leadership are also abundantly recorded in the ancient traditions. Diodorus speaks of the carousing of the Assyrian officials and troops and reports that the Assyrian king sent away his family with much treasure.[62] Maier believes that moral perversion was rampant during Nineveh's last days and contributed strongly to the nation's downfall.

(5) Nahum's prophecies concerning the final slaughter of Nineveh's citizens (3:3) and the looting of the city (2:10, 11), its utter destruction (2:11; 3:7), and the virtual disappearance of its people (3:18-19) are facts confirmed in the ancient records.[63] The essential truth of Nahum's words is the consensus of modern researchers (e.g., Layard, Thompson, and Hutchinson) as well.[64] So dramatic was the demise of Nineveh and disappearance of Assyria that Sidney Smith observes:

> The disappearance of the Assyrian people will always remain an unique and striking phenomenon in ancient history. Other, similar, kingdoms and empires have indeed passed away, but the people have lived on. . . . No other land seems to have been sacked and pillaged so completely as was Assyria; no other people, unless it be Israel, was ever so completely enslaved.[65]

While some natural factors may help to account for Assyria's final condition, such as the nation's degeneracy, the deportation of its skilled craftsmen, and the composite nature of Assyrian society,[66] the ultimate cause was the divine judgment pronounced by God's prophets, such as Nahum and Zephaniah (Zeph. 2:13-15; cf. Jer. 50:18; Ezek. 32:22-23). The specter of Assyria's disappearance haunts every great empire. Nahum's opening words concerning divine justice are

---

Temple of Ishtar at Nineveh, 1930-31," *Annals of Archaeology and Anthropology* 19 (1932): 55-73.

62. *Bibliotheca historica,* 2.26.4, 8, *LCL,* pp. 436-39.

63. *Bibliotheca historica,* 2.28.7-8, *LCL,* pp. 444-45; Wiseman, *Chaldaean Kings,* p. 61.

64. A. H. Layard (*Nineveh and Its Remains* [New York: Putnam, 1849], 1:29) remarks concerning the disappearance of the inhabitants of the land: "Those of whose works they are the remains, unlike the Roman and the Greek, have left no visible traces of their civilizations, or of their arts: their influence has long since passed away." R. Campbell Thompson and R. W. Hutchinson, "The Excavations on the Temple of Nabu at Nineveh," *Archaeologia* 79 (1929): 73-74, 106-7, detail the devastation and desolation of the site. Maier, *Nahum,* pp. 135-38, has a compendium of testimonies, ancient and modern, as to the disappearance of the Assyrians and their great capital.

65. *CAH,* 3:130-31.

66. Saggs, *The Might That Was Assyria,* pp. 129-30.

general, so that wherever a godless lifestyle so pervades a nation as to be characteristic of its people, it stands in danger of judgment. P. C. Craigie's words of warning are apropos: "If we have grasped Nahum's message, we will not volunteer to join the ranks of Nineveh's attackers; rather, we shall seek to transform the evil within the nation to which we belong."[67]

Nahum's last words contain the message that the news of Nineveh's fall has spread across the landscape (v. 19).[68] But the tidings of that event are not met with a tear; they are welcomed with a clap of hands and, perhaps, a heaving sigh.

The poet's skill continues to the very end. Once more he utilizes a rhetorical question to conclude a section, here with sobering effect. Had any escaped Nineveh's cruelty that continually threatened people all around her? The implied negative answer guarantees the universal rejoicing over Nineveh's demise. This last use of a rhetorical question (a double one, in the light of v. 18) is one of five such instances that have been woven into the book's fabric. Twice rhetorical questions introduce the poet's satirical taunt song (2:11; 3:8). Three times a rhetorical question closes a unit with striking effect: to underscore God's irresistible judgment of sin (1:6), and to emphasize Nineveh's much deserved destruction (3:7, 19).

Israel would doubtless join in that exultation and take comfort in the good news (cf. 1:7, 12, 15; 2:2). Her dreaded enemy was gone, a reminder of God's promise concerning His judgment of all Israel's foes (e.g., Gen. 12:3; Judg. 5:31). Unlike Assyria's shepherds, Israel's eternal Shepherd "slumbers not nor sleeps" (Ps. 121:3) and will yet regather her lost sheep (Jer. 23:3) so that Israel's redeemed cities can "be filled with flocks of people" (Ezek. 36:38). Moreover the divine shepherd Himself (Ps. 23:1) will be with them: "I will be their God, and they will be my people" (Ezek. 37:27, NIV). May Nahum's words, as well as those of God's prophets, teach all God's people to trust fully Him who is the shepherd and overseer of their souls (1 Pet. 2:25).

Additional Notes

3:14 A comparison of the three extended pieces of satire in Nahum yields the schema at top of pg. 109.

מִבְצָרָיִךְ . . . מֵי מָצוֹר ("water for the siege," "your defenses"): Nahum's literary prowess continues in evidence through his use of assonance. מִבְצָרָיִךְ also provides a hook to the previous subsection (cf. v. 12). The imperative חַזְּקִי ("strengthen") anticipates the repetition of the same verb in the hiphil stem in the last line of the verse. Although

---

67. P. C. Craigie, *Twelve Prophets* (Philadelphia: Westminster, 1985), 2:76.
68. For the motif of the message/messenger, see 1:15; 2:13; 3:7.

Element	2:11-13	3:8-13	3:14-19
Object of attack	Nineveh	Nineveh	Nineveh
Vehicle of attack	Metaphor of lion's den	Comparison with Thebes	Irony, simile, and metaphor
Satirical tone	Juvenalian	Juvenalian	Sarcasm
Satirical emphasis	Nineveh's rapacity	Nineveh's defenses	Nineveh's cruelty

this latter occurrence of the verb is frequently taken by expositors (e.g., Maier, R. Smith) to have the meaning "grasp/seize," "take hold of," such need not be the case. Rather, the full phrase of the last line of the verse may intend the strengthening of the 50- to 100-foot thick walls surrounding Nineveh. Such is the force of NIV "repair the brickwork." If one so construes it (cf. Neh. 5:16; Ezek. 27:9, 27), he need not choose the alternative translation of מַלְבֵּן as "brick kiln" (KJV, Keil) or "brick mold" (Cathcart, Maier), despite the attestations of such a meaning in late Hebrew and Syriac. The Hebrew word found here is best translated "brickwork" and is related to the Akkadian *libittu* ("brickwork").[69]

For טִיט ("clay"; i.e., for use in making brick; cf. Isa. 41:25) and חֹמֶר ("mortar" or [reddish] soil [note its use in parallel with לְבֵנִים, "bricks," in Ex. 1:14]) occurring together in parallel, see Isa. 41:25, where the same two verbs בּוֹא ("go") and רָמַס ("tread") are also found together, although in somewhat different fashion.[70] Thus the full taunt expressed here is to draw water for the coming siege and to strengthen the fortifications/defenses by going and kneading the clay so as to make bricks for the repair of the walls.

3:15 †שָׁם ("there"): Instead of the traditional meaning, Cathcart suggests "behold" on the analogy of Akkadian *šumma* (as attested in Amarna). Maier proposes the translation "then," citing such texts as Pss. 14:5; 36:12 (HB 36:13); 66:6. Perhaps a better solution might be to follow C. F. Whitley[71] in postulating an asseverative force for שָׁם in several contexts. Nevertheless the translation "there" is not without merit, especially if, as BDB suggests, the particle often points to a "spot in which a scene is localized vividly in the imagination."[72] In this case, disaster will strike in the very place where the workers did their reinforcing.

---

69. See *CAD*, 9:176-79.
70. For חֹמֶר and טִיט, see H. Ringgren and A. S. Kapelrud, *TDOT* 5:1-4, 322.
71. For details, see C. F. Whitley, "Has the Particle שם an Asseverative Force?", *Bib* 55 (1974): 394-98.
72. BDB, p. 1027.

Again the figure of consuming/eating is employed, here as sand-wiched repetition for dramatic emphasis.[73] As Maier points out, the terms "fire" and "sword" often appear together as a pair in connection with catastrophes. The two are also often placed together in Ugaritic.[74] Noteworthy as well is the heaping up of the letter *aleph* throughout the verse.

†הִתְכַּבֵּד† ("multiply") is probably to be construed as an infinitive absolute, anticipating the following imperative.[75]

†אַרְבֶּה† . . . יֶלֶק ("grasshopper . . . locust"): The precise identification of the various Hebrew words for locusts is debated. אַרְבֶּה (cf. Akkadian *erbu*) is generally taken to be the adult winged insect (cf. Greek ἀκρίς, Latin *locusta*), whereas יֶלֶק is often rendered "young locust" or "licker." גֹּבַי/גוֹב (v. 17) are generally conceded to refer to locusts, here in repetition to indicate a locust swarm. Other words for locust include גָּזָם ("gnawer"?) and חָסִיל ("consumer"?), both of which are found in Joel 1:4.[76]

3:16 רֹכְלַיִךְ ("your *merchants*"): The noun comes from the root *rkl*, known in South Arabic where it means "go about as a trader." This final section abounds in literary features. First the Assyrian "merchants" are compared in number to the stars of heaven (cf. Gen. 26:4), then to locusts that stay only long enough to gain their advantage and then leave. Some have seen in the mention of the merchants a reference to the Assyrians' far-flung trading enterprises. They reason as follows: The Assyrian armies had reduced the entire Fertile Crescent to political subservience. In the wake of their frequent military excursions, there would soon follow the appearance of the time-honored Assyrian merchant. Their ubiquitous presence in the vast Assyrian empire could be likened to the innumerable stars of heaven. All such commercial activities scarcely benefited their subdued trading partners, however, for when the merchants had accomplished their desired ends they would disappear, leaving a people disadvantaged and deprived of their finest goods. Although this scenario was doubtless usually the case, such was not always true. In any event the parallel with Nineveh's fleeing guards in the next verse favors the explanation given in the Exegesis and Exposition.

3:17 מִנְּזָרַיִךְ† ("your guards"): Since the following term טַפְסְרַיִךְ ("your officials"; lit. "your tablet writers/scribes") is clearly Akkadian, doubtless this term is also. Because the Akkadian root *nazāru* ("curse") scarcely makes sense here, probably the root is *naṣāru*

---

73. For further details, see Watson, *Hebrew Poetry*, p. 279.
74. See *UT*, p. 168, text no. 49, II:30-33; p. 197, text no. 137, line 32.
75. For details, see Williams, *Syntax*, pp. 38-39.
76. See also Thomas J. Finley, *Joel, Amos, Obadiah*, WEC, ed. Kenneth Barker (Chicago: Moody, 1990), p. 21.

("guard"), which has undergone regressive contiguous phonemic dissimilation. The alternating between *z* and *ṣ* is common enough in Akkadian. Certainly *naṣāru* is attested with *z* written for *ṣ* and with dissimilation via *n* (nasalization), particularly in Babylonian.[77]

†גְּדֵרוֹת ("walls") can also refer to fences or hedges.

נוֹדַד ("flee") is poal perfect 3d masc. sing. agreeing with the masc. sing. pronominal suffix in מָקוֹם ("place"). The form is a *hapax legomenon*. *Nôdad . . . nôdaʿ* provides still another example of alliteration and assonance.

3:18 †אַיָּם ("where"): The word appears in v. 17 in the MT and hence is usually translated with that verse: for example, "And no one knows where" (NIV; cf. NASB, KJV). The form can also be taken as an adverbial particle with 3d masc. pl. suffix: "Where are they?" (so Maier, who includes it with v. 17). It can also be understood as the interrogative particle אַי ("where?"), usually lengthened to אַיֵּה but here written with (enclitic?) formative *m* (cf. GKC par. 100g), much like Amarna (124:15; 131:43) *ayyami*.[78] I have followed the lead of *BHS* and some expositors (e.g., Cathcart) in translating it as an interrogative particle introducing the question contained in v. 18. Thus understood, Nahum has once again closed a literary unit with a question (cf. 1:6, 9?; 2:11; 3:7).

The parallel term "your nobles" renders it certain that רֹעֶיךָ is to be translated "your *shepherds*." Therefore, attempts to view the latter word as the plural of רֵעַ ("friend"; cf. *Pesh.*) are in error. The sequence נוּם . . . שָׁכַן ("slumber . . . be at rest") is probably chosen instead of the more common pair נוּם . . . יָשֵׁן ("slumber . . . sleep"; cf. Pss. 76:5 [HB 76:6]; 121:4; 132:4; Prov. 6:4, 10; 24:33; Isa. 5:27) to emphasize a sleep of finality, i.e., death (cf. Ps. 94:7; Isa. 26:19). The Semitic root *škn* can bear the meaning "rest" (e.g., Arabic *sakana*). The semantic range represented in the words of the MT may contain a picturesque progression. The king of Assyria's trusted officials, far from being awake to the emergency, grow drowsy and take their rest—one that will prove to be final.

†נָפֹשׁוּ ("are scattered") is doubtless from the root פּוּשׁ ("spring about"; niphal = "be scattered"). Dahood's suggestion (followed by Cathcart) to take the form in question as a piel denominative from נֶפֶשׁ ("soul"), hence נִפְשׁוּ ("expire"), is forced at best and unlikely at all in the light of the parallel image of (re)gathering, i.e., that which is

---

77. For details, see *CAD*, 10 part 1, pp. 333-34; 11 part 2, pp. 34-47. See further S. Moscati, *An Introduction to the Comparative Grammar of the Semitic Languages* (Wiesbaden: Harrassowitz, 1964), p. 59; *GAG*, par. 30b, 32a, b.

78. For this particle, see *CAD*, 1 part 1, p. 220. See also D. Cohen, *Dictionnaire des racines sémitiques* (Paris: Mouton, 1970), 1:16-17.

scattered. Cathcart's further proposal, that וְאֵין מְקַבֵּץ ("with no one to gather them") is to be understood as "there is none to remove them," is still more forced and necessitated by his repointing of *nāpōšû* to *nippěšû*. Likewise the usual understanding of the MT עַמְּךָ as "your people" is certainly preferable to Cathcart's attempt to translate the form as "your troops." The whole picture is one of a totally dispersed populace, officials and citizens alike, scattered across the countryside like sheep on the mountains with no shepherd to regather them to safety (cf. 1 Kings 22:17).

3:19 †כֵּהָה† ("healing"): The word is a *hapax legomenon*. If it is taken from the root כָּהָה ("grow faint/dim"), it may mean something like "relief." It is commonly equated with the word גֵּהָה ("healing"), also a *hapax legomenon* (Prov. 17:22). In light of the established usages of the verbal root, something like "alleviation" probably is intended. But in the light of the following לְשִׁבְרֶךָ ("for your fracture") either sense is tolerable. The masc. sing. pronominal suffix on the word for "fracture" refers to the king of Nineveh.

†נַחְלָה מַכָּתֶךָ† ("your injury is severe"): Similar phraseology is found in contexts containing שֶׁבֶר ("break") in Jer. 10:19; 14:17; 30:12. For חָלָה in the sense of an incurable sickness, see Isa. 17:11; for its use as a severe wounding, see 1 Sam. 31:3.

†רָעָתְךָ תָּמִיד† ("your evil continually"): The translation suggested here takes the word תָּמִיד as a simple adverb (cf. NASB). The NIV translation, "your endless cruelty," reflects the possibility of a broken construct chain.[79]

---

79. For this proposed construction, see D. N. Freedman, "The Broken Construct Chain," *Bib* 53 (1972): 534-36; A. C. M. Blommerde, "The Broken Construct Chain, Further Examples," *Bib* 55 (1974): 549-52; M. Dahood, *Psalms*, AB (Garden City, N.Y.: Doubleday, 1970), 3:52. For a dissenting opinion, see J. D. Price, "Rosh: An Ancient Land Known to Ezekiel," *GTJ* 6 (1985): 76-88.

HABAKKUK

Introduction to Habakkuk

HISTORICAL CONTEXT

SETTING

Taken at face value Habakkuk's short prophecy is set in a time of national upheaval characterized by gross social injustice (1:2-4) and by the imminent advent of the Babylonians (Chaldeans) as the foremost international power (1:5-11). Accordingly evangelical commentators have opted for a preexilic setting that antedates the fall of Jerusalem in 586 B.C. Three main positions have been articulated among such scholars. (1) The majority (e.g., Archer, Freeman, Hailey, R. K. Harrison, Hummel, E. J. Young) date the prophecy to the time of Jehoiakim, whose godless disposition (2 Kings 24:1-3; Jer. 26; 36) occasioned prophetic utterances of condemnation together with the threat of a Babylonian invasion (Jer. 25). (2) Others (e.g., Bullock, Laetsch, Pusey, Unger) decide for a date in the reign of Josiah before the finding of a copy of the law in 621 B.C. They argue that the desperate moral conditions denounced by Habakkuk could well be reflective of that period (cf. Jer. 1-6) and relate Habakkuk's prediction of the coming Chaldeans to the transitional nature of the period near the end of the Neo-Assyrian era. (3) Still others (e.g., Keil) defend a date in the time of Judah's most wicked king, Manasseh.[1] They cite the

---

1. Jewish tradition (*Seder Olam*) associated Habakkuk with Manasseh's reign, a position followed by many Jewish scholars, including David Kimchi. For

degraded moral and spiritual level of that time (2 Kings 21:1-16; 2 Chron. 33:1-10), an era whose debauchery was so pronounced that it drew God's declaration that He would effect a total "disaster on Jerusalem and Judah" (2 Kings 21:12).

A seventh-century date for Habakkuk's prophecy has by no means carried the day among nonevangelical scholars. The setting of the book has been variously assigned to dates between the ninth century B.C. and the Maccabean period. Complicating the question of the book's setting is the matter of its composition and compilation (see Literary Features).

An early rabbinic tradition speculated that Habakkuk was the son of the Shunammite woman who lived in the days of Elisha and King Jehoram of Israel (852-841 B.C.; cf. 2 Kings 4:16). At the other end of the spectrum, Paul Haupt decided for the Maccabean era, dating it to a time shortly after Judas Maccabeus's victory over Nicanor in 161 B.C.

Most critical scholars have suggested a date that more clearly reflects the apparent subject of the prophecy, the Chaldeans of the Neo-Babylonian era. These may be conveniently catalogued into those who favor a preexilic period and those who prefer a later period. Among the former may be cited Budde and Eissfeldt, who date Habakkuk to the later reign of Josiah (c. 625-612 B.C.). The reign of Jehoiakim (608-597 B.C.) is favored by such scholars as Albright, Bewer, Humbert, Nielsen, and von Rad. An exilic date is supported by many, including Giesebrecht, Lods, Sellin, and Wellhausen, all of whom, however, isolate certain portions of the book as being earlier prophetic material that was utilized by the author/compiler of the prophecies, who lived in the latter half of the seventh century B.C.[2] More radical is the view of B. Duhm (followed by C. C. Torrey) that the book has a fourth-century provenience. Duhm relates the book's message to the campaigning of Alexander the Great and sees in the reference to the *Kasdîm* in 1:6 a corruption of *Kittîm*, a term used to designate Cypriots or Greeks in general. He also conjectures that the word "wine" in 2:5 (*yayin*) should be read as "Greek" (*yāwān*). Interestingly enough, 1QpHab also interprets the *Kasdîm* of 1:6 as *Kittîm*, although the term probably meant the Romans.[3] Contrary to

---

helpful discussions of the background and setting of the book, see R. K. Harrison, *Introduction to the Old Testament* (Grand Rapids: Eerdmans, 1969), pp. 922-36; Otto Eissfeldt, *The Old Testament: An Introduction*, trans. P. R. Ackroyd (New York: Harper & Row, 1965), pp. 417-23.

2. Details relative to the book's compilation will be considered with the discussion of unity in the section dealing with literary context.

3. So G. Vermes, *The Dead Sea Scrolls in English* (Baltimore: Penguin Books, 1962), p. 65. See also Menahem Mansoor, *The Dead Sea Scrolls*, 2d ed.

Duhm's speculation, however, the text of the Habakkuk scroll actually reads *Kasdîm* even while interpreting it as *Kittîm*.

In the face of such diversity of opinion, final certainty as to the setting of this prophecy is elusive. The book is related to a time of internal wickedness in Judah and to an era anticipating the rise of the Neo-Babylonian empire. These factors suggest a preexilic setting. A key factor in the discussion is the precise force of 1:5-6 (q.v.). Although the case is far from settled, it seems that these data will have their fullest force if one holds to either (1) the position that sees the events described as taking place in the early period of Josiah's rule or (2) the older Jewish view that locates Habakkuk in the time of Manasseh.

Perhaps the latter suggestion has the most to commend it, particularly if it can be demonstrated that both Zephaniah and Jeremiah knew and utilized Habakkuk's prophecy (cf. Hab. 1:8 with Jer. 4:13; 5:6; Hab. 2:10 with Jer. 51:58; Hab. 2:12 with Jer. 22:13-17; Hab. 2:20 with Zeph. 1:7). According to this scenario, because Manasseh was carried away into captivity in the later part of his reign and subsequently repented and initiated several religious reforms, a date for the book shortly before the western campaigns of King Ashurbanipal of Assyria in 652 B.C. and thereafter would not be far from wrong. So understood, the book's setting is the same basic time period as that of Nahum, an era of great internal wickedness in Judah, a period denoted externally as the Pax Assyriaca, an age that antedates the rise of the predicted instrument of divine chastening, the Chaldeans, by a full generation.[4]

AUTHORSHIP

Even though the traditional setting of the book and its literary integrity can be defended with some degree of certainty,[5] the identity of the prophet Habakkuk remains a mystery. Some have sought his identity in proposed etymologies. Thus, by relating his name to the Assyrian plant called the *ḥambaqūqu* and by noting certain literary data in 2:2, Reiser theorizes that Habakkuk had been educated in Nineveh. A relationship with the root חָבַק (*ḥābaq*) "embrace" has occasioned the suggestion that Elisha gave the promise to the Shunammite who was Habakkuk's mother that "about this time next year you will embrace a son" (2 Kings 4:16). The first suggestion is spe-

(Grand Rapids: Baker, 1983), p. 93. H. Hummel (*The Word Becoming Flesh* [St. Louis: Concordia, 1979], p. 345), however, suggests the Hellenistic party or the Seleucids.

4. For details as to the historical background of the seventh century B.C. see the discussion in the Introduction to Nahum and the exposition of Hab. 1:2-4.

5. See below under Literary Context.

cious at best and the second is historically impossible.[6] So also is the
LXX tradition found in the title to the first century B.C. additions to
Daniel entitled *Bel and the Dragon* that Habakkuk was the "son of
Jesus of the tribe of Levi."[7] Equally improbable is the conjecture,
accomplished by relating Hab. 2:1 with Isa. 21:6, that "watchman"
Habakkuk is Isaiah's prophetic successor.

The later Jews were fascinated with Habakkuk not only because
of his unusual name but because of his questioning of God,[8] together
with the recording of the divine denunciation of the Chaldeans. In
addition to the above mentioned case of *Bel and the Dragon* (which in
one LXX tradition depicts Habakkuk as a Levite prophet whom the
angel of the Lord lifted up by the hair to bring him with a bowl of
boiled pottage to Daniel, who had been thrown into the lions' den),[9]
preserved among the Dead Sea scrolls is a commentary on the first
two chapters of Habakkuk (1QpHab). Written in pesher style, it proceeds by quoting a small portion of the text of Habakkuk followed by
the author's comments on the quoted material in the light of current
events. Neither of these sources helps to identify Habakkuk further
than confirming his prophetic status. Some, however, have seen in the
identification of Habakkuk as "the son of Jesus of the tribe of Levi" a
later historical confirmation of possible Levitical associations, a relationship hinted at in the musical notations in Habakkuk 3.

Was Habakkuk, then, a Levite?[10] Was he at least a prophet of the
cultus, as many (e.g., Humbert, Lindblom) confidently affirm?[11]

6. For details, see the discussion in Harrison, *Introduction*, p. 931.
7. For a valuable discussion of the additions to Daniel, see Bruce M.
Metzger, ed., *The Oxford Annotated Apocrypha*, expanded ed. (New York:
Oxford U., 1977), pp. 209-18.
8. Because of his persistent dialogue with God, Habakkuk was called "the
wrestler" by Jerome, a view that Luther later shared.
9. For the text, see Alfred Rahlfs, ed., *Septuaginta*, 6th ed. (Stuttgart: Würt-
tembergische Bibelanstalt, n.d.), 2:936-41. In the later Christian account
found in *The Lives of the Prophets*, Habakkuk is said to have come from the
tribe of Simeon.
10. Ralph L. Smith (*Micah–Malachi*, WBC [Waco, Tex.: Word, 1984], p. 93)
seems inclined to such a position: "One manuscript of *Bel and the Dragon*
says that Habakkuk was the son of Jesus of the tribe of Levi. This later
tradition that Habakkuk was of the tribe of Levi, along with the fact that
he is one of only three men in the OT to be called a prophet in the
superscription of his book, and the fact that he is presented as a prophet
in the musical chapter (3:1) of his book, suggests that he may have been a
Levite and a professional or temple prophet."
11. P. Humbert (*Problèmes du livre d'Habacuc* [Neuchatel: Secretariat de
L'Universite, 1944]) works out the details of the book so as to show its
origin among the cultic prophets of the Temple in seventh century B.C.
Jerusalem. J. Lindblom (*Prophecy in Ancient Israel* [Philadelphia:
Muhlenberg, 1962], p. 254) asserts that Habakkuk "was certainly a cultic
prophet at the temple in Jerusalem."

Though the scriptural evidence indicates that Levites functioned in a musical ministry in the Temple (1 Chron. 6:31-48; 15:16-24; 16:4-6, 37, 41-42; 23:5; 25:1-8), a fact that accords well with the musical notations in chap. 3, and although the Scriptures attest the existence of prophets who were also priests (e.g., Jeremiah, Ezekiel, Zephaniah),[12] a lack of proof makes it impossible to say more than that Habakkuk was a prophet who likely lived in Judah in the seventh century B.C. and who was burdened by what he perceived to be the divine indifference to the moral decay and spiritual apostasy that surrounded him (1:2-4). Nevertheless, these concerns reveal a great deal about Habakkuk the man. He was a person of deep spiritual longings that included a high view of God's essential power, dignity, and worth as well as of the basic importance of God's moral standards for mankind. He had a righteous hatred for sin and the resultant personal immorality and social breakdown that it caused. He was a man who was secure enough in his own spiritual condition not only to lay before his God some hard questions that perplexed him but also to respond in humility and submissiveness when those concerns were answered. In the final analysis, Habakkuk was one whose trust in God could triumph through times of testing and questioning and could find God Himself to be sufficient for life's experiences (3:16-18).

LITERARY CONTEXT

LITERARY FEATURES

The central focus of Habakkuk's prophecy is on the relation of a sovereign and holy God to a sinful world, where society is permeated by godlessness and injustice. That theme becomes apparent in its development in the perplexities (1:2-4, 12-17), petitions (3:2b), remarks (2:1; 3:2a, 16-18), and praises (3:3-15) of the prophet as well as in the divine responses (1:5-11; 2:2-20). Assuredly the truth of God's sovereign and just supervision of the affairs of the ages and all people

---

12. Even demonstrating that Habakkuk was a Levite and connected with the Temple worship at Jerusalem would not validate the current opinion of critical scholarship that finds the remnants of cultic ritual and liturgy almost ubiquitously in connection with OT prophecy. Hummel (*The Word*, p. 164) cautions: "In general, it is agreed on all sides today that in this respect the form critics greatly overstated their case, but they did establish that cult and prophecy often operated in tandem. . . . If the normative Israelite cult was Mosaic, and if prophecy was reformatory, the prophets could scarcely have been at total loggerheads with priestdom. . . . Subsequent research has confirmed that the prophets certainly speak in the temple in cultic contexts even if they held no office from the cult with which most of their audience was perfectly familiar."

according to His wise and holy purposes, directing them to their appointed end, flows through Habakkuk's prophecies. Indeed, it is this realization that gives the book a proper perspective. The theme of divine teleology is implied in the prophet's perplexities (1:2-4; 1:12–2:1) and God's replies (1:5-11; 2:2-20), where it is deliberated and defended, and also in the prophet's affirmation (3:2*a*) and rehearsal of God's greatness (3:3-15) and closing note of praise (3:16-19), where it is demonstrated and applied. Accordingly the book's theme must always be read in the light of its theological orientation.

The theme can be seen immediately in the prophet's opening characterization of the state of affairs in his day. Habakkuk can understand neither the gross sin of Judah nor God's seeming indifference to the rampant corruption he sees all around him (1:2-4).

The theme continues as Habakkuk's initial statement of perplexity is followed by the recording of God's answer to his dilemma. Much to Habakkuk's amazement, God is about to judge Judah's sin by sending the Chaldeans, a ferocious, vicious people (1:5-11). The theme next faces a test as to its equity. God's answer to Habakkuk's problem only raises a second question: How could a holy God use as an instrument of chastisement a nation that was even more wicked than Judah? For God to do so would be like making all people (including Judahites) defenseless sea creatures that fishermen (the Chaldeans) gleefully take up in their nets (conquests). Further, because such fishermen know no god but their net, how could God's holy purposes be realized? Still further, since God Himself was sending them, how could they ever be stopped (1:12–2:1)?

The book's theme finds further development in 2:2-20 as Habakkuk reveals not only God's reply to his perplexity but also some important principles of divine government. God first instructs Habakkuk to "write down the revelation," for His answer will transcend the local and temporal bounds of Habakkuk's concern (2:2-3). The Lord next puts forward the principles upon which His answer will be based—namely, that one of the purposes of His ordering of the government of earth's history is that both classes of men—the righteous and the unrighteous—may be seen in clear distinction. Not only in Judah but also everywhere else the righteous one "will live by his faith(fulness)" and the unrighteous one will perish in his godless greed (2:4-5).

The rest of the chapter is concerned with an application of these principles to the case of the Chaldeans (2:5), the bulk of it being devoted to a description of the causes for which the unrighteous Chaldeans will themselves be judged (2:6-20). Behind the changing scenes of the stage of earth's activities the author of the drama of earth's history is directing all things to their just and appointed end. Accord-

120

ingly all people are admonished to "be silent" before Him who alone is God and is "in His holy Temple" (2:20).

The theme of the book finds illustration and application in the closing chapter (3). To the double answer of God to Habakkuk's perplexities there is first appended a further divine instruction. The knowledge that God is truly sovereign and in control of all things made Habakkuk "stand in awe" of God's deeds. He humbly prayed that God, in meting out His justice, would meet His people in mercy (3:2). Habakkuk then records his contemplation of a victory psalm that recounts God's deliverance of His people from Egypt, His preservation of them through the time of their wilderness wanderings, and His triumphal leading of them in the conquest of the Promised Land (3:3-15). The rehearsal of that epic material commemorating the age of the Exodus brought a further sense of awe and humility to Habakkuk. Such a great God could be trusted to accomplish His purposes with all nations and peoples. Therefore, though calamity must come, Habakkuk would wait patiently and confidently. He would also abide in the Lord's strength for His sovereign and perfect will to be effected (3:16-19).

The composition and arrangement of Habakkuk's prophecy reflect well the basic theme of the book. The deliberation and defense of the theme in the first two chapters are given in a dialogue style, recording the discussions between the prophet and his God. The book opens with a carefully crafted unit utilizing the genre of lament (1:2-4).[13] The section contains the customary features of introductory invocation (v. 2) and a statement of the problem or crisis that precipitated the plaintiff's cry (vv. 3-4) as well as an implied petition: "God, won't you please do something about this terrible situation?" Likewise Habakkuk's second perplexity (1:12–2:1) as to God's use of the rapacious Chaldeans contains the normal elements of lament: invocation (v. 12), a statement of the problem (vv. 13-17), and a closing affirmation of confidence in God (2:1). Like the first lament it also implies a petition: "Can't you find some other agent of chastisement?"

The other participant in the dialogue—God—is introduced in two sections recording the divine answers to Habakkuk's questions. These units also show careful literary construction. In the first instance (1:5-11) God gives to Habakkuk not only a solution to his perplexity (God will send the Chaldeans to deal with Judah's sin, vv.

---

13. Walter E. Rast ("Justification by Faith," *Cur TM* 10 [1983]: 169-75) calls attention to Habakkuk's employment of the traditional forms of lament (1:2-4, 12-17) followed by response (1:5-11; 2:1-4) and suggests that Habakkuk's technique may well anticipate that of the author of 1QpHab.

5-6) but also an accompanying description of the ability of His agent of judgment to deliver the required punishment (vv. 7-11). God's second answer (2:2-20) is also given in a distinctive format: introductory formula (v. 2*a*), preliminary instructions (vv. 2*b*-3), general guiding principles (v. 4), and particular detailed application (vv. 5-20). The latter portion takes up the bulk of chap. 2 and constitutes a series of taunt songs (vv. 6-8, 9-11, 12-14, 15-17, 18-20) against the Chaldeans. The taunts are presented in the form of a series of woes, each containing several of the characteristic features of woe oracles, including invective (vv. 6, 9, 12, 15, 19*a*), threat (vv. 7, 11, 13, 16, 20), and criticism (vv. 8, 10, 14, 17, 18, 19*b*).[14]

Each major unit of chaps. 1-2 is composed such that the two perplexities of the prophet are begun with a question (1:2, 12) and each of the answers starts with an imperative (1:5; 2:2). Moreover, the two chapters are threaded together with the stitch-words מִשְׁפָּט (*miš-pāṭ*, "justice/judgment/law," 1:4, 7, 12), צַדִּיק (*ṣaddîq*, "righteous," 1:4, 13; 2:4),[15] בּוֹגְדִים/בּוֹגֵד (*bôgĕdîm/bôgēd*, "treacherous/betrays," 1:13; 2:5), and אָסַף (*'āsap*, "gather," 1:9, 15; 2:5) as well as verbs of seeing (1:3, 5, 13). Individual units in the first two chapters likewise have distinctive characteristics. Thus 1:12–2:1 is bookended with the idea of reproof, and the Lord's second reply is constructed with enclosing statements that contrast the unrighteous Chaldeans with the righteous who live by faith, mindful of God in His holy Temple (2:4, 20).

With the third chapter it is obvious that the book's central theme has received an entirely different setting. Gone is the dialogue style with its questions and answers as well as such features as lament, taunts, and woes. In their place one finds chiefly prayer and praise, and especially a long victory ode that retells in epic fashion God's leading of His people in triumph out of Egypt, through the wilderness, and into the land of promise (3:3-15). The epic poem is of particular interest in that it is composed of different Hebrew than the rest of the book. Indeed, it contains some rare words and difficult grammatical constructions not representative of standard classical Hebrew. It is apparent that the material belongs to an older stage of the language. The evidence for its archaic setting is as follows.

First are numerous cases of defective spelling in the interior of words, as pointed out by W. F. Albright.[16] Next are various early

---

14. See the chart that accompanies the exposition of Hab. 2:6-8.
15. For the concept of stitch-wording, see Richard D. Patterson, "Of Bookends, Hinges, and Hooks: Literary Clues to the Arrangement of Jeremiah's Prophecies," *WTJ* 51 (1989): 117-18.
16. W. F. Albright, "The Psalm of Habakkuk," in *Studies in Old Testament Prophecy Dedicated to T. H. Robinson*, ed. H. H. Rowley (Edinburgh: T. and T. Clark, 1950), p. 10. Albright also suggests the presence of an old energic

grammatical elements and poetic devices: (1) the lack of the definite article; (2) the *t*-imperfect used with duals or collectives (v. 4); (3) the use of the old pronominal suffix הˉ (vv. 4, 11); (4) the employment of enclitic *-m* (v. 8);[17] (5) the frequent appearance of the old preterite prefix-conjugation verbs (vv. 3, 4, 5, 7, 8, 9, 10, 11, 12, 14) in variation with the suffix-conjugation; (6) the use of the ל of possession in inverted predicate position in a nonverbal sentence (v. 6); and (7) the use of structured tricola employing climactic parallelism (vv. 4, 6*b*, 7, 8*a*, 10, 11, 13*b*) to mark major divisions (vv. 6*b*-7, 8) or subdivisions (vv. 4, 10, 11, 13*b*, 14) within the poem.

One may notice also the use of parallel expressions and set terms held in common in Ugaritic and the corpus of old Hebrew poetry: נָהָר/יָם, שָׁמַיִם/אֶרֶץ (v. 3), קֶרֶן/פָּנִים (vv. 4-5), גִּבְעוֹת עוֹלָם/הַרְרֵי־עַד (v. 6), שֶׁמֶשׁ/יָרֵחַ, סוּס/מֶרְכָּבָה (v. 8), קֶשֶׁת/מַטֶּה (v. 9), תְּהוֹם/קוֹל ,נָתַן/נָשָׂא (v. 10), חִץ/בָּרָק (v. 11). Also to be noted is the use of a vocabulary commonly found in older poetic material: חָוָה (v. 3), שָׁמַיִם ,הַר־פָּארָן ,קָדוֹשׁ ,אֱלוֹהַ (v. 6), מַטֶּה, אַף (v. 12), קוֹל ,תְּהוֹם (זֶרֶם) מַיִם (v. 10), רָגַז ,אֶוֶן (v. 7), רָכַב ,אַף (v. 8), פֶּרֶז ,רֹאשׁ (v. 14), and יָם, מַיִם רַבִּים (v. 15).[18]

No less significant is the presence of themes common to the body of Ugaritic and early Old Testament poetic literature: (1) the Lord's movement from the southland (v. 3; cf. Deut. 33:1-2; Judg. 5:4; Ps. 68:8 [HB]); (2) the presence of the heavenly assemblage (v. 5; cf. Deut. 33:2-3); (3) the shaking of the terrestial and celestial worlds at God's presence (vv. 6, 10-11; cf. Judg. 5:4-5; Pss. 18:8-9, 13-15 [HB]); 68:34 [HB]; 77:18-20 [HB]; 144:5-6); (4) the Lord's anger against sea and river (v. 8; cf. Ex. 15:8; Ps. 18:8, 16 [HB]); (5) the Lord's presence riding the clouds (v. 8; cf. Ex. 15:4; Pss. 18:11-12 [HB]; 68:5, 34 [HB]); (6) the fear of the enemy at the Lord's advance (vv. 7, 10?; cf. Ex. 15:14-16; Pss. 18:8 [HB]; 77:18-20 [HB]); (7) the Lord's fighting against the boastful (v. 14; cf. Ex. 15:9) enemy (vv. 9, 11, 13-14; cf. Ex. 15:3, 6; Ps. 77:19 [HB]) so as to deliver His people (vv. 13-15; cf. Pss. 18:38-39, 41 [HB]; 68:8 [HB] with Ex. 15:10, 12-13).[19]

---

form with emphatic ל in Hab. 3:6-7: לתחתאו, "(eternal orbits) were shattered." E. Würthwein, *The Text of the Old Testament*, 4th ed. (Grand Rapids: Eerdmans, 1979), pp. 114-15, follows the lead of K. Elliger in translating the troublesome crux as the Ugaritic word for destruction preceded by the preposition ל.

17. For enclitic *-m*, see M. Pope, "Ugaritic Enclitic *-m*," *JCS* 5 (1951): 123-28; H. D. Hummel, "Enclitic *MEM* in Early Northwest Semitic, Especially Hebrew," *JBL* 76 (1957): 85-106; M. Dahood, *Psalms*, AB (Garden City, N.Y.: Doubleday, 1970), 3:408-9.

18. For the bearing of Ugaritic research upon biblical studies, see P. C. Craigie, *Ugarit and the Old Testament* (Grand Rapids: Eerdmans, 1983), pp. 67-90, and his extensive bibliography on pp. 107-9.

19. Theodore Hiebert (*God of My Victory* [Atlanta: Scholars, 1986], p. 26) also remarks that "The image of the chariot warrior baring his bow corre-

The poetry of these verses is drawn from two separate compositions. That there are two poems here can be seen both from their differing themes and from the syntax of the respective material. The first section (vv. 3-7) describes God's leading of His heavenly and earthly hosts from the south in an awe-inspiring theophany. It is marked structurally by the repeated use of the coordinator *waw* to tie together its thought associations. The second section (vv. 8-15) constitutes a victory song commemorating the conquest itself and points to the basis of that success in the Exodus, particularly in the victory at the Red Sea. Structurally no *waw* coordinator is used, thought associations being accomplished through variations in sentence structure, including change of word order and the skillful employment of tricola.

These poems bear the marks of genuine epic,[20] employing epic themes and style throughout. The central focus is on a hero—God Himself. The first poem (vv. 3-7) relates the account of an epic journey, God's leading of His people from the southland toward Canaan, the land of promise. The poet calls attention to God's command of nature in awesome theophany (vv. 3-4), to His companions (v. 5), to His earth-shaking power (v. 6), and to the effect of all this on the inhabitants of the land (v. 7).

The second poem (vv. 8-15) transcends the bounds of the movement from Egypt to the Jordan (cf. Ps. 114:3-5), the phraseology being best understood as including God's miraculous acts in the conquest period as well. God's victories at the end of the Exodus account are rehearsed first (vv. 8-11), possibly reflecting such deeds as the triumph at the Red Sea (Ex. 15) and at the Jordan (Josh. 3-4) as well as the victories at the Wadi Kishon (Judg. 4-5) and Gibeon (Josh. 10).[21]

---

sponds with the practice of warfare in the Late Bronze and early Iron Ages as it has been reconstructed by historians and archaeologists. The bow by this time had become the principal weapon of the chariot warrior, and chariots were outfitted with bow cases and quivers to carry weapons not in use. The description of the divine warrior in Hab. 3:8-9 mounting his chariot, baring his bow (drawing it from the bow case), and firing the arrows drawn from the quiver . . . is what one would expect from an Israelite poet drawing images from the concrete world of human conflict with which the poet was familiar." See further W. F. Albright, "The Psalm of Habakkuk," pp. 8-9; W. F. Albright, *Yahweh and the Gods of Canaan* (Garden City, N.Y.: Doubleday, 1969), pp. 1-52, 183-93; U. Cassuto, "Chapter III of Habakkuk and the Ras Shamra Texts," in *Biblical and Oriental Studies*, trans. Israel Abrahams (Jerusalem: Magnes, 1975), 2:3-15, 16-59, 69-109; S. Rummel, "Narrative Structures in the Ugaritic Texts," *RSP* 3:233-84; F. M. Cross, *Canaanite Myth and Hebrew Epic* (Cambridge: Harvard U., 1973), pp. 91-194.

20. See the Excursus on Habakkuk 3.
21. The psalm in Hab. 3:3-15 thus contains a sketch of what may have constituted an early Hebrew epic commemorating God's mighty prowess in

The poet then describes the victory that gave Israel its deliverance and eventual conquest of Canaan: the triumph in Israel's exodus from Egypt (vv. 12-15).

Epic elements can also be seen in these two poems in the use of literary features common to the epic genre: static epithets, set parallel terms, and the vocabulary and themes common to the commemoration of the Exodus.[22] Thus, whether in terms of subject matter or literary style, Habakkuk's twofold psalm deserves to be recognized as an epic remnant. Habakkuk has employed epic material to illustrate and validate his thesis that God is in control of earth's unfolding history and, as in the past, He may be expected to deal justly with His covenant nation, which He has instructed to live by its faith(fulness, 2:4) and to "be silent before him" (2:20).

One might also make a reasonable case for the third chapter's being considered a *tĕpillâ*—a prayer. Indeed, many of the features common to this type of poetry (cf. Pss. 17, 86, 90, 102, 143) are present: opening cry/statement of praise, attestation of reverence/trust (v. 2*a*), petition/problem (v. 2*b*), praise and exaltation of God (vv. 3-15), statement of trust and confidence in God (vv. 16-18), and concluding note of praise (v. 19). These are developed to settle the prophet's concerns and to assure his readers that God is in control of earth's history, guiding the destinies of nations and all mankind in accordance with His holy and wise purposes.

Although a diversity of style between the first two chapters of Habakkuk and chap. 3 has been demonstrated, in a deeper sense the final chapter is a necessary corollary and conclusion to the prophet's wrestlings of the first two chapters. One wonders whether the central theophany of 3:3-15 is not only a result of the prophet's prayer (3:2) but also the anticipated outcome of the prophetic expectations (2:2, 20).

Before leaving the discussion on literary matters, note something of the richness of the literary features that Habakkuk uses. In addition to the employment of taunt songs, woe, and epic poetry pre-

---

delivering His people from Egypt and bringing them into the land of promise. The full epic, though preserved in bits and pieces in various portions of the OT, has not been inscripturated. See further Richard D. Patterson, "The Psalm of Habakkuk," *GTJ* 8 (1987): 163-94. The author wishes to thank the editors of the *Grace Theological Journal* for their permission to quote freely from that article, which has been utilized extensively for the present discussion as well as for relevant points in the exposition of Hab. 3:3-15 and the Excursus on Habakkuk 3.

22. M. P. Nilsson (*The Mycenaean Origin of Greek Mythology* [New York: Norton, 1932], p. 19) points out that "in the epical language of all peoples occurs a store of stock expressions, constantly recurring phrases, half and whole verses and even verse complexes; and repetitions are characteristic of the epic style."

viously mentioned, one may find such literary forms as the proverb (1:9; 2:6) and such literary figures as simile and metaphor (1:8, 9, 11, 14-17; 2:5, 7, 8, 15, 16; 3:4, 8-10, 11, 14, 19), allegory (2:15-16), metonymy (2:5; 3:2, 9), merismus (3:7), hendiadys (1:15?; 2:2?), hyperbole (1:6-11; 3:6, 11), paronomasia (2:19; 3:13-14*a*), personification (1:7-11; 2:5, 11; 3:1, 5, 7, 10), rhetorical question (1:12; 2:13, 18; 3:8), repetition for effect (1:15*b*-17), and synecdoche (3:7) as well as such structural devices as alliteration and assonance (1:6, 10; 2:6, 7, 15, 18; 3:2), enjambment (1:13; 2:18; 3:4, 16), gender-matched parallelism (2:5; 3:3), staircase parallelism (3:8), climactic parallelism (3:2), pivot-pattern parallelism (1:17), and chiasmus (1:2, 3, 4; 2:1, 6, 9, 14, 16; 3:3).

If Habakkuk does not reach the literary artistry of Nahum, it may be due to the nature of the prophet's spiritual odyssey that often approximates the Israelite wisdom literature in sentiment and expression. Habakkuk's wrestling with the problem of the justice of God finds its most able format in the utilization of a dialogue style that is almost narrative in quality. His familiarity with and employment of epic traditional material, however, demonstrates that Habakkuk is not without poetic sensitivity (cf. 3:16-19). A careful literary reading of his prophecy will pay rich dividends in understanding.

OUTLINE

Superscription (1:1)
I. The Prophet's Perplexities and God's Explanations (1:2–2:20)
   A. First Perplexity: How Can God Disregard Judah's Sin? (1:2-4)
   B. First Explanation: God Will Judge Judah Through the Chaldeans (1:5-11)
   C. Second Perplexity: How Can God Employ the Wicked Chaldeans? (1:12–2:1)
   D. Second Explanation: God Controls All Nations According to His Purposes (2:2-20)
      1. Preliminary instructions (2:2-3)
      2. Guiding principles (2:4)
      3. Specific applications (2:5-20)
         a. The case of the Chaldeans (2:5)
         b. The first woe: The plundering Chaldean will be despoiled (2:6-8)
         c. The second woe: The plotting Chaldean will be denounced (2:9-11)
         d. The third woe: The pillaging Chaldean will be destroyed (2:12-14)
         e. The fourth woe: The perverting Chaldean will be disgraced (2:15-17)

f. The fifth woe: The polytheistic Chaldean will be desert-
   ed by his idols (2:18-20)
II. The Prophet's Prayer and God's Exaltation (3:1-19)
   A. The Prophet's Prayer for the Redeemer's Pity (3:1-2)
   B. The Prophet's Praise of the Redeemer's Person (3:3-15)
      1. The Redeemer's coming (3:3-7)
         a. His appearance (3:3-4)
         b. His actions (3:5-7)
      2. The Redeemer's conquest (3:8-15)
         a. His power as seen at the waters (3:8-9*b*)
         b. His power as seen in the natural world (3:9*c*-11)
         c. His power as seen by the enemy (3:12-15)
   C. The Prophet's Pledge to the Redeemer's Purposes (3:16-19)
      1. A statement of the prophet's trust in the Redeemer (3:16-18)
      2. A concluding note of praise to the Redeemer (3:19)

UNITY

Although related to matters of date and authorship (q.v.), the
problem of the unity of the book is primarily literary. Recent scholarship has largely conceded that Habakkuk has been given its present
unity[23] through such things as subject matter (e.g., the downfall of
the godless and the prophet's trust in God), motifs (e.g., righteous[ness] vs. wicked[ness]), and vocabulary (e.g., [all] the nation[s]—1:5, 17; 2:5; 3:6, 16; the [whole] earth—1:6; 2:4, 20; 3:3, 5, 9;
people[s]—1:6, 7; 2:10; 3:13), but many still deny an original unity of
composition. For example, Eissfeldt acknowledges the essential authorship and resultant unity of the book but nevertheless asserts that

> we must therefore regard the book of Habakkuk as a loose collection of a
> group of songs of lamentation and oracles (i, 2–ii, 4), a series of six cries
> of woe (ii, 5-20), and the prayer of iii, which all stem from the same
> prophet Habakkuk, probably a cult-prophet, and originated in approx-
> imately the same period.[24]

Particularly worrisome to the unity of the composition has been
the identity of the wicked in 1:2-4 and 1:13-17. Earlier critical scholarship tended to solve the problem by excising 1:5-11 and relegating
it to an earlier prophetic work that supposedly had become associated with the Habakkuk material and subsequently inserted into the

---

23. For details, see Albright, "The Psalm of Habakkuk," pp. 2, 9. See also W. S.
    Prinsloo, "Die boodskap van die boek Habakuk," *Nederduits Gereformeerde
    Teologiese Tydskrif* 20 (1979): 146-51, who, however, relates the message of
    the book to a denunciation of the Assyrians.
24. Eissfeldt, *Introduction*, p. 420.

text.[25] Also troublesome was the obvious literary difference of the material in chap. 3, a chapter whose authenticity was further called into doubt by its failure to be included in 1QpHab.

As for the first problem, the identity of the wicked becomes a difficulty only by attempting to make it refer to the same group in both passages. Traditional scholarship has held that the wicked referred to in 1:2-4 are Judah's citizens but are the Babylonians in 1:13-17, those whom God was to employ in punishing the wicked Judahites (1:5-11). So viewed, 1:5-11 does not need to be deleted and the unity of the first two chapters is preserved. This is the simplest understanding and one that has enjoyed endorsement by critics of all persuasions.[26]

With regard to the problem of chap. 3, although it was not utilized by the author of 1QpHab, this may be due either to its incorporation of epic material inappropriate to the situation and purposes of the Dead Sea community or to the difficulty of its language that so obscured primary interpretation that midrashic application could scarcely proceed smoothly. Further, since as W. H. Brownlee has pointed out the authenticity of the third chapter is unquestionable, being attested sufficiently long before the date of 1QpHab, its absence from the Qumran manuscript cannot be accounted for on the basis of date.[27] Nor need its absence be attributed to matters of unity or composition. Indeed, as Eissfeldt acknowledges,

> There are in fact no substantial arguments against deriving the poem from Habakkuk, and even the fact that the Habakkuk 'Commentary' from Qumrān limits its 'exposition' to chs. i-ii and leaves ch. iii out of account, is not a decisive argument. For this does not by any means have to be taken as indicating that at the time of the composition of the commentary, *c.* 100 B.C., ch. iii did not yet belong to the book of Habakkuk. There are many other possibilities which are to be preferred to this.[28]

---

25. For details, see ibid., pp. 417-19. For a classic treatment of the liberal tradition, see W. Hayes Ward, *A Critical and Exegetical Commentary on Habakkuk*, ICC (Edinburgh: T. and T. Clark, 1912), pp. 3-6.
26. R. L. Smith (*Micah–Malachi*, p. 94) points out that such older critics as A. B. Davidson and S. R. Driver returned to this view. He observes that this position is especially attractive to those who view Habakkuk as a cultic prophet.
27. See W. H. Brownlee, *The Text of Habakkuk in the Ancient Commentary from Qumran*, JBL Monograph XI (Philadelphia: Society of Biblical Literature, 1959), p. 92.
28. Eissfeldt, *Introduction*, p. 421. Millar Burrows (*Burrows on the Dead Sea Scrolls* [Grand Rapids: Baker, 1978], 1:321-22) observes: "Many scholars have long believed that the third chapter was not a part of the original book of Habakkuk. Its absence from the scroll is consistent with this theory but does not prove it. It does not even prove that the third chapter was unknown to the Judean covenanters. Being a psalm, it does not lend

Still further, several internal data support the unity of chap. 3 with chaps. 1 and 2. (1) As noted previously, a demonstrable unity of subject matter, theme, and vocabulary exists in the book. C. Armerding has provided an extensive list of words, ideas, and themes that can be perceived in all three chapters:

> Common features include their headings (1:1; 3:1); the lament form underlying their prayers (1:2-4, 12–2:1; 3:1-2); the preoccupation with salvation, triumphantly vindicated in the final chapter (*yāša'*, 1:2, 3:8, 13 [*bis*], 18); the judgment on domestic sin through a foreign nation (1:2-11; 3:2, 14-17); the "wicked" (*rāšā'*, 1:13; 3:13) and their intent to "devour" (*'ākal*, 1:8; 3:14); the concomitant disruption of the "nations" (1:5-17; 2:5-17; cf. 3:6-7, 12); the "revelation" that forms the turning point in the prophet's intercession (2:23; 3:3-15); the resultant promise of judgment ensuing on that nation (2:3-20; 3:12-16), as on a "house" destined to be razed to its foundations (*bayit*, 2:9-10; 3:13; cf. 2:9-13; 3:13); the transformation effected by this promise, promoting both faith and patience (2:2-4; 3:16-19); the anticipation of God's universal reign (2:14; 3:3); and the common basis on the covenant, particularly Deuteronomy 28-32, that shapes the pattern outlined above.[29]

(2) A common perspective pervades the whole: the prophet interacting personally with his God (cf. 1:2-3, 5, 12-13; 2:1, 2-3, 4; 3:2, 16). Even the prophet's stance of 3:17-19 seems clearly to have been anticipated in 2:2. (3) Only with the closing verses of the third chapter is there a satisfactory conclusion to all of the prophet's uncertainties.

Though all this does not guarantee the original compositional unity of the whole book, it does argue strongly for it, particularly as these data are considered in light of its carefully crafted literary structure. One wonders whether anyone but the author could have designed the whole. Perhaps P. C. Craigie has understated the case in remarking that "despite the disparate nature of the contents there need be few doubts as to the unity of the book."[30]

OCCASION, PURPOSE, AND TEACHINGS

If the above conclusions with regard to the date and authorship of Habakkuk's prophecy are more or less accurate, the book has its origin in recounting the prophet's intense personal experience with God. Specifically it records Habakkuk's spiritual perplexities as to God's seeming indifference in an era of moral decay and spiritual

---

itself to such use as is made of the other chapters. It is even possible that the commentary was never finished." See also Edward J. Young, *An Introduction to the Old Testament* (Grand Rapids: Eerdmans, 1953), p. 264.

29. Carl E. Armerding, "Obadiah, Nahum, Habakkuk," in *EBC* (Grand Rapids: Eerdmans, 1985), 7:522.

30. P. C. Craigie, *The Old Testament* (Nashville: Abingdon, 1986), p. 196. See also Harrison, *Introduction*, p. 93.

apostasy, and God's patient responses to his prophet. The book also rehearses Habakkuk's theophanic experience that came as a climax to his spiritual wrestling and the prophet's victorious movement from a position of questioning God to one of casting himself upon his Redeemer. If Habakkuk was also a Levite or in some way connected with the Temple cultus, the book's final prayer and theophany were of such a magnitude to Habakkuk personally that he set them down in words and form intended for use in Temple worship. In any event, the whole prophecy is designed to serve as an exemplary testimony of God's continued concern for His people and His dealings in the affairs of all mankind.

As one contemplates the message and teachings of Habakkuk, it seems clear that the book has several other purposes. Some are doubtless connected with the prophet's desire to convey theological insights gained during his spiritual odyssey (see Theological Context). Habakkuk's short prophecy is also a rich mine for ethical principles, such as the availability of God for the questioning believer (1:2-4, 5; 2:1-3), God's absolute standard of holiness for personal conduct (1:12-13), God's use of human conventions and institutions to accomplish His holy purposes (1:6), God's bringing into account the actions of all nations and peoples (2:6-10), and a life of faith as a basic guide for the righteous individual (2:4).

In agreement with this latter purpose, Habakkuk also wishes to convey wise counsel to his readers. Several themes deal with divine justice, such as the problem of human sin and suffering in their relation to divine sovereignty and the problems of morality and social justice in the face of the demand for holiness.[31] These come through most forcefully in Habakkuk's second encounter with God (1:12–2:20). Here Habakkuk decries God's use of a less holy instrument (the Chaldeans) to chastise God's people for their unholy actions and is told plainly that man needs to leave such cases to God. The Lord will in turn deal with that unholy instrument, but meanwhile the righteous person is to live a life of faith (2:4) and devotion (2:20), being mindful of God's ultimate purposes (2:14).

In God's answers to Habakkuk, He gives him wise insight into the

---

31. In this regard, see the helpful comments of C. H. Bullock, *An Introduction to the Old Testament Prophetic Books* (Chicago: Moody, 1986), p. 183: "Habakkuk was bold enough to broach the subject of divine justice. Whether or not he was acquainted with Job, he nevertheless took the issue that Job had raised and probed on a personal level and dealt with it on an international plane. There is a distinct difference, however. Job defended his innocence and moral integrity, whereas Habakkuk admitted the sins of Judah."

basic issues of life for individuals and societies:[32] wealth is not in itself wrong, but unjust gain will not be tolerated (2:6-11); civic growth and prosperity are not condemnable but cannot be accomplished at the expense of mankind's rights (2:14-20); the misuse of another person to gain one's own ends is despicable (2:15-17). The individual is also reminded that anything he puts ahead of God's rightful place as the center of his life is idolatry (2:18-20). This last point serves as the culminating observation to a discussion of the spiritual and social evils for which Babylon must be judged and touches upon another major theme in the book—the problem of evil:

> Thus the problem of the book is the problem of evil—in world history, in the church, in the human heart, the realization that every human "solution" contains the seed of its own dissolution and often only exacerbates the problem. . . . Pagan dualism and fatalism could (and can) always attribute the problem to other "gods" or inscrutable forces immanent in the universe, but a monotheistic belief in one righteous and holy God must somehow reconcile the continued power of evil with His governance—and perhaps ultimately with His very existence.[33]

The issue of war forms a subpurpose in the book. Whereas Habakkuk seemingly is concerned not so much about warfare *per se* as he is about God's employment of an unholy nation against His people, the theophany of chap. 3 revealing a triumphant God in holy warfare is a reminder to Habakkuk (and to all) that extreme times call for strong measures. God Himself must at times enter human history, using such social conventions as warfare to accomplish His purpose (3:13) in order that ultimately the earth may be "filled with the knowledge of the glory of the Lord" (2:14). Such knowledge justifies neither deliberate aggression nor warfare itself as a norm for relations between peoples.[34]

As indicated above, Habakkuk wishes his experiences to be exemplary. The normal human being will be an inquisitive person, even at times calling God into question. Habakkuk had experienced honest doubts but was reminded that such an experience was not to be normative. Rather, a consideration of all the evidence, including the Person, nature, and work of God, should be a reminder that the God who will do right needs to be the God of the whole life.[35] When this is

---

32. The need for a balanced perspective with regard to the place of government is ably defended by Robert Culver, *Toward a Biblical View of Civil Government* (Chicago: Moody, 1974), pp. 156-58.
33. Hummel, *The Word*, p. 347.
34. For helpful insight into the discussion of warfare, see P. C. Craigie, *The Problem of War in the Old Testament* (Grand Rapids: Eerdmans, 1978).
35. See in this regard the helpful remarks of W. S. LaSor, David Allan Hubbard, and F. W. Bush, *Old Testament Survey* (Grand Rapids: Eerdmans,

understood the believer will respond in adoration (2:20) and faith (2:4), waiting patiently and joyfully for God's glorious (2:14) purposes to be realized both in the world and in the lives of all its inhabitants (3:16-19).

TEXT AND CANONICITY

The MT of Habakkuk contains many difficulties. In addition to the obscurities in the third chapter (in which alone Albright proposed more than three dozen "corrections"[36]), several *hapax legomena* occur elsewhere (e.g., 1:4, 9; 2:11). There are also grammatical (2:4) and scribal problems (2:16). It is small wonder, then, that the text of the LXX differs often from that of the MT. In addition, significant differences from the MT have been noted in 1QpHab. Thus Würthwein remarks: "Some sixty examples of its deviations from *M* which are more than purely orthographical (e.g., scriptio plena) are cited in the third apparatus of BHK."[37] Even so conservative a scholar as R. K. Harrison admits that "the text of the prophecy has not been particularly well preserved, and contains some obscurities, a fact that is also true of the Qumran text."[38]

On the other hand, one must not overly dramatize the textual difficulties. In addition to Albright's pioneering efforts, many have labored successfully in bringing better understanding to the consonantal text of the third chapter.[39] As for the variation between the MT and 1QpHab, though the evidence points to some fluidity in the Hebrew textual tradition (a condition that was soon altered with the adoption of the MT[40]) one must not set aside the MT in too cavalier a fashion. As Würthwein points out:

> Our main interest centers on *M*. In every instance it deserves special attention because it is based on direct transmission in the original lan-

---

1982), p. 454: "Habakkuk neither used his questions to shield himself from moral responsibilities nor shunned God's claims upon his life. . . . God's revelation of himself laid [to rest] the ghost of the prophet's doubts and gave birth to a finer faith; the redeeming God had used his questions as a means of grace to draw Habakkuk closer to himself."
36. See Albright, "The Psalm of Habakkuk," p. 10.
37. Würthwein, *Text of the Old Testament*, p. 146. Brownlee (*The Text of Habakkuk*, pp. 109-12) lists nineteen of these as major variants.
38. Harrison, *Introduction*, p. 938.
39. Although the list of authors who have worked on this portion of Scripture is filled with the names of many prestigious scholars, a critical consensus as to its reading and interpretation is far from being reached. The difficulty of the text has defied the efforts of exegetes of all theological persuasions.
40. While Würthwein (*Text of the Old Testament*, p. 15) suggests a first-century date for the standardization of the MT, F. M. Cross ("The Text Behind the

guage, and it has been handed down with great care. . . . Any deviation from it therefore requires justification. . . . The question whether *M* can be faulted either linguistically or materially is to be decided at times only after intensive investigations. Specifically, if a reading of *M* is rejected, every possible interpretation of it must first have been fully examined.[41]

When due allowance is made, then, despite the presence of a few individual textual problems one may say with R. Smith, "The Hebrew text of Habakkuk is in fair shape."[42]

If the problems concerning the text of Habakkuk are somewhat unsettling, the issue of Habakkuk's canonicity is not. The early canonization of all the OT prophetical books appears to be unquestionable. Habakkuk, as one of the twelve Minor Prophets, enjoyed full acceptance as part of the OT canon.[43] Armerding's declaration is apropos:

> Habakkuk was early grouped with the other so-called Minor Prophets in the Book of the Twelve (attested as such in Ecclus 49:10 [c. 190 B.C.]), the acceptance of which is never questioned, either in Jewish or Christian circles. Questions of the unity of the book do not seem to have affected its acceptance, and in fact there is no ancient record of a dispute over chapter 3.[44]

Text of the Hebrew Bible," *Bible Review* 1 [1985]: 12-25) is not so sure. The second-century OT Hebrew manuscripts found at Wadi Murabba'at, however, are distinctly MT. See further F. F. Bruce, *Second Thoughts on the Dead Sea Scrolls*, rev. ed. (Grand Rapids: Eerdmans, 1964), pp. 64-66.

41. Würthwein, *Text of the Old Testament*, pp. 17, 113-14. F. F. Bruce (*Biblical Exegesis in the Qumran Texts* [Grand Rapids: Eerdmans, 1959], p. 12) cautions that the author of 1QpHab may not have been so reliable in his handling of the text: "Along with this atomizing exegesis there goes at times an interesting treatment of textual variants. Where one reading suits the commentator's purpose better than another, he will use it, although he may show in the course of his comment that he is aware of an alternative reading. He has been suspected of deliberately altering the text here and there in order to make the application more pointed, but the suspicion does not amount to proof."

42. R. L. Smith, *Micah–Malachi*, p. 96.

43. See Bullock, *Prophetic Books*, pp. 34-36; M. F. Unger, *Introductory Guide to the Old Testament* (Grand Rapids: Zondervan, 1951), pp. 53-78; R. Laird Harris, *Inspiration and Canonicity of the Bible* (Grand Rapids: Zondervan, 1969), pp. 180-95.

44. Armerding, *Habakkuk*, 7:496. Harrison (*Introduction*, p. 271) includes the words of the pronouncement of the second century B.C. *baraitha* contained in the Talmudic tractate *Baba Bathra:* "The order of the prophets is Joshua, Judges, Samuel, Kings, Jeremiah, Ezekiel, Isaiah, the Twelve (Minor Prophets)." For full discussion of the early canonicity of all of the prophets, see Roger Beckwith, *The Old Testament Canon of the New Testament Church* (Grand Rapids: Eerdmans, 1985), pp. 138-80.

THEOLOGICAL CONTEXT

It was suggested earlier that one of the purposes of the book of Habakkuk was to convey theological truth. Indeed, Habakkuk tells his readers certain facts concerning God's Person and work. He informs his readers that the everlasting (1:12; 3:3, 6) God of glory (2:14; 3:3-4) is sovereign (2:20) over all individuals and nations (1:5, 14; 2:6-19; 3:3-15), guiding them according to His predetermined purpose to bring glory to Himself (2:14). God is a God of holiness (1:12-13; 2:20; 3:3) and justice (1:12-13; 2:4) who, although He judges godlessness and injustice (1:2-11; 2:5-19; 3:12-15), in mercy often tempers His righteous anger against sin (3:2, 8, 12). A God of omnipotence (3:4-7, 8-15), He works for the deliverance and salvation of His people (3:13, 18). A God of revelation (1:1; 2:2-3), He hears the cries and prayers (1:2-4, 12-17; 2:1; 3:1-2) of His own and answers them (1:5-11; 2:4-20; 3:3-15). As a result of all his experiences, Habakkuk came to learn that the issues of life and death rest with God and that the righteous individual will by faith (2:4-5) come to realize that God is sufficient for every situation (3:16-19).

The book of Habakkuk likewise gives instruction as to the nature of man's relationship with God. It demonstrates God's displeasure with immorality and injustice (1:2-11) and with such sins as greed, stealing, plundering, violence, bloodshed and murder, taking advantage of others, drunkenness, and idolatry (2:5-19). It also teaches that one can know God's salvation (3:18) through faith (2:4). Above all, the individual needs to learn to trust God and let Him be God of his whole life (3:16).

Habakkuk's prophecy also reminds the believer of the possibility of an intimate communion with God that can overcome his deepest depression and darkest seasons of doubt (1:2-4; 1:12–2:1). God hears and answers prayer (2:1-4; 3:2, 16). The believer may thus live a life of faith (2:4), walking before Him in patient trust (3:16-17) and joyful service (3:18-19).

1

The Prophet's Perplexities and God's Explanations, Part One (Habakkuk 1:1–2:1)

Habakkuk's messages deal with the problems of individual and national sin in the face of a sovereign and holy God. In the opening section (vv. 2-4) the reader is introduced to a former crisis in the prophet's spiritual experience. In contemplating the rampant immorality and social injustice that surrounded him, Habakkuk was disturbed at God's seeming indifference and inactivity. Why had a holy God not brought the needed chastisement and correction to the people of Judah?

Habakkuk's complaint occasioned a reply from a patient God. Not only would He do something, the judicial process was already underway. Although Habakkuk might find it hard to believe, it was nonetheless so. God was already raising up the ruthless Chaldeans to deal with sinful Judah (vv. 5-6).

But God's description of the Chaldeans' viciousness (vv. 7-11) raised for Habakkuk a further difficulty: How could a holy God use an unholy nation—indeed, a far more unholy people than Judah—to judge His people? (vv. 12-13). Habakkuk feared that, once set loose, such a destroyer could never be restrained, not only Judah but all nations falling victim to him (vv. 14-17). Despite his doubts, the prophet ends his remarks with a statement of his confidence in God (2:1).

From a literary standpoint, Habakkuk's first major section includes an expression of the prophet's perplexities (1:2-4; 1:12–2:1) alternating with the Lord's responses (1:5-11; 2:2-20). Habakkuk's questions are framed in the lament genre containing the commonly occurring elements of invocation (1:2, 12-13*a*), statement of the problem (1:3-4, 13*b*-17), and statement of prophetic confidence in God (2:1).

Other literary features utilized here are simile and metaphor (1:8, 9, 11, 14-17), hyperbole (1:6-11), personification (1:7-11), rhetorical question (1:12), hendiadys (1:15?), and proverb (1:9). Several structural devices also occur: alliteration and assonance (1:6, 10), enjambment (1:13), repetition for effect (1:15*b*-17), pivot-pattern parallelism (1:17?), and chiasmus (1:2, 3, 4; 2:1). The use of the stitch-words מִשְׁפָּט (*mišpāṭ*) and צַדִּיק (*ṣaddîq*), as well as verbs of seeing, must also be noted.

Immediately after the notice of the source of his prophecy (1:1), Habakkuk plunges into a rehearsal of his spiritual wrestling with God. In so doing he tells his readers of his perplexities as to the divine working and of God's answers to his questions (1:2–2:20). This chapter will consider Habakkuk's superscription (1:1), his two questions, and God's answer to the first (1:2–2:1).

SUPERSCRIPTION (1:1)

Translation

The oracle that Habakkuk the prophet saw.*

Exegesis and Exposition

Like Nahum, Habakkuk begins his messages by terming the whole an oracle, a word placed upon his heart by God that he must accurately convey to others. As did Nahum, Habakkuk assures his readers that what he was about to relate was not born of his own ingenuity but was that which God had revealed to him. Unlike Nahum, however, Habakkuk does not state that his message is specifically directed at any one individual or group of people, even though he will devote a great deal of space to a denunciation of the Chaldeans. Nor is any setting given, as in the case of Zephaniah's superscription. Rather, because Habakkuk's message is designated as that which he saw, the reader is alerted to the likelihood of the prophet's personal experiences being involved in the account.

Additional Notes

1:1 †For the significance of the word מַשָּׂא, see the additional note on Nahum 1:1. The joining of the verb חָזָה ("see") to the noun מַשָּׂא has seemed difficult to some. A translation such as "received" (cf. NIV, NJB) has often been suggested. Though emphasis is frequently placed on a prophet's delivery of a received communication (cf. Isa. 1:1), making such a translation appear to be correct, Habakkuk's stress seems to be on his own participation in the revelatory process. The reader is thus perhaps prepared for the theophany of the third chapter and reminded that God's prophet may have been an eyewitness to at least some of what God intends for him to communicate (cf. 2:2).

Nevertheless, however visionary the revelatory process might have been for the prophet, what he conveys is not merely his own impression of an event or series of events but the very words God wishes him to write (cf. Ps. 89:19 [HB 89:20]; Hos. 12:10 [HB 12:11]; Obad. 1; etc.). Such an understanding is in harmony with such texts as Isa. 30:10, which lay stress both on the prophet's reception of God's revelation and on his verbal communication of God's message to his hearers.

In contrast to those who would tend to make the prophet's participation in the revelatory process more passive,[1] the view taken here finds the prophet more active.[2] While God is held to be sovereign in revelation and inspiration, in cases of visionary experiences the prophet at times apparently sees what God intends to do, agrees with God's revealed activities (sees them from God's point of view), and conveys in his own words the very words and message that God intends to be communicated to the prophet's audience. The verb חָזָה, then, is appropriate, not only denoting what the prophet received and was passing on but also allowing for personal seeing of certain details, such as the theophany of 3:3-15.

The same root occurs in the noun חָזוֹן ("vision") in parallel with מַשָּׂא in the superscription to Nahum. There, too, though the word is used to express the words of revelation that Nahum is communicating, it may include actual visionary experiences.

---

1. See, e.g., A Jepsen, "חָזָה," *TDOT* 4:283-84.
2. For the prophet's more active role in seeing the divinely revealed vision, see R. D. Culver, "חָזָה," *TWOT* 1:274-75; G. Vos, *Biblical Theology* (Grand Rapids: Eerdmans, 1954), pp. 215-18; C. F. Keil, *The Twelve Minor Prophets*, COT (Grand Rapids: Eerdmans, 1954), 2:9; M. F. Unger, "Vision," in *Baker's Dictionary of Theology*, ed. Everett F. Harrison (Grand Rapids: Baker, 1960), p. 545. The position taken here recognizes the fact that in time the prophet's use of חָזָה came to mean something like "received."

Isaiah's prophecy, for example, contains a great deal more than visionary material, yet the whole is termed "that which he saw" (Isa. 1:1). Likewise, the noun חִזָּיוֹן ("vision") appears to mean not just "things seen" but "revelation," however it was received (cf. 2 Sam. 7:17). Accordingly the translation "saw" given here is to be understood in a neutral sense. Nevertheless, the choice of this root to describe the prophet's role in the process of divine revelation may preserve the fact that at times seeing played a major role (cf. Isa. 6:1; see also the exposition of Nah. 3:2).

A. FIRST PERPLEXITY: HOW CAN GOD DISREGARD JUDAH'S SIN? (1:2-4)

Habakkuk at once plunges into a dramatic rehearsal of a time when the impact of Judah's unchecked sin overwhelmed him. His questioning of God forms the backdrop for the examination of the relation of God's holy standards to the operation of the divine providence that follows later.

Translation

How long*, O Lord*, have I cried for help*
and You have not heard?
I cry out to You, "Violence!"
but You do not save.
³Why do You make me look at iniquity
while You behold* oppression?
Destruction and violence are before me;
there is strife, and contention abounds.
⁴Therefore, (the) law* is benumbed*
and justice* never goes forth;
Because the wicked engulf* the righteous,
justice goes out perverted*.

Exegesis and Exposition

The nature of Habakkuk's complaint to God, begun in the invocation (v. 2) and elaborated in the statement of the problem (vv. 3-4), can be better appreciated when one examines the four words he employs to describe his perception of Judahite society. חָמָס (*ḥāmās*, "violence")*, אָוֶן (*'āwen*, "iniquity"), עָמָל (*'āmāl*, "oppression")*, and שֹׁד (*šōd*, "destruction")* are strong words that contain moral and spiritual overtones. In order, they depict a society that is characterized by malicious wickedness (cf. Gen. 6:11, 13; Ps. 72:14), deceitful iniquity—both moral (cf. Job 34:36; Prov. 17:4; Isa. 29:20) and spiritual (cf. Isa. 66:3)—oppressive behavior toward others (cf. Isa. 10:1), and the general spiritual and ethical havoc that exists where such sin abounds (cf. Isa. 59:7). It is small wonder that, where such conditions persist, רִיב (*rîb*, strife") and מָדוֹן (*mādôn*, "contention") are also rife. The former root implies quarrelsome talk (Gen. 31:36) or behavior (Ex. 17:2; Prov. 17:1) and appears often in a legal setting (e.g., Prov. 25:7-10; Isa. 27:7-9); the latter is used to denote a situation where dissension is present (Prov. 6:14; 16:28; 26:20; 28:25; 29:22).

In Habakkuk's eyes, then, Judahite society was spiritually bankrupt and morally corrupt. Because sin abounded, injustice was the norm. Habakkuk describes the judicial situation in two ways: (1)

Because of the basic spiritual condition, the operation of God's law was sapped of the vital force necessary for it to guide man's ethical and judicial decisions. Accordingly righteousness did not characterize Judahite society, and justice was never meted out. (2) Because the society itself had become godless, wicked men could so hem in the attempts and actions of the righteous that whatever justice existed was so twisted that the resultant decision was one of utter perversity.

Such a perception of life and society in Judah raises the question of the historical setting involved in the prophet's description. As noted in the introduction, evangelical scholarship has suggested one of three periods to which these words might have referred: (1) the reign of Jehoiakim (608-598 B.C.), (2) the early days of Josiah (shortly after 640 B.C.), and (3) the reign of Manasseh (698-642 B.C.). In favor of the first suggestion is the known wickedness of Jehoiakim, who took advantage of his own people (Jer. 22:13-14) and also opposed all that was holy and decent, filling the land with violence and degradation (Jer. 8:18-9:16; 10:1-8; 11:1-17; 13:1-4; 23:9-40; 25:1-7; 36:1-32).

In favor of the second proposal is the known apostasy that Josiah was called upon to correct from the earliest days of his reign (2 Chron. 34:1-7) as well as the mute testimony of the Temple, which had fallen into such disrepair that its restoration called for the king's special attention. Indirect evidence comes from the widespread reforms and revival that followed upon the finding of the Book of the Law in 621 B.C. (2 Chron. 34:23–35:19).

Supportive of the third alternative is the clear scriptural indication of extreme wickedness during the reign of Manasseh. According to 2 Kings 21:1-18 and 2 Chronicles 33:11-20, that evil king not only reinstituted the loathsome Canaanite worship practices of Asherah and Baal (which Hezekiah his father had done away with) but also introduced a state astral cult. He built pagan altars in the outer courts and priests' courts and placed an Asherah pole within the Temple itself. He also indulged in sorcery, divination, and witchcraft as well as the abominable rites of infant sacrifice.[3]

Though all three views are possible and each has been espoused by evangelical scholars, the last view enjoys the support of Jewish tradition and, in light of the Lord's reply that He would deal with the situation in a way that would amaze His prophet (1:5), is perhaps the most contextually suitable. It would also demand the most prophetic foresight. Accordingly, for these reasons and those suggested in the

---

3. See further R. D. Patterson and H. J. Austel, "1, 2 Kings," in *EBC* (Grand Rapids: Zondervan, 1988), 4:277-80.

introduction, the third view will be followed provisionally in this commentary.[4]

These verses, then, underscore the prophet's consternation as to the seeming divine indifference to all the debauchery he saw around him. R. D. Culver describes some of the thinking and fears that must have accompanied Habakkuk's perplexities:

> When magistrates permit murder, theft, fornication and the like to go unchecked and unpunished, God calls the whole nation to accounting. The unpunished crimes pollute the land, becoming a growing mortgage against all, upon which God may finally foreclose, driving some inhabitants away, destroying others and permitting different peoples to dwell in the land.[5]

Habakkuk was disturbed also by God's silence with regard to his prophet's repeated cries for help and intervention.

Additional understanding on this latter point may be gained by considering the relation of Habakkuk's words to the well-known "call-answer" motif. This theme is used often in the Scriptures to assure the believer that he may call upon God for refuge and protection in times of trouble and distress (Pss. 17:6-12; 20:6-9 [HB 20:7-10]; 81:6-7 [HB 81:7-8]; 91:14-16; 102:1-2 [HB 102:2-3]; 138:8). Further, he may find guidance from God (Ps. 99:6-7; Jer. 33:2-3) and experience intimate communion with Him both in this life and in the next (Job 14:14-15; Ps. 73:23-26). The motif also touches upon God's future plans for Israel, which include full restoration to divine fellowship (Isa. 65:24; Zech. 13:7-9).

Unfortunately this motif has its negative side as well. It teaches that when sin is present, God does not answer the one who calls upon Him (Ps. 66:18). The believer must honor God with his life (Ps. 4:1-3 [HB 4:2-4]) and call upon Him in truth (Ps. 145:17-20). Where there is godless living (Isa. 56:11-12), unconcern for the needs of others (Isa. 58:6-9), or indifference to the clear teachings of the Word of God (Jer. 35:17), there is danger of divine judgment (Zech. 7:8-14). Thus the unanswered call becomes a sign of broken fellowship.[6]

In light of all of this, one wonders whether Habakkuk may have entertained the added thought that he was out of fellowship with

---

4. See also my remarks in the Introduction to Habakkuk in *Evangelical Commentary on the Bible*, ed. W. Elwell (Grand Rapids: Baker, 1989), pp. 666-67.
5. R. D. Culver, *Toward a Biblical View of Civil Government* (Chicago: Moody, 1974), pp. 93-94.
6. In a dramatic turn God is at times represented as calling out to people (Isa. 66:4), sometimes to those who only turn away from Him. Tragically, 11 times in the book of Jeremiah it is reported that God earnestly sought to meet with His disobedient people only to find that they did not keep their appointed time of communion.

God. Divine disregard of Judah's apostasy and open sin would be difficult enough to understand, but should he himself have so occasioned God's displeasure that he was not on prayer-answering ground, that might be an additional burden too great to bear. Thus viewed, Habakkuk's questions and doubts take on an extra emotional and spiritual dimension. He was an unhappy, perplexed, and greatly frustrated prophet.

Additional Notes

1:2 Although I translated the Hebrew tetragrammaton consistently as "Yahweh" in the commentary on Nahum, Habakkuk's posture as one crying to Israel's sovereign favors the traditional translation "Lord," a rendering that will be followed for consistency's sake throughout the first two chapters. יהוה will be translated "Yahweh" beginning with the epic material in 3:3.

†עַד־אָנָה ("how long"): The interrogative adverb אָן ("where") with augmented ה‪ָ‬ (â) is often combined with עַד ("for") to form, as here, a compound interrogative particle of time (cf. Ex. 16:28; Num. 14:11; Josh. 18:3; Jer. 47:6). Here it introduces the prophet's invocation. Used with a suffix conjugation, the phrase may indicate Habakkuk's past repeated cries to God. Thus Keil is probably correct in translating "How long . . . have I cried" (cf. LXX), as opposed to the usual English translations ("How long . . . will I/must I/am I to cry") that emphasize the prophet's continuing call for help.[7] Thus construed the phrase underscores Habakkuk's frustration and exasperation with the whole state of affairs.

The prophet's concern is therefore a longstanding one, so that his doubts and questionings are not those of a fault-finding negative critic or a skeptic but the honest searchings of a holy prophet of God. In contrast to other words for crying, שׁוע carries with it the idea of a cry for help. Victor Hamilton reports that the verb is used characteristically in the autobiographical first person, particularly in lament literature.[8] As to origin, Gerber suggests that the verb is a denominative from שַׁוְעָה ("cry for help"), itself drawn from the root ישׁע ("save").[9] Whether or not that can be determined, the letters in the word probably form an intentional alliterative chiasmus with תּוֹשִׁיעַ at the end of the verse. The prophet's observation, then, is that although he has cried for help for time long past calculation, no deliverance is yet forthcoming.

1:2-3 The cry *"Violence"* and the need for divine help are reminis-

---

7. Keil, *Minor Prophets*, 2:55.
8. Victor Hamilton, "שָׁוַע," *TWOT* 2:911-12.
9. See BDB, p. 1002.

cent of Job's lament (Job 9:7). Jeremiah (Jer. 6:7; 20:8) also complains of the violence and destruction of Judahite society, a charge echoed by Ezekiel (Ezek. 45:9). Zephaniah (Zeph. 3:4) points out the violating of God's law that characterized Judahite society at the inception of Josiah's reign. Such general violence naturally leaves a society in the grip of upheaval and strife (cf. Ps. 55:9 [HB 55:10]).

אָוֶן and עָמָל occur together at times to depict sin and its resulting troubles (Ps. 7:14 [HB 7:15]; Isa. 10:1), while עָמָל is employed with שֹׁד in Prov. 24:2 in describing the evil machinations and corrupt words of wicked men. The chiastic deployment of the verbs in lines 1, 2, and 4 of v. 3 is striking.

1:4 †The verb פּוּג (cf. Arabic *fāja*, "grow cool"; Syriac *pāg*, "be cold") is generally taken to mean "grow numb." It is used of Jacob's stunned reaction to the news that his son Joseph still lived (Gen. 45:26) and of the psalmist's hands stretched out to God in untiring supplication (Ps. 77:2 [HB 77:3]; cf. Lam. 2:18; 3:49). The semantic range of the verb used here with תּוֹרָה ("law") makes the tragedy of Judahite society most graphic. The operation of God's law is seen as benumbed and ineffective, much like hands rendered useless by cold, a condition (doubtless occasioned by the spiritual coldness of men's hearts) that seemed to continue with tireless regularity.

†By תּוֹרָה ("law") is meant not civil law but God's law upon which the legal enactments of society must be based if righteousness is to prevail. Thus Theodore Laetsch remarks:

> God's own Law, the constitution of the nation, the heart and soul of Judah's political, religious, and social life; God's Law, the neglect of which would inevitably bring on the ruination of God's land and people (Deut. 28:15ff.), this Law was crippled so that "judgment doth never go forth."[10]

†מִשְׁפָּט ("justice") is, as Keil points out, "not merely a righteous verdict, however; in which case the meaning would be: There is no more any righteous verdict given, but a righteous state of things, objective right in the civil and political life."[11] Indeed, as Herbert Marks observes, social justice is a key consideration in Habakkuk's prophecy.[12] Together with צַדִּיק ("righteous") it becomes the literary hook to the next section (vv. 5-11). The themes of justice and righteousness are central ones in the book and will reach a climax in Hab. 2:4. J. G. Harris appropriately states:

---

10. T. Laetsch, *The Minor Prophets* (St. Louis: Concordia, 1956), p. 318.
11. Keil, *Minor Prophets*, 2:57.
12. Herbert Marks, "The Twelve Prophets," in *The Literary Guide to the Bible*, ed. Robert Alter and Frank Kermode (Cambridge: Harvard U., 1987), p. 219.

Justice (*mšpṭ*), which . . . carried a redemptive element in its prosecution, and righteousness (*ṣdyq*) were the quintessence of the divine will. They embodied the central authority from which the coherence of the social order stemmed.[13]

Their placement in the middle two lines of the chiastic structure of the verse is probably designed for emphatic effect.

מַכְתִּיר† ("engulf") is a hiphil participle from כָּתַר ("encircle/surround"). The etymology of the root is clouded, the usual suggested cognates Aramaic/Syriac *kattar* ("wait/await") and Akkadian *katāru* (I: "band together"; II: "think") proving of little help for most Hebrew contexts (but see Job 36:2). KB-3 follows the lead of W. Leslau in relating Hebrew texts where כָּתַר clearly bears the meaning "encircle/surround" (e.g., Ps. 22:12 [HB 22:13]) to the Ethiopic (Tigre) verb *kätra* ("surround/make a hedge"; cf. Tigriña *mäktär*, "hedge").[14] KB-3 also proposes that in some cases (e.g., Prov. 14:18) the verb is a denominative from כֶּתֶר ("crown"). On the whole Leslau's suggestion appears to be the simplest, although the occurrence of the root only in the piel and hiphil stems could argue for a denominative origin of this Hebrew verb.

The image of encircling/surrounding, here either with hostile intent or overwhelming superiority, suggests the translation "engulf" given above. The NIV translation "hem in," also *ad sensum*, makes excellent sense; the NJB "outwits," however, is less tenable.

מְעֻקָּל† ("perverted"): The word is related to a root attested in Syriac ('*ăqal*, "twist") and Arabic ('*aqqala*, "bend"). The form is a *hapax legomenon*, although the related adjectives עֲקַלְקַל ("twisted," Judg. 5:6; Ps. 125:5)[15] and עֲקַלָּתוֹן ("crooked," Isa. 27:1)[16] are attested. The application of the root to the perverted justice of Judahite society is obvious.

עַל־כֵּן ("therefore") in lines 1 and 4 is another example of chiasmus.

---

13. J. G. Harris, "The Laments of Habakkuk's Prophecy," *EvQ* 45 (1973): 24-25.
14. W. Leslau, *Ethiopic and South Arabic Contributions to the Hebrew Lexicon*, University of California Publications on Semitic Philology XX (Los Angeles: U. of California, 1958), p. 18.
15. For the employment of this adjective in Judg. 5:6 where it is used of "circuitous routes," see R. D. Patterson, "The Song of Deborah," in *Tradition and Testament: Essays in Honor of Charles Lee Feinberg*, ed. John S. Feinberg and Paul D. Feinberg (Chicago: Moody, 1981), pp. 127, 131.
16. For the use of this adjective in earlier Canaanite literature (= Ugaritic '*qltn*), see C. H. Gordon, *Ugaritic Textbook* (Rome: Pontificium Institutum Biblicum, 1965), no. 67: 1:2. See also John Oswalt, *The Book of Isaiah*, NICOT (Grand Rapids: Eerdmans, 1986), pp. 490-91; E. J. Young, *The Book of Isaiah*, (Grand Rapids: Eerdmans, 1974), 2:233-35.

B. FIRST EXPLANATION: GOD WILL JUDGE JUDAH
THROUGH THE CHALDEANS (1:5-11)

To the emotional and dramatic cry of the prophet God gives a dramatic answer that will amaze him. God is already at work on the problem; He will send the Chaldeans to chastise Judah (vv. 5-6). God then supplies some additional details as to the martial abilities of the violent Chaldeans (vv. 7-11).

Translation

"Look among the nations* and observe,*
  and be utterly amazed*;
For I am doing* something in your days
  that you would not believe if* it were told (to you).
⁶For I am raising up the Chaldeans,
  that fierce and fiery* people,
that sweeps across the breadth of the earth
  to seize dwelling places not his own.
⁷He is terrifying and fearsome,
  a law and an authority to himself.
⁸His horses are swifter than leopards
  and keener* than wolves of the evening.
His cavalry* gallops on*;
  his horsemen come from afar,
  they fly like an eagle* swooping to devour.
⁹All of them are bent on violence;
  every face is set forward*,
  they gather captives like the sand.
¹⁰He scoffs at kings,
  and princes are a laughingstock to him;
he laughs at every fortress,
  he builds a siege mound and captures it.
¹¹Suddenly the windstorm pushes through and goes on;
  but he whose strength is his god will be held guilty."

Exegesis and Exposition

In his reply to Habakkuk God seizes upon the very words Habakkuk had used. The prophet had complained that he constantly had to behold evil all around him. But God Himself had seen it all—apparently with unconcern, because He had done nothing to correct either the people or the condition. God now tells Habakkuk to look, to look at the nations, to take a good look. God is already at work in and behind the scenes of earth's history to set in motion events that will change the whole situation. And when Habakkuk learns what is to happen, he will be utterly amazed. In fact, he probably will not be able to believe it.

The reason for Habakkuk's projected astonishment becomes apparent in v. 6: God will raise up the Chaldeans. Verses 5-6, revealing Habakkuk's astonishment at God's sending the Chaldeans to judge His people, are crucial to understanding the setting of the book.

"Chaldeans" translates the Hebrew כַּשְׂדִּים (kaśdîm). By the Neo-Assyrian period the term "Chaldea" was used of those tribes that lived in southernmost Mesopotamia. Many of them were designated by the word bît ("house of"), such as Bit Yakin, which was situated on the Persian Gulf. One of the most famous Chaldean kings was Merodach-Baladan, the perennial enemy of Assyria, who sent his emissaries to Hezekiah (2 Kings 20:12-19).[17] By at least 705 B.C. Merodach-Baladan took the title "King of Babylon," with the result that the terms "Chaldean" and "Babylonian" became used interchangeably in the OT (cf. Isa. 13:19; 47:1, 5; 48:14, 20).

After Sennacherib's defeat of Merodach-Baladan in 701 B.C., Chaldean resistance to Assyria continued from their power base in southernmost Mesopotamia (an area known as the sealands) and was accompanied by a frequently recurring contest for the city of Babylon. On one occasion this brought a surprise attack against Babylon by Sennacherib (689 B.C.) and on another a campaign by Ashurbanipal (652 B.C.), who eventually subdued the city in 648 B.C.

Tensions between the Assyrians and the freedom-loving Chaldeans always remained strained, and after Ashurbanipal's death the fires of revolt were again fanned. At least by the year of Ashurbanipal's passing (626 B.C.), the Chaldeans took Babylon, making it their capital and installing Nabopolassar as its king. By the end of the seventh century B.C. the Chaldeans, aided by the Medes and Ummanmanda (Scythians?), had taken all of Assyria. Afterward the allies gradually conquered the greater portion of the ancient Fertile Crescent from the borders of Elam to Egypt.[18] The Neo-Babylonian empire was to reach its height of power under Nabopolassar's son Nebuchadnezzar II (also spelled Nebuchadrezzar; 605-562 B.C.) and last until it experienced a crushing defeat at the hands of the Persians in 539 B.C.[19]

---

17. See W. S. LaSor, "Merodach-Baladan," *ISBE* 3:325-26.
18. See further the Introduction to Nahum; see also Edwin M. Yamauchi, *Persia and the Bible* (Grand Rapids: Baker 1990), p. 55.
19. See further A. Leo Oppenheim, "Chaldeans," *IDB* 1:549-50; R. D. Wilson, *Studies in the Book of Daniel* (Grand Rapids: Baker, 1972), 1:319-66; H. W. F. Saggs, *The Greatness That Was Babylon* (New York: Hawthorn, 1962), pp. 140-53.

The question naturally arises as to the relation of the Chaldean political activities to Habakkuk's prophecy. Those who argue for a date in the time of Jehoiakim (e.g., Archer, Freeman, Hailey, Hummel, Payne, E. J. Young) relate these verses and those that follow to the Chaldeans' known fighting prowess, as demonstrated in the victories at Nineveh (612 B.C.) and Haran (609 B.C.), perhaps even also at Carchemish (605 B.C.). According to this view one might argue that Habakkuk's projected amazement is what will serve as the crux of his second complaint—namely, that God would stoop to use such a ruthless people.

Those who favor a date for the book of Habakkuk in Josiah's reign (e.g., Bullock, Laetsch, Unger) emphasize the prophet's amazement at hearing about the Chaldeans, a yet relatively unproved power, the general conditions of social and religious chaos that occasioned Josiah's reforms (cf. Hab. 1:2-4 with Jer. 1-6), and the Lord's words to the prophet that He would do a work "in your days" (v. 5), which implies a degree of futurity to the prophecy.

Those who favor a setting in the reign of Manasseh (e.g., Keil) stress the documented evil of Manasseh's reign (2 Kings 21:1-18; 2 Chron. 33:1-20; cf. Hab. 1:2-4) and argue accordingly: they relate Habakkuk's incredulity to the fact that although the Chaldeans had been a troublesome source of rebellion for the Assyrians they scarcely were candidates for being a world power that could touch Judah; and they consider the expression "in your days" to be a general one that is reconcilable with the Chaldeans' efforts some 20 years later and Nebuchadnezzar's strike against Jerusalem 45 years later.

On the whole the latter two views are the most satisfactory.[20] Both rightly discount any great amazement concerning the Chaldeans by the time of Jehoiakim, for their viciousness was well known by then. Both can point to general conditions of moral and spiritual wickedness indicated by the Scriptures themselves and can deal satisfactorily with the predicted events as being accomplished "in your days." Both retain well the force of predictive prophecy, whereas the view that locates the book of Habakkuk in Jehoiakim's day must face the fact that such predictions as that of Habakkuk 1:5-11 could be given by any noninspired observer of that day.

Because the scriptural data concerning the character of Manasseh's reign are far better documented (note that the dating of Jer. 1–6 to Josiah's reign is debated), because of the closeness of subject matter and canonical position of Habakkuk with Nahum and Zephaniah, and because of the possible borrowing of Habakkuk's ma-

---

20. Even E. B. Pusey (*The Minor Prophets* [Grand Rapids: Baker, 1953], 2:165-69) finds it difficult to choose between them.

terial by Jeremiah and Zephaniah (see introduction), I tend to favor the older Jewish view that Habakkuk 1:2-11 is best related to the latter part of Manasseh's reign (c. 655-650 B.C.)

By telling Habakkuk of the Chaldeans' future prominence, the Lord reassures him of His sovereign control of the details of history. Since God's prophet will be surprised at the announcement about the Chaldeans, God goes on to supply a brief résumé of their character and potentially devastating power (vv. 6-11). They are a fierce, cruel people who will never tire in quest of their goal of conquest (v. 6b). Their successes will strike fear into the hearts of all who stand in their path (v. 7a). A terror and dread to all, they arrogantly acknowledge no law but themselves (v. 7b).

The reason for their success may be further seen in their military capabilities. Possessed of swift war horses made skillful by discipline and the experience of battle, their cavalry could cover vast distances quickly in their insatiable thirst for conquest and booty (v. 8). Not alone for spoil but seemingly for the sheer sport of it they campaigned fiercely and inflicted violence on their enemies.

Habakkuk had complained concerning the sinful violence that lay all around him (v. 2). That will be dealt with in kind and in suitable measure (cf. Isa. 24:14-23; Joel 3:7-8 [HB 4:7-8]; 2 Thess. 1:6-8). The word "violence" thus serves as more than a literary hook between the first two sections of the book: Violence was a living reality.

Contrary to Habakkuk's complaint, God assures his prophet that he sees all that comes to pass and hears the prayers and complaints of His people.[21] Habakkuk's own word is sent back to him. Has Judah done violence? It shall in turn suffer violence at the hands of a violent nation whose well-trained and battle-seasoned army will move forward with such precision that the whole striking force will march as one to achieve its objectives, at the same time taking many captives (v. 9).

No wonder, then, that enemy rulers are merely a joke to them.

---

21. God's reply to Habakkuk's charge is reminiscent of the words attributed to Aeschylus (*Fr. Incert.*, 4):

Ὁρᾷ δίκη σ' ἄναυδος οὐχ ὁρωμένη
Εὕδοντι καὶ στείχοντι καὶ καθημένῳ,
Ἑξῆς δ' ὀπάζει δόχμιον, ἄλλοθ' ὕστερον.
Οὐδ' ἐγκαλύπτει νὺξ κακῶς εἰργασμένα·
Ὅτι δ'ἂν ποιῇς, νόμιζ' ὁρᾶν δεινὸν τινα.

Justice, silent and unseen, sees you
While you sleep, while you go on your way, and while you sit down,
She stays next to you, either beside or else behind you.
Night cannot conceal the evil things that have been done;
Whatever you do, consider that there is One to be feared who sees it!

With disdain they laugh at them, move against their cities, however strongly fortified, and, using siege techniques, capture them (v. 10).

Although the language is hyperbolic throughout (vv. 6-11), in light of the ancient records it is not inappropriate. Among the many texts that could be cited concerning the Chaldeans' successful campaigning one may note the following:

> In the fifteenth year, the month of Tammuz, . . . the king of Akkad called out his army and . . . marched to Assyria where [from the month of . . . he marched about] victoriously . . . . . . of the land of Hazazu[?] quickly . . . . . . and the land of Su[ppa] he conquered, plundering from them and [taking] spoil [and prisoners] from them. In the month of Marcheswan the king of Akkad took personal command of his army and [marched] against the town of Ruggul[iti] and made an attack on the town, capturing it on the twenty-eighth day of the month of Marcheswan, not a man escaped.

> In the twenty-first year . . . Nebuchadrezzar his eldest son, the crown-prince, mustered (the Babylonian army) and took command of his troops; he marched to Carchemish which is on the bank of the Euphrates, and crossed the river (to go) against the Egyptian army which lay in Carchemish, ... fought with each other and the Egyptian army withdrew before him. He accomplished their defeat and to non-existence [beat?] them.[22]

The section also contains some striking metaphors and similes. The rapidly advancing and voracious Chaldean forces are likened to swift leopards and fearsome wolves at evening,[23] to a powerful eagle swooping down on its helpless prey, and to the simoon taking vast stores of sand as it sweeps along. The trope of the windstorm is then changed somewhat, now emphasizing the suddenness of the cessation of its fury and the implied havoc it has left behind.

The picture of Chaldean armed might is thus complete. Its armies have been portrayed as the finest and fiercest in the world, being capable of moving swiftly across vast stretches of land to strike the enemy. With his many successes in hand it is understandable that the Chaldean can be described as an arrogant bully who holds all his foes

---

22. D. J. Wiseman, *Chronicles of Chaldaean Kings* (London: The Trustees of the British Museum, 1956), pp. 61, 67. The composition and campaigning efficiency of the Assyrian army have often been described; see, e.g., H. W. F. Saggs, *The Might That Was Assyria* (London: Sidgwick & Jackson, 1984), pp. 250-68. Long years of contact with the Assyrians must have served the Chaldeans well in terms of military knowledge. L. Delaporte (*Mesopotamia*, trans. V. Gordon Childe [New York: Barnes and Noble, 1970], pp. 73-74) is doubtless correct in saying that "the Babylonian army must have been organized very like the Assyrian army in the last days of the Sargonids' empire."

23. See the additional note on Zeph. 3:3.

in contempt and mocks them. Such a one knows no god but strength (v. 10).

Habakkuk is informed, however, that God's avenging host is not without responsibility. When nations make themselves and their own strength their only god rather than acknowledging the true God, who is their sponsor, they will be held guilty for their actions. Had Habakkuk listened as carefully to the last line of God's answer as he did to the extended description of Judah's chastiser, he might have avoided the second perplexity that gripped his soul, the report of which is contained in the verses that follow (1:12–2:1).[24]

Additional Notes

1:5 †The verb נָבַט ("look/observe") had formed a critical part of Habakkuk's complaint (v. 3), and God uses the same word in His reply. It thus serves as a literary hook between the first two sections. It will figure in the next portion as well (v. 13). Further hooks can be seen in מִשְׁפָּט ("justice/law," vv. 4, 7) and חָמָס ("violence," vv. 2, 9).

†For בַּגּוֹיִם ("among the nations") LXX reads οἱ καταφρονηταί ("O despisers"), perhaps reflecting a reading בֹּגְדִים ("treacherous ones"). Paul retains the reading of LXX in his address at Pisidian Antioch (Acts 13:41), doubtless because of its familiarity there and therefore its suitability as a warning not to despise God's offer of salvation.

†I have followed the suggestion of the NIV in translating הִתַּמְּהוּ תְּמָהוּ as "be utterly amazed," a translation designed to retain the play on the root in the two imperatives in the simplest fashion. The play on verbal stems could of course reflect a contrast or progression in emphasis such as "be astonished," "be dumbfounded" as suggested by some ancient and most modern versions.

†פֹּעַל פֹּעֵל ("I am working a work"): The LXX adds the personal pronoun ἐγώ ("I") to the phrase *ad sensum*, but such is not necessary in the Hebrew text because the personal pronoun is frequently omitted in cases where the subject has already been mentioned or is sufficiently clear from the context. Here the subject has been elided *metri causa* and because the thought anticipates the הִנְנִי ("behold me," i.e.,

---

24. The Chaldeans' guilt in abusing their divine mission is reminiscent of Jehu's self-serving accomplishment of God's will (2 Kings 9-10), a mission duly condemned by Hosea (Hos. 1:4). Keil (*Minor Prophets*, 1:41) appropriately observes: "In itself, *i.e.* regarded as the fulfilment of the divine command, the extermination of the family of Ahab was an act by which Jehu could not render himself criminal. But even things desired or commanded by God may become crimes in the case of the performer of them, when he is not simply carrying out the Lord's will as the servant of God but suffers himself to be actuated by evil and selfish motives, that is to say, when he abuses the divine command, and makes it the mere cloak for the lusts of his own evil heart."

"I am") construed with the participle that occurs in the next verse.[25] The same construction occurs in 2:10 with omission of the 2d masc. sing. pronoun.

†כִּי ("if"): The conditional use of this particle is well established.[26] Alternatively the line could be translated, "you will not believe (it) when it is reported (to you)."

1:6 כִּי ("for"): The particle could also be rendered as an asseverative: "yea/indeed."[27]

הִנְנִי מֵקִים ("I am raising up"): This construction is often used to refer to future events, the details of which God is about to set in process. The following participle הַהוֹלֵךְ ("that sweeps across") also has a future time reference.

כַּשְׂדִּים ("Chaldeans"): Critical attempts to read *Kittim* and refer the term to the Greeks are devoid of manuscript support, despite 1QpHab's interpretation as *Kittim* (meaning, however, the Romans). The text of the Qumran manuscript preserves the reading of the MT.

†הַמַּר וְהַנִּמְהָר ("fierce and fiery"): Due to the play on letters and sounds in the Hebrew text the alliterative translation of the NJB has been followed. The Hebrew may be literally translated "bitter and speedy" (cf. LXX, KJV "bitter and hasty"). Since it is the Chaldeans' disposition that is being characterized here, however, most commentators and versions have opted for such renderings as "fierce" or "ruthless" for מַר and "impetuous" for נִמְהָר.

1:7 †The description of the Chaldeans added here takes the form of personification, with the nation and its people, particularly its army, being viewed in the masc. sing. Therefore, the pronoun that follows (הוּא) has been rendered accordingly. There is also an implied synecdoche here, the whole nation being reflected in the conduct of its army. Alternatively one might view הוּא as referring to the Chaldean king, the example par excellence of the Neo-Babylonian empire.

†The clause מִמֶּנּוּ . . . . יֵצֵא (lit. "from him [his justice/law and eminence] go out") is best rendered *ad sensum* "(he is) a law and authority to himself" or "(he is) his own law and authority." Thus the Chaldean knows no other law, whether divine or human, than himself and his own might (cf. v. 11). The word מִשְׁפָּט both forms a literary hook with vv. 2-4 and serves as a key stitch-word for the whole prophecy.

---

25. For details concerning the use of the subject pronoun with a participle, see A. B. Davidson, *Hebrew Syntax*, 3d ed. (Edinburgh: T. and T. Clark, 1901), par. 100a; GKC par. 106s.
26. See R. J. Williams, *Hebrew Syntax*, 2d ed. (Toronto: U. of Toronto, 1976), par. 446, 515.
27. For asseverative *kaph*, see R. Gordis, "The Asseverative Kaph in Ugaritic and Hebrew," *JAOS* 63 (1943): 176-78; Williams, *Syntax*, par. 261, 449; M. Dahood, *Psalms*, AB (Garden City, N.J.: Doubleday, 1970), 3:402-6.

1:8 †The verb חָדַד means "be sharp/keen." The difficulty of the image as applied to evening wolves has occasioned numerous suggestions such as "fiercer" (NIV, NJB), "quicker" (R. Smith; cf. LXX), "more eager to attack" (NASB marginal note). The picture probably is that of the keen sensibilities of the wolf, alert to the prey and to every situation. As applied to horses it must refer to their skill and spiritedness in battle situations.

†פָּרָשָׁיו† ("his cavalry"; cf. NIV): The noun פָּרָשׁ means "horse" or "horseman." Since Habakkuk has used סוּס for "horse" earlier in the verse and because the figure in the next line is better suited to horsemen than to horses, such is probably the intention in both instances. The translation given here follows the NIV in providing synonyms for the double occurrence of פָּרָשׁ.

†וּפָשׁוּ† ("galloping on"): I have translated *ad sensum* with the NASB (cf. NIV, NJB). The precise nuance of the verb פּוּשׁ ("spring about"; cf. Nahum 3:18) is difficult. In other places (e.g., Jer. 50:11; Mal. 3:20) it is used for the gamboling of calves. The LXX translates it "mount." R. Smith follows the lead of the text of 1QpHab in reading וּפָרְשׁוּ for the second וּפָרָשָׁיו and translates the debated lines "his horses paw the ground, they spring forward, they come from afar."[28]

†For נֶשֶׁר ("eagle") some suggest the translation "vulture" (e.g., Laetsch, NIV). Although such a translation is admissible and serves the line well, if the image of "coming from afar" is carried through, the more traditional rendering here is perhaps better. The far-reaching Chaldeans are also compared to horses and eagles by Jeremiah (Jer. 4:13; 48:40; 49:22).

1:9 †מְגַמַּת פְּנֵיהֶם קָדִימָה†: The clause is a difficult one. Ward gives it up as "untranslatable" and adds: "It is a corrupt intrusion; or, possibly represents the remnant of a member of a lost couplet."[29] Textual uncertainty is already evident in the ancient versions, whose attempts to translate *ad sensum* produced widely varying results. Modern efforts have proved no more convincing.[30] The chief difficulties center in the first and third words. The former is a *hapax legomenon* that is generally considered to be derived from the root גמם ("be

28. R. Smith, *Micah–Malachi*, WBC (Waco, Tex.: Word, 1984), p. 100. For various suggestions as to the alleviation of the difficulty, see W. H. Ward, *A Critical and Exegetical Commentary on Habakkuk*, ICC (Edinburgh: T. and T. Clark, 1911), pp. 9-11. For further discussion, see J. R. Blue, "Habakkuk," in *The Bible Knowledge Commentary*, ed. John F. Walvoord and Roy B. Zuck (Wheaton: Scripture Press, 1985), 1:1510.
29. Ward, *Habakkuk*, p. 9.
30. See, e.g., the discussions in A. R. Hulst, *Old Testament Translation Problems* (Leiden: E. J. Brill, 1960), pp. 248-49; *Preliminary and Interim Report on the Hebrew Old Testament Text Project* (New York: United Bible Societies, 1980), 5:352-53.

abundant/filled"; cf. Arabic *jamma*, "be/become abundant"). The precise nuance of the word has, however, been variously understood, some opting for the idea of eagerness (Laetsch, NASB marginal reading) on the part of the Chaldeans or the endeavor etched on their faces (Keil), others for the thought of totality (R. Smith, NEB). Accordingly the first two words are rendered "hordes" (NIV) or "horde of faces" (NASB; cf. R. Smith, "all of their faces").

Final decision as to the translation of the first word is tied to that of the third word, which has been related to the idea of advancing, hence "moving forward" (NASB), or to the figure of the east wind (NJB), a suggestion found already in 1QpHab (cf. Vg). The latter solution is favored by the following figure of the gathering of captives like sand. The NIV attempts to retain both meanings for קָדִימָה by translating "Their hordes advance like a desert wind."

Final certainty is lacking. The translation adopted here endeavors to strike a balance between the more probable meanings of the two debated words in the line and the flow of thought in the context. The disputed line builds not only on the following line with its reference to sand but the preceding line with its expression of total commitment: "All of them are bent on violence." My suggestion is that the troublesome phrase מְגַמַּת פְּנֵיהֶם is related to the figure of totality in the preceding line and that the word קָדִימָה serves to fill out the meaning of its own line and is also chosen to form a paronomasia with the following line. So construed, while yielding the sense of "pressing forward" in its own line, the force of the word's root relationship with קֶדֶם ("east wind") forms an association of ideas anticipating the figure that follows in the next line. So understood the flow of thought in the three lines may be paraphrased:

> With all of them bent on violence,
> With every face set forward,[31]
> They gather captives like the sand.

Thus the invincible Neo-Babylonian army will move forward as one unit, all of them bent on violence, all of them pressing forward as with a single face conquering and gathering captives like a colossal east wind that gathers untold quantities of sand.[32]

1:10 The twice-occurring הוּא ("he") stands in anticipatory em-

---

31. The translation given here is thus similar to that of the note in the *Traduction Oecumenique de la Bible* (Edition integrale, Ancien Testament, Paris, 1975), "*la direction de leur face vers l'avant . . .*"
32. The Babylonian kings often boasted of the taking of captives and great booty; see the several texts collected by Wiseman, *Chaldaean Kings*, pp. 51-57.

phasis and refers either to the personified Chaldean nation or its king (see the exposition of 1:7).

עָפָר ("dust") used with the verb צָבַר ("heap up") in a presumed military context probably intends a description of a siege. The building of siege mounds as a battle tactic is widely attested both in the Scriptures (e.g., 2 Sam. 20:15; 2 Kings 19:32; Jer. 32:24; Ezek. 17:17) and in the extrabiblical literature of the ancient Near East. For example, in his third campaign that eventually took him to the gates of Jerusalem, Sennacherib boasts:

> As to Hezekiah, the Jew, he did not submit to my yoke. I laid siege to 46 of his strong cities, walled forts and to the countless small villages in their vicinity, and conquered (them) by means of well-tamped (earth-)ramps, and battering-rams brought (thus) near (to the walls) (combined with) the attack by foot soldiers, (using) mines, breeches as well as sapper work.[33]

Verse 10 is marked by the frequent use (5 times) of the sound *s*, three of them occurring in successive words.

1:11 חָלַף רוּחַ ("a windstorm passes through"): Because רוּחַ is generally a feminine noun and is thus inappropriate as the subject of the masc. sing. verb here, the phrase is often translated as a simile, for example, "They sweep past like the wind" (NIV; cf. NASB). Because רוּחַ is also at times masculine (e.g., Ex. 10:13), however, it seems simplest to view it as a metaphor that is also the subject of the sentence (cf. NJB). The translation of אָז here as "suddenly," although usually rendered as a temporal particle meaning "then," "at that time," is due to the context.

אָשֵׁם ("guilty"): The relation of the last clause to what precedes is difficult. Ward decides that it yields no reasonable sense and is corrupt."[34] Keil takes אָשֵׁם as a verb and translates it "offends."[35] Others take the form to mean "become guilty" (e.g., Laetsch, R. Smith). 1QpHab reads וישם (cf. *BHS*), which has been understood by some as a form derived from שִׂים ("set"; Humbert) and by others as being from שָׁמַם ("be desolate"; G. R. Driver, Brownlee). The translation suggested above retains אָשֵׁם as an adjective in predicate relation to the following subject clause, which is introduced by the explicative particle זוּ ("the one of").[36] Thus construed the line may be rendered,

---

33. *ANET*, p. 38.
34. Ward, *Habakkuk*, p. 11.
35. Keil, *Minor Prophets*, 2:59.
36. This explicative particle is related to the Arabic *ḏ*, Epigraphic South Arabic *ḏ/ḏt*, Ugaritic, Aramaic/Syriac *d*, Old Aramaic, Phoenician *z(u/i)*, and Geez *za*. The case for its use in Hebrew is well established, as demonstrated by W. L. Moran, "The Hebrew Language in Its Northwest Semitic

"But he whose strength is his god is/will be held guilty" (cf. NASB, NJB).

C. SECOND PERPLEXITY: HOW CAN GOD EMPLOY THE WICKED CHALDEANS? (1:12–2:1)

God's answer and extended description of his agent of judgment against Judah puzzled his prophet. Habakkuk simply could not reconcile God's use of the Chaldeans, a people more corrupt than those they were to judge, to punish His people. He begins his second perplexity with an invocation in which he expresses his consternation (v. 12). Not only did God's announcement seem out of character for a holy God but the use of the Chaldeans provoked another thought. Once this plan was put into operation would not a helpless mankind always be at the mercy of these God-commissioned agents of chastisement (vv. 13-17)? Having voiced his complaint, the prophet reaffirms his confidence in God by placing himself in readiness for God's answer to his latest question (2:1). God's reply will occupy the rest of chap. 2.

Translation

Are You not from everlasting*, O Lord?
  My God, my Holy One*, we shall not die.
O Lord, You have appointed them to execute judgment*;
  O Rock, You have established them to reprove.
¹³Your eyes are too pure to look on evil;
  You cannot behold oppression.
Why do You behold the treacherous and keep silent*
  when the wicked swallow up those more righteous than
    themselves,
¹⁴and so You make men* like the fish of the sea,
  like sea creatures* without a ruler?
¹⁵He pulls all of them up with a hook;
  he draws them in his net*,
  and he gathers them into his dragnet*.
Therefore, he rejoices and is glad.

Background," in *The Bible and the Ancient Near East*, ed. G. E. Wright (Garden City, N.Y.: Doubleday, 1956), p. 69. For its existence in the ancient Hebrew poetry of the OT, see E. Lipiński, "Judges 5, 4-5 et Psaume 68, 8-11," *Bib* 55 (1974): 174-75; Patterson, "Song of Deborah," pp. 127, 131. See further Williams, *Syntax*, par. 129, 536; S. Moscati et al., *An Introduction to the Comparative Grammar of the Semitic Languages* (Wiesbaden: Otto Harrassowitz, 1964), pp. 113-14.

¹⁶Therefore, he sacrifices to his net
  and burns incense to his dragnet;
for by them his catch is abundant*
  and his food plenteous*.
¹⁷Shall he therefore* keep on emptying his dragnet*
  and continually* slay nations unsparingly?
²:¹I will stand* at my watch
  and station myself on the ramparts;
and I will keep watch* to see what He will say to me,
  and how I can reply according to my reproof.

Exegesis and Exposition

Like the previous statement of Habakkuk's perplexity (vv. 2-4), this second account is cast in a lament genre: invocation (v. 12), statement of the problem (vv. 13-17), closing declaration of the prophet's confidence in God (2:1). The section is marked by the normal elements of lament but also by the utilization of the root יכח (*ykḥ*, "reprove") as a bookending device (1:12; 2:1). This section is joined to the previous one by the stitch-words מִשְׁפָּט (*mispāṭ*, "justice, judgment") and צַדִּיק (*ṣaddîq*, "righteous"), which occur in close proximity in these sections (vv. 12, 13), and by similar employment of עָמָל (*'āmāl*, "oppression"), רָאָה (*rā'â*, "look"), and נָבַט (*nābaṭ*, "behold"; v. 13; cf. vv. 3, 5). Thus, despite the emotional trauma that gripped the prophet through this troublesome time, the record of all that transpired has been preserved and presented in a highly artistic fashion.

The section opens, as did that containing his first perplexity, with a rhetorical question (cf. v. 2). Habakkuk reminds himself of God's eternality and covenant relationship to Israel. By calling on Yahweh, Habakkuk states his awareness of the fact that God has seen it all. Despite any misgivings Habakkuk might have or will express, he makes clear his confidence in the Lord's unique eternality. As such, God alone is sufficient for the current need. He not only is the eternally existent one but also has remained Israel's covenant God since the days of the fathers (cf. Deut. 7:6; Ps. 89:1-37 [HB 89:2-38]). As T. McComiskey rightly points out, Israel's spiritual experience was to be

> an intimate relationship with God. The Lord would be their God, providing them with the protection and benefits expected in such a loving relationship. This great statement is the heart and soul of the promise because all the gracious benefits of the promise derive from the loving power and volition of God expressed in the intimate and mysterious relationship with him that the people of faith enjoy.[37]

---

37. Thomas McComiskey, *The Covenants of Promise* (Grand Rapids: Baker, 1985), p. 57.

Habakkuk also addresses God with other familiar names and titles. He is אֱלֹהִים (*ĕlōhîm*, "God"), the sovereign and preeminent one who is the creator, sustainer, and consummator of all history. Like YHWH, the name is especially linked to the patriarchs (Ex. 3:6) and Israel (Ps. 68:32-35 [HB 68:33-36]) but could be utilized also by individual believers (Ps. 63:1[HB 63:2]). Accordingly Habakkuk could rightly call the one in whom he trusted "my God."

Habakkuk also calls God "my Holy One." Because holiness is represented in the Scriptures as being the quintessential attribute of God (Ex. 15:11; Ps. 99:9; Isa. 6:3), and hence is the dynamic of the believer's ethic (Ex. 19:6; Lev. 11:44; 19:2; 1 Pet. 1:16), God is often called "the Holy One" (e.g., Job 6:10; cf. Isa. 57:15) and especially "the Holy One of Israel" (Pss. 71:22; 89:18 [HB 89:19]; and 26 times in Isaiah!). Consequently Habakkuk's addressing God as "my Holy One" is quite in line with the thinking of mainstream orthodoxy. Keil rightly observes concerning these three titles that

> the three predicates applied to God have equal weight in the question. The God to whom the prophet prays is *Jehovah*, the absolutely constant One, who is always the same in word and work (see at Gen. ii.4); He is also *Elohai, my, i.e.* Israel's God, who from time immemorial has proved to the people whom He had chosen as His possession that He is their God; and קְדֹשִׁי, the Holy One of Israel, the absolutely Pure One, who cannot look upon evil, and therefore cannot endure that the wicked should devour the righteous (ver. 13).[38]

Habakkuk also calls God a Rock.* The word found here is often used symbolically of God Himself (cf. 1 Sam. 2:2) as a place of refuge (Ps. 18:2 [HB 18:3]) for the trusting believer (Deut. 32:15). To whom else could he turn? As Laetsch remarks, "Tossed about by agonizing doubts, the prophet clings with the hands of faith to the firm, immovable Rock of Ages."[39]

Faced with the prospect of destructive judgment, perhaps even the death of the nation itself, Habakkuk cries out to Israel's God, the Holy One of her salvation who alone is her refuge in such times (cf. Deut. 32:4; Pss. 31:1-3 [HB 31:2-4]; 71:3): "we shall not die!" The precise understanding of Habakkuk's impassioned words is difficult to grasp. It has been treated in several ways. (1) The plain sense of the MT has been followed by most expositors and versions as a statement of the prophet's confidence in God's promises to Israel (e.g., Armerding, Keil). (2) Some follow the tradition of the *Tiqqune sopherim* that the older reading was "you shall not die" (e.g., Hayes, R. Smith; cf.

---

38. Keil, *Minor Prophets*, 2:64.
39. Laetsch, *Minor Prophets*, p. 325.

BHS, NEB, NJB).⁴⁰ (3) M. Dahood suggests a restructuring of the consonants of the text to read *lĕ'ōn māwet* ("the victor over death").⁴¹ (4) A. J. O. vander Wal opts for a modal use of the imperfect: "we shall not die!"⁴² (5) One could also conceivably suggest that the phrase is a question. Thus Laetsch, following the MT, translates "we shall not die?!" and ties the understanding of the prophet's words to the primeval statement of Gen. 3:15, the Abrahamic Covenant (Gen. 12:3; etc.), the predictions concerning Judah (Gen. 49:10-12), and the Davidic Covenant (2 Sam. 7; etc.). He then remarks,

> The deportation of the ten tribes (722 B.C.) had been an appalling calamity; but far more catastrophic would be the annihilation of Judah. Yet what God had just announced appeared to the prophet as the Supreme Judge's death sentence upon Judah. In horrified shock he cries out, We shall not die! . . . That cannot be, O God! That would contradict Thine own self-revelation, Thy very nature.⁴³

In addition to Laetsch's view of an implied negative answer one could suggest that the interrogative particle of the first line should be viewed as doing double duty in this line. So understood it would imply the negative הֲלֹא ("shall we not") expecting a positive reply. In this case the prophet's fear would be that, although God himself is eternal, such is not the case with Israel. Indeed, if the Chaldeans were to go on unchecked, would not Judah die and all the divine promises to Israel with it? The existence of the nation and God's own reputation were at stake.

Since the MT makes good sense as it stands, it has been followed here. Moreover, the alternate suggestions have their own problems. The second view has no manuscript support and adds little or nothing to the flow of thought. The third and fourth suggestions are conjectural. The fifth alternative, while contextually helpful, does not commend itself despite Habakkuk's use of double-duty interrogatives

---

40. This is one of 18 passages in the *Tiqqune sopherim* alleged to be scribal emendations designed to protect God's name and character. Whereas some view these "emendations" as scribal corrections of the text (e.g., R. Smith; cf. NJB, p. 156t), others view them as expressions of what the scriptural author originally intended to write but did not (e.g., Keil, *Minor Prophets*, 2:64). See further E. Würthwein, *The Text of the Old Testament*, 4th ed. (Grand Rapids: Eerdmans, 1979), pp. 15-19.
41. Dahood, *Psalms*, 3:324. See also M. Dahood, "Ugaritic-Hebrew Parallel Pairs," *RSP*, 3:18-19.
42. A. J. O. van der Wal, "Lō' Nāmūt in Habakkuk I 12: A Suggestion," *VT* 38 (1988): 480-82.
43. Laetsch, *Minor Prophets*, p. 324. In a critical note Laetsch cites with approval the words of Martin Luther: "We may regard this sentence as a question. Is it not true, Lord, that Thou art my God of old, my Holy One, so that we shall not die, but that Thou wilt use him to punish and correct us? He speaks to God in the form of questions" (p. 323).

elsewhere (1:2, 13, 17; 2:7, 18), for these are all cases of compound sentences with the same subject. Taken at face value Habakkuk's words are a statement of the prophet's ultimate confidence in God. From a literary standpoint they anticipate the closing statement of confidence at the end of the section (2:1). From a theological viewpoint they reflect Habakkuk's firm grasp of covenant truth: Despite Israel's certain chastisement, God will remain faithful to His promise to the patriarchs (Gen. 17:2-8; 26:3-5; 28:13-15), to Israel (Ex. 3:3-15; 14:1-6; Deut. 7:6; 14:1-2; 26:16-18), and to the house of David (2 Sam. 7:12-29).

Despite the prophet's confidence in God, he has reservations concerning the situation. Habakkuk has been shown that judgment and reproof* (or correction) must come, and he understands that the Lord is sending the Chaldeans for that purpose. Although he is committed to the truth of God's abiding presence with Israel and the inviolability of the divine promises, Habakkuk the man has fears. Perhaps punishment at the hands of such a vicious people will prove to be too much. How could God use such a wicked nation to execute His purposes?

These problems are detailed in the verses that follow (vv. 13*b*-17). He begins with the latter concern. Again the matter of justice surfaces in Habakkuk's thinking. While he understands the necessity of Judah's judgment and the Chaldeans' role, he cannot comprehend how a holy God can use a nation that is more wicked than the nation He desires to punish. God's prophet seizes upon words that have been the focus of God's presentation. God's eyes are too pure to see evil; He cannot look upon oppression. Habakkuk had asked whether God really saw the oppression that His prophet gazed on in Judah (v. 3). God had told him to look out at the nations for what He was going to do (v. 5). Habakkuk now tells God that having seen what God was going to do he cannot "see" how God can look on silently when a treacherous, evil,* and more oppressive nation swallows up people that at least have some semblance of righteousness. Laetsch may be correct in suggesting that by "righteous" Habakkuk intends more particularly the believing remnant within Judah:

> The prophet, of course, does not think here merely of civic righteousness. . . . He thinks here of the small remnant of such as are righteous by faith in the promised Redeemer. Yet they must suffer together with the mass of unbelieving Jews, and in like manner, the inhuman cruelties of the Chaldeans. Why does God permit, and even decree, such a judgment? How does this agree with His holiness and justice?[44]

In any case Habakkuk takes his place beside many others, such as Job (Job 7:16-21; 9:21-24; 12:4-6; 21:1-16; 24:1-16, 21-25; 27:1-12), the

---

44. Ibid.; see also the observations of Keil and Delitzsch in Keil, *Minor Prophets*, 2:65-66.

psalmist Asaph (Ps. 73), Jeremiah (Jer. 11:18-19; 12:1-4; 15:15-18; 17:15-18; 20:7-18), and Malachi (Mal. 2:17), who questioned God as to His fairness in handling the problems of evil and injustice. Like these other questioners, Habakkuk will be shown the necessity of resting fully in God (Hab. 2:4, 20).

In answer to Habakkuk's first perplexity, God had revealed that He would send the Chaldeans to deal with Judah's sin (vv. 5-6). Because the Chaldeans were relatively unknown, He supplied a résumé of their military capability (vv. 7-11). Habakkuk has a problem with both parts of God's answer to his complaint. He has indicated his displeasure in God's choice of the Chaldeans (v. 13). Now he reacts to the description of their ferocity (vv. 14-17). Granted the accuracy of God's report, has He not turned loose upon a helpless mankind a voracious force that even He would be powerless to check?

Adopting the imagery of fishing, Habakkuk portrays the scenario that God has set in motion as one of fishermen (Chaldeans), who use their sophisticated and powerful hooks and nets (Neo-Babylonian military might and methods) to catch helpless fish and creatures of the sea (the various conquered peoples). The success of these Neo-Babylonian "fishermen" will only cause them to rejoice and have their appetites whetted for still greater pleasures. Elated by the fine catches (booty) they shall take, the Chaldeans will acknowledge allegiance to neither God nor man, finding their only "religion" in their raw military power.

Habakkuk's fears were not unfounded, for the Chaldean war machine was effective enough not only to gain for them political dominance across the northern part of the Fertile Crescent and through the Levant to the borders of Egypt (Nebuchadnezzar would launch one foray into Egypt itself; cf. Jer. 43:10-11) but also to create the mighty Neo-Babylonian empire (cf. Dan. 2:37-38; 7:4) with the city of Babylon (Dan. 4:30) as the chief beneficiary. Indeed, Nebuchadnezzar's Babylon would prove to be a spectacle of opulence. Bisected by the Euphrates River, access to Babylon was gained by nine major gates. The most famous of these, the Ishtar Gate, was flanked on either side by 40-foot towers. Through it the sacred processions of Nebuchadnezzar's day proceeded to the Esagila temple via a paved street bordered by high walls decorated with brilliantly colored animals painted on a blue background. Ancient historians counted Nebuchadnezzar as the builder of the famed Hanging Gardens, heralded as one of the seven wonders of the world. Edwin Yamauchi calls Nebuchadnezzar's Babylon "the greatest city in the ancient world," and Gerald Larue declares it "one of the most beautiful."[45]

---

45. Edwin Yamauchi, "Babylon," in *Major Cities of the Biblical World*, ed. R. K. Harrison (Nashville: Nelson, 1985), p. 36; Gerald Larue, *Babylon and*

Babylon would also become a center of paganism. It would one day contain at least nine temples, the most famous of which were its ziggurat Etemenanki ("House of the Foundation of Heaven and Earth") and Esagila ("House of the Uplifted Head"), sacred to Marduk, the patron deity of Babylon. D. J. Wiseman says of the main shrine of this temple complex,

> Nabopolassar claimed to have redecorated the Marduk shrine with gypsum and silver alloy, which Nebuchadrezzar replaced with fine gold. The walls were studded with precious stones set in gold plate, and stone and lapis lazuli pillars supported cedar roof beams. The texts describe the god's gilded bedchamber adjacent to the throne room.
> Herodotus (i.183) described two statues of the god, one seated. . . . Herodotus was told that 800 talents (16.8 metric tons) of gold were used for these statues and for the table, throne, and footstool. A thousand talents of incense were burned annually at the festivals while innumerable sacrificial animals were brought in to the two golden altars, one used for large, the other for small victims.[46]

It is small wonder that the materialism and religious lust of Babylon were targets for the condemnation of Isaiah and Jeremiah, both of whom prophesied Babylon's certain fall (Isa. 21:9) and total destruction (Isa. 13:19-22; Jer. 51:24-26). Thereafter the name "Babylon" became symbolic of a misspent materialism that stands in antagonism to the things of God (cf. Rev. 17-18).

For Habakkuk the focal point of the problem lay not just in the Chaldeans' awesome success but in the fact that they were divinely commissioned warriors. It was God Himself who would raise them up (v. 6) and make expert "fishermen" of them (v. 14). Since God had thus empowered them, could He renounce His own work? Would not these "fishers of men" go on emptying and refilling their nets *ad infinitum*—conquering city after city and taking heavy booty? No, Habakkuk could not "see" any of this. Such a judgment on God's people seemed unjust and overly harsh. Once begun it might never be terminated.

Nevertheless, Habakkuk ends his complaint with a renewed statement of his confidence in God (2:1). He also reports his intention to assume the role of a watchman. As the city watchman manned his post atop the walls to look for the approach of danger (Ezek. 33:2-6) or a messenger (2 Sam. 18:24-28; Isa. 21:6-8; 52:7-10), or to keep watch over current events (1 Sam. 14:16-17; 2 Kings 9:17-20), so the

---

the Bible (Grand Rapids: Baker, 1969), p. 51. Larue's description of the splendor of the city is particularly good (pp. 51-65). For an account of the exploration and excavation of ancient Babylon, see A. Parrot, *Babylon and the Old Testament*, trans. B. E. Hooke (New York: Philosophical Library, 1958), pp. 15-67.
46. D. J. Wiseman, "Babylon," *ISBE* 1:388-89.

OT prophet looked for the communication of God's will to the waiting people (Jer. 6:17; Ezek. 3:16-21; 33:7-9; Hos. 9:8). Habakkuk would assume the role of a prophetic watchman, taking his post on the ramparts* to watch* for the Lord's reply. The word "watch" suggests an active, earnest waiting for the Lord's message; the "ramparts" (cf. 2 Chron. 8:5; 11:5) imply that just as the civil watchman assumed a particular post on the city wall (cf. Nah. 2:1 [HB 2:2]), so the prophet had his assigned post of responsibility (cf. Jer. 1:17-19; Amos 3:6-7). Keil observes:

> The words of our verse are to be taken figuratively, or internally, like the appointment of the watchman in Isa. xxi.6. The figure . . . expresses the spiritual preparation of the prophet's soul for hearing the word of God within, *i.e.* the collecting of his mind by quietly entering into himself, and meditating upon the word and testimonies of God.[47]

Habakkuk has taken issue with both the Lord's plan to judge Judah by means of the Chaldeans and with the thought of using such a vicious people at all. The prophet doubtless had given God's words careful thought and, because he could not see things from God's point of view, knew that God would have some words of correction for him. He now no longer worries about the Lord's lack of communication (cf. 1:2) but what sort of correction he will receive. He comes back to the word "reproof" with which he had begun his complaint (v. 12).

Habakkuk has expressed the fact that he understands God's intention to use the Chaldeans as his agent of reproof to Judah for their own good. Now he similarly expects divine correction to his own difficulties. Where genuine doubt and perplexities exist, God patiently brings the needed reproof (cf. Jonah 4:10-11) and correction of man's thinking (cf. Ps. 73:18-25). Such would also be Habakkuk's experience (cf. 3:17-19).

The noun תּוֹכַחַת (*tôkaḥat*) is used in one of two ways: (1) "argument" (Ps. 38:14 [HB 38:15]); or (2) "rebuke" (Ps. 39:11 [HB 39:12]; Ezek. 5:15), or "reproof that provides correction for living" (Prov. 1:23-25; 15:31-32). The meaning here could thus be either (1) "my argument" (cf. Job 13:6)—that is, what Habakkuk had just set before God (1:12-17)—or (2) "my correction/reproof" (cf. Ps. 73:14)—that is, the reproof that Habakkuk anticipates God will give him for his own good.

The critics and versions are divided as to the proper understanding here, the majority deciding for the first alternative (e.g., BDB, Craigie, Feinberg, Hayes, Laetsch, von Orelli, G. A. Smith, R. Smith, LXX, Vg, NIV, NJB, RSV) and others for the second (Armerding, Pusey, KJV, NIV marg., NKJV, NASB). Two factors must be consid-

---

47. Keil, *Minor Prophets*, 2:68-69.

ered in reaching a final choice: (1) whether the root יכח (*ykḥ*), which forms a bookending device to 1:12–2:1, is to be understood in the same way in both instances, or whether there is a repetition of the root for literary effect (such as a paronomasia); (2) the meaning of אָשִׁיב (*ʾāšîb*, "I shall reply").

Those who choose the second alternative of the use of *tōkaḥat* in this verse usually decide for an identity of meanings for the root יכח in both verses (e.g., Armerding, NASB); those who choose the first alternative do not (e.g., Keil, NIV). As for the problem of *ʾašîb* the form can be understood either as (1) the prophet's reply to himself and his people with regard to his complaint (first alternative, so Keil) or (2) his reply to his anticipated reproof (second alternative, so Armerding). The difficulty of the first position on *ʾašîb* has perhaps occasioned the Syriac translation, "He will answer" (i.e., Habakkuk waits to see how God will answer his complaint; cf. R. Smith, NJB). Another possibility is to repoint the form in the MT as a qal passive, "I shall be answered" (i.e., the way Habakkuk would be answered by God concerning his complaint).[48]

The problem of the last line of 2:1 is thus complex. Despite the weight of the majority of scholarship that favors taking *tōkaḥat* as "complaint," I am inclined to take the second alternative: "reproof." Especially telling is the probability that the root *ykḥ* is used to form an inclusio for the section 1:12–2:1. If so, it seems better to translate the root consistently rather than to adopt another explanation, such as an unprovable wordplay. Therefore, Habakkuk notes that the Chaldeans have been sent to reprove/correct the Judahites. Similarly he expects and deserves God's correction concerning his doubts and his understanding of the full scope of God's plans for the future.

Accordingly the verb *ʾāšîb* most naturally suggests Habakkuk's answers concerning God's corrective reply.[49] If all this is allowed, the suggestion of a confrontational stance by the prophet is softened. His position is thus that of a watchman in the king's service manning the ramparts and waiting eagerly for the arrival of his master's communiqué. Habakkuk expects that the message will bring correction and proper orientation to his anxieties. He is not so much challenging

---

48. For the persistence of the qal passive in biblical Hebrew see R. J. Williams, "The Passive Qal Theme in Hebrew," in *Essays on the Ancient Semitic World*, ed. J. W. Wevers and D. B. Redford (Toronto: U. of Toronto, 1970), pp. 43-50. Williams notes an analogous case with a middle weak verb occurring in Gen. 50:20 where the MT reads וַיִּישֶׂם ("he was placed") whereas the Samaritan Pentateuch renders the form as a passive (ויושם).

49. For the use of שׁוּב in a reply to an answer, see Dahood, "Ugaritic-Hebrew Parallel Pairs," 1:300-301.

God with a complaint as he is desiring to have his perplexities allevi-
ated and his viewpoint corrected.

Habakkuk also probably wanted to know God's will and wisdom
that he might respond properly to God's correction and also communicate God's intentions to others. The prophet's reaction to God's
reproof would have a telling effect on his own spiritual condition and
the effectiveness of his entire ministry. It was a crucial moment for
God's prophet, and he was to prove worthy of the test. C. Armerding
puts it well: "He revealed a mature wisdom in his determination that
this response be shaped by what God Himself would say. It is a wise
man who takes his questions about God to God for the answers."[50]
God's answer was probably not long in coming. It was to carry with it
crucial and extensive information (2:2-20).

Additional Notes

1:12 †מִקֶּדֶם means literally "from aforetime" but is usually employed in the sense of (1) "from of old" (Neh. 12:26; Ps. 77:11 [HB
77:12]; Isa. 45:21; 46:10), (2) "from most ancient times" (Ps. 74:12), or
(3) "from everlasting" (Mic. 5:2 [HB 5:1]). Any of its common meanings is possible here, and each has its advocates. Thus R. Smith favors
the first and the NJB the second. Most English versions and conservative expositors have followed the third alternative since the focus of
the passage is more on God's existence than on His past deeds (which
come into view in chap. 3). The last option is probably the correct
one.

†For the *hapax legomenon* קְדֹשִׁי ("my Holy One") *BHS* suggests
reading אֱלֹהֵי קָדְשִׁי ("my Holy God"). But the title "Holy One" here
anticipates its use in the epic psalm of the third chapter (3:3). It is
also appropriate as a basis for the ethical dimension of the present
context.[51]

The word צוּר ("rock") is often used symbolically of God Himself
(cf. 1 Sam. 2:2) as a place of refuge (Ps. 18:2 [HB 18:3]) for the trusting
believer (Deut. 32:15). סֶלַע, another word for "rock," is used similarly.[52] The image of God as a rock is applied to Christ in the NT (1 Cor.
10:4; 1 Pet. 2:6-8). *BHS* suggests reading צוּרִי ("my rock"), thus continuing the force of the suffix found earlier in the verse.

---

50. C. Armerding, "Habakkuk," in *EBC*, 7:509.
51. For extended discussions of the biblical doctrine of God's holiness, see A.
    H. Strong, *Systematic Theology* (Philadelphia: Judson, 1907), pp. 268-75;
    Stephen Charnock, *The Existence and Attributes of God* (reprint, Min-
    neapolis: Klock and Klock, 1977), pp. 446-532.
52. See further A. S. van der Woude, "צוּר," *THAT* 2:538-43; J. E. Hartley, "צוּר,"
    TWOT 2:762; R. D. Patterson, "סֶלַע," *TWOT* 2:627.

A few variant suggestions have been proposed for the latter part of the last line. The NJB and NIV translate לְהוֹכִיחַ ("to reprove/chastise") "to punish," NASB "to correct." *BHS* follows 1QpHab in reading למוכיחו ("for his chastisement"). Since the root יכח reappears in 2:1 forming an inclusio for 1:12–2:1, the translation here will be affected by its understanding in 2:1.

For יְסַדְתּוֹ ("you have established them"), LXX (ἔπλασεν) may have read the root יסר with the sense "fashion": "he/it fashioned me for his/its instrument."

1:13 †תַחֲרִישׁ ("[Why . . .] are you silent"): The asyndetic structure makes the question even more dramatic,[53] rendering the addition of the conjunction in the Qere (cf. Pesh., *Tg. Neb.*) both unnecessary and inappropriate.

The identity of the wicked here has been the subject of some controversy and has played a role in the argument over the setting of the book (see introduction). If vv. 5-11 are excised as a late interpolation (e.g., Wellhausen, Giesebrecht), one could conceivably view the wicked in vv. 4, 13 as being the same. In such a case they could be identified not only with godless Judahites but also with Egyptians (G. A. Smith), Assyrians (Eissfeldt, Weiser), or Chaldeans (Sellin, Wellhausen).[54] One could also follow Duhm in taking the wicked as the Greeks on the basis of the identification of the *Kasdim* with the *Kittim* (cf. v. 6).

By following the MT in v. 6, however, the wicked here must be the Chaldeans who are dubbed the fishermen in vv. 15-17. Thus they are not identical with the wicked in Judah of v. 4. Habakkuk's argument is therefore *a fortiori*: As wicked as the Judahites were, they scarcely matched the Chaldeans for wickedness.

---

53. I have demonstrated the use of asyndetic structure for dramatic effect as a feature of Akkadian literary composition also; see R. D. Patterson, *Old Babylonian Parataxis* (Ann Arbor: University Microfilms, 1971), pp. 165-70.
54. The case for identifying the wicked with the Chaldeans here is defended by Marshall Johnson ("The Paralysis of Torah in Habakkuk," *VT* 35 [1985]: 257-66), who theorizes that the Chaldean oppression of Judah occasioned a severe questioning of God by His prophet. Habakkuk had expected the blessing of God for the keeping of תּוֹרָה and מִשְׁפָּט in association with the Josianic reforms but instead saw only great evil and, rather than relief, the threat of increased Chaldean violence.
        For discussion of these words for evil, see M. A. Klopfenstein, "בגד," *THAT* 1:261-63; S. Erlandsson, "בָּגַד," *TDOT* 1:470-72; G. Herbert Livingston, "רָעַע," *TWOT* 2:854-56; G. Herbert Livingston, "רָשַׁע," *TWOT* 2:863-64; Robert Girdlestone, *Synonyms of the Old Testament* (Grand Rapids: Eerdmans, 1956), pp. 78-79, 80, 81-82. M. J. Erickson (*Christian Theology* [Grand Rapids: Baker, 1984], 2:564-75) presents a lively and informative discussion concerning various scriptural terms for sin.

1:14 †אָדָם ("men") is rendered as a collective noun. Several English translations (NJB, KJV, NKJV, NASB) translate the verse as though it continues the questioning begun in v. 13.

†רֶמֶשׂ ("sea creatures"): Although usually used of creeping land creatures, it can refer to gliding sea animals (cf. Ps. 104:25), the sense demanded here.

1:15 †חֵרֶם ("dragnet") and מִכְמֶרֶת ("fishnet"): The latter word can also be used of a hunter's net (e.g., Mic. 7:2), as can its cognates מִכְמָר and מַכְמֹר, both meaning "net" or "snare" (e.g., Isa. 51:20; Ps. 141:10). חֵרֶם is perhaps related to an Arabic root *harama* meaning "perforate," whereas מִכְמֶרֶת is cognate to Akkadian *kamāru* ("trap with a snare," "net").

Though precise differentiation between the two words is difficult, Armerding seems to be correct in suggesting that "they appear to correspond to the two main types of net, the throw-net and the seine, used in NT times and up to the present in Palestine."[55] In this he reflects the opinion of most expositors and versions (e.g., KJV, NIV, NJB). This view is also supported by the distinction made in the LXX, which reads respectively ἀμφίβληστρον ("casting net") and σαγήνη ("dragnet," "sweep net"), words that remain distinguished into NT times (cf. Matt. 4:18-20 with 13:47-48).[56] Keil, however, suggests that חֵרֶם refers to a net in general whereas מִכְמֶרֶת designates "the large fishing-net (σαγήνη), the lower part of which when sunk, touches the bottom, whilst the upper part floats on the top of the water."[57] His view is reflected in the NASB, which translates the terms as "net" and "fishing net." Still another opinion is put forward by A. van Selms, who calls the מִכְמֶרֶת "a net cast from the shore, which falls flat on the water and sinks by means of leaden weights," and חֵרֶם "a seine, leaded on one edge and provided with floats on the other; it is paid out from boats and gradually drawn in to the shore."[58] I have followed Armerding and the majority of scholars not only on the basis of the LXX but also because Ezekiel 47:10 seems to relate חֵרֶם to nets that are cast by fishermen standing on the shore, while מִכְמֶרֶת is mentioned by Isaiah (Isa. 19:8) as being employed by fishermen on the water.[59]

---

55. Armerding, "Habakkuk," in *EBC*, 7:507.
56. See the excellent discussion in R. C. Trench, *Synonyms of the New Testament* (Grand Rapids: Eerdmans, 1953), pp. 235-37.
57. Keil, *Minor Prophets*, 2:66.
58. A. van Selms, "Fishing," *ISBE* 2:309-11.
59. See further Fred Wight, *Manners and Customs of Bible Lands* (Chicago: Moody, 1953), pp. 215-16. M. Dahood ("The Minor Prophets and Ebla," in *The Word of the Lord Shall Go Forth*, ed. Carol L. Meyers and M. O'Connor [Winona Lake, Ind.: Eisenbrauns, 1983], p. 60) suggests on the basis of

יִשְׂמַח וְיָגִיל ("he rejoices and is glad"): The verbs are two of several words in the OT for rejoicing. While the former verb appears to emphasize the general feeling of joyfulness of disposition that a person "feels all over," the latter lays stress on the more emotional, enthusiastic, and, at times, spontaneous expression of joy. They are often used together to express total gladness, sometimes perhaps as hendiadys (cf. Pss. 14:7; 32:11; 53:6 [HB 53:7]; 1 Chron. 16:31).[60] The words appear in parallelism in Ugaritic also, often as set pairs.[61]

1:16 יִזְבֵּחַ ("he sacrifices") and יְקַטֵּר ("he burns incense"): These verbs are used in connection with the various worship services mentioned in the OT, but the former occurs only three times in contexts dealing with the proper worship of God (1 Kings 8:5; 2 Chron. 5:6; 30:22) and the latter probably never, although doubtful occurrences have been suggested in 1 Kings 22:43 (HB 22:44); 2 Kings 15:4, 35.[62] Thus Armerding correctly observes that when these verbs occur together they always have connotations of illegitimate worship; hence "the prophet was complaining that the Babylonians were clearly guilty of according to their own power the honor and strength due to God alone."[63]

†שָׁמֵן and בְּרִאָה both mean "fat." The translations "abundant" and "plenteous" are *ad sensum*. These adjectives testify to the luxurious lifestyle of the Chaldeans gained as a result of their rapacious looting. The NJB not inappropriately translates: "For by these they get a rich living and live off the fat of the land." Though the root שָׁמֵן can be employed to describe God-given prosperity (Isa. 30:23; Ezek. 34:14), like its companion adjective (cf. the masc. sing. form בָּרִיא in Ps. 73:4) it can be employed with regard to the wicked who have gained their riches through ungodly living (Jer. 5:26-28; Ezek. 34:16).

1:17 †For חֶרְמוֹ ("his dragnet") K. J. Cathcart, building on the use of the verb רִיק in Ps. 35:3, proposes a transposition of consonants to read *romḥô* ("his spear").[64] More suggestive, however, is the reading of 1QpHab חרבו ("his sword"). Yet, whereas "sword" makes good sense with the verb "empty" and whereas the two words do occur together in the OT (e.g., Ex. 15:9; Lev. 26:33; Ezek. 12:14), the MT here

recent finds at Ebla that ancient fishermen worshiped a god known as Divine Net.

60. See C. Westermann, "גיל," *THAT* 1:415-18; J. Bergman, H. Ringgren, C. Barth, "גיל," *TDOT* 2:469-75; E. Ruprecht, "שמח," *THAT* 2:829-35; B. Waltke, "שָׂמַח," *TWOT* 2:879.
61. For the occurrence of this set pair in the Keret epic, see Gordon, *Ugaritic Textbook*, no. 125: 14-15, 99. For a helpful bibliography, see Dahood, "Ugaritic-Hebrew Parallel Pairs," 1:354.
62. See, e.g., T. R. Hobbs, *2 Kings*, WBC (Waco, Tex.: Word, 1985), p. 193.
63. Armerding, "Habakkuk," in *EBC*, 7:508.
64. K. J. Cathcart, "A New Proposal for Hab 1, 17," *Bib* 65 (1984): 575-76.

preserves the imagery of fishing and the net found in the previous verses. The Chaldean "fishermen" keep emptying their loaded nets and continuing their fishing.

†וְתָמִיד† ("and continually"): *BHS* suggests the deletion of the conjunction as dittography. The conjunction is also absent from 1QpHab and Pesh. but read with the following negative: "Their sword is ever drawn to slay nations and does not spare (them)." The MT is the harsher reading and therefore probably to be retained. Its difficult syntax can be explained either by (1) understanding the Chaldeans as the subject of לֹא יַחְמוֹל (lit. "he does not spare") employed with the לֹ of reference or respect (i.e., "he shall continually have no compassion with reference to slaying the nations") or (2) viewing לֹא יַחְמוֹל as a circumstantial clause used as a substitute for an adverb ("unsparingly") while taking לַהֲרֹג as an example of the utilization of the preposition לֹ with an infinitive construct in looser subordination with a gerundive effect that virtually takes the place of a finite verb, hence "slay" with the nuance of consequence or result.[65] The latter is perhaps the better alternative.[66] Armerding suggests that a double meaning of חָמַל is intended here, noting that this verb "is used of holding back or refraining from an action, and commonly of pity as the attitude that causes one to hold back or remove from harm. Both ideas are appropriate here."[67] Thus the Chaldeans are accused of continually slaying nations without sparing and without pity.

†הַעַל כֵּן† ("shall he therefore"): No sufficient reason exists for omitting the interrogative particle with the LXX, Pesh. and 1QpHab or for viewing the MT as composed of ה (an interrogative particle) + עַל ("Most High") + כֵּן ("Just One") and translating, with Dahood, "O Most High, Just One."[68]

BDB observes that עַל־כֵּן introduces more customarily than לָכֵן ("therefore") "the statement of a *fact*, rather than a *declaration*."[69] That being the case, Habakkuk must be building his argument on the full flow of thought of these verses. He points out that because the rampaging Chaldean will gather his booty without restraint he will

---

65. For details see GKC par. 114o; 156g; Williams, *Syntax*, par. 198.
66. See similarly the translation of Keil, *Minor Prophets*, 2:65: "Shall he therefore empty his net and always strangle nations without sparing?" W. G. E. Watson (*Classical Hebrew Poetry* [Sheffield: JSOT Press, 1986], p. 220), however, retains the MT but views וְתָמִיד as an example of pivot-pattern parallelism closing the first poetic line climactically while setting the scene for the second (cf. NIV, NJB). Although attractive, such an understanding ignores the Masoretic accents, which place וְתָמִיד in the second line.
67. Armerding, "Habakkuk," in *EBC*, 7:508.
68. Dahood, "Minor Prophets and Ebla," p. 60.
69. BDB, p. 487.

"therefore" rejoice; because of his unbridled joy he will "therefore" worship only the might that has made him rich; "therefore," wonders Habakkuk, will he go on forever and unabatedly in his looting and killing? Thus the three occurrences of עַל־כֵּן are for logical (almost a veiled sorites) and dramatic effect.

2:1 †אֶעֱמֹדָה ("I will stand") is a qal cohortative of resolve or determination. The noun מִשְׁמֶרֶת, although used at times with reference to a general post (Isa. 28:8), stresses more the idea of *watching* as an activity (cf. Josh. 22:3) or as the object of such activity (cf. Deut. 11:1). Accordingly it is translated "watch" (KJV, NIV, RSV), whereas the place (but cf. Isa. 21:8) where such activity is carried on (i.e., a [guard] post; note NASB, NJB) is denoted by the cognate noun מִשְׁמָר ("guard post," Neh. 4:3). Thus the emphasis here is probably more on the activity of standing watch, the place itself being supplied in the parallel line by מָצוֹר ("ramparts").

†The verb צָפָה ("look at") is used of a careful and scrutinizing look. It was particularly suited for the duties of the watchman manning the city's walls or his tower. The participial form came to mean "watchman" (cf. 2 Kings 9:17-20). The figure of the watchman is often applied to the office and activities of the prophet (e.g., Isa. 52:7-10; Jer. 6:17; Ezek. 3:17). The imagery here is reminiscent of Isa. 21:6-8.

עַל־תּוֹכַחְתִּי ("concerning my reproof"): The phrase is probably deliberately placed to form a chiasmus with the opening עַל־מִשְׁמַרְתִּי.

2

The Prophet's Perplexities and God's Explanations, Part Two (Habakkuk 2:2-20)

For the prophet's latest perplexity (1:12–2:1) a patient God has a ready reply: He is in control of all earth's history, working through the ebb and flow of its changing historical scenes to the accomplishment of His wise and holy purposes. The challenge to Habakkuk is to respond in understanding and trust. The section begins with introductory matters (vv. 2-3), continues with basic principles that Habakkuk needs to keep in mind (v. 4), and contains a long discourse on the Chaldeans' future demise (vv. 5, 6-20).

D. SECOND EXPLANATION: GOD CONTROLS ALL NATIONS ACCORDING TO HIS PURPOSES (2:2-20)

From a literary perspective, the chapter is carefully constructed (see introduction). The central focus is on the problems that disturbed God's prophet: (1) How could a righteous God use a wicked people to chastise a people less wicked than themselves? (2) Could the rampaging of such a vicious nation ever be checked? God answers these two questions by pointing out that He is aware of the standards of righteousness attained by nations and individuals and thus will deal justly with all (v. 4). This means judgment also for the ungodly Chaldeans (v. 5), who are under His supervisory control (vv. 6-20). In relating God's reply to his perplexities, Habakkuk ties it to the previous section by his skillful use of the stitch-words צַדִּיק (ṣaddîq, "righteous[ness]," "just [one]"), בּוֹגֵד (bôgēd, "treacherous," "betrays"), and אָסַף (*'āsap*, "gathers"), each of which portrays the Lord's awareness of the clear distinctions between two classes of men and nations. The chapter, then, provides a dramatic contrast between the righteous, who live out their lives faithfully (v. 4*b*) and in humble submission to a holy God (v. 20), and the wicked, who will ultimately be punished because of their godlessness (vv. 4*a*, 5-19).

Other literary features command the reader's attention: taunt songs/woe oracles (vv. 6-8, 9-11, 12-14, 15-17, 18-20), proverb (v. 6), simile and metaphor (vv. 5, 7, 8, 15, 16), allegory (vv. 15-16), hendiadys (vv. 2, 3[?], 6[?]), metonymy and merismus (v. 5), personification (vv. 5, 11), rhetorical question (vv. 13, 18), alliteration (vv. 15, 18), assonance (vv. 2, 6, 7), paronomasia (v. 19), enjambment (v. 18), gender-matched parallelism (v. 5), and chiasmus (vv. 3, 4, 6, 9, 14, 16). Despite its difficulty of interpretation at places (e.g., v. 4; see Excursus on Habakkuk 2:4), it is a masterpiece of prophetic literature.

1. PRELIMINARY INSTRUCTIONS (2:2-3)

Before God's specific points of reply are given to Habakkuk, He has preliminary instructions for His prophet. The Lord's commands are intended to prepare Habakkuk for The revelation of crucial issues relative to the operations of divine government (v. 4) that will introduce the discussion of the whole matter of Habakkuk's concern: the disposition of the voracious Chaldeans (vv. 5, 6-20).

Translation

And the LORD answered me and said,
  "Write down the vision*
  and make it plain on tablets,
  so that the one who reads it may run.
³For the vision is a witness* to the appointed time;
  it testifies* to the end
  and will not prove false*.
If it tarries, wait for it;
  for it will come and* not be late*."

Exegesis and Exposition

In reporting the Lord's reply, Habakkuk stresses its personal nature: "The LORD answered *me.*" The prophet had laid his perplexity before the Lord, expecting divine correction (1:12–2:1). The Lord's answer was given directly to and for Habakkuk, to help him understand. But because Habakkuk doubted the principles at work in the divine activity—just as many have doubted—the Lord's answer also carried a charge, namely, that the Lord's response was to be shared with all people.

Habakkuk was told to write* the issue of the divine reply upon tablets*. If Habakkuk was literally to write down the divine dispatch, the question arises as to its extent. Various suggestions have been offered, some identifying the text of the message with v. 4 (Craigie, Feinberg), some with vv. 4*b*-5 (Brownlee, Humbert), others with all of vv. 4 and 5 (Ward), and still others deciding that the length of the communication is uncertain (e.g., Laetsch).[1]

To reach a final solution one must consider the word "tablets." Though these could be viewed as large stones, such as in the case of the Ten Commandments (Ex. 24:12; see Additional Notes), the author could intend small tablets of whatever material.[2] That the word is plural could suggest multiple copies to be hand carried by men serving as heralds that others might hear the message (cf. Jer. 51:59-64). That the heralds would carry a written dispatch rather than an oral communication would emphasize the seriousness of the divine directive. If this was the case, the message was doubtless a short one, probably encompassing no more than v. 4. But to whom would these dispatches be carried? Would they go to Judah's leaders (cf. Jer. 36), or perhaps to foreign nations (cf. Isa. 30:8)? Lack of clarity as to this latter question warns against too quickly adopting the idea of heralds carrying several tablets.

The message was to be written plainly* so that those who passed by* might be able to understand it and bear the news to others. Though the figure of reading and running may indicate the activity of a prophet (Keil) or may simply intend that all who pass by may read it (S. R. Driver, Feinberg, Laetsch), it raises again the possibility of the literary motif of a herald "whose role would thus be to 'run with the message' (cf. 1 Sam. 4:12; 2 Sam. 18:19-27; Esther 3:13, 15; 8:10, 14; Jer. 51:31)."[3] That the text reads "he who reads it may run" rather than "he who runs may read" favors strongly the motif of the herald (NIV). But because not only Habakkuk but all who read God's communication were to serve as heralds, all three of these views are in a sense complementary, the figure of the herald being adopted in order that prophets and all others might understand God's Word and carry it on to others. The message was for all.

Perhaps the simplest solution, then, to the understanding of the

---

1. For details, see W. H. Brownlee, "The Placarded Revelation of Habakkuk," *JBL* 82 (1963): 319-25.
2. The uncertainty as to the exact material is underscored by similar instructions in Isa. 30:8: "Write it on a tablet for them, inscribe it on a scroll" (NIV). The phraseology of the text in Isaiah and the problem of the extent of the message is analogous to that in Hab. 2:2-3; for details, see John N. Oswalt, *The Book of Isaiah*, NICOT (Grand Rapids: Eerdmans, 1986), pp. 550-51.
3. Armerding, "Habakkuk," in *EBC* (Grand Rapids: Zondervan, 1985), 7:511.

passage is not to press any of the details of the context beyond their more obvious intent. It is enough to see that Habakkuk is given a personalized reply. Rather than being a mere answer or correction of his thinking, God's Word is also a commission to further service. Whether or not he is literally to take tablets and write on them, he is to communicate a message of lasting importance. Everyone who reads or hears these words is to consider himself a herald of a significant communication intended for all people everywhere. Probably the precise words are to be found in verse 4, the latter part of which is of crucial significance. C. L. Feinberg observes that it "became the watchword of Christianity, is the key to the whole book of Habakkuk and is the central theme of all the Scriptures."[4]

As further preparation for that central thesis of divine government, Habakkuk is given the reason for the urgency of the message: the revelation will find its culmination in God's appointed time.* That period is reserved to God's discretion and direction. For Habakkuk this lay in the future, even though its realization was already at work in his day (1:5). Indeed, the revelation was meant to stand as a witness that testified unerringly of God's bringing His purposes to pass.

The immediate context naturally has to do with Judah's vindication and the Chaldeans' judgment (Hailey), but because this vital message that was to be shared with all (v. 4) is given as a basic truth upon which God's governing of individuals and nations is built, the outworking of the details of the appointed time would serve as a harbinger for the future. Each successive application of the message would point to the final end (Feinberg, Keil), the last appointed time when "the kingdom of the world has become the kingdom of our Lord and of his Christ, and he will reign for ever and ever" (Rev. 11:15; NIV). Then the application of the principles of the inscribed revelation will be seen to have been operative all along, a witness to God's just handling of history.

Because the appointed time lay in the future, it might seem to be delayed or perhaps postponed indefinitely (cf. 2 Pet. 3:3-4). If it seemed to tarry long, Habakkuk and all heralds were to wait patiently for its coming, for it would surely come. So it has been with all subsequent Habakkuks and heralds. As Craigie points out, each believer must keep in mind that God's time is not man's time:

> Just as, in human life, the timing of certain actions and events is of crucial importance, so it is also in the divine scheme of things. . . . The apparent lack of divine action, which may cause faith to falter, is in reality only our inability to perceive the timing of divine action. We must

---

4. C. L. Feinberg, *The Minor Prophets* (Chicago: Moody, 1976), p. 211.

try to learn Habakkuk's lesson: "If it seem slow, wait for it; it will surely come, it will not delay" (verse 3).[5]

Additional Notes

2:2 †For חָזוֹן ("vision") see the exposition of Nah. 1:1. Armerding observes that this noun is "almost invariably supersensory in nature," hence follows NIV in translating it "revelation."[6] The divine command to inscribe the חָזוֹן for all to see supports this idea; therefore to translate "Read the revelation" would not be inappropriate.

וּבָאֵר . . . כְּתוֹב ("write . . . and make plain") can be treated as hendiadys: "Write the vision plainly." The traditional translation, however, may be more emphatic: "Write . . . and (be sure to) make it plain." The second imperative may refer either to the clarity of the understanding of the message or to its legibility. The accompanying reference to the writing material favors the latter.

הַלֻּחוֹת ("the *tablets*"): Ewald suggests that the *tablets* in question were customarily erected in marketplaces. Such tablets were set up so that public notices could be written on them. Similarly, Laetsch proposes that these tablets might have been erected in any public place, including locations along highways or in temple courts. Keil and Delitzsch think that the reference is general, the definite article referring to the particular tablets that Habakkuk was to inscribe. Though this observation is valid, Laetsch's point concerning the erection of tablets has the advantage of historical parallel (cf. 1 Macc. 14:25-49). For other scriptural examples of the motif of revelation inscribed on tablets, see Isa. 8:1; 30:8; Jer. 17:1.

As for יָרוּץ ("he may run"), J. M. Holt suggests that this part of the command be taken metaphorically, the running being understood as living obediently (cf. Ps. 119:32; 1 Cor. 9:24-27; Phil. 3:13-14).[7] This proposal again raises the question of whether the command to write the revelation is to be understood literally or figuratively. The traditional interpretation takes the command to be literal and assumes that its main purpose is that of preserving (Armerding) or disseminating (Laetsch) the message. Keil opts for a figurative understanding, proposing that all of the passages dealing with prophetic activity and the writing on tablets are also to be understood figuratively:

> We therefore prefer the figurative view, just as in the case of the command issued to Daniel, to shut up his prophecy and seal it (Dan. xii.4), inasmuch as the literal interpretation of the command, especially of the

---

5. P. C. Craigie, *Twelve Prophets* (Philadelphia: Westminster, 1985), 2:92-93.
6. Armerding, "Habakkuk," in *EBC*, 7:511.
7. J. M. Holt, "So He May Run Who Reads It," *JBL* 83 (1964): 301.

last words, would require that the table should be set up or hung out in some public place, and this cannot for a moment be thought of. The words simply express the thought, that the prophecy is to be laid to heart by all the people on account of its great importance, and that not merely in the present, but in the future also.[8]

Whether literal or figurative, certainly all of the emphases that the commentators have suggested are true to the test. The message is to be clearly understood, assimilated, preserved, and propagated. The imagery of running suggests that even the most hurried passerby may see and quickly understand it (S. R. Driver) and then herald its message to others. The idea of tablets brings to mind the lasting quality and applicability of a message that is geared for an "appointed time" (v. 3).

2:3 †For MT עוֹד ("yet"), read עֵד ("witness").

†לֹא יְכַזֵּב . . . יָפֵחַ ("testifies . . . will not prove false"). The translation proposed here (cf. NIV) follows the lead of Janzen, who cites the evidence of Proverbs (Prov. 6:19; 12:17; 14:5, 25; 19:5, 9), where יפח is used in connection with the speaking of truth or falsehood.[9] In all but one of these (Prov. 12:17) it occurs in combination with כָּזָב. Common to these contexts also is the appearance of עֵד, giving a strong presumption for its reading here in the first line of the verse as suggested in the previous note.

Further support for all this comes from M. Dahood, who finds another parallel between עֵד and יפח in Ps. 27:12 that he relates to Ugaritic *yph*, "witness," "testifier."[10] Both Dahood and Janzen take *yph* as a noun rather than from פּוּחַ ("blow," "breathe") in all of the suggested instances as well as here, but the parallel with יְכַזֵּב argues strongly for a verbal form meaning "to speak" (cf. KJV, NIV), hence "testify/bear witness to." Certainly this yields a better explanation than the traditional "pants for the end" (Keil, Laetsch) or "hastens" (NASB, RSV), which seem out of place in light of the following admonition concerning tarrying.

מוֹעֵד (*"appointed time"*) is commonly used to refer to a determined time or place, its specific reference depending on context. Although it occurs in Daniel in an eschatological setting (e.g., Dan. 11:35) in

---

8. C. F. Keil, *The Twelve Minor Prophets*, COT (Grand Rapids: Eerdmans, 1954). 2:70.

9. J. G. Janzen, "Habakkuk 2:2-4 in the Light of Recent Philological Advances," HTR 73 (1980): 58-78; see also W. H. Ward, *A Critical and Exegetical Commentary on Habakkuk*, ICC (Edinburgh: T. and T. Clark, 1911), p. 14 n.

10. M. Dahood, *Psalms*, AB (Garden City, N.Y.: Doubleday, 1970), 1:169.

parallel (as here) with קֵץ ("end"), such does not prejudge a messianic interpretation for this verse (see next additional note).[11]

†כִּי־בֹא יָבֹא ("for it will come"): The LXX makes the subject to be masc. sing., whereas the noun ὅρασις that translates the subject (MT חָזוֹן) is fem. sing. This is usually understood to indicate that the translators of the LXX intended a messianic understanding here: "Wait for him, for he will surely come."[12] Corroboration of this opinion is usually sought in the citation of the LXX by the writer to the Hebrews (Heb. 10:37-38) to prove his argument concerning the need for believers to persevere in their righteous service, keeping in mind Christ's certain return.

Two matters need to be pointed out, however: (1) The author of Hebrews has changed the LXX ἐρχόμενος ἥξει ("he/it will surely come") into ὁ ἐρχόμενος ἥξει ("he who comes," or "the coming one shall come"). (2) The antecedent of the masc. sing. pronoun αὐτόν ("he/it") could be the LXX's previous masc. sing. noun καιρὸν ("appointed time"). Thus the LXX translation of v. 3 could have intended,

> Because the vision is yet for an *appointed time*,
>   and it will appear at length and not in vain;
> if *it* is late, wait for *it*,
>   for *it* will surely come, *it* will not delay.[13]

Although the messianic application of the text of the LXX by the writer of Hebrews may be a proper interpretation, nevertheless the freedom with which the NT writers employed the text of the LXX to frame their arguments calls for caution in finding an overt messianic reference in the LXX at this point.[14]

---

11. For a good discussion of the manifold uses of the term, see J. P. Lewis, "יָעַד," *TWOT* 1:387-89; G. Sauer, "יעד," *THAT* 1:742-46.
12. See Armerding, "Habakkuk," in *EBC*, 7:512; F. F. Bruce, *The Epistle to the Hebrews*, NICNT (Grand Rapids: Eerdmans, 1964), pp. 272-74; B. F. Westcott, *The Epistle to the Hebrews* (Grand Rapids: Eerdmans, 1955), pp. 347-48.
13. Nigel Turner points out that masculine pronouns can follow antecedents of other genders, so that a reference here to "vision" (ὅρασις) is not impossible; for details, see J. H. Moulton, W. F. Howard, and N. Turner, *A Grammar of New Testament Greek* (Edinburgh: T. and T. Clark, 1976), 3:312. My colleague and Septuagintal scholar Brent Sandy advises me in a personal communication that "gender differences between pronouns and antecedents are common in Greek and rarely indicative of theological importance. Since ὅρασις is separated from the αὐτόν and ἐρχόμενος by several phrases including nouns in the masculine and neuter, all of which are partially synonymous with the ὅρασις, the author is most likely enlarging the antecedents of αὐτόν to include all of the above."
14. See H. M. Shires, *Finding the Old Testament in the New* (Philadelphia:

175

†יֶאֱחַר ("be late," translating *ad sensum*):[15] The verb is placed so as to be arranged chiastically with "if it tarries" in the previous line, but the usual translation of the verb as "remain behind," "tarry/delay" appears to be at variance with the sentiment of the line. Indeed, "be late" is a related nuance and is attested for this root elsewhere in Semitic.[16]

†וְלֹא ("*and* [will] not"): The translation adopted here follows the reading of LXX, Pesh., Vg, *Tg. Neb.*, and 1QpHab.

2. GUIDING PRINCIPLES (2:4)

Habakkuk now is told the basic guiding principles upon which the operation of divine government unalterably proceeds until the coming of that final appointed time.[17] The revelation of these truths will make clear the culpability of the Chaldeans (v. 5), whose woe is pronounced in the rest of the chapter (vv. 6-20).

Westminster, 1974), pp. 24-26; J. W. Wenham, *Christ and the Bible* (Downers Grove, Ill.: InterVarsity, 1972), pp. 95-97. This is not to say that the writer to the Hebrews has misused the OT text, for God's appointed time is centered in the Messiah whether or not the LXX is a clear messianic text. Thus Keil (*Minor Prophets*, 2:70-71) remarks: "This goal was the end . . . towards which it hastened, *i.e.* the 'last time,' . . . the Messianic times, in which the judgment would fall upon the power of the world." Further, the contexts of Hebrews and Habakkuk are analogous. As Richard Milligan (*Epistle to the Hebrews*, vol. 9 of *The New Testament Commentary* [Cincinnati: Central Book Concern, 1879], pp. 293-94) observes, it appears "that our author finds in the prophecy of Habakkuk, concerning the overthrow of the Chaldean monarchy, language so very appropriate to his purpose that he here takes and applies it as his own; thereby showing that the two cases are very analogous . . . but as is usual in such cases of accommodation (see Rom. x. 6-8), he so modifies the language as to adapt it to the case in hand. The main lesson is, however, the same in both Hebrews and Habakkuk; viz.: that God would certainly come and execute his purposes at the appointed time: and that while the proud and self-reliant would of necessity perish under the righteous judgments of God, the just man's faith, if it wavered not, would certainly support him under the severest trials." Moreover, the author of Hebrews' handling of the passage may not be unprecedented, for G. Lünemann ("Critical and Exegetical Handbook to the Epistle to the Hebrews," in *Meyer's Commentaries on the New Testament* [Edinburgh: T. and T. Clark, 1882], p. 315) reports that the later Jewish theologians interpreted it as messianic.

15. See also R. Smith, *Micah–Malachi*, WBC (Waco, Tex.: Word, 1984), p. 105.
16. See D. Cohen, *Dictionnaire des racines Sémitiques* (Paris: Mouton, 1970), p. 15; *CAD* "A," 1:170.
17. W. C. Kaiser, Jr. (*Toward an Old Testament Theology* [Grand Rapids: Zondervan, 1978], p. 81), lists Hab. 2:4 as one of nine passages in the OT that record some 25 principles of morality recognized by the Jewish community.

Translation

**Behold,* the one whose desires are not upright is arrogant,
but the just will live* by his faith(fulness).**[18]

Exegesis and Exposition

God informs Habakkuk of the characteristic makeup of the wicked.[19] The latter's basic problem is an underlying selfishness that
shows itself in an arrogant and presumptuous attitude.[20] Rejecting
God, in his conceit he gives vent to affections not in line with God's
revealed standards. Therefore, it can be said that what he desires is
not upright.

The word "upright" comes from a root used of being or going
straight (cf. 1 Sam. 6:12), then of being or doing right (1 Chron. 13:4).
As a verb or adjective the root is employed in ethical or moral contexts both of God's own inherent righteousness (Deut. 32:4; 25:8; etc.)
and that of his followers who, because they fear God (Job 1:1, 8), are
declared to be upright in heart (2 Chron. 29:34; Pss. 7:10 [HB 7:11];
32:11; 36:10 [HB 36:11]; 94:15; 97:11; Prov. 11:6). Such persons conduct their lives doing what is right in God's sight (Ex. 15:26; Deut.
6:18; 12:28; 13:18; etc.).

While the upright pursue the path of righteousness before God,
the case is different with the wicked. Such individuals refuse God's
instruction and lordship and seek to gratify their own desires (Prov.
12:15; 21:8, 29; 29:27).[21]

The basic OT teaching concerning this root comes through here
also in Habakkuk: Spiritually, morally, and ethically the ungodly
presumptuously ignore the path of God's righteousness to follow the
way of selfish desires in the everyday decisions of life. There is a
distinct contrast when one considers the upright man. Because of his
righteousness (cf. Gen. 15:6; Isa. 61:10), he lives out his life in faith as
well as in faithfulness to God and His commandments. In an ultimate
sense, he alone really lives. As Delitzsch remarks:

> It is not the sincerity, trustworthiness, or integrity of the righteous man,
> regarded as being virtues in themselves, which are in danger of being

---

18. Justification for the translation given here and a full discussion of the
    data essential for the Exegesis and Exposition may be found in the Excur-
    sus on Habakkuk 2:4 found at the end of this chapter.
19. For the possibility that the text originally contained the word "wicked,"
    see n. 14 in the Excursus on Habakkuk 2:4.
20. For selfishness as the essential principle of sin, see A. H. Strong,
    Systematic Theology (Philadelphia: Judson, 1907), p. 567.
21. See further D. J. Wiseman, "יָשַׁר," *TWOT* 1:417-18; G. Liedke, "ישׁר," *THAT*
    1:790-94. See also R. Richards, "What Is Right?" *Bible Translator* 27
    (1976): 220-24.

shaken and giving way in such times of tribulation, but, as we may see in the case of the prophet himself, his *faith*. To this, therefore, there is appended the great promise expressed in the one word יִחְיֶה.[22]

Such is ever the case. By being reminded of this truth, Habakkuk can be assured that God follows a just principle of dealing with men and nations in accordance with their relationship to Him and His standards. Further, Habakkuk can be certain that God has abandoned neither that firm and fair rule nor the activities connected with being God. Is Habakkuk worried that those who are treacherous and wicked will consume those who are more righteous than they? Because God is a punisher of the godless and rewarder of life for the righteous, it is enough for Habakkuk to let God be God and live in humble trust in Him.[23] Laetsch says it well:

> Do not ask why I am using the wicked Chaldean to punish My people, righteous through faith. Leave that to Me, the all-wise God, who rules every detail of your entire life for your temporal and eternal welfare. Remain faithful, trust Me, and you shall live![24]

Additional Notes

2:4 †הִנֵּה ("lo/behold"): This particle is often used to introduce a new section or thought. As noted in the Excursus on Habakkuk 2:4, it can often be followed by אַף כִּי ("further") to form an *argumentum a fortiori*: "if . . . how much more." Such seems to be the literary purpose here (see additional note to 2:5).

Because of the difficulties inherent in v. 4, some have suggested that הִנֵּה is to be treated in a different way, as for example a noun with a definite article (הַנֶּה, *hannâ*, "the eminent man"[25]) or by combining it with the following verb as a niphal participle (הַנֶּעֱלָה).[26] But the juxtaposition of הִנֵּה . . . . אַף כִּי in succeeding sentences makes such attempts tenuous at best.

†יִחְיֶה† ("[the just/righteous] will live"): E. B. Smick emphasizes that for the OT believer faith was a totality of all of man's being and experiences, including the spiritual dimension. Accordingly a man's quality of life "is decided by a right relationship to the righteous standards of the Word of God." Thus it can be safely said, "By cleaving to God, the righteous have life (Hab. 2:4; cf. Amos 5:4, 14; Jer. 38:20)."[27]

---

22. Keil, *Minor Prophets*, 2:74.
23. M. J. Erickson (*Christian Theology* [Grand Rapids: Baker, 1984], 2:580) warns that sin has at its core a "failure to let God be God."
24. T. Laetsch, *The Minor Prophets* (Saint Louis: Concordia, 1956), p. 332.
25. P. J. M. Southwell, "A Note on Hab 2:4-5," *JTS* 19 (1968): 616-17.
26. So K. Budde, as cited by Ward, *Habakkuk*, p. 14 n.
27. E. B. Smick, "חָיָה," *TWOT* 1:280.

3. SPECIFIC APPLICATIONS (2:5-20)

The Lord now answers Habakkuk's perplexity. Building on the principles of his righteous government just revealed (v. 4), he applies them to the case of the unrighteous Chaldean. He begins with a description of the life situation of the arrogant one, a depiction that refers to the Chaldean (v. 5). Because the desires of the Chaldean are not upright, his judgment will ultimately come. A series of five woes, given in the form of the ancient taunt song, further describes the unrighteous character of the Chaldean, for which he will one day be judged (vv. 6-20).

a. The case of the Chaldeans (2:5)

Translation

Indeed*, presumption* betrays an impetuous* man,
  and he is never at rest*,
so that he enlarges his desire* like Sheol*
  and like death he is never satisfied;
he gathers to himself all the nations
  and collects to himself all the peoples.

Exegesis and Exposition

Utilizing the divine pronouncement (v. 4) and building on its principles, God's answer takes the form of an *argumentum a fortiori:* If it is true that the arrogant have ungodly desires and so, unlike the righteous, never come to enjoy the blessings of God, how much more certain is it that the qualities that accompany such an attitude will ultimately betray them!

In his sinful arrogance the wicked is betrayed by presumption. In his impetuousness he is ever restless, so that his selfish ambitions foster an unholy desire toward everyone and everything. So insatiable is his greed that it can be compared to the uncontrollable appetite of death, here personified as a voracious monster. As death and the grave continue their never-ending quest to swallow up life (until they in turn are conquered by the Life-giver, Hos. 13:14; 1 Cor. 15:55-57), so the Chaldean will swallow up all before him. In his aggression and expansion he will gather all nations and peoples under his control. Nevertheless, the underlying implication is clear: the Chaldean's selfishness and success will prove to be his undoing.

The Lord's words refer to Habakkuk's fears and reaffirm his earlier description of the Chaldeans (1:9). The Lord does not minimize the coming danger. What Habakkuk must see, however, is that given the Lord's principles of dealing with men, He will surely allow the Chaldeans to seal their own doom. As a just God He will ultimately deal with such an unrighteous nation, whose "desire is not upright in him," as it deserves.

Additional Notes

2:5 וְאַף כִּי† ("indeed"): The compound particle is employed by Habakkuk to stand in syntactic relation to the הִנֵּה of the divine pronouncement (v. 4) in order to form an *argumentum a fortiori*.[28] Laetsch observes that it "is most frequently used to introduce a climax, advancing from the lesser to the greater, 'how much more,' or an anti-climax, 'how much less.' "[29]

הַיַּיִן† (lit. "the wine"): The sudden introduction of wine as a betrayer has been questioned by many. Although some see here a reference to one of the sins that contributed to the demise of the Chaldeans,[30] other solutions have been put forward. One suggestion was made by Emerton, who proposed repointing the MT to הוֹן ("wealth"), a reading found in 1QpHab.[31] It is difficult, however, to see how wealth is more suitable to the context than wine. Houtsma[32] proposed reading הַזֵּן or הַיָּן ("proud man/presumptuous one"), while A. S. van der Woude[33] postulated a verbal form יָהִין or הֵיֵן. This idea is attractive in that the verb הוּן ("be light," hence in a derived stem probably "make light of," "presume") occurs in Deut. 1:41 where it replaces the verb עָפַל (cf. Hab. 2:4) in the earlier parallel text of Num. 14:44.

Although van der Woude's suggestion struggles with other features of vv. 4-5, Houtsma's view is both simple and contextually sound. (1) It allows the word in question to relate naturally to the following participle. (2) It anticipates the thought of its object, the impetuous man. (3) It finds support in some manuscripts of the LXX that read κατοιόμενος ("conceited").[34] (4) The rarity of an original reading הוּן here best explains a shift to the more familiar "wine" in

---

28. For details, see BDB, p. 65.
29. Laetsch, *Minor Prophets*, p. 301. Keil (*Minor Prophets*, 2:74) points out that "in the present instance it adds a new and important feature to what is stated in ver. 4a."
30. Thus Keil (*Minor Prophets*, 2:74-75) observes: "The application to the Chaldaean is evident from the context. The fact that the Babylonians were very much addicted to wine is attested by ancient writers."
31. See, e.g., J. A. Emerton, "The Textual and Linguistic Problems of Habakkuk II.4-5," *JTS* 28 (1977): 6-8.
32. M. T. Houtsma, "Habakuk II, vs. 4 en 5 verbeterd," *Theologisch Tijdschrift* 19 (1885): 180-83.
33. A. S. van der Woude, "Habakkuk 2:4," *ZAW* 82 (1970): 281-82.
34. Whereas Emerton declares that the κατοιόμενος constitutes an inner LXX corruption from an original κατοινωμένος, Brownlee decides for its originality here. See Emerton, "Textual Problems," pp. 1, 9; Brownlee, "Placarded Revelation," p. 324.

both the MT and majority of the manuscripts of the LXX, as well as the appearance of "wealth" in 1QpHab.[35] (5) It finds support in the parallel term עֻפְּלָה ("arrogant") in the argumentation of vv. 4-5. Indeed, the probability of the reflection of two rare roots drawn from parallel Pentateuchal passages (עפל, Num. 14:44; הון, Deut. 1:41) in one context is so unlikely that their appearance here is striking.

Though a plausible case can be made for the MT "wine," Houtsma's view is provisionally adopted here. Thus I suggest reading הַיַן/הַן in the sense of "presumption." So understood it forms an appropriate parallel with "arrogant" in v. 4 and provides a suitable flow to the rest of the sentence: "Presumption betrays an impetuous man."

†יָהִיר ("impetuous"): This adjective occurs elsewhere only in Prov. 21:24, where it is parallel to זֵד ("proud/insolent"). It is rendered by the LXX as καταφρονητής ("contemptuous") and by the Pesh. as marāḥā' ("willful," "presumptuous," "headstrong"). Coupled with גֶּבֶר ("man") and the following phrases it yields a picture of a strong-willed man whose presumption knows no rest, so that in his greed he enslaves all who come in contact with him. The choice of גֶּבֶר rather than other possible words for man is doubtless deliberate, emphasizing his personal strength, both physical and psychological.[36]

†וְלֹא יִנְוֶה ("he is never at rest"): The verb here is a hapax legomenon, its meaning being variously assigned chiefly on the basis of the related noun נָוֶה ("meadow/pasture") and the adjective נָוֶה ("dwelling/abiding") as well as by contextual constraints. Thus the NASB (cf. KJV, NKJV) renders it "He does not stay at home," the NJB reads "He is forever on the move," and R. Smith favors "He shall not survive."[37] The translation adopted here follows the NIV in the sense of "never takes pasture," hence "is not at rest." Possessed of a consuming ambition, the wicked is always on the move, never settling down.

†שְׁאוֹל ("Sheol"): The rendering given above (cf. NASB, NJB) transliterates the MT without implication regarding its relation to the afterlife. The word has been variously translated here as either "grave" (NIV), "death" (KJV), "hell" (NKJV), or "underworld" (LXX, Vg). The variations reflect the wide differences of opinion among OT

---

35. For the preference of the more difficult reading and the adoption of the reading that best explains the other(s), see E. Würthwein, *The Text of the Old Testament*, 4th ed. (Grand Rapids: Eerdmans, 1979), pp. 116-19; C. E. Armerding, *The Old Testament and Criticism* (Grand Rapids: Eerdmans, 1983), pp. 125-27.

36. See further R. Girdlestone, *Synonyms of the Old Testament* (Grand Rapids: Eerdmans, 1956), pp. 52-54; H. Kosmala, "גֶּבֶר," *TDOT* 2:377-82.

37. R. Smith, *Micah–Malachi*, p. 105. Among the many other suggestions of the expositors may be noted that of George Zemek, Jr. ("Interpretive Challenges Relating to Habakkuk 2:4b," *GTJ* 1 [1980]: 62): "He will not be successful."

scholars as to the concept of the afterlife in OT times and the semantic range of this word. At the very least the meaning "grave" (cf. Gen. 37:35; Ps. 16:10; Hos. 13:14) and "place of the (wicked) dead" (Pss. 49:14 [HB 49:15]; 55:15 [HB 55:16]) are established for the OT, whatever one may believe as to the concept of an OT netherworld much like that found in the literature of Israel's neighbors. I am personally convinced that Israel did not share the pagan concept of an underworld for all souls, nor did it espouse the so-called "two-compartment theory" that developed in intertestamental Judaism and the early church. That the OT teaches that at death believers could expect to live in the presence of God seems evident from the following texts: Job 14:14-15; 19:23-27; Pss. 16:10-11; 17:15; 49:14-15 (HB 49:15-16); 73:23-28; Dan. 12:2.[38]

If one were to choose a specific translation (rather than transliterating the word), the parallel with "death" in the following line would favor the NIV's "grave" (cf. Hos. 13:14 with 1 Cor. 15:54-56; see also Isa. 28:15, 18; Ps. 6:5 [HB 6:6]). Indeed, the deliberate use of gender-matched parallelism here to express merismus indicates that such is probably the author's intent.[39] The greed of the wicked Chaldean is thus linked to the eventuality of death and the grave.

†נַפְשׁוֹ ("his desire"): נֶפֶשׁ is variously translated here in the English versions as "appetite" (NASB, NJB), "greed" (RSV; cf. NIV), and "desire" (KJV, NKJV). In other contexts נֶפֶשׁ appears to refer to "throat" (Ps. 106:15) or "neck" (Pss. 57:6 [HB 57:7]; 69:1 [HB 69:2]) as well as to "soul" (Ps. 16:10) or "life" (Ps. 38:12 [HB 38:13]) or as a possible equivalent of a personal pronoun (Ps. 54:4, 5 [HB 54:5, 6]).[40] At times it seems to represent the whole person (Lev. 17:10), so B. Waltke may well be correct in deciding that "*nephesh* means the whole self, a unity of flesh, will and vitality."[41]

The translating of נֶפֶשׁ as "desire" in vv. 4-5 is an attempt to select a meaning suitable for both verses. The broad semantic range of this word, however, may indicate that all attempts to be overly precise with the meaning of נֶפֶשׁ are unnecessary.

---

38. See further Alexander Heidel, *The Gilgamesh Epic and Old Testament Parallels* (Chicago: U. of Chicago, 1963), pp. 176-223; R. L. Harris, "שְׁאוֹל," *TWOT* 2:892-93; R. L. Harris, "The Meaning of the Word Sheol as shown by Parallels in Poetic Passages," *JETS* 4 (1961): 129-35; W. G. T. Shedd, *Dogmatic Theology* (Grand Rapids: Zondervan, [n.d.]), 2:594-640; John Lightfoot, *A Commentary on the New Testament from the Talmud and Hebraica: Matthew—I Corinthians* (Grand Rapids: Baker, 1979), 3:165-72.
39. For the employment of gender-matched parallelism, see W. G. E. Watson, *Classical Hebrew Poetry* (Sheffield: JSOT Press, 1986), p. 125.
40. See H. W. Wolff, *Anthropology of the Old Testament* (Philadelphia: Fortress, 1981), pp. 10-25.
41. B. Waltke, "נֶפֶשׁ," *TWOT* 2:589.

נֶפֶשׁ serves as a stitch-word with the previous declaration of v. 4 and is repeated in v. 10. Other words/terms found in v. 5 that occur later in this section include שָׁבַע (v. 16) and the terms "nations" and "peoples" (vv. 6-8, 13).[42]

b. The first woe: The plundering Chaldean will be despoiled (2:6-8)

Habakkuk now divulges the divine estimation of the Chaldean. He gives that information in a series of woes recorded in the form of the ancient taunt song, which may be analyzed in terms of the following standard elements: invective, threat, and reason for the condemnation (see chart on p. 184).

Translation

**Will not all of them* take up a taunt song* against him with
   ridicule* and riddles* for him? They will say,
"Woe to him who realizes increase with what is not his—for how
   long?—
   and makes himself wealthy by extortion*!
[7]Will not your creditors* rise up suddenly
   and your collectors* awaken,
   and you will become spoil for them?
[8]Because you have plundered* many nations,
   all the remainder of peoples will plunder you,
   because of the shedding of human blood
   and the violence against lands, cities,
   and all who inhabit them."**

Exegesis and Exposition

The Lord informs Habakkuk that all of the nations and peoples gathered into the Chaldeans' net of conquest will take up songs against them. Using words drawn from the repertoire of wisdom literature, Habakkuk predicts the threat against the Chaldeans by means of "taunt song," "ridicule," and "riddle." All three terms indicate that the Chaldeans' former client kingdoms and victims will one day cast the Chaldeans' once-proud boasts and claims back in their teeth with cleverly devised words intended to mock them.

Each of the five woes considers one or more of the Chaldeans' sins (see chart). The first woe centers on the Chaldeans' rapacity. The language recalls their multiplying of wealth at the expense of others. Their far-reaching conquests are amply documented. After their victories over the Assyrians at Carchemish in 605 B.C., capped by their

---

42. In addition, if "wine" is to be retained in v. 5, it may anticipate the denunciation concerning drinking in vv. 15-16.

Habakkuk's Five Woes (2:6-20)

ELEMENT	1st	2d	3d	4th	5th
Invective: Woe to the:	v. 6 Plunderer	v. 9 Plotter	v. 12 Pillager	v. 15 Perverter	v. 19a Polytheist
Threat: He will be:	v. 7 Despoiled	v. 11 Denounced	v. 13 Destroyed	v. 16 Disgraced	v. 19b Deserted
Criticism: Grounded in:	v. 8 Spoiling of the nations	v. 10 Scheming against peoples	v. 14 Surety of the knowledge of God	v. 17 Stripping of man/nature	vv. 18, 20 Supremacy of God

push down the Mediterranean coast after the fleeing Egyptians (the Assyrians' supporters at Carchemish), the Chaldeans soon became masters of all Syro-Palestine. Other campaigns led Nebuchadnezzar to Asia Minor, Egypt (cf. Ezek. 29:19-21), and Arabia (cf. Jer. 49:28). Eventually the whole southern portion of the once-vast Assyrian empire lay under Chaldean control. The eagerness of the Chaldeans to take captive men and material wealth is often recorded in the Babylonian Chronicles. The following citations are typical:

> All the kings of the Hatti-land came before him and he received their heavy tribute.
> He marched to the city of Askelon and captured it in the month of Kislev.
> He captured its king and plundered it and carried off [spoil from it . . . . . .]
> In the sixth year in the month of Kislev the king of Akkad mustered his army and marched to the Hatti-land. From the Hatti-land he sent out his companies,
> and scouring the desert they took much plunder from the Arabs, their possessions, animals and gods. In the month of Adar the king returned to his own land.[43]

"How long will it go on?" Is the question Habakkuk's own plaintive cry?[44] Most expositors suggest that the question is that of the nations and peoples, perhaps out of a desire for relief from oppression (Keil), maybe out of indignation (Feinberg), or as an expression of sarcasm, the implication of which is "not for long" (Laetsch).[45] Indeed, the proud Neo-Babylonian empire would last for less than a hundred years (626-539 B.C.), its demise occurring within a generation after the death of its greatest king, Nebuchadnezzar II, in 562 B.C.

The depth of the Chaldeans' insensitivity toward others may be seen in that they add to their riches by extorting pledges from their debtors. Though such behavior would be particularly offensive to the people of Judah because it was condemned in the Torah, it would also be a violation against all mankind (cf. Job 24:3, 9-10). In any case, the charge is but an example of the Chaldeans' unjust activities and provides entrée into the following metaphor taken from the world of finance.

---

43. D. J. Wiseman, *Chronicles of Chaldaean Kings* (London: The Trustees of the British Museum, 1956), pp. 69, 71; see further H. W. F. Saggs, *The Greatness That Was Babylon* (New York: Hawthorn, 1962), pp. 134-53.
44. Instances of such exclamatory interruptions are not without scriptural precedent; see Judg. 5:21; Neh. 5:19; Joel 3:11 (HB 4:11).
45. G. A. Smith (*The Book of the Twelve Prophets*, rev. ed. [Garden City, N.Y.: Doubleday, 1929], 2:146 n. 3) deems it an intrusion by a later editorial hand.

Verse 7 reveals that those who had been so oppressed as to have even their basic necessities of life, given in honest pledge, confiscated by their Chaldean creditors now themselves become creditors. Because the Chaldeans took advantage of the nations through conquest and extortion, they will owe the nations a great deal. Thus the Chaldeans will accumulate a debt that must be repaid. One day the debt will be recalled, the nations arising suddenly and "calling in their loans." They will send collectors who will press their claims for back payment with a force equal to that of the Chaldeans' former violence. Because the term "creditors" (נשְׁכִים, *nōšĕkîm*) is related to the word for "interest" (נֶשֶׁךְ, *nešek*), Keil suggests that "there would come upon the Chaldaean those who would demand back with interest . . . the capital of which he had unrighteously taken possession, just as he had unmercifully taken the goods of the nations from them by usury and pawn."[46] Whether or not this idea is present, the law of just retribution would be applied.

The suddenness of calling in the debt predicted here came to pass. Although the Persian King Cyrus the Great spent the early days of his reign securing the subservience of neighboring peoples, he would one day be ready to move swiftly. His conquest of the Medes in 550 B.C. opened a claim to all the former Median territory, an area that composed the northern portion of the former Assyrian empire. After Lydia fell to Cyrus in 546 B.C., Cyrus quickly subdued all of mainland Asia Minor and the adjacent Greek islands. Within a few short years, then, Cyrus found himself ruler of a territory that included all of the Iranian plateau westward across the northern Fertile Crescent and on to the Greek islands off the coast of Asia Minor. The next strike would take him against the Chaldeans, who capitulated rapidly after the loss of Babylon on October 13, 539 B.C.[47] So great was the relief felt by all in that day that

> Cyrus entered Babylon not as a conqueror but as liberator. The temples were not profaned and the safety of the city was guaranteed. Cyrus took as his title 'King of Babylon, Sumer and Accad, and the four countries of the world'. He went further and claimed to have been chosen by Marduk as is shown in a Babylonian text: 'Marduk gave thought to all the lands, he saw them and sought a righteous king, a king after his own heart

---

46. Keil, *Minor Prophets*, 2:78-79; see also Laetsch, *Minor Prophets*, p. 335.
47. For details, see A. T. Olmstead, *History of the Persian Empire* (Chicago: U. of Chicago, 1948), pp. 34-58. See also Edwin M. Yamauchi, *Persia and the Bible* (Grand Rapids: Baker, 1990), pp. 72-74, 85-89; G. Buchanan Gray, "The Foundation and Extension of the Persian Empire," in CAH, 4:2-14.

whom he would lead by the hand. He called his name Cyrus, king of Anshan! and appointed him to be king over all things'.[48]

R. Ghirshman adds that

> Cyrus presented himself to the Babylonian people not as a conqueror but as a liberator and the legitimate successor to the crown. . . . He restored to their temples all the statues of the gods which Nabonidus had brought into the capital and, at the great New Year Festival, following the custom of the Babylonian kings, he took the hand of the god Bel and by this gesture legalized the new line of Babylonian kings.[49]

Some have found difficulty relating the facts of history to the statement concerning the "remainder of the peoples" who would plunder the Chaldeans. The "remainder" could refer to those "nations that remain" (NJB), either those untouched by Chaldean conquest or those that survived in some fashion. Since the Hebrew word here "always denotes the remnant which is left after the deduction of a portion,"[50] the term probably refers primarily to those peoples and nations within the Neo-Babylonian orbit that escaped annihilation. A reference to the Elamites could also be intended. The Chaldeans' campaigning had included forays against the Elamites, and nominally the Iranian plateau, though unoccupied by the Chaldeans, was part of the Medo-Babylonian alliance. Whatever its referent, the term "remainder" is probably general and is certainly not inappropriate.

The chief point, then, is that the plundering Chaldean will eventually know the effects of plunder himself. He who had so misused others, conquering, looting, and enslaving many, will himself experience the conqueror's heel and learn the sorrow of those whose men and possessions have been carried off as booty.

Habakkuk directs a further charge against the Chaldeans. In their quest for booty they would probably destroy all that was before them, be it country or city or human life itself. Too often they will shed innocent blood for the sake of their uncontrollable lust. Indeed, they will leave a trail of sorrow across the ancient Near East that would be easy to trace. Therefore, they who would shed the blood of so many and violently treat all who stand in their way would be guilty of crimes against all humanity. For that they must suffer the judgment of God. The principles in Obadiah's pronouncement against the Edomites will also take effect against the Chaldeans: "As you have

---

48. A. Parrot, *Babylon and the Old Testament* (New York: Philosophical Library, 1956), p. 121.
49. R. Ghirshman, *Iran* (Baltimore: Penguin, 1954), p. 132.
50. Keil, *Minor Prophets*, 2:79.

done, it will be done to you; your deeds will return upon your own head" (Obad. 15, NIV).

Additional Notes

2:6 †The phrase אֵלֶּה כֻלָּם (lit. "these, all of them") has stirred up controversy among the commentators. R. Smith comes to the crux of the issue:

> There is no antecedent to "these, all of them" in v 6. The "nations" and "peoples" in v 5 seem to be the antecedent. But is it logical for the pagan nations to be pronouncing "woe" on the guilty one in the name of Yahweh of hosts (v 13)? Would the nations speak about the earth being filled with the knowledge of God as waters cover the sea (v 14), or would they condemn the making of idols? Probably not. If the words of the woes are inconsistent in the mouths of the nations how do we explain "these" and "all of them" in v 6?[51]

Smith appears to favor the thought that the woes are the expression of Habakkuk himself (so also Craigie, Freeman) or perhaps of everyone (reading כֻלֹּה for כֻלָּם). F. C. Eiselen opts for Habakkuk, who is putting his words into the mouths of the nations.[52] Keil decides for the true believers among the oppressed peoples, and many (e.g., Feinberg, Hailey, Laetsch, von Orelli; cf. NJB and the note in *The NIV Study Bible*) favor the nations as such. Perhaps the whole matter is somewhat academic, the problem arising chiefly due to the literary demands of the section. Pronounced by God and communicated by His prophet, these words and those that follow will also be on the lips of the nations and peoples who will suffer at the hands of the Chaldeans.

†מָשָׁל ("taunt song"), מְלִיצָה ("ridicule"), and חִידוֹת ("riddles") are words drawn from wisdom literature. The first is a generic term that has many English equivalents. Drawn from the circles of popular wisdom, it most commonly refers to pithy generalizations on common life situations and so is translated "proverb."[53] But it can be used in negative contexts, especially in predictions of doom expressed in a derisive manner, hence a taunt (cf. Isa. 14:4; Mic. 2:4).

Whereas מָשָׁל may intend to teach by drawing comparisons between matters that must be first apprehended if its full implications are to be grasped, the riddle gives instruction through enigma (cf. Judg. 14:12-19).[54] It too can appear in a negative context (cf. Ezek.

---

51. R. Smith, *Minor Prophets*, pp. 110-11.
52. C. Eiselen, *The Minor Prophets* (New York: Eaton and Mains, 1907), p. 488.
53. See further W. McKane, *Proverbs* (Philadelphia: Westminster, 1970), pp. 22-33; A. S. Herbert, "The Parable (*māšāl*) in the Old Testament," *SJT* 7 (1954): 180-96.
54. See H. Torczyner, "The Riddle in the Bible," *HUCA* 1 (1924): 125-49.

17:2-10). מְלִיצָה is a mocking poem or satire destined to heap ridicule on the object of its scorn by allusive discourse.[55] The occurrence of all three words together in Prov. 1:8 in a neutral context demonstrates that all three literary types were familiar tools available to the sage. Here they are brought together to indicate that the Chaldean will be condemned and caricatured by many a cunning remark.

For הוֹי ("woe"), see the additional note on Nah. 3:1. לֹא־לֹו (lit. "not to him," i.e., "not his") is elliptical for "that which is not his." It forms a case of assonance with the chiastically arranged לֹו . . . הֲלוֹא of the previous lines and anticipates the הֲלוֹא of v. 7. Syntactically it serves as the object of הַמַּרְבֶּה, hence the NIV: "piles up stolen goods." עַד־מָתַי ("how long") is parenthetical and is, in a sense, an incompletely formed sentence in its own right.[56]

†עַבְטִיט ("extortion") is a hapax legomenon from the root עבט ("take/give in pledge"), itself usually considered to be denominative from עֲבוֹט ("pledge"; cf. Akkadian ebuṭṭu, "loan").[57]

Strict legislation regulated matters concerning the confiscation of pledges in the OT (cf. Ex. 22:26-27; Deut. 24:6, 10-13 with Job 22:6; 24:3, 9-10) as befitting a benevolent society in covenant relation with God. The violation of such laws was considered to be a grave moral offense (Job 22:6; Amos 2:8).[58] The Chaldean is vilified for the inhumane practice of enriching himself by confiscating things taken in pledge. Keil suggests the presence of a double entendre here based upon the composition of עַבְטִיט from עַב ("clod," "mass") and טִיט ("dirt"). So understood it would symbolize the burden that the Chaldean will place on his victim, or perhaps it indicates the vast real estate the Neo-Babylonian empire will appropriate.[59]

2:7 †נֹשְׁכֶיךָ (lit. "those who bite you" [cf. KJV]; hence, "creditors" [cf. NASB, NJB, NKJV]): Although some prefer the image of debtors who rise up against their creditors (NIV, RSV), a turn in the thought appears more likely here, the trope being that of the debtor who,

---

55. Although some have suggested a derivation of מְלִיצָה from מָלַץ ("be slippery"), the more traditional identification with לִיץ/לוּץ ("scorn") seems assured. The suggestion in the *Preliminary and Interim Report on the Hebrew Old Testament Text Project* (New York: United Bible Societies, 1980), 5:357, to render the word "irony" or "enigmatic irony" (taking מְלִיצָה with חִידוֹת), though interesting, may suggest too fixed a literary form.

56. See GKC, par. 147 n. c.

57. See *CAD* "E," p. 20; *AHW*, p. 184b. The LXX hazards a guess *ad sensum* for the entire line: "Make his yoke severely heavy."

58. See J. E. Hartley, "Pledge," *ISBE*, 3:886-87; R. de Vaux, *Ancient Israel* (New York: McGraw-Hill, 1961), pp. 171-72.

59. See Keil, *Minor Prophets*, 2:78; in this he is followed by Armerding, "Habakkuk," in *EBC*, 7:517 (cf. also Pesh., KJV).

because he has been unjustly taken advantage of, has been accumulating an obligation from his creditor. Hence, he now becomes the creditor, one who will violently press his claims through his collectors (מְזַעְזְעִים, lit. "shakers," from זוּעַ, "quake/tremble"), despoiling his former creditors.[60]

2:8 †The verb שָׁלָה ("draw out," "extort") is used as a synonym for שָׁסָה ("spoil") in the previous verse. Accordingly I have translated it "plundered" (cf. NIV, NJB, NKJV, RSV).

c. The second woe: The plotting Chaldean will be denounced (2:9-11)

Translation

"Woe to him who accrues evil gain to his house
   (in order) to set his nest on high,
   (so as) to escape* from the grasp of disaster!*
¹⁰You have plotted shame for your house
   by cutting off many peoples
   and sinning against yourself*.
¹¹Surely stones from the wall will cry out,
   and the wooden rafters* will call back."

Exegesis and Exposition

The second woe underscores the Chaldeans' capacity for cunning schemes against mankind. Building upon the imagery in the first woe, the Chaldean is portrayed as one who achieves wealth through violence and evil means. Used as a verb, the root בצע (*bṣ'*, lit. "cut/break off") means "gain one's end through violence," while as a noun it signifies "gain made by violence." Both occur here together for emphasis (cognate accusative), the picture being further strengthened by the addition of the adjective "evil." A play on the root meaning may be intended: by violently accruing unjust gain for their "house,"* the Chaldeans may have "cut off" their own "house" with evil. If so, the thought anticipates the reason for the Chaldeans' demise given in v. 10.

The verse proceeds with a reference to the Chaldeans' building projects. An implied comparison with the eagle is probably intended. If so, just as an eagle seeks security by building his nest on the uppermost cliffs, so the Chaldeans will raise high—that is, strengthen mightily—their fortifications (cf. Jer. 49:16; Obad. 4). Although Nebuchadnezzar mentions such fortifying work elsewhere, it was particularly true of Babylon, which he enclosed with two massive

---

60. The intention of the original author is nicely portrayed in the syntax here, which employs a suffix-conjugation verb after two previous prefix-conjugation verbs.

walls, the outermost of which was surrounded by a moat on its east side that stretched westward to the Euphrates on the city's northern and southern sides. The words concerning the desire to "escape from the grasp of disaster" are well illustrated in Nebuchadnezzar's chronicles:

> I brought to completion Imgur-Bel, the great wall of Babylon, the city of the great lord Marduk. At the thresholds of the city-gates I stationed strong wild-bulls of bronze, and serpents standing erect. I dug its moat and reached the bottom of the water. I built its bank with bitumen and burned brick. I had the bulwark (?) at the bank of the mighty wall built with bitumen and burned brick, like a mountain, so that it could not be moved.
>
> In order to strengthen the watchtower of Esagila, that the enemy and the destroyer might not approach Babylon, I threw around the city on the outer wall of Babylon a strong wall toward the east. I dug its moat and raised its bank with bitumen and burned brick mountain-high. By the side of Babylon I constructed a dike of great masses of earth, and surrounded it with a mighty stream of many waters like the fulness of the sea, and then I threw a swamp around this. To . . . . . the life of the people of Babylon . . . . . among the cities of Sumer and Akkad I made its name great.[61]

Nebuchadnezzar was proud of Babylon, which he made into one of the most formidable and beautiful cities in the ancient world (cf. Dan. 4:29-30). Upon entering through one of its eight ornamented gates, a visitor was able to travel about the city on wide, well-kept streets. Among the many impressive buildings were dozens of temples and, of course, Nebuchadnezzar's palace. The palace complex was lavishly furnished and enclosed with a wall 136 feet thick. In the outer course of the wall, Nebuchadnezzar had his name inscribed on each brick. The terraced hanging gardens are said to have been located in the northeast angle of the palace complex and were considered in ancient times to be one of the seven wonders of the world. It is understandable, then, that Nebuchadnezzar named his palace "The Marvel of Mankind."[62]

The woe now moves on to reveal the reason for the Chaldean's doom: his constant scheming against others. Keil puts it well: "His determination to establish his house, and make it firm and lofty by evil gain, will bring shame to his house, and instead of honour and lasting glory, only shame and ruin."[63] By cutting off—degrading and

---

61. "The Grotefend Inscription of Nebuchadrezzar II," trans. C. D. Gray, in *Assyrian and Babylonian Literature* (New York: Appleton, 1901), p. 148.
62. For details on ancient Babylon, see E. Yamauchi, "Babylon," in *Major Cities of the Biblical World*, ed. R. K. Harrison (Nashville: Thomas Nelson, 1985), pp. 36-47; D. J. Wiseman, "Babylon," *ISBE*, 1:386-89.
63. Keil, *Minor Prophets*, 2:84.

destroying—many peoples, the Chaldean will sin against himself, sealing his own judgment before God. He too will be cut off forever. As Hailey remarks,

> In "cutting off many peoples" to accomplish his end, he had sinned against his soul. God may use a ruler and nation to accomplish His purpose, but the man will be guilty of his cruel deeds, for he is responsible for the character he developed.[64]

The Chaldean was to have no lasting empire. His arrogant misuse of others and his selfish scheming against them for his own aggrandizement would one day backfire. Even the building materials in the proud city could not be silent. Though men may keep still, they who were mute witnesses to all of the Chaldean's greedy and grandiose plots could not. In a fallen Babylon would lie the collapsed edifice of the Neo-Babylonian empire:

> In the creaking of the beams connecting the "timber," the woodwork of the roof, and in the grating of the cracking stone walls (v. 11), one can hear an awesome dirge, the stones intoning the chant, the beams responding in antiphonal death song, until they also crash down into a heap of ruins and ashes. . . . *Sic transit gloria mundi.*[65]

Additional Notes

2:9 רַע ("evil") is chiastically arranged with its reappearance in the third line. בַּיִת (*"house"*) means here "family" and/or "dynasty."

†לְהִנָּצֵל ("to escape"): The *niphal* infinitive construct may be translated as a direct middle ("save himself," "escape") or as a passive ("be delivered").

†מִכַּף־רָע (lit. "from an evil hand") has been variously rendered *ad sensum* as "hand of calamity" (NASB), "power of disaster/evil" (NKJV, KJV), "clutches of ruin" (NIV), "reach of harm/misfortune" (RSV, NJB). The translation above follows Laetsch's picturesque "grasp of disaster."

2:10 †חוֹטֵא ("sin"): The translation above follows the normal significance of the verb (cf. LXX, KJV, NKJV, NASB). Some, however, point to the metonymy here and translate with the following נַפְשֶׁךָ "forfeiting your life" (cf. NIV, RSV) or paraphrase the line as "You have worked your own ruin" (NJB). The persistent problem of translating נֶפֶשׁ can be seen in the different renditions of the versions: "your soul" (NKJV, cf. KJV), "your life" (NIV), "yourself" (NASB).[66]

2:11 †כָּפִיס מֵעֵץ ("wooden rafters"): כָּפִיס is commonly considered

---

64. H. Hailey, *A Commentary on the Minor Prophets* (Grand Rapids: Baker, 1972), p. 285.
65. Laetsch, *Minor Prophets*, p. 336.
66. See the additional note concerning נֶפֶשׁ at Hab. 2:5.

to be a (main) beam of a building (cf. KJV, NKJV, NIV, NJB, RSV). The NASB, however, proposes "rafters" (cf. KB-3). Since the word is a *hapax legomenon*, its appearance with עֵץ here could conceivably imply any interior use of wood. The above translation notes the correspondence with the "stones from the (outer) walls" of the parallel line as demanding reference to a foundational framework. I have followed the suggestion of the NASB because in ancient Mesopotamia the ceiling needed wood to augment the brick walls. Thus understood, מִן introduces a genitive of material or content (i.e., "rafters made from timbers," hence "wooden rafters").

The importance of wood in Mesopotamian buildings may be seen in Nebuchadnezzar's account of enlarging the palace built by his father Nabopolassar:

> I built a structure of burned brick, and I built very high in its tower a large chamber with bitumen and burned brick for my royal dwelling-place, and joined it to my father's palace, and in a prosperous month, on a favourable day, I firmly laid its foundation in the bowels of the earth, and I raised high its turrets like a mountain. On the fifteenth day I brought to completion its construction, and I beautified the dwelling of my lordship. Mighty cedar trees from the snow-capped mountains, ashuhu trees with broad trunks, and cypress trees (with) costly stones, I laid in rows for its roofing.[67]

d. The third woe: The pillaging Chaldean will be destroyed (2:12-14)

Translation

"Woe to him who builds the city with bloodshed
   and establishes a town by injustice*!
[13]Is it not therefore* from Yahweh Sabaoth
   that people(s) toil for the sake of fire
   and nations exhaust themselves for nothing?
[14]For the earth shall be filled with the knowledge
   of the glory of the Lord,
   as the waters cover the sea.

Exegesis and Exposition

Again the discussion proceeds upon the basis of the previous woe. The image of building found in the second woe is continued in the third. Now the chief materials used in constructing the Neo-Babylonian "house" are seen for what they are: bloodshed and injustice. The Chaldeans are again (cf. v. 8) charged with the wanton shedding of blood. It is a persistent accusation (cf. v. 17). To this is added a notice

---

67. "East India House Inscription of Nebuchadrezzar II," trans. C. D. Gray, in *Assyrian and Babylonian Literature*, pp. 141-42.

of their unrighteousness. The Hebrew word suggests wrongdoing and injustice of all sorts, often taking the form of oppressive, shameful, and sometimes violent acts (cf. 2 Sam. 3:34; Mic. 3:10).[68] Such conduct is an affront to a holy and righteous God (Deut. 32:4) and marks the Chaldeans as those who, unlike the righteous who reflect God's standards, are arrogant and presumptuous. Giving way to impetuousness, they perform acts that are unrighteous.

The Neo-Babylonian inscriptions often attest the Chaldeans' preoccupation with building projects. So dedicated were they to such matters that Nabopolassar compelled his own son to do hard physical labor in the building of Etemenanki, the temple tower of Babylon.[69] Nebuchadnezzar inherited his father's passion for building, and his inscriptions recount many incidents of building projects.[70] On one occasion he proclaimed: "The building of the cities for gods and goddesses, with which the great lord, Marduk, had charged me, and to which he had incited my heart, reverently I did not cease until I finished their construction."[71] R. W. Rogers justly observes: "Nebuchadnezzar based his chief claim to posterity's remembrance upon his great works of building all over Babylonia, but especially in Babylon itself."[72]

Nevertheless, God denounces all of this splendor. He sees the atrocities by which the Chaldeans will aggrandize themselves in building lavishly endowed cities:

> Babylon's magnificent palaces, its costly temples, its grand processional street, aroused the awe and wonder of all visitors, and its mountain-high walls forced upon them the impossibility of conquering this city. Yet the Lord Jehovah was unimpressed by Babylon's strength and grandeur. He saw only the blood of untold numbers of people who were slaughtered in ruthless warfare in order to obtain the means which made these buildings possible. He saw only the iniquity, the perversity, the crookedness of the builders.[73]

---

68. The Hebrew root עוּל has been suggested as an alternative reading for the troublesome עֻפְּלָה of Hab. 2:4; see the Excursus on Habakkuk 2:4.
69. See the "Inscription of Nabopolassar," trans. P. Bruce, in *Assyrian and Babylonian Literature*, pp. 131-33.
70. See the several inscriptions of Nebuchadnezzar II in *Assyrian and Babylonian Literature*, pp. 134-57; see also R. W. Rogers, ed., *Cuneiform Parallels to the Old Testament*, 2d ed. (New York: Abingdon, 1926), pp. 363-64, 368-69.
71. "The Winckler Inscription of Nebuchadrezzar II," trans. C. D. Gray, in *Assyrian and Babylonian Literature*, p. 146. The Neo-Babylonian kings continued to be interested in building projects, particularly in temples. For several reports concerning such enterprises, see "The Stele of Nabonidus," trans. R. F. Harper, in *Assyrian and Babylonian Literature*, pp. 158-63; see also Rogers, *Cuneiform Parallels*, pp. 378-79.
72. Rogers, *Cuneiform Parallels*, p. 363.
73. Laetsch, *Minor Prophets*, p. 337.

As invective turns to threat, Habakkuk records the Lord's rhetorical question: Will not Yahweh Sabaoth see to it that all the toil* and exhausting work* spent on raising great monuments, edifices erected on bloodshed and adorned with the mortar of injustice, will come to nothing? The proud Babylonian cities will know the conqueror's torch and be reduced to emptiness. All that effort will prove to be valueless; being rewarded in the end only by fire,* it will all be in vain. Not only the Chaldean cities but also the Neo-Babylonian empire itself was destined for extinction.

> The city that is built on a foundation of iniquity and constructed at the expense of bloodshed cannot flourish; all will be for nought. Although the prophet refers to the construction of a city, his language is probably metaphorical for the construction of an empire.[74]

Jeremiah's words reinforce those of Habakkuk:

> The arrogant one will stumble and fall
>   and no one will help her up;
> I will kindle a fire in her towns
>   that will consume all who are around her.
> ·
> This is what the LORD Almighty says:
> "Babylon's thick wall will be leveled
>   and her high gates set on fire;
> the peoples exhaust themselves for nothing,
>   the nations' labor is only fuel for the flames."
>   (Jer. 50:32; 51:58, NIV)

Not only for her unbridled arrogance but also because God's purposes include a universal experiencing of His own glory* must Babylon (and all such wicked people) be judged. The words of v. 14 are adapted from Isa. 11:9. Isaiah's prophecy looks ahead to the great messianic era in all its fullness and perfection; Habakkuk uses Isaiah's prophecy to validate the pronouncement of the destruction of the Neo-Babylonian empire. Because the Chaldeans will glorify only themselves and the gods of human manufacture (whose temples they would adorn and maintain), they will scorn the living and true God and rob Him of His worship. If God is to be received fully on earth as in heaven, the earth must be filled "with the knowledge of [His] glory" (v. 14). Isaiah's prophecy is thus personalized for the Chaldeans.

The prophetic words are a reminder that all other glory-seekers shall be silenced that God may have His rightful preeminence (cf. Isa. 48:11). Accordingly God's glory must be accompanied by judgment (cf. Ezek. 39:4-24). Babylon's judgment, then, must come (cf. Isa.

---

74. Craigie, *Twelve Prophets*, 2:98.

13:19), as well as that of all future "Babylons," whom God will destroy (cf. Rev. 17-18) and over whom the Messiah will be victorious at His coming (Ezek. 38-39; Zech. 14:1-5; Rev. 19:11-21).

By God's glory is meant His magnificence. In relation to man, the word is commonly used to depict His self-manifestation by which His inner excellence becomes visible. Further, glory lies behind all of His activities. As Erickson writes, "In the ultimate sense, the purpose of God's plan is God's glory. This is the highest of all values, and the one great motivating factor in all that God has chosen and done."[75] The term is also used of the intrinsic honor that is due Him (Pss. 66:2; 79:9) and that is proper and essential for man to give (Ps. 66:7-8; Jer. 13:16). Thus for the Chaldean to honor self rather than the one God of the universe was to fail to achieve the primary purpose of man (cf. Isa. 42:8; 48:11) and therefore to be culpable before God (cf. 1 Sam. 8:7; 10:17-19; 12:19).

The glory of the Lord that filled the Tabernacle at its inauguration (Ex. 40:34, 35) and the Temple at its dedication (1 Kings 8:10-12), that attended the announcement of Christ's birth (Luke 2:9-14) and is reflected in the lives of believers who have been taken into union with Christ (2 Cor. 3:18) will one day be known and experienced by all (Isa. 59:19) who confess "that Jesus Christ is Lord, to the glory of God the Father" (Phil. 2:11). In light of all of this, Erickson's admonition is fitting:

> If we have fully understood who and what God is, we will see him as the supreme being. We will make him the Lord, the one who is to be pleased, and whose will is to be done. . . . He is the almighty and loving Lord. He has created us, not we him, and we exist for his glory, not he for ours. We will stand before him in the last judgment, not he before us.[76]

Additional Notes

2:12 †עַוְלָה ("injustice," "unrighteousness"): The root also appears as a masculine noun with little or no difference in meaning. Commenting on the masculine noun, Girdlestone remarks: "The word . . . is thought to designate the want of integrity and rectitude which is the accompaniment, if not the essential part, of wrong-doing." He goes on to point out that this noun is also translated "iniquity" in "about

---

75. Erickson, *Christian Theology*, 1:352; elsewhere Erickson says, "As the highest value in the universe, the source from which all else derives, God must choose his own glory ahead of all else. As the only infinite being, this is what he must do. To put something else in the primary place would in effect be a case of idolatry" (p. 288).
76. Erickson, *Christian Theology*, 1:300.

thirty passages" where the stress is upon "a departure from that which is equal and right."[77]

G. H. Livingston portrays something of the viciousness of these words by displaying the company they keep. At times they are parallel to words that are translated "afflict," "bloodshed," "deceitful," "iniquity," "lie," "ruthlessness," "transgression," "treachery," "violent acts," and "wickedness," while serving as antonyms to such nouns as "faithfulness," "honesty," "justice," "righteousness," and "uprightness."[78] Indeed, both the masculine and feminine nouns are clearly distinguished from צֶדֶק and צְדָקָה ("righteous[ness]"; cf. Prov. 29:27). The words, then, depict a moral quality that stands in contrast to the righteous character of God and the standard of behavior expected of His children (cf. Deut. 25:16; 32:4; Zeph. 3:13).

2:13 †The interjection הִנֵּה ("lo/behold"; cf. KJV, NKJV, RSV) is better rendered here as an emphatic particle (NASB) or regarded as a flavoring particle and left untranslated (NIV). Luther, however, is probably on the right track in translating it as an inferential particle: "*Wird's nicht also . . . geschehen?*" ("Will it not therefore come to pass?"). So viewed, the question introduces a solution drawn from the antecedent observations. Because of the Chaldeans' violent acts, will not God see to it that they (or any such nation) will exhaust themselves in vain?

†יהוה צְבָאוֹת ("Yahweh Sabaoth"): This divine title is often rendered "Lord of Hosts." It can also be translated "Lord Almighty."[79]

The synonyms יָגַע and יָעֵף ("*toil*" and "*exhaust oneself*") denote the effort and wearisome effects of hard work. The person so engaged is left with the fatigue that borders on being overcome with fainting. The Scriptures warn against the kind of labor that, like the Chaldeans, strives for wealth as an end in itself (Prov. 23:4).

The synonyms עַמִּים and לְאֻמִּים ("peoples" and "nations") also commonly occur together as parallel terms. Whereas the former speaks of a group of people considered in and of itself (or of people in general), the latter emphasizes the group considered as a whole unit.[80]

2:14 הָאָרֶץ‖ יָם ("the earth"‖ "sea"). M. Dahood proposes these two nouns as set parallel pairs whenever they occur, as here, in chiastic arrangement.[81]

---

77. Girdlestone, *Synonyms*, p. 79.
78. G. H. Livingston, "עוּל," *TWOT* 2:652-54.
79. See further the exposition of Nah. 2:13 and the additional note on 1 Kings 18:15 in R. D. Patterson and H. J. Austel, "1, 2 Kings," in *EBC*, 4:142-43.
80. See further R. L. Harris's note to G. van Groningen, "גוה," *TWOT* 1:153.
81. See also Dahood, *Psalms*, 3:346. For chiasmus functioning as closure to a stanza, see Watson, *Hebrew Poetry*, p. 205.

כָּבוֹד ("*glory*") refers to God's self-manifestation in visible and active presence among men as opposed to God's transcendence, for which יָשַׁב ("he dwelled") was used. Both stand in distinction from *Shekinah,* the late technical term for God's immanence.[82]

e. The fourth woe: The perverting Chaldean will be disgraced (2:15-17)

Translation

**"Woe to him who gives drink to his neighbors,
  pouring out* your wrath* and also* getting them drunk
  so as to look upon their nakedness!
16You will be filled with shame* rather than glory.
  Now, you drink and expose yourself!
The cup* of the LORD's right hand will come around to you,
  and utter disgrace* will cover your glory.
17For the violence you will do to Lebanon will overwhelm you,
  and your destruction of animals will terrify (you)* because of the
    shedding of human blood
  and the violence against lands, cities, and all who inhabit them."**

Exegesis and Exposition

The tie between the third and fourth woes is not as pronounced as between the first and second or the second and third. However, they do have in common a reference to a city (or town, vv. 12, 17). In reviewing the first four woes, an alternating pattern of condemnation may be observed: the first and third woes deal primarily with overt acts, whereas the second and fourth mention motives. The first and fourth woes have in common the phrase "because of the shedding of human blood and the violence against lands, cities, and all who inhabit them" (vv. 8, 17).

The fourth woe begins with an invective formed with a strong metaphor. The Chaldean is a man who gives his neighbor (strong) drink in seeming hospitality. The metaphor quickly gives way to allegory. The apparently innocent cup contains a draught of wrath, for it is designed to get its partaker drunk. Drunkenness is not alone the motive of the untrustworthy friend. Having got his neighbor drunk, he denudes him.

As invective turns to threat (v. 16) the allegory depicts the giver of

---

82. See my remarks in "Joel," in *EBC*, 7:265-66. For helpful discussions of the glory of the Lord, see G. Kittel, "δόξα," *TDNT* 2:233-37; S. Aalen, "Glory, Honour," *The New International Dictionary of New Testament Theology*, ed. Colin Brown (Grand Rapids: Zondervan, 1976), 2:44-48.

the drink as one who is forced to imbibe of his own drink and suffer the disgrace of exposure. Several familiar biblical motifs and expressions are contained in vv. 15-16. The cup as a motif of judgment is well attested elsewhere (e.g., Pss. 11:6; 75:8 [HB 75:9]; Isa. 51:17, 22; Jer. 25:15-28; 49:12; Ezek. 23:31-34). Particularly enlightening for the understanding of Habakkuk's fourth woe is Jeremiah's use of the cup to portray God's relation with Babylon (Jer. 51:6-8). For Jeremiah, Babylon is God's cup, a golden cup (cf. Daniel's head of gold, Dan. 2:36-38), which in God's hand had passed on His judgment to the nations. Those who drink of that cup lose all sense of perspective and become oblivious to the danger they are in. But Babylon will become a broken cup, for she will be smashed and never repaired.

Habakkuk makes the same point, although the image is slightly different. The Chaldean will be God's cup of judgment (cf. 1:5-11), but rather than being conscious of his privileged responsibility, the Chaldean will use his position to take advantage of others and enslave them politically and economically.

The image of shame is heightened by the double figure of drunkenness and nakedness (cf. Gen. 9:21-23). The first is condemned both by our Lord (Luke 21:34) and elsewhere in the Scriptures (e.g., Eph. 5:18). Nakedness is likened to a shameful thing (cf. Gen. 2:25 with 3:7), and he who was stripped of clothing felt degraded (2 Sam. 10:4; Ezek. 16:39; 23:29). Both figures are used elsewhere to symbolize divine judgment (Nah. 3:5, 11). All three symbols occur together in Lam. 4:21 where Jeremiah portrays the Israelites' taunt of Edom. That nation, which had so often taken advantage of Israel's misfortune, will be given the cup of judgment, become drunk, and be stripped naked.

Habakkuk thus points out that the Chaldean will pour out a cup of wrath but in turn will drink it himself. Indeed, he will drink it more deeply. The Chaldean, whose appetite was as unsatisfied as death and the grave (cf. 2:5), will now be satiated. He will have the honor of being God's "cup" of judgment. However, he will seek his own honor and wealth, using his selfishly accumulated booty to build grandiose structures and formidable cities. Accordingly he will now know the shame* he has brought on others. Therefore, he is given a sarcastic command: "Go on! Drink! . . . and expose yourself!" The last imperative is graphic. It means literally "show yourself as uncircumcised." Not even in the marks of his body could the Chaldean claim covenant relationship with Yahweh. Naked and without grounds for leniency, the Chaldean faced certain doom. As Freeman observes, "To be uncircumcised marked one as a Gentile or heathen and outside God's covenant; here it expresses God's utter contempt for Judah's oppressors and indicates the climax of their coming degradation."[83]

The cup* of judgment would now come around to the Chaldean, and his glory would be turned into disgrace.* Habakkuk has so placed this word in the development of his pronouncement that it balances the thought with which the verse began. Filled to overflowing with shame, the Chaldean's glory will be turned to utter disgrace.

The reason for which the Chaldean must drink the cup follows in v. 17. His will be a wanton disregard of the value of the natural world, the animal kingdom, and civilized humanity. Once more the subject of violence surfaces. Habakkuk had complained about the violence all about him (1:2-3), and God had warned him that still greater violence lay ahead (1:9). God had already laid the charge of violence against the Chaldeans (2:8); now he reiterates it with yet another instance of the Chaldeans' ruthless activity.

By the violence done to Lebanon some understand a figurative reference to Israel's own land. Thus Armerding remarks: "'Lebanon' is used as a symbol of Israel (2 Kings 14:9; cf. Jer. 22:6, 23) and more specifically of Israel as a victim of Babylonian aggression (Ezek. 17:3)."[84] But a literal interpretation is not impossible. The Mesopotamian kings had boasted of their exploitation of the forests of Lebanon since the earliest days.[85] Sennacherib tells of dragging cedars from there,[86] as does Nebuchadnezzar.[87] Though uncertainty exists as to the scope of the reference, Lebanon referring more commonly to a region rather than to its cedars, the enumeration of various categories of living things here argues for a veiled reference to the cedars of Lebanon (cf. Judg. 9:15; Isa. 2:13). As such they symbolized the most magnificent and best-known representation of the area's natural world (much as the redwoods do for California). They are personified here as rejoicing over Babylon's demise (cf. Isa. 14:8).

The scene shifts to the animal kingdom. It, too, will suffer violence at the hands of the Chaldeans. The natural and animal worlds are often made unwilling participants in man's sin and greed (cf. Joel 1:19-20; Rom. 8:22). It is a crime that has increasingly plagued human society. Such thoughtless conduct by the Chaldeans indicates again their godless arrogance and selfish presumption for which punishment must come. As Craigie observes, "The prophet indicates

---

83. H. Freeman, *Nahum Zephaniah Habakkuk*, Everyman's Bible Commentary (Chicago: Moody, 1973), p. 113.
84. Armerding, "Habakkuk," in *EBC*, 7:518.
85. See A. Heidel, *Gilgamesh Epic*, pp. 6-7.
86. See *AR*, 2:161-62.
87. See *Assyrian and Babylonian Literature*, pp. 141-42.

that the wanton use of violence against both the human world and the world of nature will return to haunt the perpetrators."[88]

The noun שֹׁד (šōd) is used of great devastation or destruction. It occurs at times with שֶׁבֶר (šeber, "breaking/shattering"; Isa. 51:19; 60:18; Jer. 48:35), such as in depicting the work of evil men (Isa. 59:7). Šōd is also parallel to עָמָל ('āmāl, "trouble") used of the dangers in associating with the wicked (Prov. 24:2). As is the case here, šōd parallels חָמָס (ḥāmās, "violence,") in Ezek. 45:9; Amos 3:10. Jeremiah would later echo Habakkuk's complaint with regard to the social injustice in his country (Jer. 6:7; 20:8). Habakkuk is thus assured that if the agent of God's judgment perpetrates the same wickedness he has been sent to punish, he too must receive the just judgment of God.

The fourth woe is closed with a reiteration of the charge made against the Chaldean in the first. He will have a callous disregard even for the sanctity of human life. In his quest for power he will destroy everything that stands in his way, be it lands, cities, or those who dwell in them. For this the Neo-Babylonian empire would come to know what every divinely employed agent must learn: When carrying out God's will is twisted to selfish advantage, the executor of divine justice must himself be judged (cf. 2 Kings 10:28-31 with Hos. 1:4).[89]

Additional Notes

2:15 †Three main suggestions have been given for the form חֲמָתְךָ ("your wrath"). (1) The translation just given (cf. RSV) takes the noun as חֵמָה ("[burning] anger," "rage," from יָחַם, "be hot"). (2) Some who follow this understanding of the origin of the noun suggest that it should be translated "venom" (NASB) or "poison" (NJB) as in Deut. 32:24; Job 6:4; Ps. 140:4. (3) Others believe that the word intended is חֵמֶת ("wineskin," NIV; cf. KJV, NKJV).[90] In view of the association of drinking, wrath, and cup in the OT (e.g., Isa. 51:17, 22; Jer. 25:15), the first alternative appears to be the best here. Moreover, such a view harmonizes well with a similar picture of Babylon's judgment in Jer. 51:7-8.

---

88. Craigie, *Twelve Prophets*, 2:98.
89. See further my comments and the note on 2 Kings 10:28-32 in "1, 2 Kings," in *EBC*, 4:212, 215, and the extensive discussion of J. G. Botterweck, "בְּהֵמָה," *TDOT* 2:6-12.
90. All three views have been followed in modern foreign language translations, Luther's *Die Heilige Schrift* following (1), the Italian *La Sacra Bibblia* (2), and the French *La Sainte Bible* (3). Among the ancient versions the Vg renders the MT as *fel*, which can be translated as "anger" or "venom," whereas the LXX and Pesh. go their own way or translate *ad sensum*. The *Hebrew Old Testament Text Project*, 5:359, puts forward the suggestion, "Your wine which inflames."

The 2d masc. sing. suffix has also proved troublesome. Some translations change it to a 3d masc. sing. to agree with the subject in the parallel line (e.g., 1QpHab, Vg, NJB, RSV) or add a 3d masc. sing. pronoun to the sentence (e.g., NKJV: "pressing him to your bottle"; cf. KJV) or omit the suffix altogether (LXX, *Tg. Neb.*, NIV). From a critical standpoint the difficulty of reading favors the MT.[91] Moreover, such cases of enallage are common enough in the OT.[92]

†The problem concerning חֲמָתְךָ is complicated further by controversy over the previous מְסַפֵּחַ. Some take the word to be from the root סָפַח ("join," "attach to"; cf. Ethiopic *säfḥa*, "become broad/wide"[93]), deciding for a meaning "mix in" (NASB) or "press/put to" (NKJV, KJV). Others favor the idea "pour out" (NIV, NJB), סָפַח being compared with the Arabic *safaḥa* ("pour out").[94] Still a third proposal is to emend the word to מִסַּף ("from/of the cup/bowl," KB-3, RSV).[95] Despite the uncertainty, I have followed Armerding, the NIV, and the NJB in choosing the second alternative because of the common OT usage of wrath being poured out (e.g., 2 Chron. 12:7; 34:21; Ps. 79:6; Jer. 7:20; 42:18; Ezek. 7:8; 9:8).[96]

†Still another perplexity arises in the next phrase, וְאַף שַׁכֵּר ("and also getting him drunk"). The conjunctive particle has been rendered as "even" (NASB), "till" (NIV), or "until" (NJB). Armerding offers the novel suggestion that the phrase "can be interpreted as a parallel noun in the accusative case, meaning 'and (with) anger.'"[97] This idea has the advantage of scriptural precedent in that both terms in this verse (חֵמָה and אַף) would then be words for anger that are said to be poured out (cf. Jer. 10:25; Lam. 4:11). The two even occur together at times (e.g., Jer. 7:20). Moreover, both appear together in a context of God's judgment that also uses the figure of getting the nations drunk (Isa. 63:1-6).[98]

A variation in Armerding's position would be to view the pro-

---

91. See Würthwein, *Text of the Old Testament*, p. 116.
92. See the additional note on Nah. 2:13.
93. W. Leslau, *Ethiopic and South Arabic Contributions to the Hebrew Lexicon*, U. of California Publications on Semitic Philology XX (Los Angeles: U. of California, 1958), p. 37. KB-3 suggests that the Ethiopic word may point to yet a third root with this spelling.
94. Keil (*Minor Prophets*, 2:87) emphatically denies such a meaning for סָפַח, and KB-3 does not list one. BDB postulates it as a proposed root for several nouns but does not relate Hab. 2:15 to it.
95. This solution is adopted by R. Smith, *Habakkuk*, p. 109.
96. Armerding, "Habakkuk," in *EBC*, 7:519 n.
97. Ibid.
98. For the concatenation of cup, wrath, and drunkenness (staggering/reeling), see Isa. 51:17-23.

posed noun "anger" as a compound accusative with deletion trans-formation of the pronominal suffix: thus "pouring out *your* wrath and anger." Although such a suggestion would violate the normal rules of Hebrew syntax,[99] some instances of the use of one pronoun with two connected nouns are attested in the OT (e.g., Ex. 15:2; 2 Sam. 23:5), and the resultant product of such a procedure would be similar to the omission of a pronominal suffix in parallel structure.[100]

However attractive Armerding's proposal or its variation might seem, its cumbersomeness and the rarity of the variant consideration (even the cited examples are debated), as well as the fact that Habak-kuk has already used וְאַף at the beginning of this section (2:5), make the suggestion of translating אַף as "anger" unlikely. Habakkuk proba-bly intends the particle to introduce an additional thought joined to what precedes for special emphasis.

The following infinitive absolute שַׁכֵּר likely is used adverbially to describe the manner, means, degree, or attendant circumstance whereby the outpoured wrath is to be accomplished.[101] The thought of the verse thus far may therefore be paraphrased: "Woe to him who gives his neighbor drink, pouring out your wrath and also (i.e., by, while) getting him drunk." The objective "him" is to be supplied from the preceding line.[102] As for מְעוֹרֵיהֶם ("their nakedness"), the pro-nominal suffix is masc. pl. in agreement with the collective sense in the antecedent "his neighbor(s)."

2:16 קָלוֹן ("shame," from קָלָה, "be light"), קִיקָלוֹן ("[utter] dis-grace," from קָלַל, "be slight"; cf. Akkadian *qalālu*, "be light," *qullulu*, "despised") and כּוֹס ("cup") all occur in combination in the Ugaritic literature.[103] By drawing upon well-known Canaanite precedents in making his point, Habakkuk again displays his literary skill. He fur-

---

99. See GKC, par. 105m.

100. See Dahood, *Psalms*, 3:430-31.

101. For details, see A. B. Davidson, *Hebrew Syntax*, 3d ed. (Edinburgh: T. and T. Clark, 1901), par. 87.

102. For similar instances of this syntactical feature, see Dahood, *Psalms*, 3:432-33.

103. See M. Dahood, "Ugaritic-Hebrew Parallel Pairs," *RSP*, 3:143-44. The noun קִיקָלוֹן apparently arises from progressive assimilation of conso-nant to vowel: קָלַל < *קִלְקָלוֹן < קִיקָלוֹן; see KB-3, p. 1027. Similar cases of nouns derived from the pilpel stem of this root are attested in postbiblical Hebrew; see M. Jastrow, *A Dictionary of the Targumim, the Talmud Babli and Yerushalmi, and the Midrashic Literature* (New York: Pardes, 1950), 2:1382-83. For discussions of this root and its derivatives, see C. A. Keller, "קלל," *THAT* 2:641-47; L. J. Coppes, "קָלַל," *TWOT* 2:800-801. For the use of phonetic assimilation in the Semitic languages, see S. Mosacati, ed., *An Introduction to the Comparative Grammar of the Semitic Languages* (Wiesbaden: Harrassowitz, 1964), pp. 56-58.

ther demonstrates that ability by putting the verse in chiastic structure. Laetsch suggests that קִיקָלוֹן is derived from the verb קִיא ("spit," "vomit") here used of shameful vomiting. Thus he remarks, "Dead drunk, the proud Chaldean shall lie naked on the floor in his own vomit, an object of horror and ridicule for all the world."[104]

In the Scriptures the cup is often used as a figure of God's dealings with men. It can be a symbol of His blessing (Pss. 16:5; 23:5; 116:13) or of judgment (Pss. 11:6; 75:8 [HB 75:9]; Isa. 51:17, 22; Jer. 25:15-17; 49:12; 51:7; Ezek. 23:31-34; Rev. 14:10; 16:19). The motif is also applied to Christ's finished work in drinking the cup of divine wrath against sin so that all people may be saved, as well as being utilized of the cup of eternal felicity that the heavenly host provided (Matt. 20:22-23; Mark 10:38; 14:36; Luke 22:42; John 18:11; cf. Matt. 26:27-29).

The right hand is a motif indicating honor (Gen. 48:13-14; Pss. 16:11; 110:1) or definiteness and strength of activity (Ex. 15:6; Ps. 98:1; Isa. 41:10). Its presence here adds vigor and emphasis to the threatened judgment of the Chaldeans (cf. Isa. 48:13-14).[105]

2:17 †יְחִתַּן ("will terrify") is anomalous but probably is a remnant of an old energic form of חָתַת.[106] I have followed the lead of the NIV (cf. NJB, RSV) in viewing the terror as coming upon the Chaldeans, as the parallel with the previous line appears to demand, rather than seeing the terror as being that which the Chaldeans perpetrated against the animal kingdom (cf. NASB, KJV, NKJV).

The word בְּהֵמָה ("animal") is used of cattle in general,[107] here representing the whole animal kingdom much as (the cedars of) Lebanon represents the natural world. בְּהֵמָה was also doubtless employed because of its use in contexts that contrast animal and human behavior (cf. Ps. 73:22) and because it is frequently parallel to אָדָם ("man[kind]"; cf. Gen. 2:18-20; Ps. 49: 12, 20 [HB 49:13, 21]), a combination that appears here.

---

104. Laetsch, *Minor Prophets*, p. 339; see also *Hebrew Old Testament Text Project*, 5:360-61.
105. See the helpful observations of P. Gilchrist, "ימן," *TWOT* 1:382-83.
106. For the existence of the energic verbal form in Northwest Semitic, see C. Gordon, *UT*, 1:72-73; W. L. Moran, *A Syntactical Study of the Dialect of Byblos as Reflected in the Amarna Tablets* (Ann Arbor: University Microfilms, 1967), pp. 43-49. For the utilization of the energic in Hebrew, see F. M. Cross, Jr., *Studies in Ancient Yahwistic Poetry* (Baltimore: Johns Hopkins, 1950), p. 51; D. R. Meyer, *Hebräische Grammatik* (Berlin: Walter de Gruyter, 1969), 2:100-101.
107. See the note on Joel 1:18 in Patterson, "Joel," in *EBC*, 7:244.

*f. The fifth woe: The polytheistic Chaldean will be deserted
by his idols (2:18-20)*

Translation

"Of what value* is an idol,
 that* its creator has fashioned it,
(or) an image, a teacher of falsehood*,
 that* its creator* trusts it,
 making mute idols?
¹⁹Woe to him who says to wood, 'Arise!'
 or to silent stone, 'Wake up!'
Shall it give instruction*?
 Look, it is covered with gold and silver,
 yet there is no breath in it.
²⁰But Yahweh is in His holy Temple;
 let all the earth be silent before Him."

Exegesis and Exposition

In drawing the woe oracles to a close, Habakkuk deliberately
changes the order he has previously employed by beginning with the
reason for the threatened judgment (v. 18). Then, after giving invective (v. 19*a*) and threat (v. 19*b*), he returns climactically to a further
consideration of the cause for the woe by expressing the chief lesson
to be learned from the whole discussion (v. 20). Verse 20 forms an
inclusio with v. 4 that reveals the underlying thesis and its implication for the entire section: The Lord is a just and holy God who deals
righteously with all people and is actively present in the flow of
earth's history; therefore, He is to be acknowledged as God by all.
That thesis is not only the answer to Habakkuk's second perplexity
but also serves as the basis for the Chaldean's judgment.[108]

The religious orientation of the Chaldean is now examined and
shown to be without foundation. His idolatrous polytheism is seen to
be worthless. The unit begins with a rhetorical question concerning
the Chaldean's idols. What profit is there? The answer: "None!" That
this is so is obvious from several factors. (1) His idols are man-made
and therefore can only be a source of false teaching. Whatever instruction one can glean from their worship is error. (2) Crafted by the
hand of man, idols are silent creations that can never speak. The
phrase אֱלִילִים אִלְּמִים (*'ĕlîlîm 'illĕmîm*), "mute idols," is a grotesque par-

---

108. Habakkuk's method of closure here is both climactic and carefully structured. For details, see Watson, *Hebrew Poetry*, pp. 62-65.

205

ody of אֵל/אֱלֹהִים (*'ēl/'ĕlōhîm*), the common words for the powerful and true God of revelation.[109] (3) Since idols are only man's creation, to put one's trust in them is to trust one's own creation rather than the Creator.

Before going on to give the most crucial reason for the doom of the polytheistic Chaldean, Habakkuk delivers an invective and a threat (v. 19). Having pointed out the inability of worthless man-made idols to speak, Habakkuk pronounces the Lord's woe against the devotees of idol worship. How could anyone tell a carved wooden image to arise or instruct a god fashioned of stone to awaken? Whether the reference is to general petitions or requests for information made to these idols or is intended to reflect ceremonies waking the gods practiced in some ancient cultures, the question remains: How can lifeless, speechless products of the artisans' hands give instruction? Any suggestion that such is possible is nonsense, for the fact remains that, however one may clothe them or cover them with gold and silver, the idols are not alive. The Hebrew text is emphatic: "Any breath does not exist within it!" The effect of the MT is graphically rendered by the NJB: "Look, he is encased in gold and silver,—but not a breath of life inside it!"

The condemnation of idolatry here is in harmony with that found in the other OT prophets (cf. Isa. 44:9-20; Jer. 5:7; 44:1-8; Hos. 8:4). The judgment of Babylon and its gods announced previously by Isaiah (Isa. 21:9) is repeated by Jeremiah (Jer. 50:2; 51:47-48, 52-53).

The fifth woe ends with a pronouncement that displays the vast difference between Israel's God and the gods of Babylon. Unlike those gods, who have neither life nor word of guidance for their followers (cf. Isa. 44:9-11), Yahweh the Lord of all the earth (v. 14) is a living God. He is in His holy Temple* and available to all who fear Him (cf. Deut. 4:1-40; Ps. 91:14-16). He is ever present, superintending all that comes to pass (cf. Isa. 44:6-8, 24-28). The gods of Babylon (and their devotees) can only remain silent before Him.

The invective and threat against Babylon (v. 19) thus have more than sufficient cause. Since the Chaldeans worshiped gods of their own creation (v. 18) rather than the Creator, controller, and consummator of history, their condemnation is certain. This is their most besetting sin. Because the Chaldeans worshiped self and their own selfish artifices, they will plot against the peoples around them. Their feigned friendship with them will only be a pretext to indulge their own perverted lusts. Further, they will go on to plunder the nations so that lands, cities, and their inhabitants will feel the crush of their violent oppression. The verdict is final. Habakkuk can be assured that

---

109. See H. Preuss, "אֱלִיל," *TDOT* 1:285-87.

the Chaldeans will be judged, for they will violate the standards of God (cf. vv. 4-5).

Verse 20 also has another application. Because the idolatry that leads to the neglect and rejection of God is a universal problem, all the earth is to be silent before the living God. None is to assert his independence from God but rather should worship Him in humble submission (Jer. 10:1-10), letting Him be God of the whole life (Pss. 63:1-4 [HB 63:2-5]; 73:23-28).

The universal applicability of v. 20 argues for two further considerations: (1) v. 20 is designed both to conclude the fifth woe and to bring to culmination all of the woes; (2) v. 20 is also strategically placed so as to counterbalance the thought of v. 4. There is also here a personal application for Habakkuk. God's prophet had expressed deep anxiety first over God's seeming indifference to Judah's sin (1:2-4) and then over God's method of dealing with it (1:12–2:1). He needed to learn that in the operation of divine government God proceeds in accordance with definite standards (2:4). Once he had learned that and understood the applicability of God's principles of governance to the Chaldean (2:5-19), he needed a fresh, personal resignation to the will of God (2:20). Like Job (Job 42:1-6), he needed to see God not only for what He does and gives but also for who He is. He needed to let Him be God of his whole life.

The challenge to Habakkuk is also for all people in all ages. Craigie's words of warning are well taken:

> Idolatry is essentially the worship of that which we make, rather than of our Maker. And that which we make may be found in possessions, a home, a career, an ambition, a family, or a multitude of other people or things. We "worship" them when they become the focal point of our lives, that for which we live. And as the goal and centre of human existence, they are as foolish as any wooden idol or metal image. But what we can perceive so clearly in the words of a prophet from centuries long passed, we cannot always see so clearly in our immediate life and existence. As we reflect on Habakkuk's words, we should reflect also on the nature and direction of our own lives.[110]

Craigie's admonition becomes doubly sobering for today's believer when he realizes that his body is the temple of the Holy Spirit (1 Cor. 6:19). As such it belongs to God and ought not to be profaned in thought or deed. Because the Holy Spirit indwells the believer (1 Cor. 3:16), his life should reflect that one who alone is God (2 Cor. 6:16-18) as he lives in anticipation of that glorious day when "the dwelling of God is with men, and He will live with them" (Rev. 21:3).

---

110. Craigie, *Twelve Prophets*, 2:99.

Additional Notes

2:18 †Although הוֹעִיל ("profit," "value") may be construed as a causative verb, and hence standing after the preceding מָה ("what") may be translated "What profits an idol?" (cf. Keil), the rendering adopted here follows most English translations in viewing "idol" as the subject and הוֹעִיל as inwardly transitive.[111]

פֶּסֶל is one of several basic words for "idol" in the OT. It is usually taken to mean "carved image," while the following מַסֵּכָה ("image") is customarily understood to mean "cast image."[112] Although one may not always be able to make such a distinction, the two words perhaps serve here as representative examples of idols however they are made.[113]

Still a third term for idol (אֱלִילִים) occurs here. This word lays stress on its value, for it is denounced as an empty or worthless thing. H. Preuss suggests that the word

> was created as a disparaging pun on and as a diminutive of *'el* or *'elohim* (Ps. 97:7) ("little god, godling"). This helped to bring about a conscious antithesis between *'elil* and *'el*, "the Strong One." Furthermore, it is likely that the noun *'elil* is intentionally reminiscent of the adj. *'elil*, "weak, insignificant, worthless," which we also encounter in contexts where the speaker uses scornful words (Job 13:4; Jer. 14:14; cf. Zec. 11:17; also Sir. 11:3).[114]

The alliteration with the following אֱלִלִים (*'illĕmîm*), "mute," is effective but difficult to render in English in a way that retains both its meaning and the intended audible effect. Perhaps something like "voiceless, valueless" or "mute, meretricious things" would approximate the writer's intentions.

†וּמוֹרֶה שָׁקֶר ("a teacher of lies"): In addition to its normal function as a coordinator, the conjunction can be understood epexegetically, hence left untranslated (NASB) or treated as introducing a logically subordinate clause (= "that," NIV). I have followed the NASB.

For the MT מוֹרֶה 1QpHab reads מרי, which Vermes understands to be a construct of מְרִיא ("fatling").[115] The Qumran form could also be understood as מְרִי ("rebellion").

כִּי ("that"): Both cases of this particle have been variously translated, the NIV rendering both causally, the NASB and RSV rendering

---

111. For the use of the hiphil to express inward transitivity, see GKC, par. 53d-f.
112. See the helpful classification of the various words for *idol* in the editorial note by R. L. Harris in E. S. Kalland, "גָּלַל," *TWOT* 1:163-64.
113. See the additional note concerning פֶּסֶל and מַסֵּכָה at Nah. 1:14.
114. Preuss, "אֱלִיל," *TDOT* 1:285.
115. G. Vermes (*The Dead Sea Scrolls in English* [Baltimore: Penguin, 1962], p. 240) translates the phrase in question as "a fatling of lies."

the first temporally and the second causally. The translation here follows the NJB, KJV, NKJV and several commentators (e.g., Hayes, Keil, Laetsch) in taking both particles as introducing result clauses. So construed, the question gets to the heart of the problem: "What possible profit can there be in any form of idol so that a craftsman would not only make a mute idol in the first place but then cap his foolishness by trusting in his own creation?"

2:19 דּוּמָם ("silent") emphasizes the idol's ineffectiveness with regard to speech (it is noiseless), whereas the synonym אִלֵּם ("mute") underscores its inability to speak.[116]

הוּא יוֹרֶה† ("shall it give instruction?"): יוֹרֶה is properly a verb, although some have treated it as a nominal form (e.g., NASB, NJB). The accents of the MT demand that the phrase be treated as separate from what precedes (cf. KJV). Although some have regarded it as a statement (NJB, NKJV), it is usually understood as a question. Others have omitted it as a gloss (e.g., NEB). The paronomasia with מוֹרֶה is obvious.

2:20 הַס ("keep silent"): The word is an onomatopoeic interjection with a force much like the English "hush!" (cf. Zeph. 1:7).

By הֵיכָל (*"temple"*) is probably meant not only the Temple in Jerusalem (1 Kings 8:10-11; 2 Chron. 5:13-14; 7:1-3) but also God's heavenly sanctuary (Ps. 11:4; Isa. 6:1-5; Mic. 1:2; cf. Rev. 4:2-11) from which, though it cannot contain Him (1 Kings 8:27), He hears and answers the prayers of those who know Him and seek Him (1 Kings 8:28-30; Ps. 73:17).

---

116. See A. Baumann, "דָּמָה II," *TDOT* 3:260-65.

Excursus on Habakkuk 2:4

The place of Habakkuk 2:4 in the history of biblical interpretation can hardly be overestimated. Its place in Jewish thinking is well represented by Rabbi Simlai:

> That it came to be of special importance for some Jews is indicated by *bMakk.* 23[b], which tells us that Rabbi Simlai (about A.D. 250) had asserted that the 613 commandments received by Moses had been summed up by David in eleven commandments (Ps 15), by Isaiah in six (Isa 33.15*f*), by Micah in three (Mic 6.8), by Isaiah again in two (Isa 56.1), and finally by Amos in one (Amos 5.4), but that Rabbi Nachman ben Isaac (about A.D. 350) had substituted Hab 2.4b for Amos 5.4 as the summary in one commandment.[1]

Its threefold citation in the NT (Rom. 1:17; Gal. 3:11; Heb. 10:38) attests to its basic importance to the Christian revelation. Boice rightly remarks:

> This is a great text. It could even be called *the* great text of the Bible. To understand it is to understand the Christian gospel and the Christian life. It is so important that it is picked up by the New Testament writers, twice by Paul (Rom. 1:17; Gal. 3:11) and once by the author of the Book of Hebrews (Heb. 10:38).[2]

---

1. C. E. B. Cranfield, *The Epistle to the Romans*, ICC (Edinburgh: T. and T. Clark, 1975), 1:101.
2. J. M. Boice, *The Minor Prophets* (Grand Rapids: Zondervan, 1986), 2:90.

The study of this text in Paul's expression of it in Rom. 1:17 had a remarkable impact on Martin Luther:

> There I began to understand that the righteousness of God is that by which the righteous lives by a gift of God, namely by faith. And this is the meaning: the righteousness of God is revealed by the gospel, namely, the passive righteousness with which merciful God justifies us by faith. . . . Here I felt I was altogether born again and had entered paradise itself through open gates. There a totally new face of the entire Scripture showed itself to me.[3]

Indeed, C. L. Feinberg may not be too far wrong in dubbing this text the "watchword of Christianity," the key to Habakkuk, and "the central theme of all the Scriptures."[4]

ITS CONTEXT

It is the nature of the case for crucial texts to receive great critical attention. Such is true here as well, the discussion of this verse or its NT citations in commentaries, theologies, and special studies being voluminous. Several problems are relevant to the understanding of the text, the most immediate being its relation to its context. Some (e.g., Eissfeldt; cf. *BHS*, NJB) suggest that it is closely tied to what precedes (vv. 2-3), vv. 2-4 thus forming a distinct pericope. Others (e.g., Hummel; cf. NKJV) extend this pericope backward to v. 1, while still others also include v. 5 (e.g., Humbert, R. Smith; cf. RSV). Some view Hab. 2:4 as chiefly introductory to all that follows (e.g., D. A. Koch), whereas others find the closest relationship between vv. 4 and 5 (e.g., Armerding, Keil, Laetsch; cf. NASB, NIV).

Representative of those who view Hab. 2:4 with the preceding verses is J. G. Janzen.[5] He finds the clue to his position in the word יָפֵחַ (*yāpēaḥ*, v. 3), which he takes not as a verb from פּוּחַ (*pûaḥ*, "breathe/blow") but, building on studies by Dahood and Loewenstamm[6] and considering the evidence of Prov. 6:19; 12:17; 14:5, 25; 19:5, 9, views it as a noun and translates v. 3 "For the vision is a

---

3. The citation of Martin Luther is taken from the *Preface to the Latin Writings* (*LW*, 34:336-37) as quoted by Justo L. González, *A History of Christian Thought* (Nashville: Abingdon, 1975), 3:29. See also K. S. Latourette, *A History of Christianity*, rev. ed. (New York: Harper & Row, 1975), 2:703-7.
4. C. L. Feinberg, *The Minor Prophets* (Chicago: Moody, 1948), p. 211.
5. J. Gerald Janzen, "Habakkuk 2:2-4 in the Light of Recent Philological Advances," *HTR* 73 (1980): 53-78.
6. See M. Dahood, *Psalms*, AB (Garden City, N.Y.: Doubleday, 1970), 1:169; S. E. Loewenstamm, "*Yāpîaḥ, yāpiaḥ, yāpēaḥ*," *Leš* 26 (1962-63): 205-8.

witness to a rendezvous, a testifier to the end—it does not lie."[7] Key to Janzen's interpretation is the presence in Hab. 2:3-4 of several key terms in the six texts in Proverbs:

> For in view of the collocation of key terms (*'ēd, yāpîaḥ, kizzēb, 'ĕmunâ/ 'ĕmet*) around the central concern in the six proverbs and elsewhere, only by resisting the obvious can we avoid the conclusion that the word *'ĕmunâ* in Hab 2:4b joins the three terms used earlier, *'ēd, yāpēaḥ* and *kizzēb*, to form the same four-term collocation around the same concern. But this means, unambiguously, that 2:4b refers not to the faithfulness (let alone the faith) of the *ṣaddîq*, but to the reliability of the vision.[8]

His conclusion therefore is that in vv. 2-4

> Yahweh is portrayed as vouching for the vision as a reliable witness and testifier which does not lie. But as the guarantor of the credentials of the vision as witness, Yahweh implicates himself fatefully in its reliability. This is no lying vision inspired by a lying spirit. What has been given to the prophet has not been given to deceive or to (mis)lead into destruction. This vision is reliable, such that the righteous shall *live* by it.[9]

Although Janzen's observations are helpful, only one of the key terms of Hab. 2:4 is actually used in these citations in Proverbs (אֱמוּנָה in Prov. 12:17, where it appears with צֶדֶק [*ṣedeq*, "truth"] from the same word group as the צַדִּיק [*ṣaddîq*, "righteous one"] of Hab. 2:4). Further, Janzen's three key terms of v. 3 (one of which is achieved by repointing עוֹד [*'ôd*, "yet"] to עֵד [*'ēd*, "witness/testifier"]) never occur with אֱמוּנָה (although עֵד אֱמוּנִים ["a faithful witness"] occurs in Prov. 14:5 parallel to יָפִיחַ כְּזָבִים [*yāpîaḥ kĕzābîm*, "a false witness"]). Thus in the six passages in Proverbs all four terms necessary to Janzen's theory occur in some form only once. Moreover, the אֱמוּנָה of Hab. 2:4 does not modify any of the three terms of v. 3 as in Prov. 12:17; 14:5, nor does it necessarily bear the same nuance as in the contexts in Proverbs.

Therefore, while Janzen's suggestions may help yield a satisfactory understanding of vv. 2-3, I do not believe he has demonstrated so necessary a relationship between vv. 2-3 and v. 4 that one must understand all four terms involved in the same way as his proposed understanding of the Proverbs passages. Indeed, the אֱמוּנָה of v. 4 seems tied only to its poetic line and the one preceding it, and that in a way different from the contexts in Proverbs.

Its appearance in v. 4 so close to the other three terms with which it is associated in Proverbs may simply be intended to suggest a

---

7. Janzen, "Habakkuk 2:2-4," p. 76.
8. Ibid., p. 61.
9. Ibid., pp. 59-60.

literary correspondence between Hab. 2:2-3 and 2:4. Just as God's vision testifies truthfully (=faithfully) to God's appointed end, so a righteous man lives his life in faith(fulness). Accordingly, even accepting Janzen's repointing of עוֹד to עֵד and his understanding of יָפֵחַ, one may say no more than that the passages in Proverbs may provide a literary and lexical environment for understanding the vision as a testifier and true witness to God's purposes (vv. 2-3) and possibly even a literary correspondence between vv. 2-3 and v. 4. No necessary syntactical or lexical relationship between vv. 2-3 and v. 4 can be proved. Though this does not necessarily invalidate the view that Hab. 2:4 is most closely tied to what precedes, since that view has no compelling evidence in its favor it would seem better to follow the more traditional position that relates v. 4 to what follows.

Moreover, there is much to commend a close tie of Hab. 2:4 to what comes after it: (1) The opening הִנֵּה often used as a poetic introductory formula argues for the initiation of a new thought.[10] (2) None of the key terms of v. 4 can be proved to be directly related to vv. 2-3, whereas the word נֶפֶשׁ is crucial to the application of v. 4 to the Chaldean in what follows (cf. vv. 5, 10). (3) While it might be suggested that v. 4 is a hinge verse[11] that completes the thought of vv. 2-3 and carries the discussion on to the consideration of the Chaldean in vv. 5-20, the fact that the principles enumerated in v. 4 are basic to the description of the demise of the Chaldean argues for a closer relation of v. 4 to what follows. (4) אַף כִּי (*'ap kî*) in v. 5 is designed to pick up the thought of a preceding sentence and carry it forward as an *argumentum a fortiori*: "yea, the more so," "furthermore." BDB notes that in such cases the preceding sentence is often indicated by הִנֵּה, as is the case here in Hab. 2:4. So understood it would appear that God's revelation of the principles of human behavior is the starting point for the consideration of the Chaldeans. If it is true that the wicked go on in their selfish presumption and if real life exists only with the righteous who conduct themselves faithfully before God (v. 4), the Chaldean is included in the class of the wicked whose unrighteous desires are catalogued in v. 5.

Accordingly v. 4 is best taken with what follows. Though it forms the essence of the divine revelation that is to be heralded to all, it is woven into the structure of v. 5, both verses thus serving as the basis for the woes that follow.

---

10. See W. G. E. Watson, *Classical Hebrew Poetry* (Sheffield: JSOT Press, 1986), p. 164; Dietrich-Alex Koch, "Der Text von Hab 2 4b in der Septuaginta und im Neuen Testament," *ZNW* 76 (1985): 73 n. 26. הִנֵּה can of course appear in other environments (cf. v. 19).
11. See H. van Dyke Parunak, "Transitional Techniques in the Bible," *JBL* 102 (1983): 540-41.

THE FIRST LINE

Verse 4 confronts the reader with a myriad of grammatical and lexical difficulties.[12] עֻפְּלָה (ʿuppĕlâ) has challenged the best efforts of exegetes. Most commonly the word has been related to the root עָפַל (ʿāpal, "swell") and hence as a pual participle is variously translated "puffed up" (NIV; so also *La Sainte Bible*, "enflée"; cf. *La Sacra Biblia*, "gonfia" [conceited]), "proud" (NASB), "arrogant" (BDB), or "stiff-necked/stubborn" (*Die Heilege Schrift*, "halsstarrig").

Some, citing the difficulty of the masculine singular suffixes נַפְשׁוֹ and בּוֹ, suggest an emendation to a masculine substantive such as עֹפֶל or עָפָל (*BHS*) or redivide the consonants into עָף (from עוף, "fly [away]," i.e., "perish") and לֹה, or find a relation with the Arabic ġafala ("be heedless") and translate the word "reckless" (NEB).[13] Others, feeling the need for a verb to balance יִחְיֶה in the parallel line, invert the consonants or emend the word to a form of (1) the verb עָלַף (ʿālap, "cover") translating "become weak" (Humbert), "succumb" (NJB), "draw back" (LXX), or "fail" (RSV) or (2) the verb פָּעַל (pāʿal, "do/make") with the idea of earning punishment (Rudolph).

Still others abandon the consonants of the MT and suggest a word from another root such as עַוָּל (ʿawwāl, "unjust," hence "the wicked" [Pesh., *Tg. Neb.*]) or עָצֵל (ʿāṣēl, "be sluggish," hence "slothful" [Aquila, Janzen]), while some simply translate *ad sensum* "unbelievable" (Vg) or "faithless."[14]

The problem is difficult, and some abandon any hope of solving it.[15] It seems, however, that one should follow the reading of the MT

---

12. For details, see J. A. Emerton, "Textual and Linguistic Problems of Habakkuk 2:4-5," *JTS* 28 (1977): 1-18.

13. With the Arabic root one may also compare the late Hebrew הֶעְפִּיל "be foolhardy," "act rashly"; see Marcus Jastrow, *A Dictionary of the Targumim, the Talmud Babli and Yerushalmi, and the Midrashic Literature* (New York: Pardes, 1950), 2:1100. For the division of the Hebrew noun in MT into לֹה and עָף, see Emerton, "Linguistic Problems," pp. 16-17.

14. See the *Preliminary and Interim Report on the Hebrew Old Testament Text Project* (New York: United Bible Societies, 1980), 5:356. The reading of the Pesh. and the *Tg. Neb.* underscores the possibility of an emendation to "the wicked" here, an idea supported by the occurrence of forms of the roots צדק and ישׁר together with the concept of wickedness elsewhere (e.g., Deut. 32:4; cf. Ps. 92:15 [HB 92:16]). A similar proposal is that an original עַוָּל may have fallen out due to haplography (so Wellhausen). W. H. Brownlee ("The Placarded Revelation of Habakkuk," *JBL* 82 [1963]: 322-24) suggests the retaining of the MT עֻפְּלָה but with the interpolation of a following עַוָּל and then with redivision yielding עפל העול, "the haughty is naughty"!

15. W. H. Ward (*A Critical and Exegetical Commentary on Habakkuk*, ICC (Edinburgh: T. and T. Clark, 1911], p. 14 n.) pronounces the whole line "corrupt past safe reconstruction."

due both to the criteria of textual criticism (prefer the more difficult reading[16] and consider the evidence of 1QpHab, which follows the MT: עוּפְלָה) and to the fact that the traditional text, though obscure, can be explained. Provisionally, then, the MT can be translated "arrogant" or the like.

Nevertheless, at least two other problems arise: (1) As mentioned above, the masculine singular suffixes on נַפְשׁוֹ and בּוֹ call for an appropriate singular antecedent; (2) נֶפֶשׁ may need to be translated in some way other than "soul."[17]

Taking these problems in inverse order, however broad might be the range of meanings for נֶפֶשׁ,[18] many passages are best understood in their traditional sense as the seat of moral or religious agency (i.e., the soul; e.g., Ex. 23:9; Isa. 26:8-9).[19] Therefore, the translation "soul" cannot be dismissed categorically. At this point, however, a couple of controlling factors need to be observed. נֶפֶשׁ does not elsewhere[20] occur with the root יָשַׁר, which is usually associated in a moral sense with לֵב/לֵבָב (*lēb/lēbāb*, "heart"; e.g., 2 Kings 10:15; 2 Chron. 29:34; Pss. 7:10 [HB 7:11]; 32:11; 94:15 [HB 94:16]; 97:11). Accordingly, the following בּוֹ ("in him") rather than נַפְשׁוֹ is to be understood with לֹא יָשְׁרָה ("not upright"), as most expositors suggest. Also, the use of נֶפֶשׁ in v. 5 in the sense of "appetite" or "desire" (cf. NJB, NASB) probably argues for a similar understanding in v. 4 (cf. NIV). Thus the translation of נֶפֶשׁ as "soul" in v. 4 (KJV, NASB, RSV) is probably incorrect.

Turning to the first problem, one solution to the difficulty with the masculine suffixes is to propose that the Chaldean, the subject of vv. 6-20, is to be assumed here (so Keil). This leaves the predicate adjective יָשְׁרָה to agree with נֶפֶשׁ and yields a translation something like "behold, puffed up, his soul is not straight within him."[21] Such a procedure gives tolerable sense and takes account of the apparent incongruity between the feminine עֻפְּלָה and the following masculine suffixes.

---

16. See E. Würthwein, *The Text of the Old Testament* (Grand Rapids: Eerdmans, 1979), pp. 116-17; C. E. Armerding, *The Old Testament and Criticism* (Grand Rapids: Eerdmans, 1983), p. 126.
17. See Janzen, "Habakkuk 2:2-4," pp. 62-66. H. W. Wolff (*Anthropology of the Old Testament* [Philadelphia: Fortress, 1974], p. 10) declares that "today we are coming to the conclusion that it is only in a very few passages that the translation 'soul' corresponds to the meaning of *nepeš*."
18. See the excellent discussion in Wolff, *Anthropology*, pp. 10-26.
19. Wolff (*Anthropology*, pp. 17-18) gives an inclusive list of such passages.
20. Prov. 29:10 seems to indicate that the upright is concerned for his neighbor's *nepeš* (but cf. NIV). For an excellent discussion of the difficult second line of this verse, see William McKane, *Proverbs* (Philadelphia: Westminster, 1970), p. 637.
21. C. F. Keil, *The Twelve Minor Prophets*, COT (Grand Rapids: Eerdmans, 1954), 2:71.

Additional possibilities include (1) viewing עֻפְּלָה as composed of a masculine noun of the *quṭṭāl* type ("arrogance") and a masculine singular suffix -*ōh* (rather than -*ô*),[22] here functioning as the antecedent of pronominal suffixes in a relative clause[23]—"Behold his arrogance whose desire is not upright in him" (i.e., "Behold the arrogance of him in whom his desire is not upright")—and (2) understanding עֻפְּלָה as a masculine noun with a masculine singular suffix and viewing all of the suffixes as anticipatory of the Chaldeans of the following discussion: "Behold his (the Chaldean's) arrogance; his desire is not upright in him."

Any of these explanations can yield a translation compatible with the parameters of the language and faithful to the MT. Keil's translation has the advantage of taking the text as it stands, but he must supply the antecedent for the suffixes from the demands of the context. He also fails to come to grips satisfactorily with the problem of נֶפֶשׁ, although this difficulty could possibly be solved by translating the word as "desire." The second additional view deals with נֶפֶשׁ and takes advantage of the Masoretic accents but, like Keil's proposal, faces the problem of finding a satisfactory antecedent for the suffixes. It also depends on a repointing of עֻפְּלָה. The first additional suggestion has the advantage of accounting for all the linguistic problems but at the expense of repointing the consonants of the MT.

The solution tentatively proposed here notes the seeming incongruity between the feminine substantive and the following masculine suffixes by understanding עֻפְּלָה as a predicate adjective before a relative clause with omitted particle: "Arrogant is the one whose desires are not upright" (lit. "An arrogance is he whose desire is not upright in him"). Thus construed the syntax is much like that of Isa. 41:24, תּוֹעֵבָה יִבְחַר בָּכֶם (*tôʿēbâ yibḥar bākem*), which the NIV accurately translates, "He who chooses you is detestable."[24] On the whole this seems the easiest solution and has OT literary precedent. Whatever the final solution to the difficulties in the first line, the MT can be translated as it stands, making it hasty to conclude that the text can "give no sense."[25]

THE SECOND LINE

The chief points of contention in the second line of Hab. 2:4 revolve around (1) the precise meaning of צַדִּיק (*ṣaddîq*, "righ-

---

22. For details, see GKC, par. 7b, c; 84c; 91e; cf. Hab. 3:4.
23. See GKC, par. 15e, f; the pronoun with בּ would be resumptive.
24. See further A. B. Davidson, *Hebrew Syntax*, 3d ed. (Edinburgh: T. and T. Clark, 1901), par. 143; 144 and the translation on p. 177.
25. Ward, *Habakkuk*, p. 14.

teous/just") and (2) the meaning and syntactical relationship of the following בֶּאֱמוּנָתוֹ (be'ĕmûnātô, "by his faith[fulness])." Complicating both problems is the reading of the line in the LXX and its subsequent use by the NT writers.

As for the first problem, words derived from צדק have varied meanings. The root itself appears to mean "be straight" and is largely employed in situations that denote conformity to a standard (i.e., straightness).[26] Thus the root and its word group are often used of God's activities and man's relation to God. In accordance with His righteous scrutiny God takes note of all people in their activities (Amos 5:4-7, 14; 6:12) and punishes the sin of His own (Dan. 9:14) and of all people (Ps. 9:8 [HB 9:9]). By His righteous judgment He vindicates His own (Judg. 5:11; Isa. 54:17; Mic. 7:9) and brings them salvation/deliverance (Isa. 45:21; 46:12-13), ultimately through His Righteous One (Jer. 23:6; 33:18).[27] Redeemed people can know the objective reality of right standing before a righteous God (Isa. 45:24-25; 51:7; 61:10), before whom they are to live righteous lives (Isa. 62:1-2) culminating in a kingdom of righteousness forever (Isa. 9:7; 61:1-4).

Fundamental to the use of צַדִּיק in the OT is the concept of God's own righteousness, the truth that God's decisions and actions always conform to His holy and just nature.[28] This truth is set forth in Deut. 32:4:

> The Rock, His work is perfect,
>   for all His ways are just;
> a God of faithfulness and without wrongdoing,
>   He is righteous and upright.

This important text establishes the ground of divine activity, which is essential to man's relationship to his Creator. Keil and Delitzsch remark: "As the rock, He is 'a God of faithfulness,' upon which men may rely and build in all the storms of life, and 'without iniquity,' *i.e.*,

---

26. See H. G. Stigers, "צָדֵק," *TWOT* 2:752-55. A comprehensive investigation of the root and its manifold usages may be found in K. Koch, "צדק," *THAT* 2:507-30.
27. For helpful discussions of divine righteousness, see J. B. Payne, *The Theology of the Older Testament* (Grand Rapids: Zondervan, 1962), pp. 154-61; W. Dyrness, *Themes in Old Testament Theology* (Downers Grove, Ill.: InterVarsity, 1979), pp. 53-57; Hermann Cremer, *Biblico-Theological Lexicon of New Testament Greek*, 4th Eng. ed., trans. William Urwick (Edinburgh: T. and T. Clark, 1895), pp. 183-88.
28. Geerhardus Vos (*Biblical Theology* [Grand Rapids: Eerdmans, 1954], pp. 270-76) maintains that a judicial substratum is to be observed throughout the whole assortment of contexts where צַדִּיק occurs. See also Cremer, *Lexicon*, pp. 690-92.

anything crooked or false in His nature."[29] For man, not only created in the image of God but also living in covenant relation with Him, God's Person and actions become the foundation for his conduct. God's perfection is its basis (Gen. 17:1; Ps. 78:72; Matt 5:48), His holiness its dynamic (Lev. 19:2; 1 Pet. 1:16), His truth its standard, and His love its imperative (Ps. 85:8-10 [HB 85:9-11]; Eph. 4:15).[30] The righteous man, then, is the one who makes God's righteous standards his own and lives in accordance with them.

Three of the key words in Hab. 2:4 are found also in Deut. 32:4: אֱמוּנָה, צַדִּיק, and יָשָׁר/יְשָׁרָה.[31] Habakkuk's bringing together of these words is doubtless not accidental. The effect is to make the character and culpability of the arrogant Chaldean conqueror, the object of the prophet's concern, appear all the more distinct. The basic qualities of moral responsibility and ethical behavior of men living in the presence of the sovereign judge of the earth are thus shown to be absent from Israel's chastiser. Accordingly he will be judged (cf. Isa. 45:22-25).

The second problem has to do with the precise nuance of אֱמוּנָה. Since the etymology of אמן has often been taken as the key to the meaning of אֱמוּנָה, it is perhaps best to begin there.[32] Although older commentators stated that the root idea is "be firm" and hence translated the noun as "firmness" or the like (so Keil; cf. BDB), Barr argues that the case for "be firm" cannot be demonstrated and suggests that,

---

29. C. F. Keil and F. Delitzsch, *The Pentateuch*, COT (Grand Rapids: Eerdmans, 1956), 3:468.
30. M. J. Erickson (*Christian Theology* [Grand Rapids: Baker, 1983], 1:299) points out that God's attributes control His acts and give to man a model to "relate to God by governing our actions in accordance with what the Scriptures say God is like." Cremer (*Lexicon*, p. 184) observes: "Righteousness in the biblical sense is a condition of rightness *the standard of which is God*, which is estimated according to the divine standard, which shows itself in behaviour conformable to God, and has to do above all things with its relation to God, and with the walk before Him." This aspect of the consideration of צַדִּיק, however, by no means minimizes the truth of the observation of Cranfield (*Romans*, 1:94) that "there are passages in which ṣaddîq, used of Israel or of the individual Israelite, refers to status rather than to ethical condition (see, for example, Ps 32.11 in the light of vv. 1, 2 and 5; Isa 60.21)."
31. יָשָׁר is parallel to צַדִּיק in Ps. 33:1 and to תָּם in Job 1:1, 8. It is thus a vital characteristic of the one who fears God and walks uprightly before Him (see the exposition of Hab. 2:4). Interestingly enough, forms of the two suggested emendations for the עֻפְּלָה of the first line are also found in Deut. 32:4: פָּעַל, עָוֶל.
32. The danger of assuming the presence of a root's proposed original meaning throughout the group of words that incorporate the root and/or in every context is duly treated by D. A. Carson, *Exegetical Fallacies* (Grand Rapids: Baker, 1984), pp. 26-32; see also James Barr, *The Semantics of Biblical Language* (London: SCM Press, 1983), pp. 100-106.

based on the meaning of *'mn* in the other Semitic languages, "feel secure" or "trust" would be more appropriate.[33] Jepsen, however, cautions that the absence of the root in Akkadian, Ugaritic, and Canaanite-Phoenician makes its occurrence in Hebrew the earliest, so that "if an original meaning is still generally intelligible, it must be deduced from the Hebrew, rather than from the Syriac or Arabic"[34] where the hiphil form of the verb was adopted. The matter is clouded still further by Baumgartner's listing of two roots: I. "be steady/firm/trustworthy"; II. "set in order" (a denominative from אָמֵן "keeper/guardian").[35] In sum, certainty as to an original meaning for the root escapes us.

The matter of the etymology of אמן, however, may have been over-emphasized. As Barr points out,

> Even assuming, therefore, that the 'ultimate' etymology of words of the root *'-m-n* is 'firmness', we have here an illustration of the harm of paying excessive attention to the most ultimate etymology and failing to consider what forms were current at the relevant times and what senses they bore in actual usage. Extant forms are not derived directly from the ultimate etymology or from the 'root meaning'.[36]

Thus the meaning of אֱמוּנָה and its significance for Hab. 2:4 need to be determined largely from its use in the Hebrew OT. Unfortunately here, too, a great deal of controversy has arisen as to whether this noun has an active ("trustfulness," Barr) or passive ("trustworthiness," J. B. Lightfoot[37]) sense. Jepsen appears to be on the right track in observing that אֱמוּנָה denotes "a way of acting which grows out of inner stability, 'conscientiousness.' . . . *'emunah* seems more to emphasize one's own inner attitude and the conduct it produces."[38] Thus active and passive meanings are largely merged, אֱמוּנָה for people being an "inner stability, integrity, conscientiousness, cleanliness, which is essential for any responsible service," and for God conduct that "corresponds to the nature of his deity."[39] If the active and passive meanings are both inherent in the word, God is not only trustworthy but also one who acts faithfully in accordance with His being. Similar qualities are expected of the believer, the noun prescribing "as a personal attribute of man, fidelity in word and

---

33. Barr, *Semantics*, pp. 161-87.
34. A. Jepsen, "אָמֵן," *TDOT* 1:293.
35. KB-3, 1:61-62.
36. Barr, *Semantics*, p. 187.
37. J. B. Lightfoot, *The Epistle of St. Paul to the Galatians* (Grand Rapids: Zondervan, 1957), pp. 154-56. Lightfoot, however, holds that in Hab. 2:4 the active and passive senses are blended together.
38. A. Jepsen, "אָמֵן," *TDOT* 1:317.
39. Ibid., pp. 317, 320.

deed . . . and, in his relation to God, firm attachment to God, an undisturbed confidence in the divine promises of grace."[40] For Hab. 2:4, this means that the righteous believer is one in whom God's righteous character has been reproduced; he can therefore be trusted to act faithfully toward all and especially toward God.

This emphasis is further underscored in the syntax of the clause, the Masoretic accents suggesting that בֶּאֱמוּנָתוֹ is to be taken with יִחְיֶה: "By his faithfulness (the righteous one) shall live." This observation brings into focus the problem of the LXX translation: ὁ δὲ δίκαιος ἐκ πίστεώς μου ζήσεται (*ho de dikaios ek pisteōs mou zēsetai*, "but the just shall live by my faith").[41] Though some have suggested that a fundamental difference exists between the Greek and Hebraic perceptions here concerning אֱמוּנָה, because the Hebrew noun stresses the outworking of an inner reality the LXX translators

> have rendered the word quite correctly πίστις, although by changing the suffix, and giving ἐκ πίστεώς μου instead of αὐτοῦ (or more properly ἑαυτοῦ: Aquila and the other Greek versions), they have missed, or rather perverted, the sense.[42]

Thus, aside from the change in pronouns, the LXX translators and the Hebrew author have the same perspective: faith and faithfulness can be viewed as aspects of a living reality—he who has faith will be faithful.[43]

Coupled with this truth is the fact that for the last clause of Hab. 2:4 "it is impossible to mistake the reference . . . to Gen. xv. 6, 'he believed (*he'ĕmīn*) in Jehovah, and He reckoned it to him *litsᵉdâqâh.*' "[44] Although the nature of Abraham's faith and his standing before God have been subjects of intense discussion among biblical scholars, the above study of the words and the force of the context make clear that "Abram accepted the Word of the Lord as reliable and true and acted in accordance with it; consequently, the Lord declared Abram righteous and therefore acceptable."[45] The proper

---

40. Keil, *Minor Prophets*, 2:73.
41. The LXX^A reads μου after δίκαιος. The order given above could also mean "because of faith in me."
42. Keil, *Minor Prophets*, 2:74.
43. G. J. Zemek, Jr. ("Interpretive Challenges Relating to Habakkuk 2:4b," *GTJ* 1 [1980]: 53), follows the lead of his student H. S. Bryant in translating אֱמוּנָה as "'fruit of faith': 'faithful faith' or 'steadfast trust.'" Barr (*Semantics*, p. 201) maintains that part of the problem here arises from the fact that "Hebrew usage, as far as the Old Testament evidence shows (with some possible qualification for Hab. 2:4), had developed no substantive meaning 'believing, faith' to correspond with its well known verb *he'ĕmin* 'trust, believe'—but Greek had such a word in πίστις."
44. Keil, *Minor Prophets*, 2:73.
45. A. P. Ross, *Creation and Blessing* (Grand Rapids: Baker, 1988), p. 310.

conclusion as to the matter of Abraham's righteous standing before God is summarized by Keil and Delitzsch:

> This righteousness Abram acquired through his unconditional trust in the Lord, his undoubting faith in His promise, and his ready obedience to His word. This state of mind, which is expressed in the words הֶאֱמִן בַּיהוָֹה, was reckoned to him as righteousness, so that God treated him as a righteous man, and formed such a relationship with him, that he was placed in living fellowship with God.[46]

The well-known statement concerning the patriarch's faith lies behind Habakkuk's words; consequently the idea of a genuinely righteous man with right standing before God would not be foreign to the prophet.[47] Scriptural precedent thus reinforces the blending of active and passive meanings in אֱמוּנָה. The force of the words accordingly becomes all the stronger: a genuinely righteous man will live out his faith in faithful activity.

So understood, Paul's application of Hab. 2:4b, although admittedly shifted to serve his purpose, is not as far afield as commonly charged. The development of Paul's argument in Romans demands that he took ἐκ πίστεως to modify ὁ δίκαιος rather than relating it to the verb as Habakkuk does: "The one justified by faith shall live."[48] The apostle emphasizes that man's right standing before God is not based on works (cf. Eph. 2:8), not even those of the law (cf. Gal. 3:11), but only on genuine faith.[49] This by no means suggests that Paul mishandled the words of Habakkuk's prophecy. As Everett Harrison remarks,

> Apparently he was not desirous of disturbing the form of a familiar quotation. We know that he would endorse the truth that the Christian is not only justified by faith but is also expected to live by faith in order to please God. Such an emphasis has its place, but only when the initial problem of the sinner has been met. The liberty involved in using a quotation in a way somewhat different from its original setting is necessitated by the progress of revelation.[50]

---

46. Keil and Delitzsch, *Pentateuch*, 1:213. The authors lay stress on הֶאֱמִן as meaning "trust" or "believe" (p. 212), a conclusion acknowledged (though on a different basis) by Barr.

47. See also Ps. 32:11; Isa. 60:21.

48. See Cranfield, *Romans*, 1:101-2.

49. H. A. W. Meyer (*Critical and Exegetical Hand-Book to the Epistle to the Galatians*, 5th ed., trans. G. H. Venables [New York: Funk & Wagnalls, 1884], p. 114) finds in Habakkuk's words a messianic reference. See also his cogent remarks in *Critical and Exegetical Hand-Book to the Epistle to the Romans*, 5th ed., trans. J. C. Moore and E. Johnson, trans. rev. and ed. W. P. Dickson (New York: Funk & Wagnalls, 1884), p. 53.

50. E. F. Harrison, "Romans," in *EBC* (Grand Rapids: Zondervan, 1976), p. 20.

That the NT writers were aware of Habakkuk's intended meaning seems certain by the citation of his words in Heb. 10:35-39 where, quoting the text of the LXX (though reading the pronoun "my" after "righteous one" and inverting the final two words of the verse: "My righteous one will live by faith[fulness]"), the author of Hebrews applies the outworking of the believer's faith to his living in the certain hope of Christ's coming.

> As in Habakkuk the vision was surely to come, so in Hebrews it is an assured matter that the Coming One will come and not tarry long. And if in Habakkuk's time the righteous man could be saved by his faithful and tenacious clinging to God, fidelity and fortitude are even more required of the righteous man to whom the author directs his appeal.[51]

Yet even here

> there is no fundamental difference in this respect between Paul and the author of Hebrews; but our author, reproducing this clause together with part of its context, emphasizes the forward-looking character of saving faith, and in fact includes in "faith" not only what Paul means by the word but also what Paul more often expresses by the companion word "hope."[52]

By way of summation it may be said that an analysis of all the data relative to Hab. 2:4 indicates that, unlike the righteous person who carries on his life in faithfulness to God, the wicked one goes on in his arrogance, devoid of upright desires. It is this principle that will be applied to the case of the Chaldean, whose moral and spiritual failure is catalogued in the verses that follow.

---

51. N. R. Lightfoot, *Jesus Christ Today* (Grand Rapids: Baker, 1976), p. 198.
52. F. F. Bruce, *The Epistle to the Hebrews*, NICNT (Grand Rapids: Eerdmans, 1964), pp. 274-75. Bruce's discussion (pp. 271-75) contains full data as to the critical problems in the LXX citation of Hab. 2:4. See also B. F. Westcott, *The Epistle to the Hebrews* (Grand Rapids: Eerdmans, 1955), pp. 347-48.

3
The Prophet's Prayer and God's Exaltation (Habakkuk 3:1-19)

A perplexed prophet had awaited God's instructions (2:1). They have come to him with assurance (2:2-3) and an expression of basic principles (2:4), together with application of God's working in the current crisis (2:5-19). Habakkuk has been reminded that God was in charge and that He called for submission by all, including himself (2:20).

In humble response Habakkuk turns in prayer and praise to God. He beseeches God's mercy in the midst of His righteous judgment (3:1-2). After laying bare his soul, he addresses God in a double poem of praise as the only one who can meet the needs of His people and His prophet (3:3-15). The prophecy ends on a high note. Having reviewed God's mighty actions in redeeming and caring for His people, Habakkuk responds in fear and trust that his Redeemer will bring the divine purposes to their proper conclusions (3:16-18). The final verse (3:19) sounds a triumphant chord of praise to Israel's Redeemer and puts forward Habakkuk's guide for living.

The entire chapter is a prayer psalm (see introduction) complete with opening cry, attestation of praise, petition (v. 2), a central section of twofold praise (vv. 3-15), a renewed affirmation of trust in God (vv. 16-18), and a concluding note of praise (v. 19).[1] The central portion

---

1. In his helpful excursus on chap. 3, C. Armerding ("Habakkuk," in *EBC* [Grand Rapids: Zondervan, 1985], 7:521) likewise notes this structural arrangement and views it as a large chiasmus: "introduction, v. 1 (A);

was drawn from two ancient compositions culled from an epic cycle of Israelite poems celebrating the Exodus from Egypt (vv. 3-7) and the entrance into the land of promise (vv. 8-15). Other literary features include simile and metaphor (vv. 4, 8-10, 11, 14, 19), metonymy (vv. 2, 9?), merismus (vv. 3, 7), hyperbole (vv. 6, 11), paronomasia (vv. 13-14), personification (vv. 1, 5, 7?), rhetorical question (v. 8), enjambment (vv. 8, 16), climactic parallelism (v. 2), gender-matched parallelism (v. 3), staircase parallelism (v. 8), chiasmus (vv. 3, 5), synecdoche (v. 3), and alliteration and assonance.

A. THE PROPHET'S PRAYER FOR THE
REDEEMER'S PITY (3:1-2)

Having heard and understood God's principles of judgment and their application, Habakkuk returns to the matter of Judah's judgment. Unlike the condemnation of his people with which his spiritual struggle had begun (1: 2-4), the knowledge of the severity of the divine judgment strikes fear into God's prophet. Though judicial wrath must come, Habakkuk pleads for God's mercy.[2]

Translation

A prayer of Habakkuk the prophet. On *shigionoth**.
[2]LORD, I have heard the report concerning You*;
   I stand in fear, O LORD, of Your deeds*;
in the midst of years, renew* them,
   in the midst of years, make them known,
   in ferocity*, remember compassion*.

Exegesis and Exposition

Like many of the psalms, the next section of Habakkuk's prophecy is given a heading. What follows is his prayer psalm, a composition to be set to music for use in worship. But "though its substance makes it suitable for usage in Israel's worship in general, it is also tied intimately to Habakkuk's particular experience of God which has dominated the first two chapters of the book."[3]

Habakkuk begins his prayer with a cry and statement of praise that reflect his fear of God (v. 2*a*). The choice of the word "LORD" (*Yahweh*) rather than a more general term probably emphasizes the fact that Habakkuk addresses his words to Israel's covenant God. He

---

   prayer, v. 2 (B); theophany, vv. 3-15 (C); response, vv. 16-19 (B[1]); epilogue, v. 19 (A[1])."
2. For the uniqueness of chap. 3, as well as its essential unity with chaps. 1-2, see under Literary Context in the introduction.
3. P. C. Craigie, *Twelve Prophets* (Philadelphia: Westminster, 1985), 2:102.

has heard of Yahweh's past mighty deeds. Habakkuk has in mind the theophany expressed in the epic material commemorating the Exodus, the subject of vv. 3-15. Armerding underscores the likelihood of this suggestion:

> The noun "fame" (*šema'*) is normally used of secondhand information (e.g., Job 28:22; Nah 3:19), suggesting a remoteness from the hearer's own experience to the persons or events referred to (cf. Job 42:5). The Lord's "deeds" envisaged here corroborate this sense of remoteness, being associated with his sovereign power and preeminently with his "work" (*pō'al*) at the Exodus (e.g., Num 23:23; Pss 44:1; 68:28; 77:12; 90:16; 95:9; 111:3; cf. v. 3)—a primary anchor-point of Israel's recollection, faith, and hope, as is the Cross to the Christian.[4]

Nevertheless, the past work of God also often included times of judgment for His people.

In accordance with God's message of the near chastisement of Judah, Habakkuk now prays for God's miraculous intervention. He employs a stanza-closing tricolon framed in climactic parallelism and filled with alliteration and assonance (the use of velars and the letters *z* and *r*). He asks that (as in the past) God will, in the midst of these years in which the appointed time (cf. 2:3) of God's work (cf. 1:5) of judgment is taking place, renew His deeds and thus again make known His work of redemption. With aching heart he urges God to be compassionate in the coming turmoil (cf. Ex. 34:6-7; 1 Kings 8:33-34, 46-53; 2 Chron. 6:24-25, 36-39; Isa. 54:8).

Habakkuk's prayer would be answered according to the terms of Israel's covenant with God (Deut. 4:25-31) and also the prophecies of Jeremiah (Jer. 25:1-11; 29:10-14; cf. 2 Chron. 36:22; Ezra 1:1; Dan. 9:2). His prayer and its realization stand as an earnest of God's future gathering of His people in redemptive power (Deut. 30:1-3; Ezek. 36:24-38; 37:21-28; Amos 9:14-15; Mic. 4:6; Zeph. 3:20; Zech. 10:5-12).

Additional Notes

3:1 †שִׁגְיֹנוֹת ("*shigionoth*") is derived from the verb שָׁגָה ("go astray"). Although words connected with this root are most often used in moral and spiritual contexts, this noun is employed twice as a musical notation: once in the singular (Ps. 7:1), here in the plural. Its combination with עַל ("[up]on/according to") in both places renders it certain that, like other such psalm headings, it must refer to the musical setting of the psalm. Keil observes that

> all the notices in the headings to the psalms that are introduced with '*al* refer either to the melody or style in which the psalms are to be sung, or

---

4. Armerding, "Habakkuk," in *EBC*, 7:523.

to the musical accompaniment with which they are to be introduced into the worship of God. This musico-liturgical signification is to be retained here also, since it is evident from the subscription in ver. 19, and the repetition of *Selah* three times (vers. 3, 9, 13), that our hymn was to be used with musical accompaniment.[5]

The precise understanding of the term, however, is disputed. Keil (see also Delitzsch, Laetsch, von Orelli) prefers the idea of a dithyramb with its wild, undulating, emotional setting. He also mentions the suggestion of Schmieder, who views it as a "strong, martial, and triumphal ode."[6] Armerding opts for "a vehement cry for justice against sin,"[7] whereas Watts suggests a lament.[8] The infrequency of the word's occurrence as well as the uncertainty concerning it already evident in the ancient versions has caused most English translations simply to transliterate it.[9] Blue's conclusion covers the matter well:

> It is unlikely that it refers to the content of the song, even though the Hebrew root verb may also mean "to transgress or err." But the theme is not directed to the transgressions or wanderings of Babylon and Judah; the song centers on the majesty of God. Therefore it is much more reasonable to see *shigionoth* as having a musical-liturgical significance. Another musical notation is found at the end of Habakkuk 3. Possibly this song became a part of the temple worship.[10]

For תְּפִלָּה ("prayer") see the introduction.

3:2 שִׁמְעֲךָ† ("the report concerning you"): The translation follows the NASB (cf. RSV) in taking the suffix as an objective genitive.

The translation of פָּעָלְךָ ("your deeds"; lit. "your work") follows the NIV (cf. RSV) in viewing the noun as the object of the previous verb. This preserves the parallel balance with the preceding line.

---

5. C. F. Keil, *The Twelve Minor Prophets*, COT (Grand Rapids: Eerdmans, 1954), 2:93.
6. Ibid.; see also C. L. Feinberg, *The Minor Prophets* (Chicago: Moody, 1976), p. 216.
7. Armerding, "Habakkuk," in *EBC*, 7:523.
8. J. D. W. Watts, *The Books of Joel, Obadiah, Jonah, Nahum, Habakkuk, and Zephaniah*, Cambridge New English Bible Commentary (London: Cambridge U. 1975), p. 144. See also *Preliminary and Interim Report on the Hebrew Old Testament Text Project* (New York: United Bible Societies, 1980), 5:362. The NJB renders the term "tune for dirges," perhaps reflecting a relation with the Akkadian *šegū*, "psalm of lament"; see further C. Bezold, *Babylonisch-Assyrisches Glossar* (Heidelberg: Carl Winter's Universitätsbuchhandlung, 1926), p. 265.
9. The LXX translates the term μετὰ ᾠδῆς ("with an ode"), whereas the Vg renders it *pro ignorantiis* and the Pesh. omits it.
10. J. Ronald Blue, "Habakkuk," in *The Bible Knowledge Commentary*, ed. J. F. Walvoord and Roy B. Zuck (Wheaton: Victor, 1985), p. 1517.

Hiebert calls attention to the importance of the pairing of these two verbs:

> Especially to be noted is the link between *šmˁk*, the account about Yahweh, and *pˁlk*, the content of that account. This pair of terms is linked by their semantic equivalence, their final position in parallel lines, their grammatical identity (direct objects with 2ms suffixes), and their phonetic correspondence. . . . They establish two motifs central to the poem: the hearing about the acts of God, and the response of great awe which this hearing evokes. The use of the vocative, *yhwh*, identifies at the outset the central focus of the poem, the God of Israel.[11]

The frequent proposal to attach פָּעָלְךָ to the following line ("revive thy work," NASB; cf. KJV, NKJV) makes for a choppy translation, destroys the poetic balance, and ignores the necessity for taking the form as the antecedent for the suffix on "renew/revive."

No need exists for emending יָרֵאתִי to רָאִיתִי with *BHS* (so also Ward).

†חַיֵּיהוּ† ("renew them"; lit. "renew it"): The verb can denote not only giving, calling, or creating life (Gen. 7:3; 19:32, 24; Deut. 32:39) but also reviving and renewing life (Pss. 80:19; 85:6 [HB 85:7]; 119:25) as well as preserving life (Gen. 12:12; Deut. 6:24; Ps. 22:29 [HB 22:30]). The reference here points to the redeeming work of God that is rehearsed in vv. 3-15. This conclusion is reinforced by noting the emphasis of שִׁמְעֲךָ and פָּעָלְךָ that precede.[12]

תּוֹדִיעַ in the succeeding line is reminiscent of Ps. 77:14 (HB 77:15). Since the following request for mercy also echoes Ps. 77:7-9 (HB 77:8-10), Habakkuk may be consciously drawing upon that psalm as a literary allusion by which to introduce the epic poem that follows, particularly since some of that material is reflected in Ps. 77:16-18 (HB 77:17-19). The objective pronoun in the previous line is here deleted, a common feature in Hebrew poetry.[13] This makes unnecessary the LXX ἐπιγνωσθήσῃ ("make yourself known"). The LXX apparently viewed the MT verb as niphal (תִּוָּדַע). Nor does the presence of תּוֹדִיעַ demand the reading חַיֵּיהוּ ("make it known," "declare it") in the preceding line, the sense of the MT being clear as it stands.[14]

---

11. Theodore Hiebert, *God of My Victory*, Harvard Semitic Monographs 38 (Atlanta: Scholars, 1986), pp. 60-61.
12. To the contrary, see Keil, *Minor Prophets*, 2:94-95; H. E. Freeman, *Nahum Zephaniah Habakkuk*, Everyman's Bible Commentary (Chicago: Moody, 1973), pp. 116-17; C. von Orelli, *The Twelve Minor Prophets*, trans. J. S. Banks (1897; reprint, Minneapolis: Klock and Klock, 1977), p. 252.
13. For details, see M. Dahood, *Psalms*, AB (Garden City, N.Y.: Doubleday, 1970), 3:432.
14. See W. H. Ward, *A Critical and Exegetical Commentary on Habakkuk*, ICC (Edinburgh: T. and T. Clark, 1911), p. 26; see also Hiebert, *God of My Victory*, pp. 13-14.

229

רֹגֶז ("ferocity") and רַחֵם ("compassion") are expressive words. The former comes from a root that means "to tremble/shake" (cf. Hab. 3:7), often in rage (Isa. 28:21)[15] or fear (Hab. 3:16). The noun itself occurs elsewhere only in Job, where it is employed of one's troubles (Job 3:17, 26; 14:1), the rumbling of thunder (Job 37:2), or the fierceness of the war horse (Job 39:24), and in Isa. 14:3, where it depicts Israel's oppression. Accordingly the noun here implies an action that produces a fearsome trembling, such as before a fierce storm.

The latter word signifies a warm love of great depth. A denominative from the word for "womb" and set here in emphatic position, it stresses the prophet's concern that in the midst of His judgment God will remember to have tender compassion on His people.[16]

B. THE PROPHET'S PRAISE OF THE REDEEMER'S PERSON (3:3-15)

Habakkuk has been given answers to his perplexities. Summoned to silence by God, he has broken that silence only by praying for God's mercy in the midst of judgment. He does so on the basis of his consideration of God's past redemptive acts for His people, some of which he now rehearses for all to contemplate. His prayer is continued with a psalm of praise to the God who alone can meet the needs of all people. Habakkuk draws upon older poetic material that had formed part of a body of compositions commemorating God's deliverance of His people at the Exodus and the entrance into Canaan.

The psalm consists of two distinct works (vv. 3-7, 8-15), each of which not only contributes to the corpus of epic poetry dealing with the Exodus but also is uniquely suited for adaptation into the prayer as a whole (see the Excursus on Habakkuk 3).

1. THE REDEEMER'S COMING (3:3-7)

The initial portion of Habakkuk's psalm of praise has its orientation in Israel's movement up from the Sinai peninsula through the Transjordanian countries on the way to the Jordan River crossing. The Exodus (cf. Ex. 15:1-10) and the movement to Sinai (cf. Ex. 15:11-13) have occurred; now after many years the final leg of the journey to Canaan is taking place. In these opening words God is seen

---

15. M. L. Barré ("Habakkuk 3:2: Translation in Context," *CBQ* 50 [1988]: 184-97) translates רֹגֶז as "fury" and views it as parallel to קֶרֶב, which he understands as "battle."
16. For details, see L. J. Coppes, "רָחַם," *TWOT* 2:841-43; H. J. Stoebe, "רחם," *THAT* 2:761-67.

leading the heavenly and earthly armies in their trek, a sight that strikes terror into the hearts of the citizens of that area. The poem, bookended by geographical terms (vv. 3, 7), has two stanzas (vv. 3-4, 5-7), the first of which is closed by a tricolon, the second by two tricola.

a. His appearance (3:3-4)

Translation

Eloah came* from Teman*,
  the Holy One* from Mount Paran*. (Selah*.)
His glory covered the heavens,
  and His praise* filled the earth.
⁴His brightness was like the light;
  rays* flashed from His very own hand,
  from the inner recesses of His strength*.

Exegesis and Exposition

The first poem deals with the movement from the southland. The historical perspective is variously understood, the majority opting for a relation to the theophany at Sinai (Armerding, Blue, R. Smith, von Orelli), some for Sinai as a representation of God's triumphs, whether past (G. A. Smith) or future (Keil, Feinberg) or considered as a unit (Laetsch). W. F. Albright suggests its origin in "the period following the wilderness wanderings."[17] I am convinced that the orientation of the poem is the era of the wilderness wanderings, possibly in the final movement that led to the staging area from which the assault on Canaan would be made.

The poem opens with a description of God's awesome appearance. Up from the Sinai peninsula to the south, through Edom and lower Transjordan, the heavenly entourage approaches the place from which the campaign against Canaan will be launched. The movement from the southeast is also mentioned in Judg. 5:4-5; Ps. 68:7-8 (HB 68:8-9); it seems to have been a vital element in Israel's early epic tradition. Thus Cross, having underscored its importance, laments that "the relation of this motif, the march of Conquest, to the early Israelite cultus has been insufficiently studied."[18]

---

17. W. F. Albright, "The Psalm of Habakkuk," in *Studies in Old Testament Prophecy Dedicated to T. H. Robinson*, ed. H. H. Rowley (Edinburgh: T. and T. Clark, 1950), p. 8.
18. F. M. Cross, Jr., "The Divine Warrior in Israel's Early Cult," in *Biblical Motifs*, ed. Alexander Altmann (Cambridge: Harvard U., 1966), p. 25. Cross links this motif with the idea of kingship and suggests that both were utilized in the royal cultus (pp. 27-33). See further R. D. Patterson,

The association of Yahweh with the south has in recent times been strengthened by texts discovered at Quntillet 'Ajrud on the border between the southern Negev and the Sinai peninsula. One of them reads "I bless you by Yahweh of Teiman and his *asherah*." A great deal of discussion has centered on the identification of this *asherah* and its association with Yahweh. Though many have suggested that the reference is to the name of a Canaanite goddess, the consort of Baal (e.g., Freedman), the matter is far from settled. André Lemaire offers compelling evidence that the word here refers to a sacred tree or grove, probably connected with cultic worship.[19] In addition, because of Israel's entrenched monotheism, it seems unlikely that a pagan deity would be affiliated with Yahweh as His consort, even in a splinter group far removed from the center of the Israelite cultus.

God is seen by His enemies not as Yahweh, Israel's covenant God, but as Eloah, the Creator (Deut. 32:15) and Lord of the earth (Pss. 18:31 [HB 18:32]; 114:7). God is also declared to be the Holy One (Isa. 6:3), the one who convicts of sin and judges the world (Lev. 19:1; 20:7; Jer. 50:29; 51:5), but who is Israel's Redeemer (Isa. 41:14; 43:1-3). The one whom Habakkuk had addressed in his second perplexity (Hab. 1:12) is the sovereign, holy God who had come long ago in all His glory.

Armerding suggests that the word for "glory" here, הוֹד (*hôd*), "is used primarily of kingly authority (e.g. Num 27:20; 1 Chron 29:25; Ps 45:3; Zech 6:13), revealed preeminently in the Lord's sovereignty over creation and history (cf. 1 Chron 16:27; 29:11-12; Job 40:10)."[20] If so, it admirably reinforces the names for God here. He is thus seen in all His majesty and as the one whose splendor (cf. Job 37:22-23) permeates and transcends the heavens (Pss. 8:1 [HB 8:2]; 145:4).

It is no wonder, then, that His praise is said to fill the earth. Because the word translated "praise" sometimes means "splendor,"[21] the effect is further enhanced. When one considers Him whose majestic splendor fills heaven and earth, he can but stand in awe of Him and sing His praises. This Habakkuk ultimately will do (Hab. 3:16-19).

"The Song of Deborah," in *Tradition and Testament: Essays in Honor of Charles Lee Feinberg*, ed. John S. Feinberg and Paul D. Feinberg (Chicago: Moody, 1981), pp. 130-31.

19. See, e.g., D. N. Freedman, "Yahweh of Samaria and his Asherah," *BA* 50 (1987): 241-49. Also see André Lemaire, "Who or What Was Yahweh's Asherah?" *BAR* 10 (1984): 42-51. Lemaire's article remains among the finest and most balanced in the sizable literature on this subject.
20. Armerding, "Habakkuk," in *EBC*, 7:525; see further G. Warmuth, "הוֹד," *TDOT* 3:352-54.
21. See BDB, p. 240.

In a graphic simile the brilliance of God's glory is detailed. His splendor is said to be like the light. Although the root of נֹגַהּ (*nōgah*) can be utilized of brightness in general (cf. Hab. 3:11) and Isaiah (Isa. 4:5; 60:13) employs it in describing the messianic era, it is characteristically used for the shining of the celestial luminaries (2 Sam. 23:4; Isa. 13:10; Joel 2:10; 3:15 [HB 4:15]). Ezekiel uses it to describe the radiant brightness of the glory of God (Ezek. 1:4, 28; 10:4). The psalmist also employs the root to depict the divine theophany in a context parallel to that of Habakkuk 3:4 (Ps. 18:12, 18 [HB 18:13, 29]; cf. 2 Sam. 22:13, 29). Since Ezekiel's use includes an association with fire (Ezek. 1:13, 27), and fire attended the appearance of God at Mount Sinai (Ex. 19:16-19; Deut. 5:22-26; cf. Heb. 12:18-21), many commentators assume that the references in Habakkuk and Psalm 18 are to that event. But although Deut. 33:2 connects God's glory with Sinai, it seems more likely that even there the reference is to Yahweh's departure rather than to His glory as it descends upon Mount Sinai. The association of the glory of the Lord with Sinai is unmistakable; the point here, however, may be that the same glory that was seen at Mount Sinai and traveled with the people on their journeys (cf. Ex. 40:34-38) now moves in surpassing brilliance ahead of them.

Thus the primary thrust of the passage is on the theophany.[22] The one who once appeared on Mount Sinai and who had filled the southland with His glory now fills the heavens with splendor. Dazzling rays of light stream from that radiant glory, much like those from a glowing sun. These only point, however, to their source in the inner recesses of the omnipotent one.[23] Keil puts it well:

> In the sun-like splendour, with the rays emanating from it—is the hiding of His omnipotence, *i.e.* the place where His omnipotence hides itself; in actual fact, the splendour forms the covering of the Almighty God at His coming, the manifestation of the essentially invisible God.[24]

Additional Notes

3:3 †יָבוֹא ("come"): The form is preterite. The alternating of preterite and suffix-conjugation verbs is a mark of ancient Hebrew po-

---

22. Albright ("The Psalm of Habakkuk," p. 8) suggests that the poem "was probably taken with little alteration from a very early Israelite poem on the theophany of Yahweh as exhibited in the south-east storm, the *zauba-'ah* of the Arabs; the historico-geographical background reflects the period following the wilderness wanderings."
23. Armerding ("Habakkuk," in *EBC*, 7:526) points out that "the 'hand' is repeatedly a symbol of the Lord's power . . . a 'power' manifested conspicuously in the forces of nature . . . which are 'hidden' in his storehouse."
24. Keil, *Minor Prophets*, 2:100.

etry and occurs throughout the double psalm that follows. Habakkuk will also employ it in conscious archaizing style in his concluding remarks (vv. 16-19).[25]

†Teman is the southernmost of Edom's two chief cities. Edom itself is also called Teman (Obad. 9),[26] the name stemming from a grandson of Esau (Gen. 36:11, 15, 42; Jer. 49:7, 20) whose descendants inhabited the area. (For Esau = Edom, see Gen. 25:25, 30.) Edom was formerly called Mount Seir (Gen. 36:8-9; Deut. 2:12). Paran designates not only a mountain range west and south of Edom and northeast of Mount Sinai but also a broad desert area in the Sinai peninsula. (For the juxtaposition of Seir and Paran, see Gen. 14:6.) All three terms are used as parallel names for the southern area that stretched as far as the Sinai peninsula (cf. Deut. 33:1-2a; Judg. 5:4-5).

†The musical term *selah* (cf. vv. 9, 13), probably indicating an instrumental interlude, is discussed in a helpful excursus by P. C. Craigie in *Psalms 1-50*, WBC (Waco, Tex.: Word, 1983), pp. 76-77.

3:4 †Hiebert prefers to retain קַרְנַיִם in its usual sense of "horns," pointing out a possible association with the word "strength" at the end of the verse. Such literalness does not seem necessary, however, in figurative poetry describing a theophany. In any case it makes for too rough a transition from the previous expressions. Nor is W. F. Albright's suggestion to translate "⟨Yahweh⟩ attacked like a bull(?)‖ Provided with tossing horns" particularly helpful.[27]

†עֻזֹּה ("his strength"): The spelling of the pronominal suffix reflects an older stage of the language. However, it is also attested in the later Lachish letters.[28]

b. His actions (3:5-7)

Translation

Plague went before Him,
  and pestilence went out at His feet.

---

25. See Hiebert, *God of My Victory*, pp. 77-79. See also Frank Moore Cross, Jr., *Studies in Ancient Yahwistic Poetry* (Baltimore: Johns Hopkins, 1950), pp. 54-56; Moshe Held, "The YQTL-QTL (QTL-YQTL) Sequence of Identical Verbs in Biblical Hebrew and in Ugaritic," in *Studies and Essays in Honor of Abraham A. Neuman*, ed. M. Ben-Horin, B. D. Weinryb, and S. Zeitlin (Leiden: Brill, 1962), pp. 281-90.
26. See Thomas J. Finley, *Joel, Amos, Obadiah*, WEC, ed. Kenneth Barker (Chicago: Moody, 1990), p. 362.
27. Albright, "The Psalm of Habakkuk," pp. 11-12.
28. See Z. S. Harris, *Development of the Canaanite Dialects* (New Haven: American Oriental Society, 1939), pp. 55-56. For its possible presence elsewhere in Habakkuk, see the Excursus on Habakkuk 2:4.

⁶He stood and shook* the earth;
  He looked and made the nations tremble*.
The everlasting hills were shattered;
  the eternal hills were made low
  —His eternal courses*.
⁷I looked* on Tahath-Aven*;
  the tents of Cushan were trembling,
  the tent curtains of the land of Midian.

Exegesis and Exposition

As the holy God moves His hosts forward, His agents of judgment accompany Him. Plague is there (cf. Ex. 9:15; Deut. 28:21; Amos 4:10) and also pestilence* (cf. Deut. 32:24). Both seem to be personified here as though they made up part of the heavenly retinue (cf. Deut. 33:2-3). Keil observes: "Plague and pestilence, as proceeding from God, are personified and represented as satellites; the former going before Him, as it were, as a shieldbearer (1 Sam. xvii.7), or courier (2 Sam. xv.1); the latter coming after Him as a servant (1 Sam. xxv.42)."²⁹

The first poem closes with a consideration of God's initial strikes against the enemy, the scene portrayed dramatically in a double tri-colon. Taking his stand, God throws into convulsion the age-old mountains (cf. Job 15:7; 20:4; Ps. 90:2 [HB 90:3]), the primeval paths (cf. Amos 4:13) of the one who "rides upon the heavens" (cf. Deut. 33:26; Ps. 68:33 [HB 68:34]). Whether the reference is to the hills of Transjordan, Canaan, or a widespread area of the Jordan Valley is unclear. The mention of such areas as Cushan* and Midian* would seem to favor the latter suggestion. Although tents and tent curtains are by metonymy singled out for special attention, the whole area from south to north felt the effects of God's triumphant march. The Scriptures give evidence that seismic activity accompanied the Israelites at various stages of the Exodus, especially at the time of the conquest (Judg. 5:4-5; Pss. 18:7 [HB 18:8=2 Sam. 22:8]; 114:3-6). Under such conditions it is little wonder that the inhabitants of the area were struck with terror (cf. Ex. 15:14-16).³⁰

---

29. Keil, *Minor Prophets*, 2:101.
30. Hiebert (*God of My Victory*, pp. 95-97) suggests that Kushan and Midian were not objects of God's terrifying activity but, like Habakkuk, were possibly worshipers of Yahweh who shared his awe. He finds in this suggestion "a very early date for the composition of this material" (p. 97).

Additional Notes

3:5 לְרַגְלָיו . . . . לְפָנָיו ("before him . . . at his feet") is set in chiastic arrangement.

The parallel lines have often been taken as evidence for viewing Deber as an epithet or alternative name of Resheph, the Canaanite god of *pestilence* and sterility.[31]

3:6 †וַיְמֹדֶד has customarily been translated either "measured" (RSV, KJV, NKJV; cf. NASB, "surveyed") or "shook" (NIV; cf. LXX ἐσαλεύθη). The inappropriateness of the former meaning has led most critical expositors to favor the latter here. Scholars have suggested various biforms and alloforms to account for this understanding of מדד: (1) מוּד = מוֹט ("crumble," "set in reeling motion"— Keil), (2) מוּד = נָדַד/נוּד ("move"—Hiebert; cf. מוֹט/מָטַט ["crumble"], נוּט/נָטַט ["shake"]—Margulis), and (3) Arabic *māda* ("was convulsed"; G. R. Driver).

†וַיַּתֵּר has occasioned several translations: διετάκη ("melt," LXX), "drove asunder" (KJV), "startled" (NASB, NKJV), "shook" (RSV), "made to tremble" (NIV). If the previous line is to be rendered "shook," the NIV translation is the most appropriate. If the traditional understanding of מָדַד ("measure") is retained, perhaps a root תּוּר ("spy out," "survey") might be suggested for the form here. The force of the following couplet and the dire effects of the preceding two favor a translation similar to that of the NIV for these two lines.

†הֲלִיכוֹת עוֹלָם לוֹ: The line is difficult. It has usually been translated by the English versions "His ways are everlasting/eternal." Albright suggested that the ל of the last word be combined with the first two words of v. 7 to read לתחתאן, an energic feminine plural of חְתָא with emphatic ל.[32] So constructed, the newly constituted line would be translated "Eternal orbits were shattered." While this suggestion is attractive and involves no consonantal revision, it leaves a metrical

---

31. See W. F. Albright, *Yahweh and the Gods of Canaan* (Garden City, N.Y.: Doubleday, 1969), p. 186. See also Hiebert, *God of My Victory*, pp. 92-94; John Day, "New Light on the Mythological Background of the Allusions to Resheph in Habakkuk iii 5," *VT* 29 (1979): 353-55. For the proposed Eblaite evidence, see the comments of M. Dahood in G. Pettinato, *The Archives of Ebla* (Garden City, N.Y.: Doubleday, 1981), p. 296.
32. See Albright, "The Psalm of Habakkuk," p. 15. Hiebert (*God of My Victory*, p. 21) follows Albright in this and comments on the projected *hapax legomenon* as follows: "The verb *ḥt'*, 'to crush, ruin, vanquish,' though not attested elsewhere in biblical Hebrew, is a common Semitic verb. It is present in Ugaritic literature . . . and in the Amarna correspondence. . . . Also to be noted are the Akkadian *ḥatâ* (for *ḥatā'u*), 'smash,' and the Arabic *ḥata'a*, 'to be broken, humbled' (8th form)." Both Albright and Hiebert are forced to emend the text, each doing it in a different way.

imbalance in vv. 6b and 7, which appear to have a 3/3/3 pattern. Further, the MT yields a reasonable sense as "His eternal courses." The syntax of the line is reminiscent of Num. 23:22b: כְּתוֹעֲפֹת רְאֵם לוֹ (cf. Ps. 18:8 [HB]: וַיִּתְגָּעֲשׁוּ כִּי־חָרָה לוֹ).

3:7 רָאִיתִי may be explained by recalling the similar employment of this verb in the Balaam oracles (Num. 23:9; 24:17). Indeed, the poet may have intended a deliberate pun or literary allusion to Num. 23:21: "He has not seen distress/wickedness in Jacob,‖ nor has he looked upon trouble in Israel."

The first line of v. 7 is difficult. It has frequently been taken with the first two words of the second line, leaving the last word of line two to be construed with line three. This makes for a smooth transla- tion—"I saw the tents of Cushan in distress,‖ the dwellings of Midian in anguish" (NIV)—and makes for a tolerable personification, but it leaves an unusually long pair of lines: 5/4. Despite the difficulty of the MT, it seems best to retain the more customary reading with its 3/3/3 meter.

The troublesome תַּחַת אָוֶן can be translated by the usual "in dis- tress/affliction" but may perhaps be better taken as a geographical name paralleling Cushan and Midian in lines two and three. It may have been a name employed by the Hebrew poet to describe the general area where the enigmatic Cushan (= Egyptian Kushu?) and Midian were located—that is, southern Transjordan. If so, the whole verse forms a geographic inclusio with v. 3.[33]

†*The land of the Midianites* is identified primarily with the south- ern part of Transjordan (e.g., Gen. 25:6; 36:35; Num. 10:29), and evi- dence now exists that *Cushan* was also located there. An interesting parallel to the biblical account here, including the seismic activity, is in a fragmentary inscription found at Kuntillet ʿAjrud. As pointed out by Hiebert, "the context is the battle of the divine warrior. His ap- pearance is accompanied by light (cf. Hab 3:4a), and the response to it is reflected in the convulsion of the cosmos: the mountains are melted and their peaks crushed."[34] Such an inscription from the very area where the biblical account is set is particularly significant.

---

33. תחת appears as a geographical name in Num. 33:26-27. אָוֶן-type forms occur as personal names and geographical names in the OT (e.g., Num. 16:1; Ezra 2:33; Neh. 6:2; 7:37; 11:35; Amos 1:5; cf. Gen. 36:23; 38:4, 8, 9, etc.). If תחתאון is to be taken as a geographical name, אוֹן־ may be associ- ated with a noun meaning "vigor" or "wealth" coming from a second homophonous root to that of the usual noun translated "trouble," "wick- edness," "distress." The confusion between the two words may have been viewed as a literary pun: תחתאון, "wealthy place," is seen as "in distress."

34. Hiebert, *God of My Victory*, p. 95.

2. THE REDEEMER'S CONQUEST (3:8-15)

The second poem is a victory ode that sings of the mighty strength of Israel's Redeemer. His power is displayed at the waters of testing (vv. 8-9*b*), unleashed in the natural world (vv. 9*c*-11), and viewed by the enemy (vv. 12-15). Whereas the first two sections deal in a general way with the entire Exodus event (but focus particularly on the final movement into Canaan), the final section fixes its attention on the initial stage of the Exodus. The opening stanza begins with a rhetorical question framed in staircase parallelism and set in an initiating tricolon (v. 8). The subject matter of v. 8 deals largely with God's actions in connection with water, a theme to which the poet will return in a final bookending reference to God's victory at the Red Sea (v. 15). From start to finish, Israel's God is shown to be the victor over all individuals and nations and the champion of those who follow in His train.

a. His power as seen at the waters (3:8-9b)

Translation

Yahweh, were You angry* with the rivers*,
  or* was Your wrath against the streams*
  or Your fury against the sea
when You were mounted upon Your horses,
  Your chariots of salvation*?
⁹You laid bare* Your bow;
  You were satisfied* with the club* that You commanded. (Selah.)

Exegesis and Exposition

The rhetorical question with which the second poem begins is for emphasis and vividness of effect.[35] Addressing God personally, Habakkuk asks whether His actions against the waters were born of anger. All three words for wrath here characterize God's judicial activity against anything that opposes His will. The tricolon with which the verse begins swells in intensity with the depiction of God's anger, which bursts through all resistance.

That wrath is said to be directed at the waters. Using phraseology drawn from the epic literature familiar to the people of the Levant, particularly of Syro-Palestine, Yahweh is portrayed metaphorically as Israel's mighty warrior who appears in His battle chariot (v. 8), armed with bow (v. 9*a*), club (v. 9*b*), arrows (v. 11*b*), and spear (v. 11*c*). Though the literary allusion is probably to Baal's dispatching of his

---

35. See Feinberg, *Minor Prophets*, p. 218.

238

enemy Yamm (Sea),[36] here Yahweh is shown to be the true Master over the forces of nature.

This, however, is no cosmic battle between deities representing the forces of nature; Yahweh comes as Israel's champion against human opponents. In giving His people the victory He utilizes His power over the elements to aid His people (cf. Judg. 5:19-21). Not only at the Exodus from Egypt itself (cf. Ex. 15:12-15) but also at the Jordan River Yahweh has shown Himself to be sovereign over all forces and events. Keil points out that these two episodes in Israel's history demonstrate God's control over everything "as the Judge of the world, who can smite in His wrath not only the sea of the world, but all the rivers of the earth."[37]

The reference to waters here probably intends the activities of God in connection with the entire Exodus event. The theme of water is prominent not only in the triumph at the Red Sea (Ex. 15) but also in passing through the Jordan (Josh. 3-4). Perhaps some of the early victories in the land (e.g., Judg. 4-5) are envisioned. In accordance with His promise to defend His people (Deut. 32:40-42), the God who is the Creator of the abyss and seas (Gen. 1:6-8; Pss. 24:2; 104:6; 2 Pet. 3:5) and the controller of the Flood (Gen. 6-8; 2 Pet. 3:6) and all watery domains (Job 38:8-11; Pss. 24:2; 104:7-13; 2 Pet. 3:7) moves out in the Exodus against the waters (and all His enemies) on behalf of His own. As Lord of the waters and Commander of the armies, He mounts His chariot fully armed with weapons for the fray. Thus equipped for battle He sets out to meet all obstacles, whether natural forces or human enemies.

Additional Notes

3:8 †Hiebert follows Albright in suggesting that both occurrences of the final -*m* on נָהָר are enclitic.[38] Many have pointed out the Ugaritic parallelism of *ym*‖ *nhr*.[39] Dahood also calls attention to the

---

36. See A. Cooper, "Divine Names and Epithets in the Ugaritic Texts," *RSP*, 3:375-76; for a similar treatment, see U. Cassuto, "Chapter III of Habakkuk and the Ras Shamra Texts," in *Biblical and Oriental Studies*, trans. Israel Abrahams (Jerusalem: Magnes, 1975), 2:11-12.
37. Keil, *Minor Prophets*, 2:103. Armerding ("Habakkuk," in *EBC*, 7:528) rightly observes that "Exodus and Sinai alike are the incarnation of events with universal significance."
38. For enclitic -*m*, see M. Pope, "Ugaritic Enclitic -*m*," *JCS* 5 (1951): 123-28; H. D. Hummel, "Enclitic *MEM* in Early Northwest Semitic, Especially Hebrew," *JBL* 76 (1957): 85-106; M. Dahood, *Psalms*, 3:408-9.
39. See, e.g., Cross, *Ancient Yahwistic Poetry*, p. 140; M. Dahood, "Ugaritic-Hebrew Parallel Pairs," *RSP*, 1:203.

use of סוּס ‖מַרְכָּבוֹת here.[40] The final noun has been taken by Freedman as standing at the end of a broken construct chain.[41]

†חָרָה ("be angry") is a 3d masc. sing. qal perfect verb agreeing either with יהוה ("Yahweh, were you angry?" [cf. NIV] or "Was Yahweh angry?" [cf. NASB]) or with אַף ("anger") in the parallel line, hence to be translated "burn" ("Did [your anger] burn against the rivers?"). I have followed the lead of the NIV in taking יהוה as a vocative and translating it *ad sensum*. The LXX reads ὠργίσθης ("Were you angry?"), thus making both lines formally parallel with respect to being in the second person. The enallage in the MT, however, is common enough so that such emendation is unnecessary.[42]

†The deletion in *BHS* of אִם בַּנְּהָרִים ("or against the streams") is not supported in the ancient versions. Far from being redundant, the line represents the poetic convention of employing a tricolon to demarcate the boundary of a unit.[43]

†The translation of יְשׁוּעָה as "salvation" is traditional. Despite Keil's objection, in a martial context, "victory" (RSV) or "victorious" (NIV) is also appropriate. The metonymy here is effective, God's deliverance being represented by the "chariots of salvation."[44]

3:9 †תְעוֹרֵר ("you laid bare"—i.e., the quiver full of arrows, here associated metonymically with the bow): The verbal root has been taken to be either עוּר ("be bare/exposed") or עָרָה ("lay bare"). Hiebert proposes another possible confusion:

> The confusion represented in the MT and many of the versions may be easily explained on the basis of old orthography. The consonants *t'r* in early orthography could be either a form of *'wr*, "to awaken," or of *'rh*, "to be bare," in the latter case the short preterit form of a final weak verb.[45]

---

40. Dahood, "Ugaritic-Hebrew Parallel Pairs," 1:284; for רכב, see R. D. Patterson, "A Multiplex Approach to Psalm 45," *GTJ* 6 (1985): 29-48.
41. D. N. Freedman, "The Broken Construct Chain," *Biblica* 53 (1972): 535. For added discussion as to the broken construct chain, see A. C. M. Blommerde, "The Broken Construct Chain, Further Examples," *Biblica* 55 (1974): 549-52. For a negative appraisal of the whole concept, see J. D. Price, "Rosh: An Ancient Land Known to Ezekiel," *GTJ* 6 (1985): 79-88.
42. See M. H. Pope, *Song of Songs*, AB (Garden City, N.Y.: Doubleday, 1977), pp. 303-4.
43. See W. G. E. Watson, *Classical Hebrew Poetry* (Sheffield: JSOT Press, 1986), p. 183.
44. For the motif of the divine warrior, see F. M. Cross, *Canaanite Myth and Hebrew Epic* (Cambridge: Harvard U., 1973), pp. 91-111; D. Stuart, "The Sovereign's Day of Conquest: A Possible Ancient Near Eastern Reflex of the Israelite 'Day of Yahweh'," *BASOR* 221 (1976): 159-64; Patrick D. Miller, Jr., *The Divine Warrior in Early Israel* (Cambridge: Harvard U., 1973).
45. Hiebert, *God of My Victory*, p. 25.

With the former alternative the preceding עֶרְיָה is often repointed as a piel infinitive absolute (cf. *BHS*, Hiebert), yielding "You laid quite bare Your bow."[46] עֶרְיָה could of course be retained as an internal object from the same verbal root or semantic range as the verb, here placed first for emphasis (cf. Mic. 1:11) in a double accusative construction.[47]

The verb itself can be viewed either as a 2d masc. sing. or 3d fem. sing. imperfect (prefix conjugation), the choice depending on the understanding of the parallel line. Albright decides for the former and translates "Bare dost Thou strip Thy bow";[48] Keil follows the latter course: "Thy bow lays itself bare."[49] As for the troublesome second line, Margulis laments: "The second hemistich is patently impossible."[50] No consensus as to its translation has been reached. Laetsch points out that by his day Delitzsch had counted more than one hundred different interpretations of this difficult line.[51]

That the divine warrior's weapons are taken in hand is clear from the parallel pair קֶשֶׁת ǁ מַטֶּה.[52] The use of special weapons such as lightning is familiar from the literature of the ancient Near East. Thus Ward remarks: "Syrian and Hittite art frequently represents *Adad-Ramman*, god of storm, as armed with the same weapons, while the Babylonian art gave this western god the forked thunderbolt."[53]

†For the MT שְׁבֻעוֹת ("oaths") I have followed the lead of some ancient versions (Pesh., LXX[Barb]) and many scholars in reading (with no consonantal change) שָׂבַעְתָּ ("you were satisfied"),[54] an understanding attested elsewhere in contexts dealing with fighting and weaponry. In addition to Jer. 46:10, one may note the case of Anat's fighting as recorded in the Baal cycle: "Anat fought hard and gazed (on her

---

46. Note the translation in the *Hebrew Old Testament Text Project*, 5:364: "You uncover your bow ⟨so that it is⟩ naked"; cf. RSV, "strip."
47. For details, see GKC, par. 117p, q, cc-ee.
48. Albright, "The Psalm of Habakkuk," p. 12.
49. Keil, *Minor Prophets*, 2:103.
50. B. Margulis, "The Psalm of Habakkuk: A Reconstruction and Interpretation," *ZAW* 82 (1970): 420.
51. T. Laetsch, *The Minor Prophets* (St. Louis: Concordia, 1956), p. 347. See further H. St. John Thackery, "Primitive Lectionary Notes in the Psalm of Habakkuk," *JTS* 12 (1911): 191-213.
52. See Dahood, "Ugaritic-Hebrew Parallel Pairs," 1:258. The ת in מַטּוֹת is the common Canaanite fem. sing. ending.
53. Ward, *Habakkuk*, p. 23. See also Patterson, "Psalm 45," pp. 38-39; Hiebert, *God of My Victory*, pp. 26-27.
54. Albright, "The Psalm of Habakkuk," p. 15. Albright, however, needlessly takes the following *maṭṭôt* from Epigraphic South Arabic *mṭw* ("fight"). The verb could also be pointed as a piel suffix conjugation שִׂבַּעְתָּ ("you satisfied"; cf. *BHS*).

work), she battled . . . until she was sated, fighting in the palace."[55] The NIV relates the MT consonants to שְׂבֻעַ ("heptad") and translates "many arrows." Although other versions trace the form to the verb שָׁבַע ("swear"; NASB, KJV, NKJV), some translate *ad sensum*: "You put (the arrow to) the string" (RSV; cf. NJB). Even though a final solution for the line is not forthcoming, its association with the preceding lines and the literary motif of the divine warrior make the general sense of God's actions on behalf of His people clear enough.

†The final אֹמֶר may be understood as the name of God's war club, the noun coming from a verbal root מָרַר ("drive out").[56] If so, it could be a veiled reflection of or scribal pun on Baal's war weapon Aymur ("Expeller").[57] Perhaps the simplest solution is to view the final *t* of *maṭṭôt* as a double-duty consonant, yielding the translation given above.[58]

b. His power as seen in the natural world (3:9c-11)

Translation

You split open the earth* with rivers;
   [10]the mountains saw You; they trembled.
Torrents of water swept by;
   the deep gave its voice,
   it lifted its hands on high.
[11]Sun and moon* stood still in their lofty height*,
   at the light* of Your flying arrows,
   at the flash* of the lightning, Your spear.

Exegesis and Exposition

The scene changes from preparation to engagement in battle. Continuing the motif of the divine warrior, the psalm portrays the Lord's striking with awesome force. Perhaps it is a club that is used first. As it smites the earth with titanic power, it splits the land open, the mountains crumble, and the subterranean waters and surface rivers (fed by an intense storm; cf. Gen. 7:12; 8:2; Judg. 5:21) overflow

---

55. See G. R. Driver, *Canaanite Myths and Legends* (Edinburgh: T. and T. Clark, 1956), pp. 84-85.
56. See C. Gordon, *UT*, 3:356.
57. *UT*, 2:180.
58. For the use of double-duty consonants, see I. O. Lehman, "A Forgotten Principle of Biblical Textual Tradition Rediscovered," *JNES* 26 (1967): 93; cf. Dahood, *Psalms*, 2:81; 3:371. For asyndetic subordination, see R. J. Williams, *Hebrew Syntax* (Toronto: Toronto U., 1976), p. 90; Dahood, *Psalms*, 3:426-27; A. B. Davidson, *Hebrew Syntax* (Edinburgh: T. and T. Clark, 1958), pp. 191-92. For the corresponding Akkadian construction, see W. von Soden, *GAG*, p. 219.

their natural boundaries (cf. Job 38:8-12; Judg. 5:4-5; Pss. 18:7-15 [HB 18:8-16]; 68:7-8 [HB 68:8-9]; 77:16-19 [HB 77:17-20]; 144:5-6). Hiebert rightly declares:

> The predominant image in this description of nature's response is the agitation of cosmic waters. Three of the six cola in this subsection mention the waters. Subterranean rivers erupt (v 9b); water pours from the clouds (v 10a); and the deep roars (v 10b). Just as the ancient mountains, founded firmly on the waters at creation, are shaken (vv 6, 10a), so the cosmic waters, restrained at creation behind designated boundaries, break out.[59]

The waters of the abyss (Gen. 49:25; Deut. 33:13) are said to cry out and lift up their hands, perhaps in terror (Laetsch) or prayer (Delitzsch). As a figure of battle, this doubtless refers to the force with which the waters roar from their subterranean prisons and the tossing waves that cap the surface of the waters. The imagery of a plaintiff crying to the God who alone rescues from danger may also be present. If nature is subject to the omnipotent one, surely the case is no different for mankind (cf. Pss. 19:1-4 [HB 19:2-5]; 104:31-35; 148:1-4). In any event, the figure is appropriate to the theophany associated with the culminating moments of the Exodus. Indeed, the description in vv. 9c-10 fits well the details of the crossing of the Jordan, which report a river at flood stage (Josh. 3:15) and intense seismic activity (Ps. 114:3-6).[60]

The drama of warfare continues in v. 11 with a hyperbolic description of the celestial scene. The heavenly warrior shoots His arrows and hurls His spears so that the sun and the moon appear to stand still in their courses. They are largely obscured by the darkness that attends the heavy clouds, seen only intermittently amid the flashing lightning.[61] The severity of the storm is underscored by the two tricola with which the unit ends; it is nothing less than the presence of Israel's mighty God (cf. Ps. 29).

Is there a veiled reference here to the famous "long day" of Joshua

---

59. Hiebert, *God of My Victory*, p. 98.
60. For archaeological illumination of the stopping up of the Jordan due to earthquake and the effect of seismic activity on the fall of Jericho, see J. P. Free, *Archaeology and Bible History* (Wheaton: Scripture Press, 1962), pp. 128-29; John J. Bimson, *Redating the Exodus and Conquest* (Sheffield: Almond, 1981), pp. 121-24.
61. Hiebert follows John Holladay and Patrick Miller in holding that the mention of sun and moon here not only has astrological importance but also implies their presence in the heavenly retinue: "Sun and Moon, members of the divine army, appear together in the sky in positions considered fortuitous astrologically, when the divine warrior goes into battle. As such they provide support for the attack (v 11b) launched by Yahweh" (*God of My Victory*, p. 100).

recorded in the book of Jashar (Josh. 10: 12-13), as suggested in the Targum and by several Jewish (e.g., Rashi, Kimchi) and some Christian scholars (e.g., Hailey, Pusey)? If so, the Exodus epic must have contained several songs of the conquest period. In any case, the strophe (vv. 9c-11) is appropriate not only for describing the events of the Jordan crossing and the early conquest period but also for the imagery of theophany and the theme of judgment.[62]

Additional Notes

3:9c †אֶרֶץ in the first line (v. 9c) has been understood as either the subject or the object. Because the 2d masc. sing. verbal suffix is read in the following line, it seems best to retain the traditional understanding of תְּבַקַּע as a 2d masc. sing. verb and view "earth" as its object. Thus the sentence forms a syntactical parallel with the following lines where the activity of the mountains is recorded. "Earth" parallels "mountains" in several texts commemorating this event (e.g., Judg. 5:5; Ps. 18:7 [HB 18:8]).[63]

3:10 Hiebert calls attention to the juxtaposition of suffix- and prefix-conjugation verbs in רָאוּךָ and יָחִילוּ:

> The shift from suffixal to prefixal forms here, as well as in the rest of the poem, is to be understood not as a shift between perfect and imperfect states but as the archaic use of perfect and preterit forms to convey past narrative, a practice best exemplified in Ugaritic poetry. The same sequence of these two verbs is in fact found in Ps 77:17 (r'wk mym yḥylw), part of an archaic theophany very similar to Hab 3:8-15.[64]

Hiebert also finds the influence of Ps. 77:17 (HB 77:18) in the next line, which he emends (with the support of a Hebrew fragment from Wadi Murabba'at) to read זֹרְמוּ מַיִם עָבוֹת ("clouds poured down water").[65] Though the conjecture is attractive and has the advantage of some ancient manuscript support and precedent in similar contexts (cf. also Judg. 5:4), the evidence is still too meager to set aside the MT זֶרֶם מַיִם עָבָר ("torrents of water swept by"), which has the support of the ancient versions.

For the parallelism of נָתַן || וְנָשָׂא, see the remarks of M. Dahood in

---

62. Theophany and judgment are also commonly combined in quasi-apocalyptic literature dealing with the Day of the Lord (cf. Isa. 13:10, 24:23; Joel 2:2, 10, 31 [HB 3:4]; 3:15 [HB 4:15]; Amos 5:8, 20; 8:9; Zeph. 1:15; see also Matt. 24:29; Rev. 6:12-13; 9:2).
63. Several other parallel terms common to Ugaritic and Hebrew have been suggested as present here by Dahood ("Ugaritic-Hebrew Parallel Pairs," 1:177-78, 218, 372-73): יָד || חָץ, נָתַן || נָשָׂא, תְּהוֹם || קוֹל (although the LXX may be right in finding the parallel of תְּהוֹם as רוּם).
64. Hiebert, *God of My Victory*, p. 29.
65. Ibid., p. 30.

RSP 1:218. For the collocation of קוֹל and תְּהוֹם, see Dahood's discussion in RSP 1:372-73.

3:10-11 †The lack of metrical balance at the end of v. 10 and the beginning of v. 11 has occasioned several suggestions for dividing the lines. Dahood takes רוּם with the first line of v. 10b and reads "the abyss gave forth its haughty voice."[66] Albright takes the שֶׁמֶשׁ of v. 11 with v. 10 and translates "The Exalted One, Sun, raised its arms."[67] The translation adopted here takes שֶׁמֶשׁ יָרֵחַ as a composite name, formed perhaps as a result of a deletion transformation so as to achieve the desired three poetic lines. The juxtaposition of sun and moon participating in earthly events is noted elsewhere (e.g., Josh. 10:12-13; Isa. 13:10; Joel 2:10; 3:4; etc.). The words are of course familiar set terms.[68]

This proposal does away with the problem of the lack of connection between שֶׁמֶשׁ and יָרֵחַ and any incongruity between them and the MT sing. verb עָמַד ("stand"). It also yields (with the next verse) a closing double tricolon for the subunit dealing with God's actions in the natural world (vv. 10b-11).

There is no textual support for the conjectural emendation of *BHS*, followed by some, to read "The sun forgets its rising" or the suggestion of the NEB to translate "The sun forgets to turn in its course."

3:11 †זְבֻלָה ("[their] lofty height"): *BHS* proposes a repointing to זְבֻלֹה, the resultant masc. sing. suffix thereby agreeing with יָרֵחַ. However, the MT fem. ending can be explained as agreement with שֶׁמֶשׁ, often construed as a fem. noun.

Smith calls attention to the fact that זְבֻל used here for the dwelling place of the sun and moon is usually reserved for the "exalted dwelling place of God."[69] Since sun and moon are among the heavenly retinue, they may also be viewed as being where God dwells.[70]

---

66. M. Dahood, "The Phoenician Contribution to Biblical Wisdom Literature," in *The Role of the Phoenicians in the Interaction of Mediterranean Civilizations*, ed. William A. Ward (Beirut: American U. of Beirut, 1968), p. 140.
67. Albright, "The Psalm of Habakkuk," p. 12.
68. For the use of fixed pairs of set terms, see S. Gevirtz, *Patterns in the Early Poetry of Israel* (Chicago: Oriental Institute, 1963), pp. 2-4, 10-14; Y. Avishur, "Word Pairs Common to Phoenician and Biblical Hebrew," *UF* 7 (1975): 13-47. Note, however, the caution of P. C. Craigie, "Parallel Words in the Song of Deborah," *JETS* 20 (1977): 15-22. For the participation of other celestial phenomena in earthly events, see Judg. 5:20; Isa. 60:19-20; and the remarks of P. C. Craigie, "Three Ugaritic Notes on the Song of Deborah," *JSOT* 2 (1977): 33-49.
69. R. Smith, *Micah–Malachi*, WBC (Waco, Tex.: Word, 1984), p. 114.
70. See the discussion of J. Gamberoni, "זְבֻל," *TDOT* 4:29-31; see also H. Wolf, "זְבֻל," *TWOT* 1:235.

לְאוֹר . . . לְנֹגַהּ† ("at the light . . . at the flash"): Most modern translations take the subject of these prepositional phrases to be the sun and moon of the first line of the verse (KJV, NKJV, NASB, NIV, NJB, RSV), an understanding found in some ancient versions (Vg, Pesh.) and followed by most commentators. The accents of the MT, however, indicate that the subject of the two lines in question is to be understood differently, as reflected in Ward's translation:

> For light thine arrows go forth,
> For brightness the glittering of thy spear.[71]

So perceived, the two prepositional phrases are viewed as governed by subjects in their own lines. This arrangement is also reflected in the LXX, OL, and *Tg. Neb.* and followed by Hiebert, who translates the prepositional phrases under consideration adverbially: "brightly . . . brilliantly." Middle ground in the debate is found by Keil, who takes the prepositional phrases as dependent on the previous line but views "arrow" as the subject of the following verb, which he interprets as standing in a relative clause: *At the light of Thine arrows which shoot by, at the shining of the lightning of Thy spear.*"[72]

Any of the proposed suggestions is somewhat satisfactory and yields essentially the same result. The translation given above follows the lead of Keil and the NIV in (1) relating the two lines in question closely and causally to the previous statement concerning the sun and moon and (2) taking the verb יְהַלֵּכוּ as subordinate to חֲצֶיךָ (thus "your flying arrows"), but (3) repoints the construct noun בְּרַק ("lightning of") as an absolute noun ("lightning") and (4) takes the following "spear" as apposition. Thus the celestial luminaries are obscured by the brilliance of the electric storm.

c. His power as seen by the enemy (3:12-15)

Translation

In indignation You trod upon* the earth;
    in anger You trampled* the nations.
¹³You went out for the salvation of Your people,
    for the salvation of* Your anointed.
You smote the head of the house of evil;
    laying him bare* from his lower parts to his neck (selah),
    ¹⁴You split his head with his own club*.
His warriors* stormed out;
    to scatter the humble was their boast,
    like devouring the poor in secret.

---

71. Ward, *Habakkuk*, p. 21.
72. Keil, *Minor Prophets*, 2:66.

**¹⁵You trod upon the sea with Your horses*,
heaping up* many waters.**

Exegesis and Exposition

Once again the scene is changed. With the initial phase of the attack in the natural world having been launched, Yahweh's wrath is directed at those nations that have troubled His people. If the presence of God that spread across the sky sent the earth into cataclysmic upheaval, so much the more will God's power moving through the area bring down the ungodly nations.

Habakkuk had begun his prophecy with a perplexity as to why God tolerated injustice or at least did not save the righteous from the unrighteous (1:2-3). When he was informed of God's intention to use the godless Chaldeans to bring judgment to His people (1:5-11), Habakkuk was all the more perplexed (1:12–2:1). The words of the ancient epic poem that he now considers remind him of the just nature of God. Though the Lord may employ nations and people of all sorts to do His bidding, He will ultimately deal with them on their own merits (cf. Isa. 24:1-6; 63:1-6; Jer. 50:9-13; Hos. 1:4; Nah. 3:4). Further, He will deal with them according to their troubling of His people Israel (cf. Gen. 12:3; Isa. 26:12-20; Joel 3:1-8 [HB 4:1-8]; Obad. 14-15; Zeph. 2:10).

God's indignation against the nations in this regard can mean the deliverance of His own people, as here. Indeed, salvation/deliverance was at the heart of the epic cycle concerning the Exodus (Ex. 15:2). God redeems His people out of Egypt (Ex. 15:1-10, 14-18; Hab. 3:12-15), carries them to Sinai where He reveals Himself to them (Ex. 15:11-13), and then, as their triumphant Redeemer, goes before them both to demonstrate His redemptive power to the nations and to bring His people victoriously into the land (Deut. 33:2-3; Judg. 5:4-5; Pss. 18:7-15 [HB 18:8-16]; 68:7-8 [HB 68:8-9]; 77:16-19 [HB 77:17-20]; 144:5-6; Hab. 3:3-11). That Exodus theme is perpetuated throughout the OT (e.g., Num. 23:21-24; 24:8-9, 17-19; Deut. 4:35-40; Josh. 23:3-6), especially among the prophets who build upon it in looking forward to the final salvation of Israel in a future day (e.g., Isa. 10:20-22; 25:9; 35:4; 41:11-16; 43:1-13; 49:8-26; 50:11; 52:7-10; 54:6-10; Jer. 23:5-8; 32:37-44; Ezek. 34:11-16; 36:24-38; 37:21-28; Hos. 2:14–3:5; Joel 2:31-32 [HB 3:4-5]; Amos 9:11-15; Obad. 17; Mic. 2:12-13; 4:1-7; 5:5-15; Nah. 1:13-15; Zeph. 3:8-20; Hag. 2:23; Zech. 14:3; Mal. 4:5-6).

The salvation of God's anointed* is singled out for particular attention. Although historically the term here probably has reference to Moses, it can be applied also to the ruling member of the Davidic line, whose future coming was recorded by Moses (cf. Gen. 49:10;

247

Num. 24:19). David understood his role as God's anointed (2 Sam. 7:8-29; 23:1-7), and the Scriptures from his time forward proclaim the inviolability of the far-reaching provisions in the Davidic Covenant (cf. Pss. 2; 45:2-7; 89:3-4, 19-24, 27-37 [HB 89:4-5, 20-25, 28-38]; 110; Jer. 33:19-26; Ezek. 34:20-31) that will find their ultimate realization in Israel's Messiah (Isa. 42:1-7; 48:16-17; 49:1-7; 52:13–53:12; Jer. 23:5-8; Ezek. 37:24-28; Zech. 9:9; cf. Isa. 61:1-2 with Luke 4:18-19; see further Luke 1:68-78; Acts 2:29-36; 3:24-26; 15:16-17; Rev. 11:15). Accordingly A. G. Nute's observation is well taken:

> Nor is this great statement to be confined to the events of Habakkuk's day, or to the fortunes of Israel. It is satisfied only when applied to the advent of Him of whom it was said, 'you are to give him the name Jesus, because he will save his people from their sins' (Mt. 1:21).[73]

The last two lines of v. 13 and the first line of v. 14 form a tricolon filled with problems, chief of which is the figure involved. Does God's smiting* refer to the defeat of a mythological figure (Albright, Hiebert, R. Smith), the kingdom of the ungodly (von Orelli) with Satan at its head (Laetsch, Pusey), or a wicked enemy (Fausset, Margulis) such as Pharaoh (Armerding), the Chaldeans (Feinberg, Hailey), or the Chaldeans as representative of all godless nations (Keil)? Because the primary orientation of these verses is the Exodus redemption, probably the historical reference is to Pharaoh and the armies of Egypt over whom God in Moses, His anointed, achieved the victory. The idea of a victorious Redeemer could be applied to the subsequent defeat of the enemy in the land (cf. Josh. 6; 10:12-13; Judg. 5:19-23; etc.) and to all the victories that the Lord gave to Israel (e.g., 2 Kings 19:32-36) and will yet accomplish in a future day (Ps. 110:5-6; Isa. 17:12-14; 24:21-23; 34:1-4; 63:1-6; 66:14-16, 22-24; Ezek. 38-39; Joel 3:9-17 [HB 4:9-17]; Amos 9:11-12; Obad. 19-21; Mic. 4:11-13; Zeph. 3:8-11; Hag. 2:20-22; Zech. 12:2-4; 14:1-5; Mal. 4:1-3; etc.).

Accordingly, Armerding points out that

> this verse provides further evidence of the double perspective of the chapter: the oppression in Egypt foreshadows subsequent oppression, and the deliverance at the Red Sea embodies the promise of subsequent deliverance. The term "anointed one" lends itself more readily to later usage, both with reference to the preexilic kings and in anticipation of the eschatological Messiah.[74]

Doubtless this feature of the psalm was not lost on Habakkuk. He would have found encouragement and comfort in applying the passage to the coming defeat of the Chaldeans. Thus Blue remarks:

---

73. A. G. Nute, "Habakkuk," in *The International Bible Commentary*, ed. F. F. Bruce, rev. ed. (Grand Rapids: Zondervan, 1986), p. 949.
74. Armerding, "Habakkuk," in *EBC*, 7:531.

God had destroyed Pharaoh's horsemen who pursued Israel (Ex. 14:23-28) and other leaders (Num. 21:23-25; Josh. 6:2; 8:28-29; 10-11). If God could do this, He could destroy Babylon. Belshazzar, also a "leader" in a "land of wickedness," was stripped of his power (Dan. 5:26-28, 30-31).[75]

An added problem, but one related to the first, has to do with the employment of the word רֹאשׁ (*rō'š*, "head")*. Should both occurrences of this term be applied literally to the head of an individual (Albright) or creature (Hiebert), to the upper part of a house,[76] or to the godless leader of the nations (Fausset)? Could a double reference be intended here,[77] such as *rō'š* meaning the wicked leader presented under the figure of a house (Keil, Laetsch)? Because Cassuto has shown that the controlling verb (מָחַץ) is commonly used in Ugaritic and the OT to signify a blow that a warrior gives to his enemy,[78] it seems best to understand an instance of paronomasia and differentiate the uses of *rō'š*, viewing the first as the enemy leader but the second as a literal head. So understood, the general statement (v. 13c) is taken up with the image of personal mortal combat. Yahweh first wounds (perhaps with the spear) the enemy so gravely that his body is laid open with a gaping hole (v. 13b); He then delivers the *coup mortel* to the head with His foe's own mace (v. 14a).

The referent of the poetic imagery (if one is demanded[79]) is difficult to ascertain. The poetry may simply celebrate God's general victory over Pharaoh, or it may contain a veiled reference to Pharaoh's defeat in the plague of the firstborn.

The poem closes (vv. 14b-15) with details that provide a follow-up to the previous scene. The enemy's warriors storm out against the people of God like brigands coming upon the helpless. Keil's comments on the simile are to the point: "The enemies are compared to

---

75. Blue, "Habakkuk," in *The Bible Knowledge Commentary*, p. 1520. The song itself, however, sang of the basic victory that made the eventual conquest of the land possible: the celebrated triumph at the time of Israel's Exodus (cf. Ex. 12:31-36, 50-51; Acts 7:35-36; etc.).
76. *Hebrew Old Testament Text Project*, 5:366-67.
77. For details, see A. R. Hulst, *Old Testament Translation Problems* (Leiden: E. J. Brill, 1960), p. 252.
78. U. Cassuto, "Psalm LXVIII," in *Biblical and Oriental Studies*, translated by Israel Abrahams (Jerusalem: Magnes, 1973), 1:268. See also Moshe Held, "*mḥṣ, *mḫš* in Ugaritic and Other Semitic Languages," *JAOS* 79 (1959): 169-76. For discussion of progression of meaning as a strategy for intensification, see R. Alter, *The Art of Biblical Poetry* (New York: Basic Books, 1985), pp. 63-65.
79. Hiebert (*God of My Victory*, p. 108) may be correct in affirming that "no single historical battle or enemy is singled out by the poet as is the case, for example, in Judges 5. The hymn of triumph celebrates, as do Deut 33:2-3, 26-29 and Psalm 68, the wars of conquest as a whole."

highway murderers, who lurk in dark corners for the defenseless trav-
eller, and look forward with rejoicing for the moment when they may
be able to murder him."[80] The event commemorated here may be the
Egyptians' pursuit of the fleeing Hebrews (Ex. 14:5-9). If so, the last
verse of the poem is doubly apropos: it not only sings of the miraculous deliverance of the children of Israel through the "many waters"
(cf. Ex. 15:10) of the Red Sea (Ex. 14:13-22, 29-31) but also bookends
the theme of God's action against waters with which the poem began
(v. 8).

If, as suggested above, v. 8 deals primarily with the events toward
the end of the Exodus experience, v. 15 produces the basis for the
whole chain of events: the great deliverance from Egypt.[81] The double psalm thus ends on a note of redemption. Israel's God, who
brought them through the waters of testing with a mighty power that
left all nature in convulsion and who led His people in triumph, was
the one who had been with them since the deliverance out of Egypt. A
victorious Redeemer, He could be counted on to save once more a
repentant and submissive people. This truth should prove to be a
source of assurance for a troubled prophet. "Just as God went
through the Red Sea in the olden time to lead Israel through, and to
destroy the Egyptian army, so will He in the future go through the sea
and do the same, when He goes forth to rescue His people out of the
power of the Chaldaean."[82]

Additional Notes

3:12 †תִּצְעָד ("you trod upon"): The verb occurs with יָצָא elsewhere
in the epic literature detailing God's actions on behalf of His people
during the Exodus event (Judg. 5:4; Ps. 68:7 [HB 68:8]). LXX ὀλι-
γώσεις ("you will diminish") probably represents a reading תִּצְעַר
("you will grow insignificant"), doubtless due to confusion between
the consonants ד and ר.

†תָּדוּשׁ ("you trampled") is picturesquely rendered in the Vg
obstupefacies, "you will render senseless/stupefy." The term is a key
one in the double psalm. Thus Armerding observes:

---

80. Keil, *Minor Prophets*, 2:111.
81. Ps. 114:3, 5 likewise links together both watery crossings of the Israelites,
    whereas Ps. 77:19 (HB 77:20) applies the "many waters" mentioned here
    (cf. Ex. 15:10) in connection with the Red Sea crossing to the crossing of
    the Jordan River. For the debate over the matter of whether the Hebrew
    יַם־סוּף is to be translated "Red Sea" or "Sea of Reeds," see R. L. Hubbard,
    Jr., "Red Sea," *ISBE* 4:58-61, and the extensive bibliography there. For
    the linking of the Exodus and Conquest episodes, see M. Fishbane, *Text
    and Texture* (New York: Schocken, 1979), pp. 121-40.
82. Keil, *Minor Prophets*, 2:112.

The common metaphor of threshing implies violent shaking and crushing, which also characterizes the effects on the "earth" and mountains as the Lord "strode" by (Judg 5:4-5; Ps 68:7-8; cf. 1 Kings 19:11-12; Ps 77:18-19). Thus v. 12 also recapitulates the imagery of earthquake from v. 10: in effect it resumes and integrates the content of both vv. 3-7 and vv. 8, 9-11 at the introduction to this concluding section (vv. 12-15), in which the goal of the Lord's "wrath" and salvation becomes evident whether acting on the "earth" or the "nations."[83]

The parallel pair אַף‖זַעַם appears elsewhere of God's indignation against His enemies (e.g., Isa. 30:27). Especially instructive is Isa. 10:5 where not only this pair is found but also מַטֶּה (Hab. 3:9) appears: "Woe to the Assyrian, the rod of My anger, in whose hand is the club of My wrath."

3:13 †לְיֵשַׁע ("for the salvation of") is rendered as an infinitive by the LXX: τοῦ σῶσαι ("to save"; cf. *Tg. Neb.*). On the basis of OT usage, however, one would expect an infinitival form לְהוֹשִׁיעַ, unless as Dahood suggests the MT should be repointed to read לְיֵשַׁע (yiphil infinitive construct).[84] Albright (cf. NIV) translates both cases of לְיֵשַׁע as infinitives.[85]

The appearance of the particle אֶת־ after the second לְיֵשַׁע has added to the difficulty. D. N. Freedman considers this to be an example of a broken construct chain and translates the phrase "for the salvation of your anointed."[86] The particle should probably be viewed as an instance of its use with a noun carrying an implied causative verbal force, an employment expanded from its normal function of marking the definite direct object of a verb. Its force is thus emphatic here.[87] One could also adopt Pusey's suggestion of taking אֶת as the preposition "with"; however, this would obscure the

---

83. Armerding, "Habakkuk," in *EBC*, 7:530.
84. See M. Dahood, "Two Yiphil Causatives in Hab 3¹³ᵃ," *Or* 48 (1979): 258-59. Note that ישׁע uniformly occurs in Northwest Semitic in the extensive stem; see, e.g., the Moabite Inscription, line 4, H. Donner and W. Röllig, *Kanaanäische und Aramäische Inschriften* (Wiesbaden: Otto Harrassowitz, 1966), 1:33.
85. Albright, "The Psalm of Habakkuk," p. 13.
86. Freedman, "The Broken Construct Chain," p. 535. Freedman goes on to remark: "Apparently the second phrase is a construct chain, like the first, except that the intrusive *'t* has been inserted between the construct and the absolute. Exactly what the *'t* is it may be difficult to say: it may be the emphasizing particle, normally used to identify the definite direct object of a verb (here of the action), or it may be the pronoun written defectively, used here to call attention to the pronominal suffix attached to the following noun."
87. See GKC, par. 117 1, m.

parallelism between the two lines, unless "with" is to be understood in both lines even though it appears only in the second:

> You went forth for victory with your people,
> for victory with your anointed one.[88]

The term מְשִׁיחֶךָ ("your *anointed*") has been taken as referring to the nation Israel (Ewald, Hitzig, Barker), to Israel's Davidic king (R. Smith; cf. 2 Sam. 23:1), or to the Messiah (Hailey, Keil, Laetsch, von Orelli). If the reference is primarily historical and has in view the era of the Exodus and wilderness wanderings, the term must refer to Moses. Although "Your anointed" seemingly forms a parallel to "Your people," Israel is nowhere else called by this term. Rather, "the anointed" is customarily reserved for individuals such as the high priest (Ex. 40:13) or the king (2 Sam. 23:1; note also Cyrus, Isa. 45:1). If Moses is intended, Pusey may be right in suggesting that the אֶת is to be taken as the preposition "with" (cf. Vg *in salutem cum Christo tuo*), for God promised Moses that He would be with him (Josh. 1:5; note, however, that the preposition there is עִם).[89]

3:13c-14a רֹאשׁ (*"head"*): Hiebert notes the progression of thought in the lines and so proposes deleting the first רֹאשׁ and emending מִבֵּית ("from the house of") to בָּמַת ("the back of"). He cites examples from Ugaritic and Mesopotamian literature where a warrior delivers a blow first to the body and then to the head. The proposal given in the Exegesis and Exposition likewise draws upon ancient Near Eastern literary precedent in that a blow is given first to the body of the foe and then crushingly to the head. But contrary to Hiebert, it retains the reading of the MT. This understanding has several advantages: (1) It preserves the received text with a smooth transition that moves from identifying the enemy to describing personal combat. (2) It maintains contact with the details of two-stage fighting attested in the ancient literature, such as Marduk's slaying of Tiamat first by delivering an arrow down her throat and then by a crushing blow to her skull,[90] the Egyptian Sinuhe's dispatching of his Amorite foe by an arrow to the neck followed by a deathblow with his battle-axe,[91]

---

88. See E. B. Pusey, *The Minor Prophets* (Grand Rapids: Baker, 1950), 2:217. The understanding of אֵת as "with" is also ably defended by A. R. Fausset, "Habakkuk," in R. Jamieson, A. R. Fausset, and David Brown, *A Commentary Critical, Experimental and Practical on the Old and New Testaments* (Grand Rapids: Eerdmans, 1948), 4:635-36. For additional cases of double-duty prepositions occurring only in the second parallel line, see the examples in Dahood, *Psalms*, 3:436-37.
89. For a discussion of the prepositions אֵת and עִם, see H. D. Preuss, "אֵת," *TDOT* 1:449-58.
90. See *ANET*, p. 67.
91. See ibid., p. 20.

and Baal's defeat of Yamm with a blow first to the body and then to the head.[92] (3) It has numerous interesting points of contact with stories of personal combat, such as the final blow delivered with the enemy's own weapon (in addition to the case of Sinuhe may be mentioned David's decapitation of Goliath, 1 Sam. 17:51) and the striking coincidence that the Akkadian word used for the bodily part upon which Marduk stands (Enuma Elish IV: 129), *išdu* ("foundation"), is cognate with יְסוֹד ("lower part," "foundation"; cf. NASB "thigh") found in Hab. 3:13. In light of all of this (see also the next note), no emendation of the MT is necessary.

†עָרוֹת ("laying bare") is best taken as an infinitive absolute detailing the activity of the main verb.[93] This eliminates the need for re-pointing the form as a 2d masc. sing. piel suffix-conjugation verb (cf. *BHS*), a reading suggested in the LXX and Vg. The "laying bare" (or "stripping") probably does not intend denuding the foe (cf. 2 Sam. 10:4; Isa. 20:4). The word can mean "laying bare by removal" (cf. Gen. 24:20; 2 Chron. 24:11). So construed here it would refer to taking away the weapons and defenses of the foe, so that whatever weapons or defenses he might possess would be rendered useless. A third possibility exists, however: "laying bare" could refer to severe wounding or loss of life (cf. Ps. 141:8). If so, this act is then followed by the traditional blow to the head. On the whole, the parallel with the scriptural and extrabiblical literature favors the last suggestion.

3:14 †For the MT 3d masc. sing. suffix pronoun in בְּמַטָּיו ("with his club/spear/shafts"; cf. Vg; *Tg. Neb.*) *BHS* suggests a 2d masc. sing. suffix pronoun (cf. LXX[Barb]). But the Greek tradition may be an accommodation to the previous חִצֶּיךָ in v. 11. The translation "club" is retained here (cf. v. 9), the plural being viewed as one of composition or intensification.[94]

†פְּרָזָו ("his warriors"): The word has been variously rendered as "villages" (KJV, NKJV; cf. Laetsch "villagers"), "rulers/leaders" (LXX), "throngs/hordes" (NASB, Keil, R. Smith), "warriors" (Vg, NJB, NIV, RSV). The latter idea seems most appropriate to the context here and suits as well that of another early Hebrew poem found in Judg. 5:7.[95]

---

92. See ibid., p. 131.
93. For details, see GKC, par. 75n; Williams, *Hebrew Syntax*, pp. 38-39; M. Hammershaimb, "On the So-called *Infinitivus Absolutus* in Hebrew," in *Hebrew and Semitic Studies Presented to Godfrey Rolles Driver*, ed. D. W. Thomas and W. D. McHardy (Oxford: Clarendon, 1963), pp. 85-93.
94. See Davidson, *Syntax*, pp. 18-19. BDB (p. 641) lists possible masculine and feminine plural forms for מַטֶּה. Dual ascriptions of gender are not without precedent with other nouns (e.g., שֶׁמֶשׁ); see Davidson, *Syntax*, p. 15.
95. See R. D. Patterson, "The Song of Deborah," p. 132.

The last three lines of v. 14 are obscure. Thus Hiebert laments:

> The remainder of v 14 is the lengthiest textual puzzle of the chapter. The next four words of the MT are understood very differently by the OG, and differently still by Barb. And the final four words of the MT, though confirmed by the OG and Barb, are hard to understand in the context. The disparity among the versions at this point in the poem indicates an ancient disruption in the text which may no longer be possible to correct.[96]

The position taken here suggests that there are three lines of text in a 2/3/3 pattern rather than the two lines of 3/4 as traditionally rendered. Key to understanding is the dividing of לַהֲפִיצֵנִי into two words: פּוּץ ("scatter") and צָנִיעַ ("humble") by viewing the צ as another example of a double-duty consonant. The resultant translation not only yields better sense but also parallels צָנִיעַ ("humble") and עָנִי ("poor"). So construed, צָנִיעַ would take its place alongside such words as אֶבְיוֹן in context with עָנִי.[97]

3:15 †For the figure of God treading upon the sea, see Ps. 77:19 (HB 77:20).[98] סוּסֶיךָ is an adverbial accusative absolute, which, in compressed language, complements the action of the main verb and governs the sense of the following line. The preposition of line one is also to be understood in the second line.[99]

†The LXX ταράσσοντας ("stirring up"; cf. NIV) represents a valid understanding of the MT חמר (cf. Ps. 46:4). However, the idea of the heaping up of the waters (cf. KJV, NKJV) is not inappropriate to the context, particularly as one that originates in the epic literature concerning the Exodus (cf. Ex. 15:8; Josh. 3:13, 16). *BHS* suggests the addition of בְּ to חֹמֶר (cf. Vg, *Tg. Neb.*), taking the resultant form as a preposition with a noun, "on the surge" (cf. NASB).

C. THE PROPHET'S PLEDGE TO THE REDEEMER'S PURPOSES (3:16-19)

Habakkuk ends his prophecy with affirmations of personal commitment and praise. Having been dramatically reminded of the past exploits of God against the wicked and His saving intervention on

---

96. Hiebert, *God of My Victory*, p. 43. Indeed, Margulis ("The Psalm of Habakkuk," p. 427) observes with regard to the whole verse, "This text seems to defy comprehension. It is at first sight the most seriously damaged portion of the poem." For full details as to the vast array of variant readings in this verse (especially the first four lines), see Hiebert, *God of My Victory*, pp. 43-46.
97. Suitable parallels can be found in Pss. 10:2, 8-10; 35:10; Prov. 30:14; etc.
98. For the preposition בְּ with דָּרַךְ ("tread on"), see Deut. 1:36, Josh. 14:9; Isa. 59:8; 63:2; Mic. 5:4-5.
99. For details, see Dahood, *Psalms*, 3:436.

behalf of His people, the prophet is overwhelmed. Now that he understands who God is and the principles and methods of His activities, it is enough for Habakkuk. He will trust Him through the coming hour of judgment and rejoice no matter what may happen (vv. 16-18). Borrowing phraseology from the repertoire of ancient Hebrew poetry, he closes the account of his spiritual odyssey on a high note of praise (v. 19).

From a literary perspective the passage is marked by chiasmus (vv. 16, 19) and simile (v. 19), is linked to the previous section by means of the stitch-words דָּרַךְ (dārak, "tread/walk"; v. 19; cf. v. 15) and יָשַׁע (yāšaʿ, "save/deliver"; v. 18; cf. vv. 8, 13), and is constructed with the divine name Yahweh (vv. 18, 19), the root רגז (rgz, v. 16), and the statement "I have heard" (v. 16) as bookending devices designed to form an inclusio with the opening section (v. 2) of the chapter. All this provides a unity to the chapter that allows it to form a grand liturgical psalm of prayer.

1. A STATEMENT OF THE PROPHET'S TRUST IN THE REDEEMER (3:16-18)

Translation

I heard and my inward parts* trembled,
  my lips quivered* at the sound;
decay* came into* my bones,
  and I moved with faltering footsteps*.
I will rest* during the day of distress (and)
  during the attack against the people invading us.
¹⁷When* the fig tree has not blossomed*
  and there is no fruit on the vines,
the olive crop has failed*
  and the fields* have produced no food,
the flock has been cut off* from the fold*
  and there is no cattle in the stalls*,
¹⁸I will rejoice in Yahweh,
  I will be joyful in the God of my salvation.

Exegesis and Exposition

Habakkuk had asked that God show mercy to His people in the midst of judgment and that God would make alive once more His great deeds of old (v. 2). In answer to His prophet, God had reminded him afresh of His mighty works at the time of the Exodus, as sung by the ancient poets. Had Habakkuk also been allowed a visionary glimpse of those past exploits? Many think so (e.g., Laetsch, Nute, R. Smith). Typical of these scholars is Blue, who, having suggested that the prophet was ushered into the presence of God, remarks with regard to that experience, "Obviously anyone who witnessed this amazing display of God's power would be left in awe. Habakkuk was no exception. He had asked for a show of God's might (v. 2). Little did he realize what a display it would be."[100] Whether Habakkuk was allowed to behold the theophanic splendor of old in a vision or simply visualized it himself as God impressed the words on his heart, the effect was staggering.

The prophet reports that he was so shaken by the overwhelming prospect of what he had understood that he convulsed to the depths of his being. His lips quivered, and it seemed as though his very bones were coming apart, perhaps decayed to the marrow. He reeled uncertainly on his feet, for the ground beneath him seemed to undulate incessantly. As Keil observes, "alarm pervades his whole body, belly, and bones."[101] And yet Habakkuk was to experience what Paul later declares: "Whenever I am weak, at that very moment I am strong" (2 Cor. 12:10).[102] Quickly he was flooded with the implications of all that had happened and had been revealed to him. He could take comfort in knowing that although God will chastise His people, the vicious Chaldeans will likewise undergo divine punishment. Further, he understood that what he had prayed for (v. 2) was in keeping with God's own nature: He was a God of judgment as well as of mercy (cf. Deut. 32:34-43). Therefore, when the day of distress comes for Judah, Habakkuk can rest secure in the assurance that God is in charge of everything, working it all out in accordance with His perfect will. He could also be at peace as the God of justice repays the Chaldean invaders for their crimes against Judah and all humanity (cf. Gen. 12:3; Deut. 30:7; Joel 3:1-3 [HB 4:1-3]; Nah. 1:2; 3:1-7; etc.).

Habakkuk's new resolve and trust are immediately apparent (vv. 17-18). When the time of trouble comes for Judah, disrupting the productivity of the land and the security of the cattle, Habakkuk will not only remain at peace, resting in the sufficiency of God, but will

---

100. Blue, "Habakkuk," p. 1521. T. Hiebert ("The Use of Inclusion in Habak-kuk 3," in *Directions in Biblical Poetry*, ed. E. R. Follis [Sheffield, JSOT Press, 1987], p. 133) insists that no visible theophany occurred: "The theophany is an account (*šmʿ, qwl*) which the poet has heard (*šmʿty*). The source of the account is human rather than divine, as is indicated by the fact that the divine subject of the account does not address the poet in the first person but is addressed by the narrator in the second and third persons. The poet thus locates himself within the milieu of recital. Habakkuk 3 represents the preservation and passing down of sacred traditions."
101. Keil, *Minor Prophets*, 2:113.
102. See A. T. Robertson, *Word Pictures in the New Testament* (New York: Harper, 1931), 4:266.

rejoice through it in Him who alone is his (and Israel's) Savior.[103] The words for "rejoicing*" here represent strong emotions. Habakkuk had used them previously to express his anxiety over the unbridled avarice of the Chaldeans (1:14-15). His choice of them here underscores his repentant heart and triumphant faith. Together they express his resolve not merely to rest in the Lord's will through everything that would come to pass but to rejoice fully in his saving God. Israel's covenant Lord was yet on the throne; that meant eventual blessedness for prophet and people alike (cf. Deut. 30:1-10).

Additional Notes

3:16 Several instances of chiasmus are found in vv. 16-19, two of which occur here. Thus "hearing" and "lips" are set chiastically in lines 1 and 2 to emphasize two means of sensory activity. Verse 16 is arranged so that verbs enclose the whole verse. רגז also appears chiastically in lines 1 and 4. This root is a key one in chap. 3, being found twice here and once each in vv. 2 and 7. The last line of v. 16 contains an example of enjambment.

†בְּטְנִי ("my inward parts"): the noun בֶּטֶן has several meanings, such as "belly" (KJV), "body" (NKJV, RSV), "womb." In several places it refers to the personal inner recesses (cf. Job 15:35; 32:18; Prov. 18:8; 20:27, 30; 22:18; 26:22) where a person's deepest desires lodge (Job 20:20, 23). The NIV rendering "heart," however, is not inappropriate. The translation given above follows the NASB.

†צָלֲלוּ ("quivered") is supported by the Vg: *contremuerunt*, "trembled violently," "quaked." The LXX "prayer" (cf. *Tg. Neb.*), which rests on the Aramaic root צְלָא ("pray"), scarcely makes sense in context. It surely is not the sound of the prophet's own praying that produces the trembling described in the following lines.

†יָבוֹא ("came into," "entered") is a preterite. The prophet here accommodates himself to the archaic style of the previous poems concerning the theophany.

†רָקָב ("decay") is rendered in the LXX τρόμος ("trembling"; cf. *Tg. Neb.*). Although some suggest that such an understanding might be related to Arabic *raqaba* ("observe") with a derived meaning "fear" (i.e., God),[104] it is more likely that the Greek translators are simply

---

103. Habakkuk's example of faith (he was learning the truth of Hab. 2:4) is reminiscent of the declaration of E. J. Carnell (*An Introduction to Christian Apologetics*, 4th ed. [Grand Rapids: Eerdmans, 1952], p. 82) that "faith is a resting of the soul in the sufficiency of the evidence."
104. For details, see J. G. Hava, *Al-Faraid Arabic-English Dictionary* (Beirut: Catholic Press, 1964), p. 264.

carrying on the thought that appears in the first and fourth lines. The MT is supported by the Vg *putredo* ("rottenness").

†As pointed by the Masoretes, אֲשֶׁר is the relative particle. So construed, it must be related syntactically to the two lines that follow (cf. KJV, NKJV, NASB). But to do so ruins the poetic balance, for it leaves the line with only two words and assigns four words to the next line.[105] Accordingly, the consistent 3/3 meter of the verse is upset.

To alleviate the imbalance *BHS* suggests reading אֲשֻׁרָי ("my steps"), a proposal followed by the RSV. Others simply translate *ad sensum*, e.g., "my frame" (LXX) or "my lips" (NJB). Taking the noun as the subject of the line, however, necessitates an emendation of the preceding 1st com. sing. verb. Therefore the resolution of the problem adopted here is to retain the consonants of the MT but to repoint the two words in question as אֶרְגַּז אֲשׁוּר ("I experienced a trembling [foot]step[106] [beneath me]") and translate the whole line *ad sensum*: "And I moved with faltering footsteps."

†יְגוּדֶנּוּ† . . . . אָנוּחַ ("I will rest [during] . . . [the people] invading us"): Hiebert follows S. R. Driver, who declares that "this and the next line are most obscure and uncertain, the Hebrew being in parts ambiguous, and the text open to suspicion. . . . The case is one in which it is impossible to speak with confidence."[107] The MT, however, can be explained as it stands. What is not so clear is against whom the coming calamity will be directed: Judahites (KJV, NKJV, NASB) or Chaldeans (NIV, NJB, RSV).

Because of the emotional fervor of the moment, the opening אָנוּחַ has often been considered inappropriate to the context.[108] Accordingly the verb has often been taken to mean "wait patiently" (NASB, NIV, NJB, RSV). But this is a sense that it does not bear elsewhere in the MT. Many have suggested emendations such as אֶאֱנַח ("I groaned/moaned," Hiebert, Ward) or אֲחַכֶּה ("I await," *BHS*). Nevertheless, if R. L. Harris is correct in his assessment that נוח "signifies not only the absence of movement but being settled in a particular

---

105. See further Hulst, *Translation Problems*, p. 252; *Hebrew Old Testament Text Project*, 5:369-70; Hiebert, *God of My Victory*, pp. 51-52.
106. I take the verb to be an example of an inwardly transitive hiphil (see GKC, par. 53d); the meaning of the following noun is well attested in Ethiopic (see W. Leslau, *Ethiopic and South Arabic Contributions to the Hebrew Lexicon*, U. of California Publications on Semitic Philology XX [Los Angeles: U. of California, 1958], p. 12).
107. Hiebert, *God of My Victory*, p. 52, citing S. R. Driver, *Introduction to the Literature of the Old Testament* (New York: Scribner's, 1914), pp. 96-97. Ward (*Habakkuk*, p. 25) similarly complains: "This verse requires correction to make the latter half intelligible." Hiebert's wholesale emendations are, however, less than convincing and add little to clarify the MT.
108. See e.g., Ward, *Habakkuk*, p. 28.

place (whether concrete or abstract) with overtones of finality, or (when speaking abstractly) of victory, salvation, etc.,"[109] the sense that is needed here is provided.

In the midst of conflict and distress, the prophet rests securely in the knowledge of God's purposes. It is a rest of the spirit (cf. Isa. 28:2) in full trust in the redeeming God. So construed, the *lamed* with יוֹם ("day") and the following phrase is one of specification ("with respect to")[110] or time ("during/at").[111] Thus Habakkuk will be at rest with God as the day of affliction takes its course.

With this understanding, לַעֲלוֹת in the next line can be viewed as a parallel thought: "during the going up" (to war). Although the *lamed* with עַם ("people") could be again a *lamed* of specification, it is best to take the preposition in its usual sense of "direction toward," here in the hostile sense of "against."[112] יְגוּדֶנּוּ can then be understood as occurring in subordination: "who will invade us." The verb גוּד ("invade/attack"[113]) also occurs with an energic force, as here, in Gen. 49:19, another piece of ancient poetry.[114]

Habakkuk is thus considering the total picture of distress that is to come upon his nation and the Chaldeans. If one takes the first of the two parallel lines as applying primarily to the Judahites and the second as in asyndetic parataxis with the first so as to dramatize the situation with the Chaldeans, a balance is thereby achieved. Habakkuk will take his rest both during the day of distress for his people and during the judgment of the Chaldeans, Judah's invaders[115].

3:17 כִּי ("when/while"): Because v. 17 can be understood as forming a contrast with v. 18, many translations render this particle concessively: "although" (KJV, NKJV, NASB, NIV). However, the LXX, Vg, and Pesh. treat it causally ("because"), a procedure followed by the NJB (although it renders v. 17 parenthetically).[116] The temporal use is probably to be preferred. Thus, when adversity takes

---

109. R. L. Harris, "נוּחַ," *TWOT* 2:562.
110. See Williams, *Hebrew Syntax*, par. 273.
111. See the study of M. Futato, "The Preposition 'Beth' in the Hebrew Psalter," *WTJ* 41 (1978): 68-81, especially pp. 70-72, where Futato makes a case for ל used to signify position at or during a course of action.
112. For details, see GKC, par. 119r; Williams, *Hebrew Syntax*, par. 271.
113. The LXX παροικίας μου ("my sojourn") apparently arises from a confusion of the Hebrew letters ד and ר, hence taking the root as גוּר ("sojourn").
114. For a discussion of the passage as a whole, see Cross, *Ancient Yahwistic Poetry*, pp. 128-83.
115. For a similar use of asyndetic parataxis in Akkadian, see R. D. Patterson, *Old Babylonian Parataxis* (Ann Arbor: University Microfilms, 1971), pp. 128-81.
116. LXX[Barb] omits it altogether.

place around him (v. 17), Habakkuk will put his full confidence in God (v. 18).

†תִּפְרָח† ("has not blossomed"): The verb is once again a preterite in conscious archaizing style. Together with the following suffix-conjugation verbs, it serves as the basis for the prophet's actions in the next verse.[117]

The products and resources mentioned in v. 17 were vital to Israel's economy. In addition, the fig tree and the vine had spiritual significance, for they symbolized the blessing of God upon an obedient people (cf. Hos. 2:12; Amos 4:9 with 1 Kings 4:25 [HB 5:5]; 2 Kings 18:31; see also Ps. 105:33; Isa. 36:16; Jer. 5:17; 8:13; Joel 2:19, 24; Hag. 2:19; Zech. 3:10). Likewise, olive oil and the grain of the field (as well as the cattle) were objects of God's blessing (cf. Num. 18:12; Deut. 7:13; 11:14; 28:51; 2 Kings 18:32; Jer. 31:12; Joel 2:19; Hag. 1:11). צֹאן and בָּקָר are often used together to represent the totality of cattle, both small and large.[118] Thus the failure of all these resources had serious economic and spiritual ramifications.

†כִּחֵשׁ† ("has failed"): The verb usually means "be disappointing," "deceive" (cf. NJB). Because the disappointment concerns the failure of the expected produce (cf. Hos. 9:2), the context calls for the meaning "fail," as recognized by most English translations.

†שְׁדֵמוֹת† ("fields"): Although the plural is twice used of terraced lands (2 Kings 23:4; Jer. 31:40), it was also employed with grapes and vines in Deut. 32:32; Isa. 16:8, so that "vineyard" is a likely possibility not only in these passages but also in Hab. 3:17. But the following אֹכֶל ("food") makes a final decision difficult. I have retained the traditional denotation "fields."

†גָּזַר† ("be cut off"): I follow the lead of Hiebert in understanding the form in a passive sense.[119]

†מִכְלָה† ("[sheep]fold") is probably a biform of מִכְלָא, although Keil suggests that it is a feminine form contracted from מִכְלָאָה. The MT significance is supported by the Vg and LXX[Barb] against the LXX βρώσεως ("meat/eating"), a translation probably based upon a conjectured מַאֲכָלָה (cf. Hab. 1:16).

---

117. See further W. L. Moran (*A Syntactical Study of the Dialect of Byblos as Reflected in the Amarna Tablets* [Ann Arbor: University Microfilms, 1967], pp. 28-52) and S. Schrader ("Was the Earth Created a Few Thousand Years Ago—Yes," in *The Genesis Debate*, ed. Ronald Youngblood [Grand Rapids: Baker, 1990], pp. 76-77) for discussions of this syntactical device in other settings.
118. See R. D. Patterson, "Joel," in *EBC*, 7:244.
119. For the qal passive, see R. J. Williams, "The Passive *Qal* Theme in Hebrew," in *Essays on the Ancient Semitic World*, ed. J. W. Wevers and D. B. Redford (Toronto: U. of Toronto, 1970), pp. 43-50.

†בָּרְפָתִים ("in the stalls"): The meaning of this *hapax legomenon* is assured both from the parallel lines and the ancient versions. Although the prepositions מִן and בְּ occur in parallelism here, they are not being used interchangeably.[120]

3:18 †אֶעְלוֹזָה אָגִילָה ("I will *rejoice*, I will *be joyful*"): The etymologies of these synonyms could suggest that the former lays stress on the audible singing of God's praises (cf. Ps. 149:5), whereas the latter implies physical movement (cf. Ps. 2:11). But an examination of their use in contexts in which they are closely associated does not support such a distinction (cf. Pss. 96:11, 12; 149:2, 5; Zeph. 3:14, 17), and no such contrast is apparent here.

2. A CONCLUDING NOTE OF PRAISE TO THE REDEEMER (3:19)

Translation

Yahweh is my Lord* (and) my strength;
　He makes my feet like those of a deer
　and makes me walk on the heights.*
To the director of music; on my stringed instruments.*

Exegesis and Exposition

Habakkuk closes his prophecy with a climactic tricolon that draws upon the phraseology of the epic cycle that had so greatly affected him. He declares that Yahweh is his Lord and strength (cf. Ex. 15:2). The order is significant. Whatever strength he has he owes to the one who is his strength; but basic to everything is the fact that Yahweh is his Lord and his Master, the center of his life.

Habakkuk's use of divine titles reflects his spiritual journey. God's prophet had entertained several doubts. A number of matters concerning God's working and the life of faith had haunted him. Addressing God as the covenant Lord of Israel (יהוה, *YHWH*), he had carried these problems to Him with heavy heart (1:2-4). When the Lord had answered his uncertainties in a way that left him somewhat more perplexed (1:5-11), Habakkuk reminded God (1:12) that He was not only Israel's covenant Lord (*YHWH*) but "my God (אֱלֹהַי, *'ĕlōhay*), my Holy One (קְדֹשִׁי, *qĕdōsî*)." The divine titles reminded God that, though He was the God of all things, His primary attribute is that of holiness. Therefore, although He might have the power and authority to send a

---

120. For the proposed interchangeability of מִן and ב, see Nahum M. Sarna, "The Interchange of the Prepositions *Beth* and *Min* in Biblical Hebrew," *JBL* 78 (1959): 310-16. Similar functional interchange has been suggested for several of the Hebrew prepositions, including ב and תַּחַת (cf. v. 16), for which see J. C. Greenfield, "The Preposition B . . . Taḥat . . . in Jes 57₅," *ZAW* 73 (1961): 226-28.

nation like the Chaldeans, would it be just for a holy God to use so unholy an instrument to punish His people (1:12–2:1)?

In reporting the Lord's answer to his second perplexity, Habakkuk again used the covenant designation *YHWH* (2:2). That response had made plain to Habakkuk that the Lord truly is in control of all history. Nevertheless, he uses human agency and institutions to accomplish His purposes. In so doing the distinction between the wicked on the one hand and the righteous who live by faith on the other becomes clear (2:4). Habakkuk learned that even the foremost power of the world is subject to God. Indeed, Israel's covenant Lord is the God of all people and even now is in His holy Temple to receive their acquiescence and adoration (2:20).

While the Lord's answer was satisfying to Habakkuk so that he appreciated the statement relative to the principles of God's just operations in the world, he was yet concerned for his people. Would Judah's chastisement be too severe for her to bear? Would an omnipotent God be too harsh in His punishment? Habakkuk pleaded with the Lord to show mercy amid the coming judgment. In so doing he once again employed the title *YHWH* (3:2). Much like Job (Job 38-41), what Habakkuk needed was a clear perception of how God acted. This was supplied to him through his consideration of the epic material relative to the Exodus (3:3-15). There he saw God in all His might (אֱלוֹהַ, *'ĕlôah*) and yet in His holiness (קָדוֹשׁ, *qādôš*, 3:3). It was He who delivered His people from the might of Egypt and led them to the land of promise (3:3-7). He is Yahweh, the covenant God of Israel (3:8), and as such He is Israel's Redeemer and victor (3:8-15). Yahweh, Israel's Lord and the judge of all mankind, is in charge of earth's history. He also has a righteous concern for His covenant people. Accordingly He can be counted on to deal properly with Judah's case and to fulfill His age-old promises to them.

The consideration of God in action was enough for Habakkuk:

> Habakkuk, though he did achieve a degree of intellectual understanding, came to terms with God in the experience of theophany. Though he began this encounter in dialogue and rational argument, the real turning point in his relationship with God was the result of a vision of the Living God.[121]

Gone were his fears, doubts, and perplexities. He would trust in Yahweh and rejoice in his saving God (אֱלֹהֵי יִשְׁעִי, *'ĕlōhê yiš'î*, 3:18). Israel's Redeemer was his, the Master (אָדוֹן, *'ādôn*) from whom alone he gained his strength (3:19). So near to God does Habakkuk now feel that in a bold simile he likens his spiritual climb to that of a hind

---

121. Craigie, *Twelve Prophets*, 2:103.

swiftly ascending to the mountaintops and gracefully gliding over them.

Victory at last! Israel's Lord (*YHWH*) was truly Habakkuk's own, his leader and guide. God's prophet had walked a precarious path. But lest we condemn Habakkuk too readily, we need to remember that the Lord did not do so; He merely corrected him. Ultimately Habakkuk's implanted faith bore spiritual fruit. The prophecy of Habakkuk thus not only reminds its readers of the central principles of life (2:4, 20) and of the final triumph of good through God's control of history (3:3-15) but also provides important insight into a believer's personal relationship with his God. When times of doubt and discouragement come, as they inevitably do, the believer needs to come to God, as did Habakkuk, and share his concerns with Him. Like Habakkuk, he needs to come to God's Word and get a fresh glimpse of who and what God is and so come to a place of renewed trust in the one who alone is truly God and therefore sufficient for all of life. May Habakkuk's test of faith and triumphant joy in his saving Lord be an inspiration and example to all who must travel life's road!

Additional Notes

3:19 †אֲדֹנָי ("the Lord"): The translation given above ("my Lord") follows several manuscripts of the LXX and the NJB. It involves no change of consonants of the MT and maintains the spirit of the Exodus recorded in Ex. 15:2.

If a copula is to be supplied between אֲדֹנָי and חֵילִי, it is better to retain אֲדֹנָי as a case of apposition: "Yahweh, the Lord, is my strength" (cf. RSV). The translation suggested above has the advantage of harmonizing well with the fact that other expressions in the verse are also drawn from the ancient epic corpus, "Yahweh . . . is my strength" being indebted to Ps. 18:32 (HB 18:33) and the next two lines to Ps. 18:33 (HB 18:34). Further, though not formed with the same verbs, the notice of exuitant praise found in v. 18 reflects Ex. 15:3, and חַיִל (v. 19) is found in Ex. 15:4 (though probably with a different meaning). Habakkuk's closing note of praise is thus filled with imagery drawn from the epic songs of the Exodus event.

The use of the divine name יהוה here is probably in conscious imitation of its stanza-initial position in the two ancient poems (vv. 3, 8). In addition, it serves as a stitch-word to the previous subunit (vv. 16-18) and as a bookending device with the opening portion of the chapter (v. 2).

†The usual sense of "on the heights" seems to be demanded for בָּמוֹתָי rather than seeing here the frequently suggested (e.g., Albright, Hiebert) association with Ugaritic *bmt* ("back"—i.e., of the vanquished foe). The form occurs elsewhere in the ancient poetry of Isra-

el (Ps. 18:33 [HB 18:34]= 2 Sam. 22:34, where it occurs with עָמַד ["stand"]); it is thus doubtless a frozen form based on an old genitive case.

The sentiment of the line is found in two other pieces of ancient Hebrew poetry (where, however, the Ugaritic meaning may be suitable): Deut. 32:13 and Deut. 33:13 (where it occurs, as here, with the verb דָּרַךְ). Apparently the use of עָמַד/דָּרַךְ with בָּמוֹת was part of an ancient stock phraseology for praising God for His victorious intervention on behalf of His people, even though the precise meaning of the phrase depended on the context. יַדְרִכֵנִי thus not only has important literary associations but also serves as a stitch-word to the previous subsection and provides a suitable climax to the prophet's spiritual renewal.

†The closing subscription is one of several musical notations in chap. 3 (vv. 1, 3, 9, 13) that give instructions for the possible use of Habakkuk's prayer psalm in public worship. While the term שִׁגְיֹנוֹת in the heading (3:1) appears to be an indication of the musical setting and the repeated *selah* (vv. 3, 9, 13) a note relative to a musical interlude, these final instructions are intended for the director of music (cf. 1 Chron. 15:21-22; 2 Chron. 34:12). Craigie is of the opinion that all three terms indicate that such pieces of music were part of the standard repertoire available for congregational worship.[122]

The musical experience of ancient Israel was rich and varied. Therefore, the Temple worship was highly organized (cf. 1 Chron. 6:31-48; 15:21-22; 16:41-42; 23:5; 25:1-3; etc.). Selected instruments, especially the harp and the lyre, were a prominent part of such music (1 Chron. 15:21; 25:1; Pss. 92:3; 150:3-4).[123] Thus it is not surprising that the term for "stringed instruments" found here also appears in the heading of several psalms (Pss. 4, 6, 54, 55, 61, 67, 76)[124] and is found as a singular noun in Ps. 77:6 (HB 77:7), which also contains early epic material. Keil suggests that the personal pronoun on the term here means that Habakkuk

> himself will accompany it with his own playing, from which it has been justly inferred that he was qualified, according to the arrangements of the Israelitish worship, to take part in the public performance of such pieces of music as were suited for public worship, and therefore belonged to the Levites who were entrusted with the conduct of the musical performance of the temple.[125]

---

122. P. C. Craigie, *Psalms 1-50*, WBC (Waco, Tex.: Word, 1983), p. 79.
123. For details, see D. A. Foxvog and A. D. Kilmer, "Music," *ISBE* 3:436-49.
124. Foxvog and Kilmer ("Music," *ISBE* 3:448) warn against too ready an identification with stringed instruments in every occurrence of this term (e.g., Job 30:9; Ps. 69:12 [HB 69:13]; Isa. 38:30; Lam. 5:14).
125. Keil, *Minor Prophets*, 2:116. 1 Chron. 23:5 lists about 4,000 musicians employed in the Temple worship of whom 288 apparently were master musicians (1 Chron. 25:7).

Habakkuk's joyous spiritual triumph evidenced in his proclamation of יהוה as Master of his life is reminiscent of Charles Wesley's well-known hymn:

> Rejoice, the Lord is King:
> Your Lord and King adore!
> Rejoice, give thanks, and sing
> And triumph evermore:
> Lift up your heart, lift up your voice!
> Rejoice, again I say, rejoice![126]

---

126. Charles Wesley, "Rejoice—the Lord Is King!" in *Hymns for the Family of God* (Nashville: Paragon, 1976), no. 374.

Excursus on Habakkuk 3

As noted in the Introduction to Habakkuk, the third chapter exhibits striking differences from the preceding two.[1] These factors, coupled with the presence of several musical notations (vv. 1, 3, 9, 13, 19), make clear that with chap. 3 one is dealing with material that is unique and constitutes a self-contained pericope. This observation may account for its exclusion from 1QpHab.

From a literary perspective it is likewise obvious that chap. 3 has some distinct internal differences. Thus vv. 2, 16-19 are composed in the first person and recount the prophet's own experiences and feelings, whereas vv. 3-15 are written in the third and second persons and contain epic themes drawn from the era of Israel's Exodus from Egypt and settlement in the land of Canaan. Several authors have noted that all this points to a deliberate literary methodology, vv. 2, 16-19 forming an enclosing framework for the psalmic material that intervenes. Thus Hiebert points out that "v 2 and vv 16-19 provide a literary framework for the theophany in vv 3-15" that "is itself composed of two distinct units, vv 3-7 and 8-15."[2]

---

1. In addition to the utilization of the material in my article in the *Grace Theological Journal* (see Introduction to Habakkuk, n. 21), I wish to acknowledge the helpfulness of studies by W. F. Albright, C. E. Armerding, U. Cassuto, and T. Hiebert (see the References).
2. T. Hiebert, *God of My Victory*, Harvard Semitic Monographs 38 (Atlanta: Scholars, 1986), p. 59. C. E. Armerding ("Habakkuk," in *EBC* [Zondervan: Grand Rapids, 1985], 7:521) finds a similar arrangement while treating

That such is the case can be seen from several supporting data: (1) The ideas of hearing and fearing found in v. 2 are echoed in v. 16. (2) The root רגז ("tremble") plays a prominent part in vv. 2 and 16. (3) The divine name Yahweh is used in the opening and closing sections of the chapter and is strategically placed so as to bookend the whole composition (vv. 2, 18-19). (4) The twin themes of God's awesome power and His boundless grace, though punctuating the entire chapter, are particularly featured in the framework portions.[3] All these elements are woven together by Habakkuk to demonstrate his initial concern (reflected in his opening petition, v. 2) and his satisfaction due to his perception of the character and work of God (vv. 3-15), given in his concluding testimony of praise (vv. 16-19). The material portrayed in the victory ode that forms the central section of the chapter (vv. 3-15) is suited to meet Habakkuk's own need so that, while the chapter has distinguishable units, it nonetheless demonstrates a unity of perspective.

The psalm of vv. 3-15, although it picks up themes that are present in v. 2 and carries them through to the concluding section of vv. 16-19,[4] is nevertheless distinct from those enclosing units. Particularly notable are (1) the difference in divine names, moving from Yahweh (v. 2) to Eloah and Holy One (v. 3), (2) the replacing of first-person verbs with largely third-person narrative structure, and (3) the shift of viewpoint from the prophet's fear generated by his perception of God's activity (v. 2) to a consideration of God Himself in His appearance (vv. 3-4), in His actions (vv. 5-7, 8-10*a*, 15), and in their effect (vv. 10*b*-11) in delivering God's people from their enemies (vv. 12-15).

Most distinctive of all, however, is that, while vv. 2, 16-19 contain themes and phrases that may be indebted to the material contained in vv. 3-15, they are written in a poetic style largely representative of the classical language and themes of the Psalter and prophets (cf. v. 2 with Pss. 44:1 [HB 44:2]; 85:4-7 [HB 85:5-8]; 102:12-13; Isa. 54:8; v. 16 with Ps. 37:7; v. 17 with Jer. 5:17; Joel 1:10-12; Amos 4:9; vv. 18-19 with Pss. 27:1; 46:1-5 [HB 46:2-6]; 97:12). On the other hand, vv. 3-15 reflect Israel's earliest poetry (cf. v. 3 with Judg. 5:4; Ps. 68:7 [HB 68:8]; v. 5 with Deut. 33:2-3; vv. 10-11 with Judg. 5:4-5; Pss. 18:7-15 [HB 18:8-16]; 68:7-8 [HB 68:8-9]; 77:16-19 [HB 77:17-20]; 144:5-6; vv.

---

the whole chapter as a chiasmus: introduction (v. 1), prayer (v. 2), theophany (vv. 3-15), response (vv. 16-19), epilogue (v. 19).

3. See Hiebert, *God of My Victory*, p. 61.
4. Hiebert (ibid., p. 68) calls attention to "the pattern 'trembling steps—anguish/joy—firm steps'" that unites the closing framework section to both the preceding theophanic material and the initial framework portion in v. 2.

12-15 with Ex. 15:6-10, 14-18).[5] In addition, as noted in the introduction under Literary Context, this section is filled with archaic grammatical elements, poetic devices, and themes such as that of the chariot warrior baring his bow.[6]

Though vv. 3-15 belong as a whole to a common early linguistic and literary milieu, they show some internal distinctions. Two compositions are present, each of which makes its own contribution to the corpus of the Exodus epic. Habakkuk 3:3-7 describes God's leading of His heavenly and earthly hosts from the south in an awe-inspiring theophany. Habakkuk 3:8-15 constitutes a victory song commemorating the conquest itself and points to the basis of that success in the Exodus event, particularly in the victory at the Red Sea.

Moreover, each poem is marked by literary features that give it its own distinctive integrity. Thus, both are bounded by bookending devices forming an inclusio, vv. 3-7 with geographical names that appear in the poem's opening and closing verses, and vv. 8-15 with the motifs of sea, water, and horses (vv. 8, 15). Each poem has its own internal structure. The first makes frequent use of the *waw* coordinator to bind its individual cola and words together and employs tricola to end its stanzas (vv. 3-4, 5-7). The second makes no use of the *waw* coordinator at all but connects its stanzas via variation in word order (v. 12) and the employment of stanza-beginning (v. 8) or -ending (v. 11) tricola.

Additional prominent features of the first poem include the use of stitching themes and words to unite its two subunits (vv. 3-4, 5-7) such as coming/going (vv. 3, 5) and earth (vv. 3, 6), and the heaping up of *s* sounds (11 instances) for dramatic effect. Further characteristics of the second poem include the continued use of *s* sounds for effect (26 cases), a progression in theme from that of the divine warrior's preparations (vv. 8-9) and actions in the natural world (vv. 10-11) to His activities in delivering His people (vv. 12-15), the unique placement of v. 15 so as to combine the themes of deliverance and power while forming an inclusio with the opening tricolon of the poem (v. 8), and the presence of key words and themes that stitch its two stanzas together: anger (vv. 8, 12) and salvation (vv. 9, 11, 13), earth (vv. 10, 12) and water (vv. 8, 10, 15), horses (vv. 8, 10) and weapons (vv. 9, 14),

---

5. The classic study of the corpus of ancient Hebrew literature is by Frank Moore Cross, Jr., *Studies in Ancient Yahwistic Poetry* (Baltimore: Johns Hopkins U., 1950). See also Frank Moore Cross, Jr., and David N. Freedman, *Early Hebrew Orthography* (New Haven: American Oriental Society, 1952). Other compositions reflecting this stage of Hebrew literature include Gen. 49:2-27; Ex. 15:1-18; Num. 23:7-10, 18-24; 24:3-9, 15-19, 20-24; Deut. 33:3-29; Judg. 5:2-31; Ps. 18 (=2 Sam. 22:2-51); 2 Sam. 23:1-7.
6. See Introduction to Habakkuk, n. 19.

and the repetition of verbs of going out or proceeding (vv. 11, 12, 13, 14).

Habakkuk's psalm of 3:3-15, then, is a weaving together of two poems remarkably well suited for each other. They contain complementary features, such as common items of alliteration and assonance (e.g., the *s* sound) and several key themes and words such as God's actions in the natural world (vv. 4-6, 8-11, 15), stress on the brilliance of God's glory (vv. 4, 11), use of cosmic weaponry (vv. 5, 9, 14), emphasis on earth and nations (vv. 6, 10, 12), and reference to trembling (vv. 6, 7, 10) and going out or proceeding (vv. 3, 11-14). Hiebert points out that the second poem is thus the "logical sequel to the description of his [God's] departure from his sanctuary flanked by his military attendants" in the first poem.[7] He also calls attention syntactically to the consistent employment of alternating suffix- and prefix-conjugation verbs in both poems.[8]

It is clear, then, that Habakkuk 3 is composed of four sections, the double-psalmed central portions of which are distinctive and drawn from a corpus of much older literature.[9] From a literary standpoint the two poetic compositions found in vv. 3-15 belong to the genre of epic literature and rehearse the dramatic happenings that made up the Exodus. Much as in the other literary traditions in the ancient Mediterranean and Near Eastern cultures, the Hebrew people had an epic cycle, the remnants of which can be found in those poems that sing of the era and events of Israel's Exodus. All of these poetic pieces contain not only common themes but also the same grammatical and literary features. To Hab. 3:3-15 may be added Ex. 15:1-18; Deut. 33:1-3; Judg. 5:4-5; Pss. 18:7-15 (HB 18:8-16); 68:7-8 (HB 68:8-9); 77:16-19 (HB 77:17-20); 144:5-6. Two of these passages, Hab. 3:3-15 and Ex. 15:1-18, contain extended portrayals of the Exodus experience.

Like Habakkuk's psalm, Ex. 15:1-18 gives a detailed discussion of the era of the Exodus, first singing of the Exodus itself and of Yahweh's victory at the Red Sea (vv. 1-10) and then praising the Lord for His divine leading, first to Mount Sinai (vv. 11-13) and then proleptically from Sinai to the Promised Land (vv. 14-18).

---

7. Hiebert, *God of My Victory*, p. 76.
8. See chap. 3, n. 24.
9. Thus T. Hiebert ("The Use of Inclusion in Habakkuk 3," in *Directions in Biblical Hebrew Poetry*, ed. Elaine R. Follis [Sheffield: JSOT Press, 1987], p. 122) rightly observes: "The use of inclusion in Habakkuk 3 indicates the presence of four stanzas: introductory and concluding units (Stanza I, v. 2; Stanza IV, vv. 16-19) which provide a literary framework for the theophany in vv. 3-15, which is itself composed of two distinct units (Stanza II, vv. 3-7; Stanza III, vv. 8-15)."

The two poems that compose Hab. 3:3-15 add considerable information to this event and in so doing employ epic themes and style.[10] Thus there is the central focus on a hero: God Himself. Moreover, in the first poem (vv. 3-7) the poet relates the account of an epic journey, God's leading of His people from the southland toward Canaan. He calls attention to God's command of nature in theophany (vv. 3-4), His special companions (v. 5), His earthshaking power (v. 6), and the effect of all this on the inhabitants of the land (v. 7).

The second poem (vv. 8-15) transcends the bounds of the movement from Egypt to the Jordan (cf. Ps. 114:3-5), the phraseology being best understood as including God's miraculous acts in the conquest period as well. God's victories at the end of the Exodus account are rehearsed first (vv. 8-11), possibly reflecting such deeds as the triumph at the Red Sea (Ex. 15) and at the Jordan (Josh. 3-4), as well as the victories at the Wadi Kishon (Judg. 4-5) and Gibeon (Josh. 10). The poet then directs his hearers' attention to the victory that gave Israel its deliverance and eventual conquest of Canaan: the triumph in Israel's Exodus from Egypt (vv. 12-15).

Habakkuk 3:8-15 is thus a victory psalm, a fact commensurate with the heroic tone of epic literature. As such it partakes of the same general themes that are found in other victory songs from the ancient Hebrew epic cycle. In his excellent study concerning Ex. 15:1-18 and Judges 5, A. J. Hauser isolates five key motifs that the early Hebrew victory songs have in common: (1) Yahweh as the divine hero who comes to Israel's deliverance; (2) a description of Yahweh together with action-packed scenes of God's victory; (3) the use of water imagery; (4) the mocking of the enemy; and (5) the defeat of the enemy described in terms of his fall.[11] Some of these themes can be found in Hab. 3:3-7, and all five occur in Hab. 3:8-15: (1) vv. 8, 13; (2) vv. 8-15; (3) vv. 8-11, 15; (4) v. 14; (5) vv. 13*b*-14.

Granted the epic nature and origin of Hab. 3:3-15, can the purpose for Habakkuk's incorporation of ancient poetic material into his composition be seen? Does the third chapter of his prophecy have a unity of perspective? The answer to both questions is affirmative. That there is unity in the chapter may be seen in (1) the mention in every stanza of God, the central figure of the chapter (vv. 2 [bis], 3, 8, 18, 19), and (2) the presence of key words such as רגז (vv. 2, 7, 16 [bis])

---

10. For the justification of Hab. 3:3-15 as epic and a consideration of its relation to the other epic literature of the ancient world, see R. D. Patterson, "The Psalm of Habakkuk," *GTJ* 8 (1987): 178-92. Hiebert (*God of My Victory*, p. 118) likewise terms the material epic, although he applies this terminology to the whole third chapter.

11. See A. J. Hauser, "Two Songs of Victory: A Comparison of Exodus 15 and Judges 5," in *Directions in Biblical Hebrew Poetry*, pp. 265-84.

and themes such as going/proceeding (vv. 3, 11-14, 16, 19), salvation/deliverance/mercy (vv. 2, 8, 13, 18), wrath/anger/fear (vv. 2, 6-7, 8, 12, 16), and the judgment of nations (vv. 6-7, 12-14, 16). Hiebert calls particular attention to the twin motifs "central to the poem: the hearing about the acts of God, and the response of great awe which this hearing evokes" and the prevalence of the "two characteristics of theophany, its gracious intent and its awful power to disrupt and destroy."[12]

When one considers also the shape given to the chapter by the superscription, which proclaims the composition to be a *tĕpillâ*, a prayer of praise to God that can be set to music and utilized in worship (see introduction), the question of unity is settled. Indeed, all this confirms Habakkuk's literary artistry in blending ancient epic material into his prayer psalm as a statement of exaltation to God in the midst of an opening cry and petition (v. 2) and closing affirmation of trust and praise (vv. 16-19).

It is evident, too, that the final unified composition was well suited to Habakkuk's purposes and personal needs. Habakkuk had had his perplexities resolved in the revelation of God's intentions for the nations and the divine admonition for silence. The consideration of God's actions caused him to contemplate the nature of the God who had been Israel's Redeemer all along. After Habakkuk pleads for mercy in the midst of wrath (v. 2) and reviews God's past record (vv. 3-15), his reverential trust in God is renewed. Israel's great Redeemer is his also. He will trust in such a one no matter what happens (vv. 16-19). He who had acted both in judgment and deliverance for Israel in the past can be counted on to do so once again, both for Israel and His prophet.

> The same power at whose manifestation the entire cosmos (vv 6, 9-10), nature (v 17), the peoples (v 7), and the poet himself (vv 2, 16) tremble in awe discloses itself as merciful (v 2), as a source of joy and occasion for praise (v 18), and as deliverer of salvation to the cosmos (vv 13-15), to his people (v 13), and to the poet himself (v 19).[13]

Thus Habakkuk's final prayer of praise to Israel's Redeemer stands not only as a unified composition but also as the climax to the whole prophecy.

---

12. Hiebert, *God of My Victory*, p. 61.
13. Ibid., pp. 117-18.

ZEPHANIAH

Introduction to Zephaniah

HISTORICAL CONTEXT

SETTING

Though an occasional voice of protest has been heard,[1] few scholars have failed to accept the information in the superscription that the book's author prophesied during the reign of Josiah (640-609 B.C.) as indicative of the setting of this short prophecy.[2] Rather, discussion concerning the date and background of the book has centered chiefly on the specific period within Josiah's reign. The moral and spiritual conditions mentioned by Zephaniah have been taken by many to refer to Judah's persistent apostasy and immorality despite the Josianic reform that began in earnest after the finding of the Book of the Law (2 Kings 22:8) in 621 B.C. (e.g., A. R. Fausset, C. L. Feinberg, J. Hannah, C. F. Keil, V. Reid, L. Walker). Others, however, believe that such matters as Zephaniah denounces could only be true of the earlier portion of Josiah's reign, either when the boy king was yet unable

---

1. See, e.g., L. P. Smith and E. R. Lacheman, "The Authorship of the Book of Zephaniah," *JNES* 9 (1950): 137-42. The authors see Zephaniah as the work of an apocalyptist and opt for a date of c. 200 B.C. Donald L. Williams ("The Date of Zephaniah," *JBL* 82 [1963]: 83-85) decides for a setting during the reign of Jehoiakim (608-597 B.C.), as does J. P. Hyatt, *Zephaniah*, PCB (London: Nelson, 1962), p. 642.
2. Many have suggested that individual sayings and sections may have been composed later and inserted into the final edition.

to deal with the longstanding effects of the wickedness of Judah's two previous kings, Manasseh and Amon, or when his reformation had only recently got underway (e.g., J. A. Bewer, C. H. Bullock, P. C. Craigie, F. C. Eiselen, O. Eissfeldt, H. Freeman, H. Hailey, R. K. Harrison, H. Hummel, A. S. Kapelrud, T. Laetsch, G. A. Larue, E. B. Pusey, T. H. Robinson, G. A. Smith, J. M. P. Smith, C. von Orelli).[3]

With capable scholars on both sides of the question, one is at first tempted to conclude with D. A. Schneider that "the evidence is insufficient to decide this debate."[4] In examining the internal data, however, several conclusions seem to favor the earlier period in Josiah's reign: (1) religious practices in Judah were still plagued with Canaanite syncretistic rites such as characterized the era of Manasseh (1:4-5, 9); (2) many failed to worship Yahweh at all (1:6); (3) royalty were enamored with wearing the clothing of foreign merchants (1:8) who had extensive business enterprises in Jerusalem (1:10-11); and (4) Judahite society was beset by socio-economic ills (1:12-13, 18) and political and religious corruption (3:1-4, 7, 11). All this sounds like the same sort of wickedness that weighed heavily on the heart of Habakkuk. Moreover, several of the specific sins (e.g., 1:4-5, 9; 3:4) would have been corrected in Josiah's reforms. Accordingly, I am inclined to side with those who prefer a date before 621 B.C.[5]

But how much before? Some have suggested that the political situation brought about by a Scythian raid (c. 630 B.C.)[6] occasioned both Zephaniah's response to God's call and his urgent message concerning God's impending judgment of the world.[7] However, because the evidence of such an invasion is now considered to be tenuous at best, "the Scythian hypothesis has now been almost universally abandoned."[8] Thus the search for a precise date for Zephaniah cannot

---

3. A good discussion of the setting of the book is given by F. C. Fensham, "Book of Zephaniah," *IDBSup*, pp. 983-84. Fensham also favors a date for Zephaniah early in Josiah's reign.
4. D. A. Schneider, "Book of Zephaniah," *ISBE* 4:1189.
5. If M. de Roche ("Contra Creation, Covenant and Conquest: Jer viii 13," VT 30 [1980]: 280-90) is correct in finding an allusion to Zeph. 1:2-3 in the Jeremianic passage, the case for a Josianic date is further strengthened.
6. According to Herodotus (1.41.103-6) the Scythians had plundered Ashkelon during a raid against Egypt (which ended when Psamtik I bought them off). Herodotus does not mention any invasion against Judah.
7. See, e.g., E. A. Leslie, "Book of Zephaniah," *IDB* 4:951-53; G. A. Smith, *The Book of the Twelve Prophets*, rev. ed. (Garden City, N.Y.: Doubleday, 1929), p. 40.
8. Fensham, "Zephaniah," p. 983. For a defense of the Scythian hypothesis, see *CAH* 3:295 where the somewhat fantastic elements of Herodotus's account are duly recognized as well as the probability that the supposed Scythian sack of Ashdod was as much an Egyptian enterprise as Scythian. See also R. K. Harrison, *Introduction to the Old Testament* (Grand Rapids: Eerdmans, 1971), p. 940.

be pressed too far. Nevertheless the conditions denounced by Zephaniah do seem to echo the social and religious ills decried by Habakkuk, so that if Habakkuk ministered in the mid-seventh century B.C. (see Introduction to Habakkuk) a date earlier in Josiah's reign is plausible. If so, Pusey may be on the right track:

> The foreground of the prophecy of Zephaniah remarkably coincides with that of Habakkuk. Zephaniah presupposes that prophecy and fills it up. Habakkuk had prophesied the great wasting and destruction through the Chaldaeans, and then their destruction. . . . Zephaniah . . . brings before Judah the other side, the agency of God Himself. God would not have them forget Himself in His instruments. Hence all is attributed to God.[9]

When one considers that Josiah was only eight years old when he ascended the throne in 640 B.C. and was dependent upon royal officials of questionable integrity (cf. 3:3), the cause for Zephaniah's alarm is apparent. Further, that Josiah's reforms were not instituted until the twelfth year of his reign (628 B.C.), four years after his initial spiritual awakening (2 Chron. 34:3), suggests that Zephaniah's prophetic activities may have had a salutary effect in the reformation of that era. Thus a date of 635-630 B.C. is not unlikely.

Accepting such a date means that the historical setting has advanced little beyond that of Nahum and Habakkuk. Externally the Pax Assyriaca held sway. Of that great era W. W. Hallo observes that, in addition to the Assyrian rulers' attention to administrative matters and details relative to extensive building projects,

> literature and learning too came into their own, and the vast library assembled by Assurbanipal at Nineveh is only the most dramatic expression of the new leisure. In spite of their protestations to the contrary, the later Sargonid kings were inclined to sit back and enjoy the fruits of empire.[10]

Yet it is somewhat ironic that Ashurbanipal, who had already reigned some thirty years by the time of Zephaniah and under whom the zenith of Assyrian affluence and culture was achieved, was possessed

---

9. E. B. Pusey, *The Minor Prophets* (Grand Rapids: Baker, 1953), 2:226. For the reform measures of Josiah, see R. D. Patterson and H. J. Austel, "1, 2 Kings," in *EBC* (Grand Rapids: Eerdmans, 1988), 4:281-88. Other scholars who decide for a date early in the reign of Josiah include C. H. Bullock, P. C. Craigie, F. C. Fensham, and C. von Orelli. Duane L. Christensen ("Zephaniah 2:4-15: A Theological Basis for Josiah's Program of Political Expansion," *CBQ* 46 [1984]: 678) affixes a precise date of 628 B.C. for Zeph. 2:4-15 and declares: "In its original form Zeph 2:4-15 presents a theological basis for Josiah's program of political expansion at the expense of Assyria, particularly in Philistia and Transjordan."

10. W. W. Hallo and W. K. Simpson, *The Ancient Near East* (New York: Harcourt Brace Jovanovich, 1971), p. 141.

by a personal weakness that would be mirrored in the Assyrian state itself.

> It was a defect of Ashurbanipal as a king that he had nothing in him of the great strategist, statesman, or soldier. He was as barren in political insight as he was rich in vindictiveness. It was his misfortune that he was called to be king when by inclination he was a scholastic.[11]

Because Ashurbanipal was preoccupied with the *belles lettres* that inspired him to collect the ancient texts, particularly those dealing with traditional wisdom and religious matters,[12] affairs in the empire began to show signs of the decay that would hasten its demise a scant generation after his death in 626 B.C.[13] Indeed, already by Zephaniah's day "an uneasy consciousness of impending disaster overhung the court, and not all the claims of a less and less honest history could conceal the danger on every side."[14]

Under such conditions it is small wonder that Josiah was increasingly free to pursue his reform policies, extending them even to the northern kingdom (2 Kings 23:1-25; 2 Chron. 34:32–35:19).[15] In addition, Judah could know a political and economic resurgence that it had not experienced since the days of Hezekiah.

> The time was ripe for national self-assertion expressed in the progressive steps of Josiah's reformation. . . . So Judah saw the dawning of the day of freedom, though Josiah proceeded cautiously step by step before venturing into the Assyrian province of Samaria.[16]

Leon Wood remarks:

> The three decades of Josiah's reign were among the happiest in Judah's experience. They were characterized by peace, prosperity, and reform. No outside enemies made war, the people could concentrate on constructive activity, and Josiah himself sought to please God by reinstituting matters commanded in the Mosaic Law.[17]

---

11. H. W. F. Saggs, *The Might That Was Assyria* (London: Sidgwick and Jackson, 1984), p. 116.
12. One must not assume, however, that Ashurbanipal's interests were not much more diverse. Indeed, his famed library probably held texts representative of every type of Akkadian literature, as well as business and administrative documents and correspondence. Ashurbanipal also gave attention to great building projects and the *beaux arts*. See further A. T. Olmstead, *History of Assyria* (Chicago: U. of Chicago, 1968), pp. 489-503.
13. Some ancient sources indicate that Ashurbanipal himself grew increasingly degenerate; see W. Maier, *The Book of Nahum* (Grand Rapids: Baker, 1980), p. 129.
14. Olmstead, *History of Assyria*, p. 488.
15. For the general historical situation in the latter half of the seventh century B.C., see the Introduction to Nahum.
16. John Gray, *I and II Kings*, 2d ed. (Philadelphia: Westminster, 1970), p. 720.
17. Leon Wood, *A Survey of Israel's History* (Grand Rapids: Zondervan, 1970), p. 366.

Zephaniah therefore lived in a critical time of transition. Externally, the Assyrian ship of state began to show the stress of age and, creaking and groaning in all its timbers and joints, floundered in the seas of economic and political adversity. The ancient Near East was in the grip of climactic change, for "the whole balance of power in the Near Eastern world shifted radically from what it had been for almost three hundred years. Assyria was in its death throes."[18] Internally, the relaxing of Assyrian pressure allowed Judah and its king the liberty to pursue the cause of righteousness without fear. It was an exciting and pivotal age in which to live. Zephaniah was to prove equal to its challenges. Indeed, he may well have been the Lord's catalyst for the great reformation that would sweep across the land.

AUTHORSHIP

Although some concern has been raised with regard to many passages in the book that bears his name, Zephaniah has generally been accepted as the author of a substantial core of the material of the book, particularly its first part (1:1–2:3; see under Literary Features). As for the prophet himself, Zephaniah traces his patrilineage four generations to a certain Hezekiah. Jewish (e.g., Ibn Ezra, Kimchi) and Christian commentators alike have commonly identified this Hezekiah with the king by that name. Although Laetsch is doubtless correct in stating that "Zephaniah's royal descent cannot be proved,"[19] the unusual notice concerning four generations of family lineage indicates at the very least that Zephaniah came from a distinguished family. Perhaps he was of royal descent, but current scholarship rightly prefers to be cautious. L. Walker explains:

> It has been commonly accepted that this Hezekiah was no less than the famous Judean king. This is not at all certain, however; and we have no other proof of any royal status for Zephaniah, despite the unusual mention of his great-great grandfather. Although genealogies are frequent in the OT, only Zephaniah among the prophetic books exhibits a lengthy genealogical note about the author. On the other hand, some scholars argue that since the words "king of Judah" are not added to Hezekiah's name, the reference is not to King Hezekiah. Others explain this omission on the ground that "king of Judah" follows immediately after Josiah's name. We simply lack conclusive evidence to this interesting question.[20]

Some scholars (e.g., Archer) have suggested that the time span between the birth of Hezekiah's oldest son, Manasseh (c. 710 B.C.), and

---

18. Eugene H. Merrill, *Kingdom of Priests* (Grand Rapids: Baker, 1987), p. 441.
19. T. Laetsch, *The Minor Prophets* (St. Louis: Concordia: 1956), p. 254.
20. L. Walker, "Zephaniah," in *EBC*, 7:537.

the birth of Josiah (c. 648 B.C.) is too short to allow four full generations, and others (e.g., Kapelrud) point out that Hezekiah was a common name in Judah (cf. 1 Chron. 3:23; Ezra 2:16; Neh. 7:21).

In fairness to those who believe that Zephaniah was of royal descent, however, none of these objections is conclusive. Perhaps the title "king of Judah" was omitted after Hezekiah's name out of respect for the ruling king, Josiah, to whose name it is appended. The compressed time frame may not be significant in light of the ancient custom of marriage at an early age. The argument that Hezekiah was a common biblical name is misleading in that only two other Hezekiahs are mentioned, both from the postexilic period.

Further, a case can be made for Zephaniah's royal descent. Wood observes that

> Zephaniah is unusual in tracing his lineage over four generations. Since he is the only prophet that does this, there must be a reason, and that reason apparently lies in the identity of the fourth person mentioned. The name given is Hizkiah. The significance of this may well be that King Hezekiah is in mind. . . . The lineage he gives is Hezekiah, Amariah, Gedaliah, Cushi, and Zephaniah. Comparing this with the line of Judah's kings, the following results: King Manasseh and Amariah were brothers, King Amon and Gedaliah were first cousins, King Josiah and Cushi were second cousins, and the three sons of Josiah, all of whom ruled (Jehoahaz, Jehoiakim, and Zedekiah), were third cousins of Zephaniah.[21]

In support of Wood's position it could be suggested that, if Hezekiah's son Amariah was born of a member of the king's harem, perhaps no legal recognition was accorded him,[22] so that he could have been older than Manasseh, a possibility allowing an expanded time frame from Hezekiah to Zephaniah's day. Amariah could also have been born to one of Hezekiah's daughters, who would remain unmentioned in the genealogies, and could have been older than Manasseh. Indeed, it is unlikely that Hezekiah, born in 741/40 B.C., had no children before 710 B.C. Under either scenario Zephaniah's mentioning of Hezekiah would merely indicate his justifiable pride in his descent from the great king whose memory was held in high esteem (2 Kings 18:5).[23]

In fairness to those who dispute Zephaniah's royal lineage, none of the arguments in favor of his descent from Hezekiah is conclusive.

---

21. Leon Wood, *The Prophets of Israel* (Grand Rapids: Baker, 1979), p. 321.
22. See R. de Vaux, *Ancient Israel*, trans. John McHugh (New York: McGraw-Hill, 1961), pp. 53-54.
23. S. M. Lehrman ("Zephaniah," in *The Twelve Prophets*, Soncino Books of the Bible, 12th ed., ed. A. Cohen [New York: Soncino, 1985], p. 231) points out that the name *Hezekiah* was given to several persons in the later period, doubtless due to the fame of the godly king.

As Bullock remarks: "However appealing the identification of *Hizkiyyah* with King Hezekiah, it cannot be substantiated."[24]

Whatever Zephaniah's family associations might have been, he was thoroughly at home in Jerusalem and aware of conditions there (1:10-13). A man of keen spiritual sensitivity and moral perception, he decried the apostate and immoral hearts of the people, especially those who were in positions of leadership (1:4-6, 9, 17; 3:1-4, 7, 11). T. H. Robinson remarks:

> Princes, judges, prophets, priests—all alike are faithless to their true vocation and function. It is the business of the princes to protect people—instead, they use their strength to pounce on and destroy men. It is the duty of the judges to assign property to its rightful owner— instead they cling to their causes till they have appropriated in bribes or fees all that is in question. It is the task of the Prophets to assure themselves that the oracles which they deliver are the genuine word of Yahweh—instead, they recklessly pour out unauthenticated "oracles" which can only deceive men. It is the work of the priests to distinguish between the holy and the profane, and to see that the true Divine instruction is given to the worshipper—instead, they have confused all religious distinctions and criminally distorted the revelation of Yahweh.[25]

Zephaniah denounced the materialism and greed that exploited the poor (1:8, 10-13, 18). He also was aware of world conditions and announced God's judgment on the nations for their sins (2:4-15). Above all, God's prophet had a deep concern for God's reputation (1:6; 3:7) and for the well-being of all who humbly trust in Him (2:3; 3:9, 12-13).

Zephaniah was a man for his times. He had a lively expectation of Israel's future felicity in the land of promise (3:10, 14-20). If he was a man of social prominence and therefore had the ear of Judah's leadership, it reminds all of us who read his messages that God uses people of all social strata. Zephaniah's life and ministry are a testimony that one man, yielded wholly to God, can effect great things.

LITERARY CONTEXT

LITERARY FEATURES

Zephaniah writes to inform his readers of the coming Day of the Lord. His message is twofold: (1) this day is a judgment upon all nations and peoples, including God's own covenant people, due to

---

24. C. H. Bullock, *An Introduction to the Old Testament Prophetic Books* (Chicago: Moody, 1986), p. 166.
25. T. H. Robinson, *Prophecy and the Prophets*, 2d ed. (London: Duckworth, 1953), p. 111.

their sins against God and mankind; and (2) it is a day of purification for sin, when the redeemed of all nations shall join a regathered Israel in serving God and experiencing His blessings.[26] This basic theme of judgment and its consequences is developed in two distinctive portions, the first of which serves notice of the judgment and furnishes a description of its severity (1:2–2:3) and the second of which depicts the extent and purposes of the judgment (2:4–3:20).

The early portion of Zephaniah begins with an announcement of God's intention to bring judgment upon the whole earth (1:2-3), including apostate Judah and Jerusalem (1:4-6). Thus people are urged to "be silent before the Sovereign LORD" (1:7, NIV) who, as the divine host at a sacrificial meal, has invited His guests (the nations) to partake of the sacrifice (Judah) He has prepared (1:7-9). Those who in their godless greed have taken advantage of others are warned that they will lament over their lost material gain (1:10-13). The first half of the book comes to a climactic close with a powerful description of the coming Day of the Lord and all its attendant terrors (1:14-18) and then urges its readers to assemble before the Lord and seek His help in leading a humble and righteous life (2:1-3).

Zephaniah initiates the latter portion of his prophecy with a series of divine pronouncements against the peoples who had plagued God's people: Philistines, Moabites, Ammonites, Egyptians, Assyrians (2:4-15). He then denounces Jerusalem, whose people have strayed from God to follow debased and corrupt leaders (3:1-7). Once again he issues a warning: His people must listen carefully to God's message, for His judgment is imminent and assured (3:8). The prophecy concludes by supplying the reason for the coming judgment. God will pour out His wrath not just for the sake of justice but that mankind might experience His cleansing (3:9). At a future time God will return His purified people to Jerusalem to serve Him in truth and sincerity (3:10-13). A redeemed and regathered Israel will rejoice in God and enjoy Him in everlasting felicity (3:14-20).

Thus Zephaniah, like several other OT books, is arranged as a bifid.[27] This conclusion is reinforced by considering its structural

---

26. See the helpful remarks of H. E. Freeman, *An Introduction to the Old Testament Prophets* (Chicago: Moody, 1968), p. 232.
27. For details as to bifid structure, see R. D. Patterson and M. E. Travers, "Literary Analysis and the Unity of Nahum," *GTJ* 9 (1988): 48-50. For bifid structure in Jeremiah, see R. D. Patterson, "Of Bookends, Hinges, and Hooks: Literary Clues to the Arrangement of Jeremiah's Prophecies," *WTJ* 51 (1989): 109-31. The suggestion of bifid structure here stands in contrast with the interesting discussion of B. Renaud, "Le Livre de Sophonie. La Theme de YHWH structurant de la Synthese redactionelle," *RevScRel* 60 (1986): 1-33. Renaud finds a doublet at 1:18 and 3:8 and theorizes that these are seams that indicate a threefold division of the

components. (1) The section 1:1–2:3 forms an inclusio by means of the bookending theme of God's dealing with the earth (1:2, 3; 2:2). A similar reference to the earth closes the second section (3:20). (2) The two halves of Zephaniah are arranged in complementary fashion: (a) pronouncements of judgment (1:2-6; 2:4–3:7) on the nations/earth (1:2-3; 2:4-15) and on Judah/Jerusalem (1:4-6; 3:1-7); (b) exhortations and warnings (1:7-13; 3:8); and (c) teachings concerning the Day of the Lord (1:14–2:3; 3:9-20), each of which is closed by admonitions (2:1-3; 3:14-20).

This bifid structure is accomplished by means of distinctive stitch-words. In the first portion of the book, the first stanza is linked to the second via the careful employment of the Tetragrammaton, while the second stanza is linked to the third by reference to the Day of the Lord. In the second portion of the book, judgment (3:5, 8) and the nations (3:6, 8) provide stitching between the pronouncement section (2:4–3:7) and the following exhortation (3:8); כִּי (*kî*, "because/for") links the exhortation to the added teachings concerning the Day of the Lord (3:9-13, 14-20).

Each subunit likewise displays careful stitching. Thus the pronouncement against the earth (1:2-3) is linked to that against Judah/Jerusalem by the repetition of the phrase "cut off" (1:3, 4). One may also note the use of the Tetragrammaton and themes related to the Day of the Lord throughout the second and third stanzas (1:7-13; 1:14–2:3). In the second portion of the book, the pronouncement against the nations (2:4-15) is linked to that against Judah/Jerusalem via the employment of the word "woe" (2:5; 3:1), and the two strophes (3:9-13, 14-20) of the teaching stanza are stitched together with such ideas as "scattered" (3:10, 19) and "afraid/fear" (3:13, 16) as well as the phrase "in that day" (3:11, 16).[28] The structural design is schematized in the chart on page 284.

Although Zephaniah does not display the literary genius of Nahum, several literary features are noteworthy. In keeping with his twofold purpose, two prophetic genres are evident: (1) positive prophetic sayings of hope (2:1-3; 3:9-13, 14-20); and (2) threats (judg-

---

book in which the theme of the Day of the Lord (1:2-18) moves to a consideration of the remnant (2:1–3:8) and on to a picture of the day of Israel's purification, conversion, and happiness (3:9-20).

28. Zephaniah's use of structural techniques extends to smaller units. Thus the two strophes of the final stanza of the book (3:9-20) are themselves composed of subunits, each formed according to known compositional methods. In the first strophe (3:9-13) the subunits (vv. 9-10, 11-13) are linked by כִּי אָז, whereas in the second strophe (3:14-20) they (vv. 14-17, 18-20) are delineated by such distinctive devices as bookending ("sing/singing," vv. 14, 17) and threading via first-person address (vv. 18-20).

Structure of Zephaniah

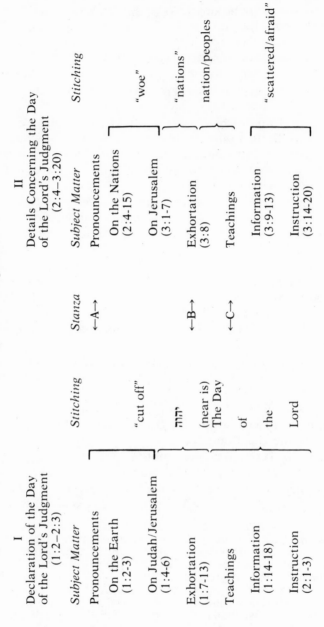

ment oracles), whether to individuals (3:1-7), Judah and Jerusalem
(1:4-6, 7-13), or the nations of the world (1:2-4; 2:4-15). Zephaniah
makes use of exhortations (1:7-13; 3:8), two instructional admonitions (2:1-3; 3:14-20, the latter of which is almost hymnic in nature),
lament (1:10-11), woes (2:4-7; 3:1-7), and pronouncements (1:2-3, 4-6;
2:4-15). Two narrative discourses giving detailed information are also
present (1:14-18; 3:9-13).

In addition, Zephaniah utilizes metaphor and simile (1:7, 11, 12;
2:1, 2, 4-7, 9; 3:3, 8, 13, 16), literary/historical allusions (1:3; 2:4, 9;
3:9-10, 18), personification (1:14; 3:14-15, 16), anthropopoeia (1:4,
12-13; 3:7, 8, 15), irony (1:11; 2:12), merismus (1:12), synecdoche
(1:16; 2:11, 13, 14; 3:6), enallage (3:7), hendiadys (3:7, 19), chiasmus
(3:19), alliteration and paronomasia (1:2, 15, 17; 2:1, 4, 7, 12(?);
3:10(?), 20), enjambment (1:9-12; 2:2, 3, 14; 3:3, 7, 8, 9, 11, 12, 18, 19,
20), and repetition and refrain (1:2, 3, 14, 15-16, 18; 2:2, 3; 3:14-15).
Several key words punctuate the prophetic material: יוֹם (*yôm,* "day"),
21 times; קָרוֹב (*qārôb,* "near"), 10 times; אָסַף (*'āsap,* "gather"), אֶרֶץ
(*'ereṣ,* "earth"), and שֵׁם (*šēm,* "name"), 5 times each; שָׁפַט (*šāpaṭ,*
"judge"), 4 times; פָּקַד (*pāqad,* "punish/visit") and קָבַץ (*qābaṣ,*
"gather/assemble"), 3 times each.

Some have suggested that Zephaniah made use of apocalyptic
genre in his teachings concerning the Day of the Lord (e.g., Freeman,
R. Smith). Thus G. A. Smith remarks:

> From this flash upon the concrete, he returns to a vague terror, in which
> earthly armies merge in heavenly; battle, siege, storm, and darkness are
> mingled, and destruction is spread upon the whole earth. The shades of
> Apocalypse are upon us.[29]

Distinguishing between apocalyptic literature and prophetic eschatology is sometimes difficult, however. Thus P. D. Hanson emphasizes that though differences exist between prophetic eschatology and
the eschatological material of apocalypse, there is also a strong element of continuity:

> Definitions attempt to specify the essential difference between prophetic
> and apocalyptic eschatology: the prophets, affirming the historical
> realm as a suitable context for divine activity, understood it as their task
> to translate the vision of divine activity from the cosmic level to the level
> of the politico-historical realm of everyday life. The visionaries, disillu-
> sioned with the historical realm, disclosed their vision in a manner of
> growing indifference to and independence from the contingencies of the
> politico-historical realm, thereby leaving the language increasingly in
> the idiom of the cosmic realm of the divine warrior and his council.
> Despite this difference in the form of prophetic and apocalyptic es-
> chatology, it must be emphasized that the essential vision of restoration

---

29. G. A. Smith, *Twelve Prophets,* p. 54.

persists in both, the vision of Yahweh's people restored as a holy community in a glorified Zion. It is this basic continuity which compels us to speak of one unbroken strand extending throughout the history of prophetic and apocalyptic eschatology.[30]

Despite the overlap and continuity between prophetic eschatology and the eschatology of apocalypse, as Hanson acknowledges, some differences do exist. Most scholars add to the above distinction by noting in the apocalyptic writers attention to such matters as details of cataclysmic changes in the physical world, cosmic settings and events, and the universal resolution of all things—particularly good and evil—in the distant future. Moreover, all such details are usually related in a series of episodic happenings. Leon Morris follows A. S. Peake in adding further that "speaking generally, the prophets foretold the future that should arise out of the present, while the apocalyptists foretold the future that should break into the present."[31]

Restraint is called for in affirming that Zeph. 1:14-18 is an apocalypse, even though some characteristics of apocalyptic language are present. It does not suit the definition of apocalypse given by John J. Collins:

> *A genre of revelatory literature with a narrative framework, in which a revelation is mediated by an otherworldly being to a human recipient, disclosing a transcendent reality which is both temporal, insofar as it envisages eschatological salvation, and spatial insofar as it involves another, supernatural world* (italics his).[32]

Thus while Zeph. 1:14-18 contains material of a sort that would one day become prominent in apocalyptic literature, it is not an apocalypse as such. Rather, it displays themes that are found in prophetic eschatology.

In harmony with other OT prophets who spoke of the Day of the

---

30. P. D. Hanson, *The Dawn of Apocalyptic* (Philadelphia: Fortress, 1975), p. 12. The aspect of continuity is also underscored by Ronald Youngblood, "A Holistic Typology of Prophecy and Apocalyptic," in *Israel's Apostasy and Restoration*, ed. Avraham Gileadi (Grand Rapids: Baker, 1988), pp. 213-21.

31. Leon Morris, *Apocalyptic* (Grand Rapids: Eerdmans, 1972), p. 62. A similar dichotomy between teleological process and eschatological redemption versus pessimism as to the course of historical events and hence the need for esoteric knowledge and sudden sovereign interposition is emphasized by John H. Hayes, *An Introduction to Old Testament Study* (Nashville: Abingdon, 1979), pp. 383-89.

32. John J. Collins, *The Apocalyptic Imagination* (New York: Crossroad, 1984), p. 4. P. D. Hanson (*Old Testament Apocalyptic* [Nashville: Abingdon, 1987], p. 32) likewise stresses that in an apocalypse "(1) a *revelation* is given by God, (2) through a *mediator* . . . (3) to a *seer* concerning (4) *future events*" (italics his).

Lord, Zephaniah sees that time as one of fearful darkness and gloominess (1:15; cf. Isa. 13:6-16; Joel 1:15; 2:2, 10), awesome earthly and celestial phenomena (1:15; cf. Isa. 13:9, 10, 13; Joel 2:30, 31; 3:14, 15 [HB 3:3, 4; 4:14, 15]; Amos 5:20; Zech. 14:1-7; 2 Pet. 3:10), and a divine wrath that brings destruction, devastation, and death (1:14-18; cf. Isa. 13:15, 16; Obad. 15, 16; Zech. 14:1-3). Zephaniah's closing messages of hope (3:9-20) are likewise in keeping with other prophecies concerning the Day of the Lord as a time of salvation and righteousness (Joel 2:32; 3:17 [HB 3:5; 4:17]; Zech. 14:2, 3) and the return of the Messiah (Zech. 14:4-7) to effect a worldwide climate of peace, prosperity, and everlasting joy (Joel 3:18, 20 [HB 4:18, 20]; Zech. 14:4-10). Zephaniah's prediction of warfare (1:16-18) is likewise mirrored in the other prophets (e.g., Isa. 27; Ezek. 38-39; Joel 3:9-17 [HB 4:9-17]; Zech. 14:1-3; cf. Rev. 19:11-21).[33]

To the extent that Zephaniah utilizes cosmic themes and extreme language he thereby anticipates later apocalyptic thought. With Zephaniah, however, we are removed from the fervor characteristic of later Jewish apocalyptic literature such as 2 Enoch, 3 Baruch, and the fragmentary apocalyptic pieces attributed to Zephaniah.[34] Indeed, Zephaniah is not so much concerned with a future that breaks into the present as he is with the unfolding of God's sovereign and ordered arrangement of history so as to bring it to its intended culmination. As Craigie observes,

> The apocalyptic aspects of the prophet's message are not so much predictions of what must happen in a future world as they are projections into the future of the potential that lies always within the human race. Insofar as Zephaniah is one of the pioneers of apocalyptic thought, we can learn from his writings. He was not, as are some modern representatives of the apocalyptic tradition, one who sat back waiting for the divine pattern of the future to unroll in a pre-ordained fashion. He perceived that the future was shaped in the present, that the horrors of apocalyptic dimensions that seem always to hover on the horizon of human history lay within the ever-present human capacity for evil, pursued to its ultimate climax. Zephaniah balanced this bleak view of human nature with a faith in God's love (3:17), by which he was able to affirm a future of hope beyond the cataclysm.[35]

---

33. For a similar concentration of apocalyptic themes in Isaiah 24-27, see Youngblood, "A Holistic Typology," pp. 216-18. See also the discussion concerning the Day of the Lord by Kenneth L. Barker, "Zechariah," in *EBC*, 7:690-92.
34. For details, see M. Rist, "Apocalypse of Zephaniah," *IDB* 4:951; N. J. Opperwall-Galluch, "Apocalypse of Zephaniah," *ISBE* 4:1189; and O. S. Wintermute, "Apocalypse of Zephaniah," in *The Old Testament Pseudepigrapha*, ed. James H. Charlesworth (Garden City, N.Y.: Doubleday, 1983), 1:499-507.
35. P. C. Craigie, *The Old Testament* (Nashville: Abingdon, 1986), pp. 200-201.

Perhaps it is most appropriate to speak of Zeph. 1:14-18 as "emergent apocalyptic."[36]

As for Zephaniah's poetic style and skill, although some have attempted to discern in the book *qinah* meter or the like, all such attempts are less than convincing. The most distinctive trait in Zephaniah's style is his penchant for repetition and wordplay, both of which are utilized extensively throughout. Accordingly Zephaniah's style is at times monotonously predictable. Nevertheless, his straightforward manner and forceful delivery capture the attention of his readers, so that J. M. P. Smith can affirm that

> Zephaniah can hardly be considered great as a poet. He does not rank with Isaiah, nor even with Hosea in this particular. . . . He had an imperative message to deliver and proceeded in the most direct and forceful way to discharge his responsibility. What he lacked in grace and charm, he in some measure atoned for by the vigour and clarity of his speech. He realised the approaching terror so keenly that he was able to present it vividly and convincingly to his hearers. No prophet has made the picture of the day of Yahweh more real.[37]

Great poet or not, Zephaniah is nonetheless to be commended for his powerful pronouncements, carefully contrived puns (e.g., 2:4-7) and striking imagery. Concerning the last point, Crenshaw calls attention to Zephaniah's "especially vivid description of the Deity wandering through the streets of Jerusalem, lamp in hand, searching for those who are overcome by a false sense of security" (1:12).[38]

Zephaniah will be best remembered for his teaching concerning the Day of the Lord. The awful effects of that message are reflected in the medieval hymn *Dies irae, dies illa,* which has been widely translated. E. P. Mackrell observes that "there are not less than 160 En-

---

36. Christensen ("Zephaniah 2:4-15," p. 682) likewise sees the beginning of later apocalyptic in Zephaniah: "For Zephaniah . . . the day of Yhwh is trans-historical. . . . The focus of attention in Zephaniah is not the judgment of Israel per se, but the vindication of Yhwh and the restoration of a righteous remnant as the true people of Yhwh (3:12-13). Zephaniah has moved beyond the events of history, in the sense of the here and now, to eschatology. . . . A number of the themes of subsequent apocalyptic literature have already begun to emerge as early as the time of Josiah, having their origin within so-called holy war traditions associated with the 'day of Yhwh,' which may well have been a rather specific setting within the cultic and political life of preexilic Israel." D. S. Russell (*The Method and Message of Jewish Apocalyptic* [Philadelphia: Westminster, 1964], pp. 90-91) also speaks of a growing apocalyptic tendency from the time of Ezekiel onward, noting Zephaniah as one such case.
37. J. M. P. Smith, *A Critical and Exegetical Commentary on Zephaniah and Nahum,* ICC (Edinburgh: T. and T. Clark, 1911), p. 176.
38. James L. Crenshaw, *Story and Faith* (New York: Macmillan, 1986), p. 277.

glish and 90 German translations of this ancient Latin hymn."[39] Perhaps the most famous is the version in the *Sarum Hymnal*:

> Day of Wrath! O Day of mourning!
> See the Son's dread Sign returning;
> Heaven and earth in ashes burning.
>
> Oh! what fear the sinner rendeth,
> When from heaven the Judge descendeth
> On Whose sentence all dependeth.[40]

H. Hummel laments concerning the almost total abandonment of Zephaniah's timeless message that

> its neglect parallels the neglect of not only end of the church year themes, but much of the Old Testament (especially the prophets) as well, and ultimately neglect of themes of Law, judgment, retribution, etc., in general. Thus our "Gospel" readily becomes "another Gospel."[41]

OUTLINE

Superscription (1:1)
I. The Announcement of the Day of the Lord (1:2–2:3)
   A. Pronouncements of Judgment (1:2-6)
      1. On all the earth (1:2-3)
      2. On Judah and Jerusalem (1:4-6)
   B. Exhortations Based on Judgment (1:7-13)
   C. Teachings Concerning the Day of the Lord (1:14–2:3)
      1. Information concerning that day (1:14-18)
      2. Instructions in the light of that day (2:1-3)
II. Additional Details Concerning the Day of the Lord (2:4–3:20)
   A. Further Pronouncements of Judgment (2:4–3:7)
      1. On the nations (2:4-15)
         a. Philistia (2:4-7)
         b. Moab and Ammon (2:8-11)
         c. Cush (2:12)
         d. Assyria (2:13-15)
      2. On Jerusalem (3:1-7)
   B. An Exhortation Based on Judgment (3:8)
   C. Additional Teachings Concerning the Day of the Lord (3:9-20)
      1. Information concerning that day (3:9-13)
      2. Instructions in the light of that day (3:14-20)

39. E. P. Mackrell, ed., *Hymns of the Christian Centuries* (New York: Longmans, Green, 1903), p. 67.
40. Ibid., p. 66.
41. H. D. Hummel, *The Word Becoming Flesh* (St. Louis: Concordia, 1979), p. 354.

UNITY

Although the first half of Zephaniah has generally been acknowledged as genuine, critical scholarship has largely impugned the authenticity and unity of the latter half. The results of critical inquiry,
however, have often been diverse, so that "literary criticism of
Zephaniah has been quite checkered and is not easy to summarize."[42]

Those who deny the authorial integrity of the book do so largely
on stylistic and thematic grounds. Given portions are said to be contrary to the spirit of the Zephaniah who prophesied dire punishment
or reflective of the viewpoint of a subsequent generation. Few critics
are as extreme in their denial of the unity of Zephaniah as L. P. Smith
and E. R. Lacheman, who consider the book to be a third-century B.C.
pseudepigraphic production.[43] Most commonly it is the third chapter
that has come under fire, largely due to its subject matter. Although
past scholars often tended to deny the entire third chapter to the
prophet (e.g., Beer, Duhm, Marti, Schwally, Stade), recent scholarship has been moderate, fixing its concerns on verses 9-20. Thus
Larue remarks:

> Attempts to include oracles of restoration and healing in the collection of
> authentic pronouncements of Zephaniah are not convincing, for not only
> do these additions remove the force of the prophetic promise of destruc-
> tion, but they reflect the mood, setting and hopes of the late Exilic peri-
> od.[44]

Indeed these verses have come under almost universal attack, with
vv. 9-10 and 14-20 being consigned to exilic or postexilic times.[45]
Even Eissfeldt, who holds largely to the unity and authenticity of the
book, has serious doubts as to these verses: "Perhaps we should therefore deny to Zephaniah not only the oracle of salvation which begins
afresh in vv. 18-20, but also vv. 14-17, and regard the latter as an
exilic or post-exilic addition."[46]

---

42. Ibid., p. 353. For details as to the critical view of the unity of Zephaniah,
    see Harrison, *Introduction*, pp. 941-43; J. M. P. Smith, *Zephaniah*, pp.
    172-74; G. A. Smith, *Twelve Prophets*, pp. 40-44.
43. L. P. Smith and E. R. Lacheman, "The Authorship," pp. 137-42.
44. Gerald A. Larue, *Old Testament Life and Literature* (Boston: Allyn and
    Bacon, 1968), p. 238.
45. Such was the earlier verdict of Budde, S. R. Driver, and J. M. P. Smith,
    and it has been perpetuated in recent times by Leslie, "Zephaniah," pp.
    952-53; J. A. Bewer, *The Literature of the Old Testament*, 3d ed. (New York:
    Columbia U., 1962), pp. 146-47. Manfred Oeming ("Gericht Gottes und
    Geschichte der Völker nach Zef 3, 1-13," *TQ* 167 [1987]: 289-300) has
    isolated what he considers to be revisions in 3:8 and 3:10 that betray a
    pro-Jewish nationalistic outlook reflecting later times.
46. Otto Eissfeldt, *The Old Testament: An Introduction*, trans. P. R. Ackroyd
    (New York: Harper & Row, 1976), p. 425.

If the third chapter has suffered at the hands of its critics, the second has fared little better. Every verse has been rejected by one scholar or another, although critical focus has centered on 2:4-15. The conclusions reached have often been confusing and contradictory. Although most have admitted the authenticity of 2:1-3, Beer questions even this, and Zephaniah's writing of parts or all of 2:3 is impugned by Duhm, Marti, Nowach, and Stade.[47] Other verses and their critics include 4-15 (Budde), 5-12 (Schwally, Sellin and Forher), 6*b-c* (Duhm), 7*a, e* (Nowach), 7*a*-10 (Beer), 7*b*-11 (S. R. Driver), 8-10 (G. A. Smith), 8-11 (Duhm, Marti, J. M. P. Smith), 8-12 (Nowach), 11 (Stade), 13-15 (Eichhorn), and 15 (Beer, Duhm, Marti, Sellin, and Fohrer). Such a catalog of opinion illustrates D. A. Schneider's contention that "although many scholars have judged that Zephaniah underwent later editing, there has been no convincing convergence of their views on any large number of verses."[48]

Probably because of the great divergence in the end product of such research

> recent critics have been more cautious, and usually prefer to think of mere amplifications of a genuine core. They point out, rightly, that the "remnant" theme was at least as early as Amos, and the frequent use of the "prophetic perfect" in Zephaniah's eschatological oracles is no more problematic than elsewhere.[49]

Indeed, the supposed exilic or postexilic point of view in chap. 3, where hope for Israel's restoration and blessing is expressed, existed side by side with pronouncements of judgment throughout the prophets. Thus R. K. Harrison has shown that "other prophecies of woe commonly concluded with an expectation of restoration and final felicity, such as are found in Amos, Micah, Nahum, and Habakkuk."[50] Moreover, as B. K. Waltke points out, the view that the themes of judgment and hope cannot come from the same era

> is inconsistent with the form of parallel prophecies in the ancient Near E. H. Gressmann wrote: "The numerous old Egyptian oracles attest to the formal unity of threat and promise as the original form. . . . Now that we are acquainted with the Egyptian oracle, it is no longer doubtful that the literary-critical school was on the wrong path" ("Prophetische Gattungen," *Der Messias*, Book II [1929], 73). The same phenomenon is attested in the Mari letters.[51]

---

47. Recently Klaus Seybold ("Text und Auslegung in Zef 2, 1-3," *Biblische Notizen* 25 [1984]: 49-54) has decided against the authenticity of 2:2*b*-3 while maintaining that 2:1-2*a* has the true ring of the prophet's concern for the poor.

48. Schneider, "Zephaniah," p. 1189.

49. Hummel, *The Word*, p. 353.

50. Harrison, *Introduction*, p. 942.

51. B. Waltke, "Book of Zephaniah," *ZPEB* 5:1051.

As for the disputed portions in chap. 2, while individual details may at present render these verses difficult to reconcile with a pre-621 B.C. date, one needs to keep in mind not only the general nature of the prophecies involved (most suggested specific applications are hazardous at best) but also that the limited sources for the recovery of precise data relative to the historical situation in any given period in the ancient Near East make dismissal of the accuracy of 2:4-15 premature.[52] The basic problem with the critical position on chaps. 2 and 3 of Zephaniah may come down, as Bullock suggests, to a presuppositional point of view:

> What we are dealing with here is a whole set of presuppositions espoused by critical scholarship, which not only disavows a strongly predictive element in the prophets, but also confidently sorts the material on the basis of vocabulary that is thought to be confined to specific periods.[53]

In light of the diversity of critical views and the demonstrated literary integrity of the book, I suggest that the case for the unity of Zephaniah is strong. Accordingly "there is no sufficient reason for denying to Zephaniah any portion of his prophecy."[54]

OCCASION AND PURPOSE

Granted the conclusions reached above, the occasion for Zephaniah's prophecy lies in the deplorable spiritual and moral condition of Judahite society in the early days of Josiah's reign. Despite Manasseh's repentance and attempts at spiritual renewal in his latter years (2 Chron. 33:10-20), things took a turn for the worse during the short reign of his wicked son Amon (2 Kings 21:19-26). Accordingly, after the assassination of his father Amon, eight-year-old Josiah found himself the head of an apostate and immoral society.

> The religious indifference and eclecticism on the one hand, and the materialistic selfishness and injustice on the other, were a natural reaction from the exalted ideas and ideals of the previous generation. The expectations and high hopes of Isaiah and his contemporaries had failed to materialize. Yahweh's people were still under the heel of the oppressor. The yoke of Assyria was as heavy and as galling as ever. In despair of deliverance through Yahweh, his followers were seeking to supplement his weakness by having recourse to other gods in conjunction with him, or were abandoning him altogether.[55]

---

52. For the general (as opposed to specific) nature of Zephaniah's prophecies, see C. F. Keil, *The Twelve Minor Prophets*, COT (Grand Rapids: Eerdmans, 1954), 2:123-24.
53. Bullock, *Old Testament Prophetic Books*, p. 170.
54. E. J. Young, *An Introduction to the Old Testament* (Grand Rapids: Eerdmans, 1953), p. 266.
55. J. M. P. Smith, *Zephaniah*, p. 177.

Fortunately for Judah, Josiah was not like his father and would soon establish an unblemished record of faithfulness to God and His law (2 Kings 23:25). Even as a young man he was sensitive to spiritual matters, and the Chronicler reports that a definite spiritual commitment at age twelve was followed by introducing thoroughgoing reform throughout the land a scant four years later (2 Chron. 34:3-7). Zephaniah may have had a part in this; his prophecies concerning the great Day of the Lord perhaps were even instrumental in the king's spiritual activities.

According to this understanding, Zephaniah's prophesying came during those early years of spiritual and social wickedness that attended the onset of Josiah's reign.

> The Book of Zeph, the early discourses of Jer, and 2 K 21-23 furnish a vivid picture of the social, moral, and religious conditions in Judah at the time Zephaniah prophesied. Social injustice and moral corruption were widespread (3 1.3.7). Luxury and extravagance might be seen on every hand; fortunes were heaped up by oppressing the poor (1 8.9). The religious situation was equally bad.[56]

Cognizant of the loss of the spiritual gains that had been made before Amon's rule and faced with conditions that would surely spell the end of Judah itself (2 Kings 23:26-27), Zephaniah speaks out for God and against wickedness. He writes to inform and warn his people of God's coming judgment not only against all the world (1:2-3), especially the nations that had oppressed God's people (2:4-15), but also against Judah and Jerusalem (1:4-6; 3:1-7). In so doing he exposes (1) the false worship practices that included the veneration of Baal and the astral deities and the syncretistic rites that emerged from attempting to blend their worship with that of Yahweh (1:4-6, 9; 3:2, 4) and (2) the corruption of Judahite society (3:1, 3, 5), especially its leaders and merchants (1:8, 10-13, 18; 3:5).[57]

Zephaniah also writes to give the people details of God's future program. On the one hand, he tells of the fearsome events of the Day of the Lord (1:14-16) that must come because of men's sins (1:17-18)

---

56. F. C. Eiselen, "Book of Zephaniah," *ISBE-1* 5:3145.
57. Many have seen in Zephaniah's condemnation of the rich a special concern for the poor. Not only are some materially poor, according to this theory, but also poor in spirit and hence shut up by faith to the provision of God, whereas the proud rich have cut themselves off from Israel's covenantal benefits. See, e.g., S. M. Gozzo, "Il profeta Sofonia e la dottrina teologica del suo libro," *Antonianum* 52 (1977): 3-37; C. Stuhlmueller, "Justice toward the Poor," *TBT* 24 (1986): 385-90; Bewer, *Literature of the Old Testament*, p. 146. N. Lohfink ("Zefanja und das Israel der Armen," *BK* 39 [1984]: 100-108), however, separates Zephaniah's concern for the poor from any spiritual equation of them with the Lord's redeemed.

and, on the other, of the Lord's undying concern (3:5, 7) for His people, especially those who are of a humble and contrite heart (2:3; 3:12). He predicts that in a future day Jerusalem will be avenged (3:19) and purified (3:11-13), its scattered people will be restored to the land (3:9-10, 19), and God's faithful ones will rejoice in the everlasting felicity that He alone provides (3:14-20).

In consideration of all that must happen in the future, Zephaniah writes to exhort and admonish the people to surrender to God (1:7) and to repent and seek Him (1:10; 2:1-3), not only to avoid the force of the Lord's fiery blast but also in anticipation of that glorious time when a redeemed and purified people will rejoice in the salvation and delights of God's love (3:14-17).

TEXT AND CANONICITY

Although critical concern has been expressed as to the authenticity of Zephaniah, its canonicity has never been called into question.[58] It was known to the author of the Apocalypse of Zephaniah (Frag. B7), accepted by Philo and Josephus, and included in the early church canonical lists. Our Lord appears to have drawn upon Zeph. 1:3 in His parable concerning the end of the age (Matt. 13:41), as did John (cf. Rev. 6:17 with Zeph. 1:14-18; Rev. 14:5 with Zeph. 3:13; Rev. 16:1 with Zeph. 3:8). In addition, the Talmud (T. B. Sanhedrin 98a) and early Christian Fathers (e.g., Clement of Alexandria, Cyprian, Augustine) cited Zephaniah as authoritative in their condemnation of man's pride and idolatry.

As for the text of Zephaniah, R. K. Harrison observes: "The Hebrew text of the prophecy has been quite well preserved, and it is only on fairly rare occasions, as for example in Zephaniah 2:2, 14; 3:7, that the LXX version is able to throw some light on the text."[59] This does not minimize the fact that the received text will be difficult to understand in places (e.g., 1:2, 14; 2:14). Nevertheless, it may be safely affirmed that "the MT is the best form of the text available, and it is probably the basis of all the versions."[60]

THEOLOGICAL CONTEXT

Zephaniah is best remembered for his presentation of God as the sovereign judge of all (1:2-3, 7, 14-18; 3:8). It is He who punishes the

---

58. See Roger Beckwith, *The Old Testament Canon of the New Testament Church* (Grand Rapids: Eerdmans, 1985), pp. 71-80; R. Laird Harris, *Inspiration and Canonicity of the Bible* (Grand Rapids: Zondervan, 1969), pp. 180-91.
59. Harrison, *Introduction*, p. 943.
60. Schneider, "Zephaniah," p. 1190.

wickedness of men (1:8-9, 17; 3:7, 11) and nations (2:4-15; 3:6), particularly those who have opposed His people (2:8, 10). Thus G. von Rad remarks that *"Zephaniah* . . . is chiefly concerned with the imminent advent of Yahweh and a universal battle against the nations on this day: but with him very much more emphasis is laid upon the resulting judgment of Jerusalem and threats against the complacent."[61] Zephaniah also shows that God is not only righteous (3:5) but also a God of love (3:17) and concern who deals justly with all (3:5*b*). D. A. Schneider points out that

> the book persistently portrays the holiness and grace of God. God's holiness appears in the contrasts between Him and the proud sinners: they pretend to rule, but God judges with inexorable power; they hold office, but the Lord gives unfailing justice (3:1-5). God's grace appears chiefly in the two passages (2:1-3; 3:11-20) that offer hope and salvation to a nation (and possibly even Gentiles) that has just been rightly condemned to complete desolation.[62]

Zephaniah also reveals a great deal concerning man's condition:

> He saw that God cannot brook haughtiness and that people's only hope lay in recognizing their own frailty. Pride is a problem rooted in human nature, and neither Judah (2:3), Ammon, Moab (v. 10), nor Nineveh is exempt. Nineveh is made to epitomize insolence, boasting "I am and there is none else" (v. 15). Such rebellion, the declaration of spiritual independence from God, is the most heinous of sins.[63]

Zephaniah focuses on the spirit of wickedness in people (1:3-6, 17; 3:1, 4). Such individuals reason that God does not intervene in human affairs (1:12) and so go on in their violence and deceit (1:9). Further, their greed occasions the oppression of those around them (1:10-11, 13, 18; 3:3). C. Lehman observes that "this book has gone to greatest depths in its exposure of sin and man's sinfulness."[64]

Nevertheless, Zephaniah holds out the hope that God will be receptive to everyone who repentantly surrenders to Him (2:1-2). Such spiritual virtues as righteousness, humility, faith, and truth receive commendation and reward from Zephaniah (2:3; 3:12-13). The Lord has a plan for the humble and faithful remnant of His people (2:2-3, 9; 3:11-13).[65] He will purify them (3:9-10), regather and

---

61. G. von Rad, *The Message of the Prophets* (New York: Harper & Row, 1965), p. 160.
62. Schneider, "Zephaniah," pp. 1190-91.
63. W. S. LaSor, D. A. Hubbard and F. W. Bush, *Old Testament Survey* (Grand Rapids: Eerdmans, 1982), p. 437.
64. C. K. Lehman, *Biblical Theology: Old Testament* (Scottdale: Herald, 1971), p. 346.
65. G. W. Anderson ("The Idea of the Remnant in the Book of Zephaniah," *Annual of the Swedish Theological Institute* 11 [1977-78]: 11-14) points out that the remnant motif can logically exist only in a context of judgment so that doom and hope are not incompatible prophetic elements. He

restore them (3:10) to their land (3:20), and give them victory over their enemies (2:7, 9). Jerusalem will be a blissful place (3:11, 18), for Israel's saving God (3:17) will bless His people (3:14-17) and in turn make them a channel of blessing to all (3:19-20).

stresses the fact that the idea of a remnant means more than mere existence; it is a "promise that those who by the mercy of God survive the judgment will by their very existence be a pledge of restoration and of God's continuing purpose of good for his people."

1
The Announcement of the Day of the Lord (Zephaniah 1:1–2:3)

Zephaniah begins his prophecy with notices of his reception of the word of the Lord, his patrilineage, and the time of his ministry (1:1). He then announces the coming of God's worldwide judgment (1:2-6) and exhorts his hearers to humble themselves before that day overtakes them (1:7-13). He closes the first major portion of his prophecy by supplying important details concerning the devastation of that coming Day of the Lord (1:14-18) and admonishes those who hear him to seek the Lord (2:1-3).

From a literary standpoint this section is marked by prophetic pronouncements (1:2-3, 4-6), a narrative with vivid descriptive detail (1:14-18), and warnings and admonitions (1:7-13; 2:1-3). It displays such literary features as alliteration and paronomasia (1:2), chiasmus and hyperbole (1:2-3), literary allusions (1:3), anthropopoeia (1:4, 12-13), metaphor and simile (1:7, 12; 2:1), lament (1:10-11), irony (1:11), merismus (1:12), personification (1:14), synecdoche (1:16), and especially a widespread use of repetition (1:2, 3, 14, 15-16, 18; 2:2, 3).

SUPERSCRIPTION (1:1)

Translation

The word of the Lord that came to Zephaniah the son of Cushi, the son of Gedaliah, the son of Amariah, the son of Hezekiah, in the days of Josiah, the son of Amon the king of Judah.

Exegesis and Exposition

The implications of the unusual recording of four generations of Zephaniah's patrilineage were discussed in the introduction (see under Setting). If Zephaniah descended from King Hezekiah, he would have had access to the royal court accorded few other prophets, an entree that might account for Josiah's early attention to Judah's spiritual condition.

Zephaniah had, however, an even higher relationship. He declares that what he is about to deliver is not the message of man but the word of the Lord (cf. Hos. 1:1; Joel 1:1; Mic. 1:1; Hag. 1:1; Zech. 1:1). Therefore, what he had to say was of supreme significance and ought to be heeded all the more earnestly.

Additional Notes

1:1 G. Gerleman suggests that in the prophetic books "the Word of the Lord" becomes a "technical term for the prophetic word of revelation."[1] He notes this usage in 225 of the 242 occurrences of the phrase in the OT. It not only identifies the source and authority of Zephaniah's prophecy but also authenticates him as God's spokesman. Because of the nature of God's Word (cf. Ps. 119) it is to be received and believed and in turn is to be mastered and allowed to master the hearts of those who receive it.

צְפַנְיָה ("Zephaniah"): The meaning of the prophet's name is usually traced to either of the two senses of the root צפן: (1) "hide," hence "he whom the Lord hides," "the Lord hides," or "hidden of the Lord" (e.g., Feinberg, Keil) or (2) "treasure," hence "Yahweh has treasured" (e.g., Opperwall-Galluch). Building on the former meaning, J. M. P. Smith proposes "Yahweh is protector." Smith suggests further that the frequent use of צפן in biblical (Ex. 6:22; Lev. 10:4; Num. 34:25; 2 Kings 25:18; 1 Chron. 6:21; Jer. 21:1; 29:24-25, 29; 37:3; 52:24; Zech. 6:10, 14) and extrabiblical names (e.g., in the Elephantine Papyri, on a Hebrew gem in the British Museum, and in Carthaginian and Assyrian inscriptions) points to the idea that it was the name of a Semitic god.[2] The form of the name *Zephaniah*, however, makes this proposal unlikely. Nor is there any demonstrable designed correspondence between the prophet's name and the message of the book (against Pusey). Whichever of the senses of the root is intended in the name (I am inclined to the first), the truth contained in the name is sufficient reason for its frequent appearance.

---

1. G. Gerleman, "דָּבָר," *THAT* 1:439.
2. J. M. P. Smith, *A Critical and Exegetical Commentary on Zephaniah and Nahum*, ICC (Edinburgh: T. and T. Clark, 1911), p. 184.

A. PRONOUNCEMENTS OF JUDGMENT (1:2-6)

In language and figures drawn from the creation and Flood accounts God's prophet warns of a universal judgment that will one day descend upon the earth and all that is on it (1:2-3). He amplifies the announcement of that judgment by applying it to God's covenant people. Because of their idolatry and apostasy, Judah and Jerusalem will find God's hand of chastisement stretched out against them (1:4-6).

1. ON ALL THE EARTH (1:2-3)

Translation

"I will utterly sweep away* everything
  from the face of the earth"
                        —the declaration of the LORD.
³"I will sweep away man and beast;
I will sweep away the birds of the air,
    (and) the fish of the sea,
    and the things that cause the wicked to stumble*;
and I will cut off man
    from the face of the earth"
                        —the declaration of the LORD.

Exegesis and Exposition

Zephaniah begins his messages with God's doubly reinforced declaration: God will destroy everything upon the face of the earth, sweeping away all life before Him whether on land, in the air, or in the water, including especially mankind and all that pertains to him. The pronouncement is solemn, its phraseology reminiscent of the Noahic flood (cf. Gen. 6:17; 7:21-23). The disaster envisioned here, however, is more cataclysmic, for although every living thing that dwelled on the land or inhabited the air died at that time the fish remained.

Zephaniah alludes also to the creation. His catalog of death is arranged in inverse order to God's creative work: man, beast, the creatures of the air, those of the sea (cf. Gen. 1:20-27). The order of creation found its climax in man, who was made in God's image and appointed as His representative. The coming destruction will begin with man, who has denied his Creator (1:6) and involved in his sin all that is under his domain. Man's sin is thus weighty, involving not only himself but his total environment (1:2-3b).

The judgment that begins with man also concludes with man. All that alienates him from his Creator and Lord will be swept away, and

299

he will be left alone to face his God. Last of all, man himself will be cut off from the land that has given him sustenance. The chiastic arrangement of the paronomasia is striking: The אֲדָמָה (ʾădāmā, "ground") had given אָדָם (ʾādām, "man") life; now the man is cut off from the life-giving ground. This wordplay, combined with the alliteration of the letters *aleph* and *mem* (both employed 12 times), makes the literary allusion all the more effective. Though the language is hyperbolic, it emphasizes the seriousness of man's sin and the universal extent of God's judgment.

Additional Notes

1:2 †אָסֹף אָסֵף ("I will utterly sweep away"): The MT puts together two verbs from different roots, אָסֹף being an infinitive absolute from אָסַף ("gather/remove") and אָסֵף a hiphil prefix conjugation verb from סוּף ("come to an end," hence here = "sweep away"). All suggested repointings of the MT are attempts to smooth out this seeming incongruity. Thus the majority of scholars tend to read two words from the root אסף (i.e., אָסֹף אָסֵף—e.g. *BHS*, Gesenius, G. A. Smith; cf. NJB).[3] Kapelrud suggests אָסֹף אֲאַסֵף ("completely/fully gather/assemble"; cf. Vg *congregans congregabo*), whereas Sabottka prefers to emend the first form to a hiphil from יָסַף ("add/do again"): אֹסִיף אָסוֹף ("I will again sweep away").[4]

Two arguments in defense of the MT are as follows: (1) the use of mixed roots is attested elsewhere (e.g., Isa. 28:28; Jer. 8:13[5]); and (2) the skilled Masoretic scribes would hardly make such a "blunder" if it were unintelligible. Not only does the difficulty of the MT argue for its retention,[6] but the LXX already recognized the incongruity, rendering the phrase ἐκλείψει ἐκλιπέτω (lit. "It will give out, let it fail"— hence, "Let there be a complete failure"). Moreover, as Keil points out, the two verbs have a "kindred meaning," the compatibility of the ideas of "gathering up things" so as to "put an end to them" being obvious.[7] The translation given above follows the MT, translating *ad*

---

3. For details, see ibid., p. 191.
4. See A. S. Kapelrud, *The Message of the Prophet Zephaniah* (Oslo-Bergen-Troms: Universitetsforlaget, 1975), pp. 21-22; L. Sabottka, *Zephanja* (Rome: Biblical Institute Press, 1972), pp. 5-7. Sabottka's proposal has the advantage of similarity to Gen. 8:21 (הָאֲדָמָה . . . . אֹסִף לֹא, "I will not again" curse "the ground").
5. GKC, par. 113w n. 3, however, lists both cases, as well as Zeph. 1:2, as textual errors.
6. See E. Würthwein, *The Text of the Old Testament*, 4th ed. (Grand Rapids: Eerdmans, 1979), pp. 113-19; C. E. Armerding, *The Old Testament and Criticism* (Grand Rapids: Eerdmans, 1983), p. 126.
7. C. F. Keil, *The Twelve Minor Prophets*, COT (Grand Rapids: Eerdmans, 1954), 2:126-27.

sensum and giving primary force to סוּף, which is repeated twice in v. 3 (cf. NIV).

As noted in the Exegesis and Exposition, these verses allude to the Flood and creation accounts. The relation to the first is underscored by Zephaniah's utilization of "from the face of the earth" (cf. Gen. 6:7; 7:4; 8:8), כֹּל ("all," "every[thing]"; cf. Gen. 6:17; 7:4; 8:19), and אֲדָמָה ("ground/land"; cf. Gen. 6:7, 20; 7:4, 8, 23; 8:8, 13, 21). Thus he may be giving a divine qualification of the promise to Noah that God would never again "curse the ground because of man" or "destroy all living creatures" (Gen. 8:21, NIV). Of course the Noahic Covenant has to do with a universal flood (cf. Gen. 9:11-16) and so may not preclude another type of universal destruction (cf. 2 Pet. 3:10). Further, the promise itself contains a qualification. Thus G. Vos remarks concerning Gen. 8:20-22: "The regularity of nature in its great fundamental processes will henceforth continue. There is, however, added to this a qualification: 'while the earth remaineth.' This pertains to the eschatological background of the deluge (cp. 1 Pet. 3:20, 21; 2 Pet. 2:5)."[8] Still further, numerous passages seem to refer to the passing away or transforming of the present earth (e.g., Job 14:12; Ps. 102:26 [HB 102:27]; Isa. 24:23; 34:6; 51:6; 54:10; Hag. 2:6, 21; Matt. 5:18; 24:35; Mark 13:31; Luke 21:33; Heb. 1:10-12; 12:26-27; Rev. 21:1). Zephaniah, however, does not appear to intend replacing the promise of Gen. 8:21[9] but rather to qualify it by demonstrating its limitations. He uses the fact and limitations of the promise as an argument *a fortiori*. If God intends to judge the whole world, how much more should Judah and Jerusalem expect to be judged (cf. vv. 4-6)? God's people ought not to misunderstand (cf. v. 12) the old promise as indicating that God cannot again intervene to judge mankind.[10]

Zephaniah's dependence on the creation account may be seen in his list of the objects of divine judgment in inverse order to their creation (Gen. 1:20-26) and the literary allusions to man and ground (אָדָם and אֲדָמָה). It seems unlikely, however, that either reversing the creative order to pre-creation conditions or canceling man's dominion over the lower creatures is being announced.[11] Indeed, the order

---

8. Geerhardus Vos, *Biblical Theology* (Grand Rapids: Eerdmans, 1954), p. 63.
9. See J. D. Watts, *Joel, Obadiah, Jonah, Nahum, Habakkuk and Zephaniah*, CNEB (Cambridge: Cambridge U., 1975), p. 156, for a dissenting opinion.
10. Some biblical scholars, however, relate Zephaniah's prophecy to a nearer historical fulfillment in 586 B.C. See, e.g., J. Barton Payne, *Encyclopedia of Biblical Prophecy* (New York: Harper & Row, 1973), pp. 440-41.
11. See M. De Roche, "Zephaniah I 2-3: The 'Sweeping' of Creation," *VT* 30 (1980): 104-9; John D. Hannah, "Zephaniah," in *The Bible Knowledge Commentary*, ed. John F. Walvoord and Roy B. Zuck (Wheaton, Ill.: Scripture Press, 1985), 1:1525.

of creation with man at its head is fixed by God and guaranteed in perpetuity (cf. Ps. 8:5-9 [HB 8:6-10]), a reality ultimately realized in Christ (Col. 1:15-20; Heb. 2:5-9). Rather, the creation account is employed by Zephaniah to remind his hearers of the continued importance of mankind.

Zephaniah draws upon both biblical sources, then, as literary precedents to underscore not only the fact of the universality of God's judgment as a principle to be applied in Judah's case but also the central place of man as a moral agent in great measure responsible for world conditions. This conclusion is reinforced by the syntax of vv. 2-6, the prefix-conjugation verbs of vv. 2-3*c* declaring God's resolve being continued by the suffix-conjugation verbs of vv. 3*d*-6 detailing the consequences of the divine purpose. Cutting off sinful man in general is thus declared along with judging God's covenant nation in particular. Indeed, the judgment of God's people is the focus of the pronouncement.

1:3 †הַמַּכְשֵׁלוֹת ("the things that cause to stumble"): The consonantal text has traditionally been understood as a noun: "ruins" (NASB), "heaps of rubble" (NIV), "stumbling blocks" (Pesh.; cf. KJV, NKJV). The following particle אֶת must then be viewed not as the marker of the definite direct object but as the preposition "with," hence "with the wicked" (NASB).

As Sabottka remarks, the word in question has been "for translators a true stone of stumbling."[12] The translation suggested here takes the MT consonantal text as a hiphil fem. pl. participle, the thought being that in God's judicial "clean sweep" not only man and his physical environment but every false religious practice that has occasioned his falling will be destroyed.[13] The idea is parallel to Jeremiah's complaint (where the hiphil participle of כָּשַׁל also occurs) that God's people "burn incense to worthless idols, which made them stumble in their ways" (Jer. 18:15, NIV). The line thus anticipates the condemnation of Judah's false religion recorded in vv. 4-6. Since man's religious practices inevitably affect his total life situation, the word may imply even more. Laetsch suggests that the term

> describes the ruined state of every social and political institution, whether of divine or human origin. . . . Every divine institution for man's welfare, matrimony (Gen. 2:18-25), government (Rom. 13:1-7), has

---

12. Sabottka, *Zephanja*, p. 8. Sabottka's own suggestion of a compound form of *mkk/mûk* ("be low," "sink," "give way") and *kšl* ("fall/stumble"), hence "I will plunge the world into ruins," is less than convincing. The LXX omits the whole phrase.
13. See also the *Preliminary and Interim Report on the Hebrew Old Testament Text Project* (New York: United Bible Societies, 1980), 5:372.

been defiled and crippled by human sin and wickedness. Every human civilization, the product of sinful man, for that very reason carries within itself the germ of decay and death. When it has run its tragic downward course (cp. Rom. 1:18-32), it will collapse and bury beneath its ruins all that in proud self-exaltation had relied on it as the salvation of the nation and the world.[14]

2. ON JUDAH AND JERUSALEM (1:4-6)

Translation

"And I will stretch out My hand against Judah
and against all who dwell in Jerusalem.
And I will cut off from this place the remnant of Baal
   —the (very) names* of the pagan priests*
together with the priests
⁵and those who bow down* upon the roofs
   to the hosts of heaven
and those who bow down and swear to the Lord
   and swear by their king*
⁶and those who turn back from following the Lord
   who neither seek the Lord nor inquire of Him."

Exegesis and Exposition

God's announced purpose to sweep away everything so that man may receive his just judgment is continued with an indication of God's ultimate intentions. He will stretch out His hand of chastisement against Judah and Jerusalem. The motif of the outstretched hand of God emphasizes God's omnipotence (Jer. 32:17) and is also used in connection with His creative power and sovereign disposition of the course of history (Isa. 14:26-27; Jer. 27:5). It is specially used of God's relations with Israel, whether in deliverance (Ex. 6:6; Deut. 4:34; 5:15; 7:19; 9:29; 26:8; 2 Kings 17:36; Jer. 32:21; Ezek. 20:33-34) or in judgment (Isa. 5:25; 9:12, 17, 21 [HB 9:11, 16, 20]; 10:4; Jer. 21:5). It is the last of these that is in view here. God's people needed to be reminded that the God of the universe and of all individuals and nations is Israel's God in particular. To Him she owed her allegiance. When such was not forthcoming, when sin and apostasy set in, Israel could expect God's outstretched hand of judgment.

The cause and course for Israel's judgment are detailed next. Zephaniah declares that God will cut off the remnant of Baalism that plagued Judah. The activities of Baal, the chief deity of ancient Ca-

---

14. Theodore Laetsch, *The Minor Prophets* (St. Louis: Concordia, 1956), p. 355.

naan, are well documented in the literature of Ugarit.[15] Baal was a god associated with the storm and fertility; his veneration together with its licentious worship rites was a constant source of temptation to Israel (cf. Num. 25:1-5; Judg. 2:13; 1 Kings 16:30-32; 18:19, 21; Hos. 13:1). Fascination with Baal had been a prime reason for the fall of the Northern Kingdom (2 Kings 17:16-18; Hos. 2:8 [HB 2:10]) and would prove to be so for Judah as well (2 Kings 17:18-20; Jer. 11:13, 17; 19:5-9).[16] Although Zephaniah's denunciation of those who worship the hosts of heaven on the rooftops is a further indication of the turn that the worship of Baal often took, the adoration of Baal and the stars was a besetting sin in Judah when Josiah came to the throne (cf. 2 Kings 21:2-3 with 2 Kings 23:4-5, 10-14; Jer. 19:3-13). Because Baal was called Baal Shamem (Baal/Lord of [the] Heaven[s]) in ancient Canaan,[17] it was inevitable that features of stellar worship would be fused with practices associated with Baal.

Although Israel's preoccupation with Baal was denounced by her prophets (1 Kings 18:20-21; Jer. 2:8, 23; 11:13, 17; 32:35; Hos. 2:13 [HB 2:15]; 11:2), the people continued in his worship, developing a dual worship of Yahweh and Baal that was compromising and syncretistic (Jer. 7:9; 23:25-29). Zephaniah's mentioning of pagan priests and regular priests shows that such worship practices were also characteristic of the religious scene of Josiah's early reign. But the day of reckoning was near, and Judah's punishment would be severe. The last vestige of Baalism will be eradicated. Indeed, the very names of the various types of priests will be erased forever.

The priests of Judah and the devotees of compromise would be punished. Zephaniah goes on to condemn those who feign allegiance to the Lord while swearing by the name of Baal their king. The prophet also singles out still a third group—those who have drawn back* from any pretense of worshiping the Lord. They seek* God neither in personal prayer nor in formal worship. They have no interest or concern for the Lord who redeemed His people (cf. Jer. 2:13, 32-35; 3:6-10; 5:2-13; etc.).

---

15. See P. C. Craigie, *Ugarit and the Old Testament* (Grand Rapids: Eerdmans, 1983), pp. 61-66; F. M. Cross, *Canaanite Myth and Hebrew Epic* (Cambridge, Mass.: Harvard U., 1973), 145-215.
16. The biblical evidence for the persistent problem of paganism in general and Baalism in particular in ancient Israel is strong. Nor is extrabiblical evidence wanting, as demonstrated in the Samaria ostraca, although some now minimize the evidence of pagan influence in such cases. See, e.g., Jeffrey H. Tigay, *You Shall Have No Other Gods: Israelite Religion in the Light of Hebrew Inscriptions*, HSS 31 (Atlanta: Scholars Press, 1986). For Baal and the OT, see K. G. Jung, "Baal," *ISBE* 1:377-79.
17. See Cross, *Canaanite Myth*, pp. 7-8; Laetsch, *Minor Prophets*, pp. 356-57; Keil, *Minor Prophets*, 2:128-29.

Additional Notes

1:4 †הַכְּמָרִים ("the pagan priests"): The Vg renders the term "temple guardians," but the Pesh. transliterates the word and the LXX omits it altogether. The English versions have handled it variously: "idolatrous priests" (NASB, NKJV, RSV), "the pagan . . . priests" (NIV), "priests" (NJB), "Chemarims" (KJV). The term occurs only twice elsewhere in the OT: (1) in Hos. 10:5 of priests who officiated in the calf worship at Bethel[18]; and (2) in 2 Kings 22:5 of priests who led in rites associated with Baal and stellar worship, priests who had been appointed by the past kings of Judah but whose offices were done away with in the reforms of Josiah. In all three cases, then, the term refers to priests outside the established priesthood of Israel and has special connection with Baalism.[19] Despite the widespread occurrence of the word in other Semitic languages, its etymology is uncertain.[20]

אֶת־שֵׁם . . . עִם הַכֹּהֲנִים† ("the names . . . with the priests"): Because the deletion of a *waw* coordinator in such a compound would be unusual, the phrase should probably be construed as apposition for emphatic amplification—even the names of the officiating priests connected with Baalism and the other false religions will be cut off.[21]

1:5 †הַמִּשְׁתַּחֲוִים ("those who bow down"): The existence of this root in Ugaritic makes certain that the form is a hishtaphel participle from חָוָה ("bow down") and not, as formerly thought, from the later Hebrew root שָׁחָה ("bend/bow"; hithpael = "prostrate oneself").[22] The action connected with the word

> may be performed before persons as a greeting or as a token of respect or submission, before Yahweh in the context of prayer or sacrifice, i.e., as a cultic action, or even (usually in the context of accusation, prohibition,

---

18. For the equation of Bethaven with Bethel in Hos. 4:15; 5:8; 10:5, see Grace I. Emmerson, *Hosea an Israelite Prophet in Judean Perspective*, JSOTSup 28 (Sheffield: JSOT Press, 1984), pp. 124-38.
19. Kimchi and Ibn Ezra identify the term as referring to "ancillary priests who ministered to Baal." See S. M. Lehrman, "Zephaniah," in *The Twelve Prophets*, Soncino Books of the Bible, ed. A. Cohen, 12th ed. (London: Soncino, 1985), p. 235. W. F. Albright (*From the Stone Age to Christianity*, 2d ed. [Garden City, N.Y.: Doubleday, 1957], p. 234) suggests that the word designates eunuch priests whose condition, according to the Mosaic law, disqualified them from service in the regular cultus. See further R. de Vaux, *Ancient Israel*, trans. John McHugh (New York: McGraw-Hill, 1961), p. 345.
20. See KB-3 2:459; J. M. P. Smith, *Zephaniah*, p. 192. For an older proposal, see A. R. Fausset, "Zephaniah," in R. Jamieson, A. R. Fausset, and David Brown, *A Commentary Critical, Experimental and Practical on the Old and New Testaments* (Grand Rapids: Eerdmans, 1948), 4:638-39.
21. See GKC, par. 154 n. 1(a).
22. Cyrus Gordon (*UT*, p. 395) suggests that the root is Egypto-Semitic.

or ridicule) before other gods, in which case it simply stands for (cultic) "worship."[23]

The twice occurring הַנִּשְׁבָּעִים is differently constructed in each instance, the first with לְ and the second with בְּ. Keil explains the distinction as follows: "The difference between the two expressions answers exactly to the religious attitude of the men in question, who pretended to be worshippers of Jehovah, and yet with every asseveration took the name of Baal into their mouth."[24]

†מַלְכָּם ("their king"): The MT has been repointed to read Milcom (the detested Ammonite deity; cf. 1 Kings 11:5, 33; 2 Kings 23:13) by the Vg, Pesh., NASB, RSV, NKJV, and NJB and the familiar Molech by the NIV. The commentators are divided, with scholars attested for each suggestion.[25] The NIV's proposal has the advantage of isolating one of the sins of Judah, whose rites were combatted by Josiah (2 Kings 23:10) along with the other practices that Zephaniah mentions here (cf. vv. 4-5 with 2 Kings 23:4-5, 12).[26] Despite the widespread endorsement of Milcom here, a reference to his worship in the Judah of Josiah's day seems unlikely. Although he was one of many gods who held a fascination for the early Israelites (Judg. 10:6), his popularity does not seem to have continued after the days of Solomon (1 Kings 11:5, 33), possibly due to the hostility between Ammonites and Israelites (cf. 2 Chron. 20:1-26; 27:5; Isa. 11:14; Jer. 49:1-6; Amos 1:13-15) and the overshadowing presence of Baalism and the fertility religion of Canaan (cf. 2 Kings 17:16-17).

The reading of the MT has much to commend it. It is followed in Rahlf's edition of the LXX and favored by the fact that the term "king" was applied to Baal.[27] Further, the context pits the worship of Yahweh against Baal and the false rites associated with him, including the syncretistic blending of Baalism with the worship of Israel's God.

1:6 הַנְּסוֹגִים ("*those who turn back*"): Although this root is used of natural movement (cf. Arabic *sāʾja*, "go and come"), the Hebrew verb is commonly employed of vacillating or faithless behavior toward

---

23. H. D. Preuss, "חוה," *TDOT* 4:249.

24. Keil, *Minor Prophets*, 2:129.

25. See Alan Cooper, "Divine Names and Epithets in the Ugaritic Texts," *RSP*, 3:450.

26. For the identity and nature of Molech worship, see my note on 2 Kings 16:3 in R. D. Patterson and H. J. Austel, "1, 2 Kings," in *EBC* (Grand Rapids: Zondervan, 1988), 4:245-46.

27. See Sabbottka, *Zephanja*, p. 24; Keil, *Minor Prophets*, 2:129; A. R. Hulst, *Old Testament Translation Problems* (Leiden: Brill, 1960), p. 253. See also M. Weinfeld, "The Worship of Molech and of the Queen of Heaven and Its Background," *UF* 4 (1972): 133-54.

people (Jer. 38:22) or God (Ps. 53:3 [HB 53:4]). When it occurs in the niphal, it denotes a willful turning of oneself away or back from someone or something. When that someone is God (cf. Isa. 59:12-13), it is a deadly condition.

לֹא־בִקְשׁוּ . . . וְלֹא־דְרָשֻׁהוּ ("they do not *seek* . . . they do not inquire of him"): The first verb lays stress on personal emotion in seeking or asking someone; the latter emphasizes the person's concern in the inquiry and hence is often used in prophetic encouragements to repentance (cf. Amos 5:4-6). דָּרַשׁ is also used of inquiring of God or consulting an oracle. The two verbs occur in parallel elsewhere in contexts dealing with seeking the Lord (e.g., Deut. 4:29; 2 Chron. 20:3, 4; Ps. 105:4).[28]

B. EXHORTATIONS BASED ON JUDGMENT (1:7-13)

In the light of the pronouncements of judgment, Zephaniah issued exhortations to Judah. Since the coming of judgment was certain, it was time for them to examine their spiritual condition. Judah's spiritual leaders and Jerusalem's leading citizens, those most responsible for the direction of God's people, ought to take particular note. In their pride and avarice they have ignored and blasphemed God. It was a time for solemn silence and sincere repentance.

The unit is made up of two strophes, each introduced by an imperative (vv. 7, 11) followed by a motive clause begun by כִּי (*kî*, "for/because/indeed," vv. 7b-d, 11b-c), and continued by an introductory phrase ("and it shall come to pass") giving additional details (vv. 8-9 and vv. 12-13).[29] Because the second imperative (v. 11) is expressed in irony concerning the grief of Judah's merchants in the future time of judgment rather than intended for the contemporary populace, vv. 11-13 continue the details of Jerusalem's punishment for which she is to "be silent" (v. 7). Accordingly v. 10 is a hinge verse that proceeds on the basis of the time framework of vv. 8-9 and predicts the lamentation of the merchants upon which the following call for wailing (v. 11) is issued. Since v. 10 partakes of the portions that precede and follow it, the section may be schematized structurally as follows:

A   A call for silence (vv. 7-9)
A.B   A report of lamentation (v. 10)
B   A call for sorrow (vv. 11-13).

---

28. For details, see G. Gerleman and E. Ruprecht, "דרשׁ," *THAT* 1:459-67; S. Wagner, "בקשׁ," *TDOT* 2:229-41, and "דָּרַשׁ," *TDOT* 3:293-307. See also the note on Nah. 3:7.
29. For a similar employment of this structure in the prophetic literature, see R. D. Patterson, "Joel," in *EBC*, 7:233-34.

Translation

Be silent* in the presence of the sovereign LORD,
   for the Day of the LORD is near;
yes, the LORD has prepared a sacrifice;
   He has consecrated His guests.
⁸"And it shall come to pass on the day of Yahweh's sacrifice*
that I will punish* the nobles*,
   and the king's sons,
and all those clothed
   in foreign clothing.
⁹And in that day I will punish all those
   who leap over the threshold*,
those who fill the houses of their masters
   by violence and deceit."
¹⁰"And on that day"—the declaration of the LORD—
   "a cry will go out from the Fish Gate,
and a wailing from the Second Quarter*,
   and a great crash from the hills."
¹¹Wail, you who live in the market district,
   for all the people of Canaan will be silent,
   all who weigh out the silver will be cut off.
¹²"And it shall come to pass at that time
   that I will search Jerusalem with lamps,
and I will punish the men
   who are indifferent*,
those who say in their hearts,
   'The LORD will do neither good nor evil.'
¹³And their wealth shall become a plunder,
   and their houses a desolation.
They shall build houses
   but not live in them;
they shall plant vineyards
   but not drink their wine."

Exegesis and Exposition

Having delivered God's pronouncement of judgment against all mankind and especially His covenant people, Zephaniah turns to exhortations. In view of the certainty and severity of coming judgment, God's prophet has some advice: "Be silent!" "Hush!" It is a call for submission, fear, and consecration.

While Yahweh is Judah's God, He is also the master of her destiny. Judah has perpetuated Israel's sin (2 Kings 17:18-20) in following Baal and other pagan practices. Accordingly the worship of Baal must have seemed a contradiction to Zephaniah. Certainly it would appear to be so to Jeremiah (Jer. 3:14), who finds in Judah's pursuit of Baal a denial of her relation to Yahweh. Thus Jeremiah condemns Judah's syncretism by playing on the word בַּעַל (ba‘al) itself.

As a verb, *bā‘al* means basically to "possess." It can also be translated "rule over" (1 Chron. 4:22) or "marry" (Deut. 24:1; Prov. 30:23; Isa. 62:4). As a noun, *ba‘al* may refer to an owner (Ex. 22:7; Job 31:39), master (Isa. 1:3), ruler (Isa. 16:8), or husband (Deut. 24:4). Theologically the root is used of God as Israel's redeemer and husband (Isa. 54:5). The covenant between God and Israel is described as a marriage in which Israel had become unfaithful (Jer. 31:32).

Building on these ideas, having pictured the covenant between God and Israel under the figure of a marriage relationship that Judah, as a wicked wife, had broken (Jer. 2:1–3:10), Jeremiah pleads with Judah to repent (Jer. 3:12-14) in order to receive God's blessing (Jer. 3:15-18). In so doing, he uses a wordplay (Jer. 3:14): "Turn (שׁוּבוּ, *šûbû*), O backsliding (שׁוֹבָבִים, *šôbābîm*) children, says the Lord; for I am married to you." Did Judah chase after Baal? Her real "Baal"— that is, her divine owner and Lord—is the only true God, her husband. Why should she seek a false master?

Zephaniah probably intends a similar wordplay in juxtaposing the denunciation of Baal with אֲדֹנָי יהוה (*’ădōnāy YHWH*, "sovereign LORD"). Judah had forsaken her rightful master (*’ādôn*) to follow another master (Baal). The folly of such conduct was now apparent. Judah's true master was about to demonstrate the powerlessness of him who was no master at all. The last remnants of Baalism would be cut off. Therefore Judah and Jerusalem should "be silent." Laetsch puts it well:

> Jehovah is the Covenant God. As such He is Lord, the supreme God, who has the right to demand what He will, and the power to enforce His will. Hush! Silence before Him! This is a call to the people of Judah to cease every manner of opposition to God's word and will, to bow down in submissive obedience, in unconditional surrender, in loving service, to their Covenant God.[30]

A further cause for fear lay in the realization that God's people stood "in the presence of" the living God whose all-seeing eye (Jer. 32:19) observes all their evil deeds and rewards them (Job 24:22-24; 34:21-22; Ps. 66:7; Amos 9:8). Judah's idolatry was loathsome in His eyes (Jer. 16:17). They had strayed far from the truth that, because Israel's God was the unseen observer not only on occasions of religious ceremony but also in every activity of life, their lives were to

---

30. Laetsch, *Minor Prophets*, p. 358.

reflect His holy character (cf. Lev. 19:1; 20:7, 22-24).[31] Contrary to their foolish thinking that God either does not see their wickedness or will not intervene, His day of judgment was at hand.

The motive for Zephaniah's call for silence follows (v. 7*b*): the "Day of the Lord." As employed by the prophets, the Day of the Lord is that time when for His glory and in accordance with His purposes God intervenes in human affairs in judgment against sin or for the deliverance of His own.[32] That time could be in the present (Joel 1:15), lie in the near future (Isa. 2:12-22; Jer. 46:10; Ezek. 13:5; Joel 2:1, 11; Amos 5:18-20), be future-eschatological (Isa. 13:6, 9; Ezek. 30:2-3; Mal. 4:1-6 [HB 3:19-24]),[33] or be primarily eschatological (Joel 3:14-15 [HB 4:14-15]; Zech. 14:1-21; cf. 1 Thess. 5:1-11; 2 Thess. 2:2; 2 Pet. 3:10-13). Zephaniah's urgent warning here is in view of imminent judgment.

Although Zephaniah delays his description of the terrors of the Day of the Lord until the next section (1:14-18), the seriousness of that time is underscored in a dramatic metaphor that adds a further motive for Judah's silence: The coming day of judgment is a sacrifice. Although the specific sacrifice is not mentioned, it was probably a type of fellowship offering (Lev. 7:11-21).[34] Instances of such sacri-

---

31. For a discussion of Israel's life viewed as being in the presence of God, see the excellent discussion of G. J. Wenham, *The Book of Leviticus*, NICOT (Grand Rapids: Eerdmans, 1979), pp. 16-18. The challenge to "do that which is right/good in the eyes of the Lord" is an often recurring theme in Deuteronomy (e.g., Deut. 6:18; 12:25, 28; 13:18; 21:9).
32. See further Patterson, "Joel," in *EBC*, 7:256-57; K. Barker, "Zechariah," in *EBC*, 7:619-20.
33. Some prophecies that seem to have a primary orientation in the future blend almost imperceptibly into the eschatological complex. They often telescope disconnected but related future events into one prophetic perspective. For details, see J. B. Payne, *Biblical Prophecy*, pp. 134-40. Prophecies often have an unfolding fulfillment that covers wide expanses of time so that their fulfillments are only progressively realized. The term *progressive fulfillment* may be used for such cases. Thus Kenneth Barker ("Progressive Fulfillment of Prophecy," paper presented at the spring meeting of the Evangelical Theological Society eastern section, April 7, 1989) demonstrates the applicability of the idea of progressive fulfillment to Joel 2:28-32 (Heb. 3:1-5) in its NT and future fulfillments. This paper is part of Barker's chapter, "The Scope and Center of Old and New Testament Theology and Hope," in the forthcoming *Israel and the Church: Essays in Contemporary Dispensational Thought*, ed. C. Blaising and D. Bock (Grand Rapids: Zondervan).
34. For details, see R. de Vaux, *Ancient Israel*, pp. 427-28; R. K. Harrison, *Leviticus*, TOTC (Downers Grove, Ill.: InterVarsity, 1980), pp. 78-80. C. R. Erdman (*The Book of Leviticus* [New York: Revell, 1951], p. 29) observes that the eating of the sacrificial feast by the offerer and his family and friends "seems to have been the supreme significance of this sacrifice." W. Eichrodt ("Prophet and Covenant: Observations on the Exegesis of Isaiah," in *Proclamation and Presence*, ed. John I. Durham and J. R. Porter

ficial feasts to which guests were invited are 1 Sam. 9:22; 2 Sam. 15:11; 1 Kings 1:9-10, 24-25; cf. Deut. 12:18; 33:19. The stipulations for such sacrificial meals are significant for Zeph. 1:7:

> The cultic celebration takes place *liphnê yhvh:* the worshippers sacrifice (*zabhach*, 1 S. 11:15), eat (Dt. 12:7), and rejoice (Dt. 12:12) "before Yahweh," i.e., within the temple precincts and in the presence of the deity. "Eating in the presence of Yahweh" means being Yahweh's guest (semantic parallels: 2 S. 11:13; 1 K. 1:25): God is the *hestiátōr*, "Host." Fellowship with Yahweh presupposes the removal of uncleanness (Lev. 7:20; 2 Ch. 30:17; Jub. 49:9), continence (1 S. 16:5; 21:5f.[4f.]), and if necessary fasting (cf. Jgs. 20:26), moral uprightness (Prov. 15:8; Hos. 8:13), and careful observance of the ritual (Lev. 7:18; 22:31f.). Only so will the sacrifice and the worshipper be acceptable to Yahweh (Ezk. 20:41; 43:27).[35]

As in the case of vv. 2-3, so here one ought not to push the identification of the various parts of the figure too far. The verse announces the conquest of Judah and Jerusalem under the metaphor of the sacrificial banquet. The sacrifice itself is Judah and Jerusalem. But who are the guests? If one sees in the metaphor a second reason for the call for silence, the guests could have been the citizens of Judah and Jerusalem. Thus the call for silence (= submission to the Lord) is issued (1) because of the awesome day of the Lord's judgment and (2) because that day can be survived only by genuine believers in Yahweh. The metaphor of the banquet (v. 7c-d) also strengthens the previous two lines while giving unity to the whole verse. The sacrifice was to be held in the presence of Yahweh (v. 7a), was at hand (v. 7b), was hosted by Yahweh himself (v. 7c), and was to be attended by His guests (v. 7d).

So construed, the metaphor of the sacrificial banquet reinforces the announcement of the Day of the Lord and provides a ray of hope in the clouds of doom. As guests called to a sacrificial feast were to come with their uncleanness removed, so the Judahites are urged to respond to the invitation of Yahweh their host. Although judgment was coming, there was still time. By acknowledging God as their master and by responding in fear to the prospect of judgment in repentance from sin and repudiation of idolatry, God's people could

---

[Macon, Ga.: Mercer U., 1983], pp. 181-82) connects this verse with Isa. 30:33, which he identifies as the covenant sacrifice at the Feast of Tabernacles.

35. B. Lang, "זָבַח," *TDOT* 4:25-26. The imagery of the sacrificial feast is also utilized by other prophets in predicting the fall of nations. Isaiah (34:6) had already depicted the judgment of Edom in similar language, while Jeremiah (46:10) will draw upon Isaiah and Zephaniah in relating the coming day of the Lord's judgments of Egypt through the Chaldeans as the Lord's sacrifice. Ezekiel (39:17-20) will mention the bidding of guests (birds, beasts) to the sacrificial slaughter in the Valley of Hamon Gog.

join a believing remnant in coming to the feast as guests acceptable to Him. There was yet hope.

The figure of the sacrificial banquet, however, also entailed a further word of caution. The alternative of being unfit for attendance carried with it an ironic twist. Guests who remained unrepentant, and hence unclean, would be disqualified and would, like those in Jehu's day (2 Kings 10:18-28), discover that they were not only invited guests* but also victims. God had summoned others (the Chaldeans) who would destroy both Judah and Jerusalem and the unrepentant people who inhabited them (vv. 8-13).

Zephaniah gives a further message with regard to that coming day (v. 8). In connection with its being a time of sacrifice hosted by Yahweh, He will visit Judah and Jerusalem, a visitation designed for chastisement. Thus the disqualified guests will be punished. Indeed, in their self-centeredness and preoccupation with the gods and goods of other nations, Israel's leadership had adopted a foreign lifestyle, including its dress. There may be a veiled threat here. Did they prefer foreign attire? They would soon see the specter of foreign uniforms throughout the land. The threat was literally carried out (2 Kings 23:31-35; 24:10-16; 25:1-21; Jer. 39:1-10; 52:4-30; cf. 2 Chron. 36:2-4, 9-10, 15-21). The verse is a vivid reminder of the responsibilities of leadership (cf. Jer. 22:1–23:39; Luke 12:47-48).

Additional charges follow (v. 9), this time leveled against all the citizens of Judah and Jerusalem. They perpetuated the custom of avoiding contact with the threshold of a temple by leaping over it. The practice had originated among the priests of Dagon during the incident of the collapse of his statue before the Ark of the Lord (1 Sam. 5:1-4). Because of the contact of Dagon's statue with the threshold, "to this day neither the priests of Dagon nor any others who enter Dagon's temple at Ashdod step on the threshold" (1 Sam. 5:5, NIV).[36] Since many superstitious beliefs revolve around thresholds, customs similar to this may have been practiced in connection with pagan worship elsewhere in Canaan, even in Judah and Jerusalem.

An alternative view suggests that the leaping over the threshold has to do with

> a violent and sudden rushing into houses to steal the property of strangers . . . so that the allusion is to 'dishonourable servants of the king, who thought that they best serve their master by extorting treasures from their dependents by violence and fraud' (Ewald).[37]

---

36. The LXX adds, "Instead they leap over it." P. K. McCarter, Jr. (*I Samuel*, AB, p. 122) remarks: "The Philistine custom seems to have survived, at least in Gaza, into the first centuries A.D."
37. Keil, *Minor Prophets*, 2:132. See also the discussion in H. Hailey, *A Commentary on the Minor Prophets* (Grand Rapids: Baker, 1972), p. 231.

This position, however, is forced to view the culprits as the leaders of v. 8 and to take the word "masters" (v. 9) as a plural of majesty to be translated as the singular "master" (i.e., the king). Not only is this understanding a less natural interpretation of the form, but it proposes that the vicious behavior of Judah's leadership is tied to the righteous king Josiah—an unlikely suggestion. Further, it must be demonstrated that a purely religious custom gave rise to a proverbial saying that could be applied to other situations. But the syntax favors the thought that v. 9 is an additional charge to that of v. 8.[38]

The view adopted here thus understands that the citizens of Judah and Jerusalem have been influenced to follow their leaders, adopting pagan customs in their worship.[39] The verse goes on to report that in the socio-economic sphere the desire to please their leaders has caused the citizenry to perpetrate deeds of violence* and deceit against the less fortunate in order to achieve their ambitions.

Further information concerning the day of the Lord's sacrifice is in v. 10. Although lamentation will come from all parts of the city, Jerusalem's greedy merchants will particularly be affected. From the Fish Gate in Jerusalem's northern wall,[40] down through the Tyropoeon Valley and the Second Quarter, areas of commercial activity, will come a great cry. Jerusalem's hills also will reverberate, filled with the horrifying clamor of havoc and destruction:

> The entire city will be filled with the noise of cries, of pitiful howling and shrieking, intermingled with the triumphant shouts of slaying, plundering enemies; while from all the hills on which Jerusalem was built will resound the crash of houses and walls and palaces and the Temple, as they are being ruthlessly smashed.[41]

Therefore Zephaniah tells the merchants to wail (v. 11). Their wealth will be taken away. Though one could hope for the lamenting that

---

38. If the people involved in the details of v. 9 were the same as those in v. 8, a simpler and more certain identification could have been given by writing הַמְמַלְאִים . . . הַדֹּלְגִים עַל הַמִּפְתָּן "who leap over the threshold . . . and fill (etc.)."

39. For support of the view adopted here, see Laetsch, *Minor Prophets*, pp. 360-61. P. C. Craigie (*Twelve Prophets* [Philadelphia: Westminster, 1985], 2:113) adds the caution that "when the path of paganism is pursued by government officials, the people may be expected to follow."

40. See W. Harold Mare, *The Archaeology of the Jerusalem Area* (Grand Rapids: Baker, 1987), p. 126.

41. Laetsch, *Minor Prophets*, p. 361. The merismus consists of mentioning selected parts of Jerusalem to represent the clamor and lamenting that will occur throughout Judah and Jerusalem by all who complain about their lost wealth. Accordingly, Zephaniah in irony tells them to go ahead and wail, for such would be their lot. Verse 10 draws the earlier charges against Judah's leadership to a close and shifts attention to its merchant class.

leads to repentance, such was unlikely. Rather, these people will lament their lost wealth. In irony Zephaniah tells them to go ahead and wail, for such will suit their lot.

The money-loving merchants are also labeled for what they are: Canaanites* and money-grubbers. The metaphor is an apt one, for like their Canaanite precursors they worshiped pagan gods and spent their lives trafficking in commercial pursuits. The merchants of Judah were no better than those of Israel (cf. Ezek. 16:29; Hos. 12:7), and both betrayed their Canaanite ancestry (Ezek. 16:3). Jesus would also warn of the perils of the pursuit of wealth (Matt. 6:24; Luke 16:19-31), and Paul would caution the church's leadership against being lovers of money (1 Tim. 3:3). Lamentably, the temptation to make merchandise of the ministry must be mastered in every generation (cf. 2 Cor. 2:17). Whereas money and wealth can be a useful resource for the advancement of the Lord's work and the rightful enjoyment of life, it must never become an end in itself (1 Tim. 6:10; Heb. 13:16) lest a grasping Canaanite bent become a snare (James 5:1-6).

Zephaniah concludes the subunit that begins in v. 11 with details concerning the coming time of wailing for Jerusalem's merchants and leaders (vv. 12-13). He reports that God's judgment will be thorough. In a brilliant figure that combines anthropopoeia and simile, the Lord is likened to a man who takes a lamp to make a diligent search* (cf. Isa. 45:3; Luke 15:8). In like manner God's instruments of invasion will seek out every corner of Jerusalem in carrying away its treasures. The prophecy of the destruction and looting of the city would come to pass in the days of Josiah's son Zedekiah (2 King 25:13-17; 2 Chron. 36:17-19; Jer. 52:17-23; cf. Josephus *Ant.* 10.9.5).

The main target of God's searching judgment is now revealed. God will punish those whose greed and self-satisfaction had grown into a settled indifference toward God and His standards.[42] The MT says literally that those who were complacent had "thickened upon their lees." Like wine left on its dregs too long and that has thus become sickeningly sweet and then spoiled,[43] so many of Jerusalem's

---

42. Irresponsibility not only has a damaging effect on men and nations but also ultimately takes its toll in divine judgment. G. Adam Smith (*The Book of the Twelve Prophets*, rev. ed. [Garden City, N.Y.: Doubleday, 1929], 2:53) well remarks: "None of us shall escape because we have said, 'I will go with the crowd,' or 'I am a common man and have no right to thrust myself forward.' We shall be followed and judged, each of us for his and her personal attitude to the movements of our time."

43. See further David J. Clark, "Wine on the Lees (Zeph 1.12 and Jer 48.11)," *BT* 32 (1981): 241-43.

citizens had remained in their apostate lifestyle so long that they had become satisfied with it and then grown indifferent to genuine piety. In their callous unconcern for anything but themselves, Judah had become "a nation hardened in iniquity equaling and surpassing the Gentiles in moral impurities, shameless vices, and self-satisfied lip service. It had become unpalatable to God, unfit for its purpose, ready to be poured away."[44]

If not in theory, at least in practice, the people of Judah behaved like full-fledged pagans. They proclaimed that God does neither good nor harm to individuals or society (cf. Isa. 41:23; Jer. 10:5).[45] To their surprise, God will demonstrate His intervention into the affairs of men. No absentee God, He will send an invading force that will search out and plunder Jerusalem. The implementation of the Lord's proclamation will come so quickly that all who have lived in pursuit of ill-gotten gain will not survive to enjoy their wealth. All that for which they have labored so hard and long will fall into the hands of others. In their preoccupation with self and riches they will lose them both (cf. Luke 12:16-21). Thus God's righteous standards will be upheld (Lev. 26:27-33; Deut. 28:30, 39). As they had been applied to Israel (cf. Amos 5:11; Mic. 6:15), so they will be applied to Judah and Jerusalem.

Whereas today's believer may applaud Zephaniah's warning to his fellow countrymen as well taken due to the apostasy, immorality, and injustice of that time, it is perhaps another matter for him to apply them to himself. But such conduct is no less culpable now than it was then. Indeed, a far more insidious danger lurks today. Apathy and inactivity abound, and these will ultimately take their toll. Craigie's warning is timeless and to the point: "Sometimes it is the apathetic and indifferent who are more responsible for a nation's moral collapse than those who are actively engaged in evil, or those who have failed in the responsibilities of leadership."[46]

---

44. Laetsch, *Minor Prophets*, p. 362.
45. J. M. P. Smith (*Zephaniah*, p. 202) observes: "Just as wine left too long in such a condition thickens and loses strength, so these men have sunk into weak self-indulgence, having lost all interest in and concern for the higher things of life and being solicitous only for their own bodily comfort and slothful ease."
46. Craigie, *Twelve Prophets*, 2:114. He concludes: "Zephaniah's words on indifference touch the conscience of multitudes, those who are not guilty of unbelief, but are equally never overwhelmed by belief. . . . The way things are is partly because that is the way we have allowed them to become. We can sit back, smug and somnolent in a desperate world, but we cannot at the same time absolve ourselves from all responsibility, and we shall eventually be caught in the very chaos we permit."

Additional Notes

1:7 †For הַס ("be silent"), see the additional note on Hab. 2:20.

קְרֻאָיו (*"his guests"*): Though the explanation adopted in the Exegesis and Exposition differs from the usual understanding of the guests as solely the Babylonians who are bidden to the sacrificial meal (Judah),[47] it has the advantage of supplying an implied plea for repentance and consecration to God. Moreover, the presence of Chaldeans alone as consecrated guests at a Judahite feast would be strange. Indeed, like Jehu's soldiers they might be there as executioners. The frequent reference (e.g., Keil, Walker) to Isa. 13:3, where the Lord's destroyers of Babylon are called "holy ones," probably has reference not to a sacrificial feast but to a consecration for holy warfare and thus has no bearing here.

1:8 בְּיוֹם זֶבַח יהוה ("on the day of Yahweh's sacrifice"): Since the Lord Himself serves as the divine host, the Tetragrammaton has been rendered by the more personal "Yahweh" rather than translating it as the customary "LORD."

†וּפָקַדְתִּי ("I will punish"): Though often translated "visit," the verb must be contextually nuanced.[48] In many cases it is employed where a superior takes action for or against his subordinates, in hostile contexts connoting "punish" (Jer. 11:22; Hos. 1:4; Amos 3:2, 14).

†שָׂרִים ("nobles"): The word refers to officials at various levels, frequently coming from leading tribal families and forming powerful advisory groups throughout Israel's history (cf. Ex. 18:13-26; 1 Kings 4:2-6; 2 Kings 24:12; 2 Chron. 35:8). The term may designate the chieftains of Israel (Num. 21:18), court officials (1 Chron. 22:17), district supervisors (1 Kings 20:14-15), city officials (Judg. 8:6), military

---

47. See, e.g., the comments by Hannah, "Zephaniah," p. 1526; Keil, *Minor Prophets*, 2:130; Laetsch, *Minor Prophets*, pp. 358-59; L. Walker, "Zephaniah," in *EBC*, 7:546-47. For alternative viewpoints as to the guests intended, see J. M. P. Smith, *Zephaniah*, p. 195. Smith believes that "the only essential feature of the figure is the picture of Judah as a sacrificial victim about to experience the punitive wrath of Yahweh. The remaining features are but accessory circumstances, necessary to the rounding out of the view, but never intended to be taken literally." The view adopted here was suggested earlier by H. Gressmann and has been put forward recently by Victor A. S. Reid, "Zephaniah," in *The International Bible Commentary*, rev. ed., ed. F. F. Bruce (Grand Rapids: Zondervan, 1986), p. 953. The view that the guests are likewise the victims is also held by T. H. Gaster (*Thespis* [New York: Harper, 1966], pp. 232-34) who, however, connects the incident with cultic themes of annual renewal that have been adopted and recast in an eschatological setting.
48. See W. Schottroff, "פקד," *THAT* 2:466-86; J. Scharbert, "Das Verbum PQD in der Theologie des Alten Testaments," *BZ* 4 (1960): 207-27; and the informative dissertation by J. B. van Hooser, "The Meaning of the Hebrew Root פקד in the Old Testament" (Harvard U., 1962).

leaders (1 Kings 2:5; 2 Kings 1:9-14; 5:1; 25:23, 26), or even religious leaders (Ezra 8:24).

The importance of the nobles in Zephaniah's day is underscored not only in their mention before the members of the royal family here but also in their prominence in the enumeration of the levels of Judahite society during the reign of Josiah (Jer. 1:18; 2:26; 4:9). Jeremiah emphasizes their importance and responsibility, using the term more than three dozen times. As for the princes mentioned in the parallel passage, if the date for Zephaniah adopted in the introduction is correct, the reference must be principally to the sons of the deceased King Amon.[49]

1:9 †הַמִּפְתָּן ("the threshold"): Something akin to this traditional meaning is demanded by its use elsewhere (1 Sam. 5:4-5; Ezek. 9:3; 10:4, 18; 46:2; 47:1).[50]

For חָמָס ("violence"), see the additional note on Hab. 1:2-3.

1:10 †הַמִּשְׁנֶה ("the second quarter") has been translated by some (NIV, NJB) in accordance with its being understood as a second or newer district of the city, perhaps as an addition to the upper Tyropoeon Valley. John Gray observes that it

> probably developed as a residential area for palace and Temple personnel after the building of the Temple. At the time of Josiah it would be located west of the palace and Temple over the depression of the upper Tyropoeon Valley.[51]

The translation "second quarter" is also given by the KJV, NKJV, NASB, and RSV (cf. LXX, Vg).

1:11 †Like הַמִּשְׁנֶה, הַמַּכְתֵּשׁ ("the market district") has been variously understood. Among the ancient versions, the LXX tradition

---

49. For the distinction between the officials and the royal sons given here, see André Lemaire, "Note sur le titre BN HMLK dans l'ancien Israel," *Sem* 29 (1979): 62. According to BDB (p. 978), the sons of the king "are never called שׂ" (שָׂרִים). J. M. P. Smith (*Zephaniah*, p. 196) rightly points out that "the reference here cannot be to the sons of Josiah, the eldest of whom was not born until six years after Josiah assumed the crown (2 K. 23³⁶ 22¹) and was not old enough to have wielded any influence until well toward the close of Josiah's long reign."

50. מִפְתָּן is defined by KB-3 as a "podium of an idol." Compounding the problem is that the more common word for threshold is סַף; see R. D. Patterson, "ספף," *TWOT* 2:631-32. The LXX apparently did not know what to do with the whole phrase: "And I will punish publicly before the gates." For additional details on the various views, see H. Donner, "Die Schwellenhüpfer: Beobachtungen zu Zephanja 1, 8f.," *JSS* 15 (1970): 42-55; J. M. P. Smith, *Zephaniah*, pp. 197-98; Sabottka, *Zephanja*, pp. 41-42; M. O'Connor, *Hebrew Verse Structure* (Winona Lake, Ind.: Eisenbrauns, 1980), p. 244.

51. John Gray, *I and II Kings*, 2d ed. (Philadelphia: Westminster, 1970), pp. 726-27. See also the note on Neh. 11:9 in *The NIV Study Bible*.

renders it in three different ways, the Vg translates it "pillars," the Pesh. transliterates it as a proper noun, and the *Tg. Neb.* identifies it as the Brook Kidron. Among modern versions, one may find "mortar" (NASB, RSV, *La Sacra Bibbia*), "hollow" (NJB), "market district" (NIV), "mill" (*Die Heilige Schrift*), or simple transliteration (KJV, Soncino, *La Sainte Bible*).

Due to its derivation from כָּתַשׁ ("pound"), it has been understood as a hollow or a place pounded out and related to a commercial district, probably in "the hollow . . . between the western and eastern hills, or the upper part of the Tyropoeon."[52] Keil suggests that the name may have been coined by Zephaniah "to point to the fate of the merchants and men of money who lived there."[53] The translation adopted here follows the NIV in giving the word a functional rendering rather than attempting a geographical or etymological identification.

כְּנַעַן ("*Canaan*"): BDB (pp. 488-89) points out that this Hebrew noun, like כְּנַעֲנִי ("Canaanite"), may often be translated "merchant," due to the Canaanites' (especially the Phoenicians') established reputation as traders.

1:12 הַקֹּפְאִים עַל־שִׁמְרֵיהֶם† ("the men who are indifferent"): Because קפא denotes "thicken/condense/congeal" and שְׁמָרִים is used of the dregs of wine (cf. Isa. 25:6; Jer. 48:11), the phrase can be translated literally as "settled on their lees" (KJV). Most modern translations, however, have rendered it according to the image it portrays. Thus the NIV reads "those who are complacent," the NASB "who are stagnant in spirit," and the NJB "the men stagnating over the remains of their wine." The translation adopted here views the sin involved as one of indifference that goes beyond the smug self-satisfaction suggested by the word "complacency" to an attitude that has hardened into deliberate disregard for the Lord and His standards.[54]

J. M. P. Smith likens God's diligent *searching* of Jerusalem to that of Diogenes equipped with a lantern in his quest for truth. This is not a search for truth, however. Smith is on target when he goes on to observe that

> the figure expresses the thought of the impossibility of escape from the avenging eye of Yahweh. . . . The figure is probably borrowed from the

---

52. G. A. Smith, *Twelve Prophets*, 2:56; see also Gray, *Kings*, p. 727. Note, however, that Barry Beitzel (*The Moody Atlas of Bible Lands* [Chicago: Moody, 1985], p. 159) locates the *maktesh* in the lower Tyropoeon Valley.
53. Keil, *Minor Prophets*, 2:133.
54. M. Rose ("'Atheismus' als Wohlstandserscheinung? [Zeph 1, 12]," *TZ* 37 [1981]: 193-208) proposes that the affluent class had become so entrenched in its wealth that it assumed God must be supportive of its lifestyle. Thus wealth was a sign of divine favor.

custom of the night-watchman carrying his lamp and may involve also the thought of the diligent search of Jerusalem that will be made by her conquerors in their quest for spoil.[55]

1:13 John T. Willis calls attention to Zephaniah's use of ABA'B' parallelism here in emphasizing that "divine punishment is able to thwart the apparent prevalence of human achievements (cf. Ezek. 27:33; 28:9; Amos 5:11)."[56]

C. TEACHINGS CONCERNING THE DAY OF THE LORD (1:14–2:3)

Zephaniah's exhortations based on the surety of the coming day of judgment are amplified with further information concerning the Day of the Lord (1:14-18). In language bordering on the later apocalyptic genre (see introduction), he tells of the coming of frightful conditions in the natural world and terrible destruction throughout the whole earth. In light of the further revelations concerning that time, Zephaniah issues instructions designed to achieve the safety and deliverance of those who repent and put their trust in the Lord (2:1-3).

1. INFORMATION CONCERNING THAT DAY (1:14-18)

Translation

The great Day of the LORD is near—
near and coming quickly*.
Listen! The Day of the LORD!
Bitter* is the cry of the warrior.
¹⁵A day of wrath is that day—
a day of distress and anguish,
a day of devastation and desolation,
a day of darkness and gloom,
a day of clouds and blackness,
¹⁶a day of trumpet and battle cry
against the fortified cities
and against the corner towers.
¹⁷"And I will bring distress to mankind
so that they will proceed like blind men,
for they have sinned against the LORD.

---

55. J. M. P. Smith, *Zephaniah*, p. 201.
56. John T. Willis, "Alternating (ABA'B') Parallelism in the Old Testament Psalms and Prophetic Literature," in *Directions in Biblical Hebrew Poetry*, JSOTSup 40, ed. Elaine R. Follis (Sheffield: JSOT Press, 1987), p. 74.

**Their blood will be poured out* like dust
and their flesh* like dung."**
**¹⁸Neither their silver nor their gold
will be able to save them
in the day of the LORD's wrath.
In the fire of His jealousy
the whole earth shall be consumed;
yea, He shall make a terrifying end*
of all the inhabitants of the earth.**

Exegesis and Exposition

Once more (cf. 1:7) Zephaniah declares that the Day of the Lord is near. He previously used that fact to provide grounds for submission to the Lord. Now he supplies added details to provide a further reason for the citizens of Judah and Jerusalem to repent and submit to God. The day is near and coming quickly.

In the description that follows Zephaniah describes conditions that will exist primarily in the final stages of the Day of the Lord. But the prophecy must be viewed as one vast event. Some matters that he mentions would soon take place at Jerusalem's fall in 586 B.C.; others would be repeated in various historical epochs (e.g., A.D. 70) until the whole prophecy finds its ultimate fulfillment eschatologically. Such prophecies (cf. Joel 2:28-32 [HB 3:1-5] with Acts 2:17-36) are progressively fulfilled, their individual segments termed fulfillment without consummation.[57] Keeping such distinctions in mind enables one to keep a clear perspective as to both the meaning of the text and the effect the prophecy must have had upon Zephaniah's hearers. However much the events detailed here may have full reference only to the final phase of the Day of the Lord, they were an integral part of the prophecy and could occur anywhere along the series. For the people of Zephaniah's time the Day of the Lord was near—very near*—and the catastrophic conditions were capable of being soon applied with tragic consequences.

In describing that time Zephaniah uses apocalypticlike themes and subject matter that occur elsewhere in prophetic passages and also utilizes a vocabulary frequently associated with them:

---

57. See further R. T. France, *Jesus and the Old Testament* (London: Tyndale, 1971), pp. 160-62; see also nn. 33 and 76 in this chapter. For a brief introduction to the problems of author-centered, text-centered, and reader-centered theories of rhetorical criticism as applied to biblical studies, see Tremper Longman III, *Literary Approaches to Biblical Interpretation* (Grand Rapids: Zondervan, 1987), pp. 19-41.

v. 14 קָרוֹב (*qārôb*, "near"; cf. Isa. 13:6, 22; Ezek. 7:7; 30:7; Joel 1:15; 2:1; 3:14 [HB 4:14]; Obad. 15),

יוֹם גָּדוֹל (*yôm gādôl*, "great day"; cf. Joel 2:11, 31 [HB 3:4]),

מַר (*mar*, "bitter"; cf. Amos 8:10)

v. 15 עֶבְרָה (*'ebrâ*, "wrath"; cf. Isa. 13:9, 13; Ezek. 7:19; 38:19),

צָרָה (*ṣārâ*, "distress"; cf. Isa. 30:6; Jer. 30:7; Dan. 12:1),

שֹׁאָה (*šō'â*, "destruction"; cf. Ezek. 38:9),

חֹשֶׁךְ (*ḥōšek*, "darkness"; cf. Joel 2:2, 31 [HB 3:4]; Amos 5:18, 20),

אֲפֵלָה (*'ăpēlâ*, "gloom"; cf. Joel 2:2),

עָנָן (*'ānān*, "clouds"; cf. Ezek. 30:3, 18; 38:9, 10; Joel 2:2),

עֲרָפֶל (*'ărāpel*, "blackness"; cf. Ezek. 34:12; Joel 2:2)

v. 16 שׁוֹפָר (*šôpār*, "trumpet"; cf. Isa. 27:13; Jer. 4:5, 19, 21; Joel 2:1, 15; Zech. 9:14),

תְּרוּעָה (*těrû'â*, "battle cry/blast"; cf. Jer. 4:19)

v. 18 בְּאֵשׁ קִנְאָתוֹ (*bě'ēš qin'ātô*, "in the fire of his jealousy"; cf. Ezek. 36:5, 6; 38:19),

כָּלָה (*kālâ*, "end/complete"; cf. Jer. 4:27),

יֹשְׁבֵי הָאָרֶץ (*yōšěbê hā'āreṣ*, "the inhabitants of the earth"; cf. Jer. 24:6; 26:9, 18; Joel 2:1; see also Rev. 3:10)

In composing his catalog of conditions that will characterize the Day of the Lord Zephaniah has drawn upon themes and vocabulary employed by Isaiah, Jeremiah, Ezekiel, and Joel, but he is particularly indebted to Joel 2:1-11:

Subject Matter	Zeph. 1:14-18	Joel 2:1-11
The Day of the Lord is near	14	1
It is a great day	14	11
A day of darkness and gloom	15	2
A day of clouds and blackness	15	2
A day of sounding trumpet	16	1
All the inhabitants of the earth	18	1[58]

---

58. The date of Joel is a matter of dispute. The tendency for most lists to be comprehensive and drawn from many sources, combined with the close correspondence in order and point of view, tends to favor the idea of Zephaniah's adapting of material from Joel rather than vice versa. (See R. D. Patterson, "Joel," in *EBC*, 7:231-33. For more details concerning the dating dispute and a different conclusion, see Thomas J. Finley, *Joel, Amos, Obadiah*, WEC, ed. Kenneth Barker [Chicago: Moody, 1990], pp. 2-9.) Conversely the demonstrably later date of Jeremiah and Ezekiel, as well as their utilization of Zephaniah's list in different settings relative to the Day of the Lord, show their dependence upon Zephaniah. C. von Orelli (*The Twelve Minor Prophets*, trans. J. S. Banks [Minneapolis: Klock and Klock, 1977 reprint], p. 267) remarks concerning the relation of this passage and Joel: "The close of the chapter (vv. 14-18) also depicts, with plain allusion to Joel, this day of retribution as one coming on all the children of men." For Zephaniah's apparent dependence on Joel elsewhere, see the note on Zeph. 2:13.

Nevertheless, Zephaniah's list of characteristic features of the Day of the Lord is no mere gathering from others. It is augmented by additions such as מְצוּקָה (*mĕṣûqâ*, "anguish," v. 15) and מְשׁוֹאָה (*mĕšô'â*, "desolation," v. 15) and filled out with new material in the latter half.[59] In sum, although Zephaniah is led by God to reiterate and recombine many thoughts concerning that day of judgment, he is also led to add fresh features. He does so with consummate literary artistry, and the effect is staggering.

What a day the Day of the Lord will be![60] So horrifying will be the conditions (vv. 14-15) that the bravest hero will shriek bitterly.[61] This is understandable, because it is the time of God's great wrath. The term for "wrath" here is suggestive of the overwhelming nature of the divine anger against sin:

> The term *'ebrâ*, when used in relation to God . . . adds the nuance of the fierceness of God's wrath (Ps 78:49) expressed in an overwhelming and complete demonstration (Isa 13:9). God's wrath burns, overflows, sweeps away everything before it (Ezk 22:21, 31). Thus on the day of the Lord's *'ebrâ*, nothing stands before it. When the day of judgment is spoken of, the reference is to God's wrath overflowing, burning, consuming all that has displeased or opposed him.[62]

Because of wrath against sin, the earth will experience great distress and anguish. Other prophets report that so severe will be the testing of the eschatological day that it will be called the time of Jacob's trouble (Jer. 30:7; cf. Dan. 12:1). Zephaniah makes a similar

---

59. Both additions are apparently adapted from Job, the first from 15:2, 24 and the second from 30:3; 38:27.
60. Although cataclysmic events are common in apocalypses, one must not assume that such details are always constituent parts of all apocalyptists' literary artistry, as some suggest. See, e.g., M. S. Terry, *Biblical Apocalyptics* (reprint; Grand Rapids: Baker, 1988), pp. 11-23. In the case of biblical prophecies that contain apocalyptic elements, it seems certain that the prophet was attempting to portray desperate changes that would take place in the physical and socio-political realms so that however much he may have utilized literary figures, one must affirm that something remarkable was going to take place. Indeed, the presence of such matters in biblical prophecy may provide a point of reference for their later application in apocalyptic.
61. Some (e.g., Sabottka, *Zephanja*, pp. 52-54) have suggested that the hero here is God Himself. For warriors in the eschatological Day of the Lord, see Joel 3:9-11 (HB 4:9-11) and Finley's (*Joel, Amos, Obadiah*, WEC, pp. 95-96) comments.
62. G. van Groningen, "עָבַר," *TWOT* 2:643. For the employment of this term with other words for divine wrath and for its prophetic application, see G. Sauer, "עֶבְרָה," *THAT* 2:205-6; for the utilization of the underlying verbal root in divine holy warfare, see G. von Rad, *Der heilige Krieg im alten Israel* (Göttingen: Vandenhoeck und Reprecht, 1965), pp. 68-75.

prediction and adds that the day will bring great anguish to all who experience it. This picture of the terror that will come upon people who have defied God may have been drawn from Job 15:23-25, where terms and themes relative to the day of darkness and the sinner's defiance of God appear together.[63] Particularly instructive are the words "distress" and "anguish" common to both passages. Ironically, Eliphaz's misdirected words against Job perhaps find a better home in criticism of the willful citizens of Zephaniah's day. Their following of paganism (1:4-6) and a self-indulgent lifestyle (1:8-13) were in open defiance of God and His standards so that they might well expect that a time of "distress and anguish" would fill them "with terror." The realization that their sin had occasioned the outpouring of God's wrath would doubtless bring anguish of soul to God's people.

Zephaniah goes on to describe conditions in the land and in nature (v. 15). Destruction will dot the landscape; everything will be a desolate waste. Once again Zephaniah draws upon phraseology employed by Job in describing a wasteland (Job 38:27) in which none can find sustenance (Job 30:3).[64] Adding to the scene of misery are conditions in the natural world. All nature is covered with clouds that form an impenetrable darkness. Although such darkness had not gripped the world of God's covenant people since early days, it will come with heavy hand upon the objects of divine wrath in the great Day of the Lord (cf. Joel 2:2).[65] It is a bleak picture at best: "No star of hope is to be seen; only 'clouds and thick darkness,' the black thunderclouds, from which flash forth the lightning bolts of the Lord's fierce wrath."[66]

From the physical world, Zephaniah turns once again to the socio-political realm (v. 16). That day will be a time of great warfare. Von Rad remarks concerning this aspect of the Day of the Lord that "the prophets expect the day of Yahweh to bring war in its train. Now the widespread employment of this concept in the prophets suggests that we are dealing with a well-established component part of es-

---

63. See further É. Dhorme, *A Commentary on the Book of Job*, trans. Harold Knight (Nashville: Thomas Nelson, 1984), pp. 218-19.
64. The paronomasia is obvious here, the second term for devastation reinforcing the first so as to depict total desolation (cf. Isa. 6:11). For the Hebrew phrase שֹׁאָה וּמְשׁוֹאָה used here and in Job, see John E. Hartley, *The Book of Job*, NICOT (Grand Rapids: Eerdmans, 1988), p. 396 n. 3.
65. All four pairs occur in the same order in Joel 2:2 (see, e.g., Finley, *Joel, Amos, Obadiah*, WEC, pp. 43-44). The first, third, and fourth were used in the scene depicting the children of Israel's encampment at Mount Sinai (Deut. 4:11), the second in the portrayal of the ninth plague against Egypt (Ex. 10:21-22).
66. Laetsch, *Minor Prophets*, p. 364.

chatological tradition."[67] Out of the distance comes the sound of the trumpet and the shout of battle cry (cf. Josh. 6:5; Jer. 4:5). Then follows the charge of the enemy army pushing into the towns of Judah (cf. Deut. 28:49-52). Not even the most stoutly fortified city will be able to withstand the advance of these agents of the Lord's judgment.[68]

Zephaniah concludes by observing the tragic cost in human life and experience that all this will effect (vv. 17-18). In accordance with His judicial purposes God will bring distress not only to Judah but also to all mankind.[69] There is a play here on words and ideas in v. 15. Because it is a day of distress and anguish, God will cause distress to man. So intense will be the conditions that people will grope like blind men. How appropriate the punishment! Because they are blind ethically and spiritually (cf. Ex. 23:8; Matt. 15:14; Rom. 2:19; 11:25; Eph. 4:18; 1 John 2:11) and have sinned against God and His commandments, God's people will incur the just penalties of the covenant (Deut. 28:28-29).[70] As Keil remarks, "This distress God sends, because they have sinned against Him, by falling away from Him through idolatry and the transgression of His commandments, as already shown in vers. 4-12. But the punishment will be terrible."[71]

The effect of these tragic conditions is further heightened in similes that liken the carnage of that day to blood poured out like worthless dust (cf. 1 Kings 20:10; 2 Kings 13:7; 23:12) and flesh treated like dung (cf. 1 Kings 14:10; 2 Kings 9:37; Jer. 8:1-3; Lam. 4:5). Human life (flesh and blood) is thus reduced to a thing of no value, with even corpses being treated as despicable refuse (cf. Jer. 9:20-22; 16:1-4; 25:32-33). The warfare* connected with the Day of the Lord will thus be both extensive and bloody.

The chapter closes (v. 18) with a reiteration of two prominent themes: (1) the self-indulgent greed of the godless wealthy and (2) the

---

67. G. von Rad, *The Message of the Prophets*, trans. D. M. G. Stalker (New York: Harper & Row, 1967), p. 98.
68. The synecdoche of citing towns and towers for the devastation of all cities and lands is an effective one. If the strongest defenses will collapse, everything will be laid waste.
69. Although some have doubted the authenticity of such universalistic pronouncements by Zephaniah, the passage is properly defended by A. S. Kapelrud, *Prophet Zephaniah*, p. 31. Von Rad (*Message of the Prophets*, p. 99) observes that "the war was now to affect all nations, even the fixed orders of creation, and even Israel herself. The event has been expanded into a phenomenon of cosmic significance."
70. For other examples of divine judicial blinding, see Gen. 19:11; 2 Kings 6:18. O. P. Robertson (*The Books of Nahum, Habakkuk, and Zephaniah*, NICOT [Grand Rapids: Eerdmans, 1990], pp. 254-56) rightly points out Zephaniah's abundant use of phraseology drawn from Deuteronomy.
71. Keil, *Minor Prophets*, 2:136.

certain judgment of all men and nations. As for the former, the wealthy have heaped up their riches at the expense of their fellow citizens in pursuit of material gain. However, it will all soon come to an end; no amount of silver or gold will be able to buy off their despoilers. Their attempt to achieve deliverance will fail (cf. 2 Kings 15:16-20; 16:17-19; 18:13-16). With regard to the latter theme, the judgment that always hangs over mankind will one day descend with sudden swiftness, and the world and all who dwell in it will experience the wrath of God. Time is running out. "The world, which had begun with such promise in creation, had gone too far; God would make an end of it all. Such was Zephaniah's vision of the *dies irae*."[72]

Though the full weight of Zephaniah's prophecy bears ultimately on the *eschaton*, because the punishment of Judah and Jerusalem was an integral part of the process, God's people might expect judgment at any time. If a godless world and its inhabitants will ultimately perish, could God's faithless nation expect any less? Hardly. No one and nothing will be able to save them on the day of the Lord's wrath. "The destruction had been determined by Jehovah and there would be no escaping the judgment against their sins."[73]

Additional Notes

1:14 † קָרוֹב וּמַהֵר מְאֹד ("near and coming very quickly"): The traditional understanding of the MT of the approach of the Day of the Lord, perhaps personified as a swift messenger or fierce soldier rushing into battle, is improved upon little by recent attempts to relate the phrase to an Egypto-Semitic term for soldier.[74] The repetition of the idea of nearness is not redundant; rather, the intentional emphasis underscores both the fact and the impending arrival of the Day of the Lord.[75]

The hermeneutical problem of multiple versus single fulfillment and the related identification of prophecies that are deemed to be

---

72. Craigie, *Twelve Prophets,* 2:116.
73. Hailey, *Minor Prophets,* p. 233.
74. For good discussions, see Sabottka, *Zephanja,* pp. 50-52; R. Smith, *Micah–Malachi,* WBC (Waco, Tex.: Word, 1984), p. 129. For details as to the term itself, see B. Couroyer, "Trois épithètes de Ramsès II," *Or* 33 (1964): 443-53; A. F. Rainey, "The Soldier Scribe in Papyrus Anastasi I," *JNES* 26 (1967): 58-60; A. R. Schulman, "Mhr and Mskb. Two Egyptian Military Titles of Semitic Origin," *Zeitschrift für die Aegyptische Sprache und Altertumskunde* 93 (1966): 123-32; Gordon, *UT,* p. 431. Sabottka calls attention to the Phoenician/Punic personal names *mhrb'l* and *b'lmhr,* which he understands as "(soldier) hero of Baal" and "Baal is the hero" respectively.
75. See W. G. E. Watson, *Classical Hebrew Poetry,* JSOTSup 26 (Sheffield: JSOT Press, 1986), pp. 278-79.

telescoped, generic, or progressively fulfilled is complex.[76] From a NT perspective the Greek verb πληρόω may at times refer to a literal, real, and necessary relationship between an OT context and the NT so that the NT text *fulfills* completely the OT meaning. More commonly, however, the NT writer cites an OT passage to establish an analogy or comparison between the OT and NT contexts, thus *filling* out more *fully* the OT context.

קוֹל† ("listen!") is taken here as an interjection (cf. Soncino). Keil calls attention to a similar employment of קוֹל in Isa. 13:4, likewise a "Day of the Lord" passage.[77]

מַר . . . גִּבּוֹר† ("bitter . . . warrior"): מַר has been taken by some with the previous clause, "the Day of the Lord is bitter" (LXX, Vg, NIV, NJB, NKJV, RSV), and by others with the last clause of the verse (KJV, NASB).[78] In the latter case it is usually taken as an adverb "bitterly" (so Soncino)[79] but can also be viewed in its normal adjectival function (lit. "bitter is he who cries, the hero"). The translation suggested here follows the MT accent in taking מַר with the last clause but points the next word as a substantive צֶרַח ("shriek/cry/battle cry").[80] In addition I view the following שָׁם not as the adverbial particle "there" but as the relative particle שֶׁ and assign the final *mem* to the following גִּבּוֹר as the prefixed preposition, thus yielding "from/of the warrior."[81]

---

76. Among important contributions in the vast literature on the subject may be cited Payne, *Biblical Prophecy*, pp. 121-40; M. S. Terry, *Biblical Hermeneutics*, 2d ed. (reprint, Grand Rapids: Zondervan, n.d.), pp. 493-99; Patrick Fairbairn, *Hermeneutical Manual* (Edinburgh: T. and T. Clark, 1858), pp. 129-36; *Prophecy* (reprint; Grand Rapids: Baker, 1976), pp. 177-96; *The Typology of Scripture* (reprint; Grand Rapids: Zondervan, n.d.), 1:368-95; C. von Orelli, *The Old Testament Prophecy of the Consummation of God's Kingdom*, trans. J. S. Banks (Edinburgh: T. and T. Clark, 1889), pp. 31-62; W. C. Kaiser, Jr., *The Uses of the Old Testament in the New* (Chicago: Moody, 1985), pp. 61-76.

77. Keil, *Minor Prophets*, 2:135. Such a use of this word is common in the OT; see KB-3, p. 1015; S. Amsler, "קֹל," *THAT* 2:631.

78. See further the *Hebrew Old Testament Text Project*, 5:350. The NEB follows an emended text and translates "No runner fast as (that day), or raiding band so swift" (cf. *BHS*). מַר is clearly read by the MT, however, and is supported by the ancient versions and the use of the word in other Day of the Lord passages (e.g., Amos 8:10).

79. See Hulst, *Translation Problems*, p. 253.

80. The existence of this noun has been postulated as well for Jer. 4:31 and Ezek. 21:27; see at KB-3, p. 987. Similarly the NJB translates צֶרַח here as "cry of war."

81. For a parallel case where שֶׁ occurs before a preposition, see Judg. 7:12. This relative particle, which was common in Akkadian, Amorite, and Phoenician, is attested in older (particularly northern) Hebrew. Although it was not often employed in standard classical Hebrew, it reappeared in later Hebrew (possibly through the influence of Phoenician), where it

A proposal by C. F. Whitley is also attractive.[82] Noting the unsuitability of the normal use of שָׁם here, he suggests treating it as an emphatic particle ("yea/indeed"), while taking מַר with the previous clause (but relating it to Ugaritic *mrr*, "be strong"). He paraphrases the whole: "The sound of the day of Yahweh is overwhelming, even the strong man cries aloud with fear." Although Whitley and I have handled matters differently, the resultant perspective is the same.

1:17-18 Von Rad suggests that the concept of the *warfare* of the eschatological Day of the Lord is an outgrowth of earlier Yahwistic traditions related to holy warfare, now extended to a universalistic perspective:

> The concepts connected with the Day of Yahweh are, therefore, in no way eschatological *per se*, but were familiar to the prophets in all their details from the old Yahwistic tradition. The prophets . . . believed that Yahweh's final uprising against his foes would take the same form as it had done in the days of old. It is beyond question that the prophetic vision of the concept of Yahweh's intervention in war became greatly intensified; for the war was now to affect all nations, even the fixed orders of creation, and even Israel herself. The event has been expanded into a phenomenon of cosmic significance.[83]

1:17 †שֻׁפַּךְ ("poured out"): Although Sabottka insists that the lack of examples of this verb in the piel necessitates viewing the form here as a qal passive, the presence of a hithpael elsewhere (Job 30:16; Lam. 2:12; 4:1), attesting the use of the D-stem in classical Hebrew, makes his pronouncement tenuous.[84]

†לְחֻמָם ("their flesh"): I take the form not as "their intestines" (Soncino; cf. NIV "entrails") but according to the Arabic *laḥm* ("meat/flesh"; cf. Job 20:23).[85]

1:18 †כָּלָה ("end") is commonly employed of divinely initiated

---

has remained with some modification until modern times. See E. Y. Kutscher, *A History of the Hebrew Language,* ed. Raphael Kutscher (Leiden: Brill, 1982), p. 32; S. Moscati, *An Introduction to the Comparative Grammar of the Semitic Languages* (Wiesbaden: Otto Harrassowitz, 1964), pp. 113-14; Z. S. Harris, *Development of the Canaanite Dialects* (New Haven, Conn.: American Oriental Society, 1939), pp. 69-70.

82. C. F. Whitley, "Has the Particle שָׁם an Asseverative Force?" *Bib* 55 (1974): 394-98. Whitley points out other possible instances of such a use of שָׁם in Isa. 48:16; Hos. 6:10; Eccles. 3:17.

83. Von Rad, *Message of the Prophets,* p. 99; see also *Old Testament Theology,* trans. D. M. G. Stalker (New York: Harper & Row, 1965), 2:122-25.

84. See Sabottka, *Zephanja,* p. 55; see also R. J. Williams, "The Passive *Qal* Theme in Hebrew," in *Essays on the Ancient Semitic World,* ed. J. W. Wevers and D. B. Redford (Toronto: University Press, 1970), p. 47.

85. See also Keil, *Minor Prophets,* 2:136. The MT form may be related to the Arabic plural *luḥûm.* The LXX and the Pesh. also read "their flesh" (cf. NASB), while the Vg suggests "their bodies" (cf. NJB "their corpses").

destruction (cf. Neh. 9:31; Jer. 4:27). It is construed here as in Nah. 1:8 (q.v.) as part of a double accusative. The syntax of this verse is like that of Isa. 10:23, in each case the object noun being modified by affixing a niphal participle:

Isaiah 10:23	Zephaniah 1:18
כִּי כָלָה וְנֶחֱרָצָה	כִּי־כָלָה אַךְ־נִבְהָלָה
"for a complete end,	"for a complete end,
and that decreed"	yea a terrifying one"
(= "a determined end")	(= "a terrifying end")

For the blending of the ideas of wrath, jealousy, and fire, see Ezek. 38:19 and the Exegesis and Exposition and Additional Notes on Nah. 1:2, 6.

2. INSTRUCTIONS IN THE LIGHT OF THAT DAY (2:1-3)

Translation

Gather together and assemble yourselves,
   O wayward* nation,
²before the decree takes effect*
   or the day passes like chaff,
before there comes upon you
   the burning anger of the LORD,
before there comes upon you
   the day of the LORD's anger.
³Seek the LORD, all you humble of the earth,
   who do His commandments;
seek righteousness, seek humility;
perhaps you will be delivered*
   in the day of the LORD's anger.

Exegesis and Exposition

In light of the horrifying spectacle of the judgment of the Day of the Lord, Zephaniah presses his fellow countrymen to gather together in repentance and humility before God. Utilizing images drawn from the process of separating straw from chaff, Zephaniah gives them a spiritual setting. He uses straw and its collection (v. 1a) to symbolize the assembling of people for the purpose of collectively repenting and thus escaping the coming destruction (i.e., to be straw, not chaff). He employs the concept of threshing (v. 1b) to point to the necessity of being broken before God rather than going on in self-indulgent waywardness. He uses the idea of chaff in connection with the speed and ease with which it is blown away: like chaff, the day of judgment was rapidly approaching (v. 2b); like chaff, wayward sinners would be destroyed in the Day of the Lord.

The word for "assemble" is related to the word for straw and its gathering. Zephaniah's hearers are told to be straw gatherers—those who are "whole grain," being of humble heart before God. Up to now they have been a wayward people (cf. 1:7-13, 18). They were not threshed;* their hearts were unbroken and had no longing for God. Thus they could not survive the coming judgment, but like chaff they would soon be swept away in the winds of God's winnowing judgment. The threat of exile was before them.[86]

Gathering together meant coming together in genuine repentance and submission to the will of God. Zephaniah's advice is akin to that of Joel 2:1-11, noted in the previous section dealing with the Day of the Lord. Joel also follows his description with a call for national repentance (Joel 2:12-14) in the fond hope (as here) that destruction may be averted.[87]

Zephaniah's plea is urgent, for God's decree was settled and would soon be put into effect. Moreover, as Zephaniah had already indicated (1:7-18), its implementation would bring with it the "burning anger of the Lord"*. Yet even here Zephaniah retains the hope that complete destruction (1:18) could be avoided. The construction "before there comes upon you the burning anger of the Lord" is unique: לֹא (*lōʾ*, "not") is inserted before the verb and after the temporal particle בְּטֶרֶם (*běṭerem*, "not yet"). Though the double negative construction is best rendered in English "before," the intended effect may have been to add a note of hope to the certainty of the coming judgment. Although the judgment is even now descending, a proper response on the people's part could perhaps ameliorate or even avert the threatened disaster—and that while the burning anger of the Lord "not yet had not come" upon them (i.e., before it could arrive).[88]

---

86. J. M. P. Smith (*Zephaniah*, p. 213) correctly points out that "everywhere that reference is made to chaff, except possibly in Is. 41¹⁵, it is as a simile of scattering (e.g., Is. 17¹³ Hos. 13³ Jb. 21¹⁸ Ps. I⁴)." If Zephaniah's point is the same, the primary force of the judgment is on the coming exile and dispersion of God's people (cf. Deut. 28:64-68).

87. Cf. Finley's comments in *Joel, Amos, Obadiah*, WEC, pp. 51-55. The note of hope suggested in the Exegesis and Exposition of Zeph. 2:1-3 stands in contrast to many who see in the context primarily doom with little hope of deliverance. Thus G. A. Smith (*Twelve Prophets*, p. 58) remarks: "Upon this vision of absolute doom there follows a qualification for the meek and righteous. They may be hidden on the day of the Lord's anger; but even for them escape is only a possibility. Note the absence of mention of the Divine mercy. Zephaniah has no gospel of that kind."

88. Although לֹא could be viewed as written for the asseverative particle לוֹ ("indeed"; see GKC par. 23i), it is best taken as the usual negative. Laetsch (*Minor Prophets*, p. 365) explains: "To the second and third בְּטֶרֶם, לֹא is added; an example of mingling of two constructions. A, before it bring forth; B, that it may not bring forth; C, before it may not bring forth."

Building on this glimmer of hope, Zephaniah urges his hearers to seek the Lord.[89] He calls primarily upon those most likely to respond—the poor, those victimized by the wealthy leaders and merchants of Judah and Jerusalem. In addition, they have kept God's commandments. Doubtless, however, Zephaniah intends all who will respond with poverty of soul in humility and submission to God.[90] He urges them to react to his pleas with the two qualities necessary for spiritual productivity: righteousness and humility*. By the first is meant those spiritual and ethical standards that reflect the nature and will of God, by the second submission to and dependence on God.[91]

To all such, then, Zephaniah holds out a ray of hope:

> The word אוּלַי "perhaps" speaks volumes. The prophet would not presume on the prerogative of Yahweh to determine who would or would not be hidden. Zephaniah, like Amos (cf. 5:15), knew that not even righteousness nor humility could guarantee a person's safety. That was all in the hand of Yahweh.[92]

Whereas Zephaniah would not presume on the divine prerogative, he brings the thought of deliverance into a lively hope. Probably this reflected his confidence that He who helps the needy will hear the prayer of the repentant and submissive (Ps. 10:12-17). "Perhaps" God will graciously deliver them as His wrath descends in judgment.

Additional Notes

2:1 הִתְקוֹשְׁשׁוּ וָקוֹשּׁוּ ("gather together and assemble yourselves"): The translation suggested here is *ad sensum*. Some attempt to read the MT as is; others seek to emend it. Thus J. M. P. Smith observes: "Various renderings have been proposed. . . . But none of these finds adequate support either in the Hebrew usage of this root, or in the related dialects, or in the Vrss. Several scholars abandon as hopeless the attempt to interpret."[93]

Because the ancient versions uniformly support the MT, it seems advisable to deal with the text as it stands. Zephaniah has utilized

---

89. For בָּקֵשׁ ("seek"), see the additional note on Nah. 3:7.
90. For "poor" as a theological term for those dependent on God, see Carroll Stuhlmueller, "Justice toward the Poor," *The Bible Today* 24 (1986): 385-90. Stuhlmueller notes its primary socio-economic reference here but sees a shift in perspective in Zeph. 3:12.
91. For righteousness, see the Excursus on Habakkuk 2:4; for humility, see R. Martin Achard, "ענה," *THAT* 2:346-50; Leonard J. Coppes, "עָנָה," *TWOT* 2:682-84.
92. R. Smith, *Micah–Malachi*, p. 132.
93. In an extensive note J. M. P. Smith (*Zephaniah*, pp. 221-222) provides a detailed discussion of these proposals and concludes that "none of these is more than a barren conjecture, providing no suitable meaning."

these denominative verbs to produce a play on ideas, their apparent derivation from קַשׁ ("straw/stubble") accounting for their selection. They anticipate the reference to chaff blown away in line two of v. 2 (as well as the figure of threshing) and provide an image that can be adapted to the socio-political and religious needs of the community. The metaphor is of judgment likened to winnowing. As one gathers the straw left from the threshing sledge and separates the grain from the chaff in the winnowing process, so the people of God will be divided into believers (straw) and unbelievers (chaff) in the coming winds of divine judgment. It was a time of spiritual harvest, and Zephaniah's countrymen needed to assemble and "gather straw."[94] In genuine repentance they needed to entreat God to save them.

†לֹא נִכְסָף† ("wayward"): Two etymologies have been suggested: (1) Akkadian *kasāpu* ("break off") and (2) Arabic *kasafa* ("cut out," thence in derived stems "disappoint," "put to shame"; cf. the Aramaic כְּסַף, "lose color," "be ashamed"). The second etymology has usually been assumed to lie behind the occurrences in Gen. 31:30; Job 14:15; Pss. 17:12; 84:2 (HB 84:3), where, however, the meaning uniformly is "long for/desire."[95]

Whether two or more different roots lie behind the verb or whether one root has taken on dialectal and contextual variation, its normal OT significance is difficult to apply here (although the Vg translates it "not lovable"). The proposed translation ("*threshed*") relies on the Akkadian cognate and relates the phrase to the agricultural symbolism of the context. As grain must be broken off (threshed) into small pieces in preparation for winnowing, so a man must be broken spiritually (cf. Pss. 34:18) [HB 34:19]; 51:18 [HB 51:19]; 147:3)[96] in submission to God if he is to be delivered. The people of Zephaniah's day, however, were "not broken." Rather, as the LXX and Pesh. suggest, they were "undisciplined/uninstructed." They displayed a willful disregard for God and his standards and sought their own path. Because a wayward person has no longing for the things of God, "wayward" seems to fit the needs of etymology and context.[97] It is also not incompatible with the use of the root elsewhere in the OT.

If the agricultural orientation is the proper one for these verses,

---

94. Laetsch (*Minor Prophets*, p. 365) calls attention to such English denominative verbs as "to berry" or "to nut."
95. See KB-3, pp. 467-68.
96. The Hebrew root in all three cases is שָׁבַר ("break [in pieces]").
97. The NASB marginal reading is "without longing." An interesting twist for understanding the negative here is supplied by Sabottka (*Zephanja*, pp. 62-63) who considers it a title for Baal and translates "O people that long for the Nothing."

Zephaniah has furnished an excellent example of a case where the figure itself carries the meaning for the context.[98] Zephaniah means that "get straw for yourself, get straw, O unbroken nation, before the decree is born or the day sweeps by like chaff (before the wind)" is to be understood as "gather yourselves in an assembly of repentance, O wayward nation, before the decree concerning the Day of the Lord takes effect, before that speedily approaching day overtakes you and like chaff you are carried away before the winds of God's judgment."

2:2 חֹק לֶדֶת בְּטֶרֶם† ("before the birth of the decree," i.e., "before the decree takes effect"): For suggested emendations, see the *Preliminary and Interim Report on the Hebrew Old Testament Text Project* (New York: United Bible Societies, 1980), 5:374-75. The metaphor here likens the time for the inception of divine judgment to that of pregnancy. Thus M. O'Connor translates "Before the womb comes to term" and explains: "The line refers to a natural term for the prophet's threat."[99]

For the phrase *"the burning anger of the Lord,"* found some thirty-three times in the OT, see the additional note on Nah. 1:6. J. T. Willis notes Zephaniah's use of ABA'B' parallelism in the closing lines of the verse to emphasize the imminence of divine punishment that urgently called for repentance.

2:3 עֲנָוָה (*"humility"*) occurs elsewhere only in 2 Sam. 22:36 where it is used of God's condescension on behalf of His people and in Prov. 15:33; 18:12; 22:4, which emphasize the importance of the fear of the Lord and lowliness of spirit as preconditions to greatness. Its derivation from עָנָה ("be afflicted/bowed down") and association with other words derived from this root reveal that inward affliction of soul and outward circumstances of affliction play a vital part in developing true humility (cf. Deut. 8:2-3; Ps. 34:6 [HB 34:7]; Prov. 16:19).[100]

תִּסָּתְרוּ† ("you will be delivered"): I take the verb as an infixed-*t*

---

98. For the statement that metaphor, as an example of a trope, constitutes meaning, see Paul Ricoeur, "The Metaphorical Process as Cognition, Imagination, and Feeling," in *On Metaphor*, ed. Sheldon Sacks (Chicago: U. of Chicago, 1979), pp. 141-57. Ricoeur's thesis is that metaphor creates meaning rather than embellishing it.
99. O'Connor, *Hebrew Verse Structure*, p. 248.
100. W. Bauder ("πραΰς," *The New International Dictionary of New Testament Theology*, ed. Colin Brown [Grand Rapids: Zondervan, 1976], 2:257) points out that *'ānî* and particularly *'ānāw* change their meaning from those who are materially poor to what becomes the self-chosen religious title of those who in deep need and difficulty humbly seek help from Yahweh alone, or have found it there. See also F. Hauck and S. Schulz, "πραΰς, πραΰτης," *TDNT* 6:645-49, who emphasize that the humble man is "one who feels that he is a servant in relation to God and who subjects himself to Him quietly and without resistance." See further the additional note on Zeph. 3:12.

form from סוּר ("turn aside") in the sense of "turn oneself aside," hence "escape," "be delivered." Many examples of infixed-*t* forms have been suggested elsewhere (e.g., Prov. 22:3; 27:12).[101] The traditional association of the word with סָתַר ("hide") is reflected in the English versions: "be sheltered" (NIV), "find shelter" (NJB), "be hidden" (NASB).

---

101. See M. Baldacci, "Alcuni nuovi esempi di taw infisso nell'ebraico biblico," *Biblia e Oriente* 24 (1982): 107-14; M. Dahood, *Psalms*, AB (Garden City, N.Y.: Doubleday, 1970), 3:388-89. For סוּר, see R. D. Patterson, "סוּר," *TWOT* 2:620-21.

2

Additional Details Concerning the Day of the Lord, Part One (Zephaniah 2:4–3:7)

The second portion of Zephaniah's prophecies (2:4–3:20) likewise is made up of pronouncements (2:4–3:7), an exhortation (3:8), and teachings (3:9-20). After his preoccupation primarily with the fate of his people in the first part of the book, Zephaniah turns his attention to the foreign nations (2:4-15). He had begun the first major portion of his prophecy by similarly considering all nations (1:2-3). Here he deals with specific nations that were mostly tied to Judah's situation geographically and politically as representatives of God's relations with the world. When he has completed his oracles against these nations, as in the first portion (1:4-6), he turns to a consideration of Judah and Jerusalem (3:1-7).

The messages against the nations are made up of the usual elements contained in such prophetic material: invective (2:5a; 3:1), threat (2:4, 5b-7, 9, 12), pronouncement (2:11, 13), taunt (2:15b), and reasons for the threatened punishment (2:8, 10, 15a; 3:2-4, 5-7).[1] This portion also contains such literary features as metaphor and simile (2:4-7, 9; 3:3), irony (2:12), synecdoche (2:13; 3:6), thematic repetition (3:1), and the use of paronomasia (2:4, 7, 12[?]), hendiadys (3:7), enallage (3:7), and literary allusions (2:4, 9).

---

1. R. Smith (*Micah–Malachi*, WBC [Waco, Tex.: Word, 1984], p. 135) follows C. Westermann in suggesting that the oracles concerning the foreign nations are a disguised salvation speech in that they imply salvation for Israel in contrast to or as a result of the judgment of the other peoples.

A. FURTHER PRONOUNCEMENTS OF JUDGMENT (2:4–3:7)

1. ON THE NATIONS (2:4-15)

Zephaniah begins his pronouncements against the nations by turning to the people on Judah's west, the Philistines (vv. 4-7), then going to those on the east, Moab and Ammon (vv. 8-11), and finally considering those on the south and north, singling out Cush (v. 12) and Assyria (vv. 13-15).

Zephaniah's prophecy against the nations is four dimensional, a convention that is, as Ronald Youngblood points out (in private communication), "in the same grand tradition of oracles against foreign nations as are Amos 1-2, Isaiah 13-23, Jeremiah 46-51, and Ezekiel 25-32." Certainly Youngblood's point is well taken. Not only is divine judgment often presented in a fourfold manner (see the additional note at 2:4), but the objects of Zephaniah's condemnation are commonly met in the other texts: Philistia (Isa. 14:28-32; Jer. 47; Ezek. 25:15-17; Amos 1:6-8), Transjordan (Moab, Ammon, Edom—Isa. 15-16; Jer. 48:1–49:22; Ezek. 25:1-14; 35; Amos 1:11–2:3), Cush and/or Egypt (Isa. 18-20; Jer. 46; Ezek. 29-32), and Assyria and/or Babylonia (Isa. 13:1–14:27; 21:1-10; Jer. 50-51).

Interesting, too, is the fact that some of the prophets, as does Zephaniah, utilize a four-directional arrangement for their prophecies. Jeremiah's geographic arrangement falls into two main sections: (1) The nations adjacent to Israel (south: Egypt, chap. 46; west: Philistia, chap. 47; east: Transjordan, 48:1–49:22; north: Damascus/Aram, 49:23-27) and (2) the nations around Babylon (southwest: Kedar and Hazor, 49:28-33; east: Elam, 49:34-39; and Babylon itself, chaps. 50-51). Ezekiel inverts Zephaniah's geographic order, considering Israel's neighbors in crisscross fashion moving from east (Transjordan, 25:1-14), west (Philistia, 25:15-17), and north (Phoenicia, chaps. 26-28) to south (Egypt, chaps. 29-32). Though other principles are at work in the case of Isaiah and Amos, Amos's prophecies do move in a geographic fashion, crisscrossing the twin kingdoms diagonally from north/northeast (Aram, 1:3-5) to southwest (Philistia, 1:6-8), and northwest (Phoenicia, 1:9-10) to east/southeast (Transjordan, 1:11–2:3) before turning to Judah and Israel themselves.[2] Daniel's use of the number four to depict the fate of the coming kingdoms of the world (2, 7) also is instructive and reflects a known literary schema that is widely attested in the an-

---

2. For a detailed discussion of Amos's prophetic arrangement, see Thomas J. Finley, *Joel, Amos, Obadiah*, WEC, ed. Kenneth Barker (Chicago: Moody, 1990), pp. 133-36.

cient Mediterranean cultures since the early part of the first millennium B.C.

a. Philistia (2:4-7)

Translation

For Gaza will be forsaken/abandoned,
   and Ashkelon will become a desolation;
Ashdod, they will drive her out at midday,
   and Ekron will be uprooted.
5Woe, you who inhabit the seacoast,
   the nations of the Kerethites;
the word of the LORD is against you,
   Canaan, land of the Philistines:
   "I will destroy you to the last inhabitant."
6And the seacoast will be a pasture land,
   shepherds' caves and sheepfolds.
7And the coastlands will belong
   to the remnant of the house of Judah;
they will find pasture on them;
   among the houses of Ashkelon
   they will lie down in the evening.
For the LORD their God will care for them
   and restore their fortunes.

Exegesis and Exposition

Zephaniah begins his messages concerning the foreign nations with words for Judah's perennial enemy to the west—the Philistines. Philistine presence in Canaan had been reported since the days of the patriarchs (Gen. 21:32) and the era of the Exodus and Conquest (Ex. 13:17; Josh. 13:2-3). The Philistines were a constant threat during the time of the judges (Judg. 3:3-4; 13-16) and the early monarchy (cf. 1 Sam. 4:1-11; 7:1-14). Although they were defeated by David in the tenth century B.C. (2 Sam. 5:17-25; 1 Chron. 20:4-5), they remained a constant thorn in the side of the Israelites throughout the days of Solomon and the period of the divided monarchy (cf. 1 Kings 15:27-28; 16:15-19; 2 Chron. 21:16-17; Isa. 14:28-32; 28:16-21; Amos 1:6-8). Though they had become vassals of Assyria in the eighth century B.C., they nonetheless enjoyed a measure of independence so that they continued to be a source of danger and irritation to the people of God (cf. 2 Kings 18:5-8; 2 Chron. 26:6-8). Even as late as the closing days of the Southern Kingdom, the Philistines were being condemned

337

by Judah's prophets (Jer. 47:1-7; Ezek. 25:15-17).[3] Accordingly Zephaniah's words of condemnation and judgment were neither unprecedented nor unexpected and doubtless would have been well received by the citizens of Judah and Jerusalem.

Adopting the literary style of Micah before him (Mic. 1:10-15), Zephaniah uses wordplay to begin his prophetic threats against the Philistine cities.[4] In the case of the first and last cities, a pun between the name of the city and the fact of its judgment is intended: Gaza (*'azzâ*) will be abandoned (*'ăzûbâ*) and Ekron (*'eqrôn*) will be uprooted (*tē'āqēr*); in the other two instances, a play on the *s* sounds in the names of the cities adds a harsh note that heightens the fact of their coming destruction and desolation: *'ašqĕlôn lišmāmâ* and *'ašdôd baṣṣāhŏrayim yĕgārĕšûhā*. These four noteworthy cities are doubtless also representative of the total destruction of Philistine territory. Likewise, the mention of their specific fate may be characteristic of the various forms that the judgment of the Philistines would take: defeat, destruction, deportation, and abandonment of cities. The reference to Ashdod's invasion at noon,* a time for rest from the midday sun, may indicate a surprise attack: "In hot countries, work is suspended during the hottest hours of the day; therefore for anything to happen then is unexpected. The prophet means that Ashdod will fall by a surprise attack (cf. Jer. XV.8)."[5]

Each of the cities experienced the horrors of invasion. Gaza was

---

3. See further K. A. Kitchen, "The Philistines," in *Peoples of Old Testament Times*, ed. D. J. Wiseman (Oxford: Clarendon, 1973), pp. 53-78; E. E. Hindson, *The Philistines and the Old Testament* (Grand Rapids: Baker, 1971); W. S. LaSor, "Philistines, Philistia," *ISBE* 3:841-46; T. Dothan, *The Philistines and Their Material Culture* (New Haven: Yale U., 1982); "What We Know About the Philistines," *Biblical Archaeology Review* 8 (1982): 20-44.

4. Only four Philistine cities are mentioned here. In the eighth century B.C. Gath was defeated by Uzziah, who destroyed its walls (2 Chron. 11:8; 26:6). It may have lain in ruins as early as Amos's day (cf. Amos 6:2) and perhaps experienced final destruction as a result of an Assyrian invasion (cf. Mic. 1:10).

5. S. M. Lehrman, "Zephaniah," in *The Twelve Prophets*, Soncino Books of the Bible, ed. A. Cohen, 12th ed. (London: Soncino, 1985), pp. 241-42. Some (e.g., Davidson, G. A. Smith) have seen in Esarhaddon's capture of Memphis "in half a day" (*AR* 2:227) a reflection of a victory at midday; the expression may have relevance here. Conversely H. E. Freeman (*Nahum Zephaniah Habakkuk*, Everyman's Bible Commentary [Chicago: Moody, 1973], p. 72) proposes: "The stronghold of the Philistines, a fortress in strength, would become so defenseless that there will be no need for a surprise attack after dark by the enemy forces, but she can be overthrown at noon, in broad daylight. An attack at noon implies contempt for Ashdod's reputation as a formidable city." For biblical parallels, see 1 Kings 20:16; Jer. 6:4.

taken by Nebuchadnezzar and became a deserted city.[6] Ashkelon was also taken by Nebuchadnezzar in 604 B.C., but it recovered and eventually became famous as a Hellenistic city and as the birthplace of Herod the Great. Ashdod and Ekron[7] likewise fell to the same Neo-Babylonian conqueror, but both are mentioned in the literature of the Hellenistic and Roman periods, which reflects Ashdod's changing fortunes and Ekron's persistence into the time of Eusebius in the fourth century A.D. As for the main fact of Zephaniah's prophecy, the capture and destruction of the cities and territory of the Philistines, there can be little doubt. Thus Nebuchadnezzar boasts:

> In the first year of Nebuchadrezzar in the month of Sivan he mustered his army and went to the Ḫatti-territory, . . .
> All the kings of the Ḫatti-land came before him and he received their heavy tribute.
> He marched to the city of Askelon and captured it in the month of Kislev.
> He captured its king and plundered it and carried off [spoil from it. . . . .]
> He turned the city into a mound and heaps of ruins and then in the month of Sebat he marched back to Babylon.[8]

Kitchen concludes:

> Ashkelon sought to resist the Neo-Babylonian advance in 604 B.C.; Nebuchadrezzar II subdued it and exiled its king in Babylon, where his sons appear in the ration-tablets along with Jehoiachin of Judah and his relations. These, with mentions of kings of Gaza and Ashdod at the Babylonian court, are the last traces of Philistia as an entity, before her final disappearance as a political unit.[9]

There may also be a clever literary play at work here. Robert Gordis,[10] building upon a suggestion of Lawrence Zalcman,[11] detects the metaphor of a deserted woman. Both scholars propose that the reason for the absence of paronomasia and the presence of, at best, weak assonance in the pronouncements against Ashkelon and Ashdod

---

6. Although there was a Gaza in NT times (cf. Acts 8:26), it appears to have been located on a different site nearer the coast.
7. For Ashdod, see M. Dothan, "Ashdod of the Philistines," in *New Directions in Biblical Archaeology*, ed. D. N. Freedman and J. C. Greenfield (Garden City, N.J.: Doubleday, 1971), pp. 17-27; J. E. Jennings, "Ashdod," in *The New International Dictionary of Biblical Archaeology*, ed. E. M. Blaiklock and R. K. Harrison (Grand Rapids: Zondervan, 1983), pp. 73-74. For Ekron, see S. Gitin and T. Dothan, "The Rise and Fall of Ekron of the Philistines: Recent Excavations at an Urban Border Site," *BA* 50 (1987): 197-222.
8. D. J. Wiseman, *Chronicles of Chaldaean Kings* (London: The Trustees of the British Museum, 1956), p. 69.
9. Kitchen, "Philistines," p. 67.
10. Robert Gordis, "A Rising Tide of Misery: A Note on Zephaniah II 4," *VT* 37 (1987): 487-90.
11. L. Zalcman, "Ambiguity and Assonance at Zephaniah II 4," *VT* 36 (1986): 365-71.

is because no verb could be found that was suitable for the needed assonance and paronomasia and that carried with it the double entendre of a woman and a city. Faced with a choice of proceeding with the metaphor or the constraints of assonance, Zephaniah chose the former. Thus the verse contains four stitches that "present an ascending scale of suffering, thus heightening the pathos of the passage" and are "to be understood as follows:

> Indeed, Gaza shall be deserted (like a betrothed woman),
> And Ashkelon will be desolate (like a deserted wife);
> Ashdod will be driven out in broad daylight (like a divorced woman),
> And Ekron will be uprooted (like a barren woman)."[12]

Although there may be some hesitation in adopting the suggestion of a metaphor in which the cities of the hated Philistines are compared to a woman, this solution to understanding the literary problems of the middle lines and the flow of thought in the whole verse is brilliant. Certainly it is in keeping with not only scriptural precedent (cf. Isa. 54:6; 60:15; 62:4; Jer. 4:29; etc.) but also Zephaniah's penchant for the use of literary allusions (cf. 1:2-3).

Zephaniah's announcement of judgment turns to invective as he pronounces a woe against those who live along the seacoast.[13] Though the term may suggest the more densely occupied portions of Philistia, J. M. P. Smith is probably correct in pointing out that it is "a fitting designation of Philistia, which lay along the Maritime Plain."[14] In making his denunciations Zephaniah calls these Philistine settlers Kerethites,* a term that reflects their Cretan origins, and their territory Canaan,* a name that indicates not only a geographic location but implies their land's similar fate of depopulation and disenfranchisement. Philistia will be judged "till there are no inhabitants left" (NJB), never again to be a threat:

> Time and again these cities were destroyed during the many wars that ravaged Palestine in the centuries following this prophecy. Pharaoh Necho devastated Philistia (Jer. 47:1-7); Alexander the Great depopulated Gaza and repeopled it from the neighborhood (Arrian, *Anabasis* II, 27). Later, Philistia became a Syrian province and in the Maccabean wars was raided and ravaged repeatedly by the Jews (1 Macc. 5:68; 10:67-89; 11:60ff.; 13:43ff.).[15]

---

12. Gordis, "Rising Tide," p. 489.
13. For הוֹי ("woe"), see the additional note on Nah. 3:1; for its use in invective in Habakkuk's extended section of taunt songs, see the exposition of Hab. 2:6-20.
14. J. M. P. Smith, *A Critical and Exegetical Commentary on Zephaniah and Nahum*, ICC (Edinburgh: T. and T. Clark, 1911), p. 216.
15. Theo. Laetsch, *The Minor Prophets* (St. Louis: Concordia, 1956), p. 368.

Whatever future hope the region had lay in its relation to the Philistines' perennial enemies, the Israelites. The prosperous seacoast district will become pastureland dotted with caves for Israelite shepherds and folds for their flocks. It will belong to the remnant* of Judah, "the object of the love and providential concern of the Lord their God who cares for and restores His people."[16]

Additional Notes

2:4 Although the mention of only four Philistine cities has been taken by some[17] as merely a suitable vehicle to represent the judgment of all of Philistia, since the prophets customarily employ groups of four to indicate totality of judgment (e.g., Jer. 15:3; Ezek. 14:21; Joel 1:2-4),[18] a technique that Zephaniah utilizes here in the wider context (2:4-15), such may not be the case. The fact that the prophets often proclaim judgment in groups of more than four cities or countries (e.g., Isa. 13-23; Jer. 46-51; Ezek. 25-32; Amos 1:3–2:5), as well as the disappearance of Gath from both biblical and nonbiblical accounts by this period, may indicate its unavailability for Zephaniah. The prophecy against the four Philistine cities may thus be intended to be understood both individually and representatively.

Several commentators have noted the occurrence elsewhere in the OT of the root *šdd* (which can be isolated in the sound of the name Ashdod) with the name Ashdod (e.g., Jer. 15:8; Ps. 91:6). Thus Lawrence Zalcman cites the comments of the Jewish scholars Rashi and Kimchi:

> "Ashdod is her name, and at noon when destruction devastates they will drive her [inhabitants] out and she will be devastated". Here the reference to Ps. xci 6 is unmistakable. Qimḥi is even more explicit: . . . Ashdod means "devastation" [*šōd*], and thus it is, as it were, paronomasia.[19]

2:5 †חֶבֶל הַיָּם ("the seacoast," or "the line of the sea"): חֶבֶל means basically "rope/cord" and is related to an Akkadian word (*eblu*) with the same meaning. It also was utilized in contexts dealing with the use of a measuring line (2 Sam. 8:2) and to indicate a unit of measured area, "district/region" (Deut. 3:4, 13, 14; Josh. 19:9). Although its employment with יָם is unique to Zephaniah (the usual term for

---

16. J. D. Hannah, "Zephaniah," in *The Bible Knowledge Commentary*, ed. J. F. Walvoord and R. B. Zuck (Wheaton: Scripture Press, 1985), 1:1530.
17. See, e.g., C. F. Keil, *The Twelve Minor Prophets*, COT (Grand Rapids: Eerdmans, 1954), 2:139-40; L. Walker, "Zephaniah," in *EBC* (Grand Rapids: Zondervan, 1985), 7:552.
18. Cf. also Amos's use of the number four in 3/4 ladder parallelism (Amos 1:3, 6, 9, 11, 13; 2:1, 4, 6).
19. Zalcman, "Ambiguity and Assonance," p. 366.

"seacoast" is חוֹף הַיָּם; cf. Jer. 47:7), the resultant term is clear. The association of the Philistines with coastal areas is mentioned also by Ezekiel (Ezek. 25:16).[20]

כְּרֵתִים ("*Kerethites*"): Apparently related to the name Crete, with which Philistine origins are partially linked,[21] its precise significance is unclear. Kerethites were included in David's bodyguard (2 Sam. 8:18; 15:18; 20:7, 20; 1 Kings 1:38, 44; 1 Chron. 18:17). The Kerethites have been considered by some to be a tribe of the Philistines,[22] by others as Cretans who first settled in Canaan during the Davidic era.[23] In any case, their close association with the Philistines is assumed both here and in Ezek. 25:16, where they are also linked with the seacoast.[24]

The term "*Canaan*," which designates geographically the land west of the Jordan (including Philistia) northward through Syria to Lebo Hamath (modern Lebweh), is probably used with the further implication of indicating "that Philistia is to share the lot of Canaan, and lose its inhabitants by extermination."[25] Canaan is thus not conterminous with Philistia, nor is Philistia identical with the modern term Palestine (except etymologically).

2:6 † כְּרֹת ("caves"): The word is variously rendered in the versions as "Crete" (LXX), "Kerethites" (NIV), "Kereth" (NEB), "resting place" (Vg), "shelters" (NKJV), "cottages" (KJV), "meadows" (RSV; cf. Soncino), "caves" (NASB). The last suggestion has been followed here, taking the root to be כָּרָה ("dig"). This seems to make the best sense in context. Whether the caves in view are "natural, dug by nature, or artificial, man-made," they are "used by shepherds and their flocks as a shelter at night or in stormy weather."[26]

---

20. See further H.-J. Fabry, "חבל," *TDOT* 4:172-79.
21. Amos links the Philistines with Caphtor, traditionally associated with Crete. Some evidence, however, suggests a possible relationship with southern Asia Minor; see A. Wainwright, "Caphtor-Cappodicia," *VT* 6 (1956): 199-210; "Early Philistine History," *VT* 9 (1959): 73-84.
22. See, e.g., A. van Selms, "Cherethites," *ISBE* 1:641.
23. M. Delcor, "Les kerethim et les cretois," *VT* 28 (1978): 409-22. See also C. Gordon, *Before the Bible* (New York: Harper & Row, 1962), p. 171.
24. The problematic "Negev of the Cherethites" (1 Sam. 30:14), as N. K. Sandars (*The Sea Peoples* [London: Thames and Hudson, 1978], p. 166) suggests, "may have lain in the hinterland of Gaza."
25. Keil, *Minor Prophets*, 2:141.
26. Laetsch, *Minor Prophets*, p. 367n. So construed, there is a paronomasia involving the root *krt*. Thus, the land of the Kerethites (כְּרֵתִים, v. 5) will become a place marked by shepherds' caves (כְּרֹת, v. 6). A similar case of paronomasia occurs in Ezek. 25:16 where the root *krt* is used of "cutting off the Kerethites" (וְהִכְרַתִּי אֶת־כְּרֵתִים).
    Among those who prefer a reference to a proper name here, C. Gordon (*Ugarit and Minoan Crete* [New York: Norton, 1966], p. 28) proposes a

2:7 שְׁאֵרִית (*"remnant"*): Zephaniah had spoken earlier of destroying the "remnant of Baal" (1:4), and Amos predicted that the "remnant of the Philistines" would perish (Amos 1:8). Here God leaves a remnant of His people, which He, the Good Shepherd, will care for (Heb. פָּקַד[27]) and restore to prosperity.[28] Elsewhere the prophets predict that God will preserve a remnant of His people, which He will regather to the land, and that they will turn to their Messiah and be blessed with everlasting felicity (Isa. 10:20-23; 11:11-16; Jer. 23:1-8; 31:11-14, 27-37; Ezek. 11:13-20; 34:20-31; 37:15-28; Amos 5:15; Mic. 2:12-13; 4:1-8; 5:7-8 [HB 5:6-7]; 7:18-20; Zech. 8:6-8; cf. Zeph. 3:9-20).[29]

Because the pronoun on עֲלֵיהֶם is masc. pl., *BHS* suggests a transposition of consonants so as to read עַל הַיָּם ("on the sea[coast]"), thus paralleling חֶבֶל in the previous line. The effect is to propose that the full territory mentioned in v. 6 is here being treated in its component parts. The masc. plurals in יִרְעוּן and יִרְבָּצוּן are construed *ad sensum*, the subject being viewed either as the shepherds of v. 6 or the individual members of the remnant presented metaphorically here as sheep (cf. Jer. 23:1-4; Ezek. 34:11-16, 20-31; 37:24-28; etc.). Thus J. M. P. Smith remarks: "The closing scene shows the former marts of trade and busy hives of men given over to the undisturbed possession of well-fed sheep, going in and out of the vacant houses at will, 'with none to make them afraid.' "[30]

b. Moab and Ammon (2:8-11)

Translation

"I have heard the insults* of Moab
and the revilings of the Ammonites,
who insulted My people
and violated* their borders.

---

reference to the Ugaritic hero "Kret . . . the eponymous ancestor of the Cretans or the Philistines in Zephaniah 2:6." The root כָּרָה apparently lies behind the decision of the *Preliminary and Interim Report on the Hebrew Old Testament Text Project* (New York: United Bible Societies, 1980), 5:375-76, to translate the form as "wells." J. M. P. Smith (*Zephaniah*, p. 218) omits the word as a "corrupt dittograph of the immediately preceding word."

27. See the additional note on Nah. 1:8.
28. For the phrase "restore their fortunes," see R. D. Patterson, "Joel," in *EBC*, 7:259.
29. For the remnant theme, see R. de Vaux, "The 'Remnant of Israel' According to the Prophets," in *The Bible and the Ancient Near East*, trans. Damian McHugh (Garden City, N.Y.: Doubleday, 1971), p. 28; G. F. Hasel, *The Remnant* (Berrien Springs, Mich.: Andrews U., 1974).
30. J. M. P. Smith, *Zephaniah*, p. 219.

⁹**Therefore, as I live,"**
  declares the LORD of Hosts, the God of Israel,
"surely Moab will be like Sodom
  and the Ammonites like Gomorrah—
overrun* with weeds and salt pits,
  and a perpetual desolation.
The remnant of My people will despoil them,
  and the remainder of My nation will inherit them."
¹⁰**This will happen to them in return for their pride,**
  for they have been insulting and arrogant
  against the people of the LORD of Hosts.
¹¹**The LORD will be terrifying among them,**
  because He will make lean* all the gods of the earth,
and the nations on every shore* will bow down to Him,
  each from his own place*.

Exegesis and Exposition

Zephaniah's pronouncements of judgment turn to Judah's eastern neighbors, the Transjordanian nations of Moab and Ammon. Like the Philistines, these nations were numbered among Israel's traditional foes. Both were descended through Lot (Gen. 19:30-38) and eventually settled east of the Jordan River (Num. 21:11, 13-15, 24; Deut. 1:15; 2:8-9, 18, 21, 37; 3:11, 16; 29:1; 32:49). Although the Lord commanded Israel to leave the Ammonites alone during the days of the wilderness wanderings (Deut. 2:19) and Israel did its best to avoid conflict with the Moabites, Israel was often forced to campaign in the area (cf. Num. 21:21-35). The Ammonites joined the Moabites in hiring Baalam to curse the Israelites (Num. 22-25), and the incident was remembered down into NT times (cf. 2 Pet. 2:15; Jude 11; Rev. 2:14). Both nations harassed the Israelites in the days of the judges (Judg. 3:12-30; 11:1-40), and Saul and David fought against them (1 Sam. 11:1-11; 14:47; 2 Sam. 8:2, 11-12, 10:1-19; 12:26-31; 1 Chron. 20:1-3).

Although relations were better during Solomon's reign so that Solomon even had Moabite and Ammonite women in his harem (1 Kings 11:1), a situation that contributed to his spiritual decline and Israel's apostasy (1 Kings 11:5, 7, 33), both nations remained antagonists of God's people. Accordingly the Israelites fought them frequently (2 Kings 1:1; 3:1-27; 2 Chron. 20:1-30; 24:26; 26:8; 27:5). Indeed, they would remain Israel's enemies to the very end (2 Kings 25:25; Jer. 40:11-14).

Both nations had been denounced by God's prophets before Zephaniah's day (Isa. 15:1–16:14; 25:10-12; Amos 1:13-15; 2:1-5) and would be again soon afterward (Jer. 48:1-47; 49:1-6; Ezek. 21:20; 25:1-7, 8-11). Therefore, no particular incident of provocation needs to be sought as the occasion for Zephaniah's prophecy, even though the activities of these nations are now known to be commensurate with the charges brought against them by Zephaniah.[31] Rather, as Keil points out, "the charge refers to the hostile attitude assumed by both tribes at all times towards the nation of God, which they manifested both in word and deed, as often as the latter was brought into trouble and distress."[32]

Zephaniah condemns both nations for their pride (cf. Isa. 16:6; 25:10-11; Jer. 48:29; 49:4), their blasphemous insults against God and His people (cf. Jer. 48:26-27; 49:1), and their atrocities and incursions against Israelite territory (Amos 1:13–2:5).[33] Not only for their vicious actions but also for gloating over their seeming successes against the Israelites, Zephaniah predicts that both nations, who often have worked together, will be treated like another well-known pair: Sodom and Gomorrah. The fertile Transjordanian steppe lands will be devastated so as to resemble the fate of the notorious ancient cities along the southeastern coast of the Dead Sea.[34] When God's judgment has been accomplished, the whole area will be turned into a perpetual wasteland, overrun with weeds and pocked by salt pits, whereas its inhabitants will be taken into captivity.

The reference to the destruction of Sodom and Gomorrah as an example of God's severe judgment of sin was familiar already by Zephaniah's day (cf. Deut. 29:23; Isa. 1:9; 13:19; Amos 4:11) and would persist (cf. Jer. 23:14; 49:14; 50:40; Lam. 4:6) into NT times (Mark 10:15; Luke 10:12; Rom. 9:29; 2 Pet. 2:6). Doubtless the story was well known to the Moabites and the Ammonites, who were also familiar with the wasteland that encompassed those once thriving cities. Indeed, the effect upon visitors to the area in modern times is still an awesome one.[35]

The very thought of weeds and salt* pits brings up visions of

---

31. See Duane L. Christensen, "Zephaniah 2:4-15: A Theological Basis for Josiah's Program of Political Expansion," *CBQ* 46 (1984): 681.
32. Keil, *Minor Prophets*, 2:143.
33. Moab's hostility toward Israel is illustrated in the well-known Mesha Stele (or Moabite Stone); see D. Winton Thomas, ed., *Documents from Old Testament Times* (New York: Harper & Row, 1961), pp. 195-99. For the text itself, see H. Donner and W. Röllig, *Kanaanäische und Aramäische Inschriften* (Wiesbaden: Harrassowitz, 1966), 1:33.
34. For light on the possible locations of Sodom and Gomorrah, see E. B. Smick, *Archaeology of the Jordan Valley* (Grand Rapids: Baker, 1973), pp. 47-51; W. C. van Hatten, "Once Again: Sodom and Gomorrah," *BA* 44 (1981): 87-92; James E. Jennings, "Bab Edh-dhra," *The New International Dictionary of Biblical Archaeology*, pp. 84-85.
35. Despite a recent resurgence, the area is still marked by its austere surroundings. See Denis Baly, *The Geography of the Bible*, rev. ed. (New York: Harper & Row, 1974), pp. 204-6.

worthlessness and desolation. Yet Ammon and Moab, who took such pride in themselves and their land and who had insulted the people of God and violated their lands, would find the source of their pride cut off and turned into just such a devastation. They who had so often taken advantage of Israel and mistreated her people would have the tables turned as the principle of appropriate divine justice was applied to their case (cf. Jer. 50:29; Obad. 15-16).

Beyond the specific judgment of Moab and Ammon lies the application of their punishment to all nations who similarly mistreat God's people and vaunt themselves against the God of the universe (cf. Gen. 12:1-3; 1 Sam. 17:26, 36, 45; 2 Kings 19:21-28; Ps. 2; Jer. 48:26; Joel 3:1-3 [HB 4:1-3]; Matt. 25:40). To such as oppose Him will come a final time of reckoning when the sovereign and omnipotent God (Deut. 10:17; Ps. 47:7-8 [HB 47:8-9]), whose awesomeness (Ps. 47:2 [HB 47:3]) is beyond measure (Ps. 89:7 [HB 89:8]) and whose strength (Ps. 89:8-13 [HB 89-9-14]) makes Him mighty in battle (Ps. 24:8), will show Himself fearsome (Ps. 76:12 [HB 76:13]) to all (Isa. 66:14-16; Ezek. 39:17-22; Joel 3:9-16 [HB 4:9-16]). Then men will learn that Israel's God alone is the one and only true God (Deut. 6:4; Isa. 42:8; 46:9). The false gods, who are no gods (Isa. 41:24), like the nations, cities, and people with whom they are identified, shall be subdued (cf. Isa. 43:11-13; 44:17-20; 46:1-2; Jer. 50:2-3; Zech. 14:9), and God alone shall be worshiped everywhere and by all (Ps. 66:1-4 [HB 66:2-5]; Isa. 2:1-5; 66:19-21; Mic. 4:1-5; Zech. 14:16-21).

Additional Notes

2:8 †חֶרְפָּה ("insult/reproach") is used of slanderous speech (Mic. 6:16) that one person uses against another (2 Chron. 32:17) or especially the disgrace that one party gives to another (Gen. 30:23; Isa. 4:1). It is often used of reproach placed upon a nation (e.g., 1 Sam. 17:26; Isa. 25:8; Jer. 31:19; Lam. 5:1; Ezek. 36:30).

The etymology of the parallel term in the second line, גִּדּוּפִים ("revilings"), denotes the act of throwing, hence idiomatically of hurling insults at one another. The two nouns are in parallel in Isa. 51:7, whereas the fem. noun גִּדּוּפָה occurs with חֶרְפָּה in Ezek. 5:15 and the two verbal roots are juxtaposed in 2 Kings 19:22; Isa. 37:23. Taken together, these two word groups form a picture of slanderous taunting that has as its object a hurtful vilifying of another.

†וַיַּגְדִּילוּ ("and [they] violated"): In the hiphil stem גָּדַל customarily is transitive, "i.e., the subject of the action and the subject of the process being brought about, viz., bringing the greatness into operation and effectiveness, are the same. . . . The intrinsically transitive hiphil of *gdl* always means 'to set oneself forth as great illegally, presumptuously, and arrogantly, to boast, to triumph over

(*'al*) others.' "[36] Accordingly it is used in contexts of judgment against the nations for mocking Israel (e.g., Jer. 48:26, 42; Ezek. 35:13). The sense here probably also carries with it not only the repeated arrogant thrusts of the Transjordanian nations into Israelite territory but also their gloating over their successes (cf. Amos 1:13).[37] Some suggest that the verb signifies the enlarging of Transjordanian borders at Israel's expense (e.g., R. Smith), while others (cf. NJB) propose that these nations boasted about their own territories.

2:9 מִקְשַׁק חָרוּל†: The first word is a *hapax legomenon* usually taken as coming from the root מֹשׁק and assumed to mean something like "possess," due to the contextual understanding assigned to the derived noun מֶשֶׁק ("possession") in Gen. 15:2.[38] Nevertheless, that meaning is somewhat difficult here, so that J. M. P. Smith (*Zephaniah*, pp. 226-27) laments concerning the whole phrase: "These two Hebrew words are obscure in meaning. The first one is found nowhere else in Hebrew, nor is any light thrown upon it by the Vrss. or the cognate languages." The usual proposal may prove to be correct, but it is also possible to view the form as an instance of enclitic *mem*, the first *mem* being attached to the previous word and the resultant form being understood as a hiphil participle from שׁוּק, meaning "overflowing," hence "overrun."[39] "Overrun" certainly provides good sense here and may not be an impossible understanding of the posited root מֹשׁק.

Although Keil (*Minor Prophets*, 2:143) affirms that the noun חָרוּל means "stinging nettle," J. M. P. Smith (*Zephaniah*, p. 227) is probably correct in observing that from its use in the OT the most likely meaning is "weeds."

Salt sometimes symbolized ruinous waste (Deut. 29:29; Job 39:6; Ps. 107:34; Jer. 17:6). Sowing the earth with salt was a mark of permanent judgment (cf. Judg. 9:45), a practice that continued into Roman times, as witnessed in the Roman sack of Carthage.[40] For the

---

36. J. Bergman, H. Ringgren, and R. Mosis, "גָּדַל," *TDOT* 2:404-5.
37. The idea of arrogant boasting is ably defended by J. M. P. Smith, *Zephaniah*, p. 226; L. Sabottka, *Zephanja* (Rome: Biblical Institute, 1972), pp. 84-85.
38. For details, see E. A. Speiser, *Genesis*, AB (Garden City, N.Y.: Doubleday, 1964), pp. 111-12.
39. J. M. P. Smith (*Zephaniah*, p. 227) suggests similarly "overgrown." For enclitic *mem*, see H. D. Hummel, "Enclitic *MEM* in Early Northwest Semitic, Especially Hebrew," *JBL* 76 (1957): 85-107; M. Pope, "Ugaritic Enclitic *-m*," *JCS* 5 (1951): 123-28; M. Dahood, *Psalms*, AB (Garden City, N.Y.: Doubleday, 1970), 3:408-9. The use of enclitic *mem* with proper nouns is attested elsewhere and may have been employed here for metrical reasons.
40. See B. H. Warmington, *Carthage* (Baltimore: Penguin Books, 1964), p. 255.

term "Lord (Yahweh) of Hosts," see the exposition of Nah. 2:13 and my note on 1 Kings 18:15.[41]

2:11 †Suggestions for the sense of רָזָה ("grow lean") here include "destroy" (LXX, Pesh., OL, NIV, Luther, *Le Sainte Bible, La Sacra Biblia*), "attend to" (Vg), "starve/famish" (NASB, RSV, KJV, Soncino), "reduce to nothing" (NKJV) and "scatter" (NJB). The commentators are likewise divided, usually following one of the suggested meanings.

Sabottka, however, breaks new ground in postulating a relation to a late Jewish-Aramaic root meaning "be strong/hard," and hence the personal name Raziel means "God Rules." He thus translates Zeph. 2:11 "he (Yahweh) will rule over the gods of the earth." The same verb in derived stems also means "throw/come against with force," a meaning that might fit the context here by taking רָזָה as a piel. A homomorphic verb (known also in Syriac) means "take secret action against," perhaps as good a conjecture as some of those proposed above.

My translation follows the use of the root elsewhere in the OT. This meaning, however, masks an allusion that now eludes us, perhaps that of impotence or death due to starvation, the idea of either being a serious affront to the nature gods of Canaan.[42] The form itself should probably be read with *BHS* as an imperfect piel. If the י of the previous כִּי is a double-duty letter, no change in the consonantal text is required.[43]

†The translation of אִיֵּי הַגּוֹיִם as "the nations on every shore" follows the NIV. מִמְּקוֹמוֹ ("from his place") has been understood as each nation serving God in/from the standpoint of his own land/place (e.g., J. M. P. Smith, Laetsch) or going from his place to Jerusalem (e.g., Keil).

c. Cush (2:12)

Translation

**"So also you, Cushites,
    are* pierced through by My sword."**

---

41. See R. D. Patterson and H. J. Austel, "1, 2 Kings," in *EBC*, 4:142-43.
42. J. M. P. Smith (*Zephaniah*, p. 229) reasons that "if the text is correct, the point of the figure lies either in the thought that by destroying the nations Yahweh will enfeeble their gods, whose existence is bound up with that of the nations worshipping them; or in the fact that in earlier times, sacrificial offerings were looked upon as the 'food of the gods' (cf. Ez. 44⁷); hence, by causing the offerings to cease, Yahweh will deprive the gods of their means of support."
43. For double-duty consonants, see I. O. Lehman, "A Forgotten Principle of Biblical Textual Tradition Rediscovered," *JNES* 26 (1967): 93-101; M. Dahood, *Psalms*, 2:81; 3:371-72.

Exegesis and Exposition

Zephaniah's news for the southern regions is an addendum to his message for the eastern nations represented by Moab and Ammon, whose judgment (vv. 8-10) anticipated that of all the nations (v. 11). Building on the concept of universal judgment in the preceding verse, Zephaniah tacks on the notice that the judgment of Cush, too, is part of the punishment that will overtake all peoples. Although according to Ezek. 29:10 Egypt's southern boundary bordered on Cush, the term could have wider implications. Therefore, as Laetsch correctly points out, by Cush is meant "what is now known as the Eastern, or Egyptian, Sudan, together with Ethiopia, Somaliland, and Eritrea. Zephaniah speaks of rivers of Cush (3:10, cf. Is. 18:1), referring to the White and the Blue Nile and their many tributaries."[44]

A touch of irony probably is intended, because doubtless Egypt is uppermost in Zephaniah's thinking here. Egypt had been defeated by its southern neighbors, and a Cushite royal house (Egypt's twenty-fifth dynasty) reigned over Egypt for more than half a century (c. 715-655 B.C.).[45] At least four of its kings ruled over all Egypt (Shabako [716-701 B.C.], Shebitku [701-690 B.C.], Taharqa [690-664 B.C.], and Tanwetamani [663 B.C.]), and their stranglehold on Egypt was broken only by the victories of Esarhaddon at Memphis in 671 B.C. and Ashurbanipal at Thebes in 663 B.C. Following the permanent withdrawal of the Cushite (or Nubian) forces, under the protection of Assyria, Egypt gradually was able to form a new dynasty (the twenty-sixth or Saite dynasty), which was to last for more than a century (c. 663-525 B.C.) and be Egypt's last flourishing kingdom.

By the time of Josiah and Zephaniah this dynasty was already in power with Pharaoh Psamtik I (c. 663-609 B.C.) at its head. Accordingly Zephaniah's use of the term "Cushites" probably served several functions: (1) that Zephaniah does not use a finite verb in denouncing the Cushites may point to the reality of their defeat—they are already slain by the sword; (2) the "sword" is actually "My sword," the Lord's own sword (cf. Josh. 5:13; Judg. 7:20; Isa. 27:1; 34:5; 66:16; Jer. 25:33; Ezek. 21:9, 13-17, 28-32; 30:24-25) moving through the earth in divine judgment;[46] (3) the term may also be a veiled reminder to the proud

---

44. Laetsch, *Minor Prophets*, p. 371. See further the helpful discussions of W. LaSor, "Cush," *ISBE* 1:839, and R. F. Youngblood, "Ethiopia," *ISBE* 2:193-94.

45. For details on Egypt's twenty-fifth (or Nubian) dynasty, see A. H. Gardiner, *Egypt of the Pharaohs* (Oxford: Clarendon, 1961), pp. 340-52; K. A. Kitchen, *The Third Intermediate Period in Egypt* (Warminster: Aris and Phillips, 1973), pp. 148-73.

46. Some suggest that the י in חַרְבִּי is an abbreviation for יהוה and hence understand here "the sword of Yahweh." See G. A. Smith, *The Book of the Twelve Prophets*, rev. ed. (Garden City, N.Y.: Doubleday, Doran, 1929), 2:63

Egyptians of their own earlier defeat at the hands of their southern neighbors, a fact that therefore could signal the possibility of a future reversal of their present fortunes; (4) the use of "Cushites" may also have avoided providing an occasion of direct antagonism with the Egyptians, with whom the political affairs of Israel (2 Kings 21:3-5) and Judah (2 Kings 23:29-35) were traditionally bound, at a time when Judah was relatively weak and its suzerain state, Assyria, was already in decline.

By Cushites, then, probably is meant the better-known Egypt (cf. Ezek. 30:1-9). As the Cushite dynasty had passed, so also would Egypt (cf. Jer. 46; Ezek. 29-32) and, one day, all earthly powers that stand in opposition to the Lord (cf. Ezek. 32:17-32).

Additional Notes

2:12 †הֵמָּה ("are") has been much discussed. Although it is true that change of persons (enallage) is characteristic of Hebrew style,[47] so that one could translate the verse "You, too, Cushites, they are (the) slain of my sword," it seems simplest to take the pronoun in its later Hebrew employment as a copula, a use that, though rare, is not unknown (cf. 2 Sam. 7:28; Ps. 44:4 [HB 44:5]; Isa. 37:16[?]).[48]

The choice of "Cushites" here (as well as in 3:10) may also reflect a conscious literary touch, constituting paronomasia on the name of Zephaniah's father (1:1). Whether "Cushite" reflects an African element in Zephaniah's patrilineage (note the similar problem in Jer. 36:14), as several have suggested, remains uncertain.

d. Assyria (2:13-15)

Translation

**And He will stretch out His hand against the north
and destroy Assyria;
and He will make Nineveh a desolation*,
dry* as the wilderness.**

---

n. 7; see also *BHS*; J. M. P. Smith, *Zephaniah*, p. 236[n]; M. O'Connor, *Hebrew Verse Structure* (Winona Lake: Eisenbrauns, 1980), p. 253.

47. See M. Pope, *Song of Songs*, AB (Garden City, N.Y.: Doubleday, 1977), pp. 303-4. Keil (*Minor Prophets*, 2:146) calls attention to similar instances in Ezek. 28:22; Zeph. 3:18; Zech. 3:8.

48. Such use is common in Aramaic/Syriac; see A. F. Johns, *A Short Grammar of Biblical Aramaic*, rev. ed. (Berrien Springs: Andrews U. 1972), p. 12; T. H. Robinson, *Paradigms and Exercises in Syriac Grammar*, 4th ed. (Oxford: Clarendon, 1962), p. 15. An alternative possibility would be to view this as an instance in which the pronoun has been attracted to כּוּשִׁים: "The Cushites . . . they are the slain of my sword." The הֵמָּה would thus be a resumptive pronoun.

¹⁴**And flocks will lie down in her midst,**
  creatures of every kind*.
The desert owl* and the screech owl*
  will lodge in the tops of her columns.
Listen!* (There is) singing in the window
(but) rubble* on the threshold,
  for He will lay bare the cedar work.
¹⁵**This was the exultant city**
  that dwelled in safety,
  that said to herself, "I am
    and there is no one else*."
What* a desolation she has become,
  a resting place for beasts!
Everyone who passes by will hiss
  and wave his hand*.

Exegesis and Exposition

Zephaniah's fourth message against the foreign powers swings around to the north. The order of his prophecies is doubtless climactic. He had delivered his messages against Judah's perennial enemies to the west and east; then he inserted a word against a traditional foe to the south. He now brings the series to a head by turning to the nation that had so long been the dominant power in the ancient Near East.

Like Nahum before him, Zephaniah announces Assyria's soon demise. God will stretch out His hand and destroy her.[49] Her capital city, Nineveh, will be rendered desolate, fit only for animals. Zephaniah urges his readers to visualize the scene with him. Inside the once impregnable walls one encounters no longer the broad streets, impressive gateways, magnificent temples and palaces, or lovely parks and gardens that once adorned the well-planned city. Only ruins and rubble remain. Signs of destruction and devastation lie all around. Where is Sennacherib's mighty palace, "which has no equal"? Where is the water that once flowed from Nineveh's aqueduct and many canals, providing the city with an ample supply and making it luxurious? Both have disappeared, leaving behind only a mound of debris and a desertlike dryness.[50]

---

49. For the motif of the outstretched hand of God, see the exposition of 1:4-6. For Zephaniah's perspective on the political crises that marked the latter half of the seventh century B.C., see Christensen, "Zephaniah 2:4-15," pp. 669-82; P. C. Craigie, *Twelve Prophets* (Philadelphia: Westminster, 1985), 2:121-22.
50. Nahum predicts that Nineveh's shortage of water would be felt already at the time of its siege; see the exposition of Nah. 3:14.

The proud royal city, once so busy and bustling with people, now houses only a creaturely kingdom. Casting his eye upward, one can see on the tops of Nineveh's many pillars not stately structures but owls—owls of every sort screeching through the lonely nights. With the morning light one is confronted with the strangest of paradoxes: from the windows of razed and gutted buildings comes the song of birds, while below them lies only the rubble of collapsed walls, fallen timbers, and broken bits of once-treasured possessions and strips of cedar paneling.

It is an eerie spectacle. The deceased metropolis is populated only by creatures and ghosts of departed grandeur. Here is the once proud and festive city whose power and wealth were beyond measure, she who was once approached with eager anticipation, respect, and fear. Now she is devoid of citizenry or visitors, and those who pass by viewing the devastation give only a sneering hiss (cf. Jer. 19:8; Mic. 6:16) or scornful wave.[51]

Like Nahum, then, Zephaniah sees no future either for Assyria or its capital. Their doom is certain and irreversible (Nah. 1:14; 2:13; 3:19). What a contrast both prophecies form with that of Jonah! If the traditional mid-eighth century B.C. date for Jonah is correct, things were vastly different in Nineveh at that time. Not only was it a weak and superstitious Ashur-Dan III who likely received Jonah's message, but a series of natural occurrences (plagues in 763 and 759 B.C. and a total eclipse in 763 B.C.) probably played a great part in securing the religious attention of the people. Their repentance at Jonah's preaching (Matt. 12:41) only confirmed God's proper concern for them.

However, conditions had changed radically. Assyria's rapacity, pride, and cruelty (Nah. 2:11-13; 3:8-19) demanded her destruction (Zeph. 2:13-15). Assyria had forfeited her place of divine service and turned against the Lord (Nah. 1:11-14). Although Jonah may have missed the Lord's intention for the Nineveh of his day (Jonah 4:1-3), Nahum and Zephaniah would not do so as they announced her certain and total demise.

This latter fact may reinforce the suggestion of Branson Woodard[52] that from a literary standpoint Jonah was in many ways a tragic figure. Woodard's proposal to treat Jonah from the perspective of tragedy rather than the more traditional stance of satire may be viewed all the more poignantly if one extends the tragic note to the

---

51. Nahum prophesies that those who learn of Nineveh's demise will not lament her passing (3:7) but will rejoice and clap their hands (3:19).
52. See his article "Death in Life: The Book of Jonah and OT Tragedy," *GTJ* 11 (1990).

verdict of history. Rather than being a city/nation for whom God is greatly concerned, Nineveh/Assyria is now viewed as one of the Lord's enemies (Nah. 1:2, 14; 3:5; Zeph. 2:13) whose hostility toward God has earned for her the forfeiture of divine privilege. Accordingly, whereas the situation in Jonah's day was not particularly appropriate for the vehicle of satire, Nahum can with due propriety apply satire to Nineveh's case (2:11-13; 3:8-13, 14-19). In contrast to Nahum, Zephaniah does not use satire but like Jonah announces Assyria's doom. Unlike the situation in Jonah's day, however, there is little hope of repentance at this message of judgment.

Zephaniah's prophetic pronouncement of Ninevah's doom is characteristically picturesque. He had compared the judgment of the cities of Philistia to the misery of the rejected woman and the destruction of Moab and Ammon to that of Sodom and Gomorrah. Once again his message is delivered in highly descriptive language. None who heard or read it could miss its force. God was about to bring down the loftiest empire the world had yet known and reduce its grand capital to rubble. Something of the reason for the demise of Assyria in general and of Nineveh in particular is given in v. 15. Nineveh has been a carefree city; unrivaled in power and unmatched in beauty, it rejoiced in its vast wealth and basked in its assurance of safety. How haughty she was! "I am—that is all there is." She needed no one and nothing else.[53]

Nevertheless, Nineveh would learn, as had one of her mightiest monarchs, that blasphemy and pride will be reprimanded by one who is mightier than she (cf. 2 Kings 19:22). Like that earlier king, when judgment has come full term she herself will be rewarded with the wages of her iniquity (cf. 2 Kings 19:37; Nah. 1:14b). Nineveh was once the gem of the Tigris, the crown jewel of the world's mightiest empire. So magnificent and beautiful were its buildings and grounds that "Nineveh's rivals were few in the ancient world."[54] Writers of another day, however, were unable to ascertain its location:

> About 200 years after its devastation, Xenophon passed by its site without realizing that the ruins were the remains of haughty Nineveh (*Anabasis* III, 4, 10-12). He calls the territory Mespila. Lucian (*Charon*, c. 23)

---

53. Note Isaiah's similar condemnation of Babylon (47:8-10). See also the exposition of Nah. 2:8-10, 11-13.
54. M. R. Wilson, "Nineveh," in *Major Cities of the Biblical World*, ed. R. K. Harrison (Nashville: Thomas Nelson, 1985), p. 186. See also *CAH* 3:76-79; A. T. Olmstead, *History of Assyria* (Chicago: U. of Chicago, 1951), pp. 326-36; H. W. F. Saggs, *The Might That Was Assyria* (London: Sidgwick and Jackson, 1984), pp. 98-99, 187-93; W. A. Maier, *The Book of Nahum* (reprint, Grand Rapids: Baker, 1980), pp. 93-98.

declares: "Nineveh has perished, and there is no trace left where it once was."[55]

Sic transit gloria mundi!

Additional Notes

2:13 מִדְבָּר† . . . שְׁמָמָה ("desolation" . . . "wilderness"): Although considerable difference of opinion exists as to the meaning of the latter term, its use in the OT indicates a wide semantic range. "Wilderness," "wasteland," "desert," and "steppeland" can each describe the author's intent in a given context. E. S. Kalland proposes three basic understandings for the type of topography involved: "Pastureland (Josh 2:22; Ps 65:12 [H 13]; Jer 23:10), uninhabited land (Deut 32:10; Job 38:26; Prov 21:19; Jer 9:1), and large areas of land in which oases or cities and towns exist here and there."[56] In the present case Nineveh's destruction will leave it uninhabited except as a refuge for animals and birds, and hence "wilderness" seems most appropriate.

The former term is one of several words drawn from the root שׁמם ("be desolate"). Zephaniah employs another of this word group in v. 15: שַׁמָּה ("desolation"). H. J. Austel observes that "in *shemāmâ* the stress is usually on the desolation itself, while in *shammâ* the emphasis is on the *spectacle* of the desolation, the reaction it causes."[57]

Both מִדְבָּר and שְׁמָמָה appear to be drawn from Joel 2:3 where they are used in describing conditions after a severe locust invasion. צִיָּה ("dry") adds dramatically to Zephaniah's picture of desolation. It occurs elsewhere with מִדְבָּר and/or שַׁמָּה to describe a waterless waste (e.g., Isa. 35:1), especially after divine judgment by means of an enemy invasion (e.g., Jer. 50:12-13; 51:43; Hos. 2:3 [HB 2:5]; Joel 2:20).[58]

2:14 כָּל־חַיְתוֹ־גוֹי† ("creatures of every kind"): The phrase has been greatly debated.[59] While it means something like "every creature of the nation," Zephaniah's point appears to be that in contrast to the

---

55. Maier, *Nahum*, p. 135. For similar prophetic messages of total judgment, see Isa. 13:19-22; 14:22-23; 34:10-15; Jer. 49:18, 33; 51:29, 36-37, 43.
56. E. S. Kalland, "דָּבַר," *TWOT* 1:181.
57. H. J. Austel, "שָׁמֵם," *TWOT* 2:937.
58. For Zephaniah's indebtedness to Joel elsewhere, see the additional note on 1:18. J. P. J. Olivier ("A Possible Interpretation of the Word *ṣiyyâ* in Zeph. 2, 13," *JNSL* 8 [1980]: 96) suggests on the basis of ancient Near Eastern malediction formulae that צִיָּה may be a technical term for "a ruined city inhabited only by wild beasts."
59. For details, see J. M. P. Smith, *Zephaniah*, p. 233; *Hebrew Old Testament Text Project*, 5:378. The construct chain here retains its old case marker (cf. Num. 23:18; 24:3, 15), apparently as a frozen form often occurring with חַיָּה (cf. Gen. 1:24; Pss. 50:10; 79:2; 104:11; Isa. 56:9).

mighty Assyrian nation that once lived in Nineveh, the nation that will inhabit the fallen city will be made up of every sort of creature. The word גּוֹי ("nation") is used in Joel 1:6 of a great army of locusts.

†קָאַת is included in the list of forbidden unclean birds (Lev. 11:18; Deut. 14:17). It occurs in Ps. 102:6 (HB 102:7) in parallel with כּוֹס ("owl") and in Isa. 34:11 where, as here, it is employed in combination with קִפּוֹד as well as with the raven and the יַנְשׁוּף, also considered to be a type of owl.

In addition to Isa. 34:11, קִפּוֹד is found in Isa. 14:23, where it forms part of the divine sentence in turning Babylon into a swampland. Suggested cognates in Syriac, Arabic, and Ethiopic all tend to indicate a porcupine (hedgehog) as the animal named here (cf. LXX), but such an identification is difficult on the basis of the words associated with swampland in Isa. 14:23 and with the list of birds in Isa. 34:11. The proposed translation "bittern" (Hitzig, G. A. Smith, Soncino) lacks support in either the ancient versions or the cognate languages.

Contemporary scholarship tends to favor a type of owl for both words.[60] The translation tentatively followed here is that of the NIV.

†קוֹל יְשׁוֹרֵר: The phrase is variously translated in the English versions that follow the MT: "their calls will echo" (NIV), "birds will sing" (NASB), "their voice shall sing" (KJV, NKJV). Keil insists that the phrase

> cannot be rendered "a voice sings," for *shōrēr*, to sing, is not used for tuning or resounding; but *yeshōrēr* is to be taken relatively, and as subordinate to קוֹל, the voice of him that sings will be heard in the window. Jerome gives it correctly: *vox canentis in fenestra*.[61]

My translation takes קוֹל as an interjection (cf. Zeph. 1:14) and understands the writer to be calling attention to the strange contrast between the sound of birds singing in the windows and the ruin encountered in the rubble along the threshold. If Keil's dictum is to be followed, it may be translated, "Listen! (There is) one who is singing." On the whole, however, the proposed translation appears simplest.

†חֹרֶב ("rubble"): In addition to the alternative reading עֹרֵב ("raven") noted above, other suggestions include חֶרֶב ("sword"—Aquila, Symmachus, Pesh.; "axe"—Sabottka) and חָרָב ("bustard"—NEB).

The final line of the verse has fared little better. Indeed, at first sight the statement does not seem to fit the previous lines well. J. M. P. Smith declares that it "has no relation to the immediate

---

60. See the helpful discussion by Sabottka (*Zephanja*, pp. 96-97), who terms them "screech owl" and "owl" respectively. See also David Clark, "Of Beasts and Birds: Zephaniah 2, 14," *BT* 34 (1982): 243-46.
61. Keil, *Minor Prophets*, 2:148.

context."[62] The MT, however, makes tolerable sense as it stands; the action of stripping bare the cedar work helps to account for the previously mentioned accumulation of debris. כִּי is best understood causally, although it could be taken as an asseverative particle;[63] אַרְזָה ("cedar work") may be understood as a collective noun;[64] and עֵרָה ("he will lay bare") is to be viewed as a verb in the piel stem employed as a prophetic perfect in the sense of "stripping off."[65]

2:15 †וְאַפְסִי עוֹד ("and there is no one else"): The final י in וְאַפְסִי is probably not a 1st com. sing. suffix, hence "besides me" as has often been proposed (NASB, KJV, NKJV), a meaning the form bears nowhere else, but is an example of *hiriq compaginis* or *paragogic yodh*.[66] אֶפֶס is frequently found in negative sentences; it also occurs elsewhere with עוֹד (e.g., 2 Sam. 9:3).

אֵיךְ ("what!"): H. Wolf reports that this word is usually used in rhetorical questions to indicate either reproach (Judg. 16:15), despair (1 Sam. 1:19), amazement (Isa. 14:4), horror (Ps. 73:19), or desire (Jer. 3:19).[67] Several of these senses could fit here.

†יָנִיעַ יָדוֹ ("he will wave his hand"): The gesture is one of contempt, but the translation "shake his fist" (NKJV; cf. NIV, R. Smith, J. M. P. Smith) may be too explicit.

2. ON JERUSALEM (3:1-7)

Zephaniah concludes his messages on judgment by turning to his own nation and to the holy city in particular.

Translation

Woe to her who is rebellious and defiled,
 the oppressive city!
²She is not obedient;
 she does not receive correction*;
she does not trust in the LORD;
 she does not draw near to her God.

---

62. J. M. P. Smith, *Zephaniah*, p. 234; G. A. Smith (*Twelve Prophets*, 2:64) omits the words altogether (cf. *BHS*).
63. So Sabottka (*Zephanja*, pp. 97-98) who, however, finds in the words בַּסַּף כִּי אַרְזָה עֵרָה an idiomatic expression of the extent of the destruction: "from the threshold right up to the cedar beams."
64. Some suggest reading אַרְזָה here, thus "her cedar work" (RSV; G. A. Smith, *Twelve Prophets*, 2:64n.2).
65. The form עֵרָה apparently lies behind the translation "will be laid bare" (RSV; cf. NJB).
66. See GKC, par. 90 1; 152s; cf. Isa. 47:8, 10.
67. See H. Wolf, "אֵי," *TWOT* 1:35 under the discussion of *'êk*.

³Her officials* in her midst are roaring lions;
  her judges* are wolves in the evening
    who leave nothing for the morning.
⁴Her prophets are arrogant,
  (they are) treacherous men*;
her priests profane the sanctuary,
  they violate the law.
⁵The LORD is righteous in her midst;
  He does no injustice.
Morning by morning He brings His justice to light,
  He/it does not fail;
  yet the unrighteous know no shame.
⁶"I have cut off nations;
  their strongholds* are destroyed.
I have made their streets desolate,
  with no one passing through;
their cities are devastated,
  with no one left—not a single inhabitant.
⁷I said, 'Surely you will fear Me,
  you will receive correction';
therefore her dwelling* will not be cut off
  with all that I have appointed for her.
However,* they eagerly remained corrupt*
  in all their deeds."

Exegesis and Exposition

In delivering his pronouncement against Jerusalem, Zephaniah utilizes the form of the woe oracle, including invective (v. 1), reason (criticism) for Judah's punishment (vv. 2-4), and implied threat (vv. 5-7).

The invective begins with a woe* in which Zephaniah calls Judah's capital a "rebellious" and "defiled" city where "oppression" is the order of the day. The three terms describe a lifestyle and social structure at variance with the character and laws of God. Each is amplified in the criticism that follows.

Invective (v. 1)	*Criticism (vv. 2-4)*
Woe to Jerusalem:	
1. The rebellious city	It accepts neither God's law nor His Person (v. 2)
2. The defiled city	Its religious leaders profane God's standards (v. 4)
3. The tyrannical city	Its civic leaders oppress the people (v. 3)

357

(1) Jerusalem is rebellious.* The Hebrew word is employed by the prophets of the rebellion of God's people against Him and His commandments (cf. Isa. 3:8; 63:10; Lam. 1:18). Thus Jeremiah charges that the people are stubborn and rebellious (Jer. 4:17) and that their leaders have kept them from fearing God, thereby causing them to turn away from God so as to miss His good purpose for them (Jer. 5:23-25). The nation has neither obeyed God nor responded to His correction (Jer. 7:21-28; cf. 11:6-8; 22:21). Ezekiel reminds his hearers of Israel's penchant for impiety (Ezek. 20:8, 13, 20). Because that sin was perpetuated in their day, it would bring God's outstretched arm and outpoured wrath against them (Ezek. 20:30-38). Zephaniah's point is much the same. He charges God's people with refusing to obey God's commandments and with unwillingness to learn from chastisement (v. 2).

Zephaniah goes to the heart of the problem by noting the cause of Jerusalem's willfulness. She has neither concern nor time for God and His standards. As J. M. P. Smith points out, "The implication is that Jerusalem has had recourse to everything and everybody but Yahweh."[68] P. C. Craigie adds: "The city's arrogance was such that it would listen to no advice and accept no words of correction. . . . It had abandoned trust in the very God that gave the city its *raison d'être*."[69]

The seriousness of Jerusalem's spiritual condition is underscored by Zephaniah's choice of word order (MT): "In the Lord she does not trust; unto her God she does not draw near." Jerusalem needed to get her priorities in order, for misplaced trust in self is no trust at all. She needed to trust in God and let Him be the focus of her life (cf. Deut. 4:5-7; Pss. 84:12 [HB 84:13]; 119:169; 125:1; Prov. 3:5-6; Isa. 26:3-4).

(2) Jerusalem is a defiled city. Zephaniah points an accusing finger at Jerusalem's religious leadership, those most responsible for the spiritual and moral fiber of the populace (v. 4). Her prophets, who should be God's spokesmen, are nonprophets (cf. Jer. 23:9-39). Their arrogance knows no bounds. Carried away by selfish conceit and personal ambition, they produce pompous pronouncements filled with idle boasting, platitudes, and lies. Craigie observes that such men abandon "the sanctity of their task . . . prostrating it to their personal ends."[70]

The priests are no better (cf. Jer. 2:8; 5:31; 6:13; 23:11). They who

---

68. J. M. P. Smith, *Zephaniah*, p. 238.
69. P. C. Craigie, *Twelve Prophets*, 2:123.
70. Ibid., 2:125. Craigie goes on to remark: "In Zephaniah's time, just as in our own, there were those persons engaged in the 'ministry of the Word' who had seen and exploited its possibilities for personal gain."

were charged with the purity of God's house and the sanctity of His law (1 Chron. 23:28; Deut. 31:9-13) have violated both. Ezekiel (Ezek. 22:26) will repeat the same charges, pointing out that conditions in his day have only worsened, for the priests willfully profane all that is sacred. As Feinberg remarks,

> Instead of teaching and upholding the law of God, they made it their business to blot out every God-given distinction between profane and holy. They belied their calling in particular after particular with the result that, instead of being magnified in His holy requirements, the Lord was profaned among them.[71]

(3) Jerusalem is a city filled with oppression.* Its source is the civic and social leadership (v. 3). With bold metaphors Zephaniah exposes Jerusalem's leaders for what they are. The nobles who serve as her officials and judges have betrayed their privileged positions. They who should be fair and impartial have become like ravenous beasts—roaring lions (cf. Prov. 28:15; Ezek. 22:25; Nah. 2:12) who take as their prey the possessions of the poor and the lives of the citizens, and wolves that prowl about in the evening gobbling up their unsuspecting prey and crushing them so thoroughly that none of their bones is left in the morning.[72] Thus justice is perverted in the insatiable greed of Jerusalem's leadership. Concerning these two groups of officials Craigie points out:

> The officials . . . used the power of their positions to gain their own ends, wielding their government office to satisfy their perpetual craving for wealth and power. . . . The only interest the judges had in the law was in the profit it could be made to bring them.[73]

In those dire days when Josiah was yet too young to deal effectively with a corrupt officialdom, the situation looked bleak indeed. With the passing of that king, who knew no peer in his concern for the law of God (2 Kings 23:25), an entrenched leadership would prevail and hasten the demise of the nation (cf. Jer. 23:1-4, 11-12; Ezek. 22:23-29). Everything rises or falls with leadership. When a nation is governed by godly individuals, their leadership provides benefits that are as welcome as a warming sun that rises at the start of a new day or comes out after a refreshing shower (cf. 2 Sam. 23:3-4). But the ship of state that is piloted by a corrupt captain is a danger to itself and all those aboard it.

---

71. C. L. Feinberg, *The Prophecy of Ezekiel* (Chicago: Moody, 1969), p. 129.
72. For a discussion of the term "wolves of the evening," see K. Elliger, "Das ende der 'Abendwolfe' Zeph 3, 3, Hab 1, 8," in *Festschrift A. Bertholet*, ed. W. Baumgartner (Tübingen: J. C. B. Mohr, 1950), pp. 158-74; Sabottka, *Zephanja*, pp. 104-5.
73. Craigie, *Twelve Prophets*, p. 174.

Zephaniah reminds his hearers of Him who is ultimately Judah's leader (vv. 5-7; cf. Jer. 23:1-8). In contrast to Jerusalem's corrupt leadership, the Lord is righteous* altogether. Unlike the wicked who know no shame, He does no iniquity. With the light of each new day He brings evidence of His unfailing justice, not only in His kindly acts of providence but, as Keil suggests, "by causing His law and justice to be proclaimed to the nation daily by prophets," who serve Him faithfully and call the nation to repentance.[74]

Something of God's righteousness may also be seen in His merciful dealings with His people in attempting to woo them back to Himself (vv. 6-7). If Judah were but to look about her, she would see the evidence. God has cut off nation after nation, not only for their sins but also on behalf of the needs of His own people. Nations and cities with their massive defenses have been destroyed and left destitute.

Doubtless Zephaniah could have pointed to many such examples (cf. Nah. 3:8). Even the Northern Kingdom of Israel had suffered such a judgment. Surely it could be expected that Judah would observe all of this and learn a lesson (cf. 2 Chron. 36:15-16). But such had not proved to be the case (cf. 2 Kings 17:6-20; Jer. 3:6-10; Ezek. 23). Rather than demonstrating a desire for repentance, Judah and Jerusalem displayed only an increased bent for shameless corruption.

The word translated "eagerly" reveals something of the degradation of late-seventh-century B.C. Judahite society. The Hebrew verb שָׁכַם (šākam, always appearing in the hiphil) is generally conceded to be a denominative from a noun meaning "shoulder." Although older translators rendered the verb "start, rise early" (e.g., BDB), more recent translators tend to favor a derived nuance such as "eagerness," "diligence," "continuity." Doubtless this is the basic idea of the verb. Nevertheless, the more traditional understanding remains helpful. Jeremiah employs the verb 11 times to picture God's eagerness to meet with His people. He rose, as it were, to be on hand at the beginning of each day, longing to meet with them—but to no avail. Zephaniah reports that the people were eager, "rose early," only to corrupt their ways further. It is small wonder that Judah's end would not be long in coming. Perhaps those who claim God as king in our generation would be well advised to "make an early start" in meeting with Him who "rises early" to meet with His people.[75]

Although this section of the book, with its attention to the judg-

---

74. Keil, *Minor Prophets*, 2:151.
75. The morning hour is often commended as an ideal time for meeting with God to find direction and strength for the day (e.g., Pss. 5:3 [HB 5:4]; 88:13 [HB 88:14]; 92:1-2 [HB 92:2-3]; 143:8; Mark 1:35).

ment of the nations and the pronouncement of woe upon Jerusalem, has not been encouraging, Zephaniah's prophesying is not yet complete. Before the final word has been said, his readers will come to understand that the day of the Lord's judgment, dark though it will be, is but the path to a brighter day.

Additional Notes

3:1 As the pronouncement against Assyria centered on Nineveh, so the message against Judah has its focus on Jerusalem. "City" (2:15; 3:1) thus serves as the stitch-word between the foreign nations prophecies (2:4-15) and the prophecy against God's people (3:1-7).

For the use of woe oracles, see the additional note on Nah. 3:1.

Victor Hamilton demonstrates that the Hebrew root for "*rebellious*" (מָרָה) is used in all but five cases of Israel's rebellion against God or His commandments, whether in word or deed. Since a word is often known by the company it keeps, Hamilton's list of Hebrew words that are used in conjunction with מרה is instructive: *sôrēr*, "stubborn"; *ʿāṣab*, "to hurt/grieve"; *māʾēn*, "to refuse"; *pāšaʿ*, "to rebel/transgress"; *nāʾaṣ*, "to scorn"; *ḥāṭāʾ*, "to sin"; *nāsâ*, "to test"; *mārad*, "to rebel"; *māʾas*, "to reject"; *ḥālal*, "to profane."[76]

As for Judah's second unsavory quality, that of being *defiled*, though the Hebrew root may be employed of defilement in general (Isa. 63:3), it is used often of religious defilement or disqualification (Ezra 2:62; Neh. 7:64; Mal. 1:7), particularly of the misdeeds of Israel's priesthood (Neh. 13:29).

The third charge against Judah is that of *oppression*. The Hebrew word יָנָה ("oppress") is utilized in a variety of ways but most frequently of intolerance toward or the suppression of the rights and privileges of others. It especially characterizes the rich and influential members of society who take advantage of the less fortunate (cf. Ex. 22:21 [HB 22:20]; Lev. 19:23; Deut. 23:16 [HB 23:17]).

3:2 †By מוּסָר ("chastisement") is meant the several instances of affliction and rebuke that God sends into the lives of His own to accomplish their correction and spiritual growth (Prov. 1:7-8; 3:11-12). Like Zephaniah, Jeremiah laments the people's failure to profit from God's chastening (Jer. 5:3; 7:28).

3:3 †For שָׂרִים ("officials/nobles"), see the additional note on 1:8. The term שֹׁפֵט ("judge") was used of those leaders of Israel to whom were entrusted civic as well as judicial responsibilities. In time the latter sense became the dominant one, especially from Samuel on-

---

76. See Victor Hamilton, "מָרָה," *TWOT* 1:526; see further R. Knierim, "מרה," *THAT* 1:928-30.

ward (cf. 1 Sam. 7:15-17; 8:1-2).[77] These two terms, along with the mentioning of prophets and priests in v. 4, served as the focal point for Ezekiel's adaptation of Zeph. 3:3-4 for his denunciation of God's people and land (Ezek. 22:25-28).[78]

3:4 †פֹּחֲזִים ("arrogant"): Conrad von Orelli observes that the Hebrew root means "to overcook"; hence, the prophets are those who boil over with personal desire.[79] Jeremiah (Jer. 23:32) uses the root to describe the prophets' deceit. He charges them with falsehood of every kind (Jer. 23:30-32).

†בֹּגְדוֹת ("treacherous"): The word carries with it not only an indication of the lying deceit of Jerusalem's prophets (cf. Jer. 28:1-17; 29:21-23) but the implication that such activity stems from a wanton disregard for God and His truth. As Keil points out, the root itself is "the classical word for faithless adultery or apostasy from God."[80]

3:5 For the concept *"righteous"* (or *"just"*), see the Excursus on Habakkuk 2:4. The term מִשְׁפָּט ("justice") used in a following line is a wordplay on שֹׁפְטֶיהָ ("her judges") in v. 3. Keil observes that the term involves more than rendering a righteous verdict; it includes "a righteous state of things."[81] For עַוְלָה ("injustice"), see the additional note on Hab. 2:12.

3:6 †פִּנּוֹת ("strongholds") was rendered "corner towers" in 1:16 and, as the key point in the defensive wall, may be the best under-

---

77. For a discussion of the West Semitic root behind the term, see A. Marzal, "The Provincial Governor at Mari: His Title and Appointment," *JNES* 30 (1971): 186-94; see also P. Fronzaroli, "*Šāpiṭu* 'una autorità tribale, con funzioni di giudice ma non esclusivamente,'" *Archivo Glottologico Italiano* 45 (1960): 51-54. For excellent discussions of the root שפט and the judicial system in earliest Israel, see R. D. Culver, *Toward a Biblical View of Civil Government* (Chicago: Moody, 1974), pp. 138-50. See also G. Liedke, "שפט," *THAT* 2:999-1009; L. J. Wood, *Distressing Days of the Judges* (Grand Rapids: Zondervan, 1975), pp. 4-6.

78. Michael Fishbane (*Biblical Interpretation in Ancient Israel* [Oxford: Clarendon, 1985], p. 463) singles out Ezekiel's use of Zephaniah as a classic case of inner biblical exegesis: "For in this case reacting to the iniquity of his time, the inspired prophet drew upon a fixed form and phraseology—learned and studied in the schools—and added to them older and idiosyncratic verbal elements which seemed to suit the situation and more exactly specify the general imagery used. By this exegetical *traditio* and older *traditum* derived from Zephaniah's prophecies came a new *traditum* in Ezekiel's hands. And by virtue of this *traditio* which wove into Zeph. 3:3-4 various authoritative phrases from legal and prophetic sources, the denunciations in Ezek. 22:25-28 acquire a double force."

79. Conrad von Orelli, *The Twelve Minor Prophets*, trans. J. S. Banks (reprint, Minneapolis: Klock and Klock, 1977), p. 274.

80. Keil, *Minor Prophets*, 2:150. See further M. A. Klopfenstein, "בגד," *THAT* 1:262-63; S. Erlandsson, "בָּגַד," *TDOT* 1:470-73.

81. Keil, *Minor Prophets*, 2:57.

standing here also. The translation above takes the term as a synec-doche and follows the NIV.

3:7 †מְעוֹנָהּ ("her dwelling"): Another case of enallage occurs here, the shift being from 2d fem. sing. to 3d fem. sing. as the sentence moves from direct to indirect address. The LXX and Pesh. apparently repointed to מֵעֵינֶיהָ ("from her eyes/sight"), a reading followed by G. A. Smith and J. M. P. Smith (cf. *BHS;* NJB; RSV). Such an understanding forces one to take the following פָּקַד in the sense of "visit" or "instruct/charge."[82] The MT, however, makes good sense as it stands. God's concern was for Jerusalem's repentance so that in the coming judgment total destruction could be avoided.

†אָכֵן ("however"): This strong asseverative particle sometimes is employed to indicate emphatic contrast, *"but indeed, but in fact,* esp. after אָמַרְתִּי *I said* or *thought,* expressing the reality, in opp. to what had been wrongly imagined."[83] Although God had made no mistake in His evaluation, looking at things from a human perspective one could have hoped that all of God's actions would have occasioned Jerusalem's repentance. The opposite had proved to be the case. The following two verbs should be taken as hendiadys: "They (all the more) eagerly corrupted (remained corrupt in) all their deeds."

---

82. See A. R. Hulst, *Old Testament Translation Problems* (Leiden: Brill, 1960), p. 255.
83. BDB, p. 38.

3

Additional Details Concerning the Day of the Lord, Part Two (Zephaniah 3:8-20)

Based on the long series of pronouncements concerning the foreign nations (2:4-15) and the city of Jerusalem (3:1-7), Zephaniah again has a strong exhortation for his people. They should wait patiently and trustingly for God to effect His worldwide judgment (3:8). The prophet goes on to give further teachings concerning the Day of the Lord, whose coming he had so vividly portrayed (1:14-18). The judgment was but part of God's plan to secure an obedient and purified people for Himself (3:9-13) who can rejoice in their divine Redeemer and sing His praises to the ends of the earth (3:14-20).

Structurally, 3:8-13 could be viewed as forming one unit, the imperative of v. 8 being continued by two motive clauses introduced by the particle כִּי (*kî*, "for/because," vv. 8, 9). The first would provide a negative reason for waiting for the Lord, the second a positive one. But the close correspondence between vv. 9-13 and 14-18 with relation to future matters, signaled by the phrase "in that day" (vv. 11, 16), argues for the transitional nature of v. 8 as a hinge verse that picks up the theme of judgment of the previous section (note מִשְׁפָּט, *mišpāṭ*, in vv. 5, 8) and provides the basis for the encouraging teaching in vv. 9-13 (note the stitching effect of the particle כִּי, *kî*, "for" in vv. 8, 9). The closing verses of the book are accomplished with striking examples of the prophet's use of repetition and refrain (vv. 14-15) and personification (vv. 14-16) designed to magnify the glad conditions associated with Zion's regathering and revivication (vv. 14-20).

B. AN EXHORTATION BASED ON JUDGMENT (3:8)

Translation

"Therefore wait for Me," declares the LORD,
  "for the day when I rise up as a witness*.
For My decision* is to gather the nations,
  to assemble the kingdoms,
    (and) to pour out My indignation* upon them—
    all My burning anger*.
Yes, in the fire of My jealousy*
  all the earth will be consumed."

Exegesis and Exposition

In light of the waves of certain judgment that will flow over the nations and wash away Jerusalem in their wake, God exhorts His people: "Wait for me." In a vivid and varied metaphor the prophet portrays a courtroom scene in which God rises first as witness (cf. Deut. 8:19; 1 Sam. 12:5; Job 16:19; Ps. 50:7; Jer. 29:23; Mic. 1:2; Mal. 3:5; Heb. 6:13) on His own behalf and before the assemblage, and then presides as judge (cf. Gen. 18:25; Judg. 11:27; 1 Sam. 2:10; 1 Chron. 16:33; Job 9:15; Pss. 7:11 [HB 7:12]; 50:6; 75:7 [HB 75:8]; Isa. 33:2) to deliver His righteous sentence (cf. Pss. 72:2; 75:2 [HB 75:3]).

The motif of God as judge is a familiar one in the OT. Indeed, God's coming to judge the earth is often declared (e.g., 1 Chron. 16:33; Pss. 9:8 [HB 9:9]; 50:4; 96:13; 98:9; 110:6; cf. Isa. 2:4; 11:3-4; Mic. 4:3). The language in Zephaniah is reminiscent of Pss. 82:8; 94:2. Here God confirms His decision to assemble all nations and peoples for judgment (cf. Isa. 13:9-11; 66:16; Jer. 25:31-33; Ezek. 36:5; 38:1–39:24; Joel 3:9-16 [HB 4:9-16]; Zech. 14:2-20).

God's intentions are here called His "indignation," His "burning anger," and "the fire of [His] jealousy," terms describing His righteous hatred of sin and concern for His holy name and reputation and for His people (cf. Isa. 66:13-16). And herein lay a message of hope. Because God's judgment of the nations was so often linked with His concern for the salvation of His people, the righteous citizens of Jerusalem could take comfort. God's justice would avenge them; could it not also mean the possibility of intervention on their behalf? In light of God's great promises (cf. Isa. 30:18-33; 33:22; 64:4 [HB 64:3]), even the exhortation "wait for me" carried a note of hope. It was "only used for waiting in a believing attitude for the Lord and His help (Ps. xxxiii.20; Isa. viii.17, xxx.18, lxiv.3)."[1] It was just such a hope that Zephaniah would deliver in the sections that follow.

---

1. C. F. Keil, *The Twelve Minor Prophets*, COT (Grand Rapids: Eerdmans, 1954), 2:153; cf. Hab. 2:3; 3:16-18.

Additional Notes

3:8 According to the Masora, this is the only verse in the OT that contains all the letters of the Hebrew alphabet, including the final forms. However, שׂ is not considered a separate grapheme from שׁ.

†לְעַד ("as a witness," lit. "for a prey/booty"; so NASB, KJV; cf. NKJV): The translation adopted here follows the LXX, the Pesh., and many scholars and versions (e.g., RSV, NEB; cf. *BHS*) in repointing the MT to read לְעֵד. In a similar vein the NIV suggests "to testify" and the NJB translates "as accuser."[2] Sabottka also repoints the MT, rendering it לְעַד and translating "from my throne."[3] In this he has followed M. Dahood and others who compare Ugaritic ʿd "throne-(room)."[4] This proposal necessitates understanding the preposition ל as "from," a meaning often found in Ugaritic.[5]

At first blush this latter suggestion seems attractive. Nevertheless, however good a case may be made for the meaning "throne" for Hebrew עד, none of the examples proposed by Dahood contains the required phrase לְעַד. Further, the meaning "from" for ל must depend on more than supposed examples of the free interchange between ל and other prepositions with the same semantic range or evidence based upon proposed contextual solutions.[6] The word for "throne" in the OT is כִּסֵּא, and the act of rising from or going down from the throne is expressed by the preposition מִן (e.g., Isa. 14:9; Jer. 3:6) or מִן in combination with עַל (e.g., Judg. 3:20; Ezek. 26:16).

In sum, however tolerable a sense "rise from the throne" may yield here, it does not find support either in normal OT usage or in the employment of the throne motif. An interesting theological translation is reflected in the Vg, which, while retaining the MT, goes off in still another direction: "in my resurrection in the future."

†מִשְׁפָּטִי ("my decision," lit. "my judgment") serves as a stitch-word with the previous section. For זַעַם ("indignation"), see the additional note on Hab. 3:12; for חָרוֹן ("burning anger"), see the additional note on 2:2. The phrase "the fire of My jealousy" occurs in 1:18. "Jealousy" often expresses God's being moved to action on behalf of

---

2. My colleague Brent Sandy reports to me that this is one of 196 times that the LXX reading is taken over the MT by the NIV.

3. L. Sabottka, *Zephanja* (Rome: Biblical Institute, 1972), pp. 113-14.

4. M. Dahood, *Psalms*, AB (Garden City, N.Y.: Doubleday, 1964), 2:81-82; 3:113; see also "Hebrew-Ugaritic Lexicography VII," *Bib* 50 (1969): 347. For Ugaritic ʿd, C. Gordon (*UT*, p. 453) proposes the meaning "throne room."

5. See Dahood, *Psalms*, 3:394-95; C. F. Whitley, "Some Functions of the Hebrew Particles *Beth* and *Lamedh*," *JQR* 62 (1972): 205-6.

6. For a cautious appraisal of the relation of the Hebrew prepositions, see M. D. Futato, "The Preposition 'Beth' in the Hebrew Psalter," *WTJ* 41 (1978): 68-81.

His own (cf. Joel 2:18), and hence the LXX and Vg translate "My zeal" here. See also the additional note on Nah. 1:2.

C. ADDITIONAL TEACHINGS CONCERNING THE DAY OF THE LORD (3:9-20)

Verses 9-20 have been traditionally considered as a distinctive unit. So construed, this section falls into two portions (vv. 9-13, 14-20) linked together by the phrase "in that day" (vv. 11, 16) and the ideas of scattering (vv. 10, 19) and being afraid/fearing (vv. 13, 16). Such a view likewise finds support from the first half of the book, which is also closed by information concerning the Day of the Lord (1:14-18) and instructions based upon it (2:1-3).

1. INFORMATION CONCERNING THAT DAY (3:9-13)

Translation

"For then will I give* to the people pure lips,
   in order that all of them may call on the name of the LORD
   (and) serve Him shoulder to shoulder*.
¹⁰From beyond the rivers of Cush*
   My worshipers* shall bring My scattered ones* as My tribute*.
¹¹In that day you will not be put to shame*
   by all your wrongdoings that you have done to Me.
For then I will remove from your midst
   your proud boasters*,
and you will never again be haughty
   on My holy mountain.
¹²But I will leave within you
   a humble and lowly people,
   and they will trust in the name of the LORD.
¹³The remnant of Israel will do no injustice;
   neither will they speak a lie,
   nor will a deceitful tongue
      be found in their mouths.
Yes,* they will feed and lie down,
   and no one will make them afraid."

Exegesis and Exposition

Structurally, vv. 9-13 provide a further reason for the exhortation to wait for the Lord (v. 8). The first reason (found in v. 8) had to do with God's determination to gather the nations for the long-awaited judgment. The second now deals with the promises of God to a humble and purified future remnant. Both reasons are introduced by the

particle כִּי (*kî*, "because/for"), the one in v. 9 being supplemented by
the temporal particle אָז (*'āz*, "then").[7] This section thus carries the
author's thoughts to information concerning a future day that will
provide the grounds for the closing admonitions of the book (3:14-20).

Zephaniah's goal in vv. 9-13 is didactic. He will provide additional information concerning the fate of God's people in the coming
Day of the Lord. It is a message of hope. As indicated previously,
critical scholarship has at times denied the authenticity of these
verses (and all of vv. 9-20) due to their strong emphasis on hope.
Verses 9-10 have seemed particularly troublesome. Thus J. M. P.
Smith remarks:

> VV. [9, 10] constitute a disturbing element within this oracle. They seem to
> be foreign to, if not also later than, their present context; . . . they man-
> ifest a totally different attitude toward the nations from that of v.[8]. In the
> latter, the nations are destined to be destroyed; here they are to be con-
> verted. . . . Still further, the elimination of vv. [9, 10] leaves a good connec-
> tion between vv. [9] and [11].[8]

Despite the critical objections, judgment and hope are often twin
themes. Certainly such is the case in our seventh-century B.C. minor
prophets. All three have strong words of judgment (Nah. 1:1-6, 8-10;
2:1-10, 11-13; 3:1-7, 8-13, 14-19; Hab. 1:5-11; 2:6-20; 3:3-7, 8-15; Zeph.
1:2-6, 7-13, 14-18; 2:4-15; 3:17-18) but also of hope and reassurance
(Nah. 1:7; Hab. 2:4-5, 3:16-19; Zeph. 2:1-3; 3:9-20). Even more significantly, all three prophets demonstrate that because judgment is an
integral part of God's teleological program designed to bless His
people and His world, it is in a sense a veiled hope.

Thus Nahum's predictions against Nineveh indicated that her
judgment was a means of deliverance for Judah (Nah. 1:11-15); the
news of Nineveh's fall was an indication of better things to come for
all people (Nah. 1:15; 2:13; 3:7, 19). Habakkuk's prophecies of the
judgment upon both Judah (Hab. 1:5-11) and Babylon (Hab. 2:6-20)
were part of God's process of allowing the character of all people to be
fully displayed (Hab. 2:4-5), while God Himself was declared in control of the disposition of the ages and every individual (Hab. 2:20;
3:3-15). Indeed, it is He who works out the salvation and blessing of
His people (Hab. 3:12-13) and all who know Him (Hab. 2:14) through
the drama of earth's history. Likewise, Zephaniah points out that
judgment can bring hope and assurance to God's people (Zeph. 2:6-7,

---

7. The close relation of vv. 8 and 9 is also indicated by the words קָנָה (v. 8) and
קָרָא (v. 9) that often occur in juxtaposition. See M. Dahood, "Ugaritic-
Hebrew Parallel Pairs," *RSP* 1:326.
8. J. M. P. Smith, *A Critical and Exegetical Commentary on Zephaniah and
Nahum*, ICC (Edinburgh: T. and T. Clark, 1911), p. 252n. See also the discussion in the introduction under Unity.

9-11). The double emphasis on judgment and hope is prominent in Zeph. 3:9-20.

Judgment and hope, then, rather than being irreconcilable themes, are two aspects of one divine perspective. Both are designed and intertwined to accomplish God's purposes. Zephaniah's concluding verses, far from being out of place, are neither unexpected nor contextually inappropriate. As. P. C. Craigie observes,

> the prophet Zephaniah thus gives us a view of the future which is part despair, part hope. . . . The source of the prophet's despair was to be found in his understanding of human nature and human states; the source of his hope was to be found in God.[9]

In these verses Zephaniah turns from judgment to its outcome— God's blessing of the people of the world. God's goal is to effect change in the hearts and lives of all. Such indeed will take place—but not just for Israel; rather, all people shall be transformed so as to call on the Lord (cf. Isa. 55:5) and serve Him as one (cf. 2 Chron. 14:16-17; Isa. 59:19-21).[10] To "call on the name of the Lord" means to invoke his name in belief, submission, and supplication (cf. Gen. 4:26; 12:8; 2 Kings 5:11).[11] All of this God's worshipers will do, and that with "pure lips." Their desire will be to serve Him in sincere devotion as one—"shoulder to shoulder." T. Laetsch observes:

> As the lips of Isaiah, the sinful member of a sinful people, had been purified by the fiery coal from the altar typifying the Cross of Calvary, so the Lord will change the impure lips of Gentile nations by the preaching of this Cross. . . . All will put their shoulder to His service in joyful gratitude for His salvation.[12]

---

9. P. C. Craigie, *Twelve Prophets* (Philadelphia: Westminster, 1985), 2:129-30. Although W. Eichrodt (*Theology of the Old Testament*, trans. J. A. Baker [Philadelphia: Westminster, 1961], 1:379n.2) rightly cautions that the reality of Israel's hope in no way minimized the seriousness and severity of her imminent judgment, it is hope through judgment that gives full force to Zephaniah's instructions to his people. From a literary standpoint, 3:9-20 forms the necessary corollary to the book's opening announcement of judgment, and taken together both passages illustrate Zephaniah's penchant for the employment of reversal as a literary technique.

10. For the Pauline perspective on the completion of the salvation of Jews and Gentiles, see the remarks of C. E. B. Cranfield, *A Critical and Exegetical Commentary on the Epistle to the Romans*, ICC (Edinburgh: T. and T. Clark, 1979), 2:572-88. For the universal hope of salvation for all people as a basic tenet of OT teaching, see P. E. Hughes, *Interpreting Prophecy* (Grand Rapids: Eerdmans, 1976), pp. 61-62; J. Barton Payne, *The Theology of the Older Testament* (Grand Rapids: Zondervan, 1962), pp. 188-94.

11. See C. F. Keil and F. Delitzsch, *The Pentateuch*, COT (Grand Rapids: Eerdmans, 1956), 1:119-20.

12. Theo. Laetsch, *The Minor Prophets* (St. Louis: Concordia, 1956), p. 377.

As proof of their new love for God, the Gentiles will bring to Him His covenant people (Isa. 66:20). From the farthest reaches of the world, wherever they have been scattered in judgment (Deut. 28:64-68), God's people will be returned to the land of promise (Deut. 4:27-31; Isa. 11:11-16) and enjoy God's richest blessings (Isa. 66:7-14). Further, all people shall know God (Hab. 2:14) and enjoy His everlasting beneficence (Isa. 2:1-4; 11:1-10; Mic. 4:1-5). Here again Zephaniah has called on earlier Canaanite literature, drawing from a context set in the contest between Yamm and Baal. In this instance, Baal was to be handed over to Yamm and sent to him as tribute:

> "Thy slave is Baal, O Yamm,
>   Thy slave is Baal [for eve]r,
> Dagon's Son is thy captive;
>   He shall be brought as thy tribute.
> For the gods bring [thy gift],
>   The holy ones are thy tributaries."[13]

The literary allusion here is rendered certain by the concatenation of words taken from that text: עֶבֶד (*'ebed*, "servant/slave"); יָבַל (*yābal*, "bring"); מִנְחָה (*minḥâ*, "tribute/offering").

The awareness of this literary setting provides the clue to solving the debate as to whether the words עֲתָרַי בַּת־פּוּצַי (*'ătāray bat-pûṣay*, "my worshipers, my scattered ones") should be taken as referring to the same group and what is the proper subject of "bring." According to one commonly held view, God's dispersed people are represented here as bringing an offering to God. Such is the verdict of the English versions, and it has the support of some expositors.[14] Other scholars (e.g., Fausset, Feinberg, Keil, Laetsch) suggest, however, that what is in view is an embassy of converted Gentiles bringing the Jews to God as an offering or tribute. In both views "my scattered ones" is taken to be in apposition to "my worshipers."

Based on the literary parallel, the scriptural indications concerning the conversion of the Gentiles, and the context, I propose that "my worshipers" is the subject of the verb "bring," "my scattered ones" is its object, and "my tribute" is a second accusative to be translated "as my tribute."[15] Thus, just as Baal was to be Yamm's servant and sent as tribute to him, so converted Gentiles who "call

---

13. *ANET*, p. 130. For the Ugaritic text itself, see *UT*, pp. 197-98, Text 137, lines 36-38. See further Dahood, "Ugaritic-Hebrew Parallel Pairs," *RSP* 3:119-20; Sabottka, *Zephanja*, pp. 121-22.
14. See, e.g., C. von Orelli, *The Twelve Minor Prophets*, trans. J. S. Banks (reprint, Minneapolis: Klock and Klock, 1977), p. 277; E. B. Pusey, *The Minor Prophets* (Grand Rapids: Baker, 1953), 2:284-85.
15. See GKC par. 117cc, ff.

upon the name of the Lord" and "serve Him shoulder to shoulder" will be "My worshipers" who will "bring My scattered ones" (the Jews) as "My tribute."

Zephaniah elaborates on all this by reporting that in that day* Jerusalem's shameful acts against God in the past will not be repeated. By then those who have done such things will have been removed, and with their departure the spirit of haughtiness will disappear. In their place God will leave* those who in true humility trust in Him[16] and will remove injustice and deception. With the godly remnant God will doubtless be well pleased, for He, as their good shepherd, will give them sustenance, serenity, and security (vv. 11-13).

Additional Notes

3:9 †אֶהְפֹּךְ ("I will give," lit. "I will [over]turn"): Known throughout the Semitic family,[17] this verb is used in the OT transitively of turning someone or something (2 Kings 21:13), overthrowing a city (Gen. 19:21, 25, 29), or transforming/changing a thing/person (Ps. 105:25). Intransitively it is employed of turning back or into something (Lev. 13:3-4; 2 Kings 5:26). Here used transitively, it takes its place in a series of statements relative to God's transforming work with regard to people (1 Sam. 10:6, 9; Ps. 105:25; Jer. 31:13; Hos. 11:8). The sentence is elliptical, the point being that the impure lips of the people will be changed to pure lips. As Keil points out, the syntax is not unlike that of 1 Sam. 10:9.[18] The translation above is *ad sensum*. The *Living Bible*'s "I will change the speech of my returning people to pure Hebrew" misses the point of the passage. The stress here is on spiritual purity, not singleness of language.

†The phrase שְׁכֶם אֶחָד (lit. "[with] one shoulder") is best taken as a figurative expression for unanimity of action or purpose (cf. RSV, NKJV, KJV: "with one accord/consent"), hence the thought "shoulder to shoulder" (NASB, NIV, NJB).[19]

3:10 †By the "rivers of Cush" is meant the distant headwaters of the Nile and its tributaries. Thus J. M. P. Smith points out that "the rivers referred to are the branches of the Nile that traverse the most

---

16. G. A. Smith (*The Book of the Twelve Prophets*, rev. ed. [Garden City, N.Y.: Doubleday, Doran, 1929], 2:71) wisely points out: "Where Churches have large ambitions for themselves, how necessary to hear that the future is destined for *a poor folk*, the meek and the honest. Where men boast that their religion—Bible, Creed or Church—has undertaken to save them, *vaunting themselves on the Mount of My Holiness*, how needful to hear salvation placed upon character and trust in God."
17. See K. Seybold, "הָפַךְ," *TDOT* 3:423-27.
18. Keil, *Minor Prophets*, 2:156.
19. The LXX translates the line picturesquely "under one yoke."

southern portion of the region; viz. the Atbara, the Astasobas, the Astapus or Blue Nile, and the Bahr-el-Abjadh or White Nile; cf. Is. 18[1-7]."[20] The phrase is a synecdoche, those of that distant region representing the farthest people of the earth.[21]

עֲתָרַי בַּת־פּוּצַי† ("my worshipers," "my scattered ones"): These words are omitted in the LXX* and the Pesh., and accordingly some suggest that they are a gloss here. However, their inclusion by the Vg and the difficulty in understanding them argue against their omission or the conjecture of a gloss. Although J. M. P. Smith declares the MT "quite . . . unintelligible,"[22] the English versions have made tolerable sense of the text: "my suppliants, the daughter of my dispersed (ones)" (RSV, KJV; cf. NKJV; so also the Vg); "my worshipers, my dispersed ones/scattered people" (NASB, NIV).

Although עָתָר ("worshiper") is a *hapax legomenon*, the verb עָתַר ("pray/supplicate") is attested. The form could also be construed as a participle: "those who worship me."[23] Adding to the difficulty is the fact that the phrase בַּת־פּוּצַי is without precedent. The usual sense of "daughter" in such cases is as a stereotyped title with a nationalistic emphasis such as "(virgin) daughter of X" (Jerusalem, Zion, etc.),[24] whereas the passive participle of פּוּץ occurs nowhere else. Nevertheless, the phrase is not totally unintelligible as an extension of its usual understanding. It can be taken to mean "the crowd or congregation consisting of the dispersed of the Lord, the members of the

---

20. J. M. P. Smith, *Zephaniah*, p. 249.
21. C. L. Feinberg (*The Minor Prophets* [Chicago: Moody, 1976], p. 234), however, suggests that the literal Ethiopia is meant. He goes on to observe that "there are some who suggest that the ones meant by the suppliants are Jews dispersed in Ethiopia. They point to the west of Abyssinia where the well-known Falashas (the word is from the same Semitic root as Philistine, meaning emigrant) live. They are said to trace their origin to Palestine and the Jewish religion. It is thought that the Abyssinian Christians were originally in part Hebrew believers. We prefer with others to understand the words 'my suppliants, even the daughter of my dispersed' as the object of the verb and not the subject. In other words, the Lord's people dispersed in Ethiopia will be brought by the Gentiles to their homeland as an offering to the Lord." (See also the additional note on 2:12.)
22. J. M. P. Smith, *Zephaniah*, p. 249. Smith emends the text to read *"The princes(?) of the daughter of Put(?)."* Sabottka (*Zephanja*, pp. 119-21) adopts a suggestion of Dahood to understand בַּת as "woven garment," emends פּוּצַי to בּוּצַי, and translates the phrase "garments of byssos" (i.e., fine linen garments).
23. Note the suggested translation in the *Preliminary and Interim Report on the Hebrew Old Testament Text Project* (New York: United Bible Societies, 1980), 5:382-83: "those who pray to me."
24. See the additional note on 3:14. See further my note on 2 Kings 19:21 in R. D. Patterson and H. J. Austel, "1, 2 Kings," in *EBC* (Grand Rapids: Zondervan, 1988), 4:269.

Israelitish congregation of God scattered about in all the world."[25] It is also possible to read the consonantal text of the first word of the phrase as בֵּית ("house of"), hence "my scattered house"—that is, the dispersed Israelites viewed as God's covenantal remnant (cf. 2 Sam. 7:11).[26] Most probably the phrase is elliptical for בַּת עַמִּי הַפּוּץ ("my scattered people"), the sense being supplied from the עַמִּים of v. 9. The phrase בַּת עַמִּי occurs often in Jeremiah.

מִנְחָתִי† ("my tribute"): מִנְחָה has been understood here as "sacrifices" (LXX; cf. Vg), "an offering made to God of any kind" (BDB), or the meal offering (Keil). The meaning "tribute" (cf. NJB, O'Connor, Sabottka) comes from the Ugaritic cognate, which is parallel to *argmn* ("tribute").[27] Although the suffix has been taken as a dative, "to me" (LXX, Vg, Sabottka), such is not necessary. The tribute will be considered to be God's proper due.

3:11 Phrases such as בַּיּוֹם הַהוּא ("*in that day*") can be used as formulae to introduce strophes or stanzas (cf. Joel 3:1 [HB. 4:1]; Amos 8:13; 9:11; Mic. 4:6; 5:9 [HB. 5:10]; 7:11-12; Hag. 2:23; Zech. 3:10; 8:23; etc.). The changed emphasis and subject matter, as well as the literary hook כִּי אָז, render it certain that the phrase introduces a subunit in this section. It also forms a linking device with the following section (cf. v. 16).

לֹא תֵבוֹשִׁי† ("you will not be put to shame"): Since the verb form is fem. sing., doubtless Jerusalem is being addressed. The verb can be taken in a subjective sense with the meaning "feel shame" (NASB) or in an objective sense meaning "be put to shame" (NIV, NKJV). The former emphasizes the forgetting of past shameful deeds against the Lord; the latter lays stress on the unlikely prospect of feeling shame ever again since its cause is removed. The latter course has been followed here because the context underscores the fact that in that future day the shameful acts perpetrated against God will no longer be practiced, for those who did such things have been removed. Although O'Connor takes לֹא as an emphatic particle ("you shall be ashamed"),[28] the force of the context and the presence of לֹא in its normal negative usage in the same verse (וְלֹא־תוֹסְפִי) make the suggestion of a rare miswriting for לוֹ tenuous.[29]

---

25. Keil, *Minor Prophets*, 2:156.
26. Thus Jeremiah speaks often of "the house of Israel," or "the house of Judah," and reports that God calls His people "my house" (Jer. 12:7).
27. See *UT*, p. 198, Text 137, lines 37-38.
28. M. O'Connor, *Hebrew Verse Structure* (Winona Lake, Ind.: Eisenbrauns, 1980), p. 259.
29. For proposed examples of לֹא written for לוֹ, see D. Rudolf Meyer, *Hebräische Grammatik* (Berlin: Walter de Gruyter, 1969), 2:173, par. 86.4; see also the comments of B. K. Waltke and M. O'Connor, *An Introduction to Biblical Hebrew Syntax* (Winona Lake: Eisenbrauns, 1990), pp. 211-12.

עַלִיזֵי גַּאֲוָתֵךְ† ("your proud boasters," lit. "the exultations of/in your pride"): The phrase is composed of a genitive of attribute and a 2d fem. sing. possessive suffix.[30] Keil observes that the phrase "is taken from Isa. xiii.3, where it denotes the heroes called by Jehovah, who exult with pride caused by the intoxication of victory; whereas here the reference is to the haughty judges, priests, and prophets (vers. 3 and 4), who exult in their sinful ways."[31] M. Dahood calls attention to the occurrence of פֶּשַׁע and גַּאֲוָה in close proximity as reflecting Ugaritic usage also.[32]

3:12 וְהִשְׁאַרְתִּי ("and I *will leave*"): Invaders customarily deported the leaders and skilled craftsmen of the lands they had conquered, leaving only the poor (2 Kings 24:14; 25:12). So God's invasion of Jerusalem leaves the עָנִי וָדָל ("humble and lowly," lit. "afflicted and poor"; cf. Job 34:28; Isa. 26:6). With regard to the first word, L. Coppes remarks: "The '*ānî*, although frequently in synonymous parallelism with '*ebyôn* and *dal*, differs from both in that it connotes some kind of disability or distress."[33] Concerning the latter he observes: "This root occurs most frequently in the adjectival form. Unlike '*ānî*, *dal* does not emphasize pain or oppression; unlike '*ebyôn*, it does not primarily emphasize need, and unlike *rāsh*, it represents those who lack rather than the destitute."[34] Together they emphasize those who made up the lower stratum of society and who were plagued by physical difficulties and social and mental torment (cf. Prov. 22:22). Here, however, these words are qualified by the statement that "they trust in the name of the Lord."

Zephaniah intends the remnant left in Jerusalem to be understood as made up of more than just the materially and socially needy. Rather, they are those who, unlike the arrogant boasters who trusted only in themselves, their accomplishments, and their possessions for which God had removed them from the midst of Jerusalem (v. 11), "recognize Yahweh as their only but all-sufficient source of strength."[35] Keil adds: "The leading characteristic of those who are bowed down will be trust in the Lord, the spiritual stamp of genuine piety."[36]

Thus the terms used here take on a theological importance that

---

30. For the genitive of attribute or quality, see A. B. Davidson, *Hebrew Syntax*, 3d ed. (Edinburgh: T. and T. Clark, 1901), par. 24c, Rem. 2.
31. Keil, *Minor Prophets*, 2:158.
32. Dahood, "Ugaritic-Hebrew Parallel Pairs," *RSP* 1:317-18.
33. L. Coppes, "עָנָה," *TWOT* 2:683.
34. L. Coppes, "דַּל," *TWOT* 1:190.
35. J. M. P. Smith, *Zephaniah*, pp. 251-52; see also Carroll Stuhlmueller, "Justice Toward the Poor," *The Bible Today* 24 (1986): 387.
36. Keil, *Minor Prophets*, 2:159.

recognizes that the saved of the world are those whose qualities of heart and mind enable them to submit to God. More than just being poor in this world's goods, they are poor in spirit (Isa. 66:2; Mic. 6:8; Matt. 5:3). It is a godly remnant unencumbered by pride and committed to the Savior. Concerning the force of these words in vv. 11-13 G. W. Anderson remarks:

> Here there are drawn together some of the themes mentioned above as linking Zephaniah with his great predecessor, Isaiah: *hybris* as the sin which particularly calls down divine judgment, humble faith as its antithesis, the creation by Yahweh of a righteous remnant which will be the recipient of Yahweh's blessing, and Zion, glorified and protected by Yahweh when he has purified and renewed her.[37]

3:13 The ethical qualities predicated for the godly remnant of Israel would be those that characterize the Messiah Himself (Isa. 42:1-4; 53:3, 7-9; Zech. 9:9; cf. Matt. 11:28-30; 12:15-21; Phil. 2:1-8).

†וְאֵין מַחֲרִיד . . . כִּי ("Yes, . . . and none shall make them afraid"): The כִּי is asseverative, as in the closing statement of 3:8. The blessings promised here are assured to those who faithfully keep God's commandments (Ps. 1:1-3; Ezek. 34:25-31; Mic. 4:4-5; 7:14). See also the additional note on 3:20.

2. INSTRUCTIONS IN THE LIGHT OF THAT DAY (3:14-20)

Translation

Sing for joy, O daughter of Zion,
** shout aloud, O Israel;**
be glad and rejoice with all your heart,
** O daughter of Jerusalem!**
¹⁵The LORD has turned aside* your judgment,
** He has turned away* your enemy.**
The LORD, the King of Israel, is in your midst;
** you will not fear* evil* anymore.**
¹⁶In that day it will be said to Jerusalem,
** "Fear not, O Zion,**
** let not your hands hang limp;**
¹⁷the LORD your God is in your midst,
** a warrior who saves*.**

---

37. G. W. Anderson, "The Idea of the Remnant in the Book of Zephaniah," *ASTI* 11 (1977-78): 387; see also the additional note on 2:7. R. L. Smith (*Micah–Malachi*, WBC [Waco, Tex.: Word, 1984], p. 142) points out that, "although the idea of God saving only the humble is magnified in the post OT era, the concept is an old one." Smith provides several examples from the Psalms and prophets that antedate Zephaniah.

He will exult over you with gladness,
  He will renew* you in his love,
  He will rejoice over you with singing."
18"I will gather* those who have been driven*
  from your appointed feasts;
(although) they were a tribute* from you,
  (they were) a reproach upon her (Jerusalem).
19Behold I will deal* at that time
  with all who oppress you;
I will rescue the lame
  and gather the outcast.
I will turn their shame* to praise
  and honor in all the earth.
20At that time I will lead you,
  even at the time I gather you;
I will surely* give you honor and praise
  among all the peoples of the earth
when I restore your fortunes
  before your eyes," says the LORD.

Exegesis and Exposition

Verses 14-20 form a closing unit of instructions concerning the Day of the Lord. The section falls into two subunits, the first constituting joyous imperatives of encouragement (vv. 14-17) based on the predictive assurances He has just given (vv. 9-13), the second providing further reasons for rejoicing given in God's own words (vv. 18-20).[38]

For Jerusalem, faced with the divine sentence against her, Zephaniah has words of instruction that will doubtless be carried out: sing for joy*; shout aloud*; be glad and rejoice*. The commands are happy ones, heaped up to underscore the great expectation of the joyous times that lay beyond the immediate punishment. As Laetsch remarks, "Jerusalem is to be glad and rejoice 'with all the heart,' with joy flowing from the very seat of life, true, sincere, living joy."[39] In that coming day there will be singing and shouting, together with joy and rejoicing such as had never been known before. Although the command is aimed at the future Jerusalem, no doubt the message would not be lost on the godly worshipers of Zephaniah's own day.

---

38. For literary keys to the structure of vv. 14-20, see the additional note on 3:17.
39. Laetsch, *Minor Prophets*, p. 380.

The immediate reason for that renewed felicity is revealed. It is twofold: (1) externally, God will have ended the period of Jerusalem's judgment by defeating all her enemies; (2) internally, God Himself will be in her midst as the everlasting King.[40] The Lord, Israel's righteous judge, deems her punishment completed and Jerusalem's correction accomplished. Accordingly, the judicial sentence may be commuted and God can now deal with His agents of chastisement. He will turn them away from His city and people and will judge them for their sins. Moreover, Yahweh, Israel's King (Isa. 44:6), will dwell in His royal city. Cleansed by long ages of corrective judgment, Jerusalem will now be made permanently holy by the presence of the Holy One of Israel (cf. Isa. 54:4-8; 57:14-19; 62:10-12; Ezek. 48:35; Joel 3:17, 21 [HB 4:17, 21]).[41]

The promise of release from fear is accompanied by words of encouragement not to let either fright or anxiety grip their hearts (vv. 16-17). Zion's citizens will at last be free of the all-too-common fear that left their hands hanging limp* in despondency, paralyzed from terror. Each will remind the other of God's abiding presence. He, the sovereign Lord of the universe and Israel's heavenly warrior*, has delivered them from their enemies, effected their redemption, and now lives among them in glory.

Such assurances form a striking contrast with Zephaniah's earlier prophecy that the Day of the Lord would be filled with such horror that even the bravest of warriors would cry out bitterly (1:14). Unlike those whose limit of strength and courage will be reached, Israel's champion and Redeemer will prove to be a "victorious warrior" (NASB) who shows Himself "mighty to save" (NIV). Such a one is Israel's defender in her midst—hers alone. Such a thought is so awe-inspiring that it bears repeating (cf. v. 15). What inexpressible happiness and rejoicing (cf. v. 14) that will bring!

Adding to the scene of jubilation is the fact that God will exult over His redeemed people with hymns of gladness (cf. Isa. 54:7-17). Therefore, His people will bask in the glow of His love (cf. Isa. 54:1-6). It is a grand prospect for Israel and one that should be a source of encouragement for all people: "Though the promise belongs to the

---

40. For the universal and local aspects of the divine title "King," see Daniel Block, *The Gods of the Nations*, Evangelical Theological Society Monograph Series No. 2 (Jackson: Evangelical Theological Society, 1988), pp. 47-52.
41. Subsequent revelation makes clear that this will be realized when the Messiah reigns in His everlasting glory (Jer. 23:5-8; 33:14-26; Ezek. 34:21-31; 36:22-38; 37:21-28; Zech. 2:10-13 [HB 2:14-17]; 14:1-11; cf. Phil. 2:9-11; Rev. 11:15; 19:6-16; 21:2-3).

literal Israel, it also belongs to the spiritual. And it should cause the fearful believer to take courage, and 'lift up the hands that hang down.' "[42]

When I was in Israel shortly after the Six-Day War of 1967, I was told repeatedly by those I met that their watchword was "No fear." In a far greater way, Zephaniah prophesies of a coming day when, with God in her midst, Israel will never again fear any harm.

In a climactic finish to all that he has prophesied, Zephaniah reveals the personal promises of Israel's Redeemer. Though from a literary standpoint vv. 18-20 provide a further reason for the commands concerning rejoicing in v. 14, their force must not be missed: God Himself is speaking. What an encouragement these words must have been to the beleaguered remnant of Zephaniah's day! "He wanted to place a strong hope before the believing remnant . . . since His judgment was imminent and His restoration mercies remote. The prophet, in spite of dark days, wanted the repentant to grasp firmly God's promises for comfort and strength."[43]

The Lord's opening assurance (v. 18) stands in stark contrast to His pronouncements at the beginning of the book. Unlike that earlier announcement of God's gathering of the nations together so as to sweep them from the face of the earth (1:2-4), the Lord will gather up those who have been driven away from Jerusalem and therefore from the opportunity to partake of Israel's periods of festivity. In God's providence His sinning people had been punished by being carried away into exile as booty to their conquerors. This had been a shameful reproach to God's name and to that of the holy city. Now, however, judgment has given way to hope. God will regather His chastised and cleansed people in order to lead them home. Herbert Marks appropriately calls attention to the effective use of wordplay here:

> The Hebrew stem *'sf* has two nearly antithetical senses, on the one hand "ingathering," on the other "removal" or "destruction," and the prophet's message, like the fate of Judah, is suspended between them. The promises of salvation culminate in the "ingathering" in 3:18 . . . but this is only the merciful counterpart of the threatened decreation with which the opening doom on Judah began.[44]

---

42. A. R. Fausset, "Zephaniah," in R. Jamieson, A. R. Fausset, and David Brown, *A Commentary Critical, Experimental and Practical on the Old and New Testaments* (Grand Rapids: Eerdmans, 1948), 4:650.

43. J. D. Hannah, "Zephaniah," in *The Bible Knowledge Commentary,* ed. J. F. Walvoord and R. B. Zuck (Wheaton: Scripture Press, 1985), 1:1534.

44. Herbert Marks, "The Twelve Prophets," in *The Literary Guide to the Bible,* ed. Robert Alter and Frank Kermode (Cambridge: Harvard U., 1987), p. 216.

A threefold promise follows in v. 19: (1) God will now deal with Israel's enemies, for their time of judgment has come (cf. Isa. 54:17-21; 66:15-16); (2) He will rescue and gather up His helpless and dispersed people; (3) He will turn Israel's former shame into praise and honor that will fill the whole earth (cf. Deut. 26:19; Isa. 62:7; Mic. 4:6-8). So great are these latter two thoughts that Zephaniah repeats them in v. 20, at the same time emphasizing Israel's own festive future: "Verse 20 is generally regarded as a repetitious gloss, but perhaps Zephaniah, like other preachers, found the repetition of a particularly exciting truth too tempting to avoid!"[45]

The certainty of Israel's newly acquired felicity is assured: the Lord gathers up His scattered people and brings them home. The metaphor is that of the good shepherd. It is a familiar figure in the OT, one that Zephaniah had utilized previously (cf. 2:6-7; 3:13). Indeed, God revealed himself to be Israel's shepherd (Gen. 48:15; Pss. 23:1; 80:1 [HB 80:2]) who sees to her daily provision (Ps. 23:3; Amos 3:11) and rescues her in time of need (Ezek. 34:11-16; Zech. 9:15-16). He guides His sheep in the way they should go (Isa. 40:11).

Likewise, Israel's Messiah will shepherd Israel as His flock (Ezek. 34:22-24). Though He must suffer for the sheep (Zech. 13:7; cf. Isa. 52:13–53:12), He will ultimately triumph (Zech. 14:1-8) and reign over His regathered people in fulfillment of all the covenant promises made to them (cf. Gen. 12:1-7; 13:14-17; 15:7-21; 17:1-8; 2 Sam. 7:16-19; Pss. 2:6-9; 89:3-4, 20-37 [HB 89:4-5, 21-38]; 110:1-6; Isa. 9:6-7; 11:1–12:6; 54:10; Jer. 23:5-8; 31:31-34; 33:14-26; Ezek. 37:22-28; etc.).

It is no surprise, then, that Christ would later affirm that He was the Good Shepherd who would lay down His life for the sheep (John 10:11-18). Subsequently the NT writers would teach that Jesus is the Great Shepherd, who both sees to the maturity and well-being of His sheep (Heb. 13:20-21; 1 Pet. 2:25) and, as the Chief Shepherd, will come again for His flock (1 Pet. 5:4).[46]

---

45. Victor A. S. Reid, "Zephaniah," in *The International Bible Commentary*, rev. ed., ed. F. F. Bruce (Grand Rapids: Zondervan, 1986), p. 957.
46. For a standard premillennial interpretation of Zeph. 3:20, see H. E. Freeman, *Nahum Zephaniah Habakkuk*, Everyman's Bible Commentary (Chicago: Moody, 1973), pp. 89-90. For poetic sentiment concerning Christ's triumphant return, one may note the words of Thomas Kelly ("Look, Ye Saints, the Sight Is Glorious!" in *Immanuel Hymnal* [New York: Macmillan, 1939], No. 188):

Look, ye saints, the sight is glorious!
See the Man of Sorrows now,
From the fight returned victorious!
Every knee to Him shall bow: Crown Him!
Crowns become the Victor's brow!

Zephaniah closes his prophecy on the highest of notes. Not only is that which he has just recorded (vv. 18-20) "the word of the Lord" but the whole prophecy is as well (1:1; cf. 1:2, 3, 10; 2:9; 3:8). God himself has spoken. The hymn writer's response reflects what is in the heart of every believer:

> How firm a foundation, ye saints of the Lord,
> Is laid for your faith in His excellent Word!
> What more can He say than to you He hath said,
> To you who for refuge to Jesus have fled?[47]

Additional Notes

3:14 וְעָלְזִי שִׂמְחִי . . . הָרִיעוּ . . . רָנִּי ("*Sing for joy . . . shout aloud . . . be glad and rejoice*"): L. Walker calls attention to the piling up of verbs of similar meaning here as an expression of strong emphasis.[48] The future scene of God's blessing will be one of boundless joy. הָרִיעוּ is in the masc. pl. because Israel is being considered with regard to its individual citizens; the city and state, personified as a woman, is appropriately addressed with the fem. sing. imperative. The term "daughter of Zion/Jerusalem," familiar as a stereotyped phrase with nationalistic emphasis,[49] probably gives the idea of representing Zion and Jerusalem as the author of the community of the faithful. The use of personification, anthropopoeia, and metaphor in vv. 14-16 is striking.

3:15 פִּנָּה† . . . הֵסִיר ("turned aside . . . turned away") constitutes a play on ideas.[50] While the first verb indicates the removal of the source of stress, the second emphasizes their being sent away. Since the objects of the verbs are "judgment" and "enemy" respectively, the scene may be that of a courtroom where God the judge has overturned the sentence against His people and sent away their enemies. Such an understanding does away with critical conjecture that since the parallelism of the passage demands a word for a person to bal-

---

47. The text of this hymn is listed as "K" in Rippon's *Section of Hymns*, 1787. For a contemporary hymn setting, see *The Hymnal for Worship and Celebration*, ed. Tom Fettke and Ken Barker (Waco, Tex.: Word, 1986), No. 275.
48. L. Walker, "Zephaniah," in *EBC*, 7:564n. See also the interesting study of Ihromi, "Die Häufung der Verben des Jubelns in Zephanja iii 14f., 16-18: *rnn, rwʿ, śmḥ, ʿlz, śwś* und *gîl*," *VT* 33 (1983): 106-10.
49. See H. Haag, "בַּק," *TDOT* 2:334-35.
50. For the verb סוּר, see R. D. Patterson, "סוּר," *TWOT* 2:620-21. The verb פָּנָה may have been chosen as a deliberate echo of the earlier פִּנּוֹת ("strongholds") in Zeph. 1:16; 3:6; for the verb itself, cf. Arabic *fanî* ("pass away") and Geez *fännäwä* ("send away").

ance the noun "enemy," one should probably read מְשֹׁפְטַיִךְ ("your judges/rulers").[51]

Zephaniah has previously brought up the themes of judgment and justice (2:3; 3:5, 8), so their presence here is not without precedent. God has served as witness against all the world and also as its judge (3:8). He is Jerusalem's righteous judge (3:5) who will deliver those who humbly practice His judgments and statutes (2:3). Now that there is a purified and humble remnant in the city, He may freely terminate her sentence and remove those He had sent to execute her punishment. In keeping with the forensic tone of the context, Israel's many enemies are viewed collectively as one adversary. Therefore, אֹיְבֵךְ is acceptable as it stands in the MT without resorting to the widely suggested change to אֹיְבָיִךְ.[52]

†לֹא־תִירְאִי ("you will not fear"): Some Hebrew MSS, followed by the LXX and Pesh. (cf. BHS, KJV, NKJV), read לֹא תִרְאִי ("you will not see"). But the weight of Hebrew manuscripts favors the MT, a reading reflected in the Vg. Accordingly most newer translations follow the MT (cf. NIV, NASB, NJB).[53] "Fear" also provides a play on the notion of Israel's failure to demonstrate proper fear in the midst of God's chastisement (cf. 3:7). The message concerning fear also anticipates the emphases of the next two verses.

†רָע ("evil"): Any disaster, injury, or adverse circumstance—even God's judicial punishment—could be considered as evil by those who experienced it. The word also has been translated in the English versions as "disaster" (NASB, NKJV) and "harm" (NIV).

3:16 אַל־יִרְפּוּ (*"let not [your hands] hang limp"*): Although the Hebrew root means basically "be slack," it is used in a wide variety of situations and contexts. As a verb it is employed idiomatically with "hands" several times. Twice it appears with the idea of the alleviation or cessation of divine judgment (2 Sam. 24:16; 1 Chron. 21:15), once of failing to help (or abandoning) another (Josh. 10:6), and several times of losing one's courage or of being discouraged (e.g., 2 Sam. 4:1; 2 Chron. 15:7; Jer. 38:4). In some cases discouragement turns to fear (Neh. 6:9; Ezek. 21:7 [HB 21:12]) with the result that the prophets often speak of hands hanging limp in fear (Isa. 13:7-8; Jer. 6:24-25;

---

51. See the *Tg. Neb.*; cf. *BHS*. For a full discussion, see J. M. P. Smith, *Zephaniah*, pp. 256, 261[n].

52. See the LXX, Vg, Pesh., *Tg. Neb.*, BHS. For אֹיֵב as an adversary at law, see Job 9:15; 13:24; 33:10; cf. 1 Kings 21:20. For the term itself, see E. Jenni, "אֹיֵב," *THAT* 1:118-22; H. Ringgren, "אָיַב," *TDOT* 1:212-18. It remains to be asked only whether the adversary here could be God Himself (cf. Isa. 63:10; Lam. 2:4-5).

53. Among modern foreign-language Bibles taking a similar position may be cited *Die Heilige Schrift* and *La Sacra Biblia*.

50:43; Ezek. 7:17-18). That is the understanding here, as the parallel with the vetitive "do not be afraid" ("fear not") makes clear.

3:17 גִּבּוֹר ("*warrior*"): In the OT גִּבּוֹר is employed most frequently "in connection with military activities, especially as a designation for a warrior, either a man who is eligible for military service or is able to bear arms, or one who has actually fought in combat, who has already distinguished himself by performing heroic deeds."[54] God is called El Gibbor, "The Mighty God" (Isa. 10:21),[55] and, as Israel's hero and warrior par excellence, He gains the victory (Ps. 24:8-10; Isa. 42:13; Hab. 3:8-15) and delivers His people (Ex. 15:2; Ps. 68:17-20 [HB 68:18-21]). Although Israel was saved by the Lord (Deut. 33:29), their physical deliverance was an outward sign of God's spiritual relation to them (Ezek. 37:20-28).

†Although I have rendered the hiphil prefix-conjugation form יוֹשִׁיעַ according to its normal imperfect usage (here functioning after "warrior" in an elliptical construction to form a relative clause with adjectival force[56]), it could be construed as an unusual transitive so that the whole phrase is translated "a hero/warrior, he saves."[57]

†The MT יַחֲרִישׁ ("he will quiet [you]") has been explained variously as (1) keeping silent about or covering up people's sins (Henderson, Maurer, Rashi), (2) God's silence due to the overwhelming depths of His love (A. B. Davidson, Fausset, Feinberg, Keil, von Orelli), (3) God's preoccupation with planning Israel's good (Graetz, Nowack), (4) God's resting in His love (Laetsch, R. Smith), (5) a means for the believer to cultivate in his heart peace and silence (Luther, L. Walker), and (6) God's singing out of the joy of His loving concern (O'Connor). In addition, a relation to the Akkadian *erēšu* ("to desire/crave") might be suggested.[58]

Though one is always hesitant to abandon the MT reading,[59] the incompatibility of the thought of the clause thus formed by יַחֲרִישׁ with the two parallel clauses that surround it makes attractive the search for alternative possibilities. Among the many proposed alternative readings,[60] perhaps the best is that of *BHS* to read יְחַדֵּשׁ ("he

---

54. H. Kosmala, "גָּבַר," *TDOT* 2:374; see also J. Kuhlewein, "גבר," *THAT* 1:400.

55. For this title applied to Israel's Messiah, see Isa. 9:6 (Heb. 9:5).

56. See Davidson, *Syntax*, par. 44b, Rem. 3.

57. For such hiphil transitives, see GKC, par. 53d, e, f.

58. Still other ideas have been proposed. Thus, Sabottka (*Zephanja*, pp. 132-34) follows Dahood in taking חָרַשׁ in the sense of "devise artfully," "improvise," "compose"; see further R. Smith, *Micah–Malachi*, p. 143n.17a.

59. See E. Würthwein, *The Text of the Old Testament*, 4th ed., trans. E. F. Rhodes (Grand Rapids: Eerdmans, 1979), pp. 111-19.

60. See the *Hebrew Old Testament Text Project*, 5:384. Note that some suggest dropping the phrase entirely (e.g., Buhl, Marti).

will renew [you]"). This involves a simple consonantal change of ר to
ד. In accepting a change from *r* to *d* it would also be possible to
redivide the words in the clause to read: יַחַד יֵשֵׁב אֲהֵבָתוֹ ("let the one
who inhabits his love rejoice," i.e., "let him whom God loves rejoice").[61] The verb חָדָה ("rejoice") would then be parallel to the other
clauses of the verse. Moreover, Zephaniah has employed the participial form of יָשַׁב in a similar genitive relationship previously
(2:15).[62] So construed the phrase would constitute Zephaniah's parenthetical remark, a prophetic technique attested elsewhere (e.g.,
Joel 3:11 [HB 4:11]).[63] Final certainty is wanting here. I have followed
the lead of several ancient (LXX, Pesh.) and modern (NJB, RSV) versions and many scholars (e.g., Buhl, S. R. Driver, Duhm, Hitzig, G. A.
Smith) in reading יְחַדֵּשׁ. J. M. P. Smith, who also adopts this reading,
observes that there are many different interpretations of what this
means, such as

> he will do new things (*cf.* Is. 43¹⁹) the like of which have not heretofore
> been known; or, he renews his love; or, he renews himself in his love;
> or, . . . through the manifestations of favour inspired by his love for thee,
> he will restore thee to pristine vigour and glory, giving thee newness of
> life.[64]

Although the renewing of God's love toward His people appears to be
more harmonious with the ideas of God's delighting in and rejoicing
over Israel, found in the parallel lines of v. 17, it must be admitted
that the MT reading is not altogether inappropriate, the thought of
quieting being perhaps related to Israel's fear in v. 16.

בְּרִנָּה ("with singing") is positioned last in the clause and in the
verse so as to form an inclusio with רָנִּי in v. 14. Verses 14-17 thus
compose a strophe within the final stanza. The second strophe to
follow is marked by a shift to first-person address and the presence of
the temporal marker בָּעֵת הַהִיא ("at that time," vv. 19, 20) rather than
the בַּיּוֹם הַהוּא ("in that day," v. 16) of the first strophe.

3:18 †נוּגֵי מִמּוֹעֵד׃ נוּגֵי has generally been taken to be a niphal participle from יָגָה ("to suffer," "be grieved") with attenuation of וֹ to וּ,

---

61. Confusion between ד and ר is a source of frequent textual corruption; see
Würthwein, *Text of the Old Testament*, p. 106. For the jussive of חָדָה, see Job
3:6; GKC, par. 75r.
62. יָשַׁב is used elsewhere in the OT with similar emphases, e.g., "(You are)
the one who inhabits the praises of Israel" (Ps. 22:3 [HB 22:4]; cf. NIV,
however, which follows *BHS* in construing the participle with the first
colon).
63. See my comments on Joel 3:11 (HB 4:11) in R. D. Patterson, "Joel," in
EBC, 7:262.
64. J. M. P. Smith, *Zephaniah*, p. 257. For still other suggestions among those
who adopt this reading, see Walker, "Zephaniah," in *EBC*, 7:563.

here meaning "sorrows."[65] However, J. M. P. Smith follows a widely suggested emendation in reading כְּיוֹם and joining the full phrase to v. 17: "He will exult over thee with shouting as in the days of a festival."[66] Those who accept the MT propose something like "the sorrows of the appointed feasts" ("I will remove from you").[67] This makes tolerable sense, but the phrase and whole clause must also be related to the full verse. This has proved to be no easy task, with some declaring the rest of the verse "unintelligible."[68] Even so conservative a scholar as Keil admits, "Every clause of ver. 18 is difficult."[69] Small wonder, then, that the verse has received widely differing textual, lexical, and syntactical treatment from the ancient and modern versions and the commentators.

The solution proposed here is built around two pivotal points: (1) the verb under consideration must be understood in the sense of "depart" or "drive out/take away"; (2) the noun מַשְׂאֵת in the succeeding clause should be rendered "tribute/payment." Validation of the former point comes from one of two lines of evidence. (1) If the verb is from the root יָגָה, its meaning should be related to one found in the hiphil stem, "drive/thrust out," and hence here in the niphal participle, "those driven out."[70] (2) The verb in question may really be נוג ("depart"), a verb attested in the Ugaritic Keret Epic:

| *wng mlk lbty* | And depart, O king, from my house; |
| *rḥq krt lḥẓry* | withdraw, O Keret, from my court.[71] |

Evidence for the latter point also falls along two lines: (1) the meaning "tribute/payment" is well known in other examples in Northwest Semitic literature;[72] (2) such a meaning is also found in the OT:

| Therefore, because you have imposed a tax[73] upon the poor (man) | לָכֵן יַעַן בּוֹשַׁסְכֶם עַל־דָּל |
| and taken a tribute of grain from him | וּמַשְׂאַת־בַּר תִּקְחוּ מִמֶּנּוּ (Amos 5:11) |

---

65. See GKC, par. 69t; cf. Lam. 1:4.
66. J. M. P. Smith, *Zephaniah*, p. 257; see also pp. 258, 262. See further the LXX, Pesh. and *Tg. Neb.*; cf. NJB, RSV.
67. NIV; cf. NASB, NKJV, KJV.
68. So J. M. P. Smith, *Zephaniah*, p. 258.
69. Keil, *Minor Prophets*, 2:162. For full details, see the *Hebrew Old Testament Text Project*, 5:384-86; J. M. P. Smith, *Zephaniah*, pp. 262-63.
70. This possibility is acknowledged by G. A. Smith, *Twelve Prophets*, p. 73n.4.
71. *UT*, 251, *KRT*, lines 131-33.
72. For details see *KAI*, 2:84; 3:15.
73. The verb here may be שָׁבַס; see H. R. Cohen, *Biblical Hapax Legomena in the Light of Akkadian and Ugaritic* (Missoula, Mont.: Scholars Press, 1978), pp. 49, 95-96[nn265-68].

Utilizing these data it is possible to make good sense of the MT, as it stands, as constituting a further divine promise. God will regather those who, due to Jerusalem's sin, were carried away as booty for the Chaldean army, a fact that stands as a reproach upon the holy city. As for מוֹעֵד ("appointed feasts"), Jack Lewis remarks:

> . . . *mô'ēd* must be thought of in a wide usage for all religious assemblies. Jerusalem became the city of assemblies (Isa 33:20; cf. Ezk 36:38) which were characterized by great rejoicing and were deeply missed during times of exile (Zeph 3:18; Lam 1:4).[74]

3:19 †הִנְנִי עֹשֶׂה† ("behold I will deal"): The construction הִנֵּה with the participle in future contexts lays stress on the certainty and immediacy of the action.[75] At that future time envisioned here, God will deal vigorously and swiftly with those who afflict His people. The verb עָשָׂה ("do/make") followed by the particle אֶת־ is often used in the sense of "deal with" (e.g., Jer. 21:2; Ezek. 22:14; 23:25, 29). Zephaniah used this verb previously in proclaiming the speedy end of the world in the Day of the Lord (1:18). God's effective power is underscored both there and here.

†בָּשְׁתָּם† ("their shame"): The syntactical relation of the form is disputed.[76] Because the preceding prepositional phrase "in all the earth" contains a definite article, it would be grammatically anomalous as part of that construction (i.e., "In all the land of their shame"; but cf. the Vg). Some (e.g., NASB, RSV) have solved the difficulty by seeing a case of enjambment and relating בָּשְׁתָּם to the controlling verb of the clause: "I will turn their shame (into praise and renown)."[77] Others have viewed the form relatively: "Whose shame hath been in all the earth" (Soncino; cf. Ewald) or "In every land where they were put to shame" (NKJV; cf. KJV, von Orelli).

Among other proposals have been (1) that of Keil to treat בָּשְׁתָּם as epexegetical, "i.e. of their shame,"[78] (2) that of the LXX to view the form as a verb, a procedure that involves a restructuring of the text that relates the material involved to v. 20, "And they shall be

---

74. Jack Lewis, "יָעַד," *TWOT* 1:389. A verb נוג with the meaning "drive out/depart" also fits well the case of Lam. 1:4 where the MT בְּתוּלֹתֶיהָ נּוּגוֹת is rendered by the LXX αἱ παρθένοι αὐτῆς ἀγόμεναι ("her virgins are led away"). For the use of מוֹעֵד as either "appointed time" or "place," see G. Sauer, "יעד," *THAT* 1:743-44.

75. See GKC, par. 116m, p.

76. For details, see the *Hebrew Old Testament Text Project*, 5:386.

77. Such a procedure involves taking the final *mem* on the verb as an enclitic. For details, see Sabottka, *Zephanja*, p. 139. For שִׂים with the meaning "turn/change/transform," see M. Dahood, "Hebrew-Ugaritic Lexicography X," *Bib* 53 (1972): 399-400.

78. Keil, *Minor Prophets*, 2:163.

ashamed at the time when I deal kindly with you," and (3) that of M. Dahood to take the form as the object of the verb but to view the final *mem* on the verbal form as a type of *dativus commodi*, "And for them I shall transform their humiliation."[79] Because of the grammatical difficulties here, some simply omit the form (Pesh.) or treat it as a corrupt dittography occasioned by the בְּשׁוּבִי אֶת־שְׁבוּתֵיכֶם of v. 20 (*BHS*, NJB).

On the whole, the difficulty seems best solved by relating the phrase to the controlling verb, "I will turn their shame to praise and honor." This view has the advantage of recognizing the presence of the phrase in some ancient texts. It also finds further support in the juxtaposition of the ideas of "name" and "shame" in the same Ugaritic epic material noted in the problem at Zeph. 3:10-11:

bšm tg'rm 'ttrt	Athirat rebuked him by name,
bt laliyn b['l]	"Be ashamed, O Aliyan Ba'al,
bt lrkb 'rpt	Be ashamed, O Rider on the Clouds."[80]

The primary thrust, then, appears to be that the Lord will change His people's shame to a name (i.e., honor) and praise. By separating the twin objects of the verb so widely, the author emphasizes the inclusive nature of the Lord's action: Both they and their shame will be transformed to objects of honor and praise.

3:20 For בָּעֵת הַהִיא אָבִיא ("at that time I will lead"), J. M. P. Smith follows Buhl in suggesting an emendation to בָּעֵת הֵיטִיבִי ("in the time when I do good [to you]"; cf. LXX, Duhm).[81] The LXX reading, however, may depend on its own handling of the relationship of vv. 19 and 20 (see previous note). In any case, other textual data do not support it, nor does the context necessitate it.

†The translation of וּבָעֵת קַבְּצִי אֶתְכֶם as "even at the time I gather you" takes the *waw* as explicative.[82] The use of בָּעֵת with the infinitive construct (here followed by an accusative complement) rather than a verb to express a temporal clause may be explained on the analogy of similarly formed nominal clauses used as a genitive (cf. Gen. 2:17; Jer. 2:7; Neh. 9:27). Thus, "at the time of my gathering you" becomes

---

79. Dahood, "Lexicography X," 399-400; for this employment of the pronominal suffix with verbs, see GKC, par. 117x; Davidson, *Syntax*, par. 73, Rem. 4.

80. *UT*, p. 180, Text 68, lines 28-29. For the term "rider on the clouds," see R. D. Patterson, "A Multiplex Approach to Psalm 45," *GTJ* 6 (1985): 37n.35. See also Dahood, "Ugaritic-Hebrew Parallel Pairs," *RSP* 3:308-9; Dahood draws attention to a similar problem in Ezek. 34:29.

81. J. M. P. Smith, *Zephaniah*, p. 263.

82. For *waw* explicative, see R. J. Williams, *Hebrew Syntax*, 2d ed. (Toronto: U. of Toronto, 1976), p. 71, par. 434; D. W. Baker, "Further Examples of the WAW EXPLICATIVUM," *VT* 30 (1980): 129-36; Dahood, *Psalms*, 3:402.

"at the time (when) I gather you." The clause could also be an instance in which בְּעֵת functions as a compound preposition followed by an infinitive construct with a pronominal suffix to express a temporal clause: "at the time (when) I shall gather you" (cf. NASB, NJB, RSV).[83] Thus, there is no need to view the construction here as a case of ellipsis, the eliding of the הַהִיא after וּבָעֵת occasioning the change of the imperfect אֲקַבֵּץ to the infinitive קַבְּצִי (cf. *BHS*). As J. M. P. Smith remarks, "It is difficult to see how so easy and natural a reading as this . . . one could have given way to the rarer idiom suggested by the MT, which bears the stamp of originality."[84]

†כִּי ("surely"): The Hebrew particle is emphatic here as in vv. 8 and 13.[85] For the phrase "when I restore your fortunes," see the note at 2:7. The singular שְׁבוּתְכֶם, read by the LXX, Pesh., Vg and fourteen Hebrew MSS for the MT plural, is widely accepted by OT scholars (cf. *BHS*).

---

83. Note the similar function of מִדֵּי with the infinitive construct to mean "as often as" (lit. "out of the abundance of"); see BDB, p. 191.
84. J. M. P. Smith, *Zephaniah*, p. 263.
85. For emphatic כִּי see R. Gordis, "The Asseverative Kaph in Ugaritic and Hebrew," *JAOS* 63 (1943): 176-78; Dahood, *Psalms*, 3:402-6; Williams, *Syntax*, par. 261, 449; Waltke and O'Connor, *Hebrew Syntax*, p. 670.

Index of Authors

Achard, 330
Albright, 116, 122, 124, 127, 132,
    231, 233, 234, 236, 239,
    241, 245, 248, 249, 251,
    263, 305
Allen, 73
Alter, 91, 249
Amsler, 326
Anderson, 295, 296, 376
Archer, 15, 18, 115, 146, 279
Armerding, 12, 28, 33, 45, 49, 50,
    56–57, 72, 76, 85, 95, 97,
    98, 129, 133, 156, 161, 162,
    163, 165, 166, 171, 173,
    175, 181, 189, 200, 202,
    212, 216, 225–26, 227, 231,
    232, 233, 241, 248, 251,
    267, 300
Austel, 60, 91, 98, 354
Avishur, 245

Baker, 39
Baldacci, 333
Baly, 345
Barker, 19, 25, 287, 310, 387

Barr, 219–20, 221
Barré, 230
Barth, 166
Bauder, 332
Baumann, 209
Beckwith, 14, 133, 294
Beer, 290, 291
Beitzel, 318
Bergman, 166, 347
Bewer, 10, 11, 23, 116, 276, 290
Bezold, 228
Bimson, 243
Block, 378
Blommerde, 112, 240
Blue, 151, 228, 231, 249, 255, 256
Boice, 211
Borger, 88
Botterweck, 39, 201
Brown, 252
Brownlee, 128, 153, 171, 180, 215
Bruce, F. F., 133, 175, 233
Bruce, P., 194
Bryant, 221
Budde, 116, 178, 290, 291
Buhl, 383, 384

Bullock, 5, 53, 115, 130, 133, 146, 276–77, 281, 292
Burrows, 128

Calvin, 19
Carnell, 257
Carson, 219
Cassuto, 124, 239, 249
Cathcart, 13–14, 19, 27, 32, 34, 35, 36, 39, 40, 41, 48, 51, 57, 65, 67, 69, 70, 71, 73, 78, 87, 90, 91, 98, 99, 100, 101, 109, 111, 166
Charnock, 163
Christensen, 277, 288, 345, 351
Clark, 314, 355
Clifford, 86
Cohen, 111, 176, 385
Collins, 286
Cooper, 34, 239, 306
Coppes, 79, 203, 230, 375
Couroyer, 325
Craigie, 5, 47, 108, 123, 129, 131, 161, 171, 173, 188, 195, 201, 207, 245, 262, 264, 276, 277, 287, 304, 313, 315, 325, 351, 358, 359, 370
Cranfield, 211, 219, 222, 370
Cremer, 218, 219
Crenshaw, 288
Cross, 124, 132, 204, 231, 234, 239, 240, 259, 269, 304
Culver, 131, 137, 140, 362

Dahood, 32, 42, 71, 72, 73, 91, 123, 157, 166, 167, 174, 229, 236, 239, 240, 241, 242, 244–45, 251, 252, 254, 347, 348, 367, 369, 371, 373, 375, 383, 386, 387, 388
Davidson, 48, 56, 65, 92, 128, 150, 203, 217, 242, 253, 375, 383, 387
Day, 236
Delaporte, 148
Delcor, 342

Delitzsch, 177–78, 218, 219, 222, 228, 243, 370
de Roche, 276, 301
de Vaux, 62, 189, 280, 305, 310, 343
Dhorme, 323
Donner, 97, 251, 317, 345
Dothan, 338, 339
Driver, G. R., 51, 153, 236, 242
Driver, S. R., 72, 73, 104, 128, 171, 174, 258, 290, 291, 384
Duhm, 78, 116, 164, 290, 291, 384
Dyrness, 218

Ehrlich, 41, 72, 77
Eichhorn, 291
Eichrodt, 310, 370
Eiselen, 188, 276, 293
Eising, 65, 98
Eissfeldt, 115, 116, 127, 128, 164, 212, 276, 290
Elliger, 123, 359
Emerton, 178, 180, 215
Emmerson, 305
Erdman, 310
Erickson, 164, 178, 196, 219
Erlandsson, 164
Ewald, 7, 173, 252, 312, 386

Fabry, 342
Fairbairn, 326
Fausset, 248, 249, 252, 271, 305, 371, 379, 383
Feinberg, 161, 171, 172, 185, 188, 212, 228, 231, 238, 248, 275, 298, 359, 371, 373, 383
Fensham, 276, 277
Finley, 110, 234, 321, 322, 323, 329, 336
Fishbane, 250, 362
Fisher, 51
Fitzmyer, 92
Fohrer, 13, 53, 291
Foxvog, 264
France, 320

Free, 243
Freedman, 112, 232, 240, 251,
    269
Freeman, 5, 6, 75, 115, 146, 188,
    200, 229, 276, 282, 285,
    338, 380
Fronzaroli, 362
Futato, 99, 259, 367

Gamberoni, 40, 245
Gardiner, 96, 349
Gaster, 25, 41, 51, 65, 316
Gelio, 78
Gerleman, 298, 307
Gevirtz, 245
Ghirshman, 187
Giesebracht, 116, 164
Gilchrist, 204
Girdlestone, 39, 40, 164, 181, 197
Gitin, 339
Gonzalez, 212
Gordis, 42, 150, 339, 340, 388
Gordon, 71, 100, 110, 143, 166,
    204, 242, 305, 325, 342,
    367, 374, 387
Gozzo, 293
Graetz, 383
Gray, 25, 186, 191, 193, 194, 278,
    317
Greenberg, 71
Greenfield, 261
Gressman, 316

Haag, 381
Hailey, 115, 146, 172, 188, 192,
    244, 248, 252, 276, 312,
    325
Haldar, 13, 32, 51, 73, 77
Hallo, 277
Hamilton, 106, 141, 361
Hammershaimb, 253
Hannah, 275, 301, 316, 341, 379
Hanson, 285–86
Harper, 194
Harris, J. G., 143
Harris, R. L., 133, 182, 197, 208,
    258, 259, 294
Harris, Z. S., 99, 234, 327

Harrison, E. F., 222
Harrison, R. K., 115, 118, 276,
    290, 291, 294, 310
Hartley, 163, 189, 323
Hasel, 345
Hauck, 332
Haupt, 5, 13, 116
Hauser, 271
Hava, 257
Hayes, 156, 161, 209, 286
Heidel, 34, 182, 200, 212, 215
Held, 15, 234, 249
Henderson, 383
Hengstenberg, 19
Herbert, 188
Hiebert, 123, 229, 234, 235, 236,
    237, 240, 241, 243, 244,
    246, 248, 249, 252, 256,
    258, 260, 263, 267, 268,
    270, 271, 272
Hillers, 32, 92, 101
Hindson, 340
Hitzig, xvi, 252, 355, 384
Hobbs, 166
Holladay, 243
Holt, 173
Horst, 51
Houtsma, 180
Howard, 175
Hubbard, 131, 250
Huey, 51
Huffmon, 58
Hughes, 370
Hulst, 71, 151, 249, 258, 306,
    326, 363
Humbert, 13, 116, 118, 153, 171
Hummel, 50, 115, 117, 119, 131,
    212, 239, 276, 289, 290,
    291, 347
Humphrey, 146
Hutchinson, 107
Hyatt, 275

Jamieson, 252
Janzen, 174, 212–14, 215, 216
Jastrow, 50, 203, 215
Jenni, 382
Jennings, 339, 345

Jepsen, 137, 220
Johns, 350
Johnson, 164
Jung, 304

Kaiser, 176, 326
Kalland, 208, 354
Kapelrud, 109, 276, 280, 300, 324
Keil, 19, 21, 40, 48, 55, 71, 73,
    77, 83, 98, 115, 137, 141,
    142, 146, 149, 153, 156,
    157, 158, 161, 162, 165,
    167, 171, 172, 173, 174,
    176, 178, 180, 186, 187,
    188, 189, 191, 202, 208,
    209, 220, 221, 228, 229,
    233, 235, 236, 238, 239,
    241, 246, 248, 249, 250,
    252, 253, 256, 260, 264,
    275, 292, 298, 300, 304,
    306, 312, 316, 318, 324,
    326, 327, 341, 342, 345,
    347, 350, 355, 360, 362,
    366, 370, 372, 375, 383,
    385, 386
Keller, 203
Kilmer, 264
Kitchen, 96, 338, 339, 349
Kittel, 198
Klopfenstein, 164, 362
Knierim, 361
Koch, 212, 214, 218
Kosmala, 159–60, 383
Kramer, 70
Kuhlewein, 383
Kutscher, 327

Lacheman, 275, 290
Laetsch, 19, 64, 69, 115, 142, 146,
    151, 152, 153, 156, 157,
    158, 161, 171, 173, 174,
    178, 180, 185, 186, 188,
    192, 194, 204, 209, 212,
    228, 231, 241, 243, 248,
    249, 252, 253, 255, 256,
    279, 303, 304, 309, 313,
    315, 316, 323, 329, 331,

    340, 342, 348, 370, 371,
    377, 383
Lambdin, 98
Lambert, 32
Laney, 16
Lang, 34
Langdon, 49
Lange, 7
Larue, 276, 290
La Sor, 131, 145, 295, 338
Latourette, 212
Layard, 70, 107
Lehman, 15, 72, 242, 280, 295,
    305, 338, 348
Lemaire, 232, 317
Leslau, 143, 202, 258
Leslie, 276, 290
Lewis, 175, 386
Liedke, 177, 362
Lightfoot, 182, 220, 223
Lindblom, 118
Lipinski, 154
Livingston, 164, 197
Lods, 116
Lohfink, 293
Longman, 320
Luckenbill, 34
Lünemann, 176
Luther, 19, 118, 157, 197, 201,
    212, 383

McCarter, 312
McComiskey, 155
McKane, 188, 216
Mackrell, 289
Maier, 5, 8, 19, 20, 25, 27, 35, 40,
    41, 45, 59, 62, 64, 66, 67,
    71, 75, 76, 77, 79, 83, 88,
    90, 98, 101, 103, 106, 107,
    109, 110, 111, 278, 353,
    354
Mansoor, 116
Mare, 313
Margulis, 236, 241, 248, 254
Marks, 73, 142, 379
Marti, 290, 291, 383
Martin, 16

Marzal, 362
Maurer, 383
Merrill, 279
Metzger, 118
Meyer, 204, 222, 374
Miller, 240, 243
Milligan, 176
Moran, 47, 153, 204, 260
Morris, 286
Moscati, 111, 154, 203, 327
Mosis, 347
Moulton, 175
Mowinckel, 13
Muilenburg, 67

Nielsen, 116
Nilsson, 125
Nowach, 291, 383
Nute, 248, 255

O'Connor, 317, 332, 350, 374,
  383, 388
Oeming, 290
Olam, 115
Olivier, 354
Olmstead, 186, 278, 353
Oppenheim, 51, 145
Opperwall-Galluch, 289, 298
Oswalt, 143, 171
Ottosson, 69

Parrot, 101
Parunak, 90, 214
Patterson, 18, 30, 34, 51, 52, 57,
  60, 63, 68, 72, 78, 84, 88,
  92, 97, 98, 100, 105, 122,
  125, 139, 140, 143, 154,
  163, 164, 197, 198, 201,
  204, 231–32, 253, 259, 260,
  271, 277, 282, 306, 307,
  310, 317, 321, 343, 348,
  373, 381, 384, 387
Payne, 146, 218, 301, 310, 326,
  370
Peake, 286
Pelser, 51
Pettinato, 236

Pfeiffer, 11
Pope, 39, 50, 79, 123, 239, 240,
  347, 350
Preuss, 44, 206, 208, 252, 306
Price, 112, 240
Prinsloo, 127

Rahlfs, 118
Rainey, 325
Rast, 121
Reid, 275, 316, 380
Renaud, 282
Richards, 177
Ricoeur, 30, 332
Ringgren, 109, 166, 347, 382
Rist, 318
Robertson, A. T., 79, 256
Robertson, O. P., 324
Robinson, 276, 281, 350
Rogers, 194
Röllig, 97, 251, 345
Ross, 221
Rudolph, 73, 215
Rummel, 124
Ruprecht, 166, 307
Russell, 288

Sabottka, 300, 302, 306, 322, 325,
  327, 331, 347, 355, 356,
  367, 371, 373, 374, 383,
  386
Saggs, 13, 69, 84, 87, 106, 107,
  145, 148, 185, 218, 353
Sandars, 342
Sandy, 175, 367
Sarna, 261
Sauer, 175, 322, 386
Scharbert, 316
Schmider, 228
Schneider, 276, 291, 294, 295
Schottroff, 316
Schrader, 47, 260
Schulman, 325
Schulz, 332
Schwally, 290, 291
Sellin, 5, 13, 53, 116, 164, 291
Seybold, 291, 372

Shedd, 182
Shires, 175
Simpson, 277
Smick, 26, 178, 345
Smith, G. A., 11, 161, 164, 185,
 231, 276, 285, 290, 291,
 300, 314, 318, 329, 349,
 355, 356, 363, 372, 384,
 385
Smith, J. M. P., 5, 10, 11, 18, 32,
 34, 41, 50, 51, 57, 58, 67,
 69, 71, 74, 78, 89, 90, 109,
 288, 290, 291, 292, 298,
 300, 305, 315, 340, 343,
 347, 348, 350, 354, 356,
 358, 363, 369, 373, 375,
 382, 384, 385, 387, 388
Smith, L. P., 275, 290
Smith, R. L., 13, 101, 118, 128,
 133, 152, 153, 156, 161,
 163, 181, 188, 202, 212,
 231, 245, 285, 325, 329,
 335, 347, 356, 376
Southwell, 178
Speiser, 347
Stade, 290, 291
Stigers, 218
Stoebe, 230
Stonehouse, 58
Strong, 163, 177
Stuart, 240
Stuhlemueller, 293, 330

Terry, 322, 326
Thackery, 241
Thomas, 345
Thompson, J. A., 72
Thompson, R. C., 106, 107
Tigay, 304
Torczyner, 188
Travers, 16, 63, 84, 105, 282
Trench, 165
Turner, 175

Unger, 115, 133, 137, 146

van der Wal, 157
van der Woude, 163, 180

van Groningen, 197, 322
van Hatten, 345
van Hooser, 316
van Selms, 165, 342
Vermes, 116, 208
Vetter, 78
von Orelli, 188, 228, 229, 231,
 248, 276, 277, 321, 326,
 362, 371, 383, 386
von Rad, 13, 116, 295, 322, 324,
 327
von Soden, 242
Vos, 15, 50, 137, 218, 301

Wagner, 48, 93
Wainwright, 342
Walker, 275, 279, 316, 341, 381,
 383
Waltke, 166, 182, 291, 374, 388
Ward, 128, 151, 153, 171, 174,
 178, 215, 217, 229, 241,
 246, 258
Warmington, 347
Warmuth, 232
Watson, 33, 61, 67, 78, 79, 86, 87,
 101, 110, 167, 182, 197,
 205, 214, 240, 325
Watts, 228, 301
Weinfeld, 306
Weiser, 164
Wellhausen, 116, 164, 215
Wenham, G. J., 52, 310
Wenham, J. W., 152
Wesley, 265
Westcott, 175, 223
Westermann, 166, 335
Whitley, 327, 367
Wight, 165
Williams, D. L., 275
Williams, R. J., 42, 48, 87, 99,
 110, 150, 154, 162, 167,
 242, 253, 259, 260, 327,
 387, 388
Willis, 319
Wilson, 145, 353
Wintermute, 287
Wiseman, 48, 104, 107, 148, 152,
 160, 177, 185, 191, 339

Wolf, 245, 356
Wolff, 182, 216
Wood, 278, 280, 362
Woodard, 352
Würthwein, 123, 132, 133, 157,
    181, 202, 216, 300, 383,
    384

Yadin, 62

Yamauchi, 145, 159, 186, 191
Yoder, 26
Young, 19, 115, 129, 143, 146,
    292
Youngblood, 286, 287

Zalcman, 339, 341
Zemek, 181, 221

Selected Index of Scriptures

Genesis

1:20-26	301
1:20-27	299
2:25	199
6:17	299, 301
7:21-23	299
9:21-23	199
12:1-3	346
12:3	108, 247, 256
15:6	177, 221
17:1	219
17:2-8	158
19:11	324
26:3-5	158
28:13-15	158
49:10	247

Exodus

3:13-15	158, 262
6:6	303
14:1-6	158, 383
14:13-22	250
14:20-31	250
15:1-10	230, 249
15:1-18	270, 271
15:2	58, 261
15:3, 4	263
15:6-10	269
15:11	156
15:11-13	230, 247
15:12-15	247
15:14-16	235
15:14-18	247, 269
19:6	156
20:4-5	22
20:7	19
22:26-27	189
23:8	324
34:6-7	29
34:14	22
40:34, 35	196
40:34-38	233

Leviticus

7:11-21	310
11:44	156
19:1	232, 310
19:2	156, 219
20:7	232, 310
20:22-24	310
26:13	49
26:27-33	315

Numbers	
14:44	181
23:7	19
23:9	237
23:21	237
23:22	237
24:4, 16	19
24:17	237
24:19	247-48
25:1-5	304
31:1	24
Deuteronomy	
1:12	19
1:41	181
4:5-6	358
4:23-24	22
4:25-31	227
4:27-31	371
4:29	307
4:34	303
5:8-9	22
5:15	303
6:4	346
6:13-15	22
6:18	310
7:6	155, 158
7:19	303
8:2	332
10:17	346
12:18	311
12:25	128, 310
13:18	310
14:1-2	158
21:9	310
24:6	189
25:16	197
26:15	76
26:16-18	158
26:19	380
28:28-29	324
28:30	315
28:39	315
28:49-52	324
29:23	345
29:29	347
30:1-10	257
30:7	256
32:4	156, 197, 218-19
32:13	264
32:15	163, 232
32:22	36
32:34-43	256
32:35	24
32:41	89
33:1-2	234
33:2	233
33:2-3	235, 247, 268
33:13	264
33:19	311
33:26	235
33:27-29	55
Joshua	
1:5	252
3:15	243
6:24	97
10:12-13	244
10:13	24
24:19-20	22
Judges	
2:13	304
3:12	326
3:22	89
5:4	244
5:4-5	231, 234, 235, 243, 247, 268
8:21	108
9:45	347
10:6	306
14:12-19	188
18:27	97
1 Samuel	
2:2	156, 163
4:12	171
5:1-4	312, 317
9:22	311
10:6, 9	372
17:26, 36, 45	346
17:45	76
24:21	45
31:3	112

2 Samuel

7:8-29	248
7:12-29	158
10:15	153
15:11	311
23:3-4	359

1 Kings

1:9-10	311
1:24, 25	311
8:10-12	196
8:28-30	209
13:2	7
14:10	324
16:30-32	34
17:1	7
18:19, 21	304
20:10	324
20:16	338

2 Kings

4:16	117
5:17	19
6:18	324
9:37	324
10:18-22	312
10:28-31	201
13:7	324
17:16-17	306
17:16-18	304
17:18-20	304
18:5	280
18:13–19:8	44
18:19	4
18:19-27	171
18:28-32	84
19:21-27	84
19:21-28	44, 346
19:22	346, 353
19:32	153
19:32-36	44
19:37	353
21:1-11	4
21:1-16	116
21:1-18	139
21:2-3	304
21:12-15	4

21:16	4
21:19-26	292
22:5	305
22:8-13	4
23:1-7	248
23:1-25	278
23:4-5	304, 306
23:10	306
23:10-14	304
23:12	306, 324
23:25	293, 359
23:26-27	293
25:7	100

1 Chronicles

3:23	280

2 Chronicles

11:8	338
20:3, 4	307
26:6	338
32:1-23	4
33:1-9	4
33:1-10	11
33:10-20	292
33:11-20	139
33:19	4
34:1-7	139
34:3	277
34:7	293
34:23–35:19	139
36:15	76

Ezra

2:16	280

Nehemiah

1:3	97
2:3, 13, 17	97
3:16	70
5:16	109
7:21	280
9:31	328
11:9	317

Esther

3:13, 15	171

8:10, 14	171	11:6	199
8:13	24	16:10-11	182
		17:6-12	140
Job		17:15	182
2:11	93	18:2	163
6:10	156	18:7	235, 237
7:16-21	158	18:7-15	243, 247, 268
9:7	142	18:17	45
9:21-24	158	18:31	232
12:4-6	158	18:32	263
14:12	301	18:33	263, 264
14:14	15	24:8	346
15:2	322	24:8-10	343
15:23-25	323	27:1	268
15:24	322	31:1-3	156
19:23-27	182	31:5	29
20:23	327	33:20	366
21:11	16	34:6	332
21:18	329	34:18	331
22:6	189	35:18, 28	16
24:1-16	158	37:7	268
24:21-25	158	37:37-40	37
24:22-24	309	44:1	268
27:1-12	243	45:1, 13	15
27:9-10	189	46:1-5	268
30:3	322, 323	47:2, 7-8	346
34:21-22	309	49:14-15	182
37:22-23	232	50:4	366
38:8-12	243	51:18	331
38:27	322, 323	55:9	142
39:6	347	58:11	16
39:23	89	59:13	15
42:1-6	207	66:1-4	346
		66:2, 7-8	196
Psalms		68:7-8	231, 243, 247
1:1-3	376	68:17-20	383
1:4	329	68:33	235
4:1-3	140	69:6	15
5:3	360	71:3	156
7:9	15	71:22	156
7:17	16	73:17	209
7:28	15	73:18-25	161
8:1	232	73:23-28	182
8:5-9	302	75:8	199
9:8	366	76:5	111
9:9	29	76:12	346
10:12-17	230	77:7-9	229
11:4	209	77:14, 16-18	229

77:16-19	247, 268	147:17	36
77:17	244	147:17-20	37
77:17-20	243	149:2, 5	261
77:19	254		
78:72	219	Proverbs	
79:5	22	1:7-8	361
81:6-7	140	1:8	189
82:8	366	3:5-6	358
84:12	358	3:11-12	361
85:4-7	268	6:4, 10	111
85:8-10	219	6:19	212
88:13	360	12:15	177
89:1-37	155	12:17	212
89:7, 8-13	346	14:5, 25	212
89:18	156	16:19	332
91:14-16	140	17:22	112
94:2	366	19:5, 9	212
94:7	111	21:8, 29	177
96:11, 12	261	21:24	181
96:13	366	22:22	375
97:12	268	24:33	111
98:9	37, 366	25:21-22	24
99:6-7	140	28:15	359
99:9	156	29:27	177
102:1-2	140, 360		
102:12-13	268	Ecclesiastes	
102:26	301	3:17	327
105:4	307		
105:25	372	Isaiah	
107:34	347	1:9	345
110:6	366	2:1	19
113:1	36	2:1-4	371
114:3-6	235, 243	2:1-5	346
114:7	232	2:4	366
118:14	58	2:7	72
119:132	173	2:13-14	34
121:3	108	3:7	19
121:4	111	4:2	55
125:1	358	5:1-7	58
132:4	111	5:25	303
138:8	140	5:27	111
139:23-24	15	6:1-5	209
143:8	360	6:3	156, 232
144:5-6	243, 247, 268	8:1	173
145:17-20	140	8:17	366
147:3	331	9:6	383
147:5	32-33	9:12	17, 21, 303
147:7-9	37	10:5	251

10:20-23	343	40:9-11	46
10:21	383	41:14	232
10:23	328	41:25	109
11:1-10	371	42:1-4	376
11:3-4	366	42:8	346
11:9	195	42:11	19
11:11-16	343, 371	42:13	383
12:2	58	43:1-3	232
13:1	20	43:11-13	346
13:6-16	287	44:9-20	45, 206
13:7-8	73, 382	44:17-20	346
13:9-11	366	44:28	7
13:19	145, 196, 345	45:1	7
13:19-22	160	45:3	314
14:4	19, 188	45:15	100
14:22	45	45:22-25	219
14:26-27	303	46:1-2	346
17:11	112	46:9	346
17:13	329	47:1, 5	145
18:1	349	48:11	195, 196
19:8	165	48:14, 20	145
21:6	118, 168	48:16	327
21:9	160	51:6	301
22:5	72	51:7	346
23:16-17	90	51:17, 22	199, 201
24:1	72	51:17-23	202
24:1-6	247	51:19	93
24:14-16	55	51:22–52:1	49
24:14-23	147	52:1-10	46
24:21-23	76	52:7	14, 15, 46-47, 52, 56
24:23	301	52:7-10	168
25:4	40	53:3, 7-9	376
26:3-4	358	54:1-6	378
26:12-13	247	54:4-8	378
26:19	111	54:4-17	23
28:29	300	54:6	340
30:8	171, 173	54:7-17	378
30:10	137	54:8	268
30:18	366	54:10	301
30:18-33	366	54:17-21	380
30:23	166	56:11-12	140
33:9	34	57:14-19	378
33:22	366	57:15	156
34:1-10	76	58:6-9, 11-12	140
34:6	301, 311	59:17	22
37:4	19	59:19	196
37:16	75	60:15	55, 340
37:23	346	61:1-7	42

61:2	24	7:21-28	358
61:10	147	7:28	361
62:1-6	202, 247	8:1-3	324
62:4	340	8:13	300
62:7	380	8:18–9:16	139
62:10-12	378	9:20-22	324
63:4	24	10:1-8	139
64:3	366	10:1-10	207
64:4	366	10:25	202
65:24	140	11:1-17	139
66:2	376	11:6-8	358
66:4	140	11:13, 17	304
66:7-14	391	11:18-19	159
66:13-16	366	12:1-4	159
66:14-16	346	13:1-4	139
66:15-16	380	13:11	45
66:16	366	13:22	91, 92
66:19-21	346	13:26	27, 85, 91
66:22	45	15:3	341
		15:5	93
Jeremiah		15:15-18	159
1:17-19	161	16:1-4	324
1:18	317	16:17	309
2:1–3:5	22	17:1	173
2:8	358	17:6	347
2:26	317	17:15-18	159
3:14	309	17:21, 22	19
4:9	317	18:15	302
4:13	117	19:3-13	304
4:17	358	19:5-9	304
4:24	35	20:7-18	159
4:26	36	20:8	142, 201
4:27	328	21:5	303
4:29	340	22:1–23:39	312
4:31	326	22:13-14	139
5:3	361	22:13-17	117
5:7	206	22:21	358
5:16	117	23:1-4	359
5:17	268	23:1-8	343, 360
5:23-25	358	23:3	108
5:26-28	166	23:9-20	139
5:31	358	23:9-39	358
6:4	338	23:11	358
6:7	142, 201	23:11-12	359
6:13	358	23:14	345
6:17	161, 168	23:20-32	362
6:24-25	382	23:29	36
7:20	202	25:1-7	139

25:1-11	227	51:17	199
25:15	201	51:22	199
25:15-28	199	51:24-26	160
25:31-33	366	51:26	36
25:32-33	324	51:31	171
27:1-10	49	51:57	105
27:5	303	51:58	117, 195
28:1-17	362	51:59-64	171
28:10-12	49		
29:10-14	227	**Lamentations**	
29:21-23	362	1:4	386
30:7	322	4:5	324
30:18	55	4:6	345
31:11-14	343	4:11	202
31:13	372	4:21	199
31:23	55		
31:27-37	343	**Ezekiel**	
32:17	303	3:16-21	161
32:21	303	3:17	168
32:24	153	5:13	22, 24
32:44	55	5:15	346
33:2-3	140	7:17-18	383
35:17	140	9:3	317
36:1-32	139	10:4, 18	317
38:20	178	11:13-20	343
40:1, 4	100	14:21	341
44:1-8	206	16:35-42	22
46:1–51:58	336	16:37	85
46:5	71	16:37-39	92
46:9-10	95	16:38	24
46:10	241, 311	17:2-10	188-89
46:21	71	17:17	153
46:25-26	6	20:8	13, 20
48:26	346	20:30-38	358
49:12	199	20:33-34	303
49:14	345	21:15	89
50:2-3	346	21:27	326
50:9-13	247	22:23-29	359
50:11	151	22:25	359
50:17, 18	6	22:26	359
50:18	75, 107	23:10	92
50:29	232, 346	23:25	22
50:32	195	23:31	34
50:40	345	25:16	342
50:43	383	25:32	337
51:5	232	27:9	109
51:6-8	199	27:10	99
51:7-8	201	27:27	109

29:17-20	6
30:18	49
33:7-9	161
34:11-16	343
34:14, 16	166
34:20-31	343
34:25-31	376
36:5	366
36:6-7	22
36:38	108
37:15-28	343
37:20-28	383
37:27	108
38:1–39:24	366
38:17-23	22
38:18-19	24
38:19	328
38:22-23	107
39:17-20	311, 346
39:25-29	22
45:9	142
46:2	317
47:1	317
47:10	165
48:35	55, 378

Daniel
2:26	19
4:10	19
4:29-30	191
11:35	174
12:1	322
12:2	182

Hosea
1:2	90
1:4	201, 247
1:4-5	7
2:3	85, 92
2:6, 15	90
2:8	304
2:9-10	92
2:12	58
6:10	327
6:11	55
8:4	206
8:7	105
9:8	161

10:5	305
11:8	372
13:1	304
13:3	329
13:14	182

Joel
1:2-4	321, 341
1:10, 12	35, 268
1:19-20	200
2:1-11	321, 329
2:2-11	103
2:2	323
2:3	354
2:4	88
2:5	88, 89
2:6	72
2:12-14	329
2:13	29
2:18	368
2:20	354
3:1	55
3:1-3	256, 346
3:1-8	247
3:3	100
3:7-8	147
3:9-11	322
3:9-16	346, 366
3:9-17	287
3:11	384
3:17	52, 378
3:18	287
3:18-20	46
3:20	287
3:21	378

Amos
1:1	19
1:4	110
1:8	343
2:7	50
2:8	189
3:6-7	161
4:9	58, 268
4:11	345
4:13	75
5:1	19
5:4, 14	178

5:11	315	1:6	14, 106, 108, 111, 332
5:20	287	1:7	15, 16, 108, 369
6:2	338	1:7-8	14, 16
9:8	309	1:7-10	14
9:12	50	1:8	8, 14, 106, 343
9:14	55	1:8-10	14, 369
		1:9	16, 111
Obadiah		1:10	8, 97, 106, 107
1	19	1:11	7, 16
11	100	1:11-12	14
14-15	247	1:11-14	352
15	187-88	1:11-15	369
15, 16	287, 346	1:12	6, 8, 14, 16
		1:14	8, 14, 16, 106, 352, 353
Jonah		1:15	8, 14, 15, 16, 86, 101, 108
1:2	84		
4:1-3	352	2:1	11, 14, 105, 161
4:10-11	161	2:1-10	369
4:11	16	2:2	6, 8, 14, 108
		2:3	11
Micah		2:3-5	7
1:1	19	2:3-7	14
1:2	209	2:4	89
1:4	36	2:5	7, 89
1:7	90	2:6	7
1:10-15	338	2:7	106
2:4	188	2:8	10, 14
4:1-5	346, 371	2:9	7, 89, 106, 107
4:3	366	2:10	107
4:4	58	2:11	6, 107, 108, 111
4:4-5	376	2:11-12	7, 8
4:6-8	380	2:11-13	8, 14, 15, 16, 352, 353, 369
5:2	7		
6:8	376	2:12	7, 359
6:15	317	2:13	6, 8, 14, 16, 97, 99, 106, 348, 352, 369
7:14	376		
		3:1	6, 8, 361
Nahum		3:1-7	15, 256, 369
1:1	14	3:2-3	7
1:1-6	369	3:3	106, 107
1:2	14, 256, 353, 368	3:4	6, 7, 8, 247
1:2-3	14	3:4-6	15
1:2-4	16	3:4-7	8, 16
1:2-6	16	3:5	8, 76, 79, 101, 199
1:2-10	8, 11	3:5-6	16
1:3	14, 15, 16	3:5-7	14
1:4	8	3:7	99, 107, 108, 111, 369
1:4-6	14	3:8	63, 108, 360

3:8-10	8, 14	2:14	131, 132, 136, 369
3:8-13	15, 353, 369	2:20	117, 122, 132, 134, 369
3:8-19	352	3:1-2	104
3:11	6, 8, 107, 199	3:2	121, 134, 268
3:11-13	7	3:3	134, 163
3:11-19	14	3:3-4	134
3:12	6, 8	3:3-7	369
3:13	8, 76	3:3-15	28, 120, 122-25, 134,
3:14	7, 8, 351		369
3:14-17	15	3:4-7	134
3:14-19	353, 369	3:6	35, 134
3:15	76, 106	3:8	134
3:15-17	8	3:8-15	134, 369, 383
3:16	6, 8	3:11	89
3:16-18	7	3:12	134, 367
3:17	8, 107	3:12-13	369
3:18	8, 151	3:12-15	134
3:18-19	11, 76, 107	3:13	131, 134
3:19	8, 15, 16, 46, 76, 108,	3:16	134, 268
	352, 369	3:16-17	134
		3:16-19	132, 134, 369
Habakkuk		3:17	268
1:1	134	3:18	134
1:2-4	120, 121, 134, 155	3:18-19	134, 268
1:2-11	134		
1:5	134	**Zephaniah**	
1:5-11	49, 120, 121, 134, 369	1:1	381
1:6	6, 7	1:2, 3, 10	381
1:8	117	1:2-3	293, 294
1:9	200	1:2-4	379
1:12	134, 232	1:2-6	369
1:12-17	134	1:3	294
1:12–2:1	120, 121, 122, 134	1:4	383
1:13	134	1:4-5	276
1:14	134	1:4-6	281, 293
2:1	118, 134	1:6	276, 281
2:1-4	134	1:7	117, 209, 294
2:2-20	120, 122	1:7-13	369
2:4	122, 132, 134, 211-23	1:8	253, 276, 281
	362	1:8-9	295
2:4-5	134, 369	1:9	276, 281, 293, 295
2:4-20	134	1:10	254
2:5-19	134	1:10, 11	276, 295
2:6-19	134	1:10-13	281, 293
2:6-20	369	1:12	288, 295
2:8	200	1:12-13	276
2:10	117	1:14	355, 378
2:12	117, 362	1:14-16	293

1:14-18	286-88, 294, 369
1:17	281, 295
1:17-18	293
1:18	276, 281, 295, 354, 367
2:1-2	295
2:1-3	294, 369
2:2	367
2:2-3	295
2:3	281, 294, 295, 382
2:4-7	288
2:4-15	281, 293, 295, 369
2:6-7	369, 380
2:7	296, 376, 388
2:8	295
2:9	295, 296, 381
2:9-11	370
2:10	247, 295
2:12	373
2:13	63
2:13-15	75, 105, 107
2:15	84
3:1	293, 295
3:1-4	276, 281
3:1-7	293
3:2	293
3:3	277, 293, 295
3:3-6	295
3:4	142, 276, 293, 295
3:5	293, 294, 295, 382
3:6	295, 381
3:7	276, 281, 294, 295, 382
3:8	294, 381, 382
3:8-17	22
3:9	281
3:9-10	294, 295
3:10	281, 296, 349
3:11	276, 295, 296
3:11-13	294, 295
3:12	294, 332
3:12-13	281, 288, 295
3:13	197, 294, 380
3:14	261, 373
3:14-17	294, 296
3:14-20	281, 294
3:17	261, 295, 296
3:17-18	369
3:18	296, 386
3:19	294
3:19-20	296
3:20	296, 376

Haggai

2:6, 21	301

Zechariah

7:8-14	140
8:2-3	22
9:9	376
12:1	19
13:7-9	140
14:1-5	196
14:1-7	287
14:2-20	366
14:4-10	287
14:9, 16-21	346

Malachi

1:1	19
2:17	159
2:20	151

Matthew

4:18-20	165
5:3	176
5:18	301
5:48	219
6:24	314
11:28-30	376
12:15-21	376
12:41	352
13:41	294
13:47-48	165
15:14	324
18:21-25	31
18:19	24
24:35	361
25:1-13	23
25:40	346

Mark

10:15	345
13:5	360
13:31	301

Luke
2:9-14	196
2:10	52
10:12	345
12:16-21	315
12:47-48	312
16:19-31	314
21:33	301
21:34	119

John
10:11-18	380

Acts
2:17-36	320
4:12	50
5:41	50
10:30	52
13:41	149

Romans
1:17	211, 212
2:19	324
3:26	29
8:22	200
9:29	345
10:9-15	46
10:15	14
11:25	324
12:19-20	24

1 Corinthians
6:15-19	23
6:20	24
9:24-27	173
10:4	163
15:54-58	182

2 Corinthians
2:17	314
6:6	31
6:15	44
11:1-4	23

Galatians
3:11	211, 222
5:22	31

Ephesians
2:8	212
4:15	219
4:18	324
4:26-27	25
5:18	199
5:25-27	23

Philippians
2:1-8	376
2:11	196

Colossians
1:15-20	302

1 Timothy
3:3	314
6:10	314

Hebrews
1:10-12	301
2:5-9	302
10:35-39	223
10:37-38	175
10:38	211
12:26-27	301
13:16	314
13:20-21	380

James
5:1-6	314

1 Peter
1:16	156, 219
2:6-8	163
2:25	108, 380
3:20	31
3:20-21	301
5:4	380

2 Peter
2:5	301
2:6	345
3:3-4	172
3:9-15	29
3:10	287, 301
3:15	31

1 John		Revelation	
2:11	324	6:17	294
3:1-3	24	11:15	172
4:7-12	31	14:5	294
		16:1	294
		19:7	23
3 John		19:11-21	196, 287
7	50	21:1	301

Selected Index of Hebrew Words

אֱמוּנָה	218, 219–23	יפח/פוח	174, 212–14
אֲשֶׁר	77–78, 258	כהה	112
בַּעַל	24, 25–26	כָּרֹת	342
בֶּטֶן	257	כסף	331–32
בְּלִיַּעַל	43, 44, 47–48	כשל	67–68
בצע	190	מִדְבָּר	354
בקש	93, 101, 307	מדד	236
בשׂר	51–52	מוג	35
גָּאוֹן	57–59	מִכְמֶרֶת	165
גלה	91	מֹכֶרֶת	90
דַּל	375	מַכְתִּיר	143
דרש	307	מַכְתֵּשׁ	317–18
הוֹי	86–87	מִנְזָר	110
הפך	372	מִפְתָּן	313, 317
זכר	67	מִרְעֶה	76–77
חֶבֶל	341–42	משׂא	19, 20, 136–37
חוּצָה	66	מִשְׁנֶה	317
חָזוֹן	19–20	מִשְׁפָּחָה	91
חמד	72	מִשְׁפָּט	142–43, 150, 155, 164,
חנק	79		365, 367
חסה	39–40	נֹא אָמוֹן	97
חצב	69–70	נֹגַהּ	246
חֵרֶם	165	נוה	181
חֹשֵׁב	47	נוח	258–59
יְאֹר	97–98	נטר	26–27
יכח	162, 164	נקה	31–32

נֶפֶשׁ	182–83, 216, 217	רגז	271
סוּפָה	33	רֹגֶז	230
סכך	68–69	רזה	348
עַבְטִיט	189	רְחוֹב	66
עָנִי	375	רַחֵם	230
עֲפֵלָה	215–16	רֹכֵב	33–34
עָתָר	373–74	רֹכֵל	316
פָּארוּר	72–73	רַעַשׁ	88
פוג	142	שָׂרִים	316–17
פוח/יפח	174, 212–14	שְׁאוֹל	181–82
פוש	151	שְׁאֵרִית	343
פְּלָדָה	65–66	שִׁגָּיוֹן	227, 228, 264
צַדִּיק	155, 158, 169, 213, 217–19	שֹׁד	201
		שְׁדֵמָה	260
צִיָּה	354	שֵׁם	109
צפה	57, 168	שְׁמָמָה	354
קָאַת	355	שַׁעַר	69
קוֹל	88, 326	תּוֹכַחַת	161–62
קלל	51	תּוֹרָה	142, 164
קפוֹד	355